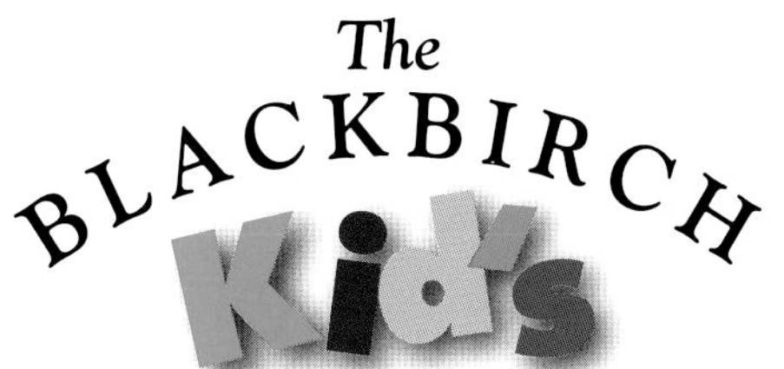

VISUAL REFERENCE OF THE UNITED STATES

More than 2,500 graphs, charts, maps, and photos that cover the most important and interesting facts about every state in our country!

By the Editors of Blackbirch Press
Maps, Charts, and Graphs by Bob Italiano

San Diego • Detroit • New York • San Francisco • Cleveland
New Haven, Conn. • Waterville, Maine • London • Munich

For more information, contact
The Gale Group, Inc.
27500 Drake Rd.
Farmington Hills, MI 48331-3535
Or you can visit our Internet site at http://www.gale.com

The Blackbirch Kid's Visual Reference of the United States Staff
Publisher: Bruce S. Glassman
Editorial Director: Marla Felkins Ryan
Production Manager: Jay Price
Production Artist: Suzette Diaz
Production Editor/Photo Research: Carol Buckley
Editorial: Kristen Woronoff
Book Design/Layout: Calico Harrington
Indexer: Kathleen Rocheleau

LIBRARY OF CONGRESS CATALOGING-IN-PUBLICATION DATA

Kid's visual reference of the USA / by the editors of Blackbirch Press.
p.cm.
Summary: An alphabetical presentation of brief statistics and pictorial information about each of the United States, as well as U.S. territories and possessions.
ISBN 1-56711-659-0 (alk. paper)
1. U.S. states — Miscellanea — Juvenile literature. 2. United States — Miscellanea — Juvenile literature. 3. U.S. states — Pictorial works — Juvenile literature. 4. United States — Pictorial works — Juvenile literature. [1. U.S. states. 2. United States — Miscellanea. 3. United States — Territories and possessions — Miscellanea.] I. Title: Kid's visual reference of the United States of America. II. Blackbirch Press.
E180.K48 2003
973 — dc21 2002004239

Printed in China
10 9 8 7 6 5 4 3 2 1

Color Key

 Alaska/Hawaii
 Northeast
 Midwest
 South
West
Territories/Possessions

TABLE OF CONTENTS

Iowa

Louisiana

Massachusetts

Nevada

Oregon

South Dakota

Texas

Vermont

A Look at the 50 States
Pages 6-15

In most of the pages of this book, you will see fascinating information about each of the 50 United States. Each state's section will include a detailed state map; quick at-a-glance information on population, capital city, state size, and much more; pie charts, bar graphs, and other maps; fun facts about state firsts and state history; as well as text on each state's unique geography, history, and people.

Before the sections on the individual states begin, however, you will find *A Look at the 50 States*—10 pages that compare all states to each other. These pages feature the broad categories of state size, population, temperature and climate, as well as other interesting categories. In this section, you can get the "broad perspective" on all the states first—before you delve into the state-specific portions of this book.

So, turn the page and start reading. By the time you're done, you'll be an expert on all the facts that make these United States one of the most awe-inspiring countries in the world!

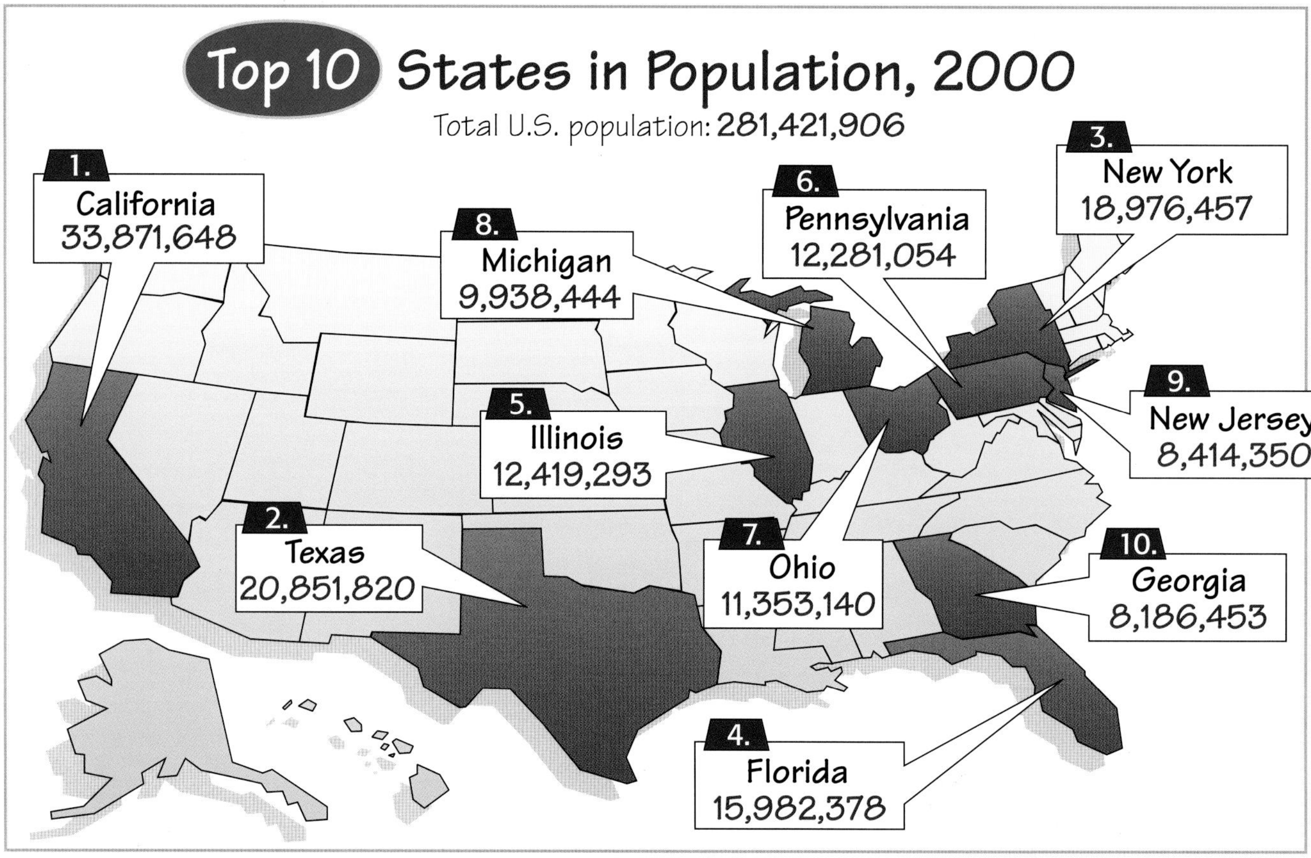

Top 10 States in Population, 2000

Total U.S. population: 281,421,906

1. California 33,871,648
2. Texas 20,851,820
3. New York 18,976,457
4. Florida 15,982,378
5. Illinois 12,419,293
6. Pennsylvania 12,281,054
7. Ohio 11,353,140
8. Michigan 9,938,444
9. New Jersey 8,414,350
10. Georgia 8,186,453

SOURCE: Based on data from Bureau of the Census, U.S. Department of Commerce

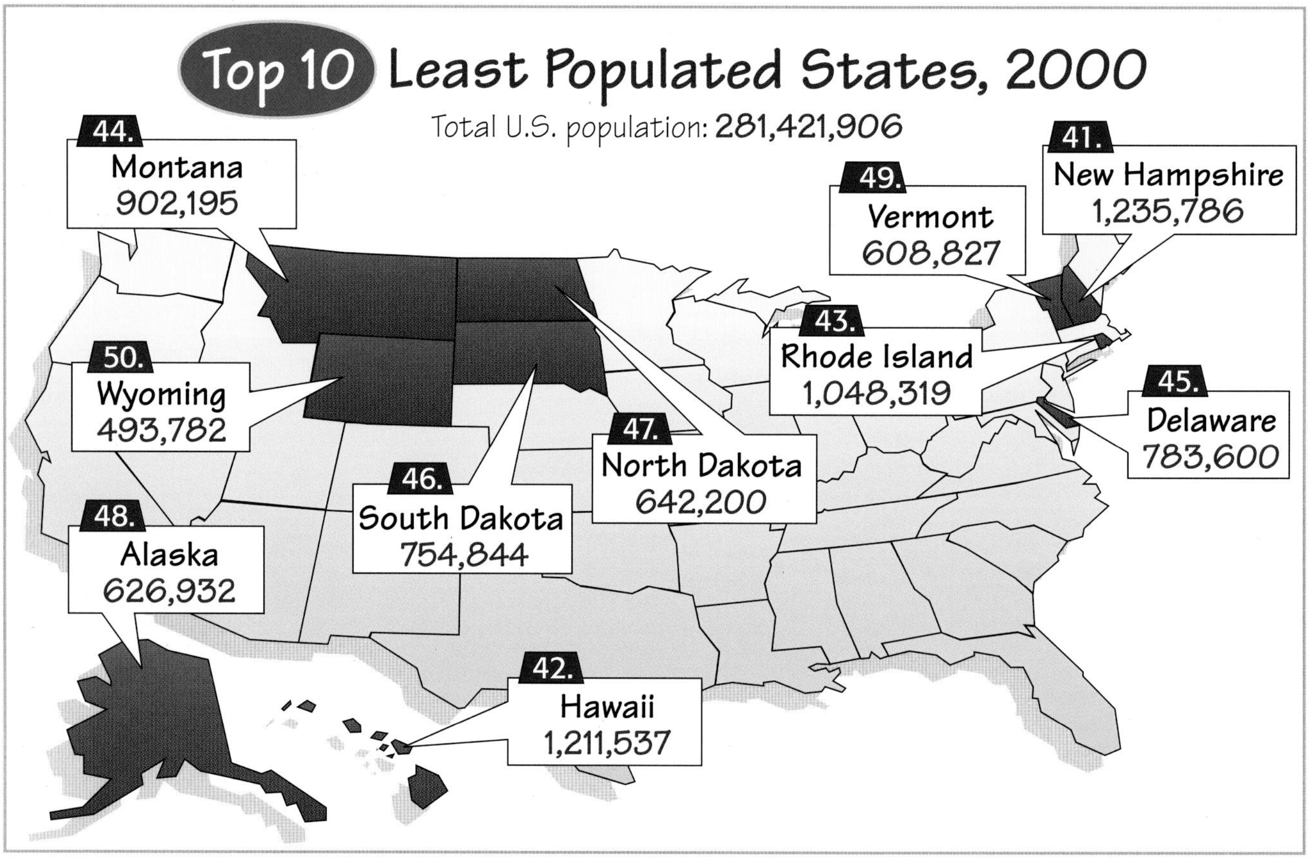

Top 10 Least Populated States, 2000

Total U.S. population: 281,421,906

41. New Hampshire 1,235,786
42. Hawaii 1,211,537
43. Rhode Island 1,048,319
44. Montana 902,195
45. Delaware 783,600
46. South Dakota 754,844
47. North Dakota 642,200
48. Alaska 626,932
49. Vermont 608,827
50. Wyoming 493,782

SOURCE: Based on data from Bureau of the Census, U.S. Department of Commerce

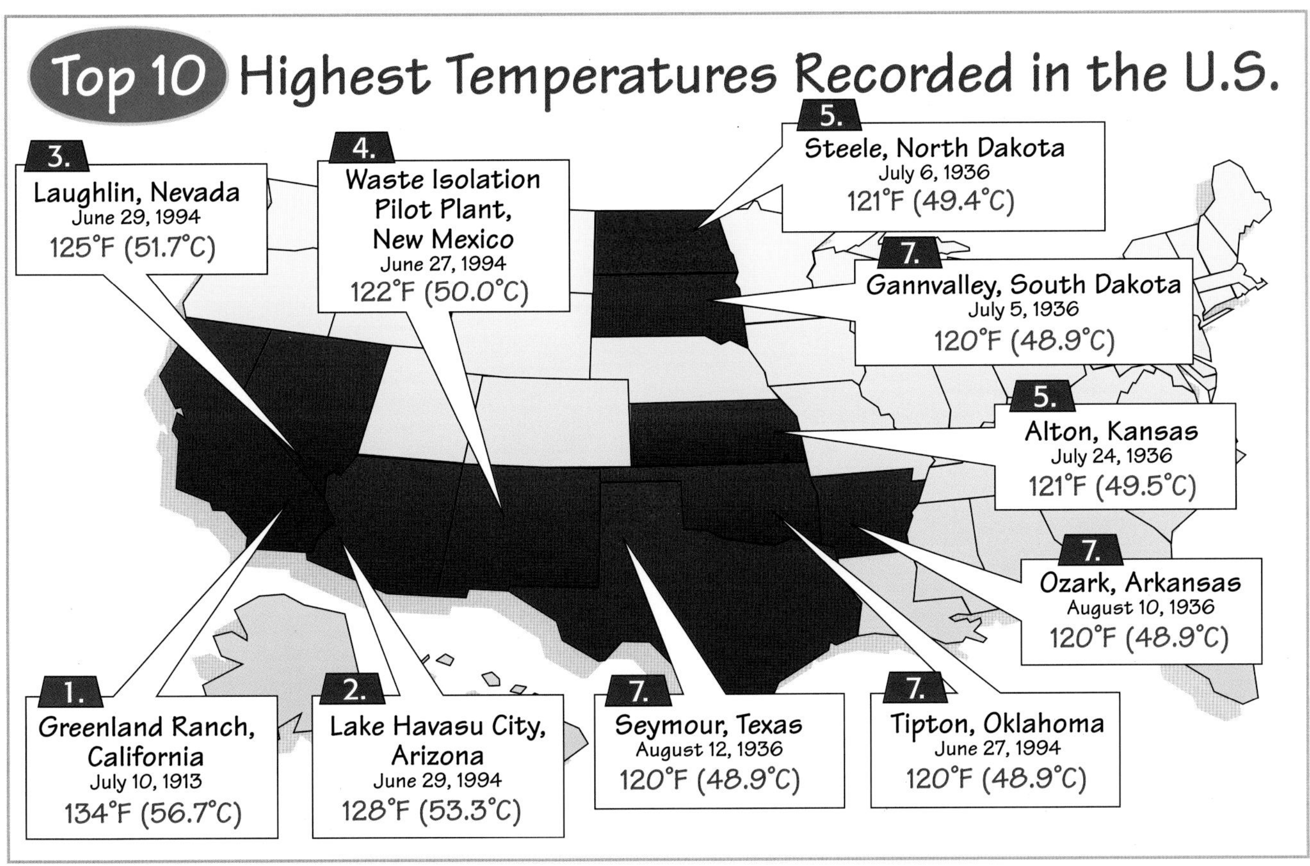

SOURCE: National Climatic Data Center

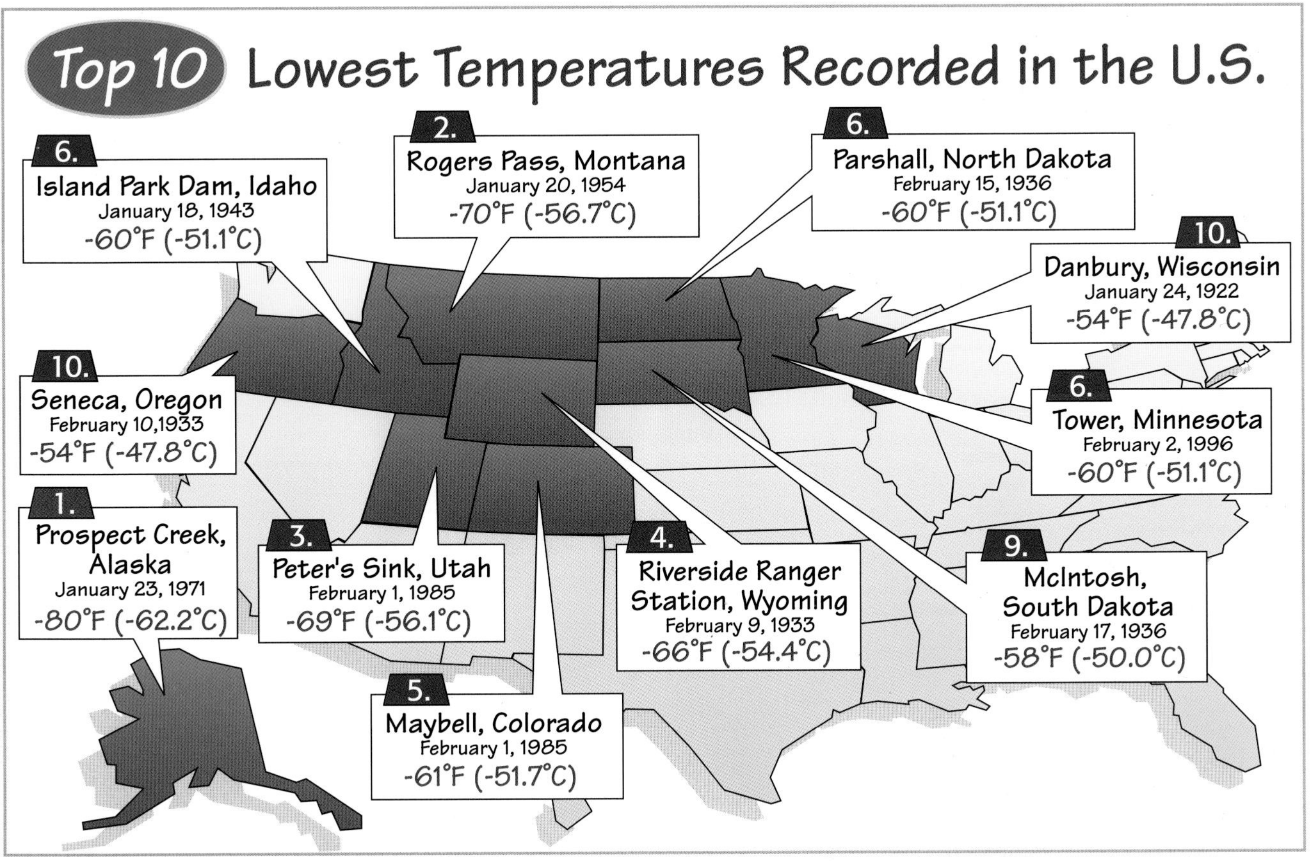

SOURCE: National Climatic Data Center

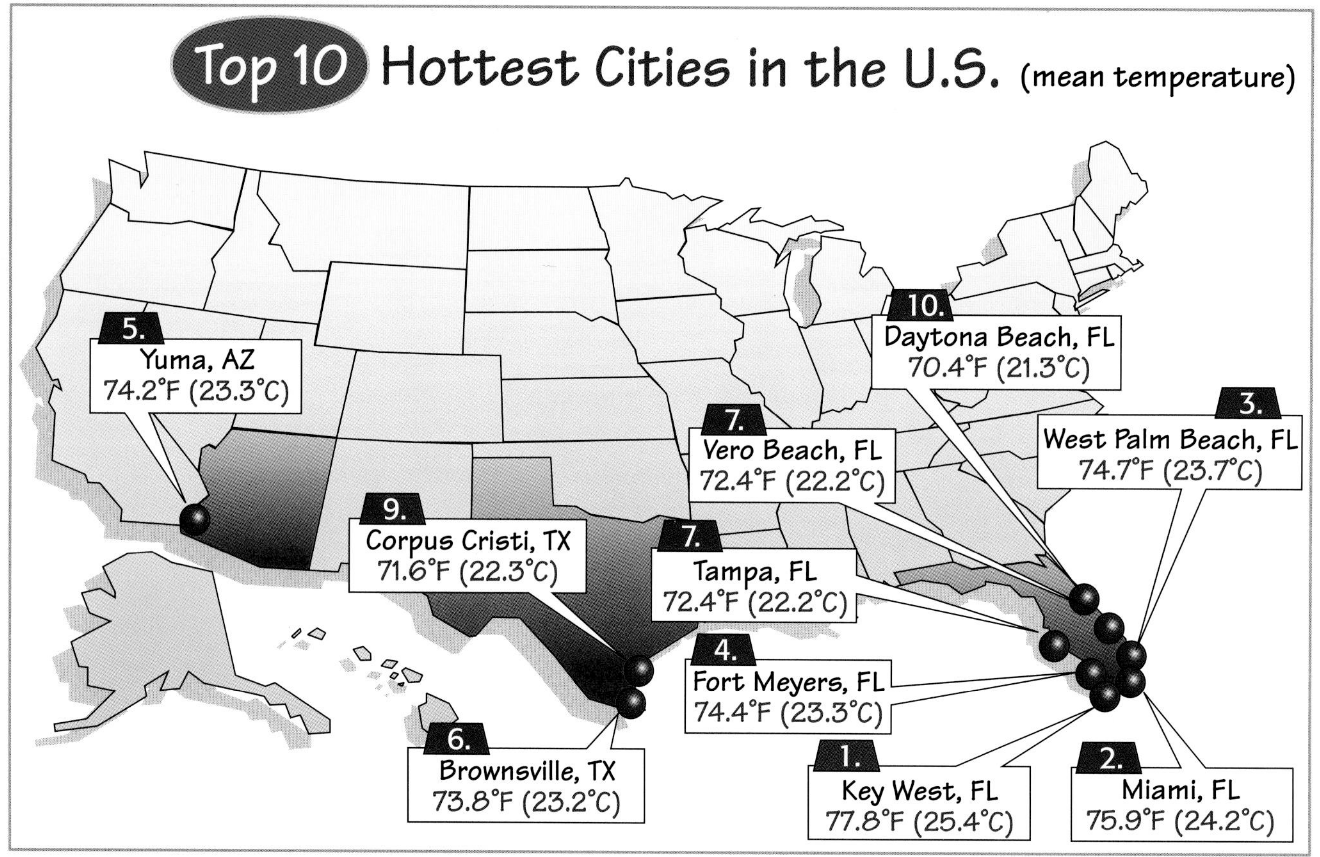

SOURCE: National Climatic Data Center

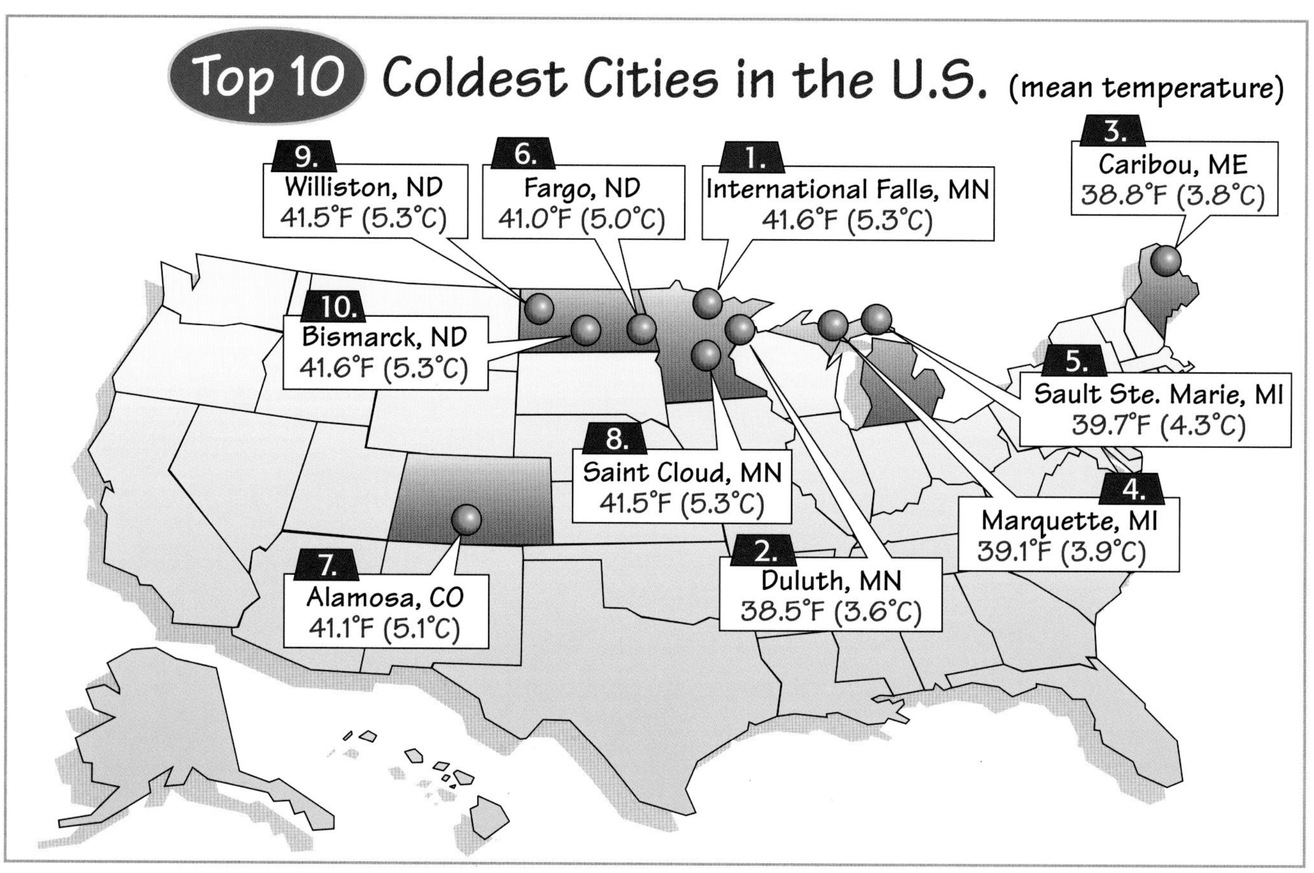

SOURCE: National Climatic Data Center

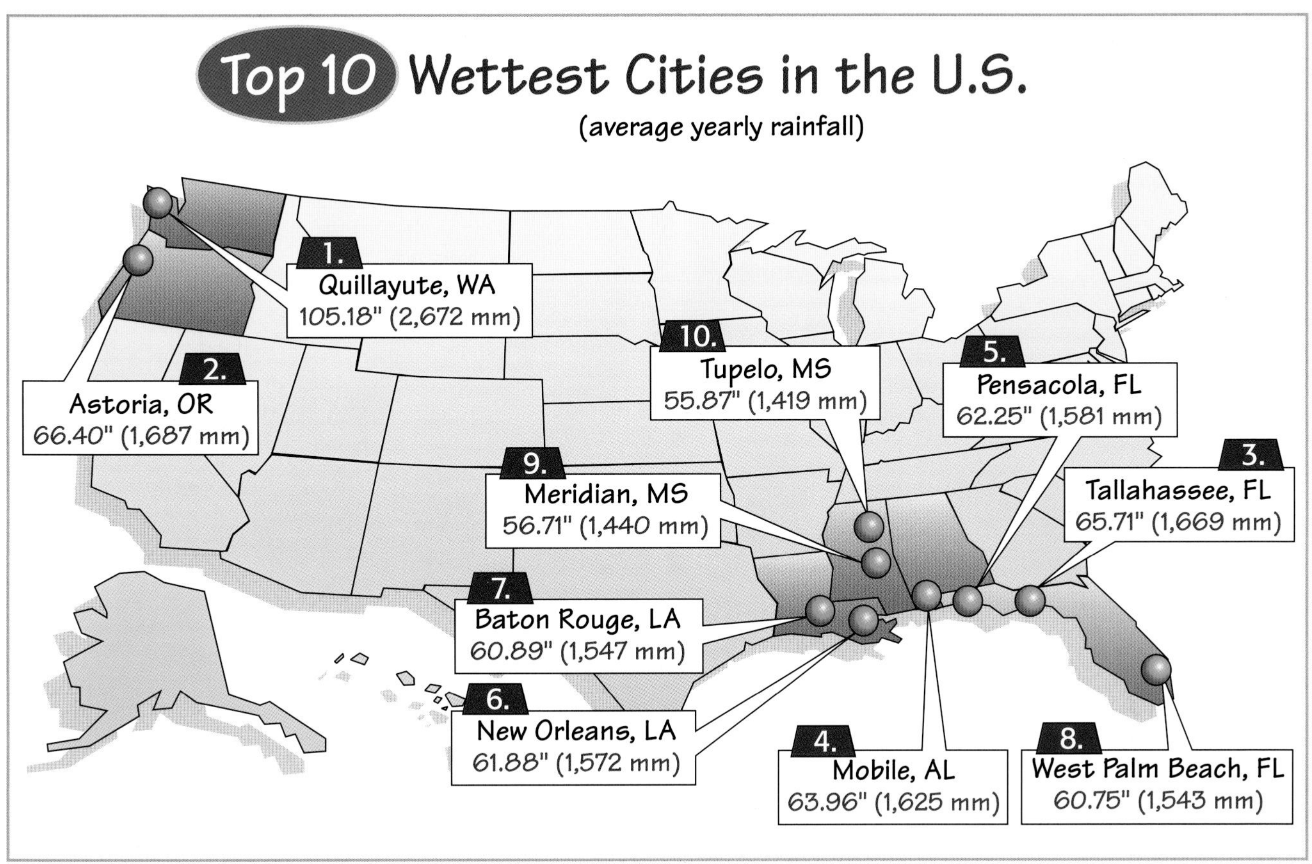

SOURCE: National Climatic Data Center

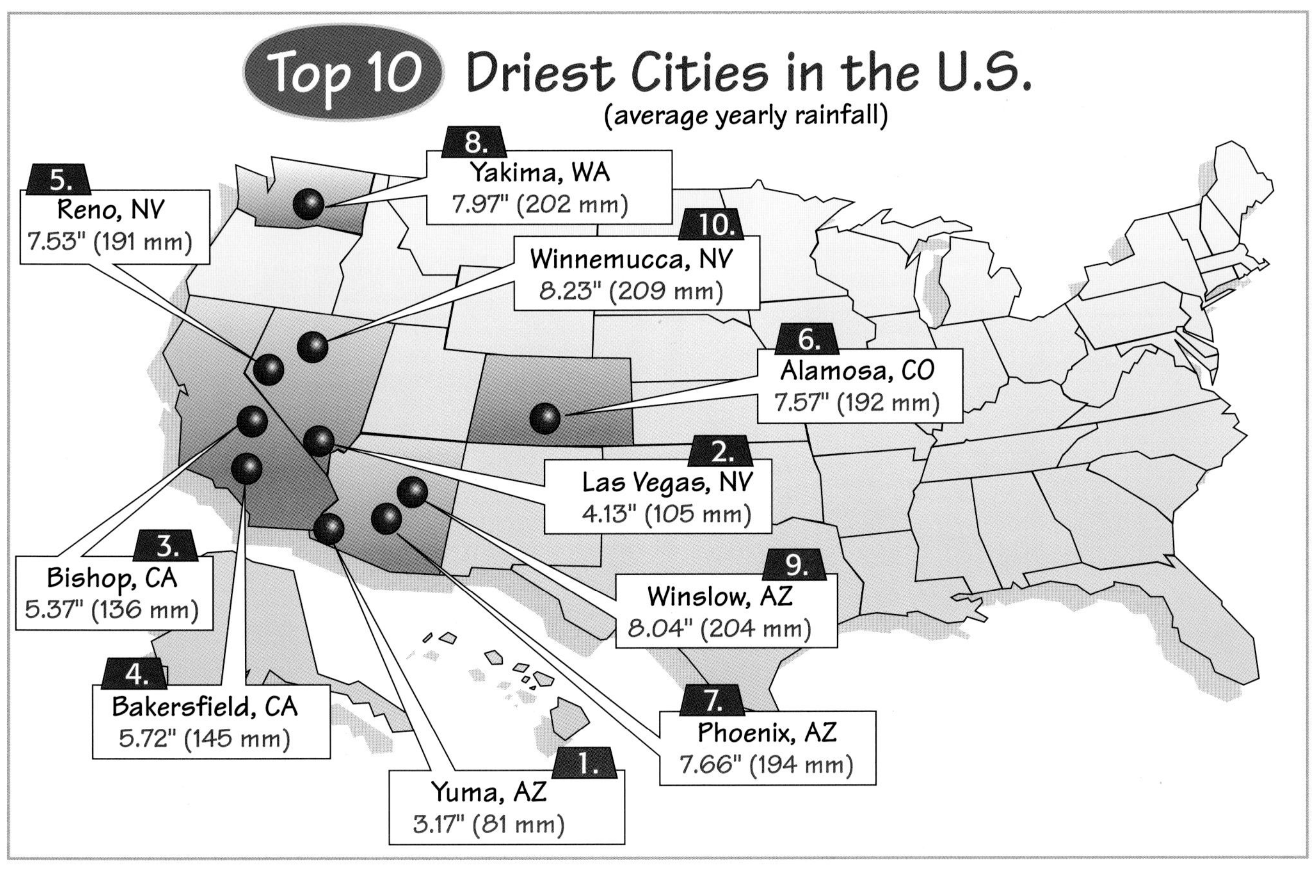

SOURCE: National Climatic Data Center

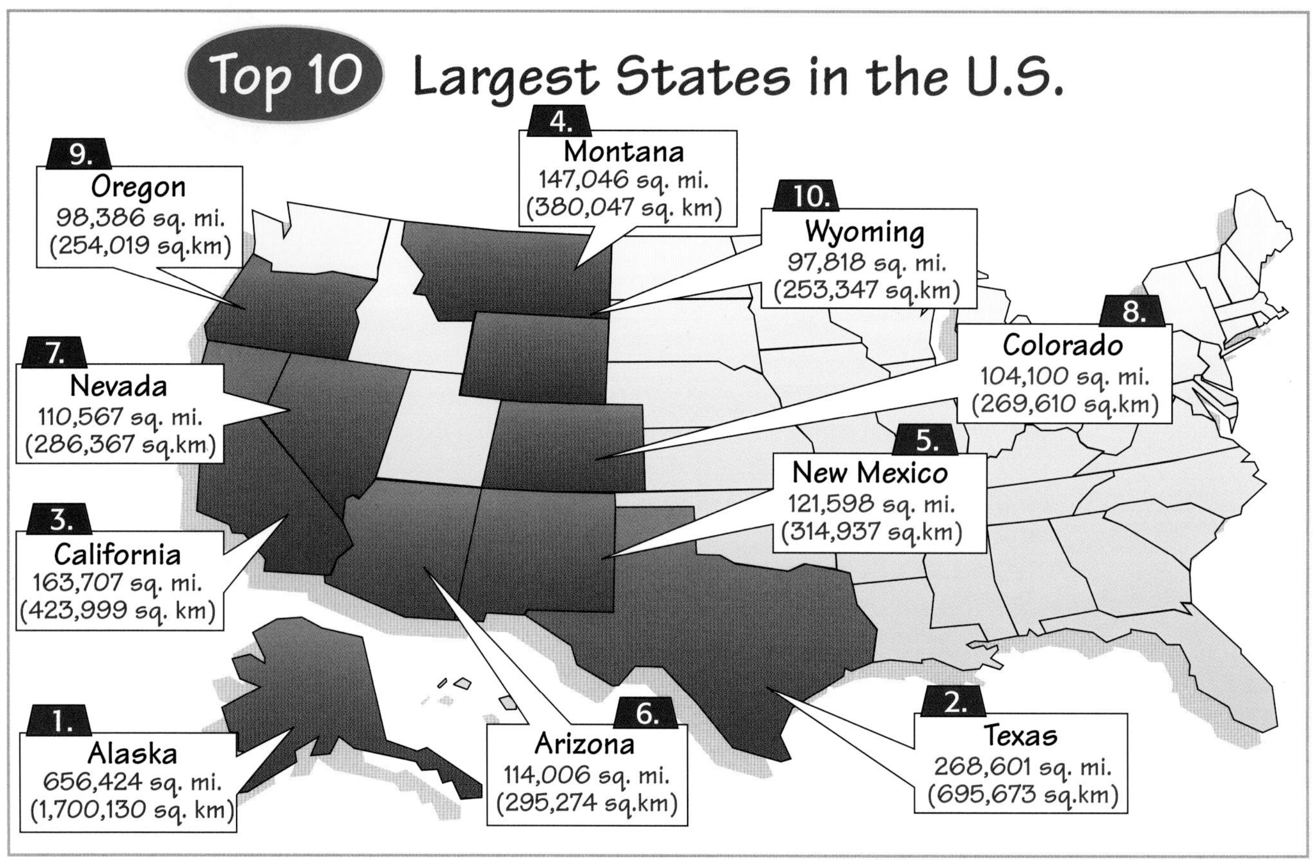

SOURCE: Based on data from Bureau of the Census, U.S. Department of Commerce

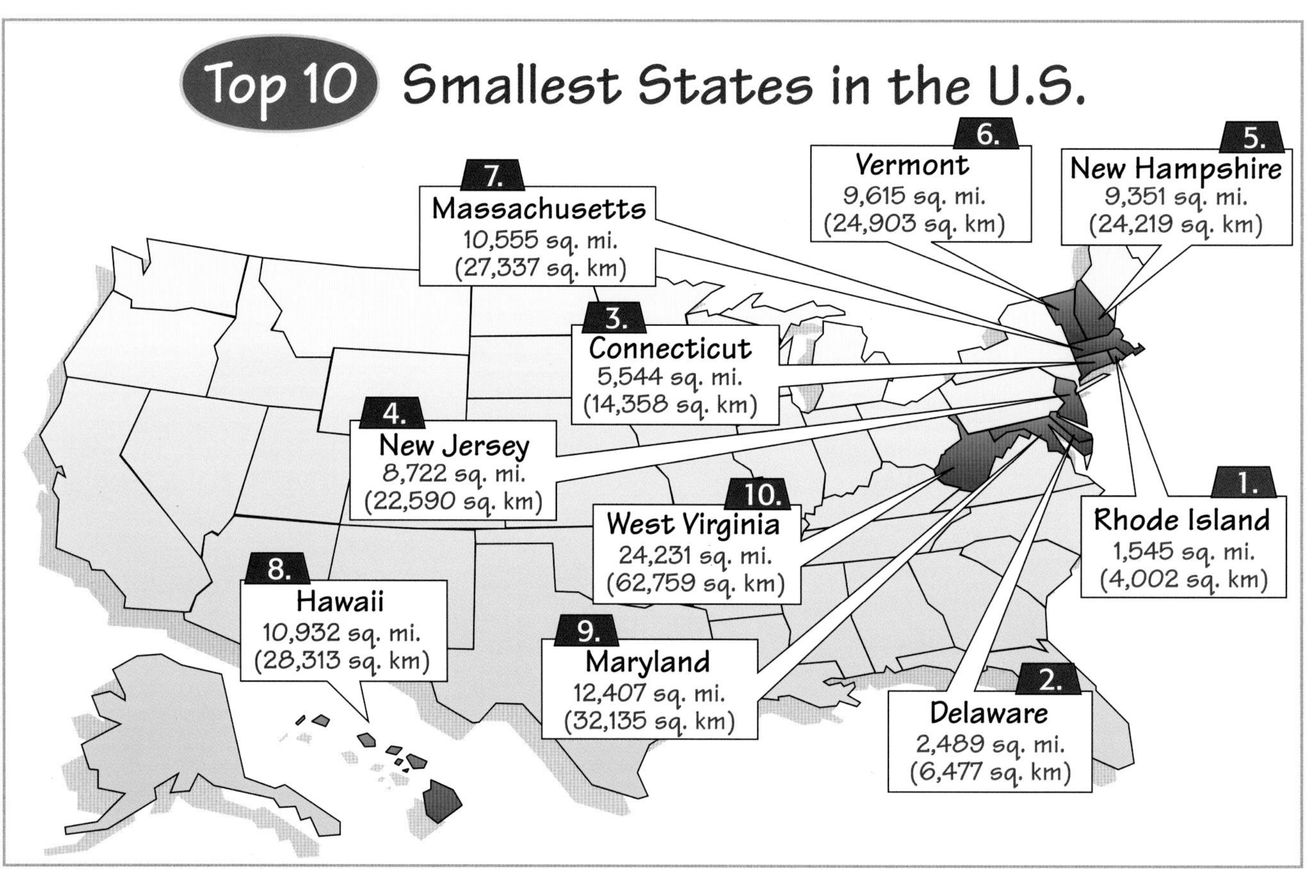

SOURCE: Based on data from Bureau of the Census, U.S. Department of Commerce

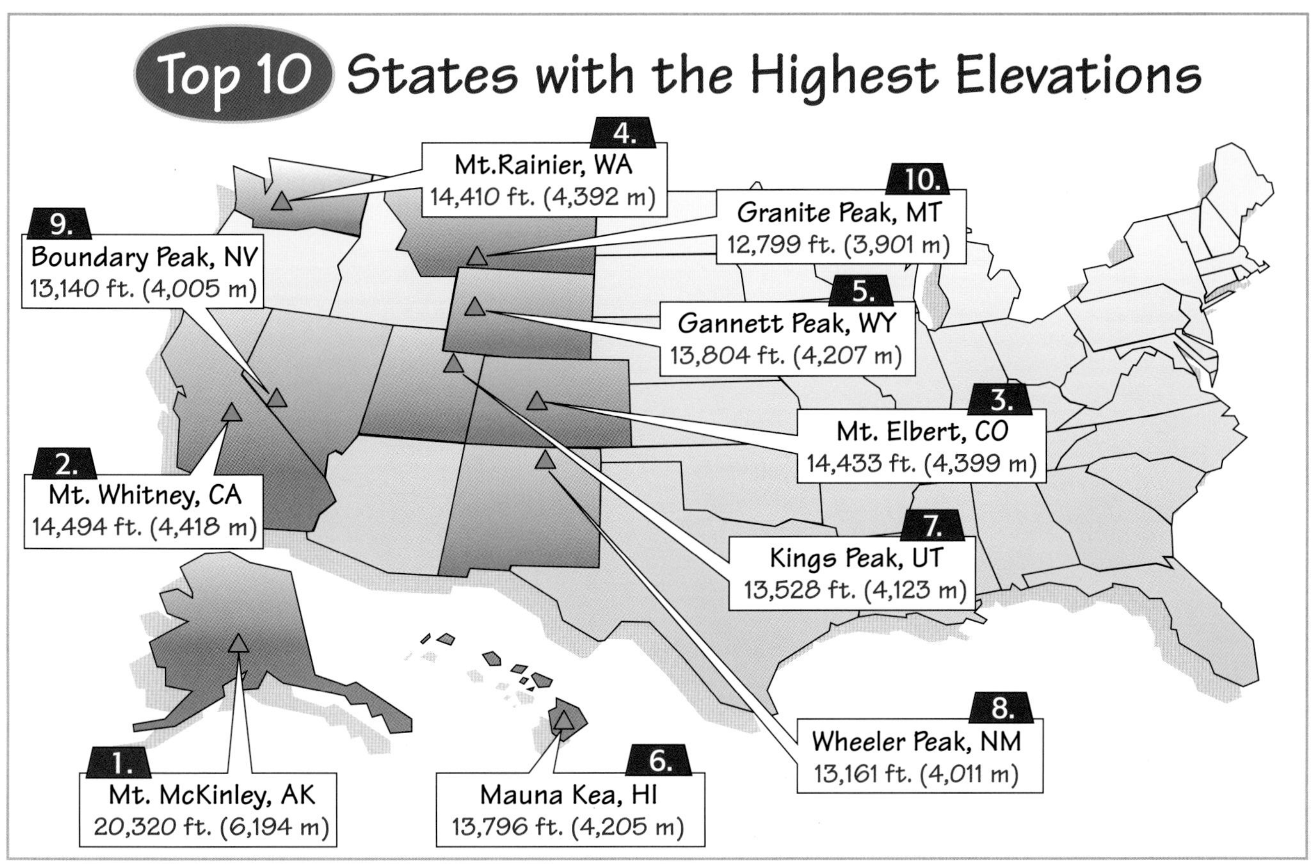

SOURCE: U.S. Geological Survey

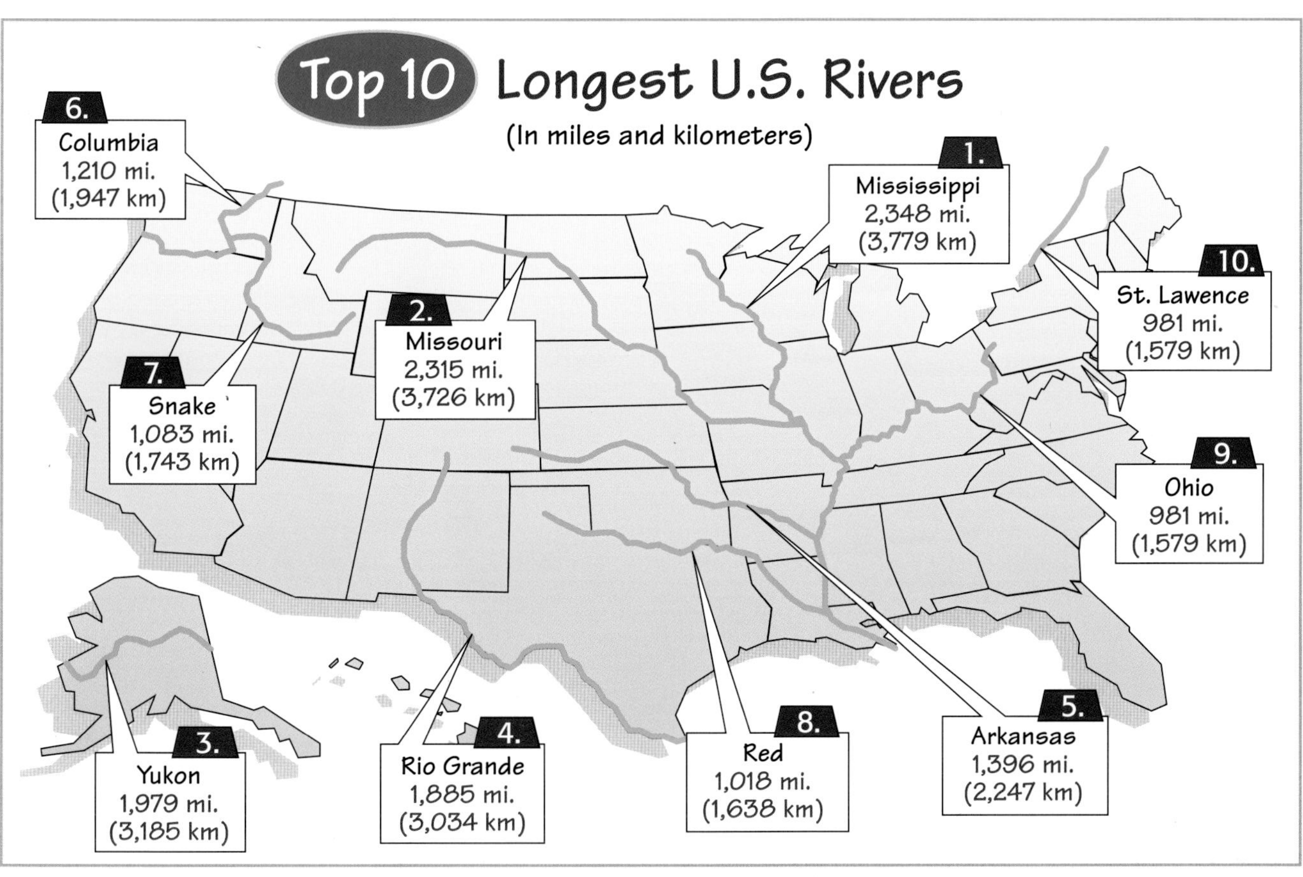

SOURCE: National Oceanic and Atmospheric Administration, *Distances Between United States Ports,* 1987

Top 10 Busiest U.S. Airports

(Number of passengers in 2000)

10.
San Francisco International, CA
16,664,000
9.
Minneapolis-St. Paul International, MN
16,710,000
7.
Wayne County, Detroit,MI
16,930,000
8.
McCarran International, Las Vegas, NV
16,739,000
2.
O'Hare International, Chicago,IL
30,888,000
5.
Denver International, CO
17,643,000
4.
Los Angeles International, CA
25,110,000
6.
Phoenix Sky Harbor International, AZ
17,239,000
3.
Dallas/Fort Worth International, TX
27,841,000
1.
Hartsfield International, Atlanta, GA
38,256,000

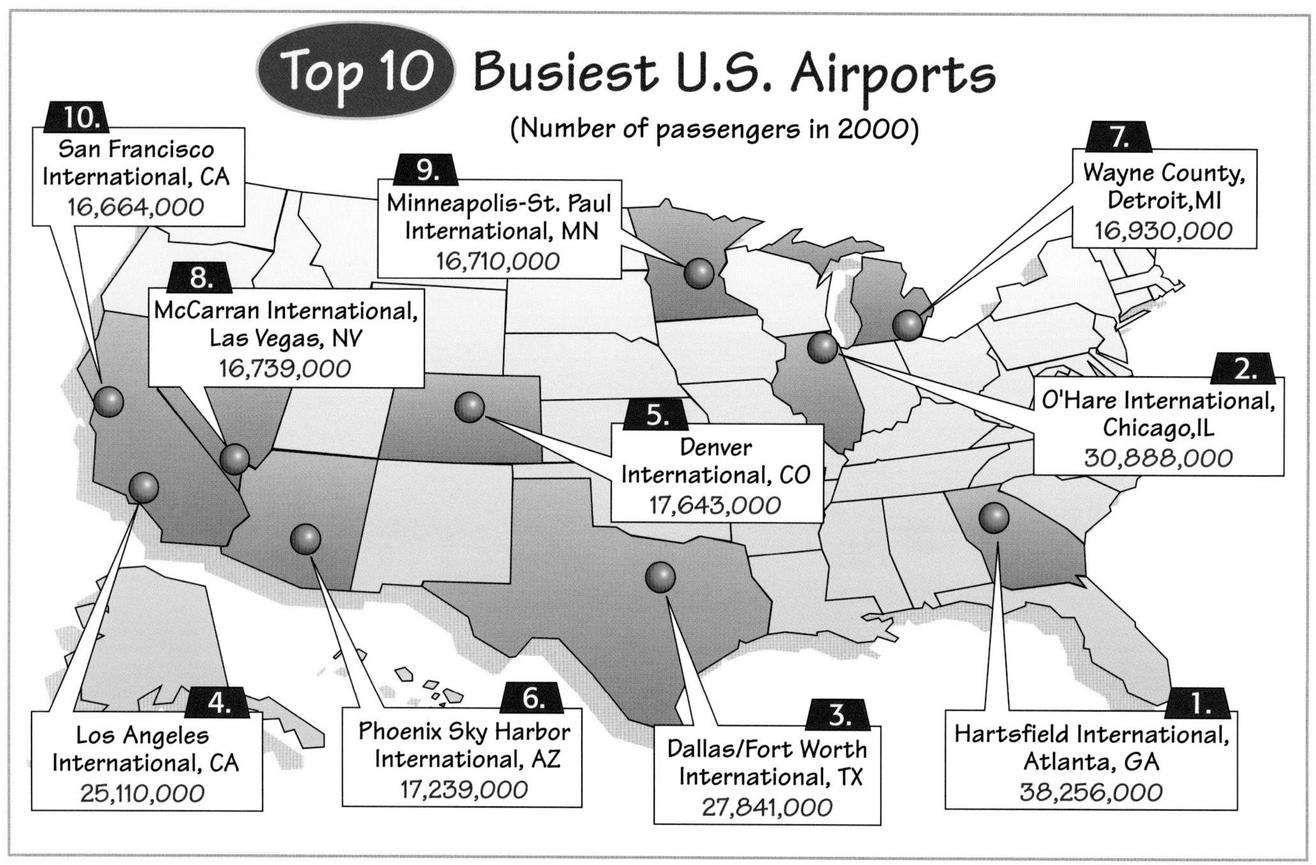

SOURCE: U.S. Bureau of Transportation Statistics

Top 10 States in Land for Recreation and Conservation

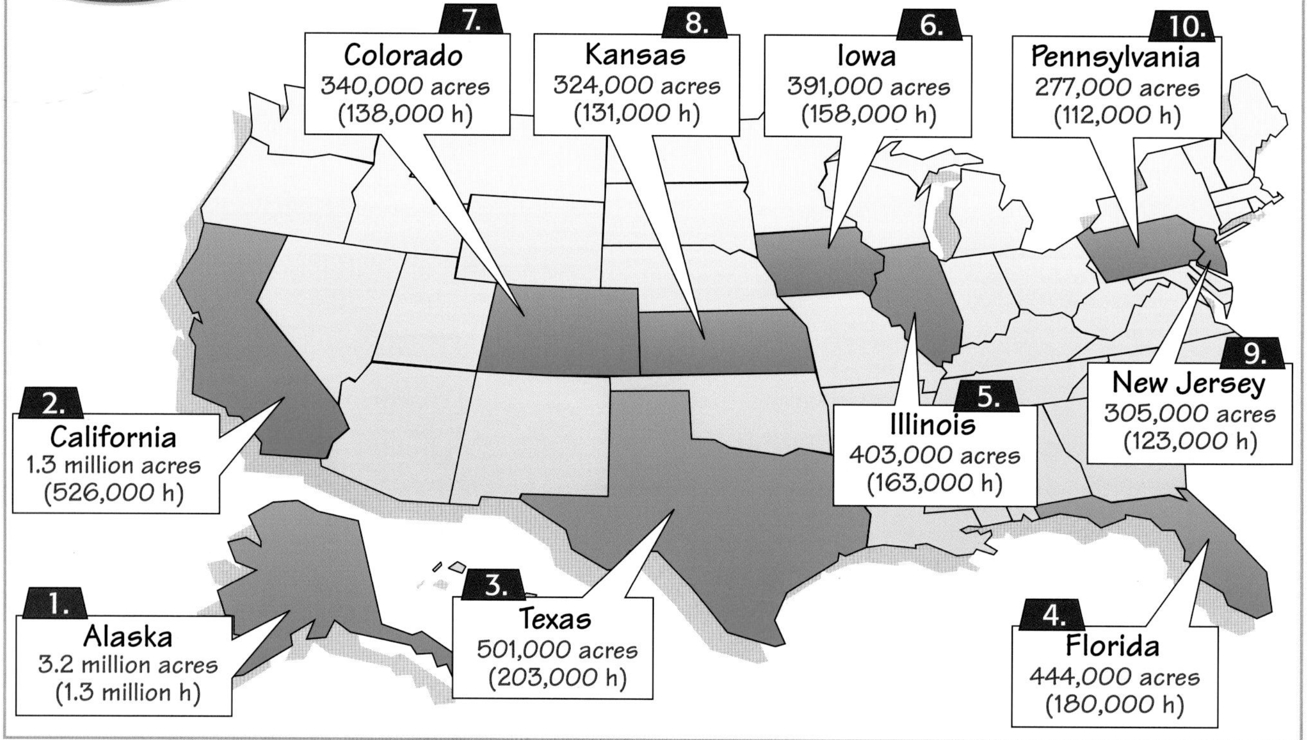

7.
Colorado
340,000 acres
(138,000 h)
8.
Kansas
324,000 acres
(131,000 h)
6.
Iowa
391,000 acres
(158,000 h)
10.
Pennsylvania
277,000 acres
(112,000 h)
2.
California
1.3 million acres
(526,000 h)
5.
Illinois
403,000 acres
(163,000 h)
9.
New Jersey
305,000 acres
(123,000 h)
1.
Alaska
3.2 million acres
(1.3 million h)
3.
Texas
501,000 acres
(203,000 h)
4.
Florida
444,000 acres
(180,000 h)

SOURCE: National Association of State Park Directors

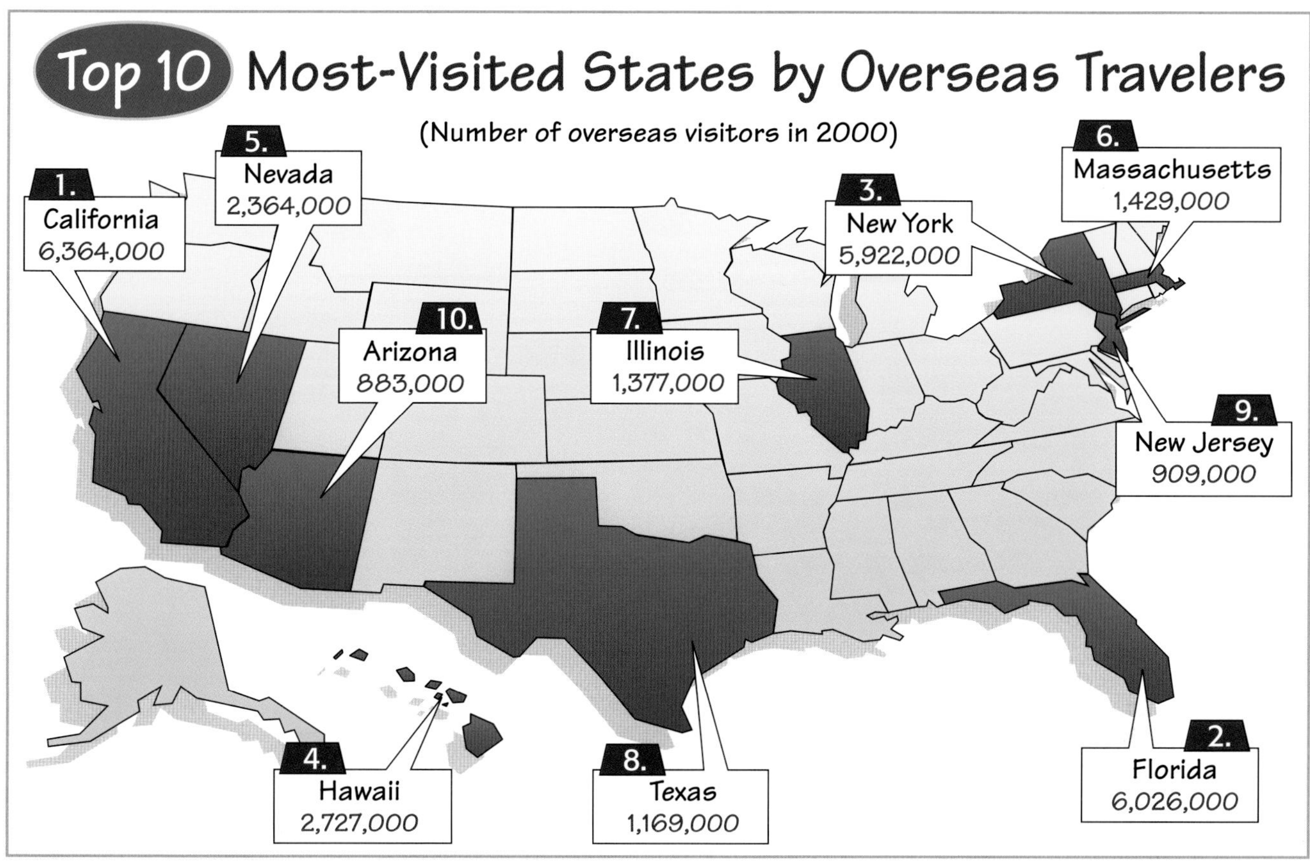

SOURCE: U.S. Department of Commerce

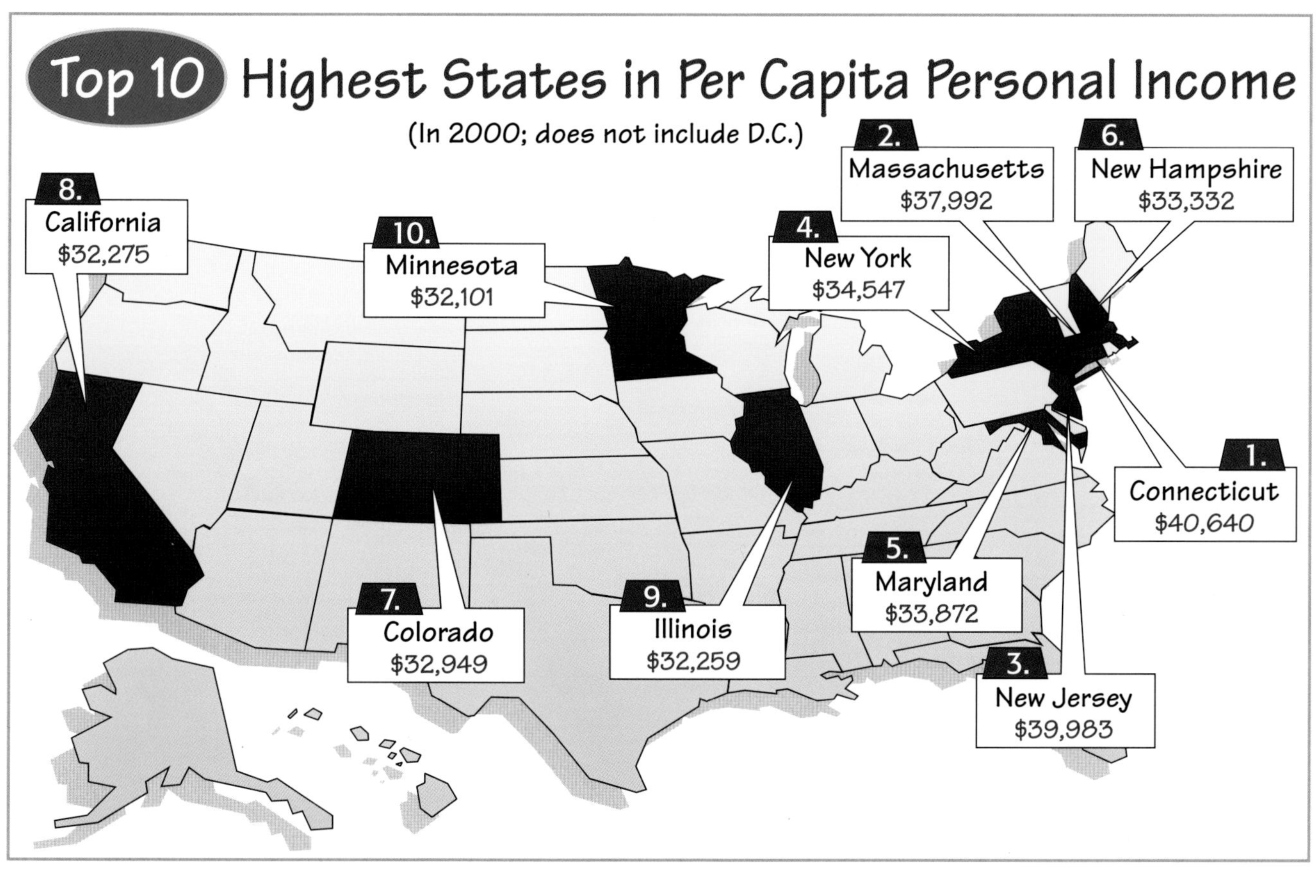

SOURCE: U.S. Bureau of Economic Analysis

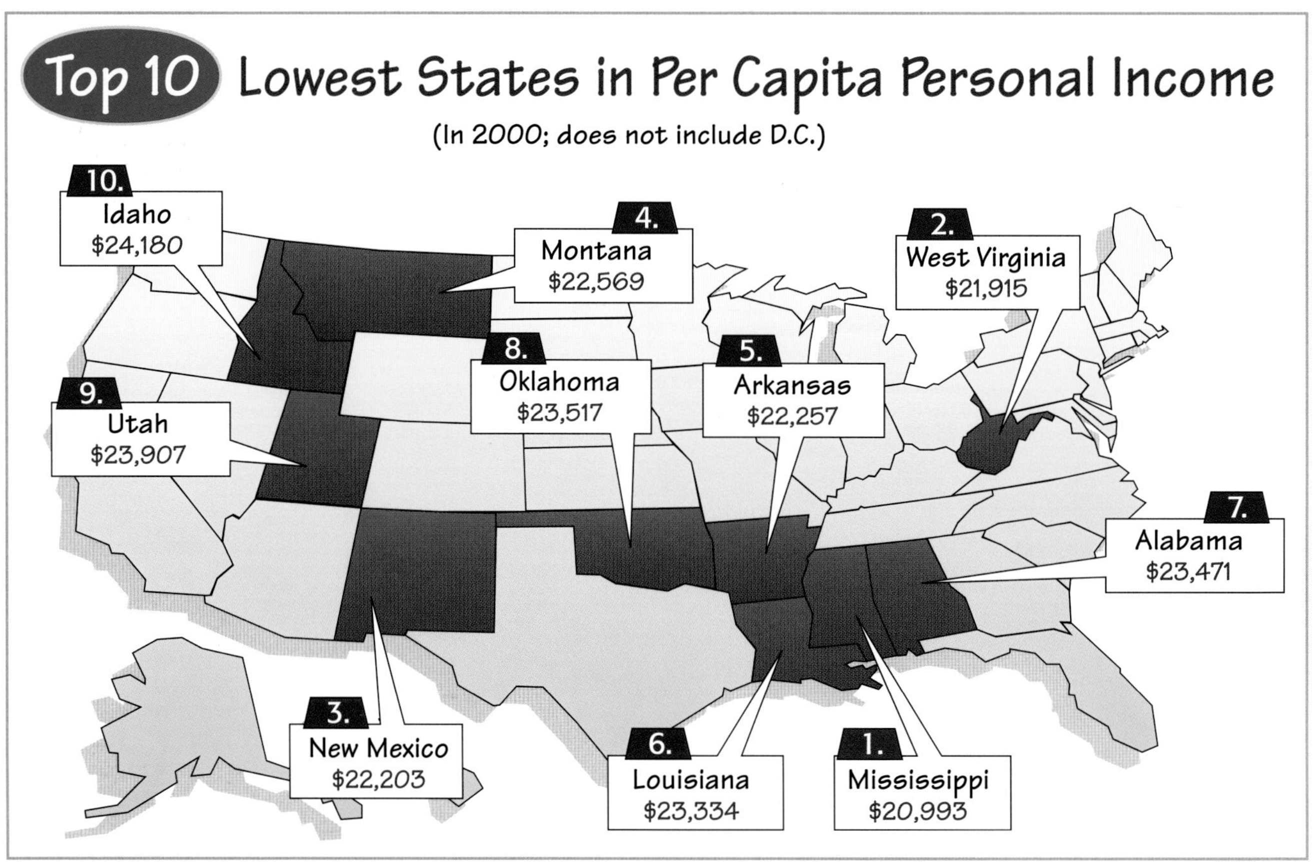

SOURCE: U.S. Bureau of Economic Analysis

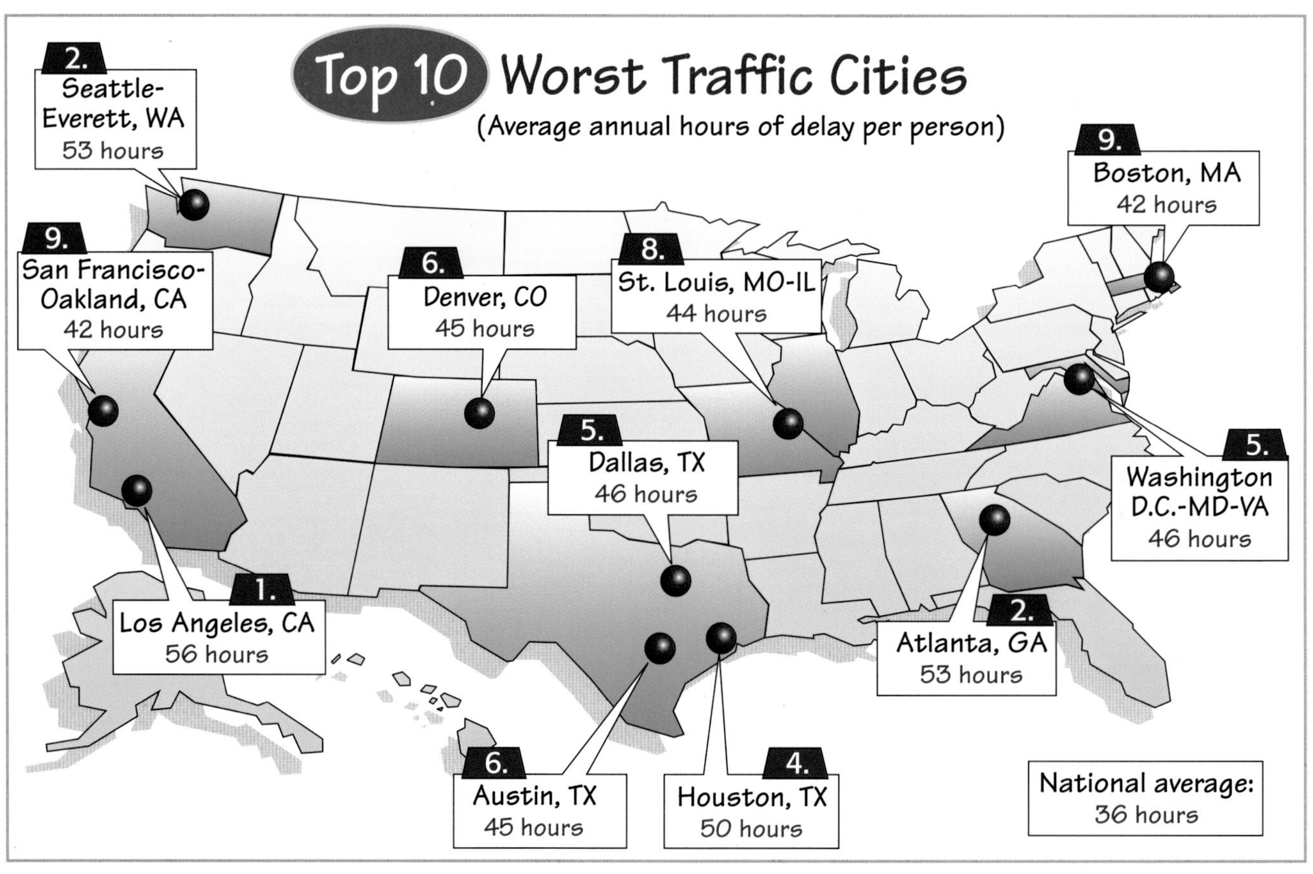

SOURCE: Texas Transportation Institute, 2001

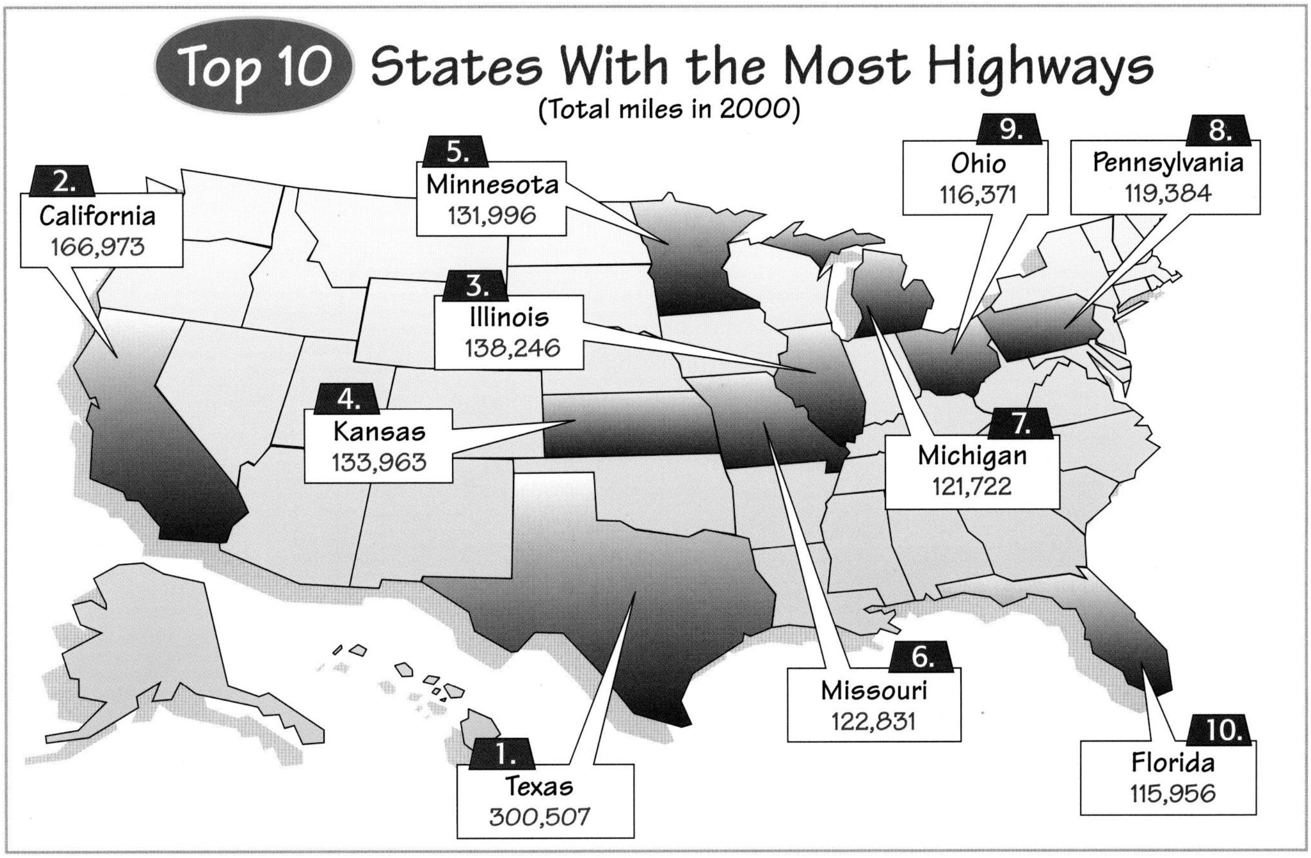

Top 10 States With the Most Highways
(Total miles in 2000)

1. Texas 300,507
2. California 166,973
3. Illinois 138,246
4. Kansas 133,963
5. Minnesota 131,996
6. Missouri 122,831
7. Michigan 121,722
8. Pennsylvania 119,384
9. Ohio 116,371
10. Florida 115,956

SOURCE: U.S. Federal Highway Administration, *Highway Statistics,* annual

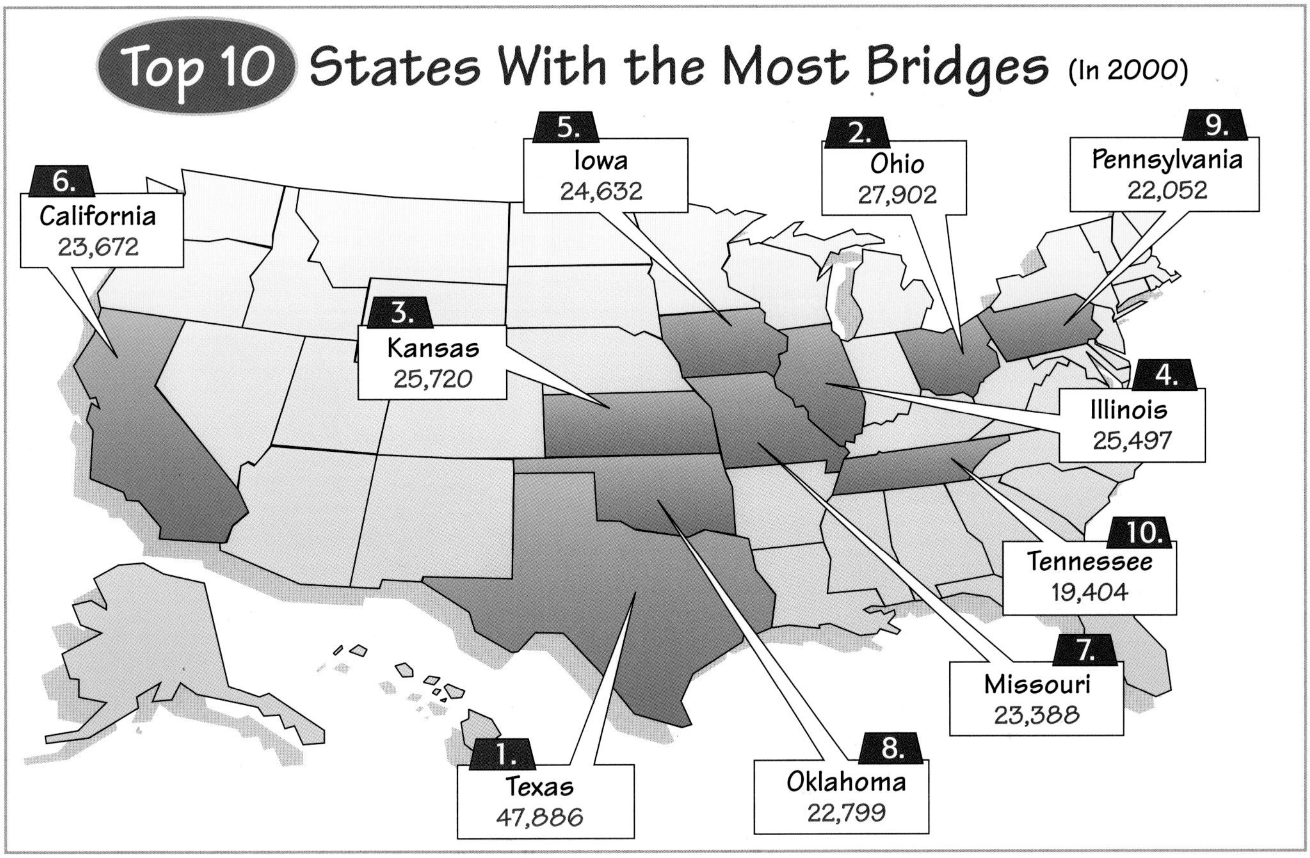

Top 10 States With the Most Bridges (In 2000)

1. Texas 47,886
2. Ohio 27,902
3. Kansas 25,720
4. Illinois 25,497
5. Iowa 24,632
6. California 23,672
7. Missouri 23,388
8. Oklahoma 22,799
9. Pennsylvania 22,052
10. Tennessee 19,404

SOURCE: U.S. Federal Highway Administration, Office of Technology

Alabama

We dare defend our rights.

Land area rank *Largest state (1)* 30 *smallest state (52)*

Population rank *Most people (1)* 23 *fewest people (52)*

At a Glance

Name: *Alabama* comes from the word *Alibamu*, the name of a Native American tribe that lived in the area. The name may mean "to clear the vegetation."

Nicknames: Heart of Dixie, Camellia State, Yellowhammer State

Capital: Montgomery

Size: 52,237 sq. mi.

Population: 4,447,100

Statehood: Alabama became the 22nd state on December 14, 1819.

Electoral votes: 9 (2004)

U.S. Representatives: 7 (until 2003)

State tree: Southern longleaf pine

State flower: camellia

State saltwater fish: fighting tarpon

Highest point: Cheaha Mountain, 2,407 ft.

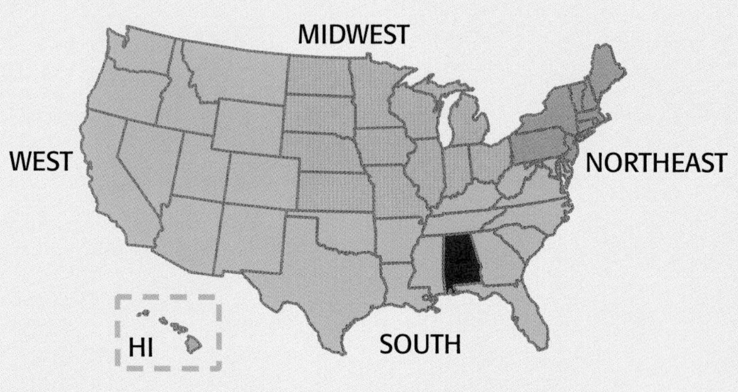

The Place

Alabama is located in the heart of the Deep South. The Appalachian Mountains end in the northern part of the state, which is covered by forested hills. In the south, these hills become smaller and give way to rich grasslands. Alabama's coast on the Gulf of Mexico has both sandy beaches and bayous, which are swampy streams.

Although the state's warm climate is ideal for farming, Alabama was one of the first southern states to become industrialized.

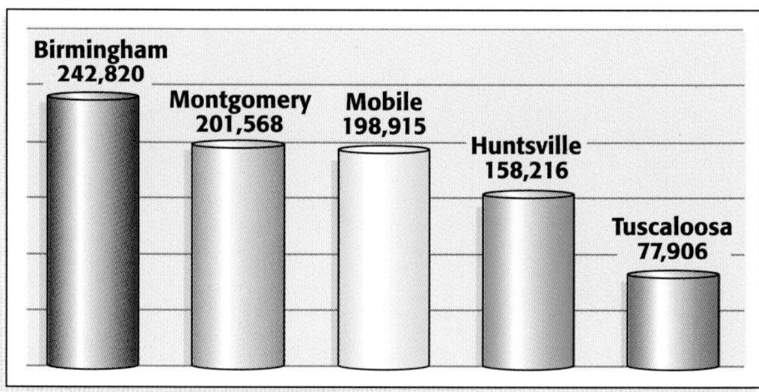

Major Cities

The Mizell Mansion, constructed in Ozark, Alabama, in 1912, was built in the same architectural style as many pre–Civil War plantation homes.

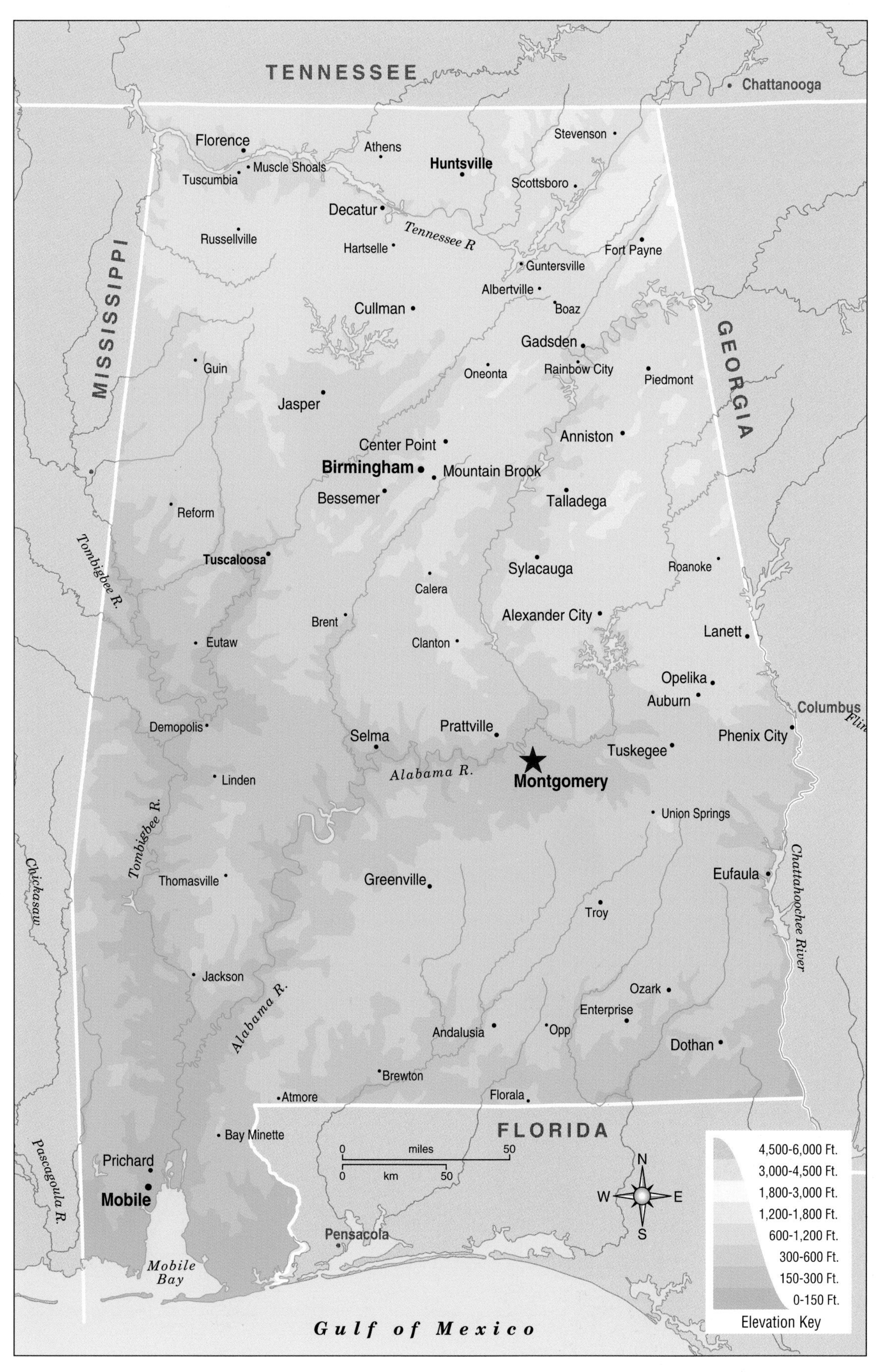
TENNESSEE
Chattanooga
MISSISSIPPI
GEORGIA
FLORIDA
Florence
Muscle Shoals
Tuscumbia
Athens
Huntsville
Stevenson
Scottsboro
Decatur
Tennessee R
Russellville
Hartselle
Fort Payne
Guntersville
Albertville
Boaz
Cullman
Gadsden
Guin
Oneonta
Rainbow City
Piedmont
Jasper
Center Point
Anniston
Birmingham
Mountain Brook
Bessemer
Talladega
Reform
Tombigbee R.
Tuscaloosa
Sylacauga
Roanoke
Calera
Brent
Alexander City
Eutaw
Clanton
Lanett
Opelika
Auburn
Columbus
Demopolis
Selma
Prattville
Phenix City
Tuskegee
Linden
Alabama R.
Montgomery
Union Springs
Tombigbee R.
Chickasaw
Thomasville
Greenville
Eufaula
Chattahoochee River
Troy
Jackson
Alabama R.
Ozark
Enterprise
Andalusia
Opp
Dothan
Brewton
Atmore
Florala
Bay Minette
Pascagoula R.
Prichard
Mobile
Mobile Bay
Pensacola
Gulf of Mexico
miles
0
50
0
km
50
N
W
E
S
4,500-6,000 Ft.
3,000-4,500 Ft.
1,800-3,000 Ft.
1,200-1,800 Ft.
600-1,200 Ft.
300-600 Ft.
150-300 Ft.
0-150 Ft.
Elevation Key

Fort Morgan, on Mobile Bay, was the site of a major Union army victory in the Civil War.

The Past

Alabama's history stretches back at least 8,000 or 9,000 years, to the time when cliff-dwelling Native Americans inhabited Russell Cave, near Bridgeport.

The first Europeans to reach Alabama were the Spanish, who are believed to have sailed into Mobile Bay in 1519. Hernando de Soto explored inland portions of the state in 1540. Later, the French built the first permanent European settlement in Alabama, at Fort Louis de la Louisiane, in 1702. In 1763, the British took control of the area through the Treaty of Paris.

When the United States gained its independence in 1783, Britain was forced to give up the colony. Most of the area became part of the new American nation, except for the Mobile Bay area, which was under Spanish rule. In 1813, the United States gained control of the Mobile region, and in 1819, Alabama became the 22nd state.

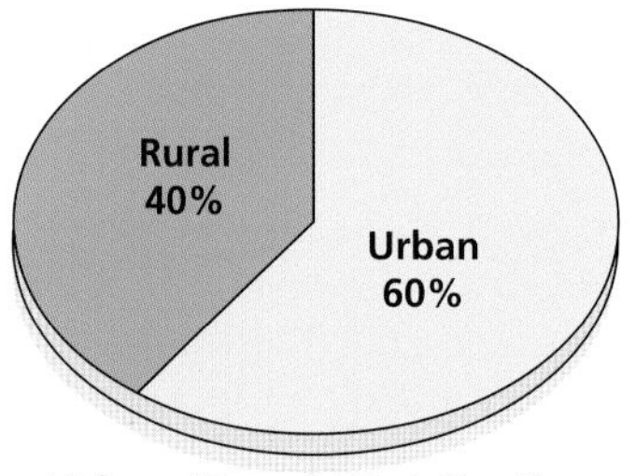

Urban/Rural Distribution

Alabama rose to importance during the American Civil War. Montgomery was declared the capital of the Confederate States of America, which was the new union formed by the Southern states. (The Confederate capital was later moved to Richmond, Virginia.)

Facts and Firsts

- ★ In 1886, Montgomery became the first U.S. city to use electric streetcars for transportation. Montgomery is known as the Pittsburgh of the South because of its steel production, factories, and railroad yards.
- ★ The Berman Museum in Anniston has a collection of about 1,500 weapons that once belonged to such famous figures as Napoléon I and Jefferson Davis, president of the Confederacy.
- ★ George Washington Carver, a scientist who did a great deal of research in Alabama, discovered more than 300 uses for peanuts and more than 100 uses for sweet potatoes.

Before and after the Civil War, Alabama's economy depended primarily on the cotton industry. In 1915, however, the boll weevil, which infests cotton plants, began to destroy crops. Farmers were forced to find other ways to make a living. Some began to raise livestock and grow crops besides cotton. Others turned to industry and built factories that manufactured a number of products, including steel.

State Smart

Alabama is home to the world's largest motorcycle museum, the Barber Vintage Motorsports Museum in Birmingham, which has a collection of more than 700 motorcycles.

Alabama again became the focus of American attention during the 1950s when Rosa Parks, an African American woman, refused to give up her bus seat to a white male passenger. Her action set off the civil rights movement, which eventually gave African Americans equal legal rights in the United States.

Many Americans in Alabama and throughout the country fought to keep the South racially divided. On September 15, 1963, a bomb exploded in the Sixteenth Street Baptist Church in Birmingham, which had been a local center for the civil rights movement in Alabama. The bomb killed four young girls. In 1965, Martin

Below: *In 1965, Martin Luther King Jr. led a march in Alabama to support civil rights.*
Above right: *Barber Vintage Motorsports Museum*

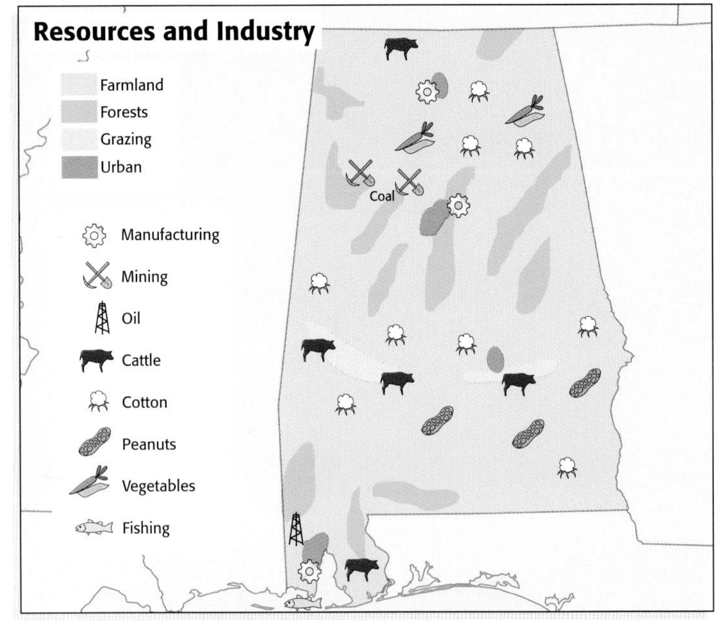

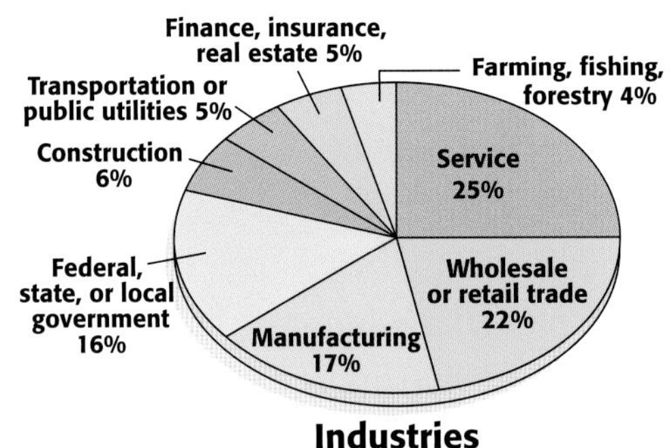

Luther King Jr., the most famous American civil rights leader, led a march from Selma to Montgomery to protest segregation (legal divisions between African Americans and whites).

The Present

Service is the largest industry in Alabama. Farming is still important, however, and Alabama continues to grow crops, including cotton and peanuts. Manufacturing also contributes to the state's economy.

Innovative rockets and space technology are produced in Huntsville, which is known as Rocket City, USA. The city is home to the Redstone Arsenal and the George C. Marshall Space Flight Center, where scientists built the *Saturn 5* rocket that took the first astronauts to the moon.

Many people visit Alabama to experience its history and enjoy its sandy beaches along the coast. Every year, visitors interested in history come to see the former Confederate capital and tour the area's many pre–Civil War homes.

Other places of historic interest include Helen Keller's childhood home and Russell

Below left: *This replica of the space shuttle is located at the U.S. Space and Rocket Center in Huntsville.*
Below right: *A youngster plays in the sand of Orange Beach on the Gulf of Mexico.*

Born in Alabama

★ **Hank Aaron**, baseball player

★ **Nat "King" Cole**, musician/entertainer

★ **W.C. (William Christopher) Handy**, blues songwriter

★ **Mae Jemison**, astronaut

★ **Helen Keller**, author/educator

★ **Coretta Scott King**, civil rights activist

★ **Harper Lee**, author

★ **Jesse Owens**, track star

★ **Rosa Parks**, civil rights activist

★ **Condoleeza Rice**, professor, diplomat, national security adviser

Above: *Helen Keller;* below: *Mae Jemison*

Cave. There are also picturesque state parks throughout Alabama. In northern areas, reservoirs attract thousands of fishing enthusiasts each year. Because of Alabama's French past, its annual Mardi Gras celebration is also one of the state's most interesting and popular events.

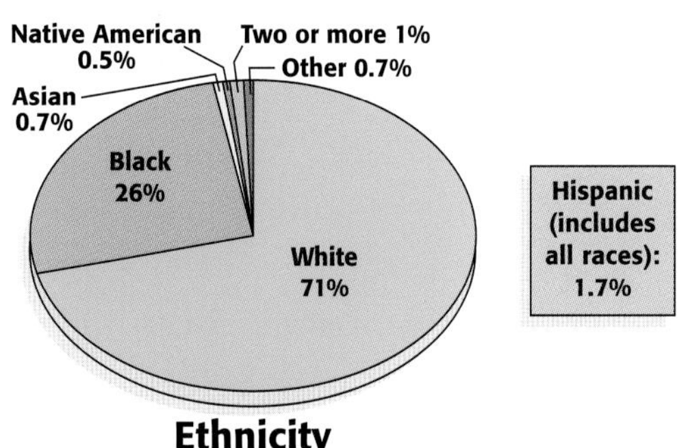

Ethnicity

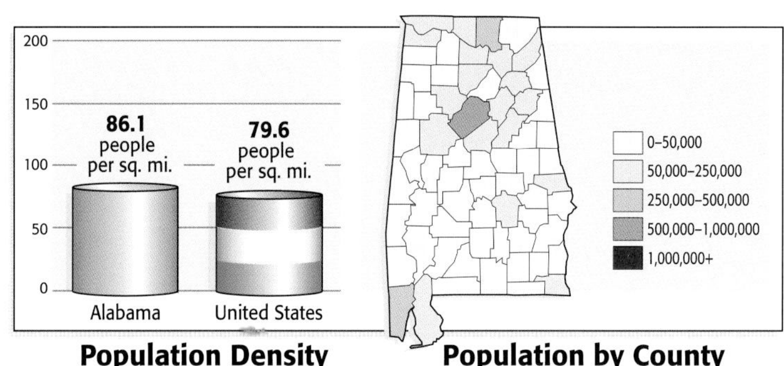

Population Density **Population by County**

Ivy Green, childhood home of Helen Keller, in Tuscumbia

Alaska

North to the future.

Land area rank 1
Largest state (1) — *smallest state (52)*

Population rank 48
Most people (1) — *fewest people (52)*

At a Glance

Name: *Alaska* comes from an Aleut word meaning "great land."
Nicknames: Last Frontier, Land of the Midnight Sun
Capital: Juneau
Size: 615,230 sq. mi.
Population: 626,932
Statehood: Alaska became the 49th state on January 3, 1959.
Electoral votes: 3 (2004)
U.S. Representatives: 1 (until 2003)
State tree: Sitka spruce
State flower: forget-me-not
State marine mammal: bowhead whale
Highest point: Mount McKinley, 20,320 ft.

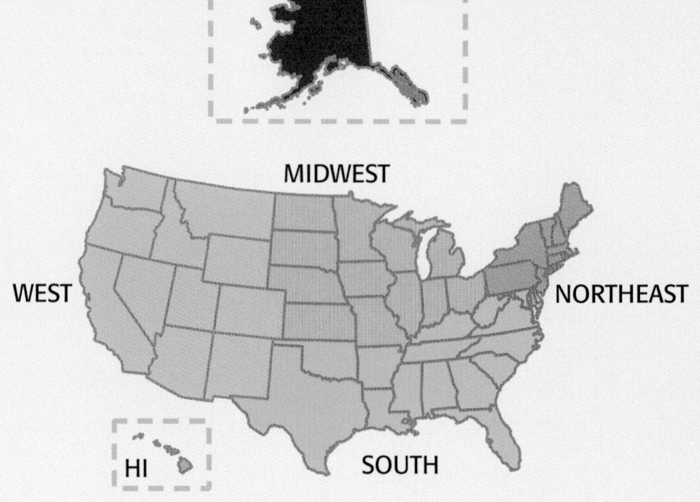

The Place

Alaska is the country's largest state. It lies far north of the continental United States and west of Canada. Alaska's three main natural regions are the Coast Ranges, the Interior, and the Arctic.

The Coast Ranges region runs along Alaska's Pacific coast and includes high mountains and many islands. The Interior region is relatively low. The Arctic region contains continuous permafrost, or frozen ground, as well as large deposits of coal, petroleum (oil), and natural gas. During the summer, this area serves as calving grounds for hundreds of thousands of caribou and as nesting grounds for many birds.

Temperatures in Alaska vary greatly according to area. Temperatures remain moderate near the coast, while the interior experiences large differences between winter and summer temperatures. Arctic Alaska is cool year-round and receives very little rain or snow.

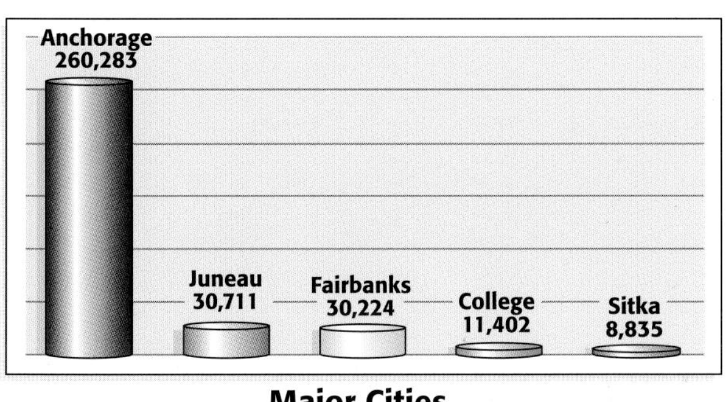

Major Cities

Alaska has very few residents and has remained one of the most isolated states in the country. Alaska's petroleum and gas deposits, extensive forests, and minerals make it one of the most economically valuable states.

Opposite: *The Coast Ranges surround Anchorage, Alaska's most populous city.*

Inuit people, descendants of Alaska's first settlers, fish in kayaks around 1929.

THE PAST

The first people to reach Alaska came over a land bridge that once connected Alaska's western tip to Asia. In 1741, Vitus Bering, a Danish adventurer working for Russia, explored parts of Alaska's mainland and several islands. Alaska was still mostly unknown in 1867, when the United States bought it from Russia. In the late 1890s, however, more than 30,000 people rushed into Alaska determined to find gold.

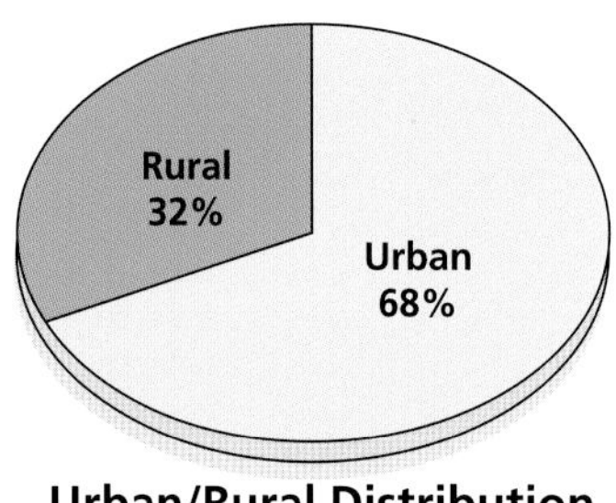

Urban/Rural Distribution

Alaska became a state on January 3, 1959. After the state's gold was

Facts and Firsts

- ★ Alaska is the largest state of the United States. It is almost one-fifth the size of all the rest of the states combined. Rhode Island, the smallest state, could fit inside Alaska 425 times.
- ★ Mainland Alaska's westernmost tip, Cape Prince of Wales, is only 53 miles from Russia.
- ★ During the summer, the sun shines for extended hours; in Anchorage, the sun does not set until approximately 10:42 P.M.
- ★ There are more than 100,000 glaciers in Alaska.
- ★ Approximately 25 percent of all oil produced in the United States comes from Alaska.
- ★ Alaska's capital, Juneau, is the sole capital city in the United States accessible only by boat or plane.
- ★ The United States paid $7.2 million for Alaska in 1867, which is two cents per acre.
- ★ The Aleutian islands of Agattu, Attu, and Kiska were the only parts of North America occupied by Japanese troops during World War II.

State Smart

Alaska, along with its islands, has the longest shoreline of any state. Alaska boasts a total of 33,904 miles of coastline.

depleted, interest in Alaska declined until 1968, when a large oil and gas deposit was discovered near Prudhoe Bay on the Arctic coast. Since then, many other major oil and natural gas deposits have been found in Alaska. In 1977, the nearly 800-mile-long Trans-Alaska Pipeline, which carries Alaskan oil throughout the state, was completed.

In 1989, the oil tanker Exxon *Valdez* ran aground in Prince William Sound, causing the biggest oil spill in U.S. history and a major ecological disaster.

Right: *An otter swims in water polluted by the* Exxon Valdez *oil spill.* Below: *An Inuit family poses in front of their dwelling in the early 1900s.*

Above left: *Walker Glacier is one of many that attract scientists and adventurers to Glacier Bay Park and Preserve.*
Above right: *Wolves are native to the Alaska wilderness.*

THE PRESENT

Alaska is famous for its size, beauty, and natural resources. Alaska contains the largest known North American oil field.

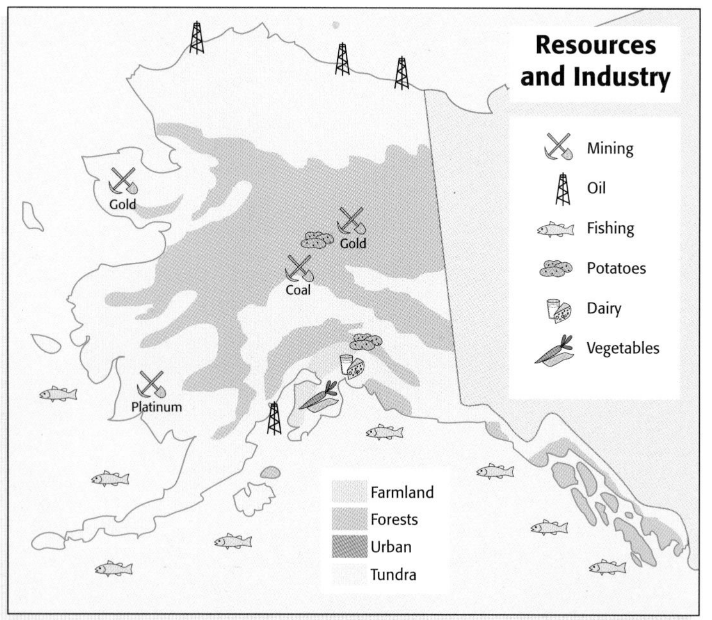

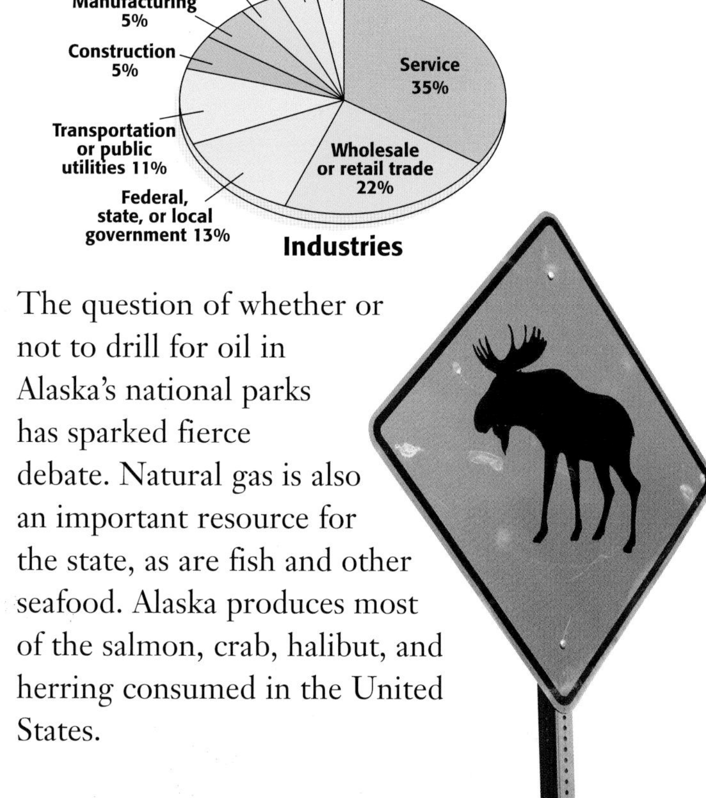

The question of whether or not to drill for oil in Alaska's national parks has sparked fierce debate. Natural gas is also an important resource for the state, as are fish and other seafood. Alaska produces most of the salmon, crab, halibut, and herring consumed in the United States.

Born in Alaska

- ★ **Irene Bedard**, actress
- ★ **Benny Benson**, child designer of state flag
- ★ **Scott Gomez**, hockey player
- ★ **Virgil F. Partch**, cartoonist
- ★ **Elizabeth Peratrovich**, political activist
- ★ **Curt Schilling**, baseball player

Irene Bedard

Despite its industrial and commercial importance, Alaska remains the state with the lowest population density. Alaska's scenery and wilderness make it a popular tourist destination. However, the state has remained closely tied to its past. Alaska is home to a number of different Native American groups, and dogsled racing is the official state sport.

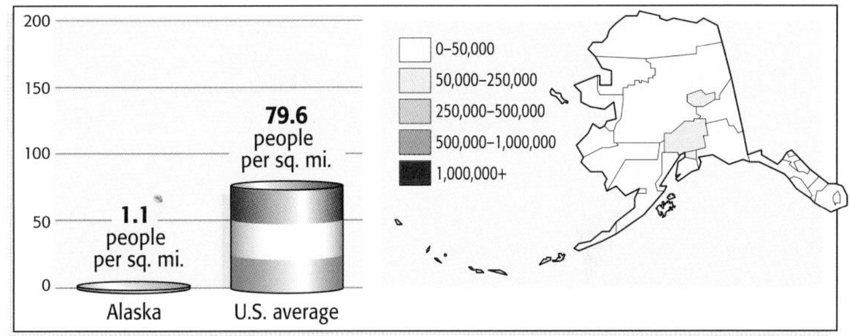

Population Density **Population by County**

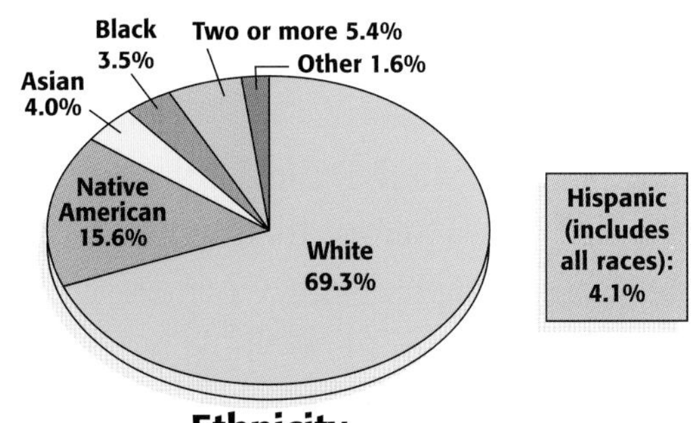

Ethnicity

Alaska's natural beauty, sense of history, and untouched wilderness have earned the state the nickname the Last Frontier.

Native American children enjoy a show at the Barter Island recreation center.

Arizona

Ditat Deus (God enriches).

Land area rank *Largest state (1)* — 6 — *smallest state (52)*

Population rank *Most people (1)* — 20 — *fewest people (52)*

At a Glance

Name: *Arizona* comes from the Native American word *Arizonac,* which means "little spring" or "young spring."

Nickname: Grand Canyon State

Capital: Phoenix

Size: 114,006 sq. mi.

Population: 5,130,632

Statehood: Arizona became the 48th state on February 14, 1912.

Electoral votes: 8 (2004)

U.S. Representatives: 6 (until 2003)

State tree: paloverde

State flower: saguaro cactus blossom

State bird: cactus wren

Highest point: Humphreys Peak, 12,633 ft.

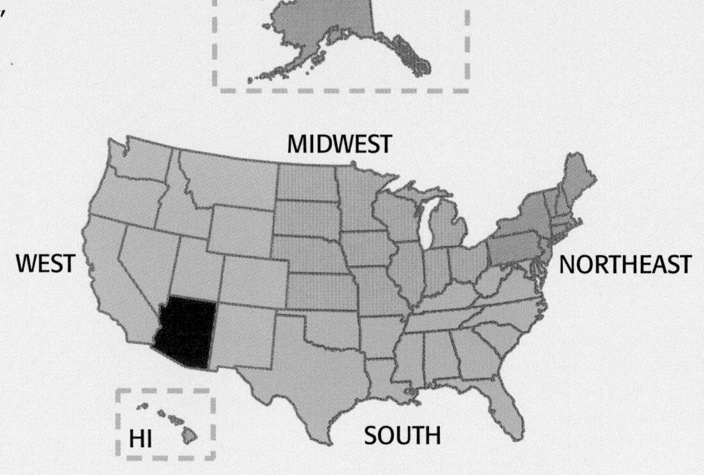

The Place

Arizona is located in the southwestern region of the United States. Its northeastern corner forms part of the Four Corners, where Utah, Colorado, New Mexico, and Arizona meet. Four Corners is the only place in the United States where a person can simultaneously stand in four different states.

Much of Arizona consists of desert, including the famous Painted and Sonoran Deserts. These regions have a dry climate that is hot in the summer and warm in the

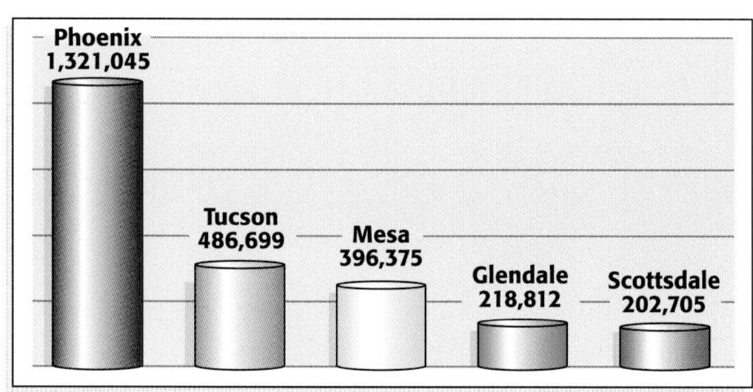

Major Cities

Cathedral Rock at Red Rock Crossing towers over the Oak Creek, which winds its way through the town of Sedona in Northern Arizona.

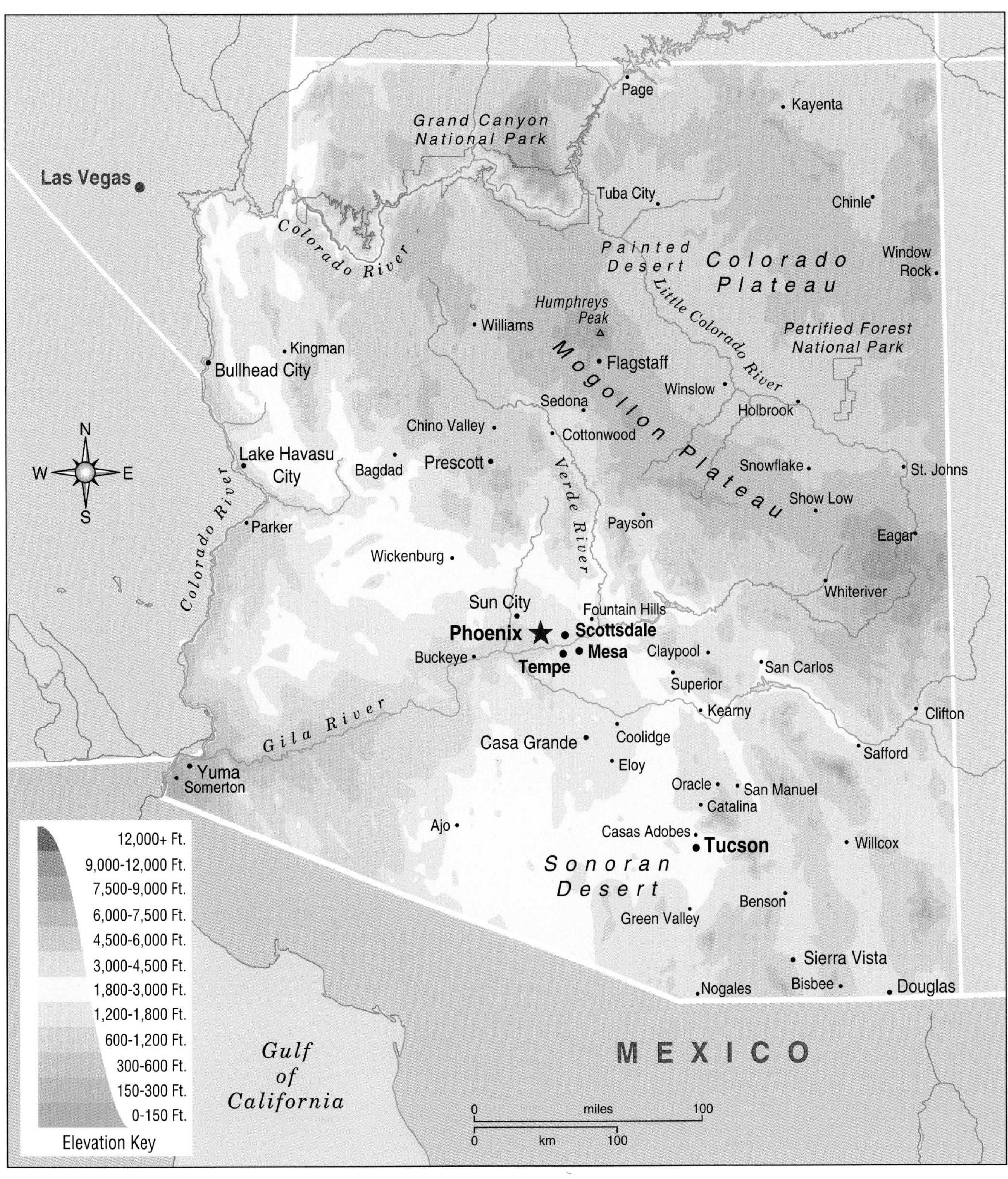

winter. Many of these areas are irrigated with water from Arizona's large rivers, including the Colorado River, and the lands are used for farming.

Other areas of Arizona are mountainous and are home to some of the largest ponderosa pine forests in the United States. The climate is cooler in these parts of the state. Arizona has large deposits of minerals, including gold, silver, and copper.

Chiricahua Apache girl, granddaughter of Cochise

The Past

Human remains dating back about 12,000 years have been found in Arizona. Many native civilizations flourished there, including the Hohokam and the Anasazi, who built complex cliff dwellings between 1100 and 1300. Apache and Navajo peoples migrated to Arizona during the 1400s.

Spanish explorers first arrived in 1539. Franciscan friar Marcos de Niza was the first Spaniard to visit Arizona in his search for the mythical Seven Cities of Cíbola. A year later, explorer Francisco Vásquez de Coronado arrived. In the following years, Spanish missionaries settled the land.

As part of Mexico, Arizona remained under Spanish rule until Mexico was granted independence from Spain in 1821. In 1848,

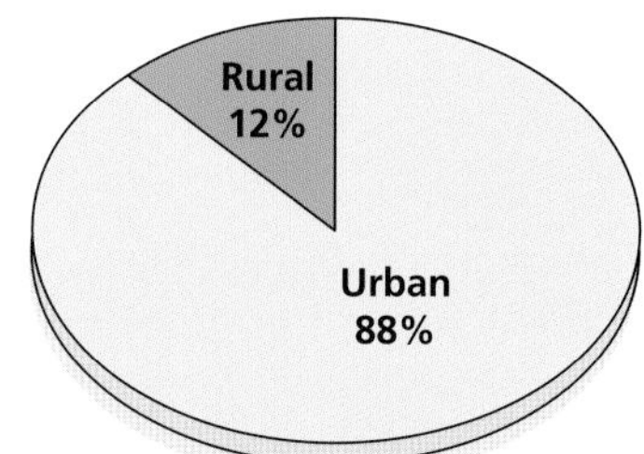

Urban/Rural Distribution

Facts and Firsts

- ★ Arizona has the third-largest Native American population in the United States.
- ★ Kykotsmovi is believed to be the oldest inhabited village in the United States. The Hopi people built this settlement during the 1100s.
- ★ Tucson, the astronomy capital of the world, has more telescopes than anyplace else. The largest solar telescope in the world is located in Kitt Peak National Observatory in Sells.
- ★ Arizona is the home of some of the country's most famous landmarks, including Grand Canyon National Park, the Painted Desert, the Petrified Forest, and the Sonoran (or Gila) Desert.
- ★ Arizona produces more copper than any other state; the copper covering atop the Arizona state capitol building is equivalent to 4.8 million pennies.

after the Mexican War, the United States won most of Arizona from Mexico. The United States bought the rest of the territory in 1853 as part of the Gadsden Purchase.

Once the territory became part of the United States, several wars broke out between frontiersmen and Native Americans. These wars did not end until 1886, when Apache leader Geronimo surrendered. The territory became a state on February 14, 1912.

State Smart

Arizona has more tribal land reserved for use by Native Americans than any other state—approximately 20 million acres, more than one-quarter of the state's total area.

Above: *This cliff dwelling, known as the White House, is located in Canyon de Chelly.*
Below: *Geronimo*

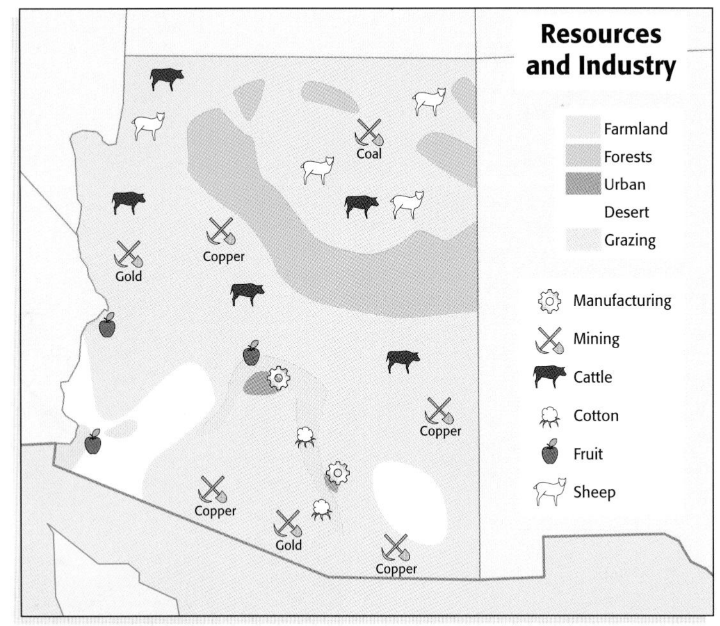

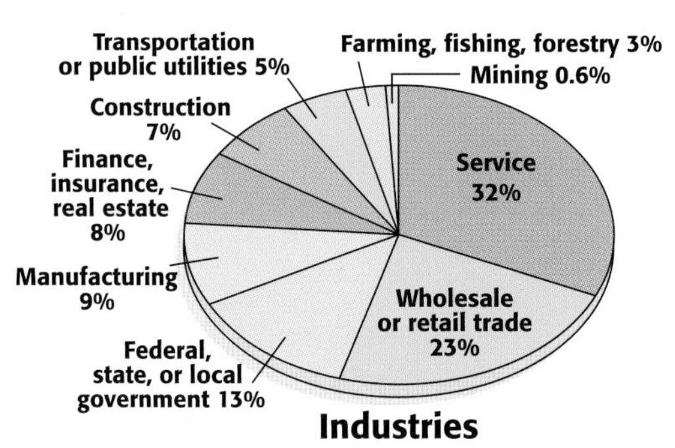

The Present

When Spanish explorers first arrived in Arizona in the 16th century, they found a dry region that was covered with deserts and mesas. Today, Arizona is a modern, industrial state that manufactures many electrical, communications, and aeronautical items.

Irrigation from Arizona's large rivers, including the Colorado, has transformed some of the state's desert regions into rich farmland. Cotton, vegetables, and sorghum are important crops. In the mountainous regions, farmers raise cattle and sheep.

Many businesses are located in downtown Tucson, shown here at sunset.

Born in Arizona

★ **Lynda Carter**, actress

★ **Cesar Chavez**, labor leader

★ **Cochise**, Apache chief

★ **Geronimo** (Goyathlay), Apache leader

★ **Barry Goldwater**, politician

★ **Charles Mingus**, jazz musician and composer

★ **Carlos Montezuma**, doctor and Native American spokesman

★ **Stevie Nicks**, singer

★ **Linda Ronstadt**, singer

★ **Kerri Strug**, gymnast

Above: *Charles Mingus;* below: *Cesar Chavez*

Above: *Arizona attracts hikers year-round.*
Right: *The Grand Canyon at dawn*

Arizona's scenery, landmarks, and warm climate make it a popular tourist destination. The Grand Canyon, the Painted Desert, and the Petrified Forest attract thousands of people each year. The state's rich heritage and history also attract visitors.

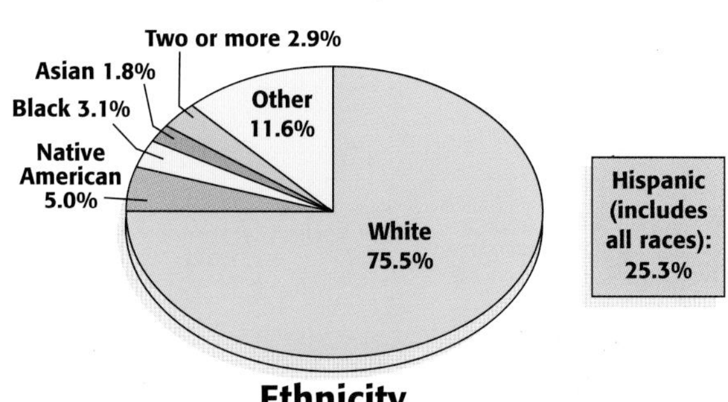

Ethnicity

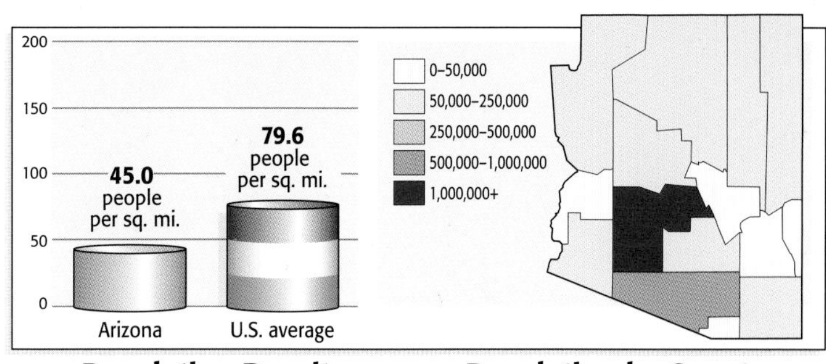

Population Density

Population by County

Arkansas

Regnat populus (Let the people rule).

Land area rank
Largest state (1)
Population rank
Most people (1)

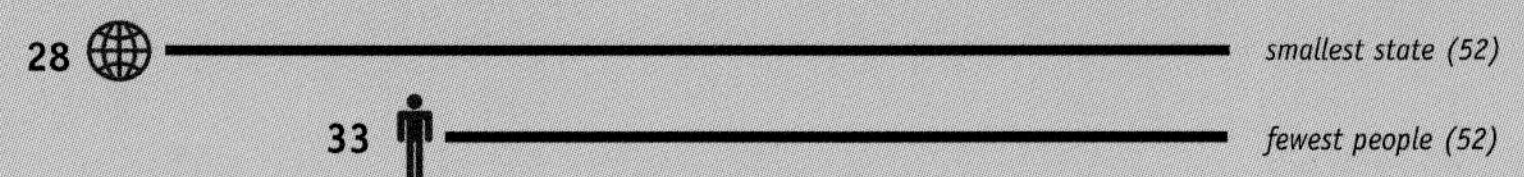

At a Glance

Name: The word *Arkansas* is from the French name for the Quapaw tribe, the *Arkansa*, and the region the tribe inhabited.
Nicknames: Natural State, Razorback State, Land of Opportunity
Capital: Little Rock
Size: 53,182 sq. mi.
Population: 2,673,400
Statehood: Arkansas became the 25th state on June 15, 1836.
Electoral votes: 6 (2004)
U.S. Representatives: 4 (until 2003)
State tree: pine
State flower: apple blossom
State bird: mockingbird
Highest point: Magazine Mountain, 2,753 ft.

The Place

Arkansas is located on the borders of the southern and central parts of the United States. The Ozark Plateau and Ouachita Mountains in the northern and western parts of the state are mountainous and densely forested. The southern and eastern parts of the state are lower in elevation. The Mississippi River forms the eastern border of the state and makes this region suitable for agricultural use. The West Gulf Coastal Plain, in the south and southwestern portion of the state, is low in elevation and has pine forests, natural gas and

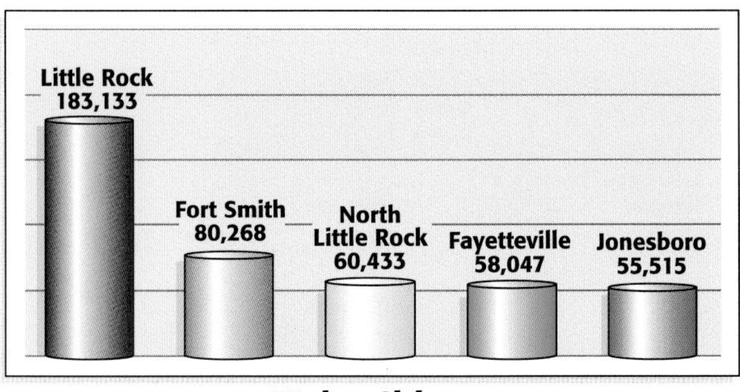

Major Cities

A view of the state capitol in Little Rock, on the Arkansas River

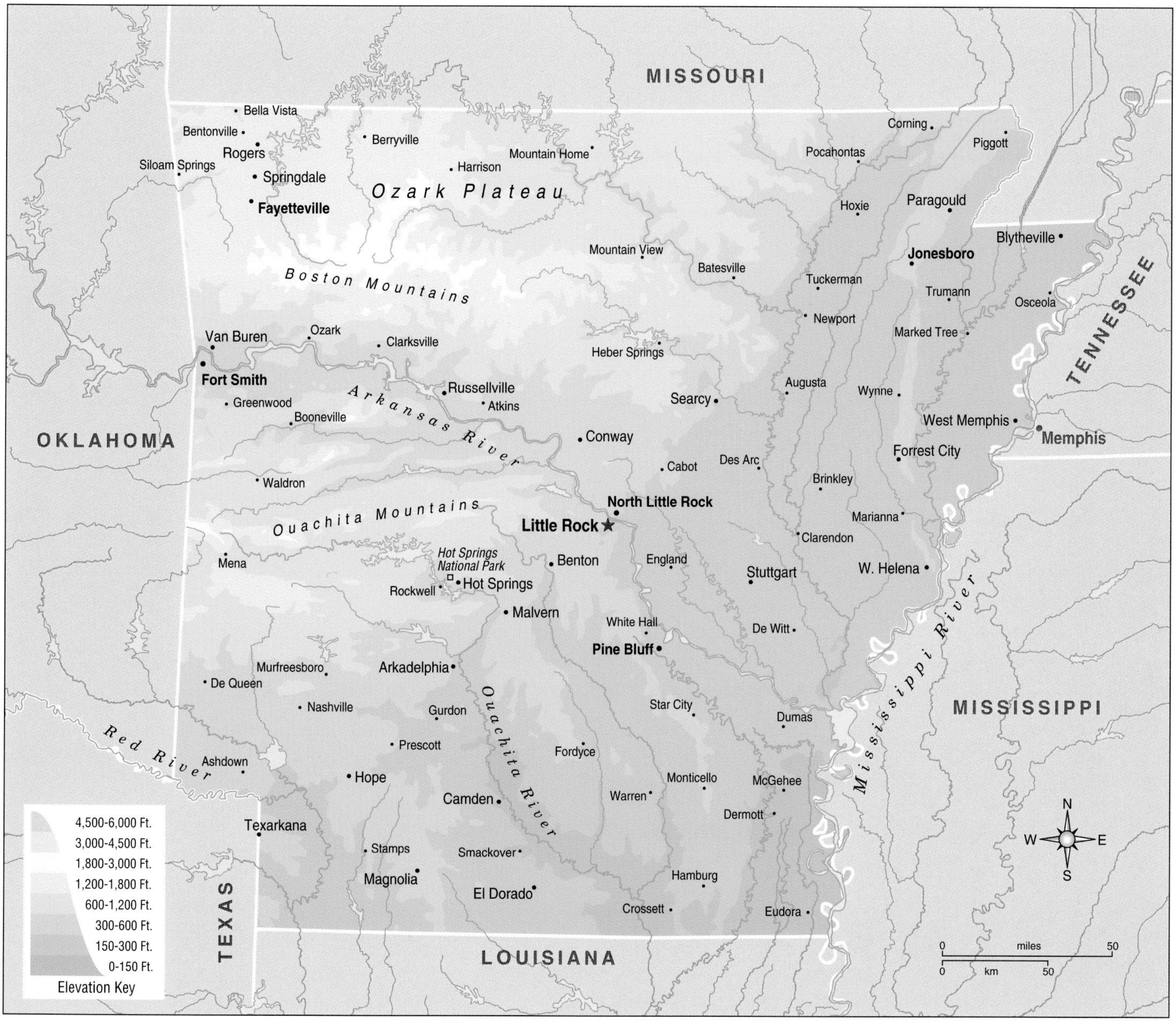

petroleum deposits, and beds of bromine salts.

Arkansas has many lakes and rivers. The largest is the Arkansas River, which flows southeast across the state. Natural springs are also common around the Ozark Plateau and Ouachita Mountains. Summers in Arkansas are hot and humid while winters are cool, especially in the mountains.

Lake Ouachita extends into Ouachita National Forest and is known for its clear water.

Spanish explorer Hernando de Soto came to Arkansas in search of gold.

The Past

Native Americans have been living in Arkansas for approximately 12,000 years. The first Europeans to explore the state were Spaniards. In 1541, Hernando de Soto searched for gold and silver deposits in Arkansas. In 1682, French explorers claimed the Louisiana Territory, which included Arkansas. French colonists settled the region and began to exploit its natural resources, including trees and animal furs.

Spain gained control of the Louisiana Territory in 1762 through a series of wars. In 1800, the region returned to French rule, until the United States bought the territory through the Louisiana Purchase of 1803.

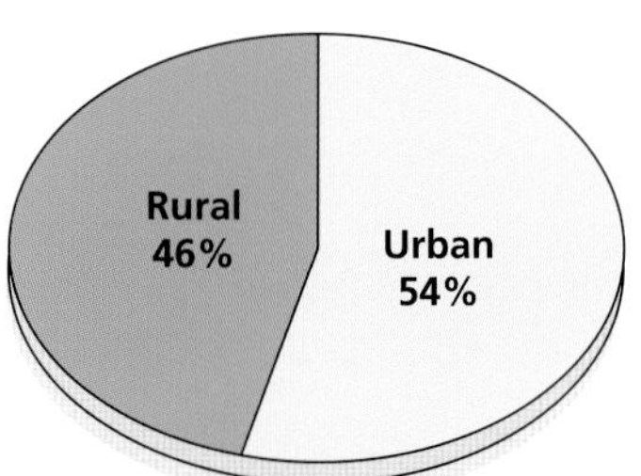

Urban/Rural Distribution

Facts and Firsts

- ★ Arkansas is home to 50 state parks, 6 national parks, 2.5 million acres of national forests, seven national scenic byways, and three state scenic byways.
- ★ Arkansas's hot springs are nationally known. Some famous Americans, including President Franklin D. Roosevelt, baseball player Babe Ruth, and gangster Al Capone, visited Hot Springs National Park.
- ★ Buffalo National River is one of the few free-flowing rivers in the continental United States.
- ★ Arkansas has the country's only active diamond mine, Crater of Diamonds State Park, which is located near Murfreesboro. There, tourists and prospectors alike can mine for diamonds and other precious gems, including amethysts, garnets, jaspers, agates, and quartz crystals.
- ★ Texarkana is divided by the Arkansas-Texas state line. The city has two governments—one for the Arkansas side and one for the Texas side. The Texarkana post office building straddles the state line, standing in both states.

The Fordyce was a famous bathhouse in Hot Springs from the 1920s to '40s.

In 1836, Arkansas was admitted to the Union as a slave state. When the Civil War broke out, Arkansas eventually seceded (withdrew) from the Union and joined the Confederate States of America.

State Smart

Arkansas is home to the largest retail headquarters in the United States: that of Wal-Mart, located in Bentonville. In 2000 Wal-Mart had sales of more than $200 billion.

Toward the end of the 1800s, Arkansas began to expand rapidly. Railroads were built, and timber became a leading industry. The state remained mostly agricultural, however, until the 1950s, when manufacturing became more important and Arkansas quickly became industrialized.

Fort Smith housed Confederate soldiers during the Civil War.

H. B. Mollhausen

Lith of SARONY MAJOR & KNAPP New York

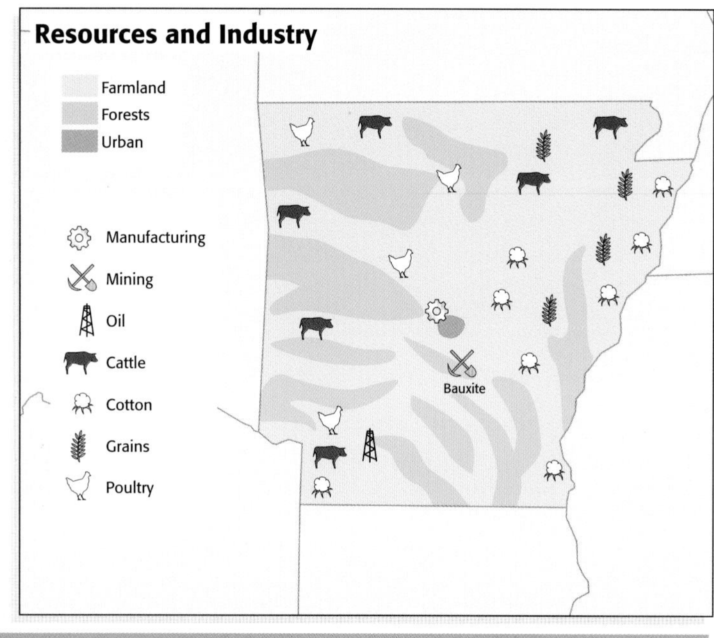

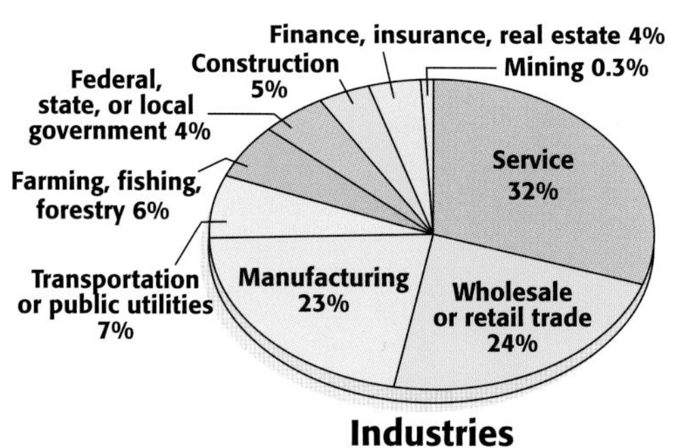

The Present

Arkansas is a popular vacation spot. The state's lakes, rivers, and rugged Ozark Mountains make it an ideal location for boating, fishing, water sports, and hiking. Arkansas's many hot springs are also well-known attractions.

Despite its tourist attractions, Arkansas is primarily an industrial state. Food processing is the state's most important industry, but electrical manufacturing is also notable. Agriculture is still significant, and Arkansas leads the country in rice production and the raising of chickens. Cotton and soybeans are also common crops, and lumber and wood product industries flourish.

Below left: *Hikers view the Ozarks from Whitaker Point in Newton County.* Below right: *A family relaxes on a dock at Lake Chicot State Park.*

Born in Arkansas

- ★ **Helen Gurley Brown**, editor
- ★ **Glen Campbell**, singer
- ★ **Johnny Cash**, singer
- ★ **Eldridge Cleaver**, black activist
- ★ **William Jefferson Clinton**, U.S. president
- ★ **Jay Hanna "Dizzy" Dean**, baseball player
- ★ **James W. Fulbright**, U.S. senator
- ★ **John Grisham**, author
- ★ **Douglas MacArthur**, general
- ★ **Mary Steenburgen**, actress

Above: *Eldridge Cleaver;* below: *Mary Steenburgen*

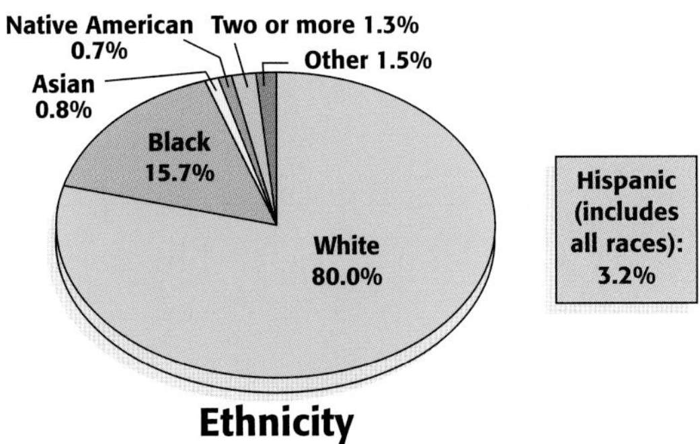

Ethnicity

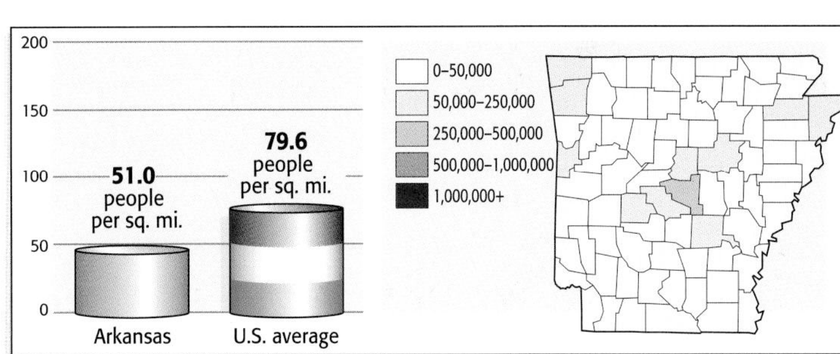

Population Density

Population by County

Arkansas's large deposits of bauxite, an ore used to make aluminum, make mining another key industry. The state also has deposits of natural gas and petroleum.

Despite Arkansas's rapid industrialization, the state's citizens have not forgotten their early folk customs. Folk festivals and county fairs, including the Arkansas State Fair and Livestock Show, bring Arkansans together. The town of Mountain View, the Folk Capital of America, preserves the original pioneer lifestyle, and attracts many visitors to the Ozark Folk Center State Park.

An old general store in south central Arkansas displays folk crafts, including a quilt.

California

Eureka (I have found it).

Land area rank *Largest state (1)* 3  *smallest state (52)*

Population rank *Most people (1)* 1 *fewest people (52)*

At a Glance

Name: California is named after Califia, a mythical island paradise described by Garci Ordonez de Montalvo in his 16th-century novel *Las Sergas de Esplandian*.

Nickname: Golden State

Capital: Sacramento

Size: 158,869 sq. mi.

Population: 33,871,648

Statehood: California became the 31st state on September 9, 1850.

Electoral votes: 55 (2004)

U.S. Representatives: 52 (until 2003)

State tree: California redwood

State flower: golden poppy

State reptile: California desert tortoise

Highest point: Mount Whitney, 14,494 ft.

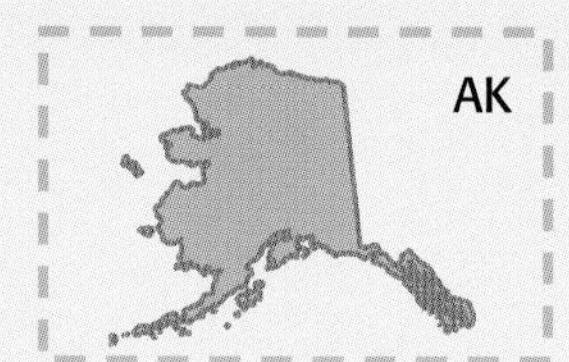

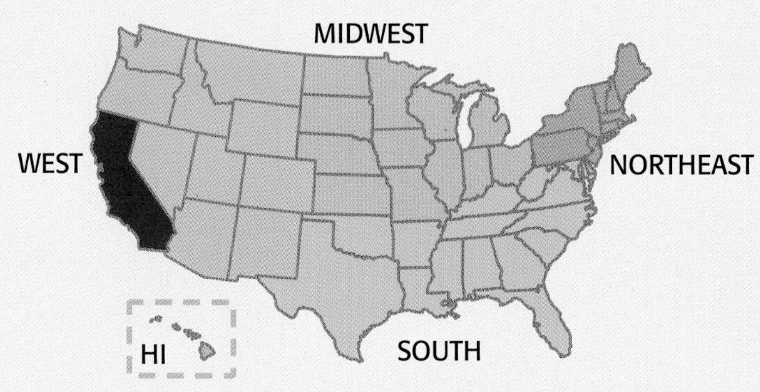

The Place

California is known for its geographical diversity and extremes. It is the third-largest state in area, after Alaska and Texas. It contains the highest point in the continental states—Mount Whitney—and also the lowest point—Death Valley. Much of California is mountainous and forested, but there are also farmlands and extensive desert areas, including the Mojave, and Colorado Deserts.

City	Population
Los Angeles	3,694,820
San Diego	1,223,400
San Jose	894,943
San Francisco	776,733
Sacramento	407,018

Major Cities

Napa Valley and the San Andreas Fault are in the Coast Ranges chain of mountains.

La Jolla, a suburb of San Diego, is known for its beautiful coastline and beaches.

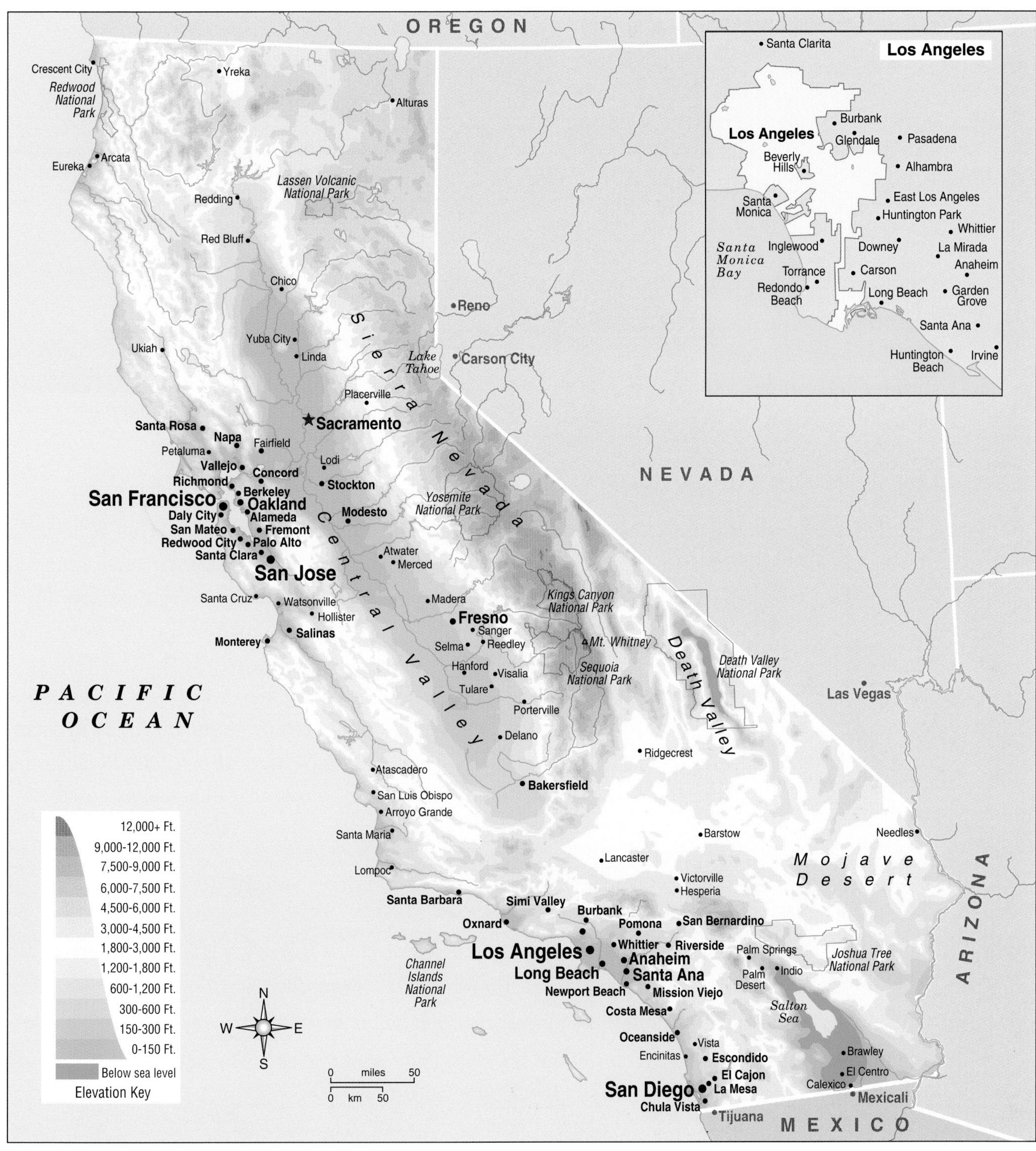

Many of the seismic activities and earthquakes that occur throughout the state originate in this area. The Cascade Mountains contain at least one active volcano, Lassen Peak.

California has large areas of fertile farmland. The state's best farmland is in the Central Valley, located between the Coast Ranges and the Sierra Nevada mountains.

California's 840-mile coastline is world famous. Two of its most popular harbors are in San Diego and San Francisco.

California is home to many unique species of plants and animals as a result of its diversity of climates and landscapes. Barriers to migration routes, such as rivers, mountains, and deserts, led to the evolution of many isolated species and varieties of animals.

Northern parts of the state experience cool and mild weather conditions, while the southwestern coast is warmer. The southeastern part of the state, home of the Mojave and Colorado Deserts, is dry and hot in spring and summer, but cold in winter.

Immigrants from China helped build the California Pacific Railroad.

The Past

California's history is as diverse as its geography. For thousands of years, hundreds of Native American tribes lived in this region. When the Spanish began to explore the Americas, they arrived in the Baja Peninsula (the peninsula south of California) to look for a mythical water route across North America.

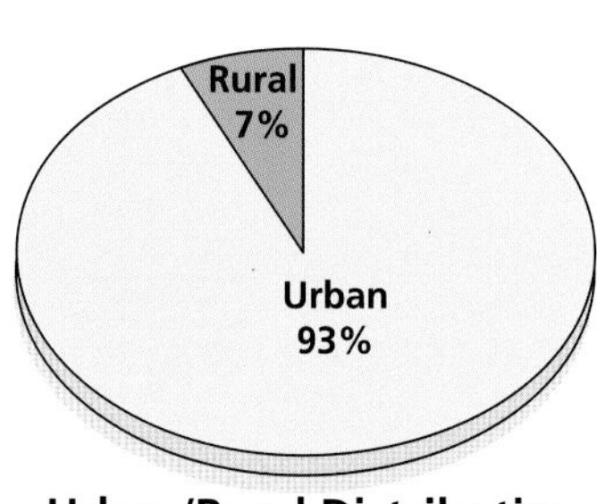

Urban/Rural Distribution

Juan Rodriguez Cabrillo continued the search to the north and arrived in California in 1542. The Spanish founded many Catholic missions, but they turned the territory over to Mexico in 1822 when Mexico won its independence from Spain. In 1812, Russian settlers also reached California from Alaska and established

Facts and Firsts

- ★ California has more residents than any other U.S. state—almost one out of every eight Americans lives there. California is also the most urban state—93 percent of its population lives in cities.
- ★ More goods are manufactured in California than in any other state.
- ★ California has the largest economy of any state. If its economy were ranked against those of all the countries in the world, it would be in the top 10 largest economies.
- ★ More than 500,000 seismic tremors are detected in California annually.
- ★ The bristle cone pine, found in Inyo National Forest and native to California, is the oldest known living tree species in the world. Some of the trees in the forest are more than 4,600 years old.
- ★ In 1853, Levi Strauss invented blue jeans in California. He made some pants out of the canvas tents he had unsuccessfully tried to sell to gold rush prospectors. Unhappy with canvas, Strauss later made the pants out of denim.

Fort Ross. Mexico had difficulty controlling the province, and California was close to independence when the Mexican-American War broke out.

At the end of the war in 1848, the United States acquired California from Mexico. In the same year, James W. Marshall discovered gold in Coloma, which set off the gold rush. This discovery eventually brought 300,000 men and women to California in search of gold or new jobs in California's booming economy.

California rapidly became one of the most diverse states as thousands of immigrants from Mexico, Europe, and China came in search of gold. Shortly afterward, in 1850, California was admitted to the Union as the 31st state. In 1869, the first transcontinental railroad was completed, which joined California to the East Coast. In 1906, a severe earthquake—one of the worst in California's history—struck San Francisco. The earthquake and the fires it sparked caused widespread damage and forced residents to rebuild the city.

As California entered the 20th century, important changes began to shape the state's destiny. In 1908, the first motion picture to be made completely in Los Angeles, *In the Sultan's Power*, was produced. California eventually became the world's motion picture industry leader.

State Smart

Death Valley is the lowest point in the United States. In some areas, this valley is more than 282 feet below sea level.

During the Great Depression of the 1930s, California became legendary as a land of plenty, and drew 10,000 people a month from the drought-stricken plains states, as described in John Steinbeck's novel *The Grapes of Wrath*.

In 1935, the first statewide irrigation system began to transport water. The system brought water to the great Central Valley, which soon became the leading agricultural area in the United States. After the end of World War II in 1945, California's population continued to grow, as the aerospace and electronics industries brought more people.

The 1906 San Francisco earthquake left much of the city in ruins.

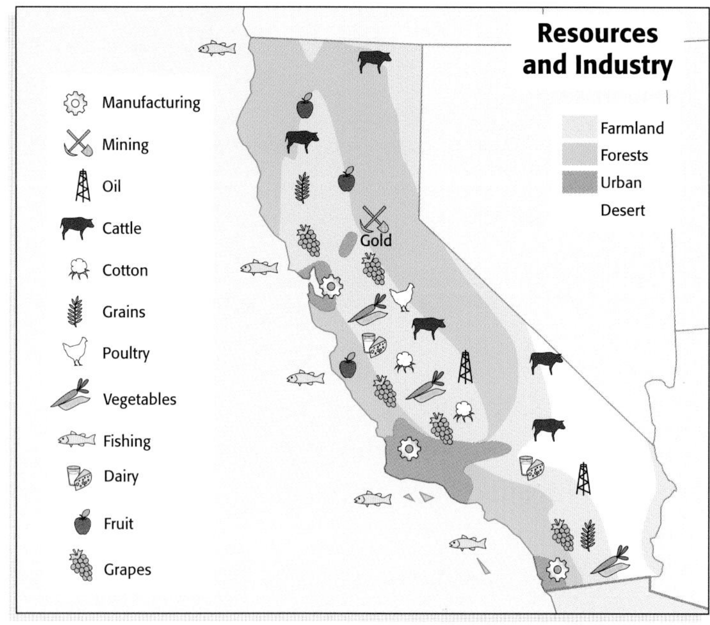

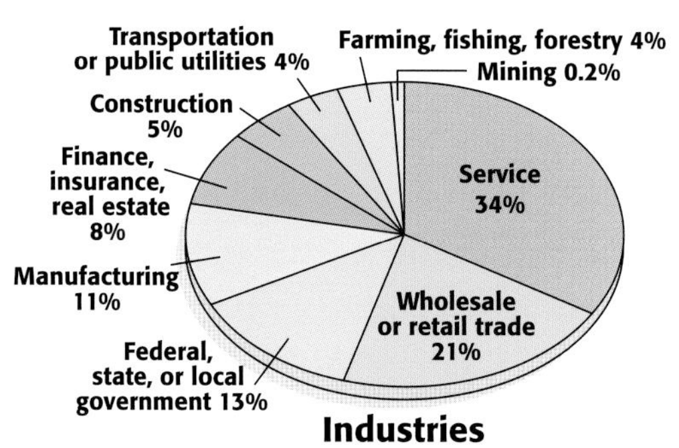

In Silicon Valley in 1977, the Apple II personal computer, the first personal computer with color graphics, was brought to market. The personal computer revolutionized business, and continues to bring people to the state to work in high-tech industries.

The Present

California has a diverse population, geography and economy. More immigrants settle in California than in any other state. In addition, the motion picture and television industries, known all over the world, are concentrated in California.

California is home to a large aerospace manufacturing industry as well as electrical and electrical equipment manufacturers. These companies produce televisions, radios, telephones, semiconductors, printed circuit boards, lighting fixtures, and many other electronic products. Computer and computer software manufacturers in Silicon Valley make up another crucial portion of California's economy. The Napa Valley region produces most of the grapes used to make American wine. On nonirrigated land, many farmers raise cattle.

Below left: *A vineyard in Sonoma.* Below right: *Sand dunes at Death Valley National Monument*

Born in California

★ **Shirley Temple Black**, actress, ambassador
★ **Dave Brubeck**, musician
★ **Julia Child**, chef
★ **Joe DiMaggio**, baseball player
★ **Robert Frost**, poet
★ **Tom Hanks**, actor
★ **William Randolph Hearst**, publisher
★ **Anthony M. Kennedy**, jurist
★ **Jack London**, author
★ **Richard M. Nixon**, U.S. president
★ **Isamu Noguchi**, sculptor
★ **George S. Patton Jr.**, general
★ **Robert Redford**, actor
★ **Sally K. Ride**, astronaut
★ **William Saroyan**, author
★ **John Steinbeck**, author
★ **Adlai Stevenson**, politician
★ **Kristi Yamaguchi**, ice skater

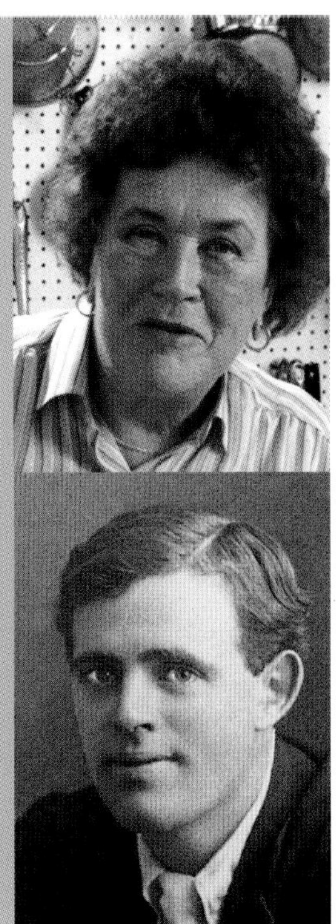

Above: *Julia Child;* below: *Jack London*

California's natural resources also support its varied economy. California's lush forests make lumber an important industry. Minerals, oil, and natural gas are also sources of wealth.

Tourism is another leading industry in California. The state's varied natural beauty and generally mild climate draw millions of visitors annually for outdoor activities. Attractions such as theme parks and motion pictures are also popular.

Boogie boarding is a favorite hobby in California.

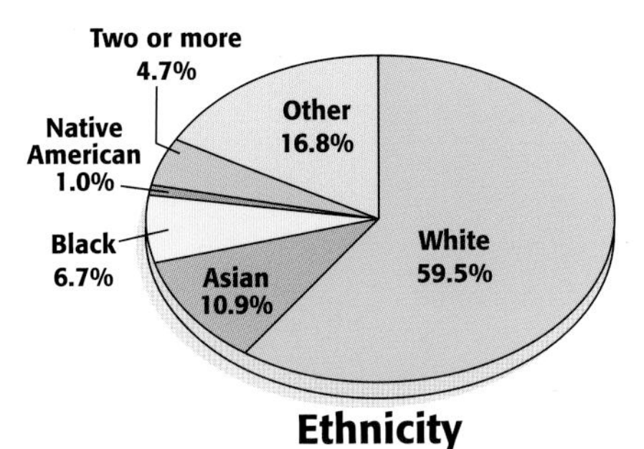

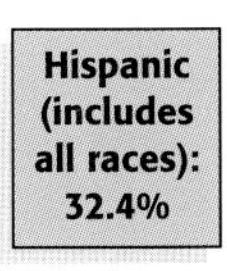

Ethnicity

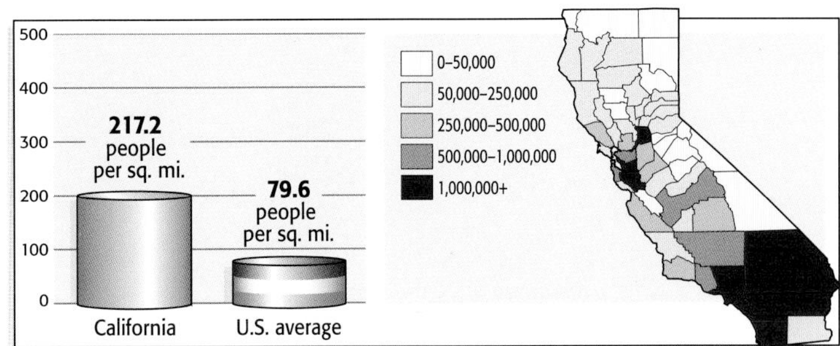

Population Density **Population by County**

Colorado

Nil Sine Numine (Nothing without providence).

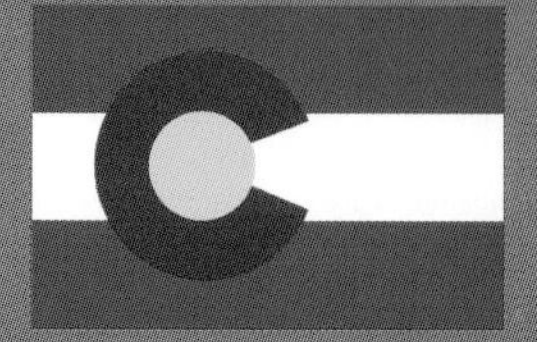

Land area rank
Largest state (1) 8 ———— *smallest state (52)*

Population rank
Most people (1) 24 ———— *fewest people (52)*

At a Glance

Name: *Colorado* is a Spanish word that means "colored red." The name was first given to the Colorado River by Spanish explorers because it flows through red stone canyons.

Nickname: Centennial State

Capital: Denver

Size: 104,100 sq. mi.

Population: 4,301,261

Statehood: Colorado became the 38th state on August 1, 1876.

Electoral votes: 9 (2004)

U.S. Representatives: 6 (until 2003)

State tree: Colorado blue spruce

State flower: Rocky Mountain columbine

State animal: bighorn sheep

Highest point: Mount Elbert, 14,433 ft.

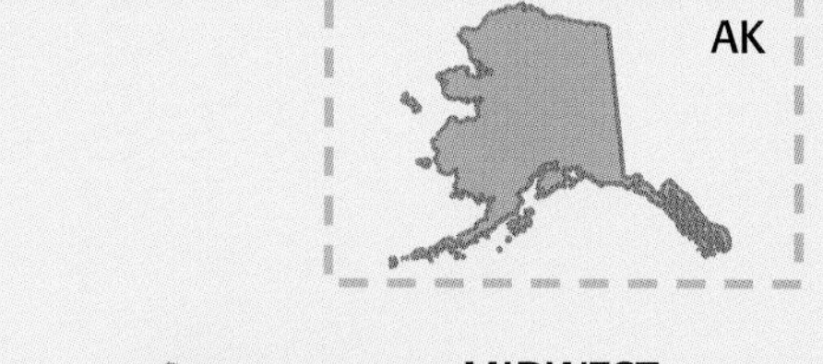

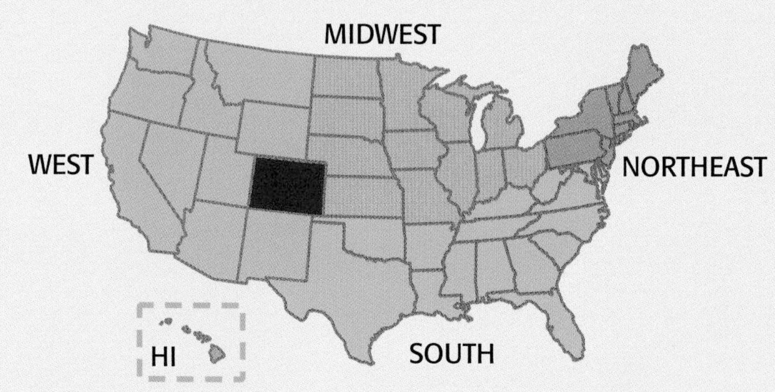

The Place

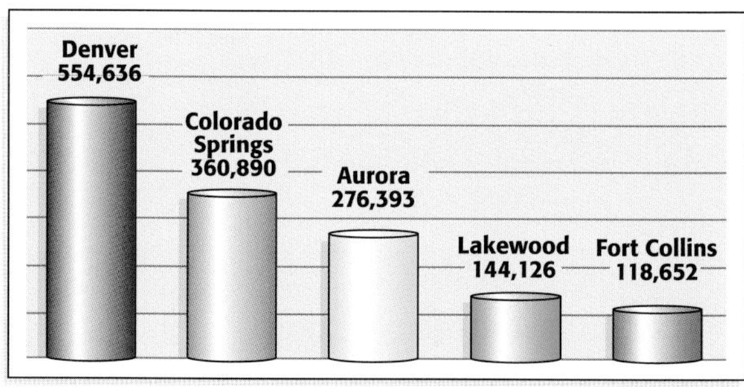

Major Cities

Colorado is located partly in the Rocky Mountains. Because the western portion of the state is mountainous, Colorado has the highest average elevation of any state. More than 800 of its peaks are higher than 10,000 feet, and more than 50 are higher than 14,000 feet.

The western half of the state is separated from the eastern half by the Continental Divide, the high point of the Rocky Mountains that runs from north to

The mountains of western Colorado give the terrain a rugged beauty.

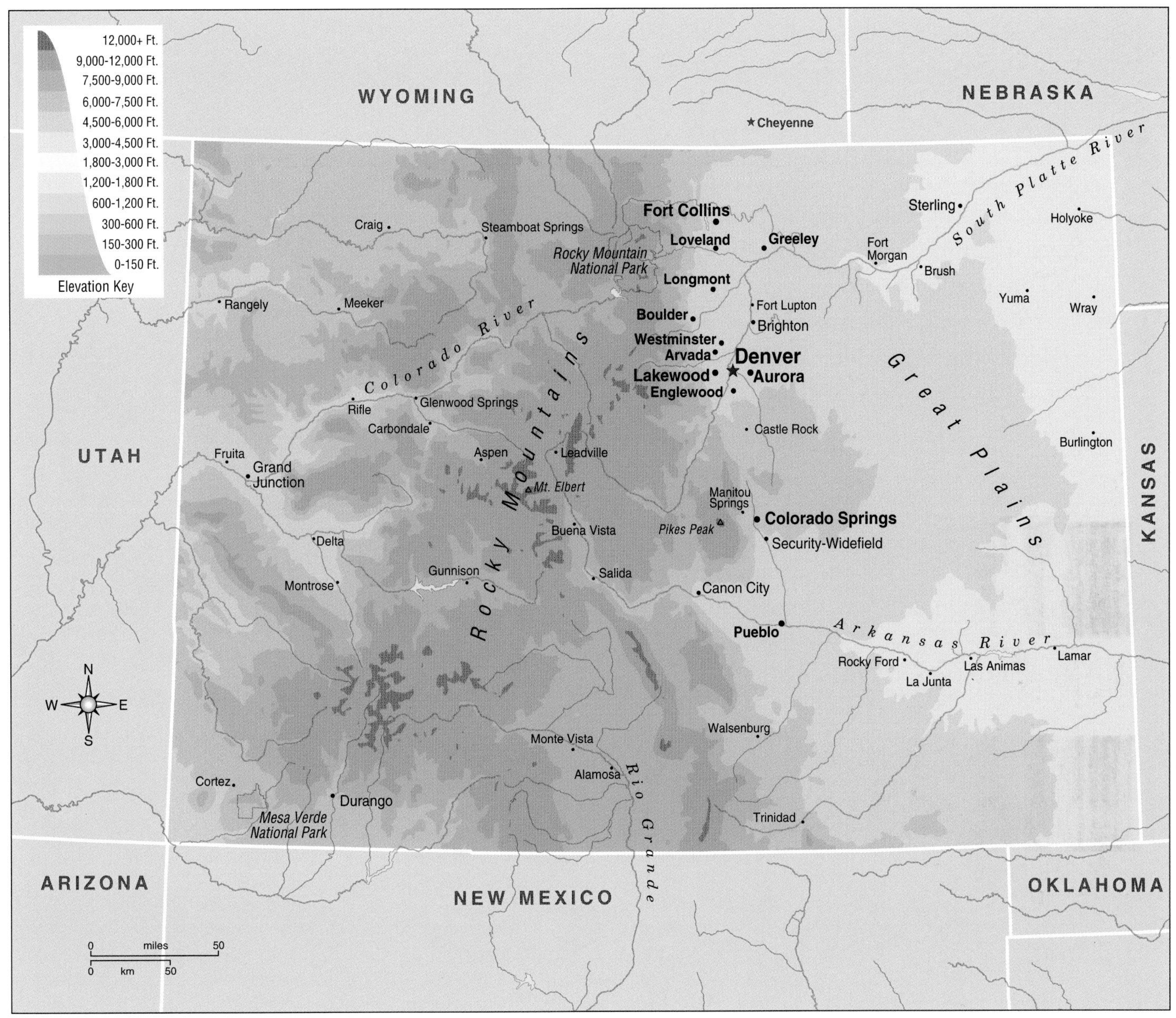

south and separates the waters that flow west into the Pacific Ocean from those that flow east. The eastern half of the state, an area of plains and prairies, is part of the Great Plains region. This area becomes gradually higher as it slopes to meet the Rockies in the west, and it is good farming and cattle-raising land.

The alpine terrain of the western mountains is full of towering peaks, wide valleys, jagged canyons, high plateaus, and deep basins. Six major rivers flow through Colorado. The Colorado River is the most important one because it supplies hydroelectricity and water for irrigation. Over many years, the Colorado River carved out the Grand Canyon (in Arizona) in its southwest journey to the Gulf of California.

Colorado's weather is typically cool and pleasant in summer, and winters are very snowy. Colorado is rich in many minerals, including gold, silver, uranium, coal, molybdenum (used in making steel), and petroleum.

The Past

Evidence of Colorado's long geographical history can be seen in Great Sand Dunes National Monument. For thousands of years, prevailing southwesterly winds blew over the San Juan Mountains and down over the Rio Grande flood plain, picking up sand particles on the way. These particles were then deposited at the east edge of the river valley as the wind moved upward to cross the Sangre de Cristo Mountains. This process continues today as the wind changes the shape and sand patterns of the dunes daily.

Colorado has a long human history, stretching back before

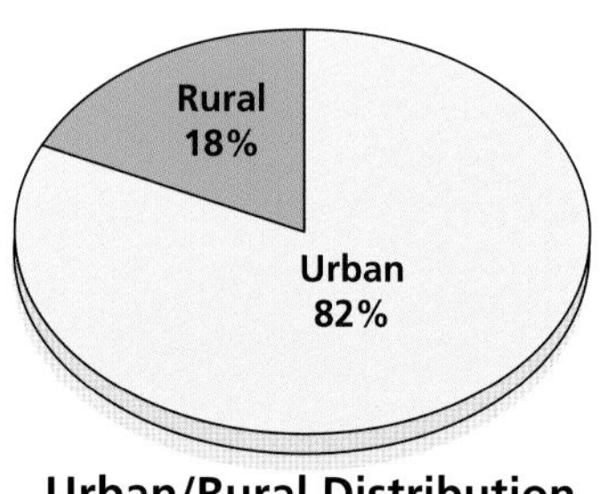

Urban/Rural Distribution

A child climbs a kiva ladder at Mesa Verde National Park.

Facts and Firsts

- ★ Colorado's southwest corner is part of the Four Corners. There, the borders of Colorado, Arizona, New Mexico, and Utah all touch. This is the only place in the United States where four states meet.
- ★ Colorado is home to the world's highest suspension bridge, the Royal Gorge Bridge, located near Cañon City. The bridge crosses the Arkansas River at a height of 1,053 feet.
- ★ Great Sand Dunes National Monument, located outside Alamosa, has the tallest sand dune in America.
- ★ Mesa Verde National Park contains more than 4,000 cliff dwellings, as well as a four-story city, created by the Ancestral Pueblo people between 600 and the late 1200s.These Native American inhabitants gradually abandoned the cliffs by 1300.
- ★ Katherine Lee Bates was inspired to compose the song "America the Beautiful" after climbing to the top of Pikes Peak, the most famous mountain in Colorado. Pikes Peak is 14,110 feet above sea level.
- ★ Denver annually hosts the world's largest rodeo, the Western Stock Show.
- ★ Denver is one of several American cities that claim to be the home of the original cheeseburger. A Denver monument reads, "On this site in 1935, Louis E. Ballast created the cheeseburger."
- ★ The Colorado state capitol building is decorated with beulah red marble from the town of Beulah. No more of this marble exists; all of it known in the world was used in the construction of the capitol.

the year 600, when Native Americans constructed cliff dwellings and cities in what is now Mesa Verde National Park, near Cortez. Although these people, known as Anasazi, mysteriously vanished from the cliffs by 1300, Colorado was home to many Native American groups when the Spanish arrived there in the 1500s.

Eastern Colorado became a U.S. territory in 1803 as a part of the Louisiana Purchase. That agreement with France gave the United States all of France's former territories north of Mexico and south of Canada. The central part of the state became a territory in 1845. Western Colorado was added after the United States acquired it, along with other territory, from Mexico in the Mexican-American War, which ended in 1848.

State Smart

Colorado has the highest average elevation—6,800 feet above sea level.

Gold was discovered in Colorado in 1858, and a rush of fortune seekers and settlers began to populate the area. When Colorado became a full-fledged state on August 1, 1876, it was an important agricultural and mining region.

Anasazi people built these cliff dwellings at Mesa Verde.

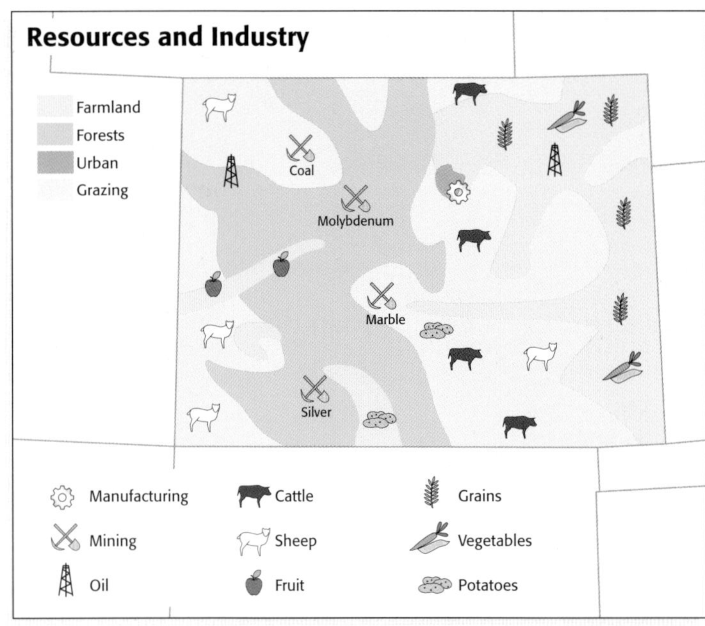

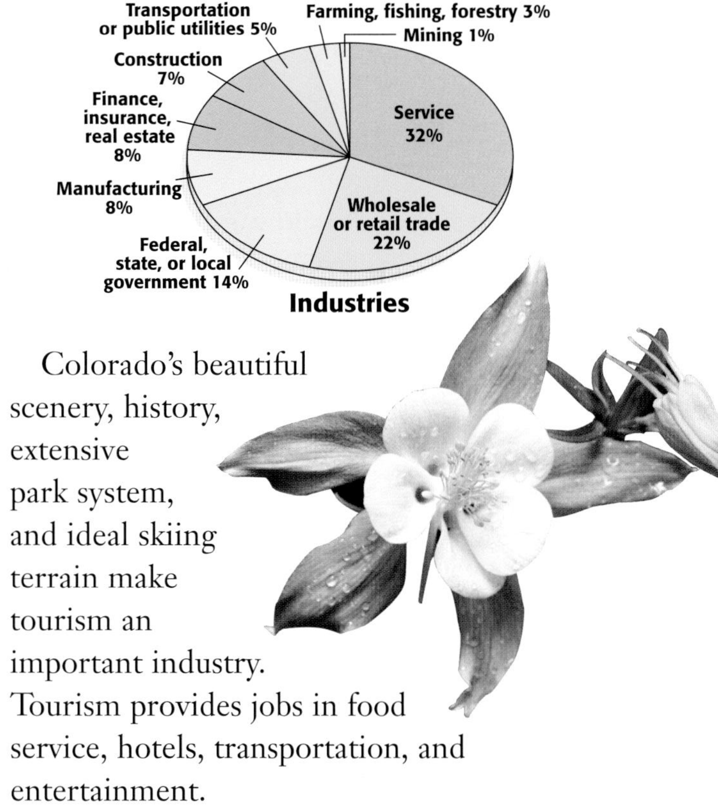

The Present

The eastern part of Colorado is still an important agricultural area where many fruits and vegetables grow on irrigated land. Cattle are raised in nonirrigated areas, and beef is another of Colorado's chief products.

Colorado's beautiful scenery, history, extensive park system, and ideal skiing terrain make tourism an important industry. Tourism provides jobs in food service, hotels, transportation, and entertainment.

Although Colorado's past economy was based on mining and agriculture, the state's economy now centers on high technology

Below left: *The absract architecture of the U.S. Air Force Academy Cadet Chapel, in Colorado Springs, attracts many visitors.* Below right: *Children view the historic interior of the state capitol in Denver.*

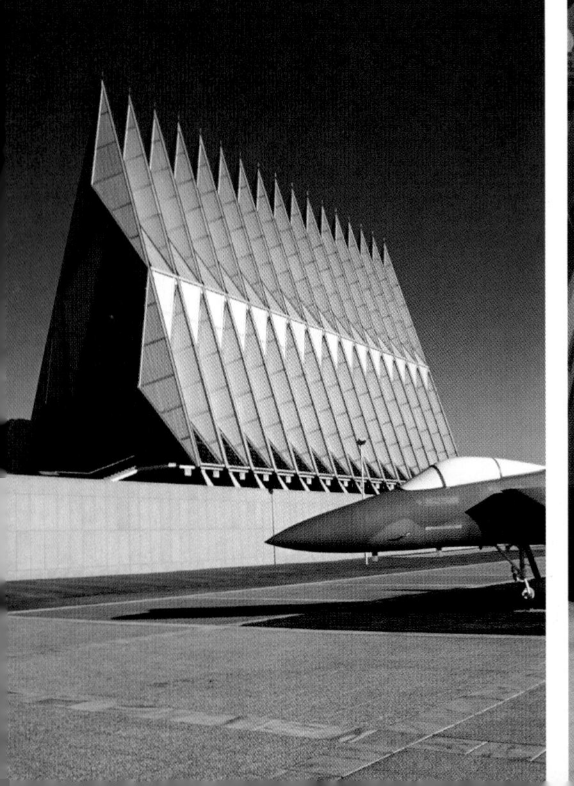

Born in Colorado

- ★ **Tim Allen**, actor and comedian
- ★ **M. Scott Carpenter**, astronaut
- ★ **Lon Chaney**, actor
- ★ **Mary Coyle Chase**, playwright
- ★ **Chipeta**, Native American negotiator
- ★ **Jack Dempsey**, boxer
- ★ **Douglas Fairbanks**, actor
- ★ **Eugene Fodor**, violinist
- ★ **Willard Libby**, scientist
- ★ **Ouray**, Ute chief
- ★ **Florence Sabin**, scientist
- ★ **Lowell Thomas**, commentator and author
- ★ **Dalton Trumbo**, screenwriter and novelist
- ★ **Byron R. White**, jurist
- ★ **Paul Whiteman**, conductor

Above: *Mary Coyle Chase;* below: *Byron R. White*

and the service industries. While Colorado is a modern, industrial state, its residents strive to preserve its history and natural splendor for future generations.

The Durango & Silverton Narrow Gauge Railroad offers visitors a chance to experience Colorado's natural beauty.

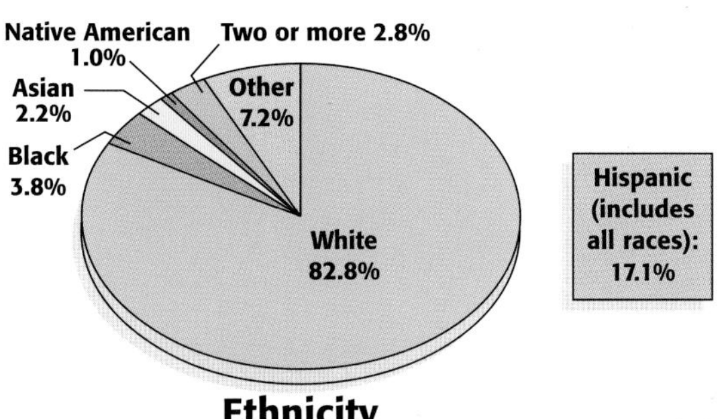

Ethnicity

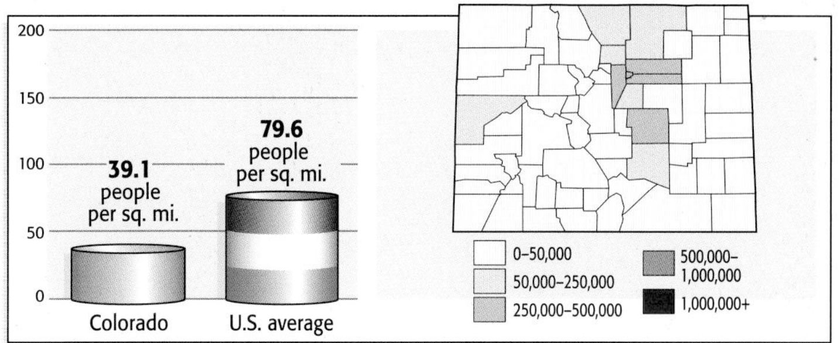

Population Density

Population by County

Connecticut

Qui Transtulit Sustinet (He who transplanted sustains).

Land area rank *Largest state (1)* — 48 — *smallest state (52)*

Population rank *Most people (1)* — 29 — *fewest people (52)*

At a Glance

Name: *Connecticut* comes from an Algonquian word meaning "place beside the long tidal river."

Nicknames: Constitution State, Nutmeg State

Capital: Hartford

Size: 5,544 sq. mi.

Population: 3,405,565

Statehood: Connecticut became the fifth state on January 9, 1788.

Electoral votes: 7 (2004)

U.S. Representatives: 6 (until 2003)

State tree: white oak

State flower: mountain laurel

State animal: sperm whale

Highest point: Mount Frissell, 2,380 ft.

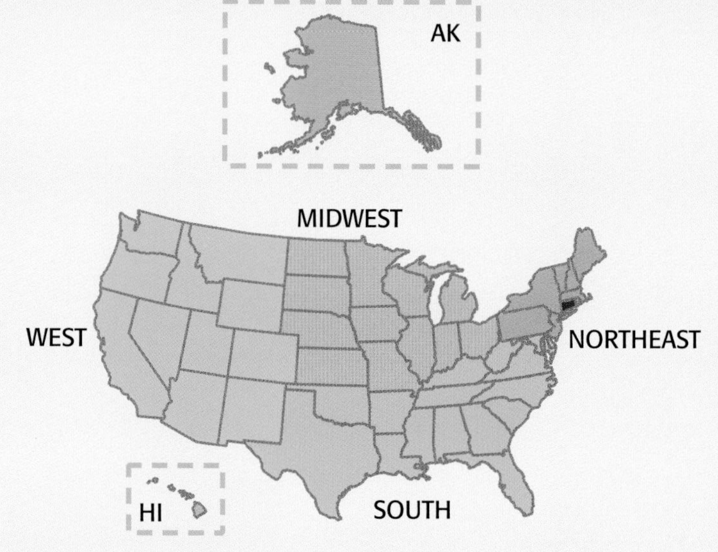

The Place

Connecticut is the third-smallest state and forms the southern portion of New England. Connecticut has rolling hills and mountains to the north and west and 250 miles of shoreline to the south along Long Island Sound. Elevations are highest in the northwest corner of the state.

Connecticut has many lakes, streams, and rivers. The Connecticut River flows south from upper New England, cuts through the middle of the state, and ends in Long

Historic Mystic Seaport, on Long Island Sound

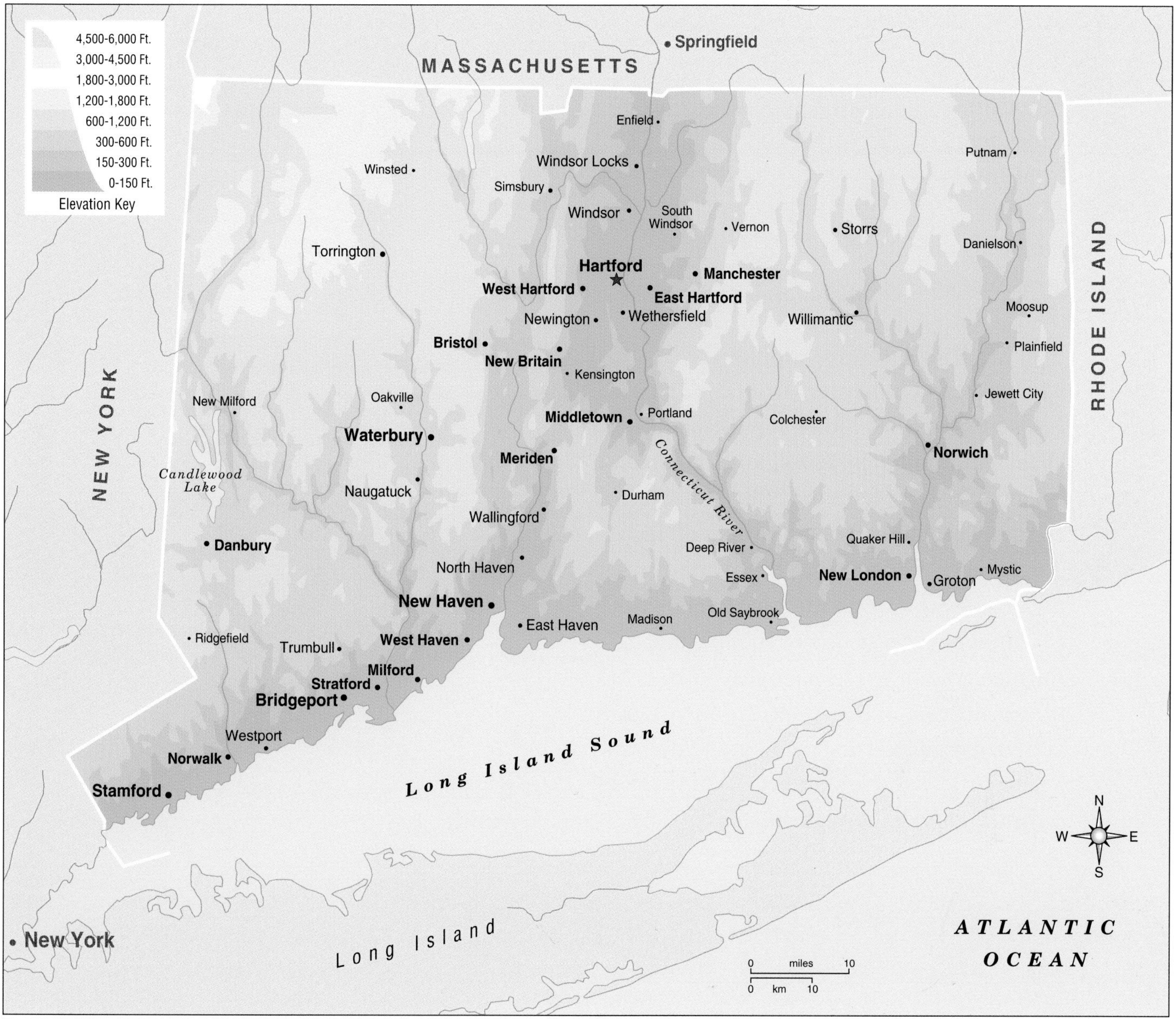

Island Sound. The valleys in the central part of the state are agricultural areas, although much of Connecticut's soil is too stony for farming.

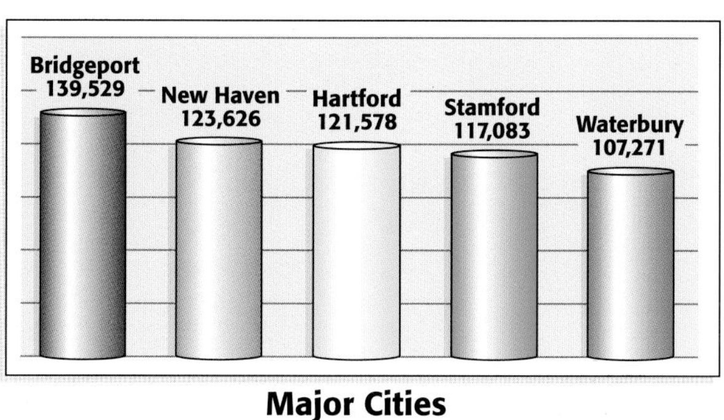

Major Cities

Connecticut has a climate that does not range to great extremes. The state's weather is warm in the summer and cold and snowy in the winter. Connecticut's climate is milder than that of the more northerly New England states.

Connecticut does not have many natural resources, but forests are plentiful, and sand and gravel are important exports.

The Past

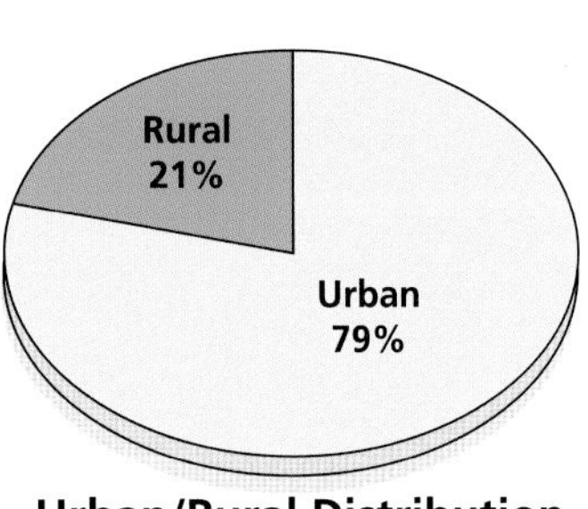

Native American tribes that lived in the area for hundreds of years named the region. The first Europeans to explore the territory were the Dutch. Settlers from the Massachusetts Bay Colony quickly followed. While still under British rule, Connecticut became the first state to create its own charter, the Fundamental Orders of 1639. This earned Connecticut one of its nicknames, the Constitution State.

Connecticut was one of the original thirteen colonies. The state played an important role in the American Revolution as a major supplier for the Continental army.

After the war, Connecticut became a key industrial and manufacturing state. The

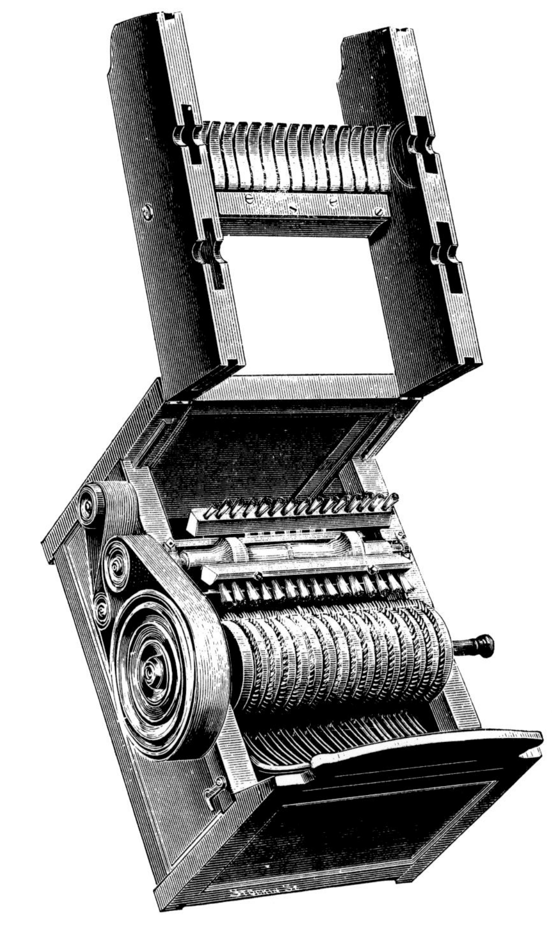

Eli Whitney invented the cotton gin in Connecticut in 1794.

Facts and Firsts

- ★ In 1728, the first American steel mill opened in Simsbury, Connecticut.
- ★ Connecticut native Noah Webster wrote the first American dictionary, which was published in 1806.
- ★ New Haven was the first place in the world to have a telephone exchange. The exchange opened on January 28, 1878. New Haven also had the first telephone book, which was published the same year the exchange opened and contained only 50 names.
- ★ The oldest public library in the country is the Scoville Public Library, in Scoville.
- ★ The hamburger (1895), Polaroid camera (1934), helicopter (1939), and color television (1948) were invented in Connecticut.
- ★ The world's first nuclear-powered submarine, the USS *Nautilus*, was built in Groton in 1954.
- ★ Pez candy is manufactured in Orange.
- ★ In 1999, Connecticut was the state with the highest per capita income (money earned per person). In 2000, New Jersey surpassed it for the first time in many years.

State Smart

Connecticut's* Hartford Courant *is the oldest continuously published newspaper in the United States. Thomas Green started the publication in 1764.

state's strong rivers provided it with an inexpensive energy source for its many mills. When Connecticut's economy shifted from farming to manufacturing, demand for ready-to-wear clothing helped the textile industry to grow.

Connecticut residents also invented a number of useful products, including the portable typewriter and the can opener. Other significant items from Connecticut were the cotton gin, invented by Eli Whitney in 1794; the first sewing machine invented by Elias Howe in 1846; and the first artificial heart invented by Dr. Robert K. Jarvik in 1982.

Connecticut mills and factories were also known for their brass, clocks, silverware, locks, guns, and tools. Although the days of the old mills have passed, Connecticut remains a leading industrial state today.

The Tapping Reeve in Litchfield was the first law school in the American colonies.

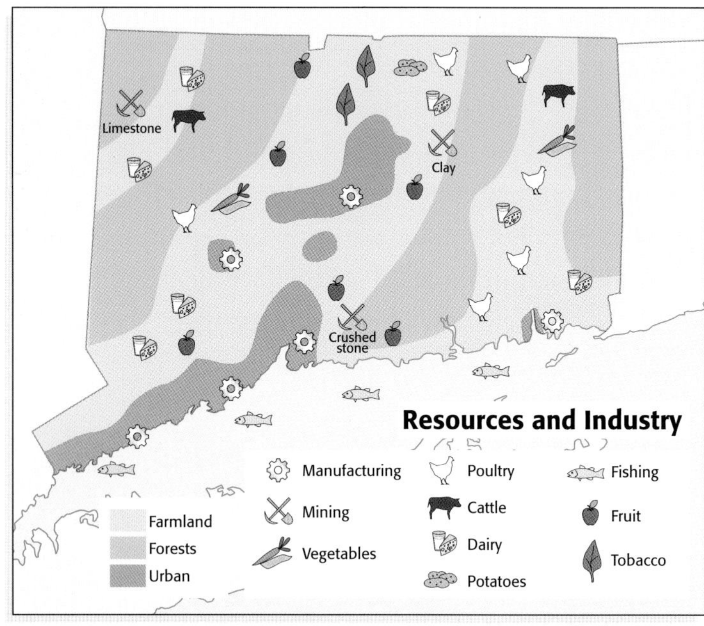

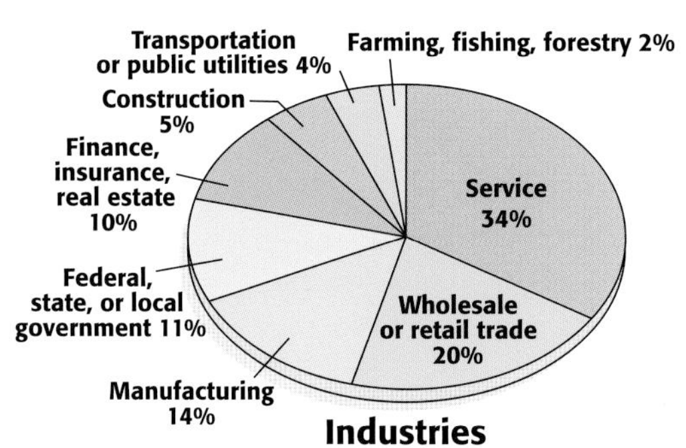

The Present

Connecticut has retained a strong sense of history. The state offers a blend of urban and rural areas that include both large cities and small farming towns. The farms produce dairy foods, poultry, fruits, and vegetables. Tobacco is the state's most valuable crop.

Connecticut is home to many of the nation's insurance companies. Hartford is known as the Insurance Capital of the World. Other Connecticut cities produce weapons, helicopters, jet engines, and submarines.

Yale University, founded in 1701, is the third-oldest institution of higher learning in the United States. Its library is the oldest library still operating in Connecticut. Many people visit Connecticut every year to tour its historic small towns, fish and camp in Connecticut's rural areas, or take in the colorful foliage of a Connecticut autumn.

Below left: *Schoolchildren visit salt marshes on Barn Island.* Below right: *Helicopters such as those used by the Coast Guard are manufactured in Connecticut.*

Born in Connecticut

- ★ **Dean Acheson**, statesman
- ★ **Ethan Allen**, American Revolutionary War soldier
- ★ **Benedict Arnold**, American Revolutionary general
- ★ **(Phineas Taylor) P.T. Barnum**, showman
- ★ **Henry Ward Beecher**, clergyman
- ★ **John Brown**, abolitionist
- ★ **George W. Bush**, U.S. president
- ★ **Samuel Colt**, weapons manufacturer
- ★ **Charles Goodyear**, inventor
- ★ **Nathan Hale**, American Revolution officer
- ★ **Dorothy Hamill**, ice skater
- ★ **Katharine Hepburn**, actress
- ★ **Charles Ives**, composer
- ★ **Edwin H. Land**, inventor, photographic pioneer
- ★ **John Pierpont Morgan**, financier
- ★ **Rosa Ponselle**, opera singer
- ★ **Adam Clayton Powell, Jr.**, congressman
- ★ **Meg Ryan**, actress
- ★ **Benjamin Spock**, pediatrician
- ★ **Harriet Beecher Stowe**, author
- ★ **Noah Webster**, lexicographer

Above: *Harriet Beecher Stowe;* middle: *Edwin H. Land;* below: *Meg Ryan*

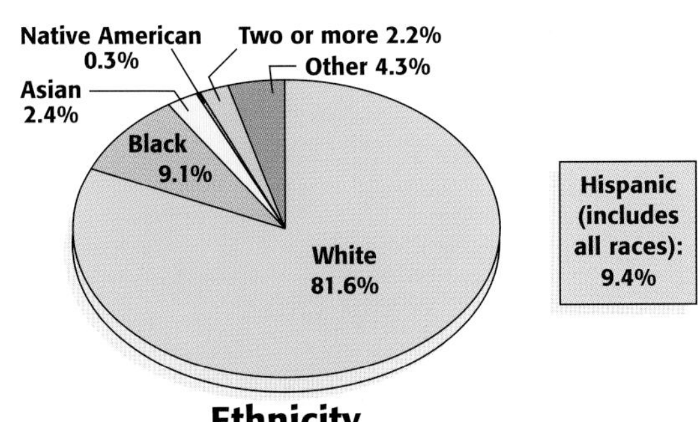

Ethnicity

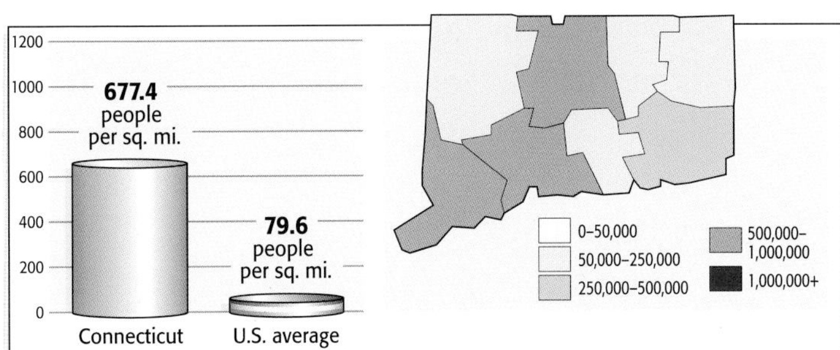

Population Density

Population by County

The library at Yale University in New Haven. Yale was founded in 1701.

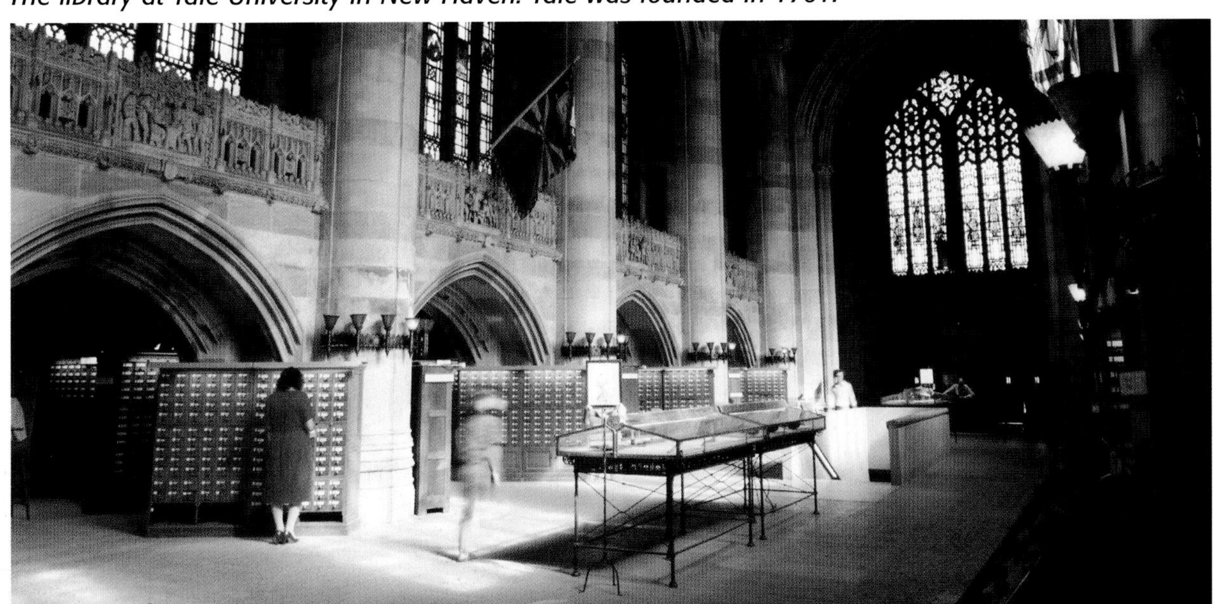

Delaware

Liberty and independence.

Land area rank
Largest state (1)

Population rank
Most people (1)

At a Glance

Name: The name *Delaware* comes from the Delaware River and Bay, which were named for Sir Thomas West, Baron De La Warr, the first governor of Virginia.

Nicknames: First State, Diamond State

Capital: Dover

Size: 2,396 sq. mi.

Population: 783,600

Statehood: Delaware became the first state on December 7, 1787.

Electoral votes: 3 (2004)

U.S. Representatives: 1 (until 2003)

State tree: American holly

State flower: peach blossom

State insect: ladybug

Highest point: Ebright Azimuth, 448 ft.

The Place

Delaware is the second-smallest state and is located in the Mid-Atlantic region of the country. Delaware's coastline is 28 miles long. The state is situated close to many of the nation's largest cities, including Baltimore, Philadelphia, and New York, and the nation's capital, Washington, D.C.

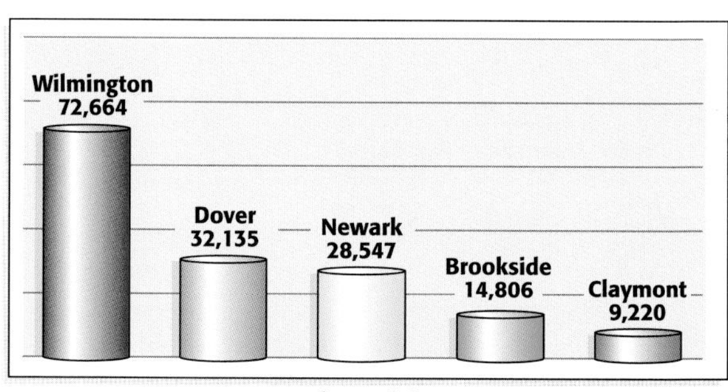

Major Cities

The Delaware River forms the boundary between Delaware and New Jersey.

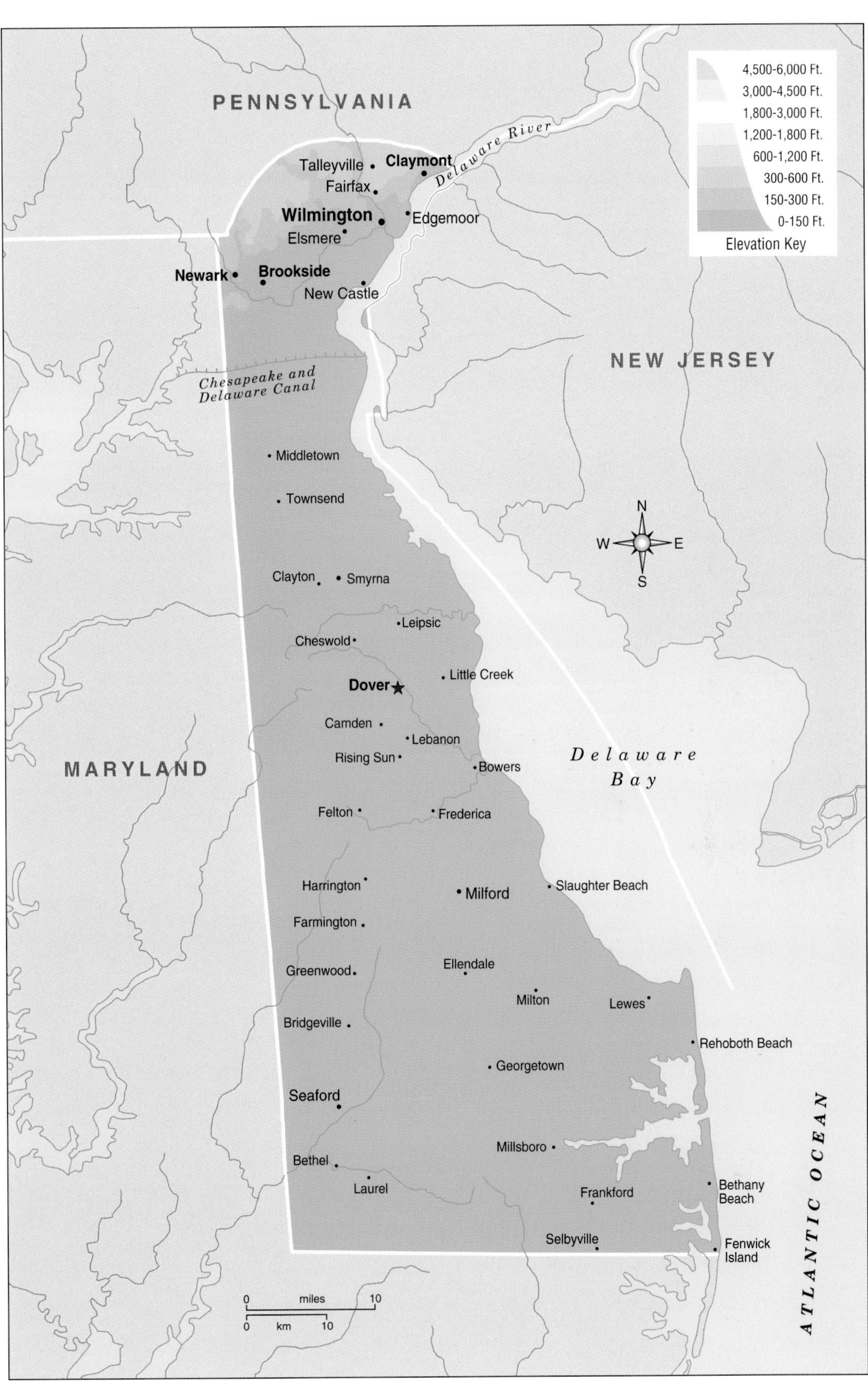

Delaware shares the DelMarVa Peninsula with Maryland and Virginia.

Most of the state is low, flat, coastal terrain. The northern area of the state, part of the Piedmont region, is covered with rolling hills and valleys. Much of Delaware is excellent agricultural land. A 30,000-acre swamp runs along Delaware's southern boundary.

The Delaware River is the state's largest river. Lakes and streams are important to Delaware's transportation and economy. Stone, sand, gravel, and clay are the state's most important mineral resources. About a third of Delaware is thickly forested. Delaware's climate is generally humid with hot summers and mild winters, although temperatures along the coastline are more stable and temperate.

Log cabins were erected by the Swedes who founded Fort Christina in 1638.

Facts and Firsts

- ★ Delaware is known as the First State because it was the first to ratify (approve) the U.S. Constitution, on December 7, 1787.
- ★ Nylon was invented in the Du Pont factories in Seaford.
- ★ The first beauty pageant in the United States, which later became the Miss America Pageant, was held at Rehoboth Beach in 1880. Inventor Thomas A. Edison was one of the three judges.
- ★ Swedish and Finnish settlers built the country's first log cabins along the Delaware River.
- ★ Delaware was an important stop along the Underground Railroad. Delaware resident Thomas Garrett reportedly helped more than 2,000 fugitive slaves escape to safety.
- ★ The Thousand Acre Marsh is northern Delaware's largest freshwater tidal wetland. Analysis of a fossilized pollen sequence from the mucky bottomland determined the swamp's age at 10,000 to 12,000 years old.
- ★ Barratt's Chapel was built in 1780 and was one of Delaware's first churches. The chapel is known as the Cradle of Methodism and is the oldest Methodist house of worship still standing in the United States.

The Past

Many different peoples have occupied Delaware throughout its history. For centuries, the area was the home to several Algonquian tribes, including the Delaware and Nanticoke. Europeans first reached Delaware in 1631 when the Dutch settled near the city of Lewes. During the next 50 years, Delaware fell under Swedish, Dutch, and then English control.

In 1664, England took control of the area, then gave it to William Penn, the founder of the colony of Pennsylvania, in 1682. Although Delaware was known as Pennsylvania's Three Lower Counties, it was relatively independent from the main colony, and fought as a separate state in the American Revolution.

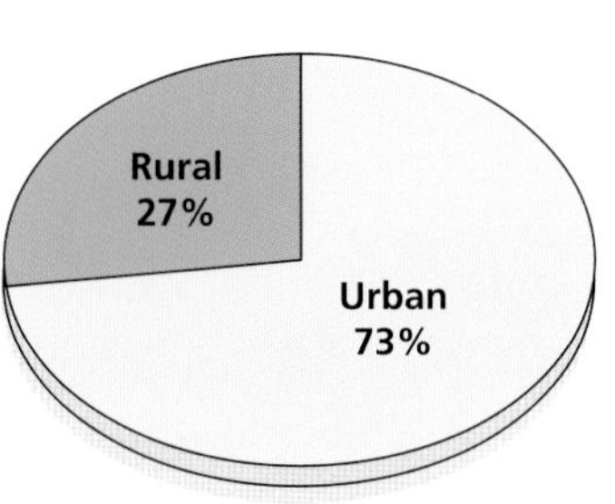

Urban/Rural Distribution

State Smart

Old Swedes Church, in Wilmington, is the oldest church in the United States still in its original form. It was built as a Swedish Lutheran Church in 1699.

In 1802, Delaware's industrial future was sealed when E.I. Du Pont opened the first Du Pont factory, a gunpowder mill at Wilmington. In 1935, Wallace Carothers of the DuPont Company invented nylon. Since then, Delaware has become increasingly industrialized and many companies and industries locate in the state because it has low taxes.

Fort Delaware, located on Pea Patch Island in the Delaware River, housed Confederate prisoners during the Civil War.

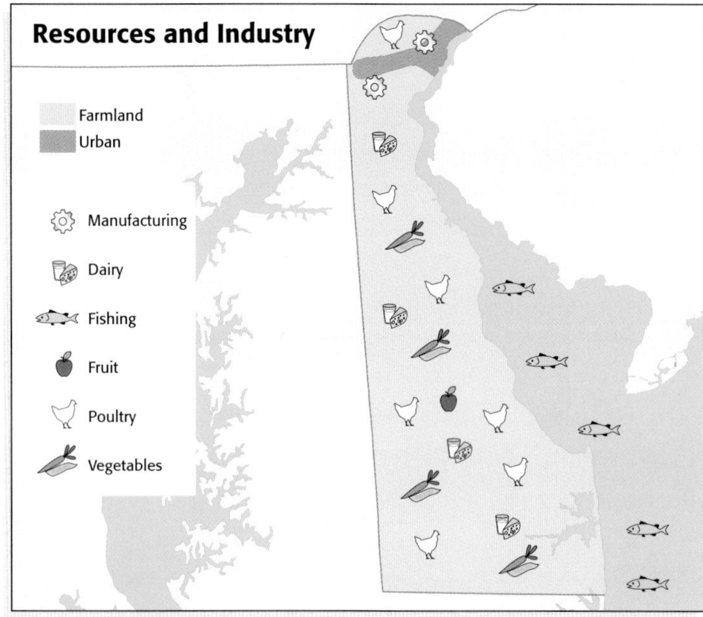

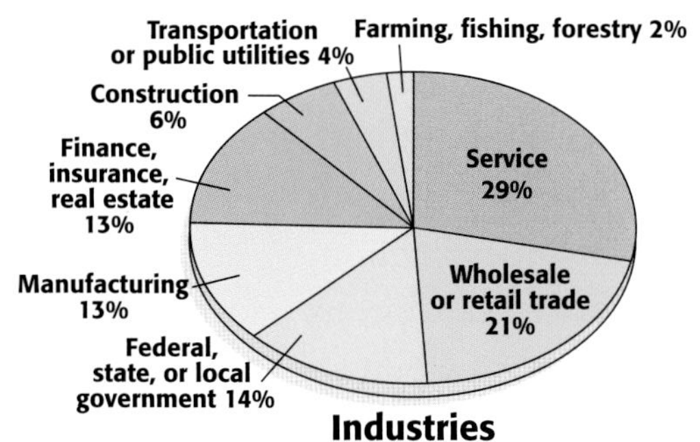

The Present

Delaware is home to more than 200,000 different businesses because it is so corporation friendly. Many chemical-producing corporations are located in Delaware. The Du Pont Company is the largest of these and employs the most people.

Other Delaware companies manufacture vulcanized fiber, textiles, paper, medical supplies, metal products, machinery, machine tools, and automobiles. In the city of Wilmington, banking is an important industry.

Delaware's good soil makes it competitive agriculturally. Chicken raising is Delaware's principal type of animal farming. Fishing and dairy farming are also common.

Today, Delaware has a strong base in chemical manufacturing that began with the Du Pont Company in 1802.

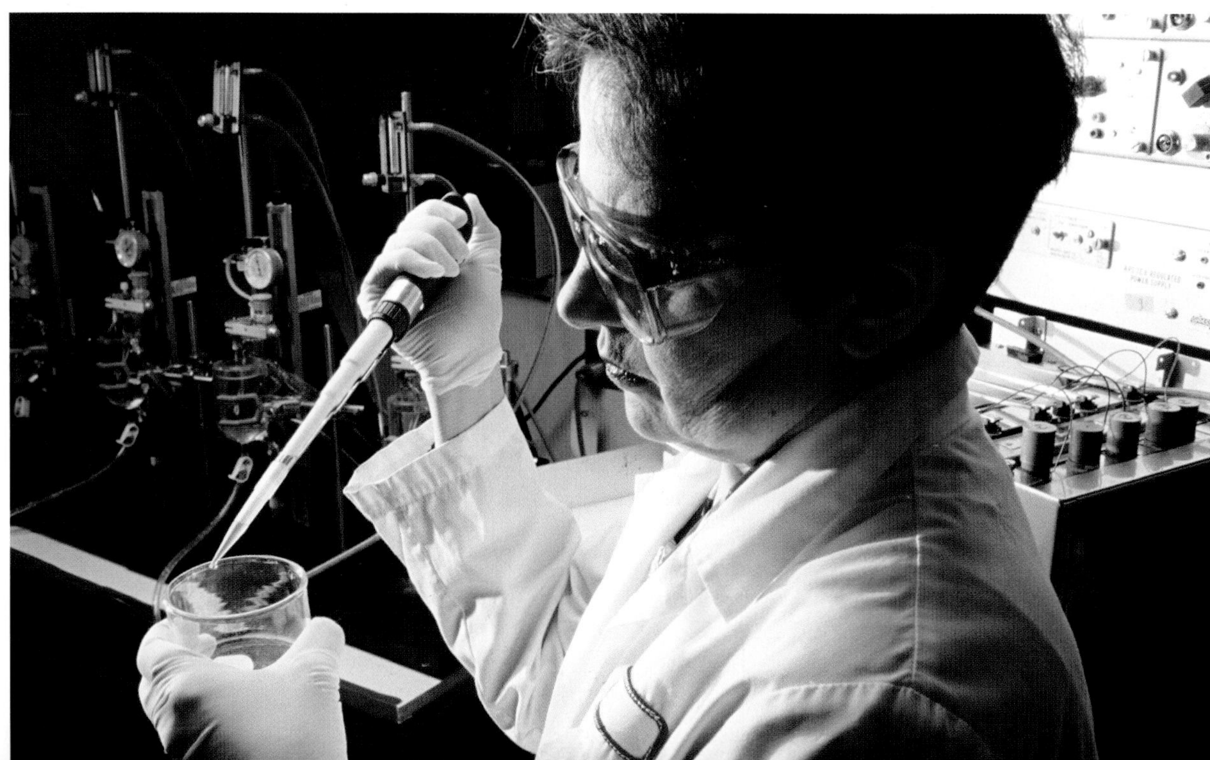

Born in Delaware

- ★ **Robert Montgomery Bird**, playwright
- ★ **Henry S. Canby**, editor and author
- ★ **Annie Jump Cannon**, astronomer
- ★ **Oliver Evans**, inventor
- ★ **Henry Heimlich**, surgeon and inventor
- ★ **Pierre S. Du Pont**, chemist and industrialist
- ★ **Howard Pyle**, artist and author
- ★ **Caesar Rodney**, patriot, signer of Declaration of Independence
- ★ **Elizabeth Shue**, actress

Howard Pyle reads to his daughter.

Delaware farms produce a variety of crops, including corn, soybeans, potatoes, and hay.

Each year, thousands of people visit Delaware's historic homes, some of which were built before the American Revolution.The Delaware coastline is also a popular vacation spot. Water-sport and fishing enthusiasts enjoy the state's many scenic lakes and rivers.

A couple performs a folk dance during the Winterthur Country Fair at the Winterthur Museum and Gardens.

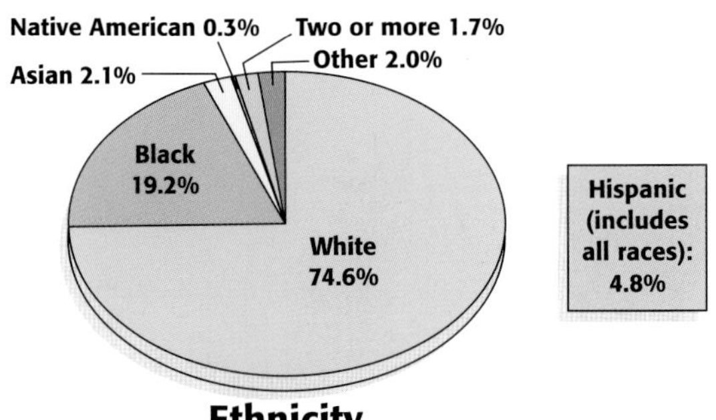

Ethnicity

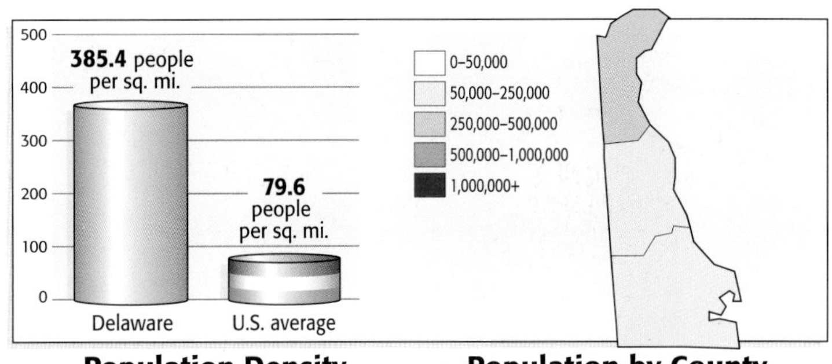

Population Density

Population by County

Florida

In God we trust.

Land area rank *Largest state (1)* — 23 — *smallest state (52)*

Population rank *Most people (1)* — 4 — *fewest people (52)*

At a Glance

Name: Spanish explorer Ponce de León named Florida when he landed there on Easter Sunday in 1513. He called the place *Pascua Florida*, which means "flowery Easter" in Spanish.

Nickname: Sunshine State

Capital: Tallahassee

Size: 59,928 sq. mi.

Population: 15,982,378

Statehood: Florida became the 27th state on March 3, 1845.

Electoral votes: 27 (2004)

U.S. Representatives: 23 (until 2003)

State tree: sabal palmetto

State flower: orange blossom

State marine mammal: manatee

Highest point: Britton Hill, 345 ft.

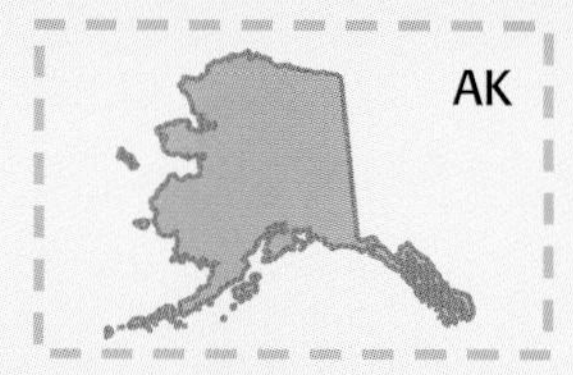

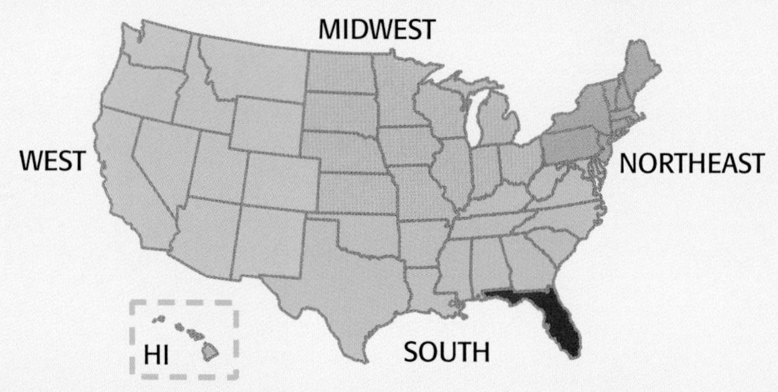

The Place

Florida is a long peninsula surrounded by water on three sides. To the west is the Gulf of Mexico; to the east is the Atlantic Ocean. Only Alaska has a longer coastline than Florida.

The northwestern part of the state is called the Panhandle and lies along the Gulf of Mexico. The southernmost tip of

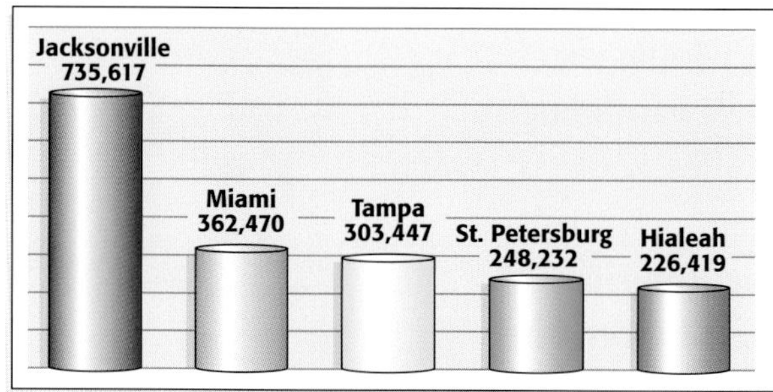

Major Cities

Miami, a center for business and tourism, is surrounded by water.

Florida is less than 100 miles from the island nation of Cuba. The Everglades, a region of swamps and wetlands, cover most of southern Florida.

Most of Florida's terrain north of the Everglades is level or rolling. More than half the state is forested. Lake Okeechobee is the largest lake in Florida and covers 680 square miles (1,768 square km). It is the second-largest natural freshwater lake in the United States. Many other small lakes are scattered throughout central Florida. Florida is also famous for springs from which clear water flows.

Seminole chief Osceola led the Seminole people in resistance against white settlers.

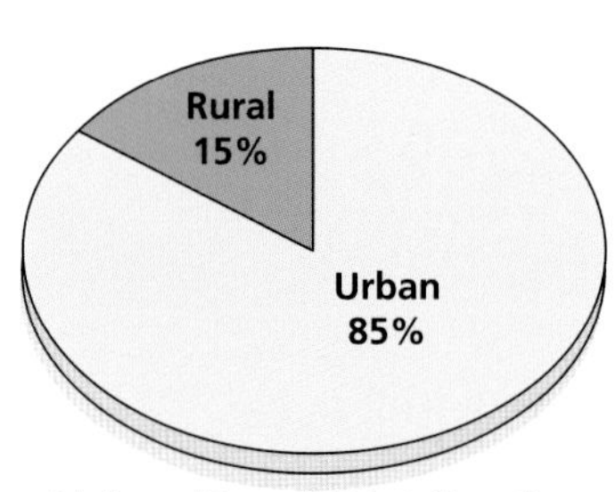

Urban/Rural Distribution

Florida's climate is subtropical except in the south, where it is tropical. Summers are hot, humid, and sunny, while winters are generally mild. This climate is excellent for many types of agriculture.

Limestone is the state's most plentiful mineral, but Florida also has the largest deposits of phosphate in the United States. Mineral sands are also important to Florida's economy.

The Past

Ponce de León claimed the region for Spain in 1513 during his search for the mythical Fountain of Youth. In 1565, Pedro

Facts and Firsts

- ★ Florida is the southernmost of the continental United States.
- ★ One of only two naturally round lakes in the world is in DeFuniak Springs.
- ★ Fort Lauderdale's 185 miles of local waterways helped earn it the nickname the Venice of America.
- ★ The Florida Keys, a series of islands off the coast, extend more than 150 miles from Florida's southernmost tip.
- ★ Every year, more people go to Orlando than to any other city in the United States to visit the many amusement parks located there.
- ★ All American spaceflights are launched from Cape Canaveral, including the *Apollo 11* flight that carried astronauts to the moon for the first time.
- ★ Clearwater has the highest per capita (per person) rate of lightning strikes of any place in the United States.
- ★ Gatorade, a popular sport drink, was invented in Florida and named after the University of Florida's mascot, the Gators.
- ★ In 1944, Benjamin Green, a pharmacist from Miami Beach, invented suntan lotion by cooking cocoa butter.

Menéndez de Avilés founded St. Augustine, the site of the first permanent European settlement in North America. Although the Spanish settled and built missions in the northern area of what later became the state of Florida, portions of the region fell under British control around 1763.

The territory did not become part of the United States until 1821, when Spain sold it to the United States. Florida was the site of fighting between settlers and Native Americans. This fighting, known as the Seminole Wars, ended in 1842. The United States established control of the region, and Florida became a state in 1845.

When the Civil War began, Florida seceded from the United States with the rest of the South. It was readmitted to the Union in 1868.

State Smart

Key West is the warmest city in the United States, with an average temperature of 77° F (24° C).

In the late 19th and early 20th centuries, areas of swampland were drained to expose the fertile soil beneath for farming. This new land stimulated the first of several population booms in southern Florida when people came to the area with hopes of getting rich by farming or by buying and selling real estate. Florida quickly became

Castillo de San Marcos, which the Spanish began to build in 1672, protected both St. Augustine and the route treasure ships took back to Spain.

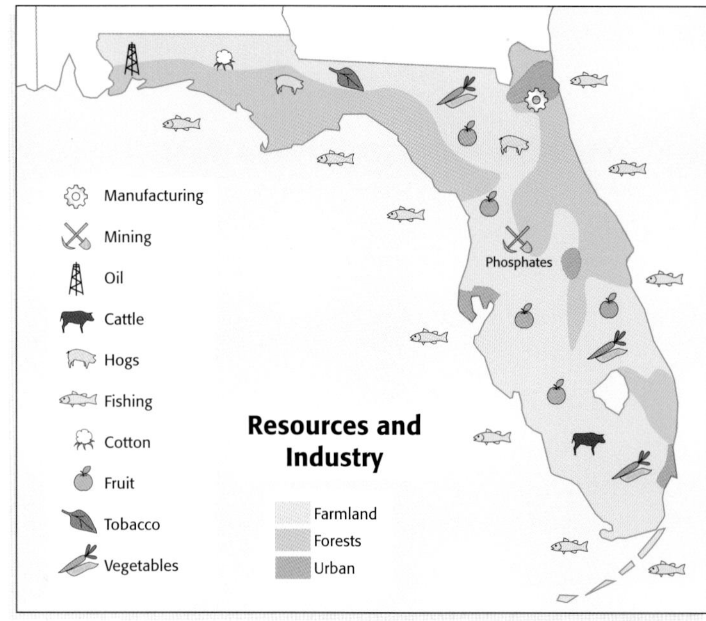

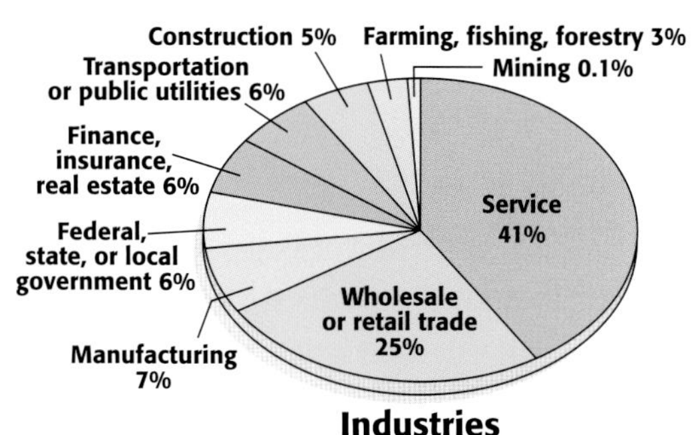

prime agricultural land, but after great fires in 1939, studies of the Everglades concluded that most of the southern part was unfit for cultivation.

As early as the 1870s, residents from northern states traveled south to spend the winter months in Florida to enjoy the state's natural beauty and mild climate. Steamboat tours on Florida's winding rivers were a popular attraction for these visitors. One hundred years later, in 1971, Florida tourism got a big boost when Walt Disney World opened in Orlando.

The Present

Florida's biggest industry is tourism. Some of the popular attractions located in Florida include Walt Disney World, Sea World, Everglades National Park, and Kennedy Space Center. The large theme parks in the Orlando area, as well as other attractions, annually bring more than 40 million

Below left: *Tourists relax on the beach at Clearwater.* Below right: *The space shuttle takes off from Cape Canaveral.*

Born in Florida

- ★ **Julian "Cannonball" Adderley**, jazz saxophonist
- ★ **Fernando Bujones**, ballet dancer, choreographer
- ★ **Faye Dunaway**, actress
- ★ **Zora Neal Hurston**, writer
- ★ **Jim Morrison**, singer
- ★ **Sidney Poitier**, actor
- ★ **A. Philip Randolph**, labor leader
- ★ **Joseph W. Stilwell**, army general

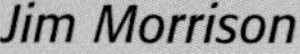
Jim Morrison

visitors from the United States and countries around the world.

Florida's warm temperatures and sandy beaches also contribute to its popularity with vacationers. Florida's service industries provide food, communication, utilities, medical care, entertainment, housing, and transportation to tourists and the state's growing population. These service industries form the foundation of Florida's economy.

The warm climate and long growing season allow farmers to grow fruits and vegetables, especially citrus fruits, year-round. Florida grows almost two-thirds of the nation's oranges and three-fourths of its grapefruit.

Many other industries help round out Florida's diverse economy. Banking and business services are quickly growing industries. Many Floridians raise cattle. Florida also manufactures aerospace and aircraft equipment and electrical equipment, such as telephones and X-ray machines.

Key Largo sits between Florida Bay and the Everglades National Park and is rich in natural wildlife.

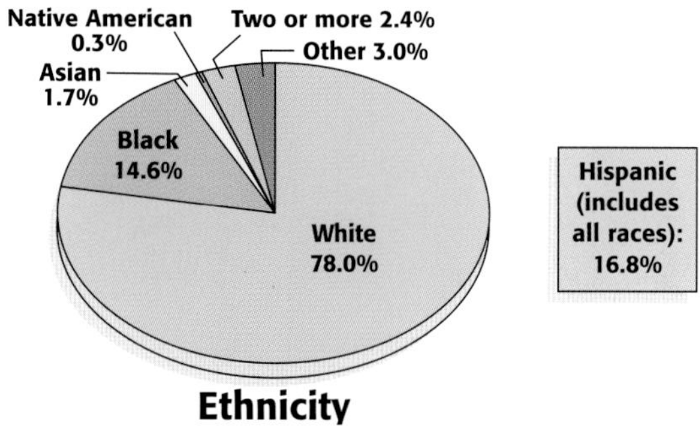

Ethnicity

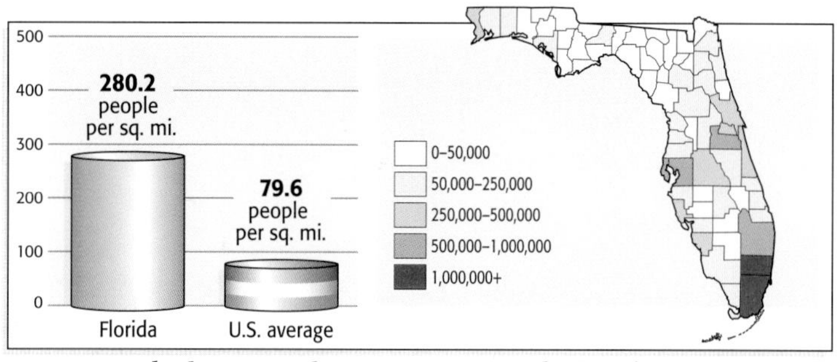

Population Density **Population by County**

Georgia

Wisdom, justice, and moderation.

Land area rank *Largest state (1)* — 24 — *smallest state (52)*

Population rank *Most people (1)* — 10 — *fewest people (52)*

At a Glance

Name: Georgia was named for King George II of England.

Nicknames: Peach State, Empire State of the South

Capital: Atlanta

Size: 58,977 sq. mi.

Population: 8,186,453

Statehood: Georgia became the fourth state on January 2, 1788.

Electoral votes: 15 (2004)

U.S. Representatives: 11 (until 2003)

State tree: live oak

State flower: Cherokee rose

State fish: largemouth bass

Highest point: Brasstown Bald, 4,784 ft.

The Place

The northern half of Georgia is covered with high mountains that form part of the Appalachian chain, which extends through the eastern United States. Georgia's most fertile soil is in the Appalachian valleys, which makes them important agricultural regions. The land becomes increasingly flat as it stretches toward the Atlantic Ocean and Florida.

About 65 percent of the state is thickly forested, especially the mountainous regions. Georgia's climate is generally mild with warm, humid summers and short winters. Temperatures are cooler in the mountains. Some of Georgia's natural resources are its rivers, extensive forests, and many minerals, including clay, granite, and marble. The statue of Abraham Lincoln in the Lincoln Memorial in Washington, D.C., was carved from Georgia's white marble.

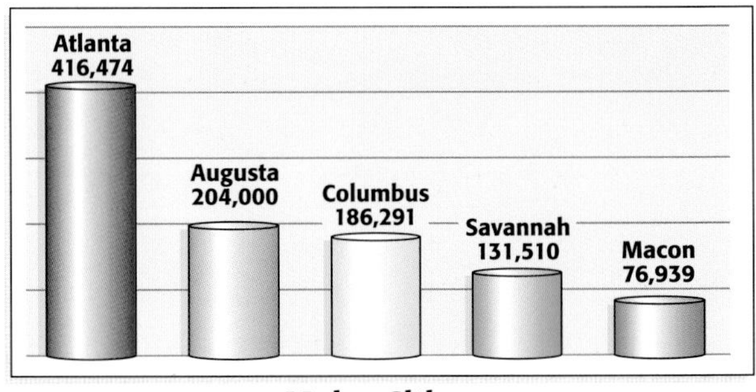

Major Cities

Atlanta, Georgia's capital, is a commercial, financial, and cultural center.

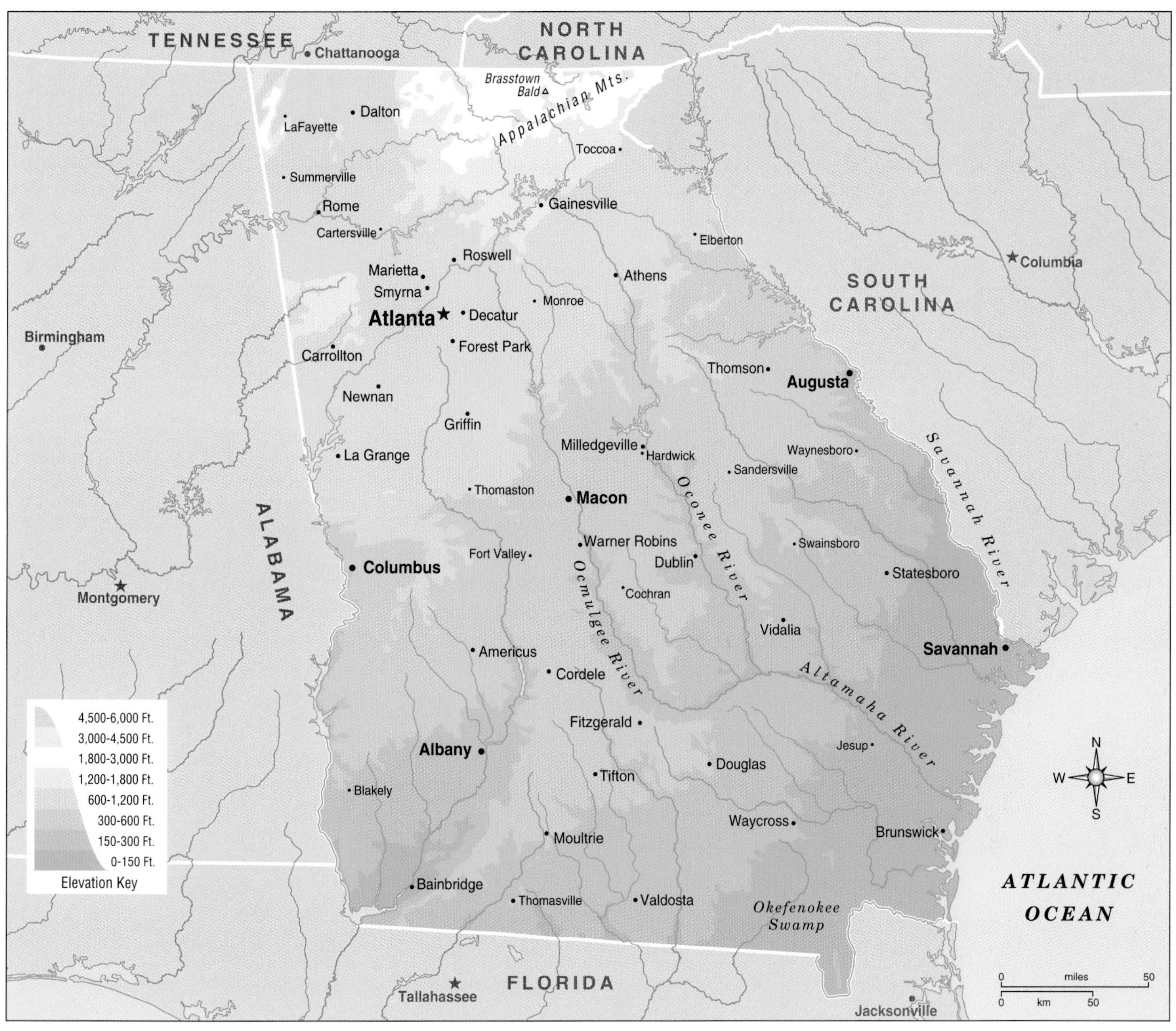

THE PAST

Georgia's first inhabitants were Creek and Cherokee peoples. The first Europeans to explore the area were Spanish missionaries, who founded Santa Catalina in 1566. The British also claimed the region. James E. Oglethorpe founded the first permanent settlement in Georgia at Savannah in 1733. Georgia became a refuge for English debtors and victims of religious persecution.

During the American Revolution, Georgians helped the American Continental army by raiding the British armory in Savannah and giving the weapons to the American revolutionaries. After the war, Georgia became the fourth of the original thirteen colonies to ratify the U.S. Constitution and become a state.

During the 1830s, Georgia expelled much of its Native American population.

The Cherokee were forced by the U.S. government to leave their homes in Georgia and travel west. The route came to be known as the Trail of Tears.

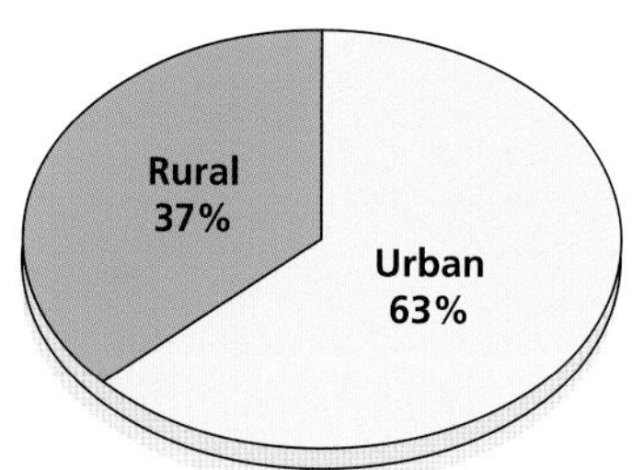

Urban/Rural Distribution

In 1838, the last of the Cherokee Indians were forced to move to Indian Territory in Oklahoma in a cross-country march that became known as the Trail of Tears. During the Civil War, Georgia left the Union to fight as a southern state. Much of the state was damaged during William Tecumseh Sherman's famous March to the Sea, when the Civil War general and his men destroyed everything in their path from Atlanta to Savannah.

After the Civil War, Georgia's economy began to expand. The cultivation of cotton, which had dominated the economy, began to decrease and production increased on a variety of crops including peaches and peanuts, and manufactured goods.

After slow economic growth at the beginning of the 20th century, Georgia became one of the most industrialized southern states. Following World War II, Georgia's industrial growth accelerated, and Atlanta became known as a commercial,

Facts and Firsts

- ★ Georgia is the largest state east of the Mississippi.
- ★ Georgia produces more peanuts, pecans, and peaches than any other state.
- ★ Vidalia onions, one of the sweetest types of onion in the world, are grown only in Vidalia and Glennville.
- ★ The world's largest college campus is at Berry College in Rome.
- ★ Dr. John S. Pemberton invented the soft drink Coca-Cola in Atlanta in May 1886.
- ★ The *Cherokee Phoenix*, the nation's first known newspaper written in a Native American dialect, began publication in New Echota in 1828.
- ★ In 1943, Georgia became the first state to allow 18-year-olds to vote.

State Smart

Georgia produces more than 1.3 billion pounds (590 million kg) of peanuts every year—more than 50 percent of the nation's total peanut output.

financial, and cultural center for the Southeast. In 1996, Atlanta's progress was highlighted when the city hosted the Summer Olympic Games.

Left: *Lori Harrigan pitched a gold medal game for the U.S. Women's softball team in the 1996 Summer Olympics in Atlanta.* Below: *The images of three prominent Confederate figures (from left to right) Jefferson Davis, Robert E. Lee, and Thomas J. "Stonewall" Jackson are carved, 400 feet above the ground, into the granite of Stone Mountain.*

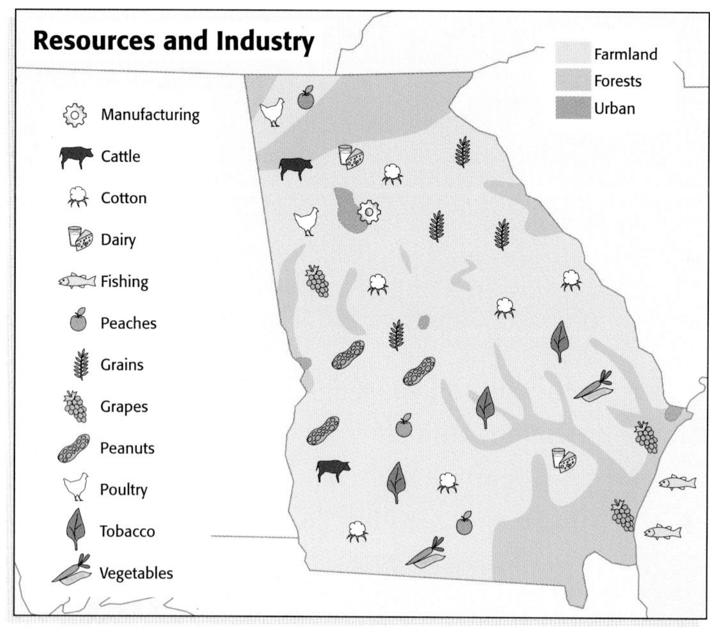

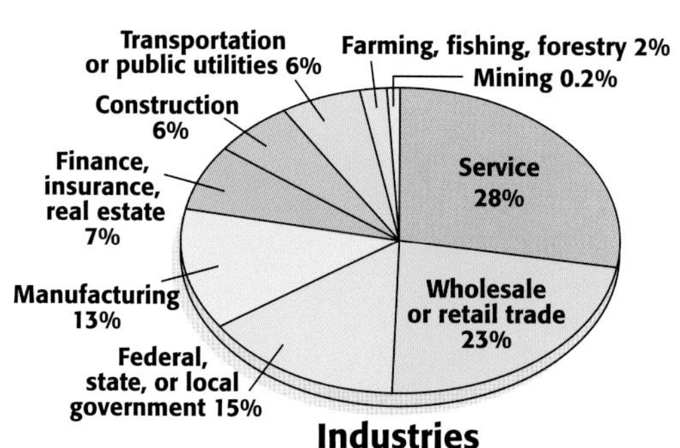

The Present

Before the Civil War, Georgia was famous for cotton produced on its many plantations, and agriculture remains an important part of the state's economy. In addition to peaches and pecans, Georgia farms grow large amounts of soybeans, tobacco, corn, and wheat. Tourism also contributes to the state's economy, as many tourists come to Georgia to visit the historic plantations, antebellum homes, and farms on the Antebellum Trail in the northeast part of the state.

Georgia is also a business-oriented state. Atlanta, the capital, is a center of trade, finance, and transportation. Many businesses, such as Coca-Cola, Georgia-Pacific, United Parcel Service, and Delta Air Lines have headquarters in Georgia.

Georgia has a strong manufacturing industry. Georgia produces more textiles than any other state except North Carolina, and the city of Dalton manufactures more carpet than any other city in the nation. Georgia also has many productive paper

Below left: *A paper mill, Savannah.* Below right: *Bulloch Hall, in Roswell on the Antebellum Trail, was built in 1840.*

Born in Georgia

- ★ **Conrad Aiken**, poet
- ★ **Erskine Caldwell**, writer
- ★ **James E. Carter**, U.S. president
- ★ **Ray Charles**, singer
- ★ **Ty Cobb**, baseball player
- ★ **Ossie Davis**, actor and writer
- ★ **James Dickey**, poet, novelist
- ★ **Rebecca Latimer Felton**, first woman appointed U.S. senator
- ★ **Oliver Hardy**, comedian
- ★ **Harry James**, trumpeter
- ★ **Jasper Johns**, painter, sculptor
- ★ **Martin Luther King Jr.**, civil rights leader
- ★ **Juliette Gordon Low**, U.S. Girl Scouts founder
- ★ **Carson McCullers**, novelist
- ★ **Johnny Mercer**, songwriter
- ★ **Margaret Mitchell**, novelist
- ★ **Elijah Muhammad**, black nationalist, religious leader
- ★ **Jessye Norman**, soprano
- ★ **(Mary) Flannery O'Connor**, author
- ★ **Osceola**, Seminole leader
- ★ **Jackie Robinson**, baseball player
- ★ **Clarence Thomas**, jurist
- ★ **Alice Walker**, author

Top: *Jackie Robinson;* middle: *Jimmy Carter;* bottom: *Alice Walker*

mills, and its factories build cars and aerospace equipment for the transportation industry.

Georgia is called the Empire State of the South because it is home to so many important industries.

Peaches are so plentiful in Georgia that women residents are sometimes referred to as Georgia Peaches.

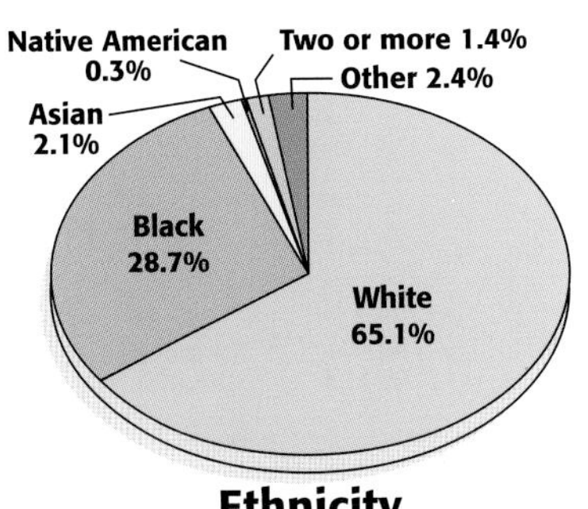

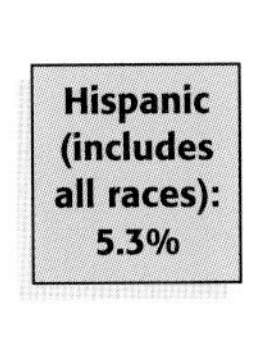

Ethnicity

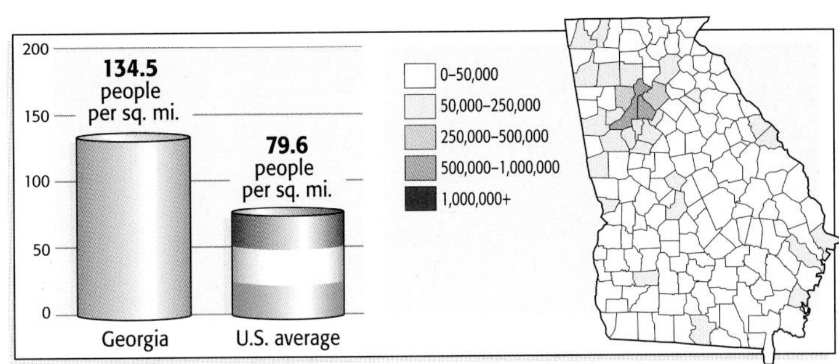

Population Density

Population by County

Hawaii

The life of the land is perpetuated in righteousness.

Land area rank
Largest state (1)

Population rank
Most people (1)

At a Glance

Name: The origin of the name *Hawaii* is uncertain. The islands may have been named after Hawaii Loa, the chief who has traditionally been believed to have discovered them, or they may have been named after Hawaii or Hawaiki, the traditional home of the Polynesians.

Nickname: Aloha State

Capital: Honolulu

Size: 6,459 sq. mi. (16,793 sq km)

Population: 1,211,537

Statehood: Hawaii became the 50th state on August 21, 1959.

Electoral votes: 4 (2004)

U.S. Representatives: 2 (until 2003)

State tree: kukui (candlenut)

State flower: yellow hibiscus

State bird: Hawaiian goose

Highest point: Mauna Kea, 13,796 ft. (4,205 m)

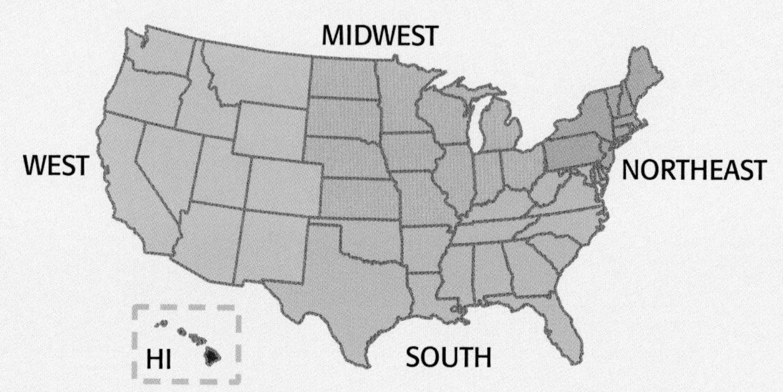

Honolulu, on the island of Oahu is the largest city in the Hawaiian Islands.

The Place

Hawaii is the world's longest island chain, with 124 islands. Hawaii is located 2,090 miles (3,344 km) west-southwest of San Francisco, California. Each island is made up of at least one primary volcano, although many islands are composites of more than

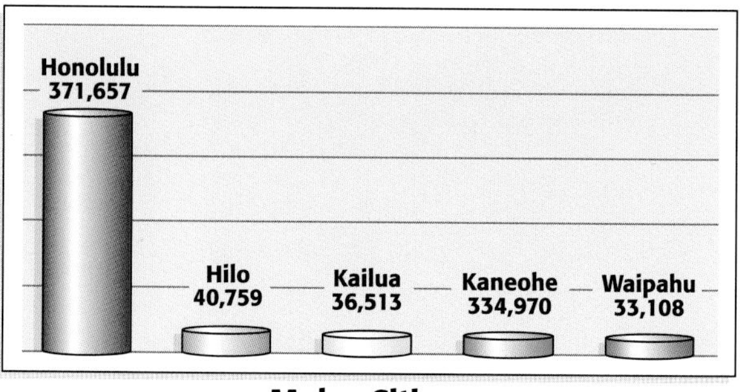

Major Cities

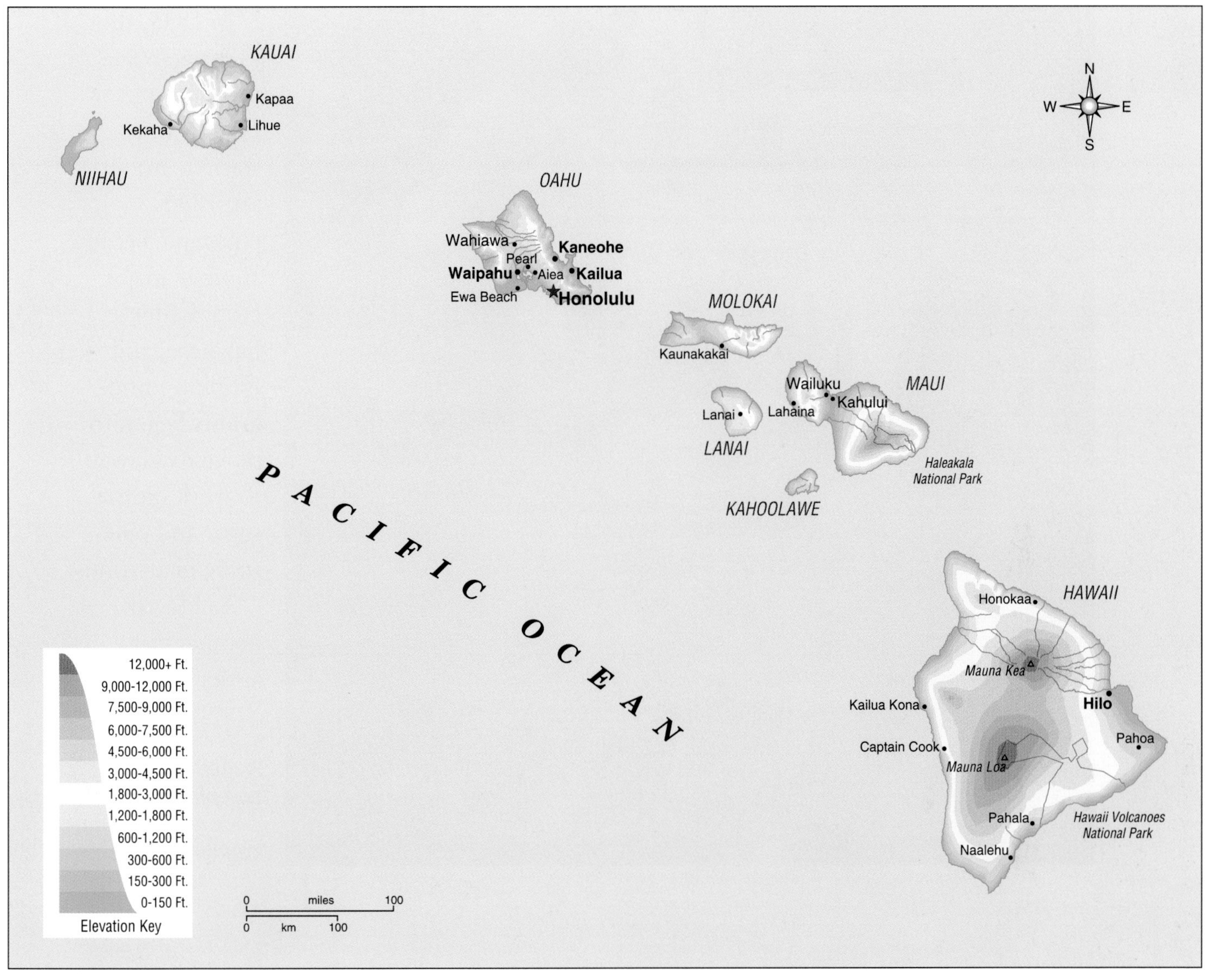

one. The eight largest Hawaiian islands are Hawaii, Kahoolawe, Maui, Lanai, Molokai, Oahu, Kauai, and Niihau. Of these eight, only Kahoolawe has no permanent inhabitants. The island of Hawaii is the largest. Honolulu, the state capital, is on Oahu.

The remaining islands consist of islets of rock in the middle of the chain, as well as coral and sand islands in the northwest.

The climate on the eight main islands is rainy and warm. Most of these islands have fertile soil, which enables their inhabitants to grow many kinds of tropical products.

Hawaii has few natural resources. It also has little native wildlife, but most of its animals and plants are unique in the world.

The Past

Hawaii's past is as colorful as its landscape. Polynesians, who sailed in canoes from other Pacific Islands sometime between A.D. 300 and 600, first settled the islands. The first European to explore Hawaii was British captain James Cook, who landed there in 1778. When Cook arrived, Hawaii was a monarchy controlled by Polynesian kings.

In 1835, the first sugarcane plantation in Hawaii was started, and in the 1880s pineapple became another major crop. Chinese, Japanese, and Filipino immigrants began to move to Hawaii to work on the sugar and pineapple plantations.

As Hawaii became more agriculturally

A mother and son play an ancient Polynesian counting game.

Facts and Firsts

- ★ Hawaii is the only state formed entirely of islands and not attached to continental North America.
- ★ From east to west, Hawaii is the widest state.
- ★ Hawaii has its own time zone, Hawaiian Standard Time. It is two hours behind Pacific Standard Time.
- ★ Hawaii is the only state that was once a royal kingdom. Today, Iolani Palace on the island of Oahu is the only royal palace in the United States.
- ★ The Hawaiian Islands were formed thousands of years ago by volcanoes that erupted under the sea. The islands are the tops of these undersea volcanoes.
- ★ Hawaii grows more than one-third of the world's supply of pineapple, and it is the only state that grows coffee.
- ★ The Hawaiian alphabet has only 12 letters—A, E, I, O, U, H, K, L, M, N, P, and W.

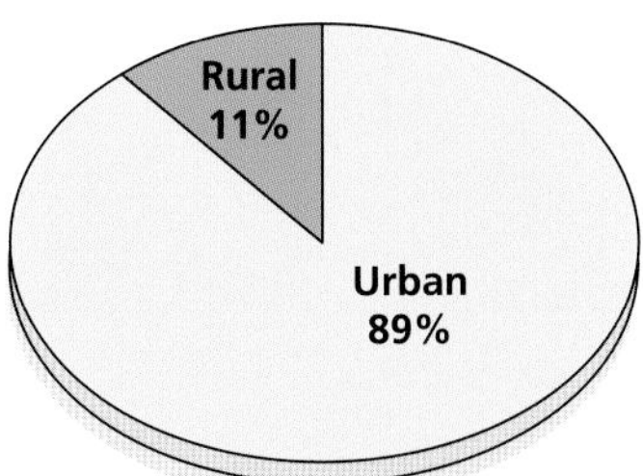

Urban/Rural Distribution

> ## State Smart
> ***Mount Waialeale, on the island of Kauai, is the wettest place on earth. Approximately 460 inches (1,168 cm) of rain falls there each year.***

valuable, U.S. involvement in its business and politics increased. In 1893, the last Hawaiian queen was removed from the throne, and Hawaii became a republic. In 1900, Hawaii became a U.S. territory. During World War I, the U.S. military built a naval base at Pearl Harbor. Years later, the Japanese attack on Pearl Harbor on December 7, 1941, drew the United States into World War II. Only after the war, when Hawaiians had proved their loyalty to the United States in a number of battles, was the territory admitted as a state.

This memorial honors Americans who lost their lives in the Japanese attack on Pearl Harbor.

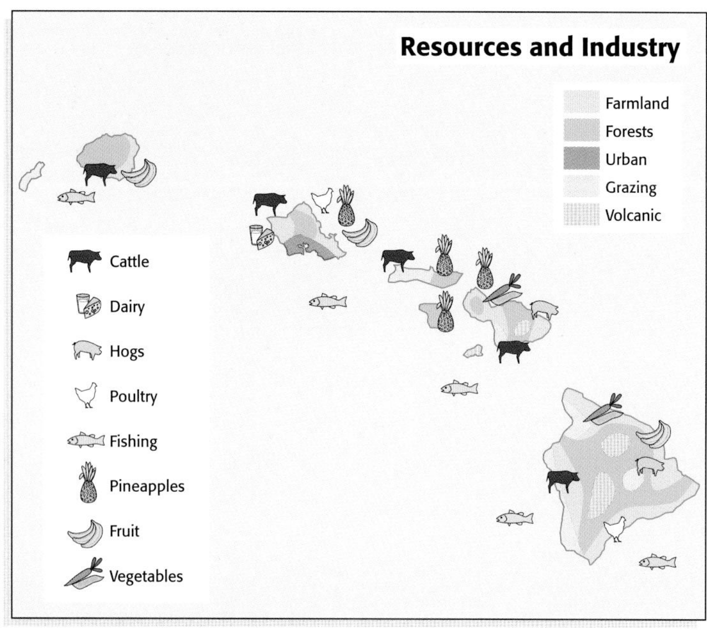

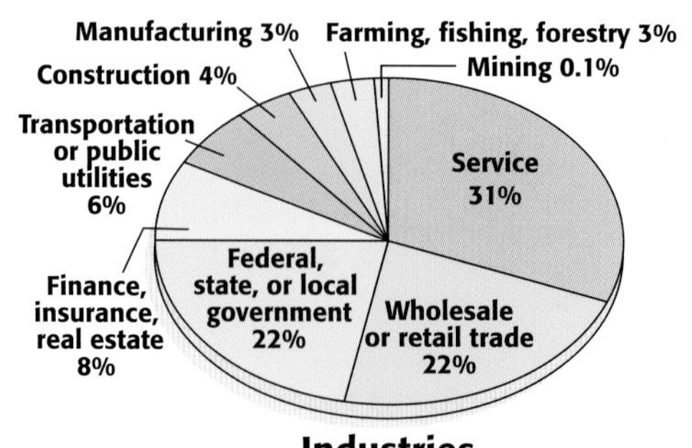

The Present

Today, tourism is Hawaii's most important industry. More than 6 million people visit the islands every year. Hawaii's beaches, mixture of cultures, and warm climate draw people from a variety of countries.

Tourism, however, presents Hawaii with a number of challenges. The state must balance the needs of its many tourists with its own ecological necessities. Many of Hawaii's native animal and plant species are endangered, and the expansion of tourism puts Hawaii's land at further risk.

Pineapple is an important crop, and the islands also grow coffee, bananas, sugar, flowers, and macadamia nuts. Aquaculture—the raising of fish and shellfish—is expanding. Manufacturing, especially food processing such as sugar refining and pineapple processing, help round out Hawaii's economy.

Above: *Pineapple is an important Hawaiian crop.*
Below: *An agricultural valley on the island of Kauai.*

Born in Hawaii

- ★ **Salevaa Atisanoe** (Konishiki), sumo wrestler
- ★ **Tia Carrere**, singer and actress
- ★ **Jean Erdman**, dancer and choreographer
- ★ **Hiram L. Fong**, first Chinese American senator
- ★ **Don Ho**, entertainer
- ★ **Duke Paoa Kahanamoku**, Olympic swimming champion
- ★ **George Parsons Lathrop**, journalist and poet
- ★ **Bette Midler**, singer and actress
- ★ **Ellison Onizuka**, astronaut
- ★ **Harold Sakata**, actor

Above: *Duke Paoa Kahanamoku;* below: *Bette Midler*

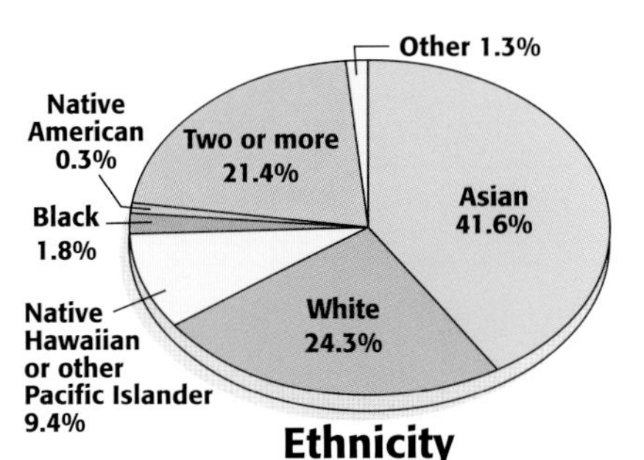

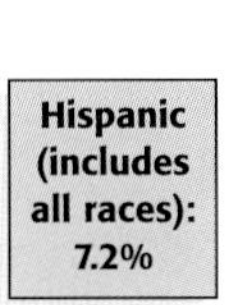

Ethnicity

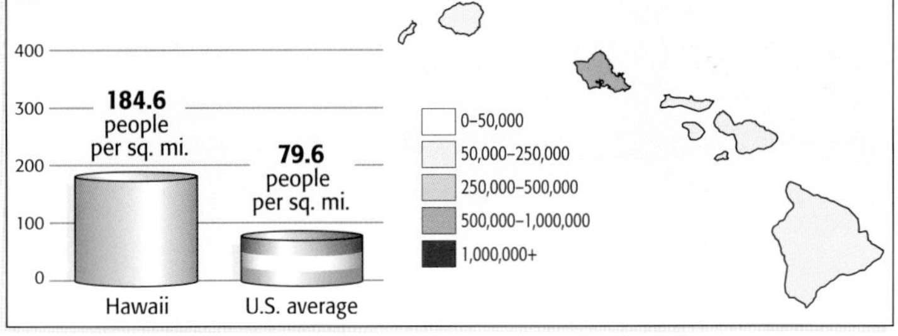

Population Density

Population by County

Surfers visit Waimea, the north beach of Oahu, because of the Banzai Pipeline, a set of high and extremely tubular waves that can be quite dangerous.

Idaho

Esto Perpetua (It is perpetual).

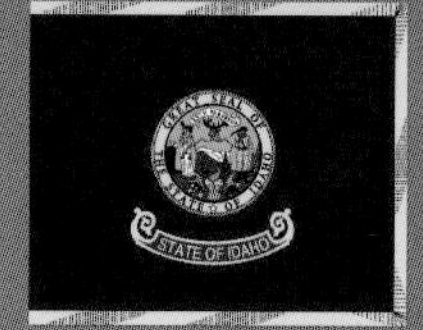

Land area rank *Largest state (1)* — 14 — *smallest state (52)*

Population rank *Most people (1)* — 40 — *fewest people (52)*

At a Glance

Name: The meaning of the name *Idaho* is unknown, although it is believed to be of Native American origin.

Nickname: Gem State

Capital: Boise

Size: 83,574 sq. mi. (217,292 sq km)

Population: 1,293,953

Statehood: Idaho became the 43rd state on July 3, 1890.

Electoral votes: 4 (2004)

U.S. Representatives: 2 (until 2003)

State tree: western white pine

State flower: syringa

State horse: Appaloosa

Highest point: Borah Peak, 12,662 ft. (3,859 m)

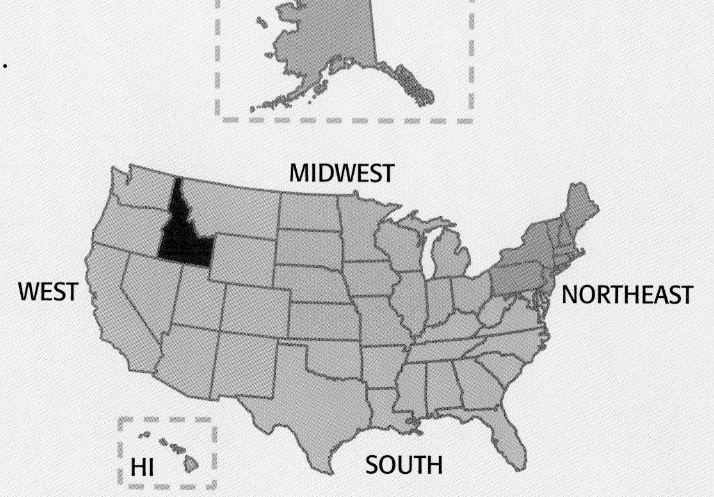

The Place

Idaho is famous for its rugged scenery. The eastern part of the state is known as the Panhandle and is covered by the Rocky Mountains. This area has mineral deposits, lush pine forests, and deep gorges.

Southwest of the mountainous Panhandle region is a flatter area along the Snake River. Part of this fertile plain was formed by lava seeping through cracks in the earth.

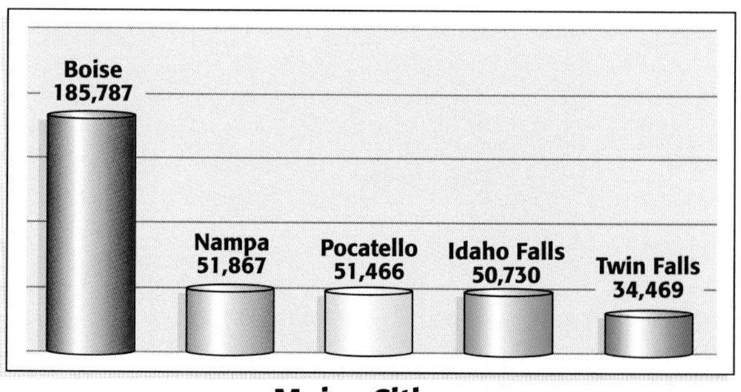

Major Cities

Farmers grow a variety of crops in this part of the state. The southwestern portion of

Boise is built on a fertile plain near the Snake River.

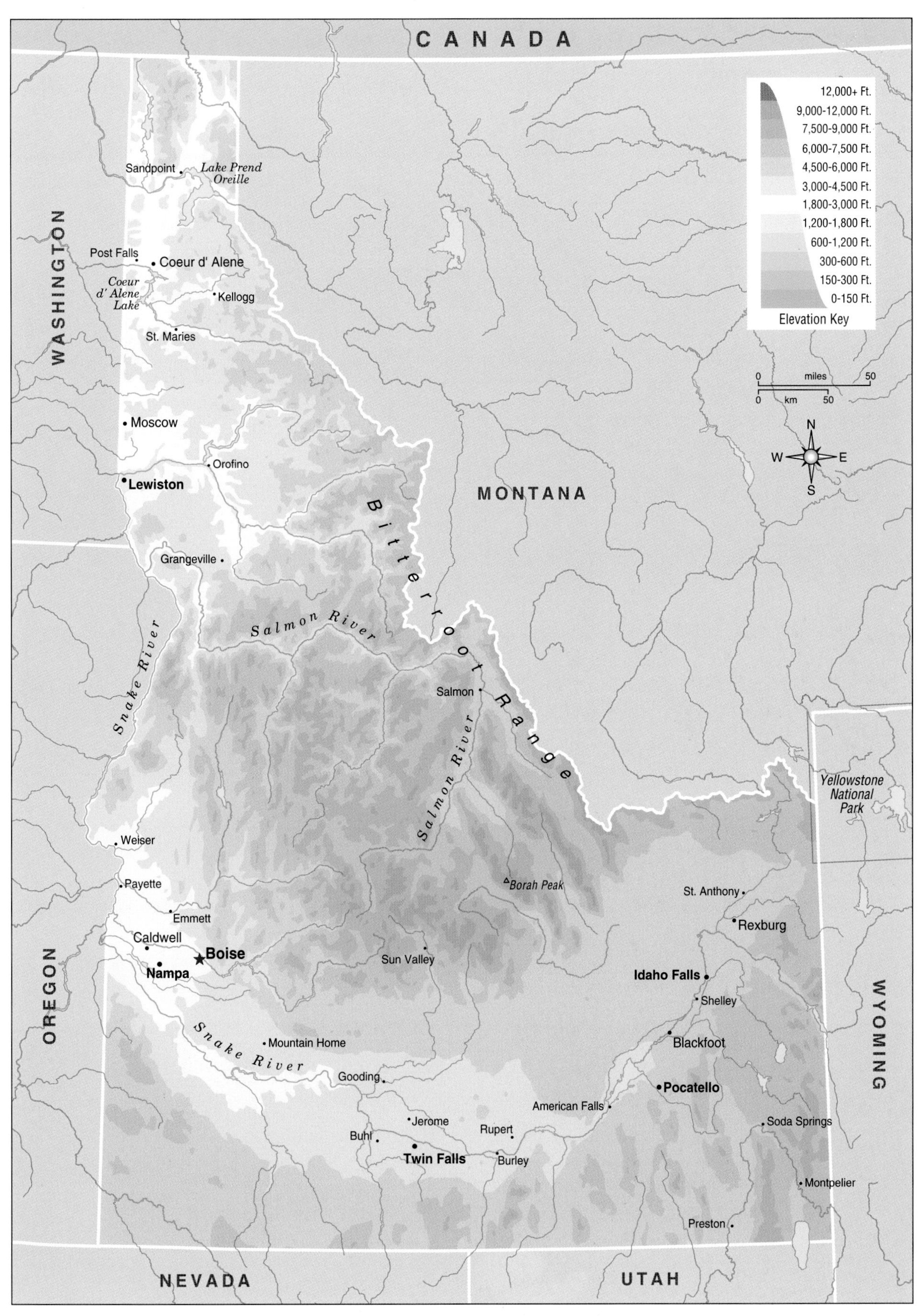
CANADA
WASHINGTON
MONTANA
OREGON
WYOMING
NEVADA
UTAH
Sandpoint
Lake Prend Oreille
Post Falls
Coeur d' Alene
Coeur d' Alene Lake
Kellogg
St. Maries
Moscow
Orofino
Lewiston
Grangeville
Bitterroot Range
Salmon River
Snake River
Salmon
Yellowstone National Park
Weiser
Payette
Emmett
Caldwell
Boise
Nampa
Borah Peak
Sun Valley
St. Anthony
Rexburg
Idaho Falls
Shelley
Blackfoot
Pocatello
Mountain Home
Gooding
American Falls
Jerome
Rupert
Buhl
Twin Falls
Burley
Soda Springs
Montpelier
Preston
12,000+ Ft.
9,000-12,000 Ft.
7,500-9,000 Ft.
6,000-7,500 Ft.
4,500-6,000 Ft.
3,000-4,500 Ft.
1,800-3,000 Ft.
1,200-1,800 Ft.
600-1,200 Ft.
300-600 Ft.
150-300 Ft.
0-150 Ft.
Elevation Key
0 miles 50
0 km 50
N
W
E
S

the state is much drier and more suitable for grazing cattle and sheep.

Idaho's climate is relatively mild. Mountains protect the state from cold Canadian air, while warmer air from the Pacific keeps temperatures relatively stable. Winter in Idaho is snowy, and summer is cool.

Idaho's many natural mineral deposits include silver, phosphate, and molybdenum. The state's powerful rivers, rich soils, and thick forests are its most valuable resources.

The Lewis and Clark expedition stopped at Indian Graves Lookout, on the Lolo Trail in northern Idaho in 1805.

The Past

Remains of Native American civilizations more than 10,000 years old have been found in Idaho. The Nez Percé and Shoshone tribes, among many others, made their home in Idaho at one time. In 1805, Meriwether Lewis and William Clark explored the region during their expedition to the western United States. Soon after their visit, settlers began to trickle into the state. In 1860, E.D. Pierce's discovery of gold in Orofino Creek set off a gold rush

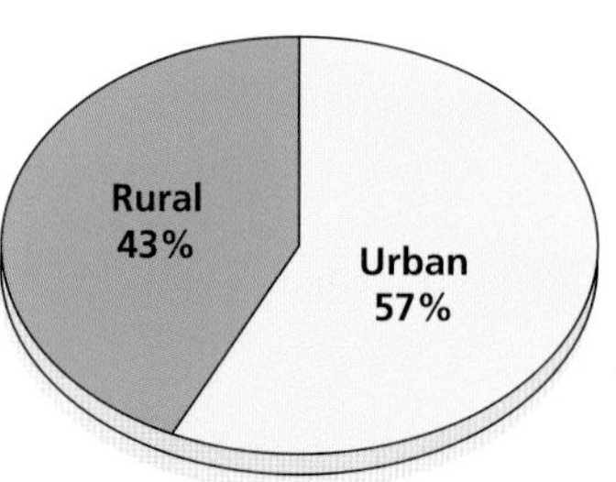

Urban/Rural Distribution

Facts and Firsts

- ★ Sun Valley was the nation's first ski resort.
- ★ Hell's Canyon, along the Snake River, is the deepest gorge in North America. On average, it is more than 1 mile (1.6 km) deep.
- ★ More than 3 million gallons of steaming mineral water pour through Lava Hot Springs every day.
- ★ The oldest standing building in the state is the Cataldo mission, built in the mid-1800s by Jesuit priests and members of the Coeur d'Alene tribe.
- ★ The highest fire lookout in the Boise National Forest sits on Trinity Mountain at an elevation of 9,500 feet (2,896 m).
- ★ Idaho has many ghost towns, including Silver City, Yankee Fork, Gold Dredge, and the Sierra Silver Mine.
- ★ The only captive geyser in the world is in Soda Springs. It was discovered while searching for a hot water source for a swimming pool. It is now capped, controlled by a timer, and erupts every hour on the hour.

State Smart

The Snake River Birds of Prey National Conservation Area is the largest bird of prey (raptor) habitat in the United States. About 2,500 raptors live there.

that brought thousands of settlers to the region. Railroads built in the 1870s helped increase Idaho's population, and mining became an important industry.

Agriculture began to expand at the beginning of the 20th century, when irrigation made more of Idaho's land suitable for farming. Idaho's farmers helped supply food for the country during the shortages of World War I. During World War II, factories were built to process much of the food grown in the state, and Idaho's food-processing industry grew. Increased tourism and manufacturing also helped build Idaho's economy.

Above: *Children in traditional Basque clothing at a festival in Idaho.*
Below: *Miners, such as these men in the Chance lead mine near Coeur d'Alene, made up much of Idaho's population in the early 1900s.*

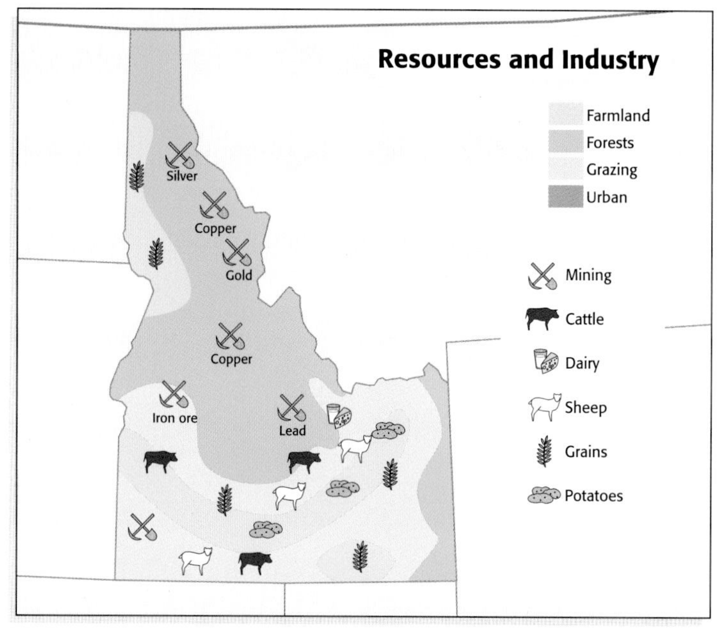

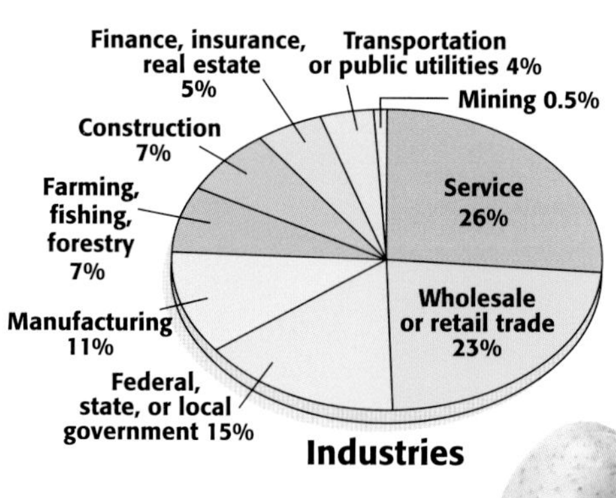

The Present

Idaho has many important natural resources, including timber, water, and minerals, but today tourism and manufacturing account for much of the state's revenue. Idaho's Rocky Mountains ski resorts, such as Sun Valley, and other unspoiled areas nurture one of Idaho's newest businesses—the tourist trade. Idaho's lakes and rivers are popular fishing areas for visitors.

Electrical equipment and food processing are Idaho's most valuable types of

Idaho's unspoiled wilderness brings tourists to the state.

Born in Idaho

- ★ **Gutzon Borglum**, Mt. Rushmore sculptor
- ★ **Carol R. Brink**, author
- ★ **Frank Church**, U.S. senator
- ★ **Harmon Killebrew**, baseball player
- ★ **Ezra Pound**, poet
- ★ **Sacagawea**, Shoshonean guide
- ★ **Picabo Street**, skier
- ★ **Lana Turner**, actress

Gutzon Borglum

manufacturing. The food-processing industry prepares many of Idaho's crops, such as potatoes, sugar beets, and wheat, for sale throughout the United States. The electrical equipment industry makes many of the parts needed in Idaho's computer industry. While manufacturing is important, the raising of sheep and cattle is essential to the economy in Idaho's drier regions.

The manufacturing industry is transforming Idaho into an urban state, but cattle and dairy goods are the leading agricultural products in rural areas. Mining, once a major source of income, is still important and produces phosphates, gold, silver, molybdenum, antimony, lead, zinc, and other minerals.

Dairy farming is an important activity in rural Idaho.

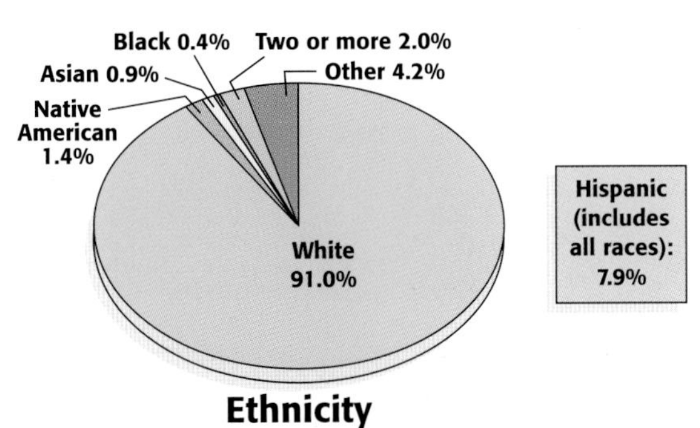

Ethnicity

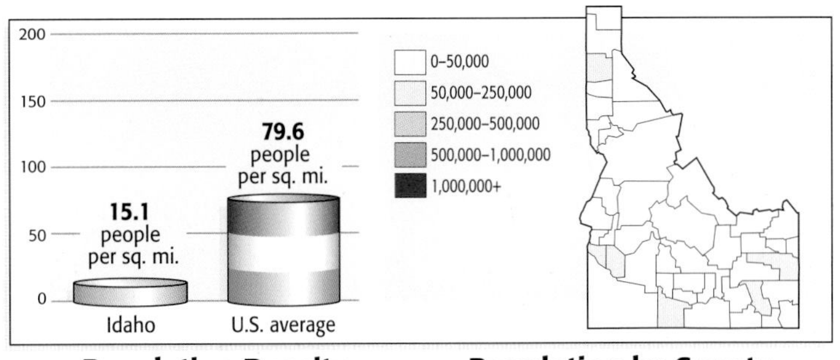

Population Density

Population by County

Illinois

State sovereignty, national union.

Land area rank *Largest state (1)* 25 *smallest state (52)*

Population rank *Most people (1)* 5 *fewest people (52)*

At a Glance

Name: *Illinois* is an Algonquian word meaning "tribe of superior men."

Nickname: Prairie State

Capital: Springfield

Size: 57,918 sq. mi. (150,007 sq km)

Population: 12,419,293

Statehood: Illinois became the 21st state on December 3, 1818.

Electoral votes: 21 (2004)

U.S. Representatives: 20 (until 2003)

State tree: white oak

State flower: native violet

State animal: white-tailed deer

Highest point: Charles Mound, 1,235 ft. (376 m)

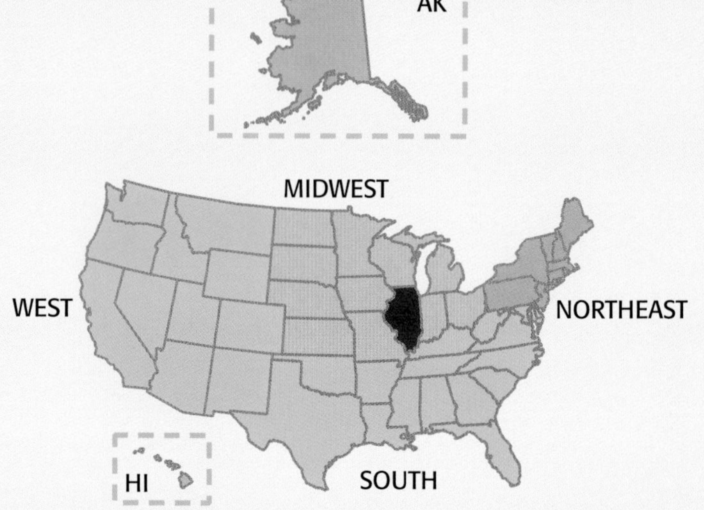

The Place

Illinois is often called the Prairie State because much of the state is covered by gently rolling plains. Most of these plains were created when glaciers leveled the midwestern portion of the country thousands of years ago. Illinois's plains are rich agricultural lands suitable for growing a variety

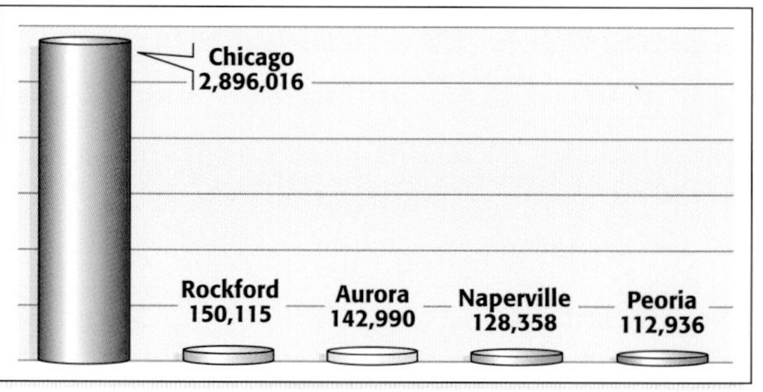

Major Cities

Ancient rock formations in the Garden of the Gods Recreational Area in southeastern Illinois provide perches for hikers to view the Shawnee National Forest.

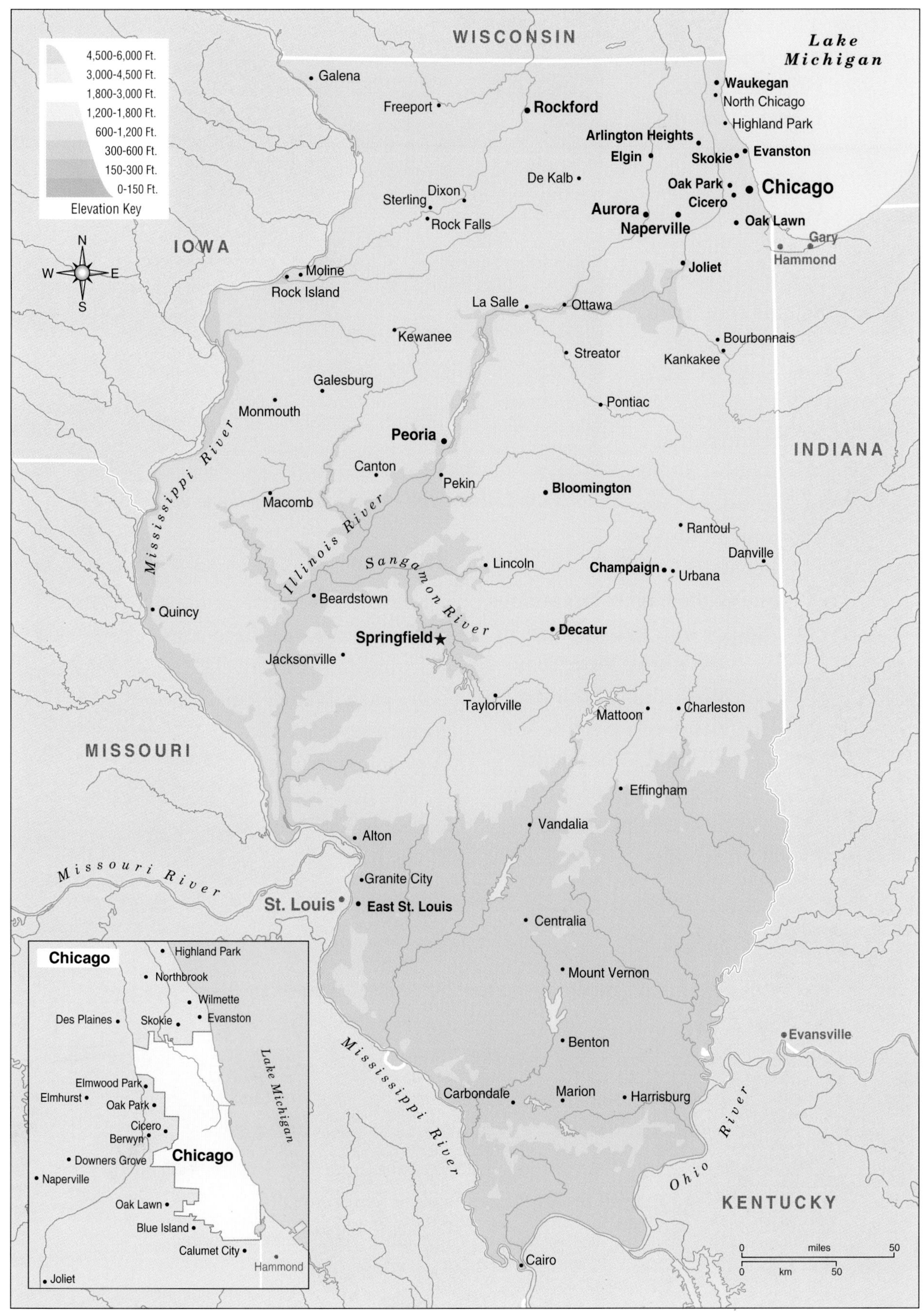
WISCONSIN
Lake Michigan
IOWA
INDIANA
MISSOURI
KENTUCKY
4,500-6,000 Ft.
3,000-4,500 Ft.
1,800-3,000 Ft.
1,200-1,800 Ft.
600-1,200 Ft.
300-600 Ft.
150-300 Ft.
0-150 Ft.
Elevation Key
N
W
E
S
Galena
Freeport
Rockford
Waukegan
North Chicago
Highland Park
Arlington Heights
Elgin
Skokie
Evanston
De Kalb
Oak Park
Chicago
Cicero
Sterling
Dixon
Rock Falls
Aurora
Naperville
Oak Lawn
Gary
Hammond
Moline
Rock Island
Joliet
La Salle
Ottawa
Kewanee
Bourbonnais
Streator
Kankakee
Galesburg
Monmouth
Pontiac
Peoria
Canton
Pekin
Bloomington
Macomb
Mississippi River
Illinois River
Sangamon River
Rantoul
Danville
Lincoln
Champaign
Urbana
Beardstown
Quincy
Springfield
Decatur
Jacksonville
Taylorville
Mattoon
Charleston
Effingham
Vandalia
Alton
Missouri River
Granite City
St. Louis
East St. Louis
Centralia
Mount Vernon
Evansville
Benton
Carbondale
Marion
Harrisburg
Ohio River
Cairo
0 miles 50
0 km 50
Chicago
Highland Park
Northbrook
Wilmette
Des Plaines
Skokie
Evanston
Elmwood Park
Elmhurst
Oak Park
Cicero
Berwyn
Chicago
Downers Grove
Naperville
Oak Lawn
Blue Island
Calumet City
Hammond
Joliet

of crops. The southern part of the state is known as the Shawnee Hills and is more hilly and forested than the plains region. Illinois has 63 miles (101 km) of shoreline on Lake Michigan, one of the Great Lakes. Chicago is Illinois's largest city and the site of the state's chief port.

Summers in Illinois are hot, while winters can be very cold. The Lake Michigan shoreline region is the coldest and snowiest area of the state. Tornadoes have killed more people in Illinois than in any other state.

Illinois has one of the largest bituminous, or soft, coal deposits in the world. More than two-thirds of the state lies over a gigantic soft coal bed. The south-eastern part of the state is rich in petroleum deposits.

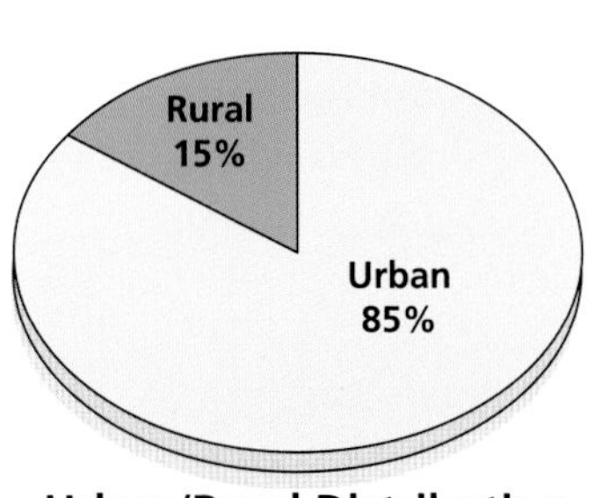

Urban/Rural Distribution

Abraham Lincoln lived in this Springfield home with his wife and children.

The Past

Thousands of burial mounds created by prehistoric Native American cultures still exist in Illinois today. The descendants of these early Native Americans eventually formed several tribes that make up the Algonquian family.

The first Europeans to see Illinois were probably Father Jacques Marquette and Louis Jolliet (1673), who were exploring

Facts and Firsts

- ★ In 1865, Illinois became the first state to approve the 13th Amendment to the Constitution, which made slavery illegal.
- ★ In 1885, the world's first metal-framed skyscraper, the Home Insurance Building, was built in Chicago.
- ★ The first successful nuclear fission reaction took place at the University of Chicago in 1942, when Enrico Fermi and other scientists proved that it is possible to produce heat using the materials graphite and uranium.
- ★ The first McDonald's restaurant opened in Des Plaines in April 1955.
- ★ The Chicago Public Library, with more than 2 million books, is one of the largest public libraries in the world.

the Mississippi River region for the French governors of Canada. The French began to settle the region, but war broke out with the British, who claimed all the land west of their American colonies on the East Coast. The British won the Illinois territory in 1763. During the Revolutionary War, the Americans took control of Illinois from the British, and the area remained a U.S. territory until its statehood became official in 1818.

Black Hawk, center left, a famous Sauk chief born in Illinois, was part of the Algonquian family.

After statehood, many people began to settle in the northern part of Illinois, and the city of Chicago grew. In 1825, the Erie Canal opened a transportation route to the Midwest from the east, and by 1830 the state's population had tripled. Illinois gained fame during the Civil War because President Abraham Lincoln spent most of his life there, and Union general Ulysses S. Grant was living in Illinois when the war began in 1861.

The post–Civil War construction of railroads stimulated the growth of industry and attracted many European immigrants to Illinois. Manufacturing and farming in Illinois exploded. Chicago quickly became the center of the meat-packing industry.

The discovery of new oil fields in southwestern Illinois in 1937 brought an oil boom to the state. Illinois quickly became one of the richest midwestern states, and Chicago grew to be a manufacturing center as well as a leading site for scientific research. The state's rapid expansion also produced negative consequences, including pollution and traffic problems.

State Smart

The Sears Tower in Chicago is the tallest building in the United States. It is 1,450 feet (442 m) tall and cost $160 million to build.

Visitors to Chicago can view the Sears Tower by taking a boat tour of the city's architecture.

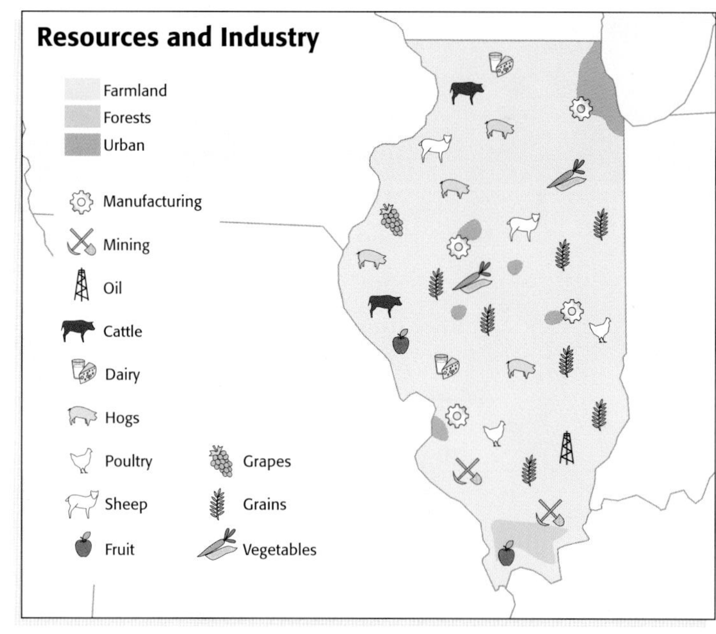

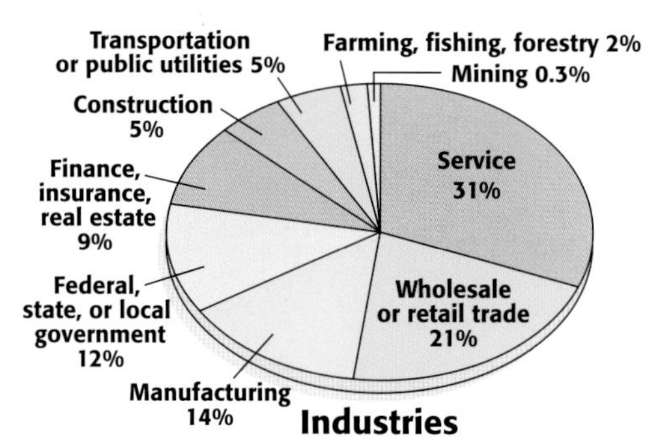

The Present

Chicago, one of the largest cities in the world, is home to about half of Illinois's total population. The city is also an industrial and transportation center. Many major companies, including McDonald's, Sears Roebuck, and United Airlines, have their corporate headquarters in the area. Chicago is the second most important manufacturing area in the nation. It is also the international center for the study of atoms.

Below left: *O'Hare Airport in Chicago is one of the busiest airports in the world.* Below right: *Amish farmers in east central Illinois rely on corn as one of their best crops.* Above right: *LaSalle Street is in the heart of downtown Chicago.*

Born in Illinois

- ★ **Jane Addams**, social worker
- ★ **Ray Bradbury**, author
- ★ **Christine Brewer**, opera singer
- ★ **William Jennings Bryan**, lawyer, politician
- ★ **Edgar Rice Burroughs**, author
- ★ **Raymond Chandler**, author
- ★ **Hillary Rodham Clinton**, U.S. senator and first lady
- ★ **Miles Davis**, musician
- ★ **Walt Disney**, film animator and producer
- ★ **Bobby Fischer**, chess player
- ★ **Betty Friedan**, feminist
- ★ **Benny Goodman**, musician
- ★ **John Gunther**, author
- ★ **Black Hawk**, Sauk chief
- ★ **Ernest Hemingway**, author
- ★ **Wild Bill Hickok**, scout
- ★ **Frederick Maytag**, inventor, manufacturer
- ★ **Bill Murray**, actor
- ★ **Ronald Reagan**, actor, U.S. president
- ★ **Carl Sandburg**, poet
- ★ **Sam Shepard**, playwright

Top to Bottom: *Betty Friedan, Ernest Hemingway, Ronald Reagan*

Illinois is a leading agricultural state as well, with about three-quarters of its land devoted to farming. The most important crop is corn, followed by soybeans, wheat, and hay. The raising of hogs and cattle is also a significant contributor to Illinois's agricultural economy. The state's coal and petroleum resources help to diversify its economy.

Comiskey Park is the home of the Chicago White Sox.

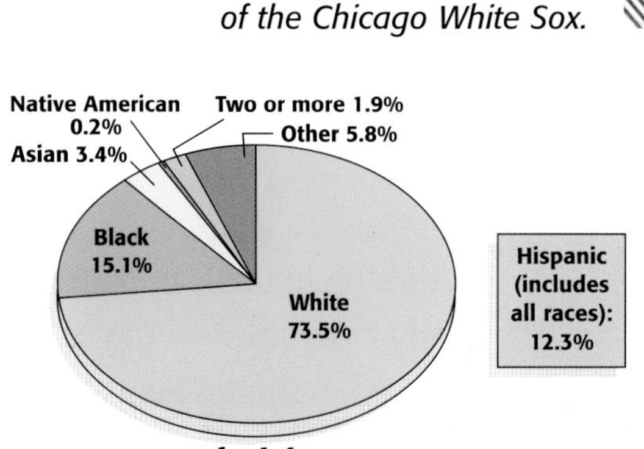

Ethnicity

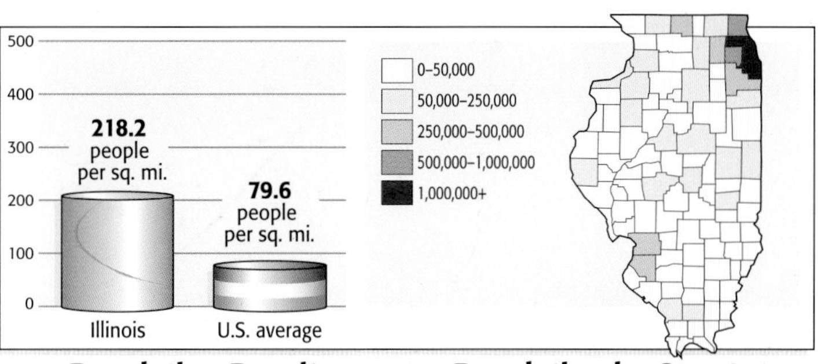

Population Density

Population by County

Indiana

Crossroads of America.

Land area rank
Largest state (1)
38 — *smallest state (52)*

Population rank
Most people (1)
14 — *fewest people (52)*

At a Glance

Name: *Indiana* means "land of Indians."
Nickname: Hoosier State
Capital: Indianapolis
Size: 36,420 sq. mi. (94,328 sq km)
Population: 6,080,485
Statehood: Indiana became the 19th state on December 11, 1816.
Electoral votes: 11 (2004)
U.S. Representatives: 10 (until 2003)
State tree: tulip poplar
State flower: peony
State bird: cardinal
Highest point: Wayne County, 1,257 ft. (383 m)

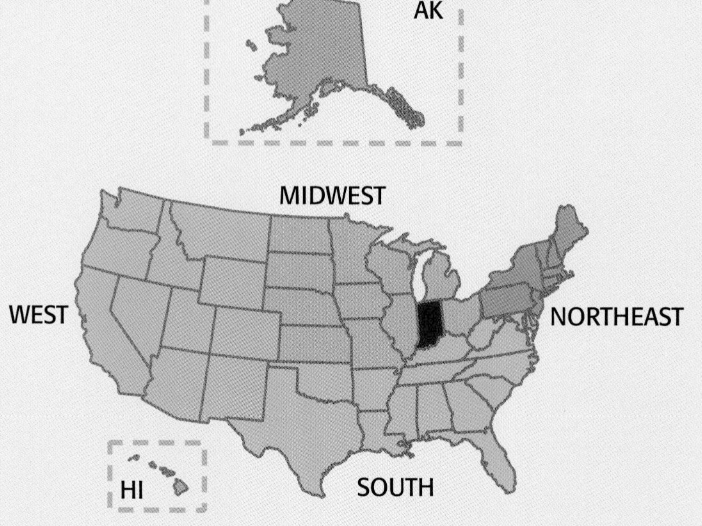

The Place

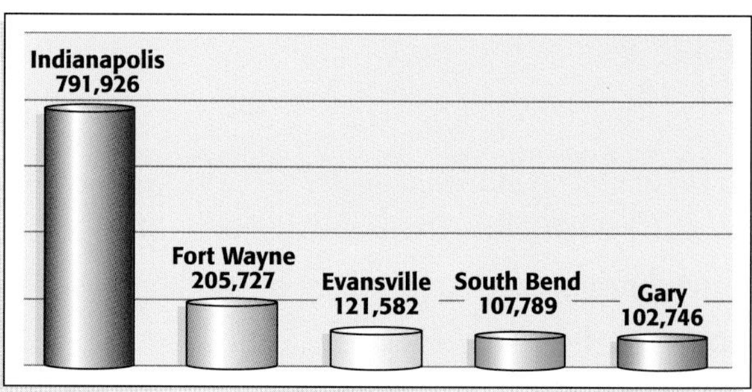

Major Cities

Indiana, the smallest of the agricultural Midwest states, is made up of three main regions. The Great Lakes Plains are found in northern Indiana, along the state's border with Lake Michigan. This region has large sand dunes, which give way to more fertile land to the south. The center of the state is covered by the Till Plains, a region of fertile soil perfect for farming. The southernmost part of the state is covered by rolling hills and contains deposits of coal and petroleum. Indiana is also abundant in clay and limestone, and the state's rich soil is its most valuable resource.

Indiana's climate varies by region. In general, Indiana's weather is humid, with warm summers and mild winters. The

Citizens of Madison on the banks of the Ohio, in southern Indiana, call it "the most beautiful town in the Midwest."

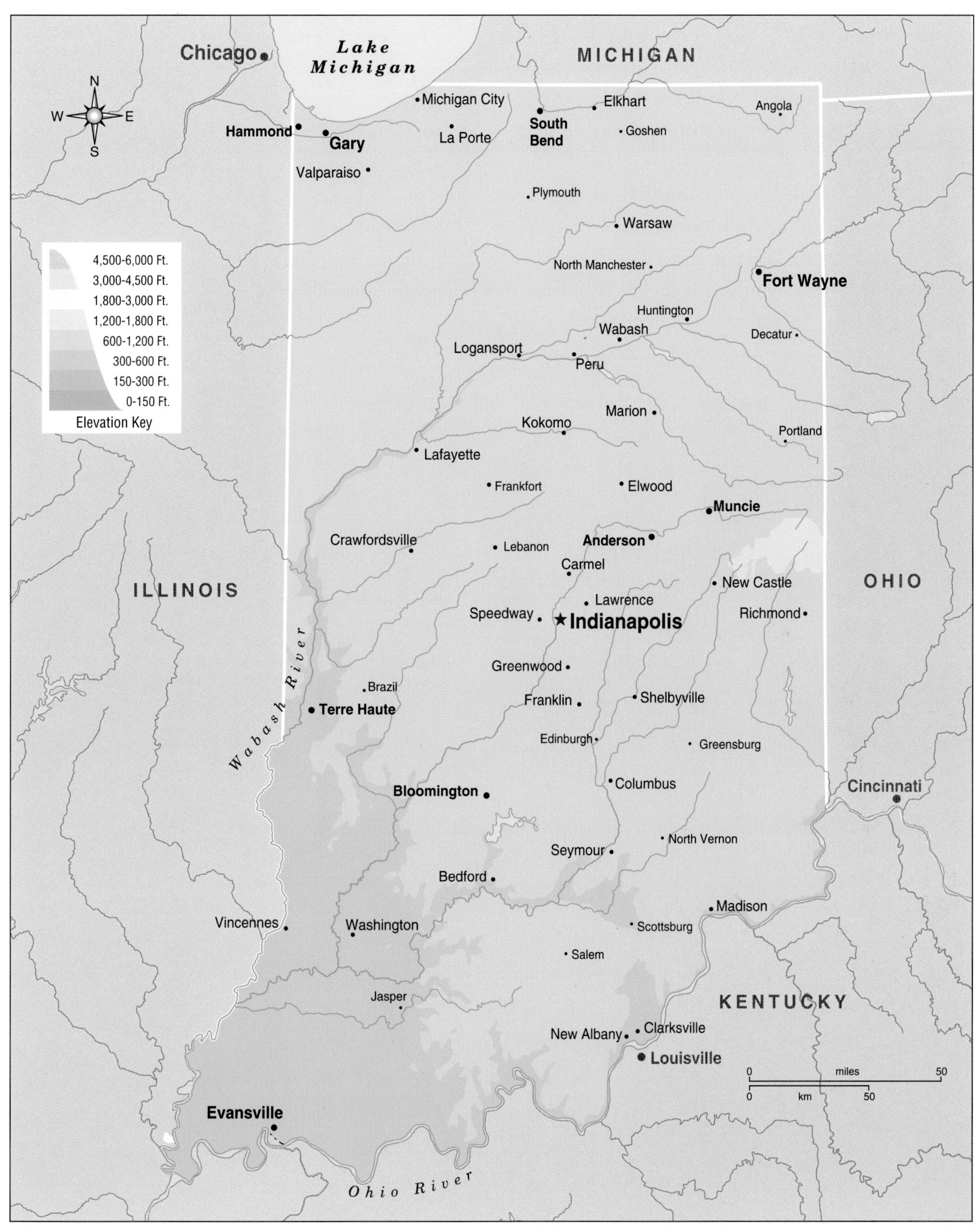

weather in the Great Lakes Plains is the least extreme of all the regions, because winds from Lake Michigan warm the area in the winter and cool it in summer.

The Past

The first known inhabitants of Indiana were prehistoric Native American tribes who built earthen mounds throughout the area.

In 1679, French explorer René-Robert Cavelier, Sieur de La Salle, explored the region while searching for a water route from Canada to the Pacific Ocean. Shortly after, French fur trappers and settlers began to move south from Canada and crossed Lake Michigan into Indiana. In 1763, the French lost control of the region to the British, who claimed all the land west of the original 13 colonies. During the Revolutionary War the Americans took control of the area, and in 1787 Indiana became part of the region known as the Northwest Territory.

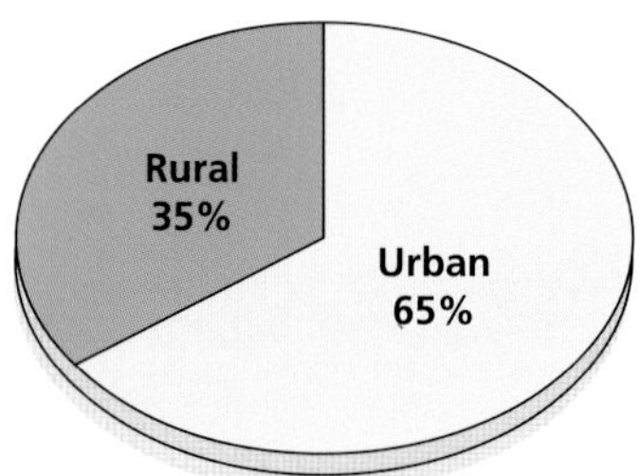

Urban/Rural Distribution

In 1816, after a series of wars with Native Americans living in the area, Indiana officially became a state. The state's economy, which was dismal in its early years, improved during the 1850s with the construction of

The defeat of Native Americans at the Battle of Tippecanoe in 1811 led the way to Indiana statehood.

Facts and Firsts

- ★ Abraham Lincoln spent much of his youth in Spencer County. His family moved there when he was seven years old.
- ★ The first professional baseball game was played in Fort Wayne on May 4, 1871.
- ★ The first long-distance auto race was held in Indianapolis in 1911. This race eventually became the famed Indianapolis 500.
- ★ The Empire State Building, the Pentagon, the U.S. Treasury, and the capitols of 14 states have been built using limestone from huge deposits mined in southern Indiana.
- ★ Indiana has more miles of interstate highway per square mile than any other state.
- ★ Every Christmas, the town of Santa Claus receives more than a half-million letters for remailing.

State Smart

The Children's Museum of Indianapolis is the largest children's museum in the United States. The building has an area of 356,000 square feet (33,068 sq m) and draws about one million visitors every year.

railroads. Manufacturing developments paved the way for large industrial growth. The Studebaker company of South Bend became the largest wagon manufacturer in the country, and Richard Gatling invented the first practical machine gun in Indianapolis in 1862.

Around the beginning of the 20th century, Standard Oil built a large oil refinery near Lake Michigan, and the United States Steel Corporation (now USX) constructed a large plant in the same area. Indiana's

Ray Harroun drove his car, Marmon Wasp, *to victory in the first Indy Speedway Race in 1911.*

industries continued to grow throughout the century, despite a downturn during the Great Depression of the 1930s and another during the 1980s. Indiana's agriculture and manufacturing industries revived again at the beginning of the 1990s.

The Children's Museum of Indianapolis

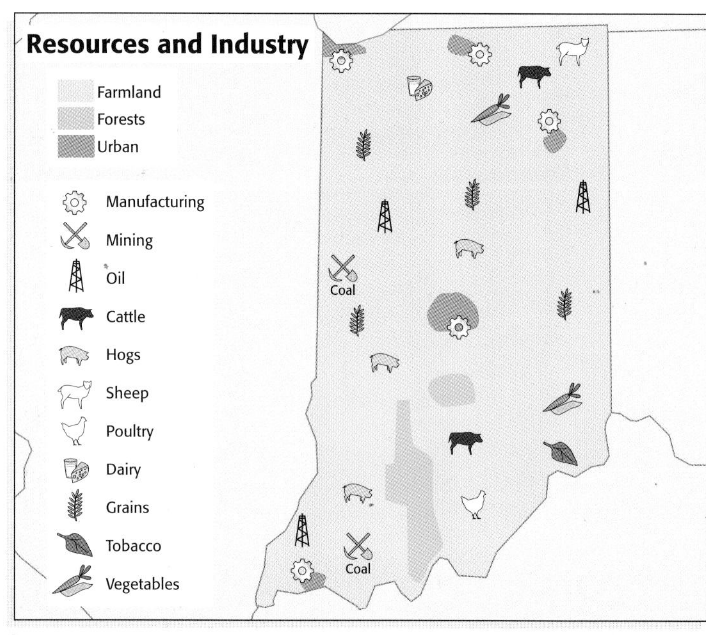

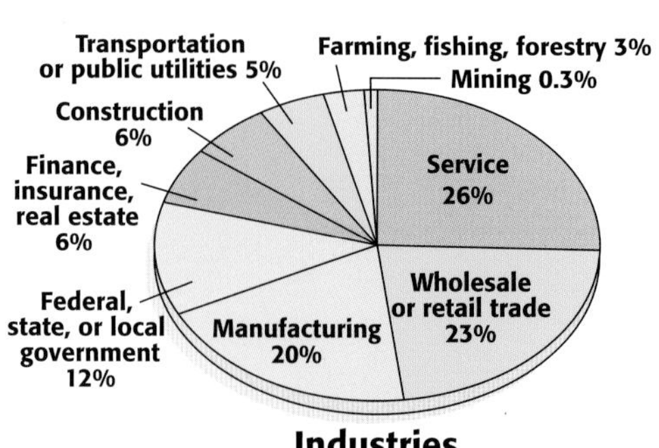

The Present

Indiana ranks among the top 20 states in manufacturing and agriculture. Although it is geographically the smallest of the Midwest states, it has a large population that is fueled by its many industries.

Indiana's chief agricultural product is corn; the center of the state is part of the Midwestern Corn Belt. Indiana farmers also grow large amounts of soybeans and raise hogs.

Manufacturing, however, contributes the most to Indiana's economy, with oil refineries and steel mills yielding most of the state's gross product. While Indiana companies

Below left: *Molten steel is milled in northwestern Indiana, where steel manufacture provides work.* Below right: *A farmer shows his tall stalks of corn in Mount Vernon, Indiana.*

Born in Indiana

- ★ **Larry Bird**, basketball player
- ★ **Bill Blass**, fashion designer
- ★ **Jim Davis**, cartoonist
- ★ **James Dean**, actor
- ★ **Theodore Dreiser**, author
- ★ **Michael Jackson**, singer
- ★ **David Letterman**, television show host
- ★ **Jane Pauley**, broadcast journalist
- ★ **Cole Porter**, songwriter
- ★ **J. Danforth "Dan" Quayle**, U.S. vice president
- ★ **James Whitcomb Riley**, poet
- ★ **Ned Rorem**, composer
- ★ **Harland Sanders**, founder of Kentucky Fried Chicken restaurants
- ★ **Twyla Tharp**, dancer and choreographer
- ★ **Harold C. Urey**, physicist
- ★ **Kurt Vonnegut**, author
- ★ **Wilbur Wright**, aviator

Above: *Larry Bird;* below: *James Dean*

also produce a number of chemicals and pharmaceuticals, the traditional manufacture of automobiles and automobile parts remains the major industrial activity.

A river barge transports goods from Indiana on the Ohio River.

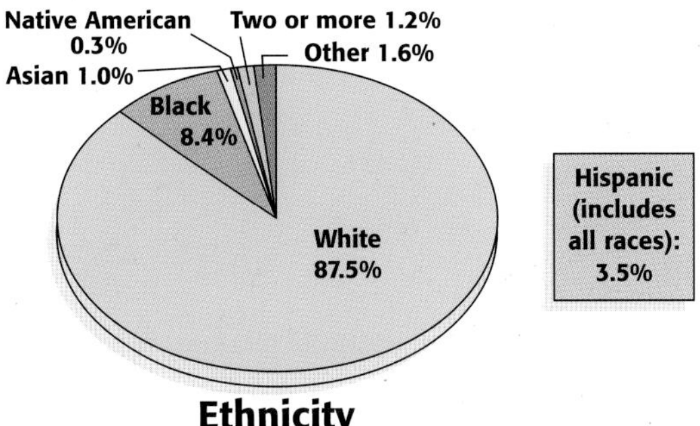

Hispanic (includes all races): 3.5%

Ethnicity

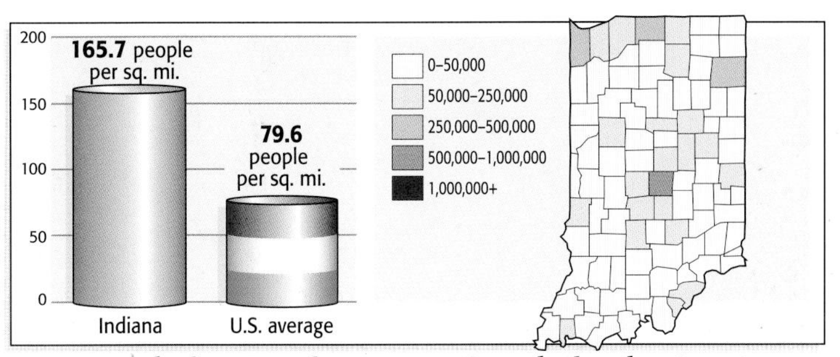

Population Density

Population by County

Iowa

Our liberties we prize, and our rights we will maintain.

Land area rank *Largest state (1)* — 26 — *smallest state (52)*

Population rank *Most people (1)* — 30 — *fewest people (52)*

At a Glance

Name: *Iowa* is believed to have come from a Native American word meaning "this is the place" or "the beautiful land."

Nickname: Hawkeye State

Capital: Des Moines

Size: 56,276 sq. mi. (145,755 sq km)

Population: 2,926,324

Statehood: Iowa became the 29th state on December 28, 1846.

Electoral votes: 7 (2004)

U.S. Representatives: 5 (until 2003)

State tree: oak

State flower: wild rose

State bird: eastern goldfinch

Highest point: Osceola County, 1,670 ft. (509 m)

The Place

Approximately 11,500 years ago, during the last Ice Age, Iowa was covered by glaciers. These huge mounds of ice, rock, and dirt carved the state into three distinct areas. The first is a glacier-leveled region in northern and central Iowa, that has some of the most fertile soil in the Midwest.

Iowa has some of the most fertile land in the Midwest.

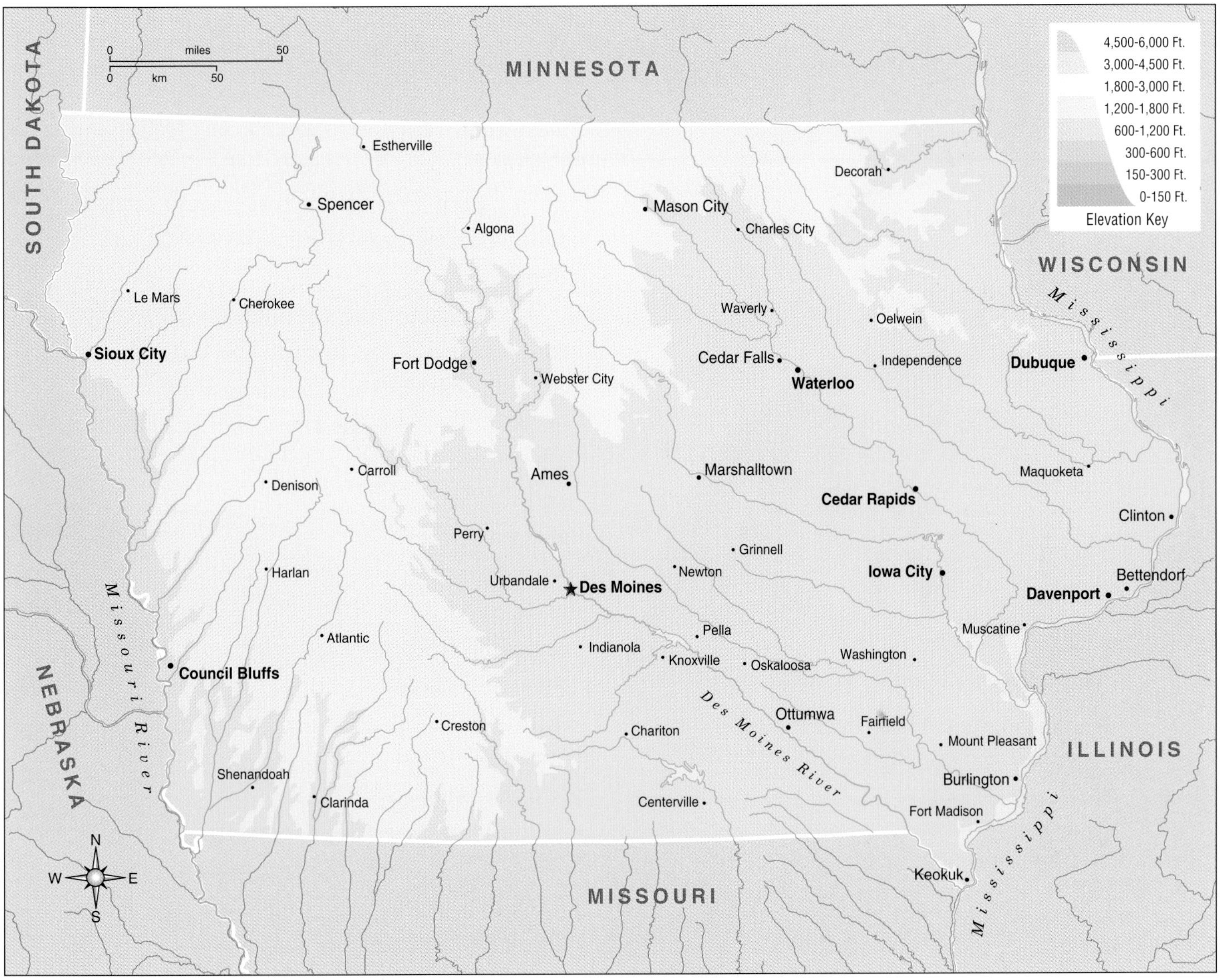

Uneven soil deposits resulted in beautiful lakes and characteristic swamps in this region. The southern portion of Iowa is much like the north, although the glaciers that once filled this area did not leave the land as rich or as flat as the northern and central parts of the state. The northeastern portion of Iowa was crossed by only one glacier, which left most of the area's original hills intact. The northeastern corner of Iowa is covered with pine trees and cliffs.

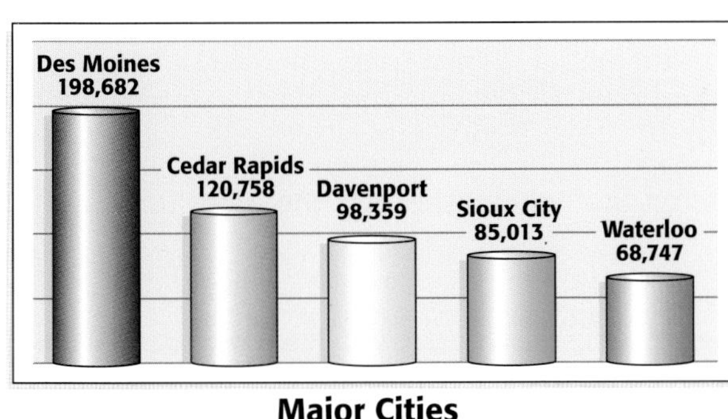

Major Cities

The powerful Mississippi and Missouri Rivers form Iowa's eastern and western borders. In their valleys are some of the best hardwood forests in Iowa.

Iowa's climate is extreme and can change quickly from day to day. Winter in Iowa is cold and snowy, while summer is usually hot.

Black Hawk was a forceful chief who led 200 warriors and their families across the Mississippi, from Iowa to Illinois, to reclaim lost lands.

THE PAST

Like many other midwestern states, Iowa was once inhabited by prehistoric Native Americans who constructed earth mounds to bury their dead. More than 10,000 of these mounds remain throughout Iowa.

The first Europeans to reach the area were the French explorers Louis Jolliet and Father Jacques Marquette, who arrived in 1673. A few French fur traders and settlers followed, but France gave the region to Spain in 1762.

The French later regained control, only to sell present-day Iowa to the United States as part of the Louisiana Purchase in 1803. In 1832, the region suffered during a brief war between the U.S. government and the Sauk and Fox tribes, who did not want to be relocated from their homeland in Illinois to unsettled Iowa.

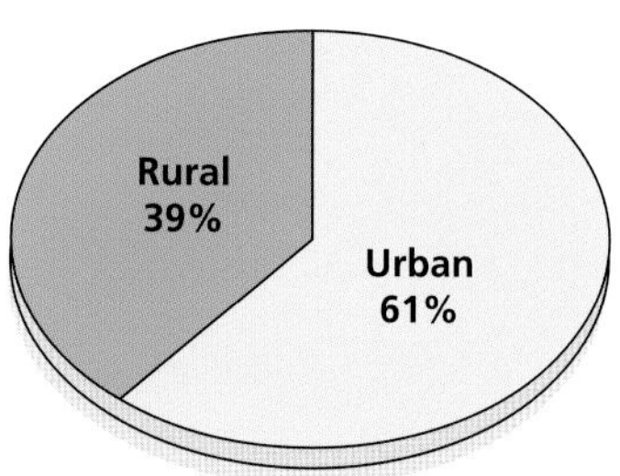

Urban/Rural Distribution

Iowa came to be known as the Hawkeye State in honor of Chief Black Hawk, the leader of the Native American protesters. Iowa officially became a state on December 28, 1846.

The growth of railroads in the 1870s and the large-scale construction of roads during World War I helped Iowa's agriculture

Facts and Firsts

- ★ Wright County has the highest percentage of grade A topsoil in the nation.
- ★ Iowa is the only state with east and west borders that are formed by water. The Missouri and Mississippi Rivers mark Iowa's borders.
- ★ Herbert Hoover, Iowa native and 31st president of the United States, was the first president born west of the Mississippi River.
- ★ The campers and motor homes known as Winnebagos are manufactured in Winnebago County.

This envelope from the Civil War era proclaimed Iowa's loyalty to the Union.

industry expand. Iowa's economy suffered during the Great Depression of the 1930s, but the high demand for food during World War II helped the state recover. Food processing and the production of farm equipment grew in importance.

During the 1980s, Iowa again suffered from serious economic problems as its crops became less valuable, but the state recovered and continued to expand.

State Smart

Iowa grows more corn than any other state—about 1.65 billion bushels, most of which is used for livestock feed.

Several locomotives are stored at the roundhouse of the North Yards railroad station in North McGregor, Iowa, in 1870. Their endurance and speed made it easier to get Iowa produce to market.

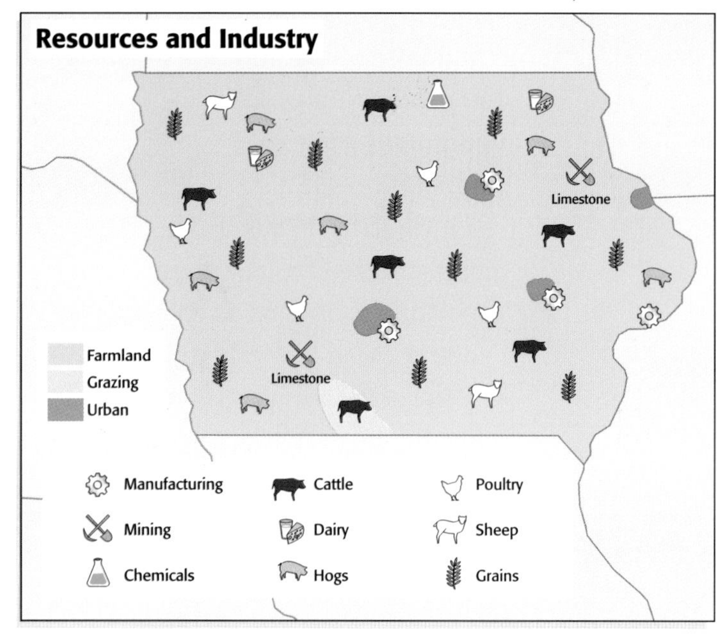

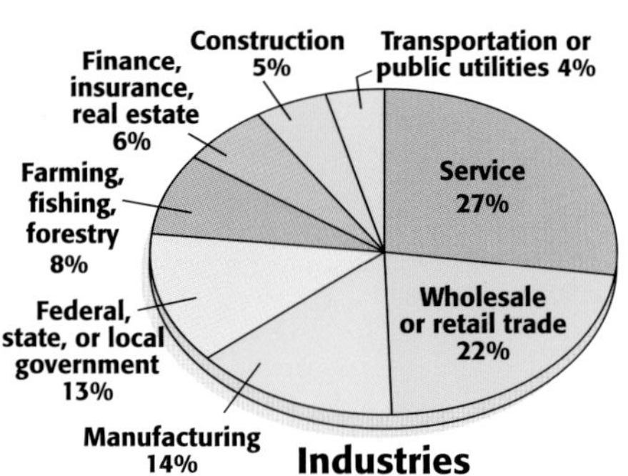

The Present

Iowa has changed a great deal during the last century. Though Iowa was once a primarily agricultural state that depended on corn as its main crop, today the state's manufacturing industries compete with its farms in economic importance. Although 93 percent of Iowa's land is used for farming, only about 10 percent of its inhabitants live on farms.

Iowa produces about 7 percent of the nation's food supply. The state grows a wide variety of crops, including soybeans and oats. Many farmers also raise hogs and cattle for meat and dairy products.

The capital, Des Moines, has become a national center for many insurance

Below left: *Iowa-born artist Grant Wood created the well-known painting "American Gothic."*
Below right: *Des Moines is home to insurance companies and other types of businesses.*

Born in Iowa

- ★ **Leon Bismarck "Bix" Beiderbecke**, jazz musician
- ★ **Norman Borlaug**, plant pathologist, geneticist
- ★ **Johnny Carson**, television entertainer
- ★ **William Frederick "Buffalo Bill" Cody**, scout, showman
- ★ **Mamie Doud Eisenhower**, first lady
- ★ **George H. Gallup**, poll taker
- ★ **Herbert Hoover**, U.S. president
- ★ **Ann Landers**, newspaper columnist
- ★ **John L. Lewis**, labor leader
- ★ **Glenn Miller**, bandleader
- ★ **Wallace Stegner**, writer, environmentalist
- ★ **Abigail Van Buren**, newspaper columnist
- ★ **John Wayne**, actor
- ★ **Meredith Wilson**, composer
- ★ **Grant Wood**, painter

Above: *"Buffalo Bill" Cody;* below: *Mamie Eisenhower*

companies, as well as food processing and farm equipment factories. Many kinds of electrical equipment, including home appliances, are also manufactured in the state.

A young girl sleeps next to her prize cow at the Iowa State Fair.

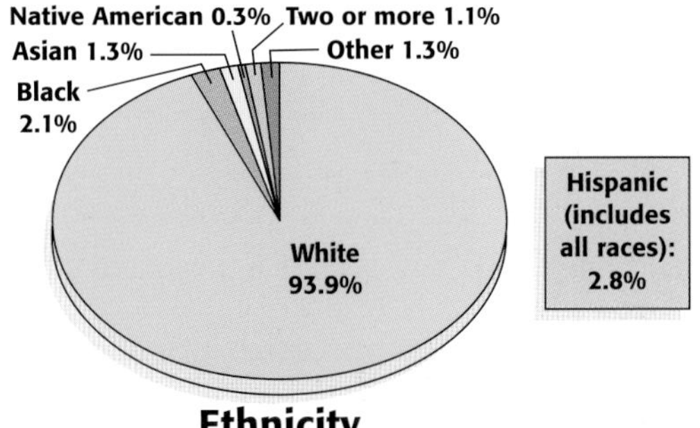

Ethnicity

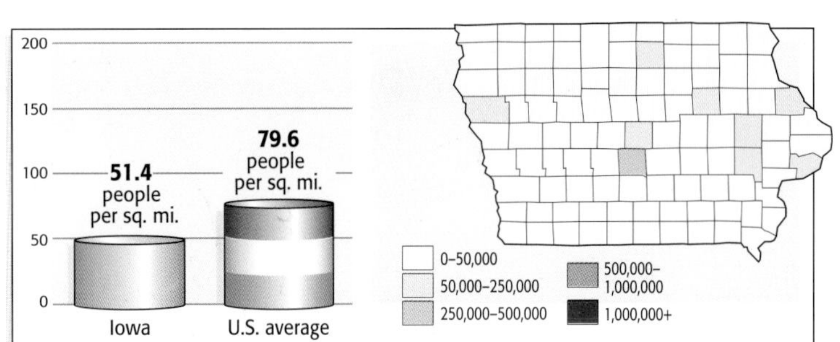

Population Density

Population by County

Kansas

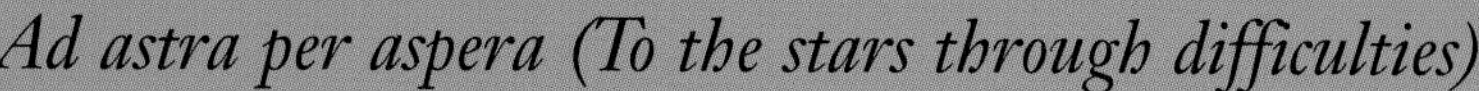

Ad astra per aspera (To the stars through difficulties).

Land area rank *Largest state (1)* — 15 — *smallest state (52)*

Population rank *Most people (1)* — 32 — *fewest people (52)*

At a Glance

Name: *Kansas* is from a Sioux word meaning "people of the south wind."

Nickname: Sunflower State, Jayhawker State

Capital: Topeka

Size: 82,282 sq. mi. (213,110 sq km)

Population: 2,688,418

Statehood: Kansas became the 34th state on January 29, 1861.

Electoral votes: 6 (2004)

U.S. Representatives: 4 (until 2003)

State tree: cottonwood

State flower: native sunflower

State animal: American buffalo

Highest point: Mount Sunflower, 4,039 ft. (1,231 m)

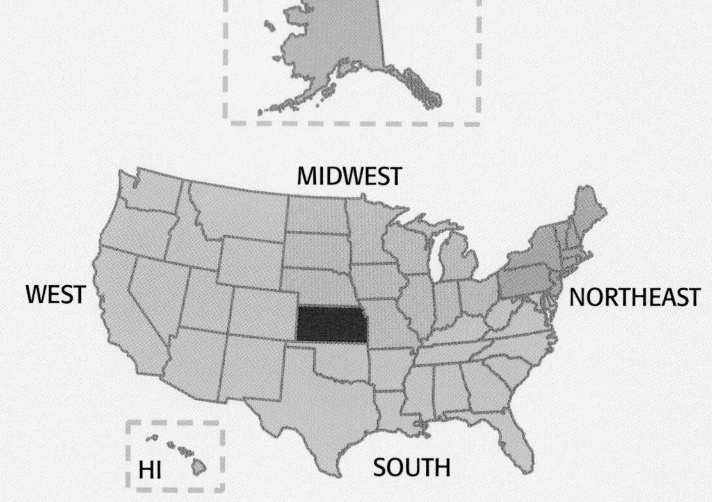

The Place

Kansas is made up of both level and rolling plains, which increase in height in the western part of the state. The western portion, which is part of the Great Plains, is the driest region in Kansas. The southeastern part of the state is generally flat land that is valuable for grazing cattle.

Kansas has vast areas of flat plains.

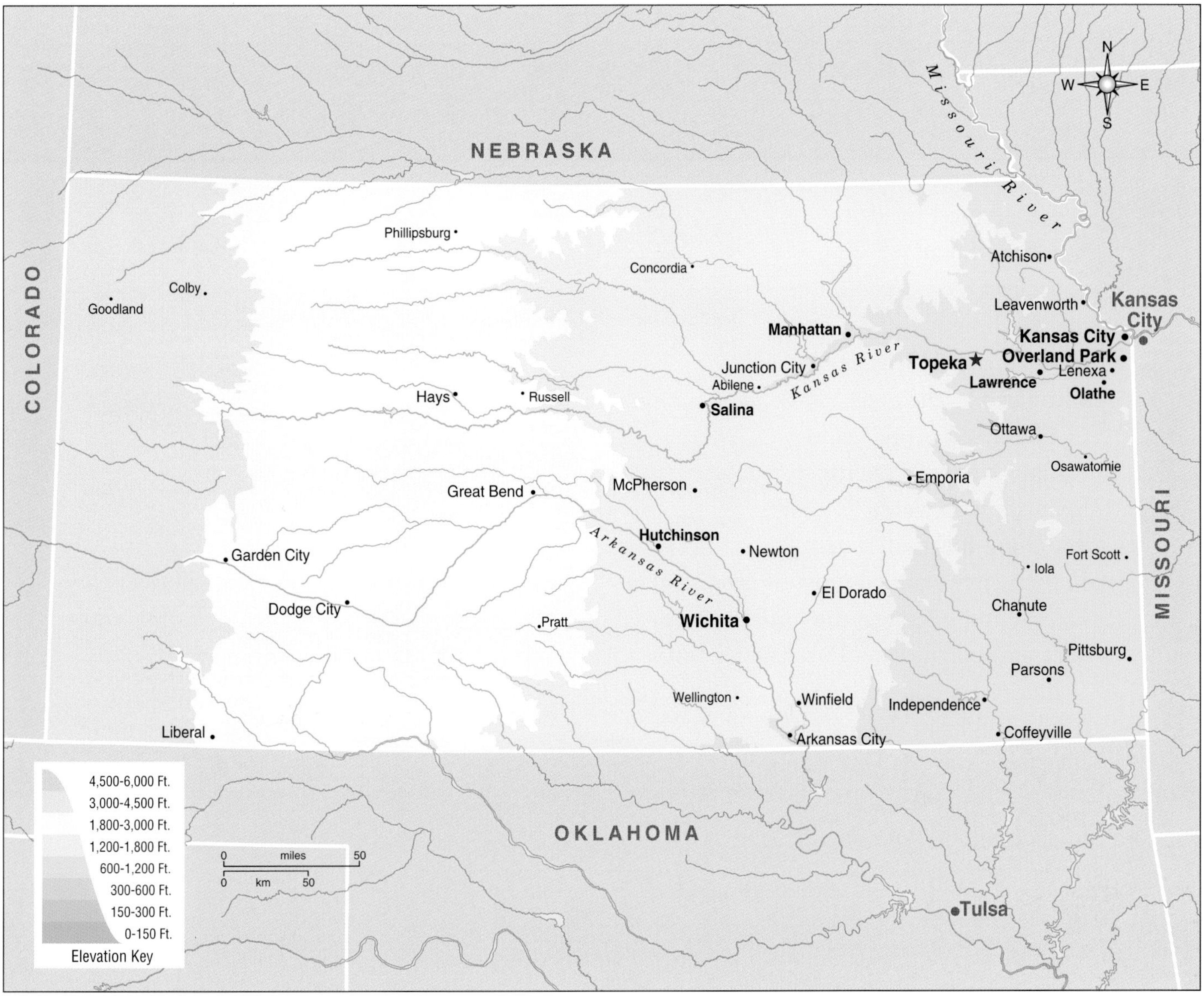

The northeastern region, which is also level, was covered by glaciers during the last Ice Age. These glaciers left behind rich deposits of soil that have since been cut and crisscrossed by rivers. Many different kinds of trees grow in the river valleys.

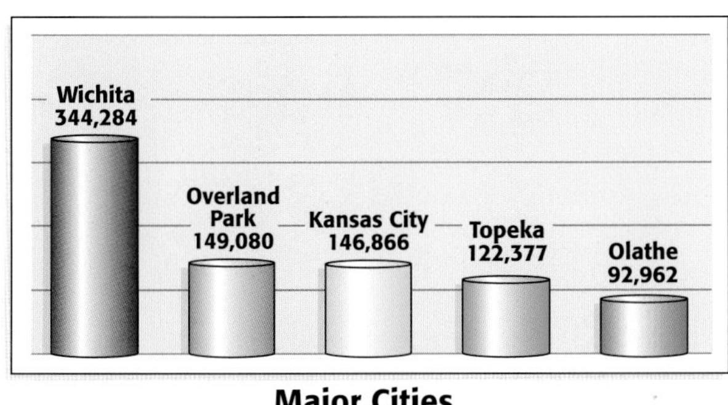

Major Cities

Kansas's climate is much more variable than its land. The state experiences cold, snowy winters and hot summers. During the winter, cold air from the north chills the state, while hot winds from the south bring intense heat during the summer. From day to day the weather can change rapidly, and residents of Kansas often have to protect themselves from blizzards and hail in winter and powerful thunderstorms and tornadoes in summer.

The Past

Before Kansas became heavily settled, large herds of buffalo roamed its prairies. These buffalo provided food for a number of Native American tribes, including the Kansa, Osage, Pawnee, and Wichita, who lived in the area.

This political cartoon from the 1850s depicts the conflict over slavery in Kansas.

The first Europeans to explore Kansas were the Spanish, who were searching for gold. The French later claimed most of present-day Kansas and sold it to the United States as part of the Louisiana Purchase in 1803.

Before Kansas became a state, however, it was caught in the national fight over slavery. During the 1850s, many people who wanted to build a railroad from the East to California began to push for former western territories to become official states. Congress had trouble deciding whether to admit Kansas as a free or slaveholding state, so it allowed residents of the Kansas territory to vote for themselves. Soon, people from all over the country began pouring in and casting votes, and the region became known as "Bloody Kansas" as settlers fought each other in violent skirmishes over their votes. After many slaveholding Southern states withdrew from the Union, Kansas was officially admitted into the Union as a state in 1861.

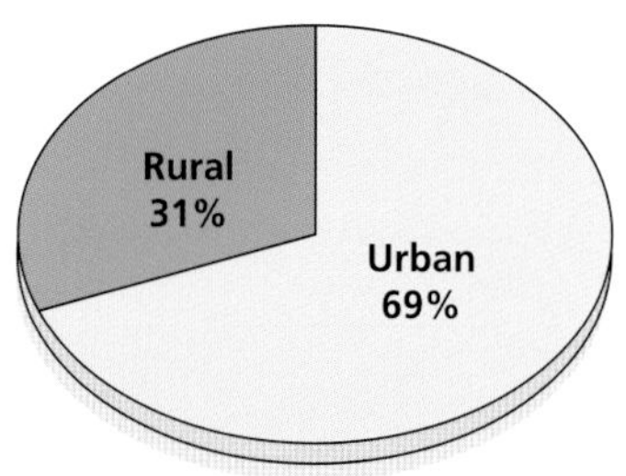

Urban/Rural Distribution

During the 1870s, railroads were built through Kansas and the era of the cattle towns began. Ranchers and cowboys from Texas drove their cattle north to Kansas to be shipped

Facts and Firsts

- ★ The geographical center of the contiguous United States lies in Smith County.
- ★ Dodge City is the windiest city in the United States.
- ★ Kansas has North America's largest population of wild grouse, commonly known as prairie chickens.
- ★ In 1909, William Purvis and Charles Wilson of Goodland invented the helicopter.
- ★ The international fast food chain Pizza Hut began in Wichita.

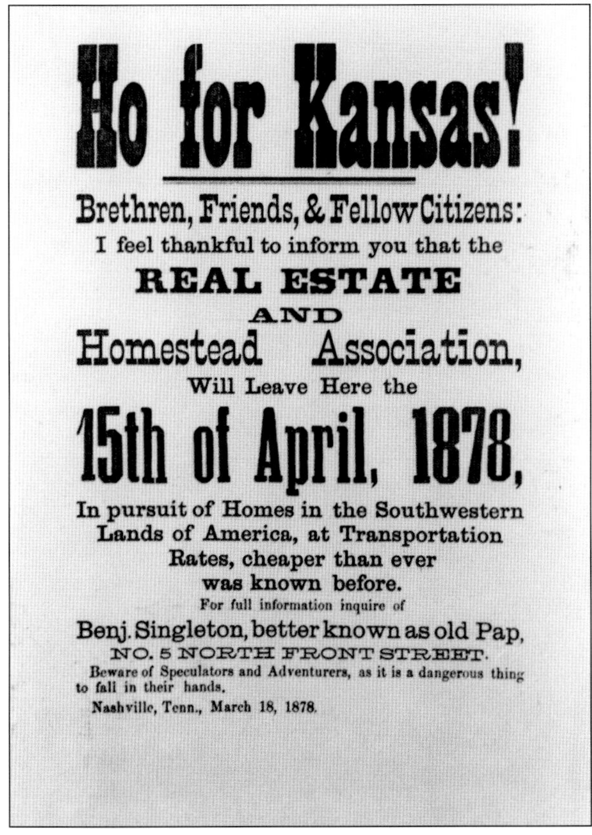

Ho for Kansas!

Brethren, Friends, & Fellow Citizens:
I feel thankful to inform you that the
REAL ESTATE
AND
Homestead Association,
Will Leave Here the
15th of April, 1878,
In pursuit of Homes in the Southwestern Lands of America, at Transportation Rates, cheaper than ever was known before.
For full information inquire of
Benj. Singleton, better known as old Pap,
NO. 5 NORTH FRONT STREET.
Beware of Speculators and Adventurers, as it is a dangerous thing to fall in their hands.
Nashville, Tenn., March 18, 1878.

Poster calling Southern blacks to emigrate to free state of Kansas.

State Smart

The first woman mayor in the United States, Susanna Salter, was elected mayor of the town of Argonia in 1887.

east by railroad. Legendary lawmen, including "Wild Bill" Hickok and Wyatt Earp, tried to keep order in the cattle towns of Dodge City and Wichita. Cowboys clashed with farmers who wanted to build fences and grow corn and wheat. In the end the farmers won, and Kansas became the "breadbasket" of the United States, so-called because so much wheat for bread was grown there.

During World War II, the aviation industry began to produce airplanes and airplane parts in the city of Wichita. Other industries in Kansas expanded, and the state became increasingly urban.

During the 1980s, Kansas, like many other agricultural states, suffered from a number of economic problems. Prices for crops—especially wheat—fell, adversely affecting Kansas farmers. The state's economy improved by the end of the 1980s.

Arapaho, another tribe that lived in Kansas, dry buffalo meat in front of their tepees at Fort Dodge, in 1870.

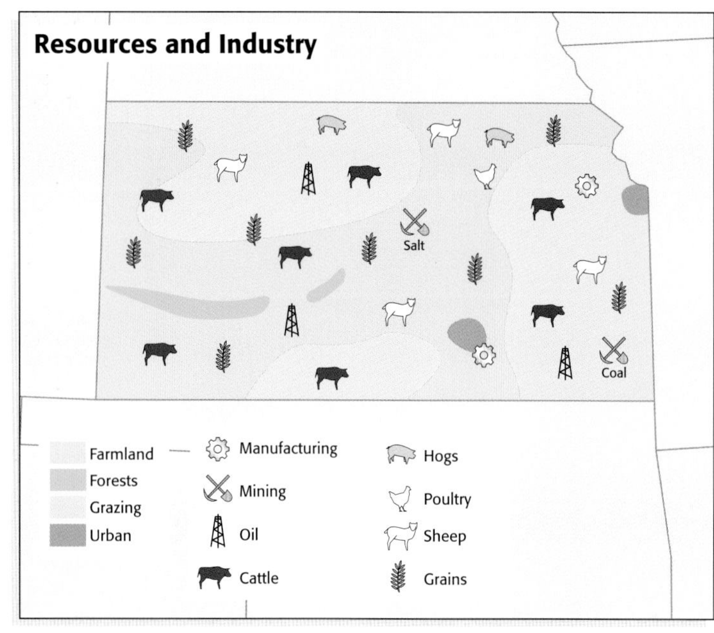

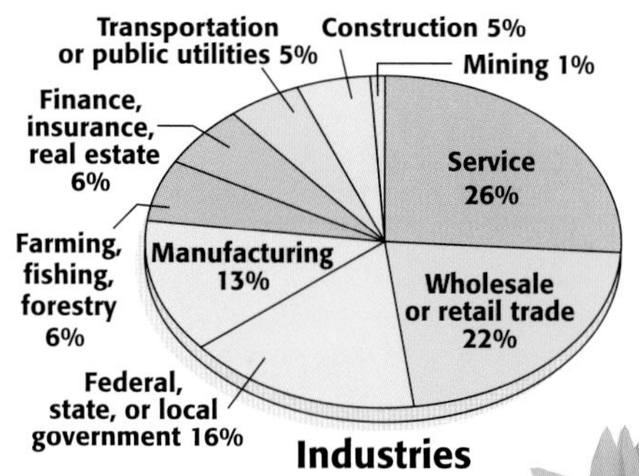

The Present

Kansas produces most of the nation's wheat, and its mills grind wheat into flour that is shipped all over the world. Kansas farmers also grow grain sorghum and hay for animal feed. Other major products include beef cattle and hogs.

Manufacturing is Kansas's most significant industry. Wichita is a center of the light-airplane industry, and more than 60 percent of the nation's aircraft is produced there. Food processing, to prepare many of the crops grown in Kansas to be sold around the world, is another major industry.

Below left: *The best grain sorghum wins prizes at the Kansas State Fair in Hutchinson, because it is an important crop.*
Below right: *Airplane manufacturing is an important industry in Wichita.*

Born in Kansas

- ★ **Gwendolyn Brooks**, poet
- ★ **Walter P. Chrysler,** auto manufacturer
- ★ **John Steuart Curry**, painter
- ★ **Robert Dole**, U.S. senator
- ★ **Amelia Earhart**, aviator
- ★ **William Inge**, playwright
- ★ **Walter Johnson**, baseball player
- ★ **Buster Keaton**, comedian
- ★ **Stan Kenton**, jazz musician
- ★ **Jim Lehrer**, broadcast journalist
- ★ **Edgar Lee Masters**, poet
- ★ **William Allen White**, journalist

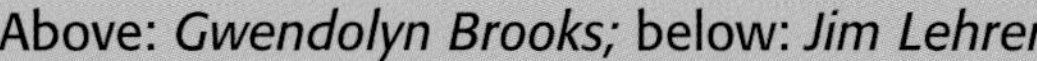

Above: *Gwendolyn Brooks;* below: *Jim Lehrer*

Kansas grows the most wheat in the nation.

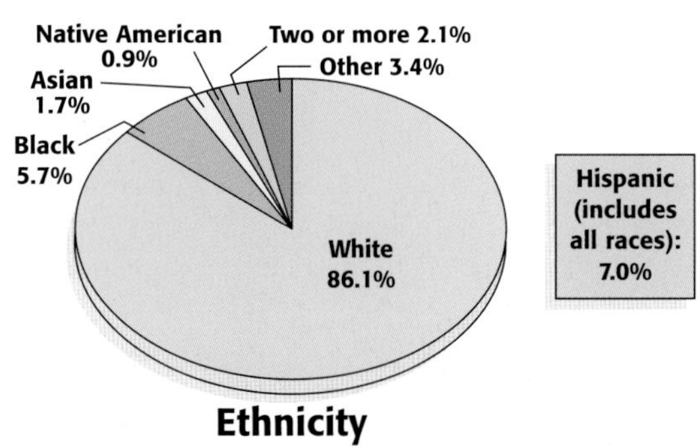

Ethnicity

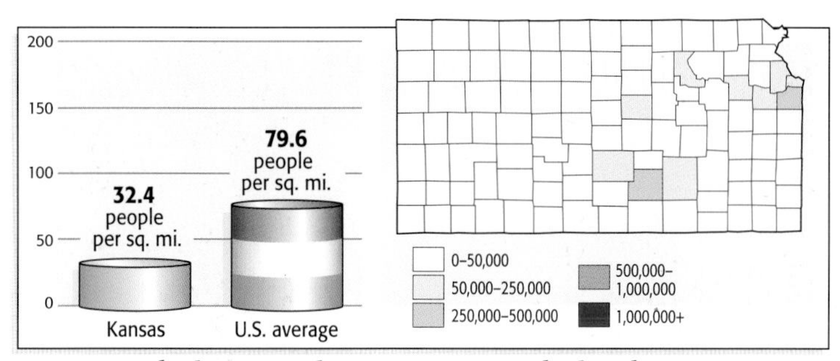

Population Density

Population by County

Kentucky

United we stand, divided we fall.

Land area rank
Largest state (1)
Population rank
Most people (1)

37 — *smallest state (52)*
25 — *fewest people (52)*

At a Glance

Name: *Kentucky* is from the Iroquois word *Ken-tah-ten*, which means "land of tomorrow."
Nickname: Bluegrass State
Capital: Frankfort
Size: 40,411 sq. mi. (104,665 sq km)
Population: 4,041,769
Statehood: Kentucky became the 15th state on June 1, 1792.
Electoral votes: 8 (2004)
U.S. Representatives: 6 (until 2003)
State tree: tulip poplar
State flower: goldenrod
State animal: gray squirrel
Highest point: Black Mountain, 4,145 ft. (1,263 m)

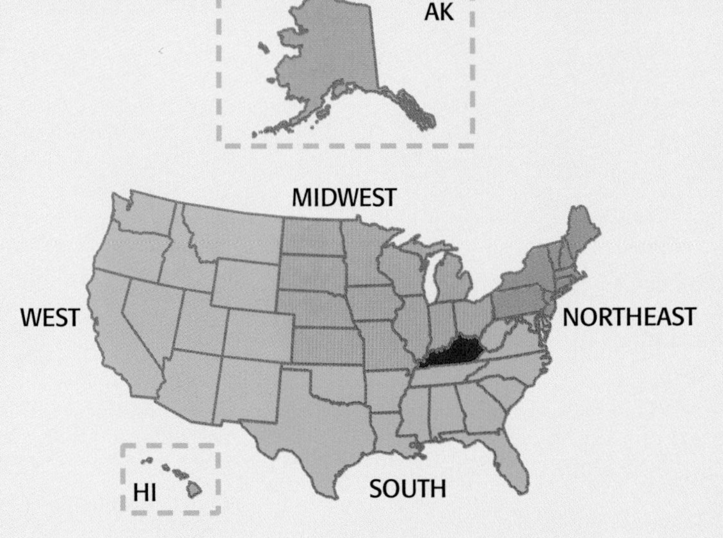

The Place

Kentucky is located in the south central United States and is bordered by seven states: Indiana, Ohio, West Virginia, Virginia, Tennessee, Missouri, and Illinois. The Mississippi River forms Kentucky's

The bluegrass area of Kentucky is known for its horse farms.

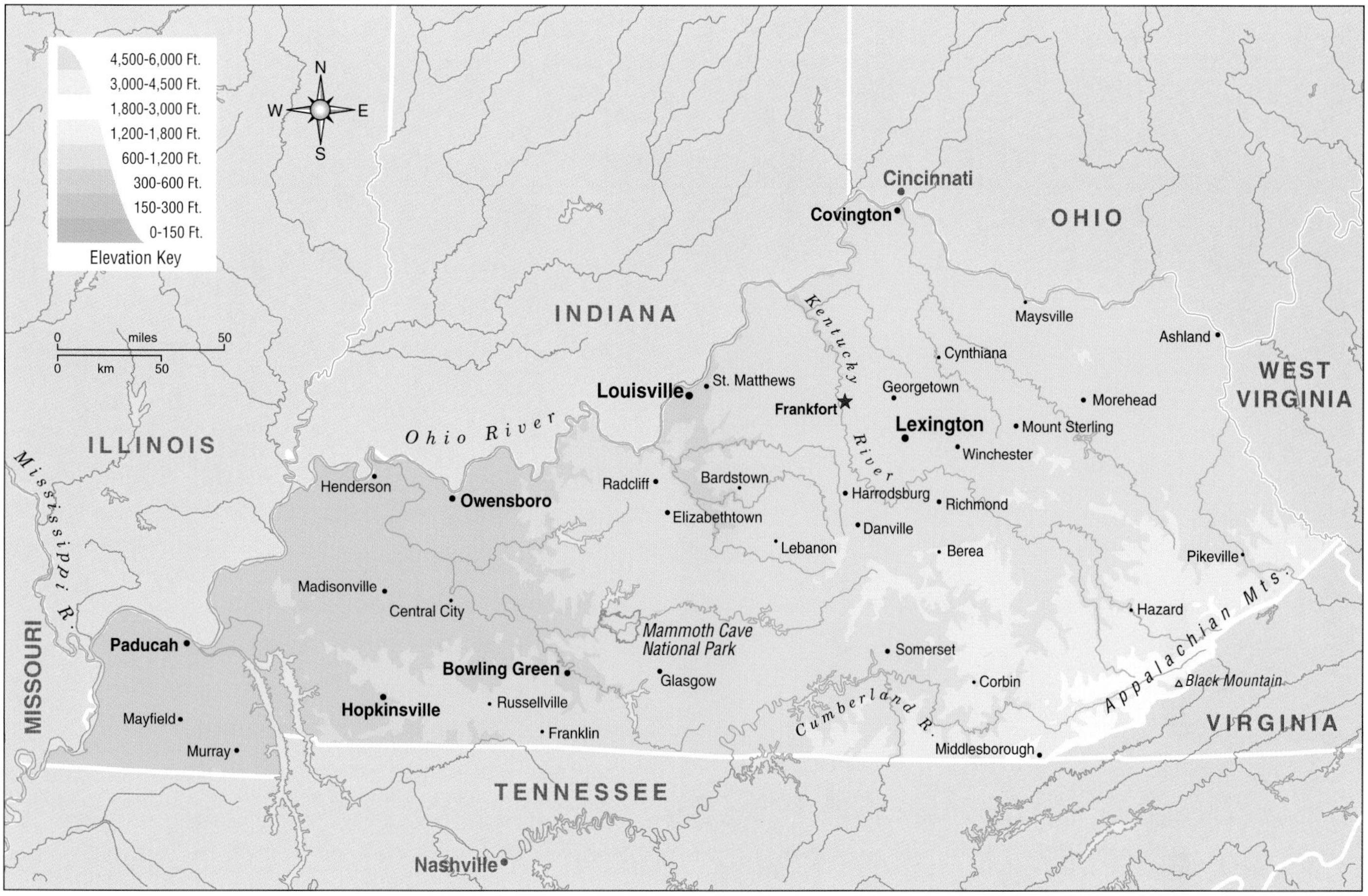

western border, and the state's eastern border lies in the Appalachian Mountains.

The eastern part of the state is mountainous and forested and has several large coal deposits. The Bluegrass Region, in the north central part of the state, is an area of gently rolling hills covered by the grass that gives the region its name. Some tobacco and corn is grown there. Most of Kentucky's famous thoroughbred horse farms are located in this region.

About two-thirds of the state's coal reserves are located in the northwestern region. To the south are the Mississippi floodplain and more gently rolling farmlands, as well as some of the longest cave systems in the world.

Forests cover about half of Kentucky. The state's climate is warm and rainy, with humid summers and cool winters. Most snow falls in the southern half of the state.

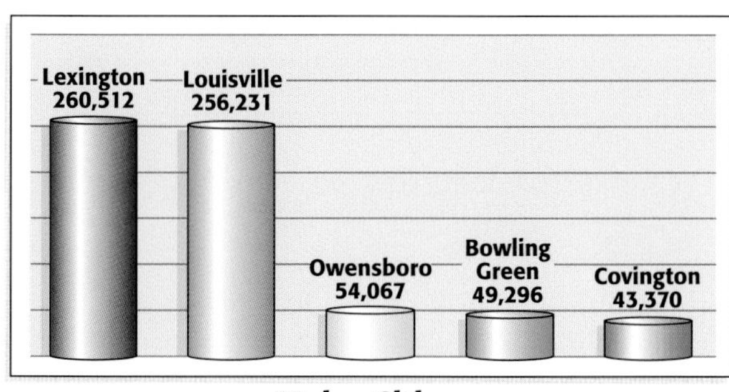

Major Cities

The Past

When British, French, and American explorers arrived in the Kentucky area in the 1600s and 1700s, they found many different Native American tribes living

Kentucky coal miner and his family, 1929

there. In 1774, James Harrod led a group of settlers from Pennsylvania into Kentucky and established the first permanent white settlement, Harrodsburg. The Native Americans, including Cherokee, Delaware, Iroquois, and Shawnee, were not willing to give up their land to the settlers without a fight. They waged war against the newcomers. Pioneers, including the legendary Daniel Boone, defended the settlers from the Native Americans.

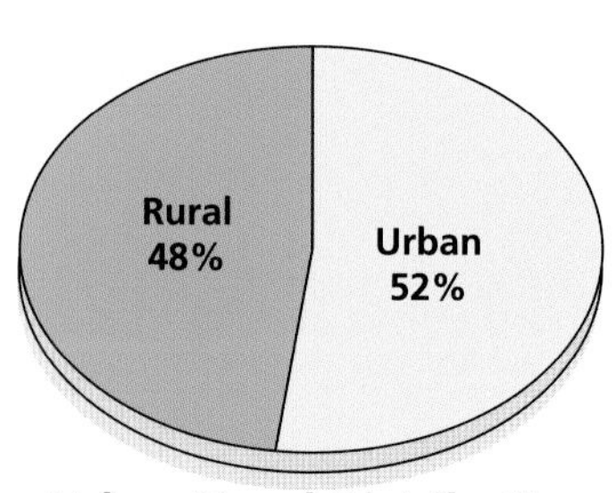

Urban/Rural Distribution

Kentucky became a U.S. territory and later, in 1792, a state. After Kentucky became a state, its population increased and more areas of farmland were opened to settlement. Farmers grew hemp and tobacco,

Facts and Firsts

- ★ Bluegrass is not really blue—it is green. In the spring, bluegrass produces bluish-purple buds. When a large number of these buds grow close together in a field, they give a blue cast to the grass.
- ★ Middlesboro is the only city in the United States built inside a meteor crater.
- ★ The Kentucky Derby, first run in 1875, is the oldest continuously held horse race in the United States. Each May, thousands of spectators come to the Churchill Downs racetrack in Louisville for the "run for the roses"—the blanket of roses presented to the winning horse and jockey.
- ★ In 1887, Kentucky schoolteacher Mary Towles Sasseen Wilson held the first observance of Mother's Day. Mother's Day received national recognition in 1914. On May 9 of that year, President Woodrow Wilson signed a resolution that recommended Congress and the executive branch of the federal government observe Mother's Day. The next year, Wilson proclaimed Mother's Day an annual national observance.
- ★ In 1893, two Louisville sisters, Mildred Hill and Patty Hill, created the song that became "Happy Birthday to You."
- ★ The largest amount of gold in the world, more than $6 billion in the form of gold bullion, is stored underground at Fort Knox.

as well as corn, rye, and other grains used to manufacture alcoholic beverages. Horse breeders began to move into the Bluegrass Region for its rich soil and grass.

Slavery was central to the state's agricultural economy. The abolition of slavery after the Civil War hurt Kentucky's horse breeding and tobacco industries; the state's growth and economic progress slowed. Agriculture in Kentucky suffered again during the Great Depression of the 1930s, when residents began to move from farms to the cities in search of work.

The demand for food and war materials during World War II helped Kentucky restore its economy. After the war, manufacturing grew, and Kentucky began to shift from an agricultural to an industrial economy. During the 1960s, coal mining expanded greatly, and the construction of new highways increased tourism throughout the state.

State Smart

Mammoth Cave, which stretches for more than 300 miles (483 km), is the world's longest known system of caves and underground passages.

Below: *Harrodsburg was the first white settlement in Kentucky.* Above: *Grave of Kentucky pioneer Daniel Boone in Frankfort.*

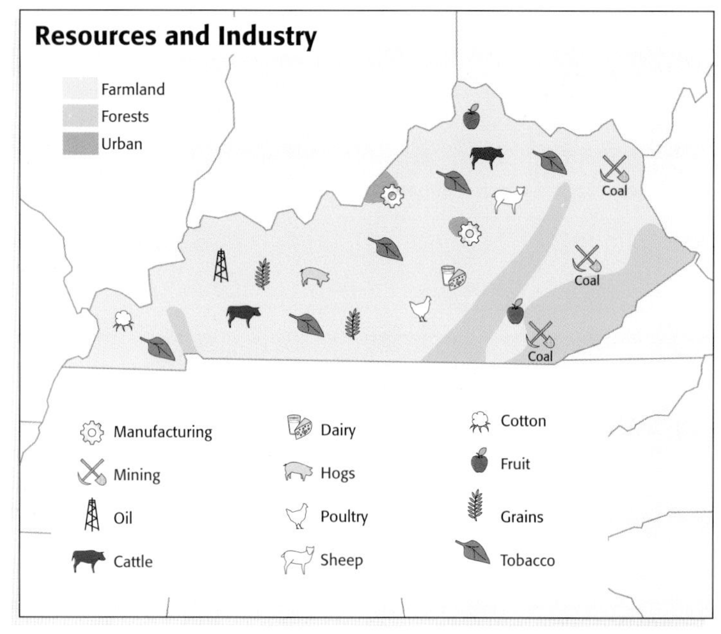

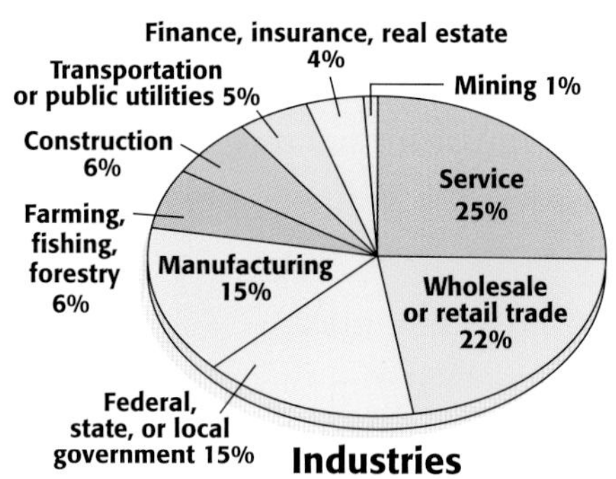

The Present

Kentucky has long been known for its tobacco, racehorses, and whiskey. Today, Kentucky produces more burley tobacco and bourbon whiskey than any other state.

Huge deposits of coal and other mineral resources have made the state an important mining center. Manufacturing, too, has made Kentucky into an urban, industrial state. Automobiles and automobile parts are now the most valuable of Kentucky's manufactured goods. Other goods manufactured there include aircraft parts, pharmaceutical products, paints, industrial cleaners, elevators, typewriters, and printers.

Tourist attractions such as Cumberland Falls, Mammoth Cave, and Land Between the Lakes make Kentucky a popular vacation spot. The Kentucky Derby also attracts tourists from all over the world.

Below left: *Louisville at night.* Below right: *Thoroughbred horses race at the Keeneland track outside of Lexington in preparation for the Kentucky Derby.*

Born in Kentucky

- ★ **Muhammad Ali**, boxer
- ★ **Louis D. Brandeis**, jurist
- ★ **Christopher "Kit" Carson**, scout
- ★ **George Clooney**, actor
- ★ **Rosemary Clooney**, singer
- ★ **Jefferson Davis**, president of the Confederacy
- ★ **Johnny Depp**, actor
- ★ **Naomi Judd and Wynonna Judd**, singers
- ★ **Abraham Lincoln**, U.S. president
- ★ **Diane Sawyer**, broadcast journalist
- ★ **Robert Penn Warren**, novelist

Above: *Abraham Lincoln;* below: *Diane Sawyer*

Above left: *Tobacco is dried in drying barns before it is prepared for market.* Above right: *National Bridge State Park in the Daniel Boone National Forest attracts many visitors to eastern Kentucky.*

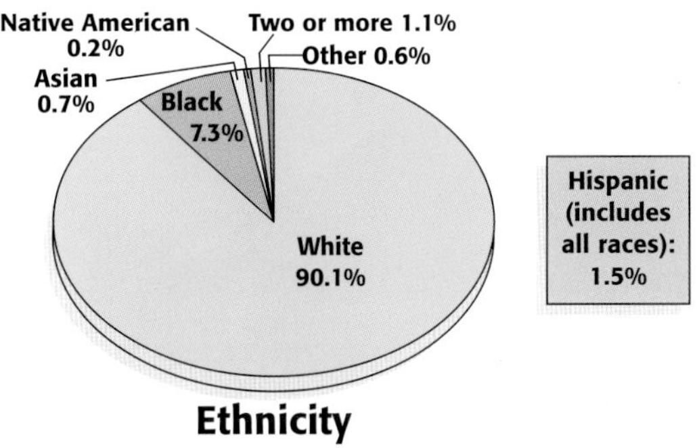

Ethnicity

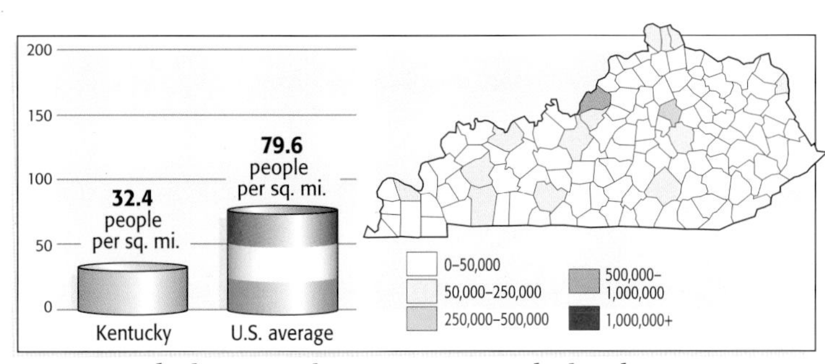

Population Density **Population by County**

Louisiana

Union, justice, confidence.

Land area rank *Largest state (1)* — 31 — *smallest state (52)*

Population rank *Most people (1)* — 22 — *fewest people (52)*

At a Glance

Name: Louisiana was named for King Louis XIV of France.

Nickname: Pelican State

Capital: Baton Rouge

Size: 47,751 sq. mi. (124,153 sq km)

Population: 4,468,976

Statehood: Louisiana became the 18th state on April 30, 1812.

Electoral votes: 9 (2004)

U.S. Representatives: 7 (until 2003)

State tree: cypress

State flower: magnolia

State crustacean: crayfish

Highest point: Driskill Mountain, 535 ft. (163 m)

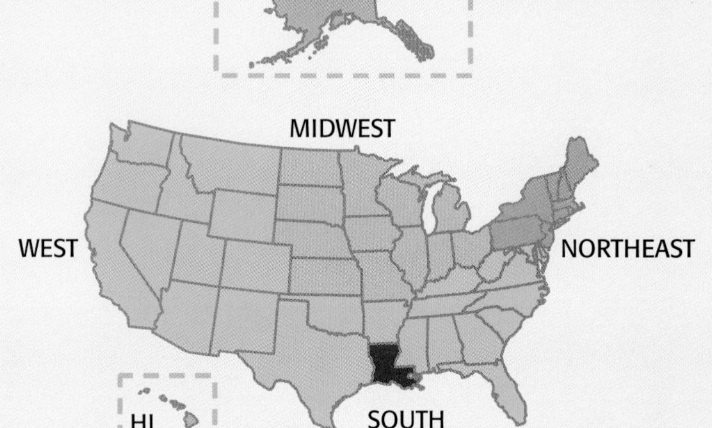

The Place

Louisiana is a southern state that lies at the mouth of the Mississippi River, where the river empties into the Gulf of Mexico. New Orleans, Louisiana's largest city, is a major international port on the river. At one time,

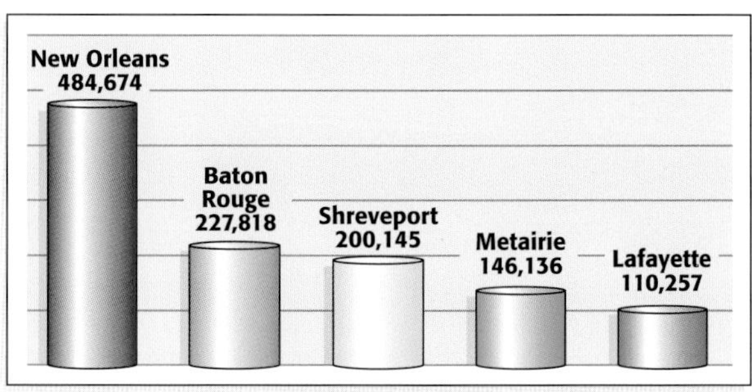

Major Cities

The French Quarter of New Orleans is known for its lacy wrought iron ornamentation.

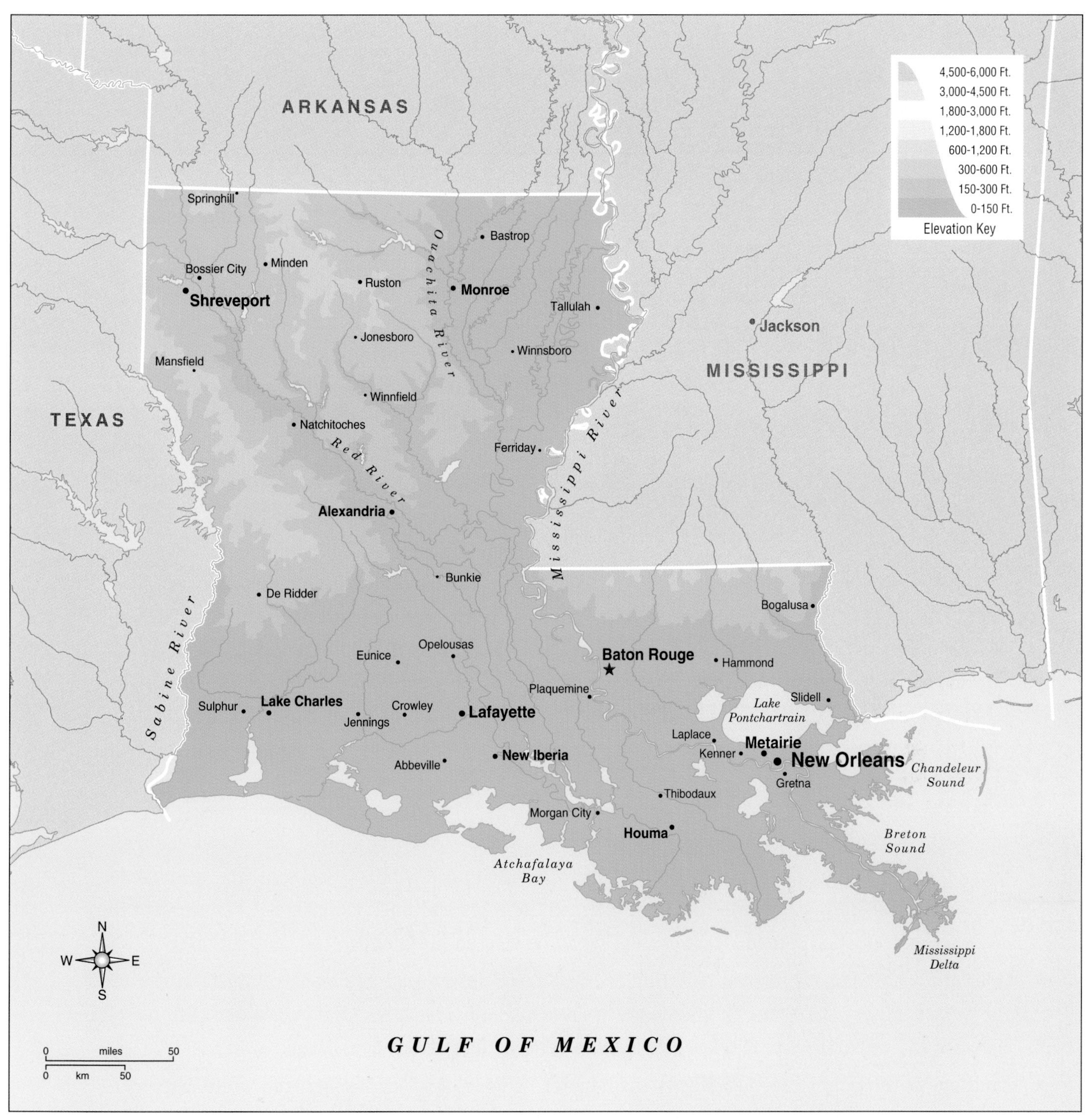

Louisiana was nothing more than a bay on the Gulf of Mexico. The state was formed over thousands of years as soil deposits from rivers, including the Mississippi, piled up to form solid land. As a result, most of Louisiana is low, fertile land.

The Mississippi Delta—the triangular area at the mouth of the river—has the richest soil in the state. In the northwestern part of the state where it borders Texas, there are about 60 miles (96 km) of prairie. To the north of this grassy region, in the

Andrew Jackson was welcomed by New Orleans residents after the Battle of New Orleans, fought during the war of 1812.

area where Louisiana borders Arkansas, the land begins to slope upward and reaches its highest point at Driskill Mountain. Almost half of the state is forested with trees such as cypress, magnolia, and oak.

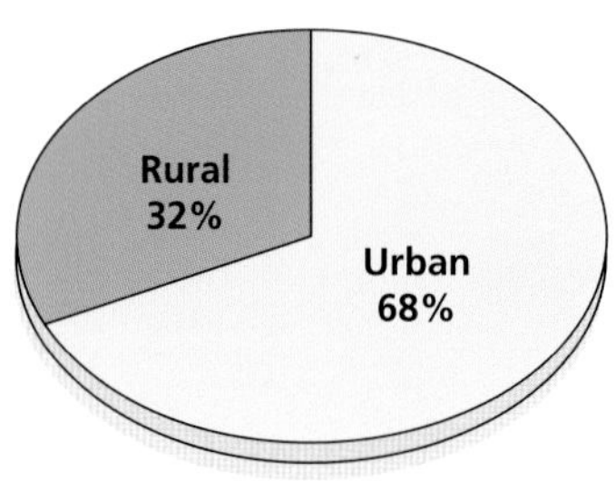

Urban/Rural Distribution

Louisiana has the third-longest ocean shoreline of any state, after Alaska and Florida. The coast has constant problems with erosion, because salt water kills the freshwater grasses that live in Louisiana's river marshes.

Louisiana's weather is subtropical. Temperatures and humidity are high all year, and the state receives about 57 inches of rain every year.

Facts and Firsts

★ The Battle of New Orleans, fought during the War of 1812 between the United States and England, actually took place two weeks after the war had officially ended. Andrew Jackson, who commanded American forces during the battle, did not learn of the war's end until more than a month after the peace treaty had been signed. Jackson went on to be elected president of the United States in 1828.

★ Louisiana's most famous festival is Mardi Gras, which was introduced by French colonists in the 1700s. The phrase *mardi gras* means "fat Tuesday" in French. Mardi Gras marks the end of a traditional period of feasts and celebration that takes place before Lent, a time of self-denial and fasting.

★ Louisiana is the only state that follows the Napoleonic Code, a set of laws written while Emperor Napoléon Bonaparte governed France.

★ Louisiana has the highest population of Cajuns of any state. Cajuns are the descendants of Acadians, a group of French-speaking settlers who lived in Nova Scotia, Canada. They were forced to leave Nova Scotia because they would not pledge allegiance to the king of England after England took control of Canada.

★ Louisiana is the only state that is not divided into counties. Instead, Louisiana is divided into 64 parishes.

The Past

Europeans reached the area of present-day Louisiana in the early 1500s, when the Spanish first explored the region. French colonists from Canada, however, officially claimed the area for the king of France in 1682.

This young Confederate soldier from Louisiana died in the Civil War.

Spain and France alternately controlled parts of Louisiana until 1803. In that year, the United States bought the entire territory from France. The Louisiana Purchase included more than 885,000 square miles of land and more than doubled the size of the United States. Soon after, the land acquired in the purchase was divided into smaller regions. One of these regions, the Territory of Orleans, became present-day Louisiana.

After Louisiana joined the United States, it emerged as a leader among the southern states. New Orleans was one of the most important trading cities in the country, and steamboats traveled up and down the Mississippi River to bring goods and people to the inland states to the north.

Louisiana's huge cotton and sugar plantations depended on slavery, and Louisiana fought on the side of the South during the Civil War. Although the war damaged Louisiana's economy, the postwar construction of railroads quickly revived the state. Furthermore, the discovery of oil and natural gas at the beginning of the 1900s helped the state expand industrially throughout most of the 20th century.

In the 1960s, the National Aeronautics and Space Administration (NASA) began construction of the Saturn rocket (which launched astronauts to the moon in 1969) in New Orleans. Louisiana's manufacturing industries continued to grow until the end of the 1980s, when low oil prices slowed its economy.

> **State Smart**
>
> ***Louisiana's Superdome is the largest indoor arena in the United States. It covers 13 acres (5.3 ha) and can hold up to 95,000 people (with floor seating added).***

NASA engineers based in New Orleans experimented with the design of the Saturn 5 *rocket in 1968.*

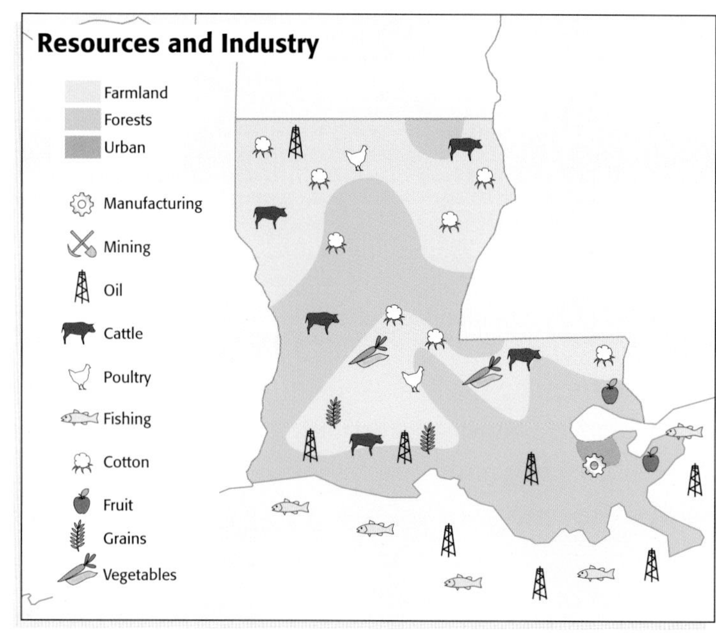

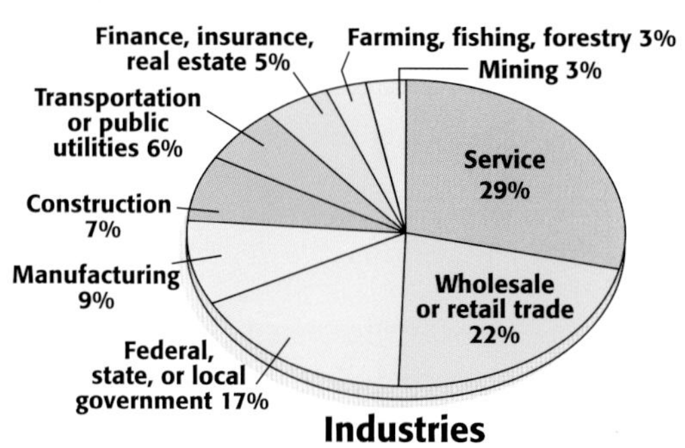

The Present

Since the 1980s, tourism has helped boost Louisiana's economy. People come from all over the United States to experience Louisiana's unique mixture of cultures, especially during the Mardi Gras celebration. Spanish, African, and French influences from Louisiana's past are still evident today. They are reflected in the state's architecture, the French and Spanish words that remain in the local dialects, and the state's spicy Cajun and Creole cuisine.

Visitors to Louisiana's stately pre–Civil War homes and gardens can glimpse the lifestyle that once existed on the state's many wealthy plantations. Louisiana is known as the Cradle of Jazz, because it was the birthplace of New Orleans–style jazz. This music grew out of Louisiana's African-Creole heritage during the first half of the

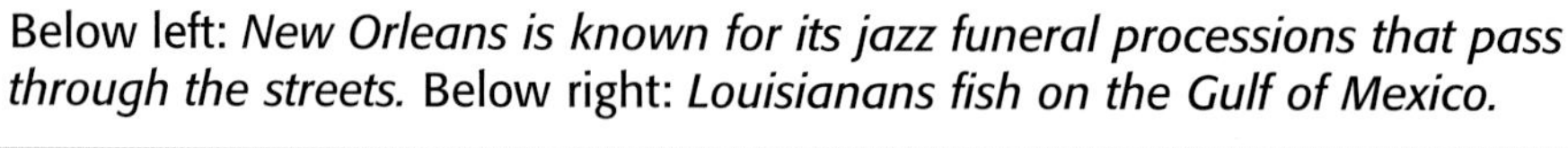

Below left: *New Orleans is known for its jazz funeral processions that pass through the streets.* Below right: *Louisianans fish on the Gulf of Mexico.*

Born in Louisiana

- ★ **Louis "Satchmo" Armstrong**, musician
- ★ **Truman Capote**, writer
- ★ **Kate Chopin**, writer
- ★ **Van Cliburn**, concert pianist
- ★ **Fats Domino**, musician
- ★ **Bryant Gumbel**, television newscaster
- ★ **Lillian Hellman**, playwright
- ★ **Mahalia Jackson**, gospel singer
- ★ **Jerry Lee Lewis**, musician
- ★ **Huey P. Long**, politician
- ★ **Wynton Marsalis**, musician
- ★ **Ferdinand Joseph La Menth "Jelly Roll" Morton**, musician and composer
- ★ **Huey Newton**, African American activist
- ★ **Anne Rice**, author
- ★ **Britney Spears**, singer
- ★ **Edward Douglas White**, jurist

Above: *Wynton Marsalis;* below: *Anne Rice*

20th century and influenced such famous musicians as Louis Armstrong and Jelly Roll Morton. Many music lovers visit New Orleans to retrace the history of jazz.

Louisiana is becoming a more urban, industrial state as its commercial trade grows. The industries that process the state's oil and natural gas deposits are critical to Louisiana's economy. Much of the state's income comes from oil refineries. The mining and processing of oil and gas, however, have caused pollution that has created environmental problems.

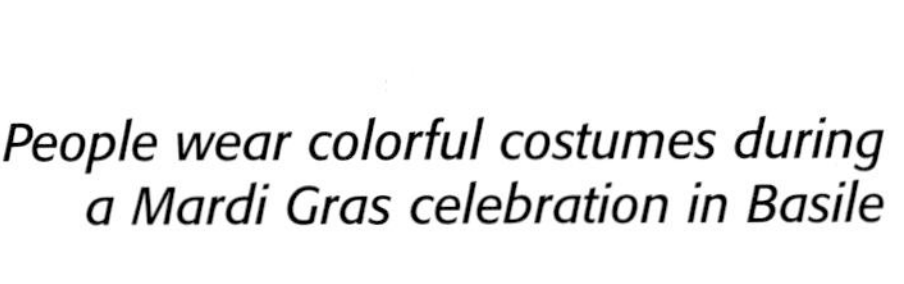

People wear colorful costumes during a Mardi Gras celebration in Basile

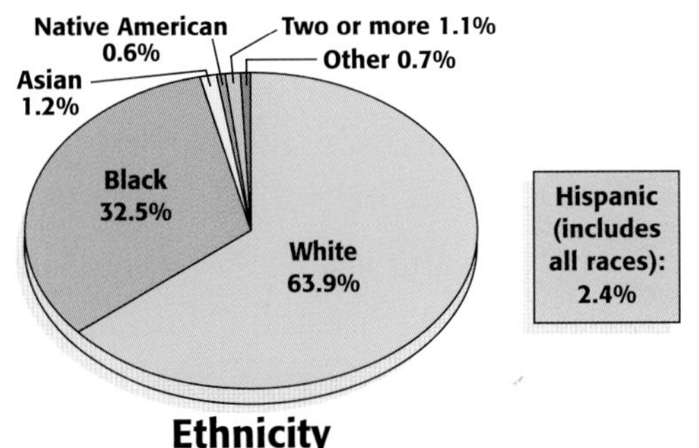

Ethnicity

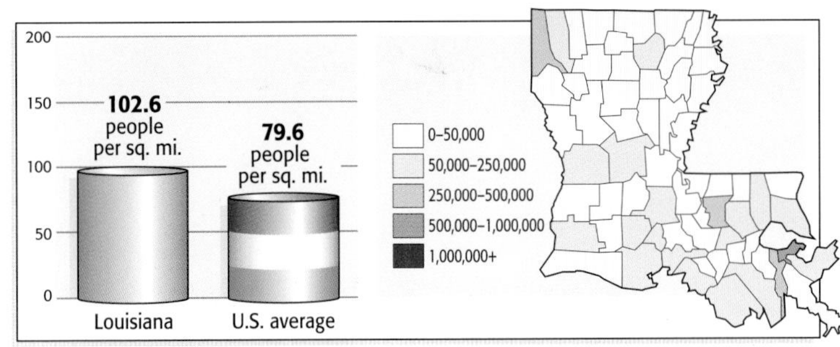

Population Density

Population by County

Maine

Dirigo (I direct)

Land area rank
Largest state (1)

Population rank
Most people (1)

At a Glance

Name: *Maine* probably comes from the word *mainland*. Early English explorers used the phrase "the main" to distinguish Maine from its offshore islands.

Nickname: Pine Tree State

Capital: Augusta

Size: 33,265 sq. mi. (87,727 sq km)

Population: 1,274,923

Statehood: Maine became the 23rd state on March 15, 1820.

Electoral votes: 4 (2004)

U.S. Representatives: 2 (until 2003)

State tree: eastern white pine

State flower: white pinecone and tassel

State cat: Maine coon cat

Highest point: Mount Katahdin, 5,267 ft. (1,606 m)

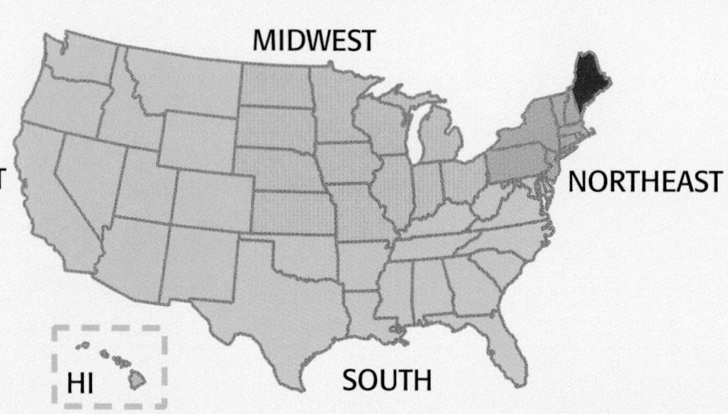

The Place

Maine forms the northeastern tip of New England and shares approximately half of its border with Canada. Maine's Atlantic coastline is famous for its bays, coves, and inlets. Most of the land along the shore is flat, but it gets higher in the central and southern regions of the state, which have areas of rich soil and good farmland.

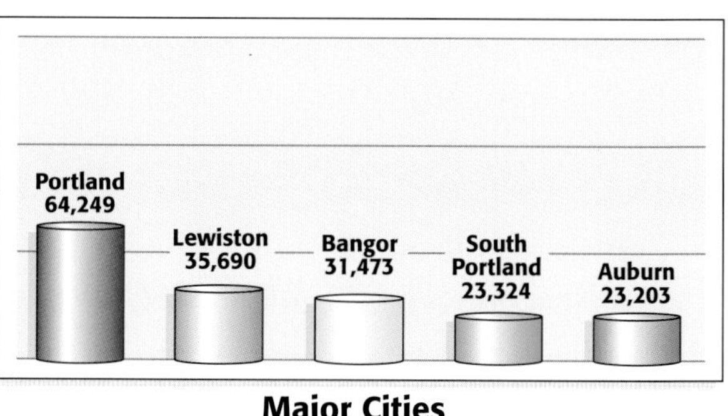

Major Cities

Maine's northwest is covered by the White Mountains, part of the Appalachian Mountain chain. The northern and central parts of the state are dotted with ponds and lakes, and about 90 percent of Maine is forested. Maine produces many different kinds of minerals and mineral products, including

Maine is known for its rugged coastline and historic lighthouses.

limestone, granite, slate, copper, zinc, lead, sand, and gravel.

Because of its location on the northeast coast of the country, Maine is one of the coolest states. It lies to the north of where the Gulf Stream, a warm current of air from Europe, ends. As a result, Maine has cold, snowy winters and cool summers.

In this painting, Leif Eriksson approaches the coast of Vinland (his name for America). The exact location of Vinland is not certain.

THE PAST

Historians believe that the Norse mariner Leif Eriksson and a group of Vikings explored Maine around A.D. 1000, a time when the only other inhabitants of the region were Native Americans. The first true European settlement, however, did not begin until the 1620s, when different groups of English settlers moved into the region. In general, these settlers lived peacefully with the Native Americans, which included several Algonquian tribes.

In 1677, Maine became a part of the Massachusetts Bay Colony. Many Maine patriots fought in the Revolutionary War. In 1785, a movement began for Maine's separation from Massachusetts and admission to the Union, but it was not until after the War of 1812 that the movement gained strength. In 1820, Maine became an independent state as part of the Missouri Compromise. Maine entered the Union as a free state, while Missouri

Facts and Firsts

- ★ With a total land area of 33,265 square miles, Maine is larger than all of the other five New England states combined.
- ★ Maine lies the farthest east of any state. Eastport is the eastern most city in the United States.
- ★ Maine borders only one other state.
- ★ Maine's Acadia National Park is the second most-visited national park in the United States.
- ★ In June 1775, the first naval battle of the Revolutionary War was fought between the British and the American colonists off the coast near Machias.
- ★ Maine produces at least 98 percent of all of the nation's blueberries, 50 percent of the nation's lobsters, and 90 percent of all the nation's toothpicks.
- ★ In 1964, U.S. senator Margaret Chase Smith of Maine was the first woman ever to seek the presidential nomination from a major political party.

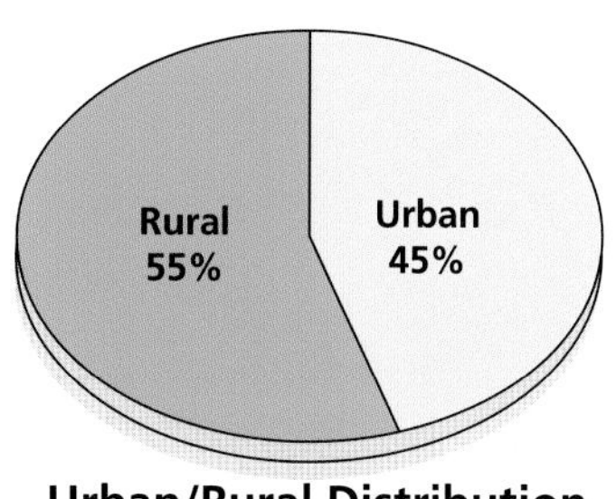

Urban/Rural Distribution

entered as a slave-holding state, thereby maintaining the balance of free and slave states in Congress. Maine strongly supported the Union cause during the Civil War.

After the war, Maine's textile and power industries began to develop, while small farms began to disappear. During the 1920s, the production of paper products from Maine's extensive forests became more important to the state's economy. During World War II, Maine produced ships, shoes, and food for American troops.

During the second half of the 20th century, tourism began to grow, as did the lumber and food-processing industries. Maine's growth was slowed during the 1970s and 1980s by overcutting in state forests and overfishing in its waters. Air and water pollution also became problems.

State Smart

Maine harvests more lobsters than any other state. More than 47 million pounds (21.3 million kg) were harvested in 1998.

Above: *Children pose at a Memorial Day parade in Ashland, Maine, during World War II.* Below: *Augusta, Maine's capital, developed from a trading post established in 1628, on the Kennebec River.*

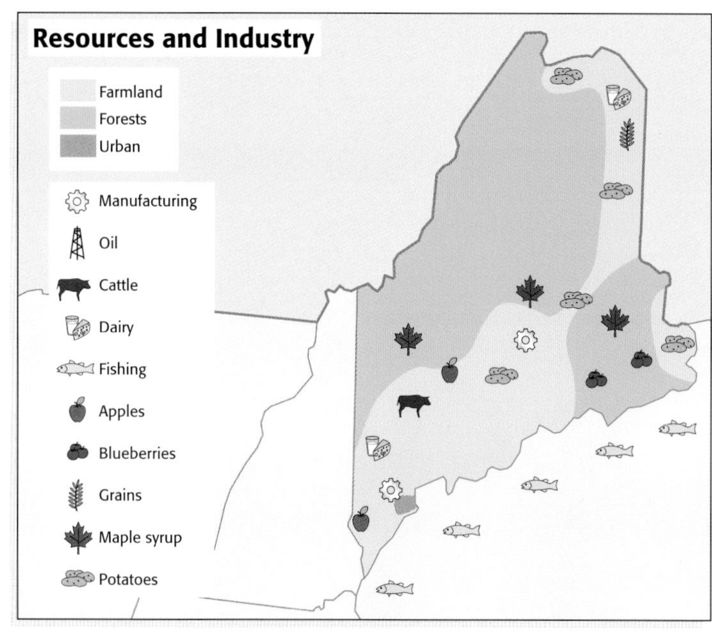

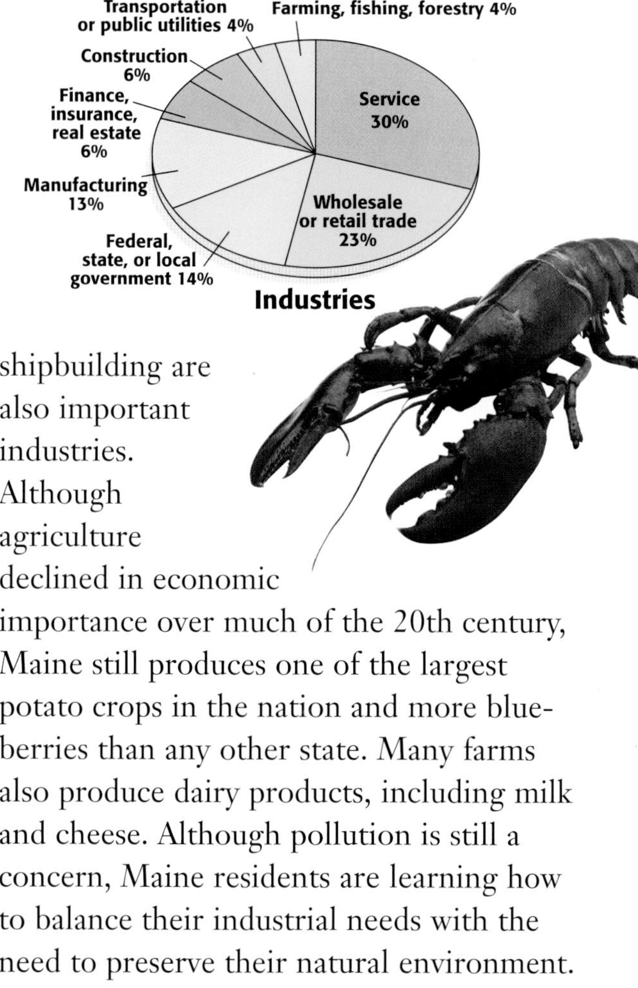

The Present

Maine is sometimes called Vacationland because of its popularity as a tourist destination. Maine's rugged coastline, historic lighthouses, scenic lakes, and White Mountains ski resorts attract millions of tourists every year.

Paper production, electronics, and shipbuilding are also important industries. Although agriculture declined in economic importance over much of the 20th century, Maine still produces one of the largest potato crops in the nation and more blueberries than any other state. Many farms also produce dairy products, including milk and cheese. Although pollution is still a concern, Maine residents are learning how to balance their industrial needs with the need to preserve their natural environment.

Below left: *Specially painted lobster buoys are used to mark a lobsterman's territory in the water.*
Below right: *A destroyer is launched at Bath Iron Works in Bath, Maine, in 1999.*

Born in Maine

- ★ **Dorothea Dix**, civil rights reformer
- ★ **John Ford**, film director
- ★ **Marsden Hartley**, painter
- ★ **Sarah Orne Jewett**, author
- ★ **Henry Wadsworth Longfellow**, poet
- ★ **Stephen King**, author
- ★ **Linda Lavin**, actress
- ★ **Edna St. Vincent Millay**, poet
- ★ **Marston Morse**, mathematician
- ★ **Edwin Arlington Robinson**, poet
- ★ **Margaret Chase Smith**, politician

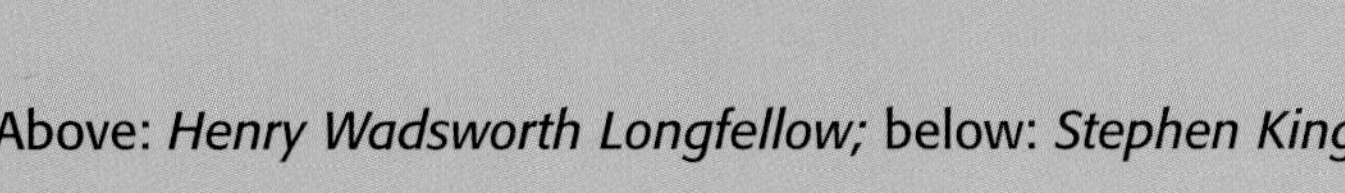

Above: *Henry Wadsworth Longfellow;* below: *Stephen King*

Above left: *Maine is the only state to have a large moose population.* Above right: *A Maine blueberry-picker takes a break from work.*

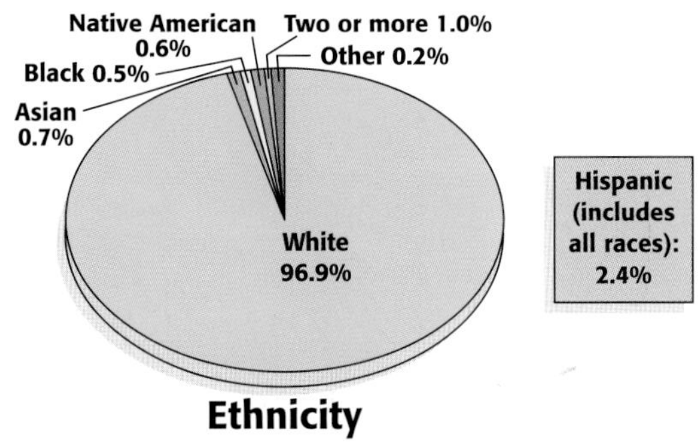

Hispanic (includes all races): 2.4%

Ethnicity

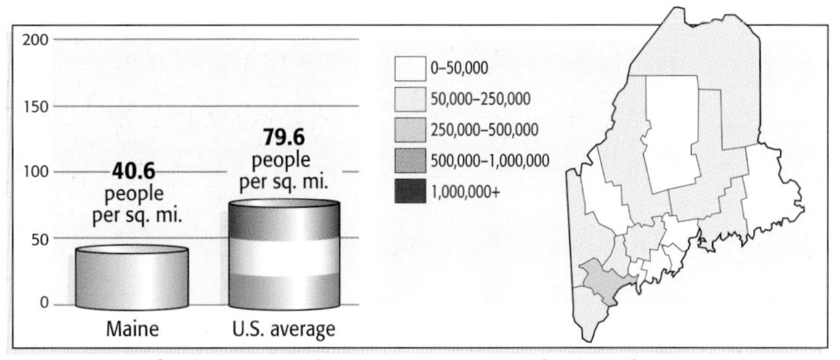

Population Density

Population by County

Maryland

Fatti maschii, parole femine (Manly deeds, womanly words).

Land area rank *Largest state (1)* — 42 — *smallest state (52)*

Population rank *Most people (1)* — 19 — *fewest people (52)*

At a Glance

Name: Maryland was named in honor of Henrietta Maria, queen consort of King Charles I of England.

Nicknames: Free State, Old Line State

Capital: Annapolis

Size: 12,297 sq. mi. (31,972 sq km)

Population: 5,296,486

Statehood: Maryland became the seventh state on April 28, 1788.

Electoral votes: 10 (2004)

U.S. representatives: 8 (until 2003)

State tree: white oak

State flower: black-eyed Susan

State bird: Baltimore oriole

Highest point: Backbone Mountain, 3,360 ft. (1,024 m)

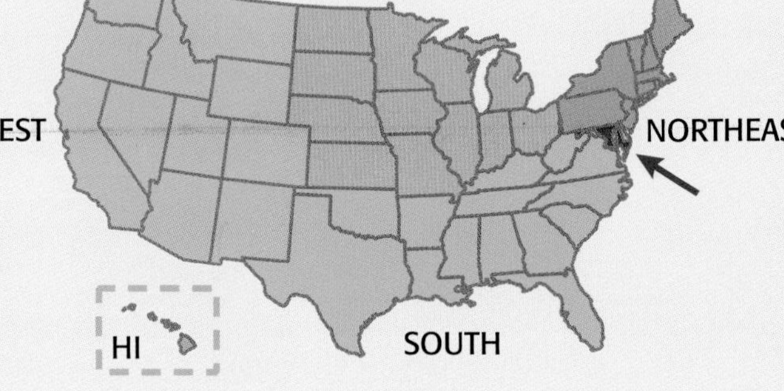

The Place

Maryland is located in the northeastern corner of the southern states. Maryland's northern border runs along the Mason-Dixon Line, the traditional boundary between the North and the South. Maryland is split by the Chesapeake Bay, an inlet of the Atlantic Ocean. Maryland has

Baltimore is a historic port on the Chesapeake Bay.

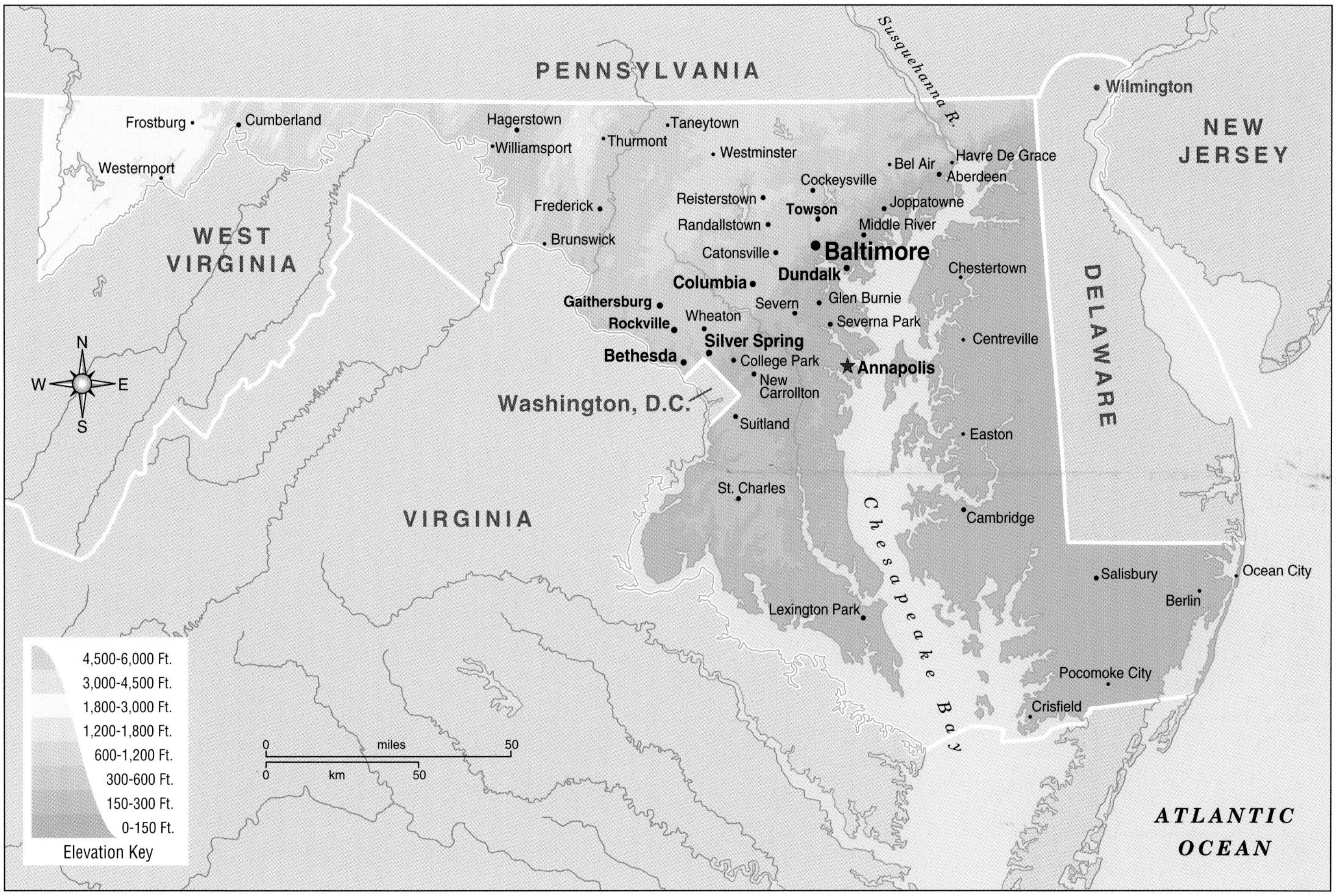

several ports along the bay, including Baltimore, the state's largest city, and Annapolis, the capital.

The portion of Maryland east of the Chesapeake Bay is known as the Eastern Shore, and the part west of the bay is called the Western Shore. Both coastlines are generally low and flat, but much of the Western Shore is hilly to mountainous, with some fertile valleys. Most of Maryland's soil in the west, except for areas along the shoreline, is good for farming. About 40 percent of the state is forested. Maryland has several lakes, all of which are man-made.

Maryland experiences humid weather conditions, with hot summers and generally mild winters. The state's mountainous northwest can be considerably cooler than shore areas. Rain is frequent throughout the state, and more snow falls in the mountains than elsewhere.

Maryland produces large amounts of crushed stone, which is used in construction. The state also has several coal, natural gas, limestone, and marble deposits.

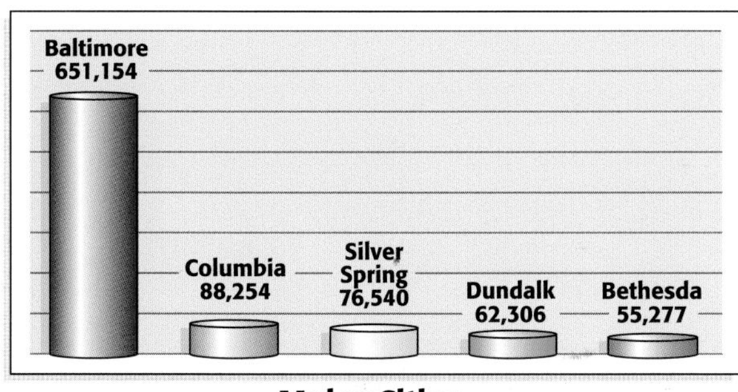

Major Cities

The Past

Native Americans have lived in Maryland for more than 10,000 years. When Spanish and English explorers first sailed into the Chesapeake Bay 400 years ago, they found several different Algonquian tribes there. Colonists began to settle in the area in 1631, when the first trading post was opened.

King Charles I gave Maryland to the Calvert family.

In 1632, King Charles I of England gave most of Maryland to Cecilius Calvert, Lord Baltimore. The Calvert family governed the area until the Revolutionary War, except for a brief few years. Tobacco was a valuable crop, and the colony's population grew rapidly. Maryland was also known for its religious tolerance.

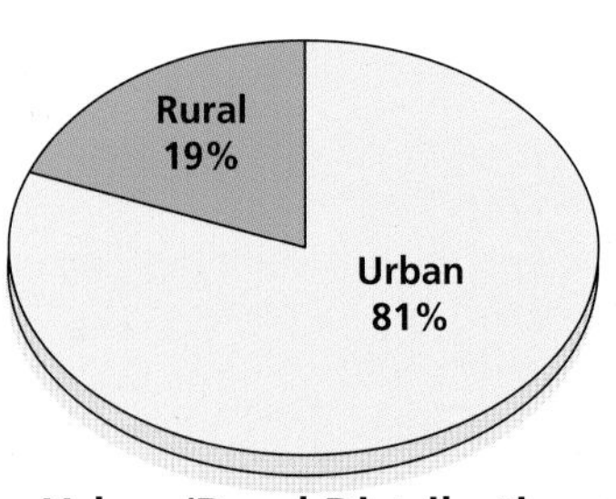

Urban/Rural Distribution

During the American Revolution, Maryland residents built cannons and ships in Baltimore for General George Washington's Continental army. Maryland approved the Constitution on April 28, 1788, and became the seventh state of the Union. In 1791, Maryland

Religious tolerance was practiced at St. Mary's City, the first capital of Maryland, and now the site of a living museum.

Facts and Firsts

- ★ In 1696, King Williams School, the first free school in the United States, opened in Annapolis.
- ★ The Maryland State House is the oldest state capitol building still in legislative use.
- ★ In 1791, Maryland gave up land for the nation's capital—Washington, D.C.
- ★ According to legend, Francis Scott Key, a Maryland lawyer, wrote "The Star-Spangled Banner" as he watched the British bombardment of Fort McHenry in Baltimore Harbor in September 1814.
- ★ In 1902, Maryland became the first state to enact a workers' compensation law to support people injured on the job.

donated land for the new nation's permanent capital. The capital was looted and burned by the British during the War of 1812. During the Civil War, Maryland remained in the Union even though it was a slaveholding state. Many of Maryland's residents, however, chose to fight for the Confederate cause.

After the war's end, Baltimore's commercial importance grew and it became known as one of the cultural centers of the nation. Maryland factories and shipyards flourished throughout most of the 20th century, although the state, like the rest of the nation, suffered economically during the Great Depression of the 1930s.

During World War II, manufacturing activity increased greatly in Maryland. Baltimore and other cities drew large numbers of workers from nearby states, the population began to expand quickly, and the state became increasingly urban. By the 1960s, the quality of Maryland's roads, transportation systems, schools, and housing had declined. During the 1960s and 1970s, however, many new bridges, roads, airports, houses, and schools were built to meet the growing needs of the state. In 1985, Maryland began an ongoing project to clean up pollution in the Chesapeake Bay.

State Smart

The Peabody Conservatory of Music, founded in Maryland in 1857, is the oldest music school in the United States.

The Battle of Antietam, the bloodiest battle of the Civil War, took place in Maryland.

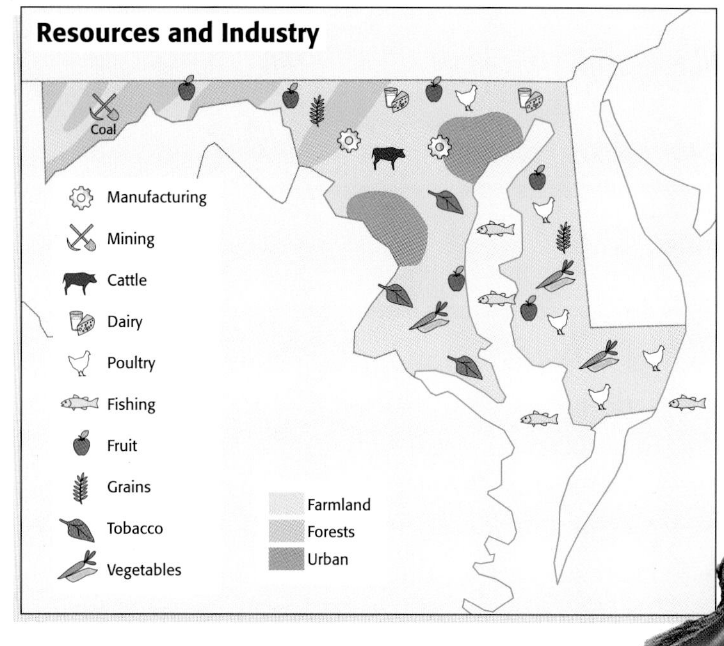

Transportation or public utilities 4%
Farming, fishing, forestry 2%
Mining 0.1%
Finance, insurance, real estate 8%
Service 34%
Construction 6%
Manufacturing 6%
Wholesale or retail trade 21%
Federal, state, or local government 17%

Industries

The Present

Maryland's location on the Chesapeake Bay has helped it to become and remain one of the most important commercial and shipping states in the nation. Manufacturing is strongest in the Baltimore and Washington, D.C., areas, where industries such as food processing and chemical production flourish.

Maryland is the site of several government bureaus and offices, including the U.S. Naval Academy in Annapolis and Goddard Space Flight Center in Greenbelt.

Maryland is not only a manufacturing and industrial state. Approximately one-third of Maryland is farmland. Many of the state's approximately 13,000 farms produce broilers, or young chickens, which are Maryland's most valuable farm product.

Below left: *Crabs are a favorite Maryland food.* Below right: *Students at the U.S. Naval Academy in Annapolis perform field exercises.*

Born in Maryland

- ★ **John Wilkes Booth**, actor and assassin of Abraham Lincoln
- ★ **Tom Clancy**, author
- ★ **Frederick Douglass**, abolitionist
- ★ **Philip Glass**, composer
- ★ **Billie Holiday**, jazz-blues singer
- ★ **Johns Hopkins**, financier
- ★ **Francis Scott Key**, author of the national anthem
- ★ **Thurgood Marshall**, jurist
- ★ **H.L. Mencken**, author
- ★ **Charles Willson Peale**, painter
- ★ **Frank Perdue**, farmer and businessman
- ★ **Babe Ruth**, baseball player
- ★ **Upton Sinclair**, author
- ★ **Harriet Tubman**, abolitionist
- ★ **Frank Zappa**, singer

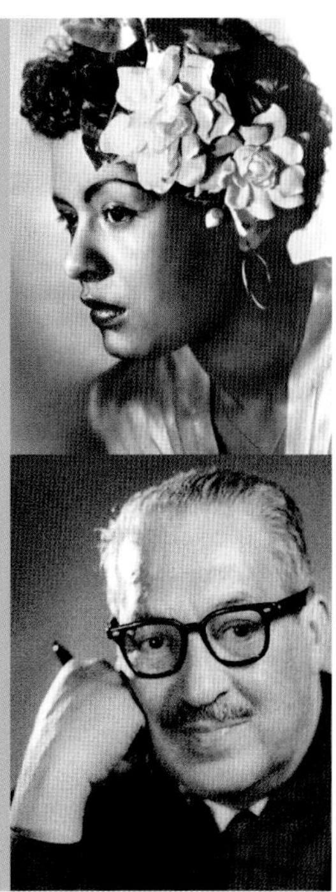

Above: *Billie Holiday,* below: *Thurgood Marshall*

Dairy farms are also important to the state's agricultural economy. Maryland's other farms grow ornamental shrubs and flowers, soybeans, corn, wheat, and many other crops.

Maryland has a thriving fishing industry. Valuable catches include blue crab, bluefish, catfish, clams, flounder, mackerel, striped bass, and white perch.

Maryland is famous for its beautiful horse country.

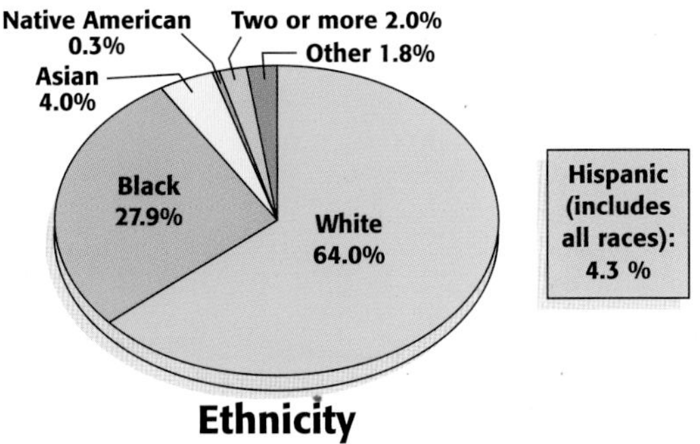

Ethnicity

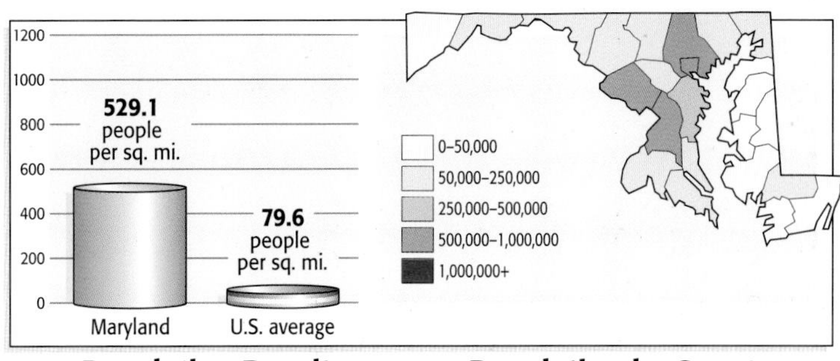

Population Density

Population by County

Massachusetts

Ense petit placidam sub libertate quietem (By the sword we seek peace, but peace only under liberty).

Land area rank *Largest state (1)* — 45 — *smallest state (52)*

Population rank *Most people (1)* — 13 — *fewest people (52)*

At a Glance

Name: Massachusetts was named for the Massachusett, a Native American tribe whose name means "at or about the great hill."

Nicknames: Bay State, Old Colony State

Capital: Boston

Size: 8,262 sq. mi. (21,398 sq km)

Population: 6,349,097

Statehood: Massachusetts became the sixth state on February 6, 1788.

Electoral votes: 12 (2004)

U.S. representatives: 10 (until 2003)

State tree: American elm

State flower: mayflower

State fish: cod

Highest point: Mount Greylock, 3,491 ft. (1,064 m)

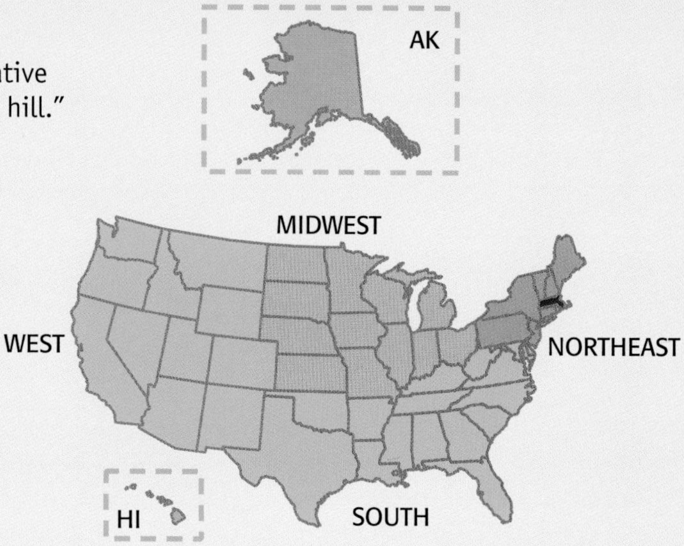

The Place

Massachusetts is one of the six New England states. Although Massachusetts is the sixth-smallest state in the country, it is the third most densely populated. It has a long coastline, which includes the Cape

This historic colonial mansion in Salem inspired Massachusetts-born author Nathaniel Hawthorne to write the classic novel The House of Seven Gables.

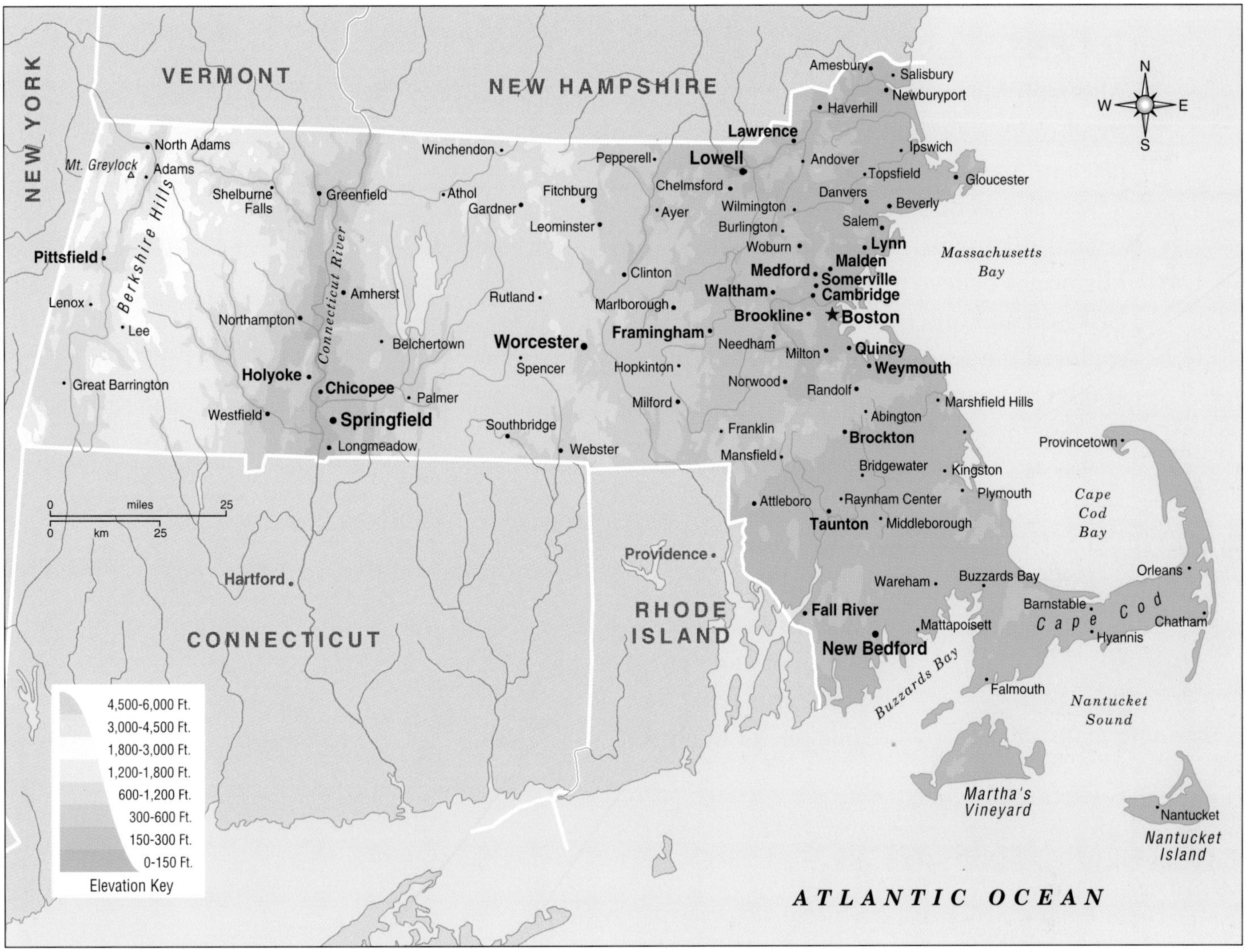

Cod peninsula. Land along this shore is low and dotted with glacial deposits from the last Ice Age more than 10,000 years ago.

Most of Massachusetts is hilly or mountainous. The Berkshire Hills, in the western part of the state, are an extension of the Green Mountains of Vermont. The Taconic Mountains, which form the western edge of Massachusetts, continue into Vermont. The Connecticut River flows through Massachusetts and divides the state almost in half. Along the banks of the river is some of the richest soil in the state. Mineral deposits found in the state include marble and granite.

Massachusetts has cool weather in the winter and warm weather in the summer. The western part of the state is much cooler than the eastern, and the coastal region enjoys the mildest weather. The western mountains can receive up to 75 inches of snowfall annually.

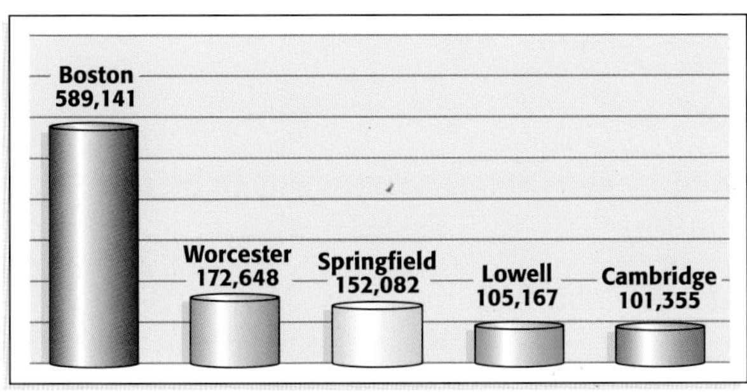

Major Cities

THE PAST

English settlers who established Plimouth Plantation named it after Plymouth, England.

Although Massachusetts is a small state, it occupies a key place in American history. The area was once home to several Algonquian tribes. Historians believe that Leif Eriksson and other Vikings explored the area around A.D. 1000. On September 16, 1620, the first group of Pilgrims sailed to America from Plymouth, England, and established a settlement. More settlers followed, and Massachusetts became one of the most powerful of all the British colonies in the New World.

Rural 16%
Urban 84%

Urban/Rural Distribution

During colonial times, Boston was a busy seaport. Rebellious acts by Massachusetts residents, such as the Boston Tea Party,

Facts and Firsts

- ★ Pilgrims in Plymouth first celebrated Thanksgiving in 1621.
- ★ Boston Common, the first public park in America, was established in 1634 as a military training field and a cattle pasture.
- ★ Harvard University, the first college in North America, was founded in 1636 at Newtowne, which was later renamed Cambridge.
- ★ In 1780, Massachusetts drafted its first state constitution. Today, that constitution is the oldest still in use in the nation.
- ★ The first game of basketball was played in Springfield in 1891.
- ★ In 1895, William M. Morgan, a director of the YMCA in Holyoke, invented the game of volleyball.
- ★ In 1897, Boston became the first U.S. city to build a subway system.
- ★ The Fig Newton cookie was named after the town of Newton.
- ★ The Cape Cod National Seashore was the first land purchased by the federal government to be made into a national park.
- ★ Four U.S. presidents were born in Norfolk County: John Adams, John Quincy Adams, John Fitzgerald Kennedy, and George Herbert Walker Bush.

were instrumental in starting the American Revolution, and much of the early fighting took place on Massachusetts soil. On February 6, 1788, Massachusetts ratified the Constitution and became the sixth state in the Union.

During the War of 1812, textile mills opened throughout the state. The whaling industry, which produced oil for many different household uses, also expanded.

During the Civil War, Massachusetts residents had strong antislavery feelings and helped the Union cause by sending troops and building ships. After the war, the state's industries continued to expand, and immigrants from all over the world poured into Massachusetts to work in its mills and factories.

Massachusetts suffered along with the rest of the nation during the Great Depression of the 1930s. Its economy recovered during World War II, when its factories and shipyards built boats and produced supplies for the war effort. After the war, space and rocket research and the production of electronics equipment replaced traditional industries such as textiles and shoemaking.

State Smart

Boston Lighthouse in Boston Harbor is the oldest lighthouse in the United States. First lit in 1716, it was destroyed by the British during the American Revolution and rebuilt in 1783.

Basketball was first played in Massachusetts

An abolitionist addresses a sympathetic crowd in Boston Common in the 1860s.

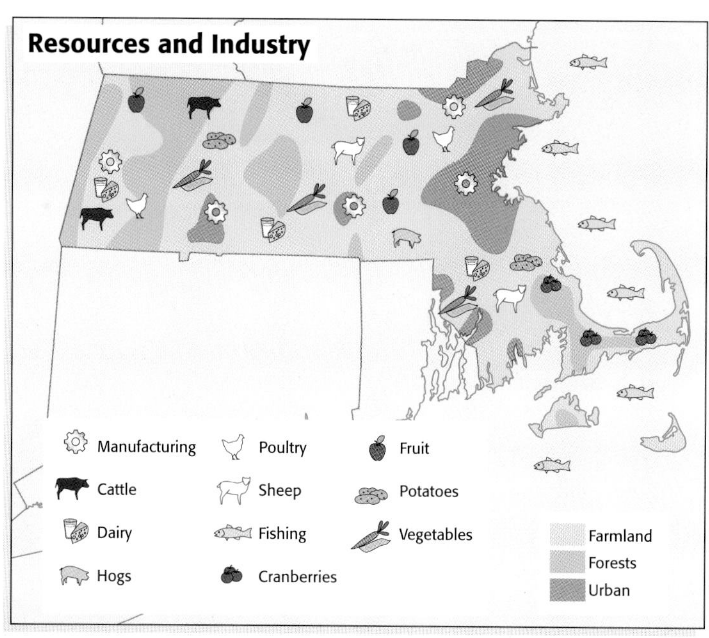

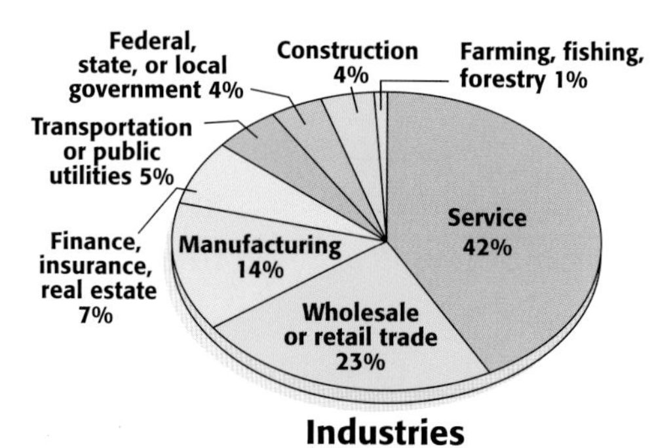

The Present

Boston is a center of trade and finance, with several banks and insurance companies headquartered there. The city remains a leading New England port, and shipping contributes significantly to Boston's economy. Massachusetts companies manufacture products such as scientific instruments, electronic equipment, computers, and military communications systems.

Below left: *Old Sturbridge Village re-creates life in the 1800s.* Below right: *Boston at night.* Above: *Beach on Martha's Vineyard*

Born in Massachusetts

- ★ **John Adams and John Quincy Adams**, U.S. presidents
- ★ **Samuel Adams**, patriot
- ★ **Horatio Alger**, author
- ★ **Susan B. Anthony**, women's suffragist
- ★ **Clara Barton**, founder of the Red Cross
- ★ **Leonard Bernstein**, conductor
- ★ **George H.W. Bush**, U.S. president
- ★ **John Singleton Copley**, painter
- ★ **e.e. cummings**, poet
- ★ **Bette Davis**, actress
- ★ **Cecil B. DeMille**, film director
- ★ **Emily Dickinson**, poet
- ★ **Ralph Waldo Emerson**, philosopher and poet
- ★ **Benjamin Franklin**, statesman and scientist
- ★ **Robert Goddard**, creator of modern rocketry
- ★ **John Hancock**, statesman
- ★ **Nathaniel Hawthorne**, novelist
- ★ **Oliver Wendell Homes**, jurist
- ★ **Winslow Homer**, painter
- ★ **Elias Howe**, inventor
- ★ **John F. Kennedy**, U.S. president
- ★ **Amy Lowell**, poet
- ★ **James Russell Lowell**, poet
- ★ **Horace Mann**, educator
- ★ **Cotton Mather**, clergyman
- ★ **Edgar Allan Poe**, author
- ★ **Samuel F.B. Morse**, painter and inventor
- ★ **Dr. Seuss (Theodore Geisel)**, author and illustrator
- ★ **Henry David Thoreau**, author
- ★ **Barbara Walters**, television commentator
- ★ **James McNeill Whistler**, painter
- ★ **John Greenleaf Whittier**, poet

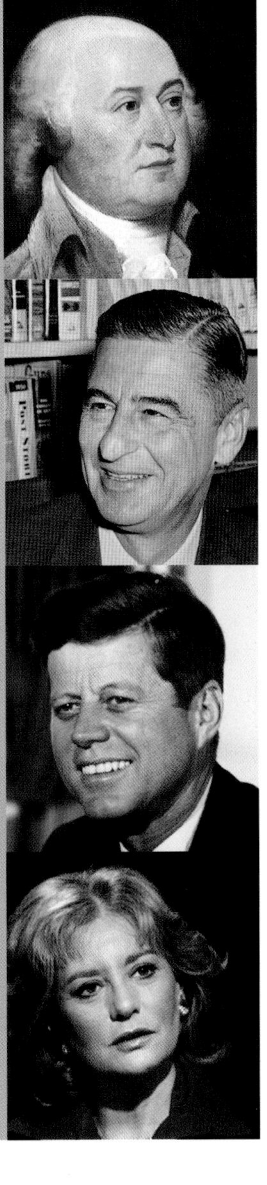

Top to bottom: *John Adams, Theodore Geisel, John F. Kennedy, Barbara Walters*

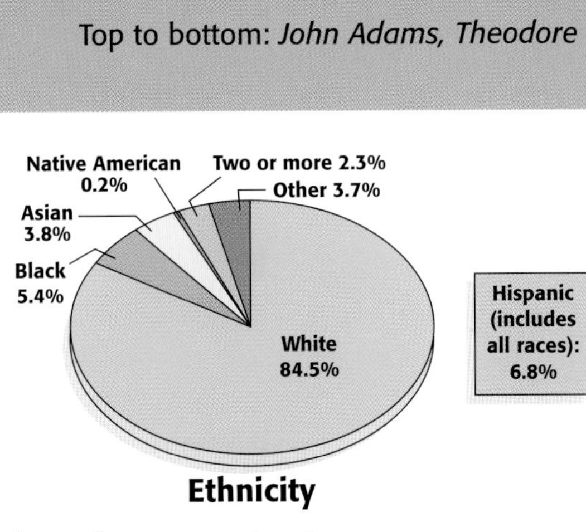

Ethnicity

Massachusetts maintains a strong sense of history. More than 25 million tourists visit the state each year. Some of the most popular attractions include the Freedom Trail in Boston and the historic sites of Lexington and Concord. Old Sturbridge Village is a historic attraction that depicts life in the first half of the 19th century using period houses, stores, and schools. Cape Cod and the Berkshires are popular vacation spots and attract visitors from all over the country.

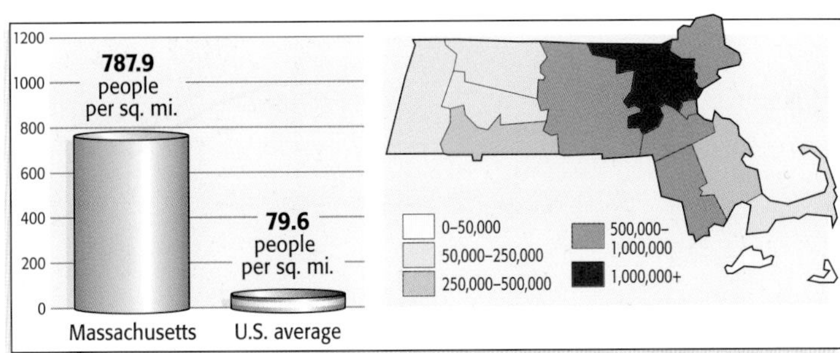

Population Density **Population by County**

Michigan

Si quaeris peninsulam amoenam, circumspice (If you seek a pleasant peninsula, look about you).

Land area rank *Largest state (1)* 11 — *smallest state (52)*

Population rank *Most people (1)* 8 — *fewest people (52)*

At a Glance

Name: Michigan comes from a Native American word that means "great or large lake."

Nicknames: Wolverine State, Great Lakes State

Capital: Lansing

Size: 58,513 sq. mi. (151,548 sq km)

Population: 9,938,444

Statehood: Michigan became the 26th state on January 26, 1837.

Electoral votes: 17 (2004)

U.S. representatives: 16 (until 2003)

State tree: white pine

State flower: apple blossom

State insect: dragonfly

Highest point: Mount Curwood, 1,980 ft. (604 m)

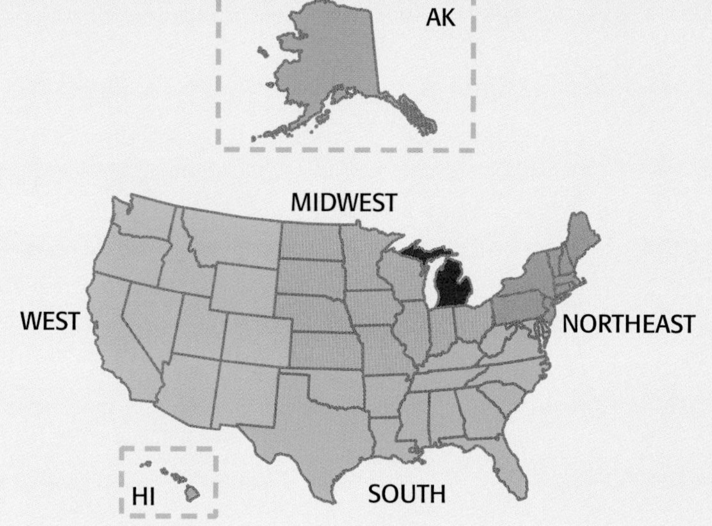

The Place

Michigan is one of the Great Lake states. The Great Lakes separate Michigan into the Upper and Lower Peninsulas. The Mackinac Bridge, one of the world's longest suspension bridges, connects the two areas.

The western half of the Upper Peninsula is the most mountainous part of Michigan.

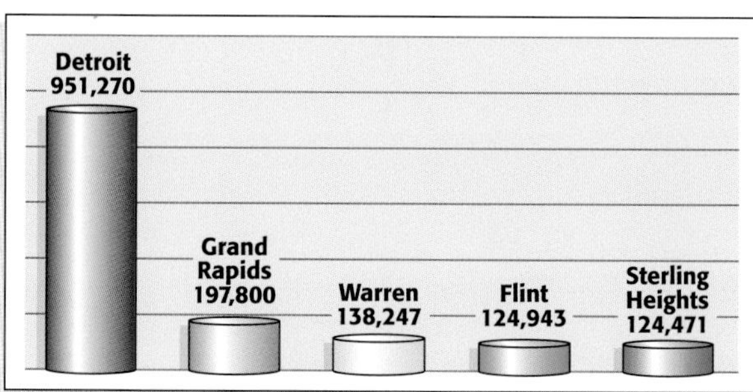

Major Cities

Detroit is home to several automobile companies.

This region is covered by dense forests, rivers, and waterfalls, and has some of the best copper and iron deposits in the country.

The rest of the state is a fairly level plain. The land is swampy in the eastern part of the Upper Peninsula and fertile in the southern half of the Lower Peninsula. Most of the farms in the state are located in that area, which has the richest soil, as well as valuable oil and natural gas deposits.

The Great Lakes often influence Michigan's weather. Its climate is generally moist and humid, and summers are warmer in the southern part of the state. Northern Michigan receives more snow than southern regions of the state.

The Past

When French Canadian explorers from Quebec first traveled into Michigan in search of furs and a water route to the Pacific Ocean, they found more than 15,000 Native Americans living in the area. When they found no route to the West, the French established the city of Detroit in 1701 and began to trade furs with the local tribes.

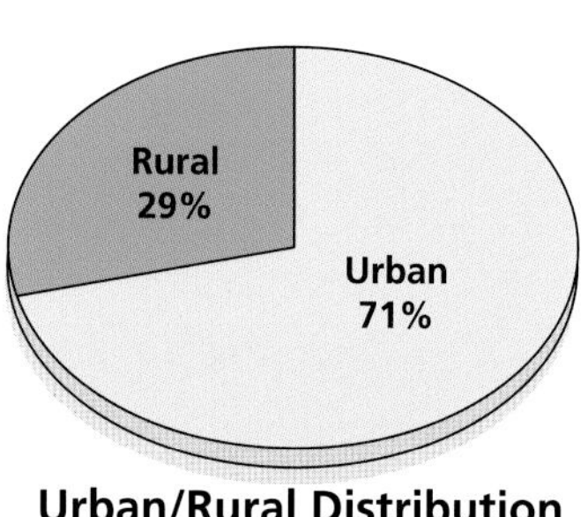

Urban/Rural Distribution

When the British took control of Canada, Michigan became a British territory. The English settlers who moved to the region were more interested in trading furs than in settling the region. Because of the

Detroit-born Chief Pontiac allied himself with the French against the British during the French and Indian Wars.

Facts and Firsts

- ★ Michigan is the only state that touches four of the five Great Lakes: Erie, Huron, Michigan, and Superior. It has the longest freshwater shoreline in the world and more general shoreline than any other state except Alaska.
- ★ Rogers City contains one of the world's largest limestone quarries.
- ★ Although Michigan is known as the Wolverine State, there are no longer any wolverines there.
- ★ Michigan was the first state to guarantee every child the right to a free high school education.
- ★ Michigan established the first state university, the University of Michigan, in 1817.
- ★ In 1879, Detroit was the first city in the nation to be issued telephone numbers to make calling easier.
- ★ Michigan has the only floating post office in the world. It is aboard the *J.W. Westcott II*, a boat that delivers mail to ships.
- ★ Michigan produces more automobiles and parts than any other state.

profitable fur trade, the British refused to surrender Michigan to the United States until 1796, many years after the Revolutionary War ended.

In 1825, completion of the Erie Canal connected the area around the Great Lakes with New York. The canal provided a valuable transportation route from the Atlantic coast to the western territories. As a result, more settlers began to move into Michigan.

In 1837, Michigan became the 26th state in the Union. Mining was an important industry in the Upper Peninsula, and iron and steel factories sprang up along the Great Lakes. The lumbering industry grew in the years after the Civil War. The state's population doubled over the next thirty years, and agriculture became more important as new settlers cleared the land for farming.

During the early 1900s, industrialization expanded as the Olds Motor Works and the Ford Motor Company built automobile plants in Detroit. The Great Depression of the 1930s hurt these companies and many others, but Michigan began to recover during World War II, when the state's automobile industry shifted to the production of tanks, airplane equipment, and other materials for the U.S. military.

Nationwide economic slumps in the 1950s, 1960s, and early 1980s hurt Michigan's automobile sales. The automobile industry suffered, and unemployment rose dramatically.

State Smart

Marquette is the snowiest city in the United States. An average of 130 inches (330 cm) of snow falls there every year.

Michigan prospered after the Erie Canal connected the Great Lakes to New York in 1825.

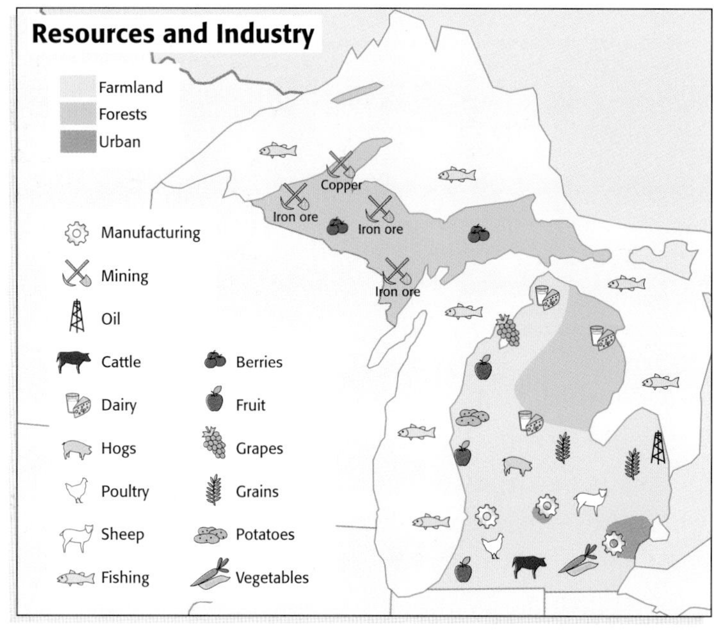

Industries

Transportation or public utilities 4%
Farming, fishing, forestry 2%
Mining 0.2%
Construction 5%
Finance, insurance, real estate 7%
Service 29%
Manufacturing 18%
Wholesale or retail trade 22%
Federal, state, or local government 12%

The Present

Detroit remains the leading producer of automobiles and automobile parts in the United States. Automobiles are also manufactured in Flint and Lansing. During recent decades, however, the state has tried to lessen its dependence on the automobile industry, and has encouraged the development of other types of manufacturing, including steel and food-processing plants.

Michigan is also one of the leading agricultural states, and raises some of the nation's largest apple and cherry crops. Mining also continues to balance the state's

Below left: *A scientist at the University of Michigan performs research, using the metal platinum.*
Below right: *Participants in the annual Labor Day Bridge Walk cross the five-mile-long Mackinac Bridge, which connects the Upper and Lower Peninsulas of Michigan.*

Born in Michigan

- ★ **Ellen Burstyn,** actress
- ★ **Bruce Catton,** historian
- ★ **Roger Chaffee,** astronaut
- ★ **Francis Ford Coppola,** film director
- ★ **Henry Ford,** industrialist
- ★ **Julie Harris,** actress
- ★ **Earvin "Magic" Johnson,** basketball player
- ★ **Charles A. Lindbergh,** aviator
- ★ **Madonna,** singer
- ★ **Terry McMillan,** author
- ★ **Jason Robards,** actor
- ★ **Diana Ross,** singer
- ★ **Steven Seagal,** actor
- ★ **Bob Seger,** singer
- ★ **Tom Selleck,** actor

Above: *Charles Lindbergh;* below: *Magic Johnson*

economy—only Minnesota produces more iron ore than Michigan. In addition, Michigan produces natural gas, petroleum, salt, sand, and crushed gravel.

Michigan's many lakes and forests, and its beaches along the Great Lakes, have also helped to make it a leading tourist destination. Tourists visit Michigan to hike, swim, and fish in the lakes that dot the countryside.

Children build sand castles at Porcupine Mountains State Park, on the shores of Lake Superior.

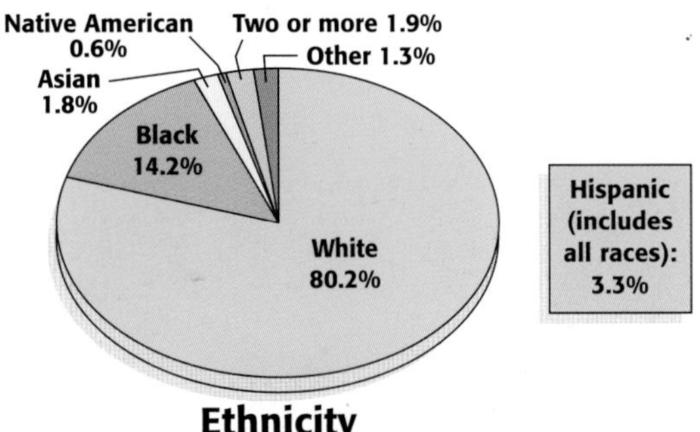

Ethnicity

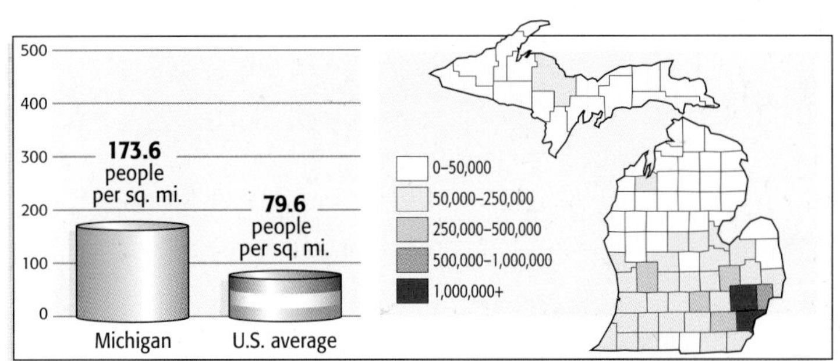

Population Density

Population by County

Minnesota

L'etoile du nord (The star of the north).

Land area rank *Largest state (1)* 12 — *smallest state (52)*

Population rank *Most people (1)* 21 — *fewest people (52)*

At a Glance

Name: Minnesota is from Sioux words that mean "sky-tinted water."

Nicknames: North Star State, Gopher State

Capital: St. Paul

Size: 84,397 sq. mi. (218,587 sq km)

Population: 4,919,479

Statehood: Minnesota became the 32nd state on May 11, 1858.

Electoral votes: 10 (2004)

U.S. representatives: 8 (until 2003)

State tree: red pine

State flower: pink and white lady's slipper

State bird: common loon

Highest point: Eagle Mountain, 2,301 ft. (701 m)

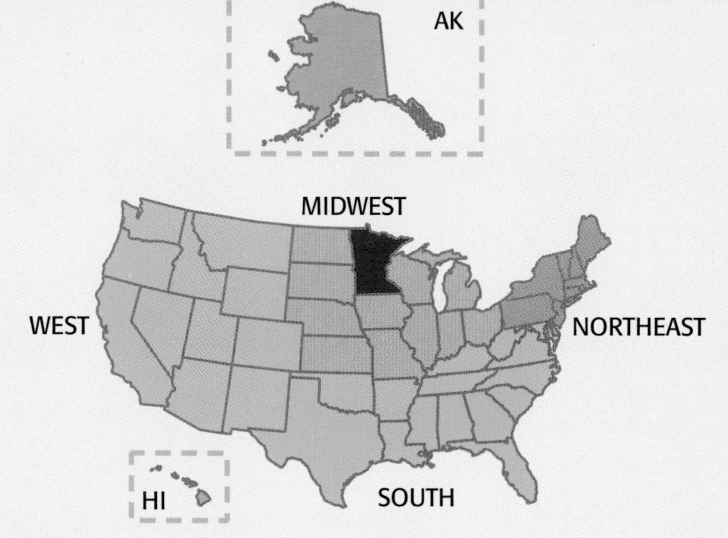

The Place

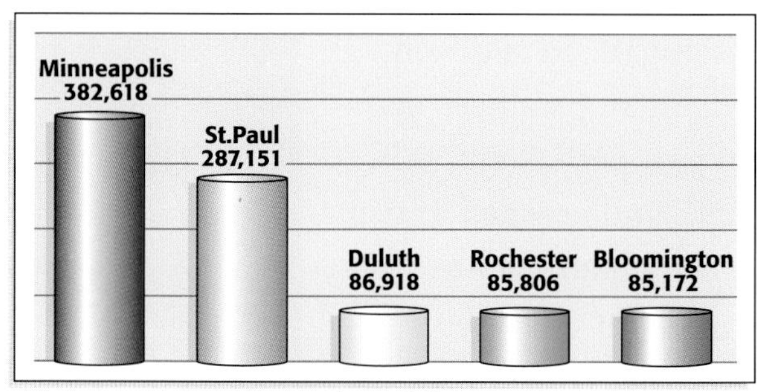

Major Cities

Minnesota is one of several large agricultural states in the Midwest. Lake Superior forms part of Minnesota's eastern border. Less than 20,000 years ago, large glaciers covered the land. These glaciers flattened much of the terrain into low, rolling hills. In many places, the glaciers left behind rich soil. Depressions in the ground left by the

Lakes cover more than 20 percent of Minnesota.

glaciers became marshes, lakes, and swamps. These lakes cover more than 20 percent of the state.

About 35 percent of Minnesota's land is forested with trees such as balsam fir, pine, spruce, and white birch. Minnesota has valuable deposits of granite, iron ore, and manganese, which is an important element in making steel.

Winters are cold and snowy, especially in the northeastern part of the state, which can receive up to 70 inches of snowfall a year. Summers are generally warm.

Chippewa rock paintings that are five hundred to a thousand years old have been found in northern Minnesota.

THE PAST

The first Europeans to explore Minnesota were French fur traders. When they arrived in the 1600s, they found Minnesota settled by Sioux and Chippewa. The French continued to trade valuable animal furs in Minnesota even after France lost control of the area to Spain.

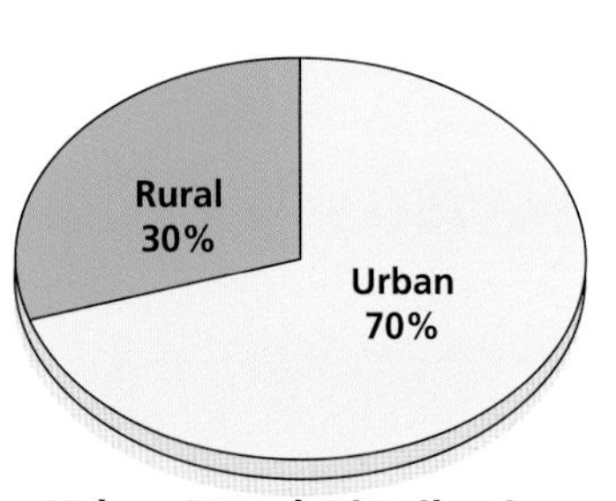

Urban/Rural Distribution

The region was under Spanish, British, and French rule at different times. Minnesota finally became part of the United States in 1803 through the Louisiana Purchase, a land purchase from

Facts and Firsts

★ Because of its numerous lakes, Minnesota has 90,000 miles of shoreline—more than California, Florida, and Hawaii combined.

★ Many popular consumer items originated in Minnesota, including the stapler, masking tape and Scotch tape, Wheaties cereal, and the Green Giant brand of vegetables.

★ Frank C. Mars introduced the Milky Way candy bar in Minneapolis in 1923.

★ The Hormel Company of Austin created SPAM, a meat product, in 1937. A SPAM museum in Austin features a towering wall of SPAM, built of 3,390 cans, in its lobby.

★ In 1980, Scott and Brennan Olson, two Minnesota students, designed the first set of Rollerblades, skates with inline wheels instead of a blade. They created Rollerblades so they could practice hockey all year round.

★ The world-famous Mayo Clinic, located in Rochester, is a leader in medical treatment.

★ The Mall of America, located in Bloomington, is the largest retail space in the country. It is larger than 78 football fields and has more visitors every year than Walt Disney World, Graceland, and the Grand Canyon combined.

France that more than doubled the size of the United States.

Lumber became an important industry, and lumberjacks came to Minnesota to take advantage of the state's thick forests. When the government signed a treaty with the Sioux and took over their lands in 1851, settlers began to pour into the region and establish farms. In 1858, Minnesota became the nation's 32nd state.

During the Civil War, Minnesota was the first state to offer troops for the Union army. After the war's end, railroads across the state were completed, and mills that produced huge amounts of flour were built throughout Minnesota's farmland. In the 1870s, settlers from Europe, especially the Scandinavian countries of Norway, Sweden, and Finland, arrived in the state.

In the 1880s, iron ore was discovered, and Minnesota quickly became a mining center. The production of grain, lumber, and minerals for the U.S. military during both World War I and World War II supported the state's economy through the middle of the 20th century.

By the 1950s, Minnesota's best deposits of iron ore had been greatly depleted, and worldwide demand for the ore had dropped. Minnesota companies began to develop aerospace equipment, chemicals, computers, electronic equipment, and heavy machinery. The state became more urban as many residents moved from farms to the cities, and Minnesota strengthened its role as a trade and finance center for the

State Smart

International Falls is the coldest city in the United States. The city has an average temperature of 36.8° F (2.6° C).

Children dance at a Swedish festival in Minneapolis. Scandanavian settlers arrived in Minnesota in the 1870s.

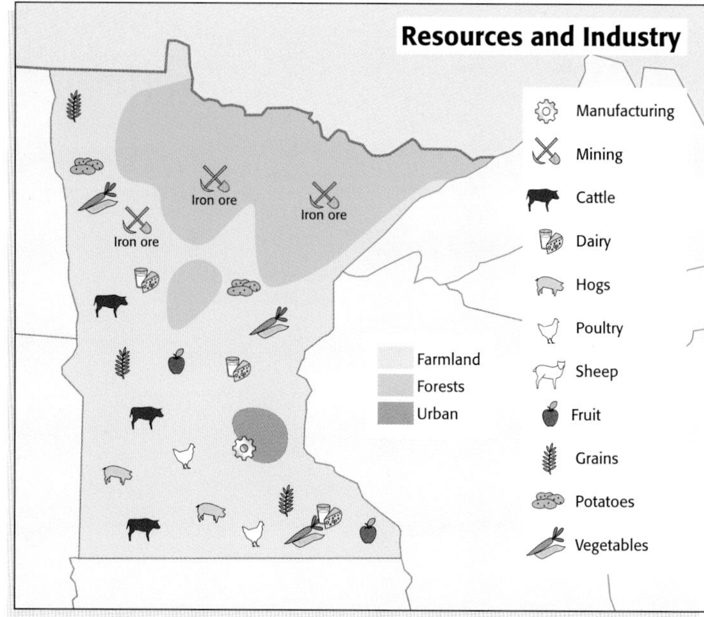

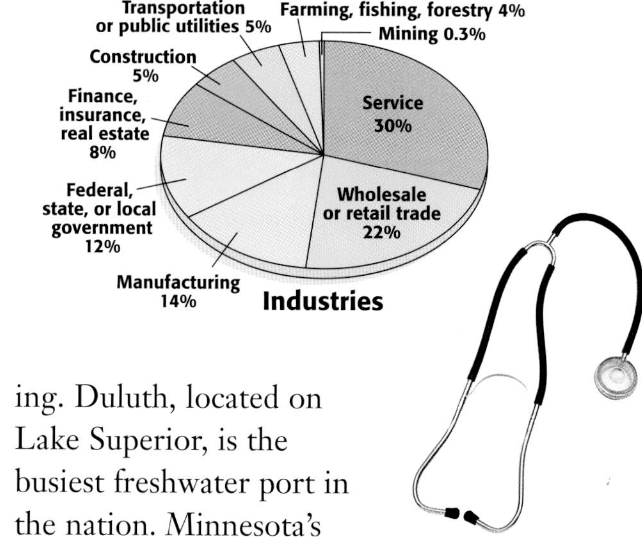

Midwest. In the 1980s, Minnesota began to explore ways to both protect its environment and continue to develop its mineral resources.

The Present

Today, Minnesota's cities are important centers of trade, business, and manufacturing. Duluth, located on Lake Superior, is the busiest freshwater port in the nation. Minnesota's Twin Cities, St. Paul and Minneapolis, are home to several large computer companies as well as some of the nation's largest banks and insurance firms.

Agriculture remains part of Minnesota's economy. More than half of the state is farmland, and Minnesota is one of the leading producers of dairy products. The state also produces corn, hogs, soybeans, and wheat. Manufacturing associated with

A showboat glides on upper reaches of the Mississippi River near the Twin Cities, St. Paul and Minneapolis.

Born in Minnesota

★**William O. Douglas**, jurist
★**Bob Dylan**, singer and composer
★**F. Scott Fitzgerald**, author
★**Judy Garland**, singer and actress
★**J. Paul Getty**, oil executive
★**Cass Gilbert**, architect
★**Hubert H. Humphrey**, U.S. senator and vice president
★**Jessica Lange**, actress
★**Sinclair Lewis**, author
★**Roger Maris**, baseball player
★**Charles H. Mayo**, surgeon
★**Eugene J. McCarthy**, senator
★**Kate Millett**, feminist
★**Walter F. Mondale**, U.S. vice president
★**Jane Russell**, actress
★**Charles M. Schulz**, cartoonist

Above: *F. Scott Fitzgerald;* below: *Judy Garland*

agriculture is also an important source of Minnesota's income; throughout the state, many dairy-processing and meat-packing plants thrive, as well as flour mills and grain producers. The mining of iron ore in the state's northern region, although it has changed over the last century, continues to round out Minnesota's economy.

Grain stored in grain elevators at Duluth, a major U.S. port, is conveniently located for shipping on Lake Superior.

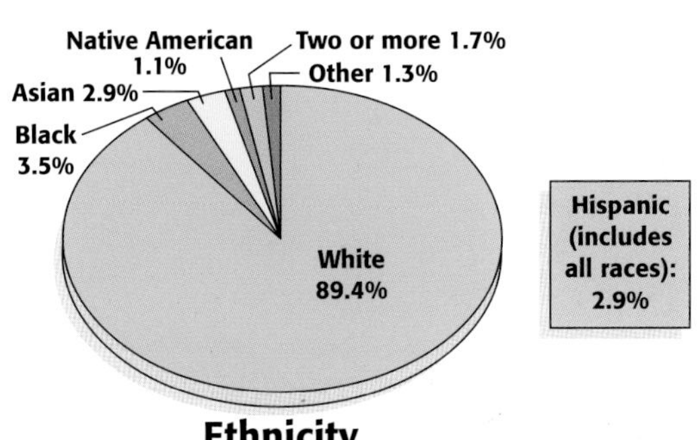

Ethnicity

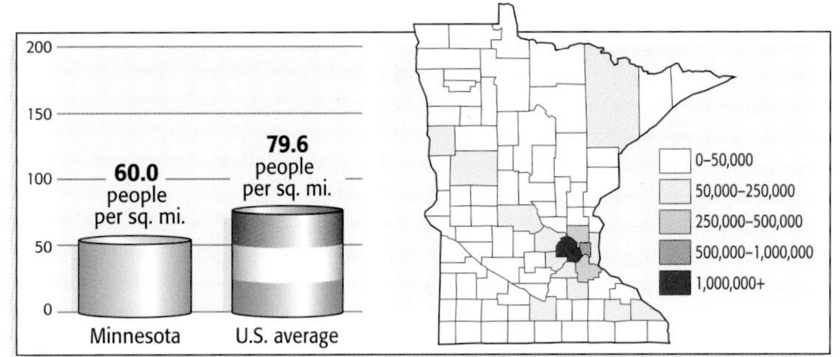

Population Density

Population by County

Mississippi

Virtute et armis (By valor and arms).

Land area rank
Largest state (1)
Population rank
Most people (1)

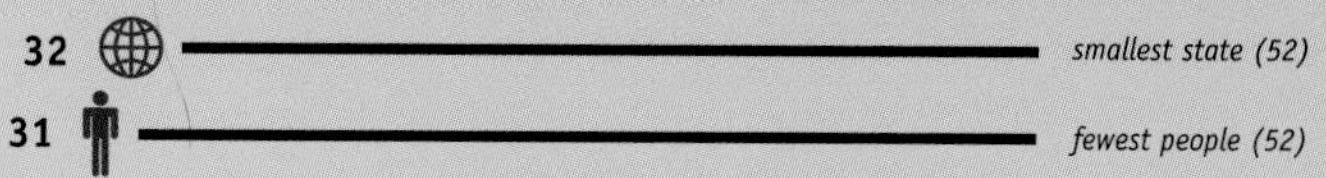

At a Glance

Name: Mississippi comes from a Native American word that means "father of waters."
Nickname: Magnolia State
Capital: Jackson
Size: 47.695 sq. mi. (123,530 sq km)
Population: 2,844,658
Statehood: Mississippi became the 20th state on December 10, 1817.
Electoral votes: 6 (2004)
State representatives: 5 (until 2003)
State tree: magnolia
State flower: magnolia
State fish: black bass
Highest point: Woodall Mountain, 806 ft. (246 m)

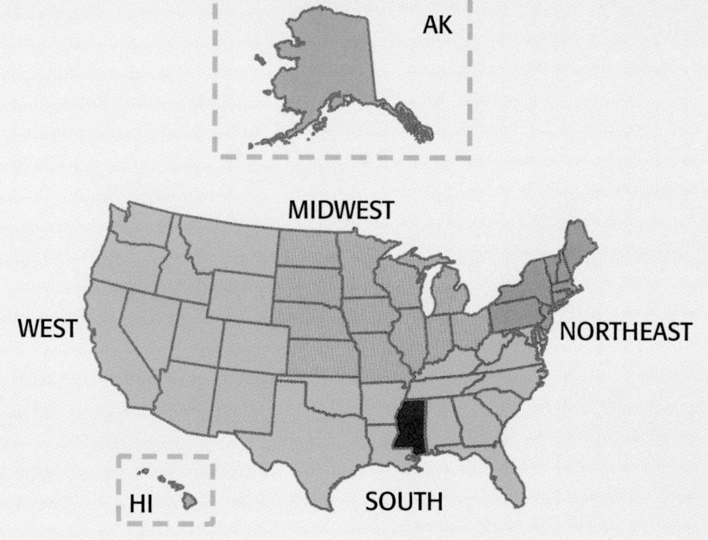

The Place

Mississippi is located in the Deep South and was named after the Mississippi River, which forms most of its western border. Part of the Mississippi River Delta, the triangular area around the mouth of the river, forms the western corner of the state. The Mississippi has also left behind many

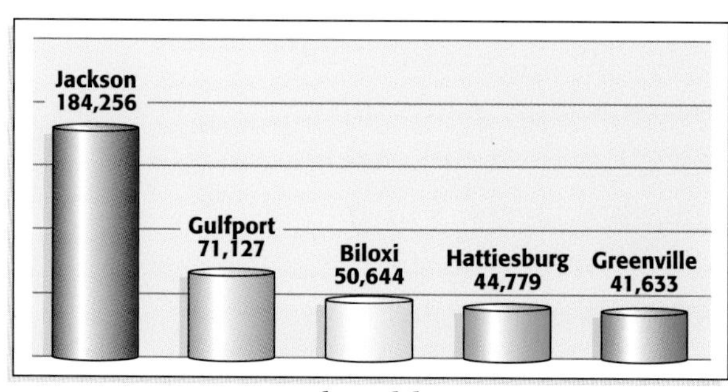

Major Cities

The Mississippi River forms the western border of the state of Mississippi.

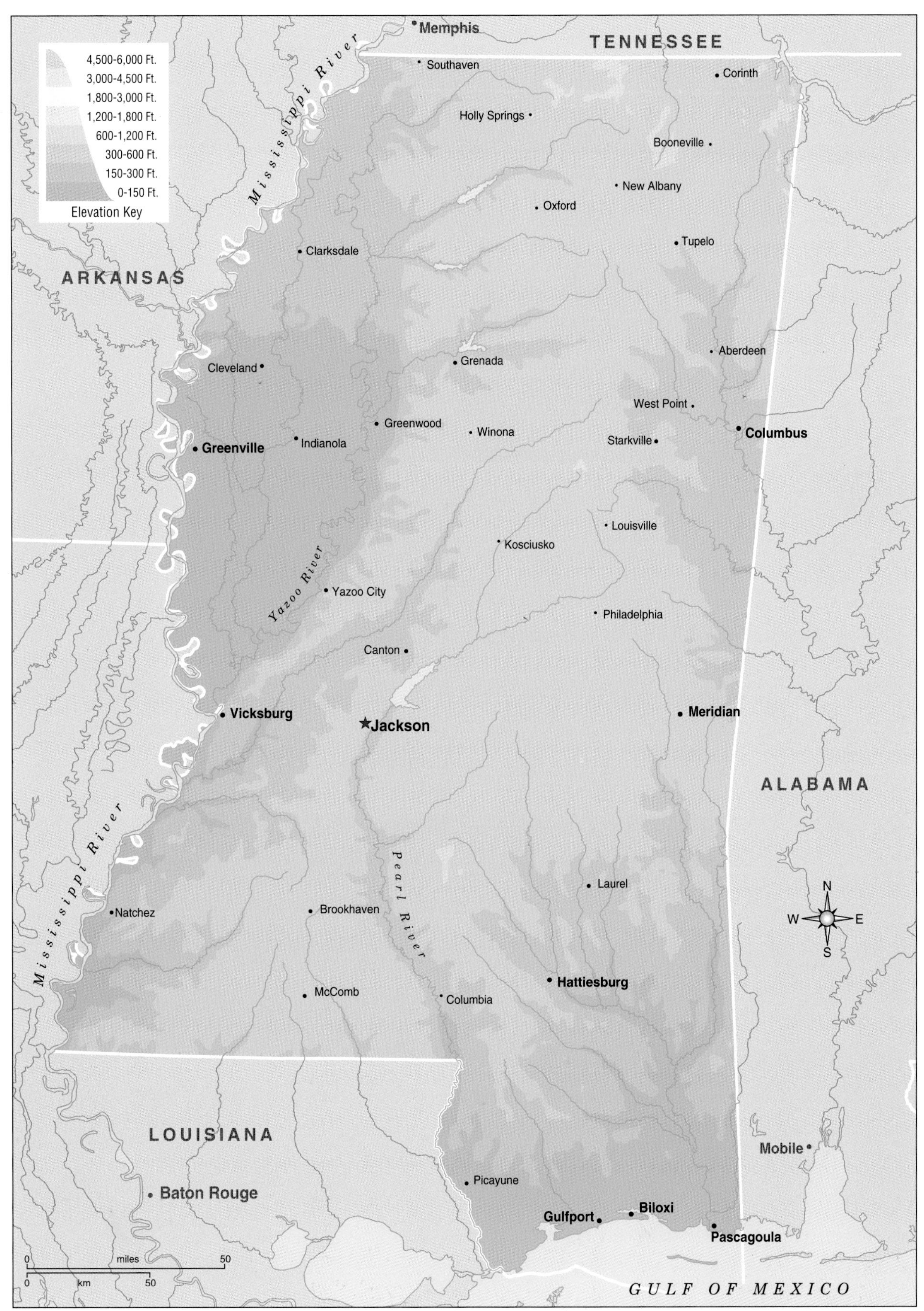

4,500-6,000 Ft.
3,000-4,500 Ft.
1,800-3,000 Ft.
1,200-1,800 Ft.
600-1,200 Ft.
300-600 Ft.
150-300 Ft.
0-150 Ft.
Elevation Key
Memphis
TENNESSEE
Southaven
Corinth
Holly Springs
Booneville
New Albany
Oxford
Tupelo
Mississippi River
Clarksdale
ARKANSAS
Aberdeen
Cleveland
Grenada
West Point
Greenwood
Winona
Starkville
Columbus
Greenville
Indianola
Louisville
Kosciusko
Yazoo River
Yazoo City
Philadelphia
Canton
Vicksburg
Jackson
Meridian
ALABAMA
Pearl River
Laurel
Natchez
Brookhaven
N
W
E
S
Hattiesburg
McComb
Columbia
LOUISIANA
Mobile
Picayune
Baton Rouge
Biloxi
Gulfport
Pascagoula
0
miles
50
0
km
50
GULF OF MEXICO

Union soldiers laid siege to Vicksburg during the Civil War.

oxbow (crescent-shaped) lakes that were once curves in the river.

The rest of the state is covered with gently rolling hills, forests, and prairies. The Black Belt, so named for the deep color of its soil, is in north-eastern Mississippi. The Gulf of Mexico, with its sandy beaches, forms Mississippi's southern border.

Many different crops grow well in Mississippi because of its warm, humid climate. Summers are long and cooled by winds from the Gulf of Mexico, and winters are short and mild. Hurricanes sometimes occur in late summer and early fall.

The Past

Spanish explorer Hernando de Soto first sailed down the Mississippi River in 1541 and found members of the Chickasaw, Choctaw, and Natchez Native American tribes living in the Mississippi region. He did not find gold as he had hoped, so he left the area and did not establish any settlements there.

Later, French colonists from Canada became the first white settlers in Mississippi. They brought in the first

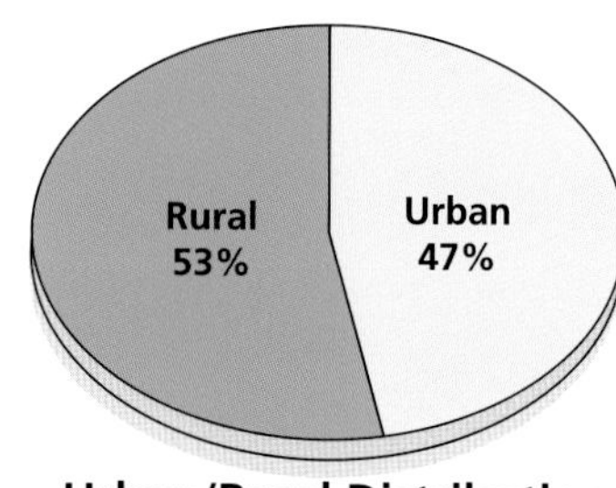

Urban/Rural Distribution

Facts and Firsts

★ The rarest kind of North American crane, the Mississippi sandhill crane, is found only in the grassy savannas of Jackson County. This four-foot-tall bird has a six-foot wingspan.

★ In 1834, Captain Isaac Ross founded the African country of Liberia when he freed all the slaves on his Lorman plantation and paid for their transportation back to Africa.

★ During the Civil War, more people from Mississippi died than from any other state. Of the 78,000 Mississippians that fought in the Confederate army, more than 59,000 were wounded or killed in battle.

★ The world's first human lung and heart transplants were performed at the University of Mississippi in 1963 and 1964.

The Lyceum at the University of Mississippi (nicknamed Ole Miss) was built in Oxford, Mississippi, in 1840.

State Smart

The University of Mississippi has the country's largest collection of blues music—more than 50,000 recordings.

slaves from Africa in 1719 to work in their rice and tobacco fields. The French lost the region to England after the British helped the Native Americans take back control of their land during the French and Indian War. After the American Revolution, the British surrendered the area to the United States, and Mississippi became a state in 1817.

By 1832, most of the Native Americans had been forcibly removed to Oklahoma Territory, and settlers moved west into the region to farm the newly available land. Cotton plantations quickly were built all over the state. During the Civil War, Mississippi residents fought on the Southern side to maintain their right to use slave labor on their vast plantations.

After the Civil War, the loss of revenue from cotton caused the economy to suffer, but the construction of railroads provided access to the state's pine forests, and lumbering became an important industry. During World War II, the shipbuilding industry prospered.

Agriculture grew until the 1960s, when machines began to replace human labor on farms. During the latter half of the 20th century, Mississippi worked to attract new industries that would employ many of the workers no longer needed on farms. During the 1980s and 1990s, unemployment rose and low-income households increased in number.

Women welders kept the shipbuilding industry going during World War II.

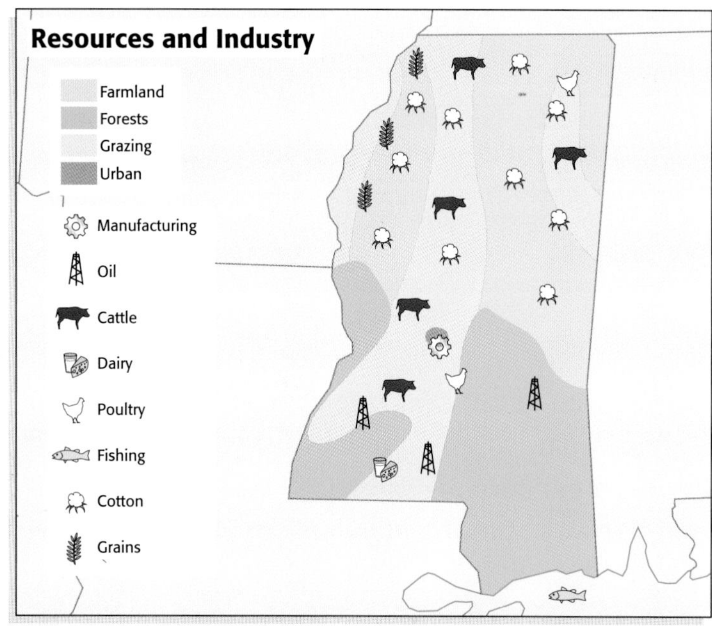

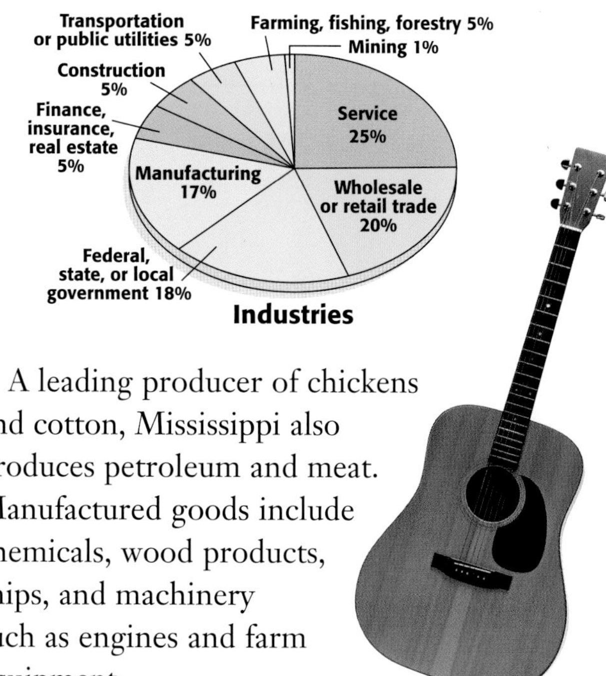

THE PRESENT

Mississippi suffers from high unemployment rates and low wages. During the last two decades, Mississippi has had one of the lowest average family incomes of any state. The state has attempted to attract new industries in an effort to improve its economy.

A leading producer of chickens and cotton, Mississippi also produces petroleum and meat. Manufactured goods include chemicals, wood products, ships, and machinery such as engines and farm equipment.

Cities along the Mississippi River are important trade and business centers. Many telecommunications and financial services companies have offices in river cities, including Jackson. Stennis Space Center in Hancock is a rocket-testing site for the

Mississippi children at play in Metcalf

Born in Mississippi

- ★ **Jimmy Buffett**, singer and songwriter
- ★ **Bo Diddley**, musician
- ★ **William Faulkner**, author
- ★ **Morgan Freeman**, actor
- ★ **Jim Henson**, puppeteer
- ★ **James Earl Jones**, actor
- ★ **B.B. King**, musician
- ★ **Willie Morris**, author
- ★ **Elvis Presley**, singer and actor
- ★ **Jerry Rice**, football player
- ★ **LeAnn Rimes**, singer
- ★ **Sela Ward**, actress
- ★ **Eudora Welty**, author
- ★ **Tennessee Williams**, playwright
- ★ **Oprah Winfrey**, talk show host and actress

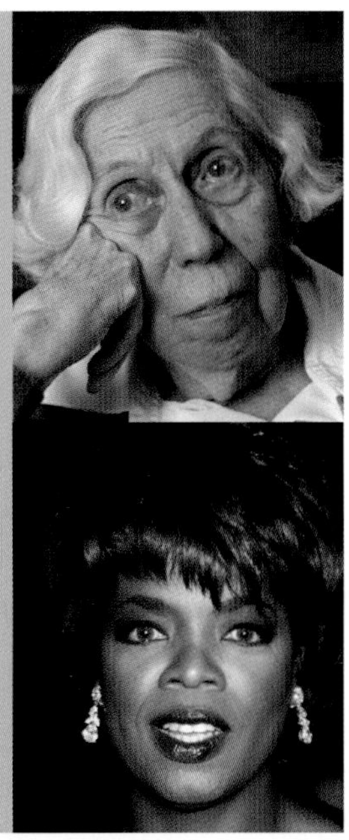

Above: *Eudora Welty;* below: *Oprah Winfrey*

National Aeronautics and Space Administration (NASA).

Mississippi's Gulf Coast, with its white beaches, is a popular tourist destination, and tourism provides a significant source of revenue. Casino gaming has also become a profitable industry in the state.

Jackson, Mississippi, attracts many companies to its business district.

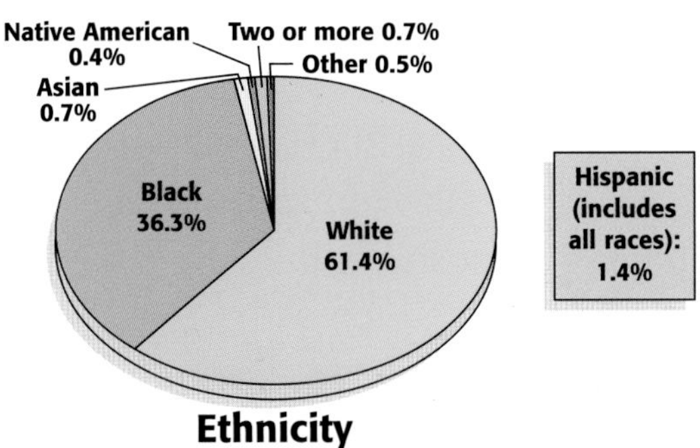

Hispanic (includes all races): 1.4%

Ethnicity

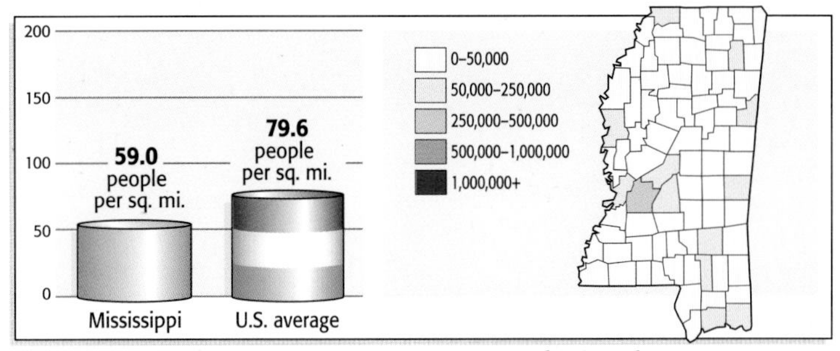

Population Density

Population by County

Missouri

Salus populi suprema lex esto (The welfare of the people shall be the supreme law).

Land area rank *Largest state (1)* — 21 — *smallest state (52)*

Population rank *Most people (1)* — 17 — *fewest people (52)*

At a Glance

Name: Missouri is the name of a Native American tribe and means "town with the big canoes."

Nickname: Show Me State

Capital: Jefferson City

Size: 69,709 sq. mi. (180,546 sq km)

Population: 5,595,211

Statehood: Missouri became the 24th state on August 10, 1821.

Electoral votes: 11 (2004)

U.S. representatives: 9 (until 2003)

State tree: dogwood

State flower: hawthorn

State insect: honeybee

Highest point: Taum Sauk Mountain, 1,772 ft. (540 m)

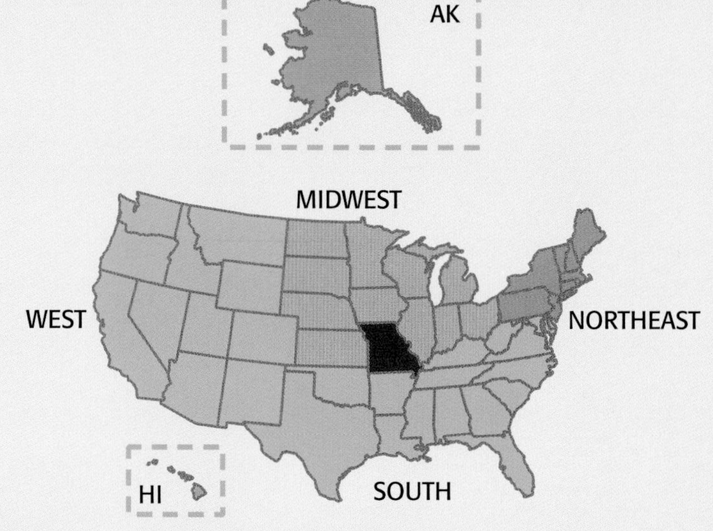

The Place

Missouri is a fertile Midwest state. The Mississippi River forms Missouri's eastern border, while the Missouri River forms part of its western border before continuing through the center of the state.

Missouri's north and west are made up of rolling plains. North of the Missouri River, these plains were flattened by the glaciers that covered much of the Midwest during the last Ice Age more than 11,500 years ago. These glaciers also left behind a rich top layer of soil in this area.

Forested hills and fast-flowing streams abound in the Ozarks and the St. Francois mountains of southern Missouri. Southeastern Missouri is part of the Mississippi Alluvial Plain and has some of the richest soil in the state.

The Gateway Arch in St. Louis commemorates the nation's westward expansion.

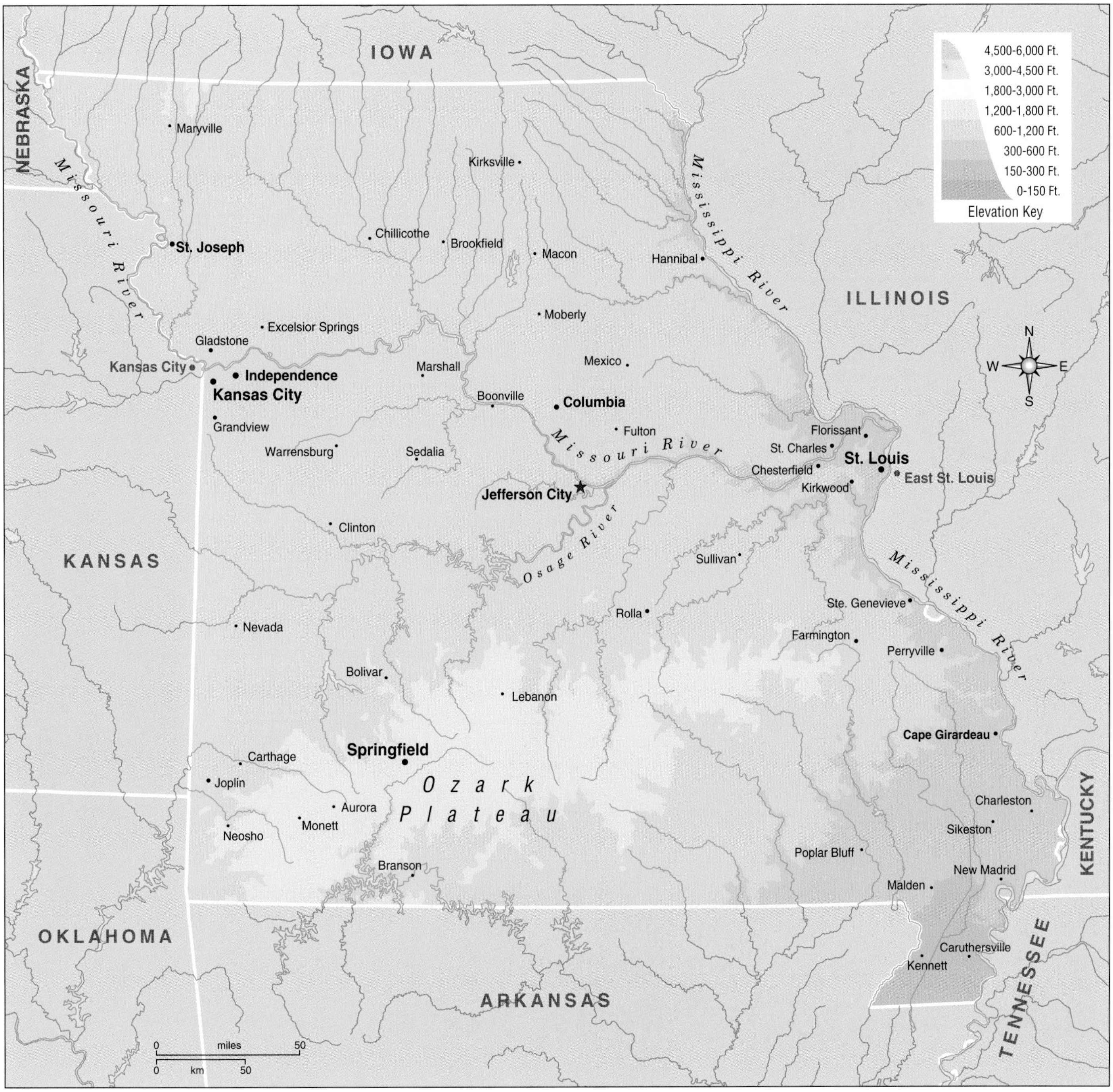

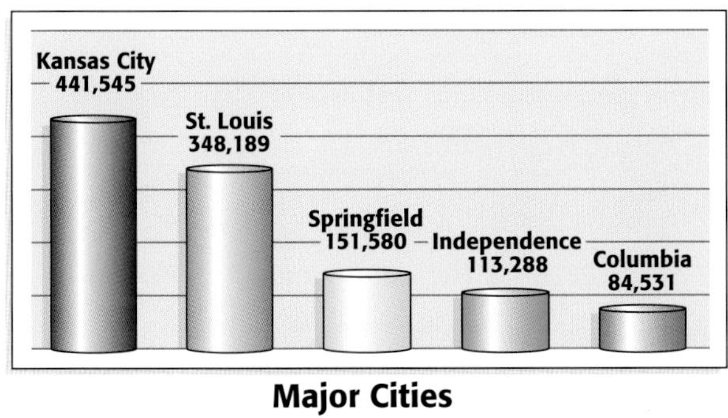

Major Cities

Summers and winters are milder in Missouri's high areas than in the low-lying plains. The southeastern corner of the state receives the most precipitation.

Lead is Missouri's most abundant mineral, and the state also produces copper, silver, and zinc. About half of the state contains coal deposits, and iron ore is found in the eastern Ozarks.

Meriwether Lewis and William Clark explored the Missouri region after the Louisiana Purchase.

THE PAST

Native Americans lived in Missouri for hundreds of years before Europeans settled there. Some of the earthen mounds they built as graves can still be seen in parts of the state. When Europeans reached the area in 1673, they found Osage, Fox, and Sauk tribes living there.

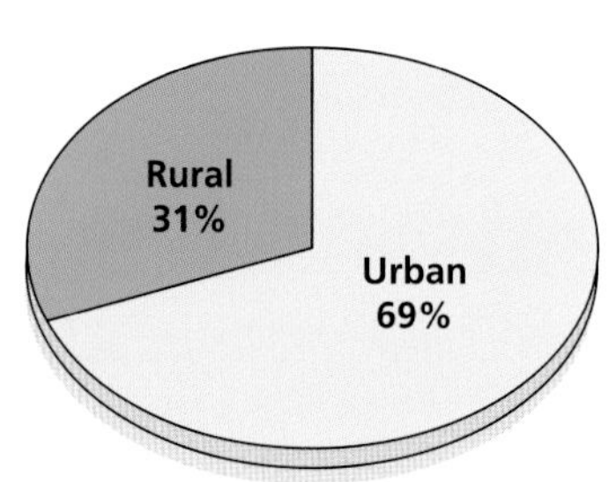

Urban/Rural Distribution

The first Europeans to travel to Missouri were the French explorers Jacques Marquette and Louis Jolliet, who were in search of a water route to the West. French fur traders and missionaries who followed the explorers established the first white settlements, including St. Louis in 1764.

During the French and Indian War, France gave all its land west of the Mississippi to Spain, an ally against Britain. The Spanish encouraged settlers to come west to the region. In 1800, the French won back the territory, but sold it to the United States in 1803 as part of the Louisiana Purchase.

Missouri became a state in 1821. Through the Missouri Compromise, Missouri entered the Union as a slaveholding state while Maine entered as a free state, which maintained the balance of slave and free states in the U.S. Congress.

Missouri quickly became a gateway to the West. Both the Oregon Trail and the Santa Fe Trail started in Independence. The Oregon

Facts and Firsts

- ★ Both Missouri and Tennessee border eight states, more than any other states.
- ★ Jefferson City, the capital of Missouri, was named for Thomas Jefferson, the third president of the United States.
- ★ Kansas City has more miles of boulevard than Paris and more fountains than any other U.S. city.
- ★ In 1865, Missouri was the first slaveholding state to free its slaves.
- ★ In 1904, the ice-cream cone was invented at the World's Fair in St. Louis. An ice-cream vendor ran out of cups and asked a nearby waffle vendor to roll waffles into cones to hold the ice cream.
- ★ The tallest documented man, Robert Pershing Wadlow from St. Louis, was 8 feet, 11.1 inches tall.

Trail was one of the overland routes used by settlers during the westward expansion of the United States. The Santa Fe Trail connected Mexico with Missouri and was an important trade route.

After the Civil War, St. Louis and Kansas City became significant centers of trade, although the fur trade and the Santa Fe Trail declined in importance. During World War I and World War II, many new industries moved into the area and began to manufacture supplies and process food for the U.S. military.

During the 1950s and 1960s, the discovery of iron ore deposits and the growth of industry and tourism boosted the state's economy. Many families moved from cities to suburbs. Missouri was forced to take initiatives to redirect more business and revenue to St. Louis and Kansas City. During the 1980s, farms suffered during a nationwide drop in agricultural prices, but most recovered by the mid-1990s.

State Smart

The Gateway Arch in St. Louis, at 630 feet (192 m) tall, is the largest human-made monument in the United States.

Pioneers stocked covered wagons with their most precious goods for the long ride, from Independence, Missouri, across the Oregon Trail, to new lands.

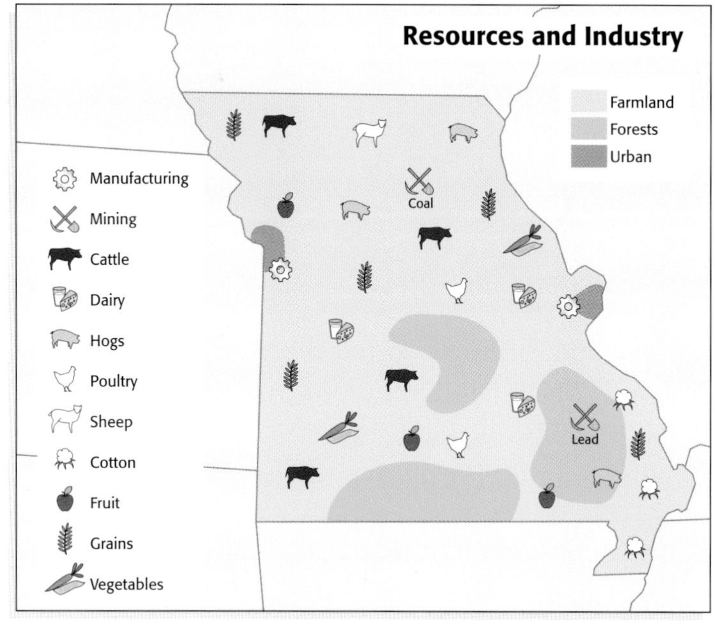

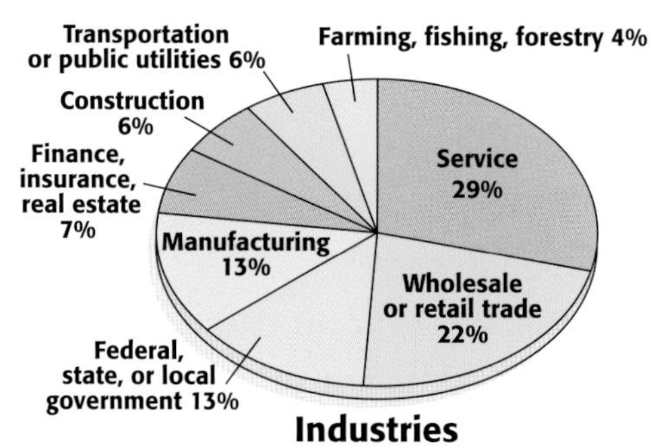

The Present

Missouri has faced a number of problems in recent decades, including water pollution and soil erosion caused by new land development. The state has lacked adequate funds to support public programs such as schools, roads, and welfare. To increase revenue, a state lottery was initiated in 1986.

Despite these challenges, Missouri's economy is strong and the state remains a major center for trade and travel. Many kinds of goods are shipped along the Missouri and Mississippi Rivers daily, and St. Louis and Kansas City are the sites of some of the Midwest's busiest airports and the nation's most important trucking and railroad centers.

Below: *The Ozark Mountains in western Missouri are a popular tourist destination.*
Above right: *St. Louis teenager*

Born in Missouri

- ★ **Robert Altman**, film director
- ★ **Maya Angelou**, poet
- ★ **Burt Bacharach**, songwriter
- ★ **Josephine Baker**, singer and dancer
- ★ **Yogi Berra**, baseball player
- ★ **William S. Burroughs**, author
- ★ **Sarah Caldwell**, opera director and conductor
- ★ **Martha Jane Canary ("Calamity Jane")**, frontierswoman
- ★ **George Washington Carver**, scientist
- ★ **Walter Cronkite**, television newscaster
- ★ **T.S. Eliot**, poet
- ★ **Eugene Field**, poet
- ★ **John Goodman**, actor
- ★ **Betty Grable**, actress
- ★ **Jean Harlow**, actress
- ★ **Coleman Hawkins**, jazz musician
- ★ **Al Hirschfeld**, artist
- ★ **Edwin Hubble**, astronomer
- ★ **Langston Hughes**, poet
- ★ **Frank James and Jesse James**, outlaws
- ★ **James C. Penney**, merchant and founder of J.C. Penney Co.
- ★ **John Joseph Pershing**, general, U.S. Army
- ★ **Vincent Price**, actor
- ★ **Ginger Rogers**, dancer and actress
- ★ **Sara Teasdale**, poet
- ★ **Harry S. Truman**,U.S. president
- ★ **Mark Twain (Samuel Clemens)**, author
- ★ **Dick Van Dyke**, actor

Top to bottom: *Mark Twain, George Washington Carver, Langston Hughes, Maya Angelou*

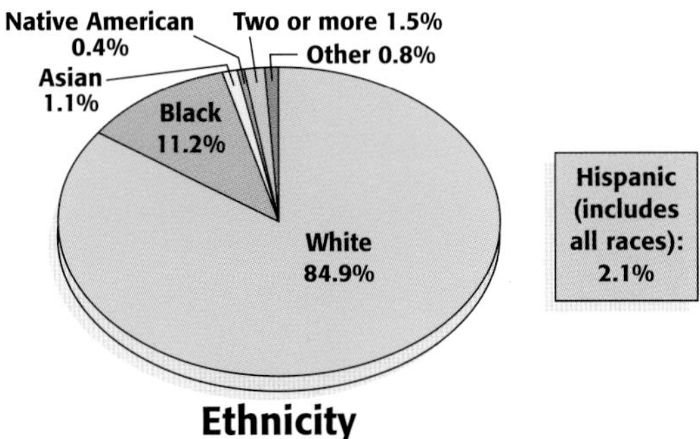

Ethnicity

Missouri farms grow grains and soybeans and raise beef cattle and hogs. Manufacturing associated with agriculture (such as meat processing and fertilizer production) is important to the state's economy. Missouri companies manufacture products such as airplanes, barges, railroad cars, truck and bus bodies, and truck trailers.

Missouri encourages tourism, which is a billion-dollar industry for the state. The Ozark Mountains are one of the Midwest's most popular vacation destinations, and St. Louis, Springfield, and Kansas City are common convention sites.

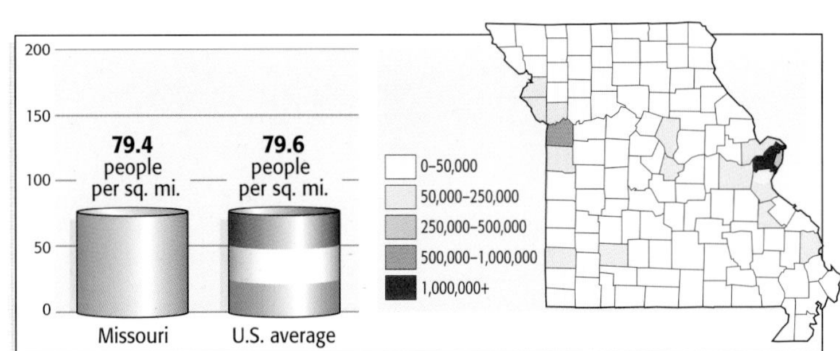

Population Density **Population by County**

Montana

Oro y plata (Gold and silver).

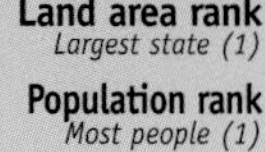

Land area rank
Largest state (1) 4 — *smallest state (52)*

Population rank
Most people (1) 44 — *fewest people (52)*

At a Glance

Name: Montana comes from the Spanish word *montãna*, which means "mountainous."

Nicknames: Treasure State, Big Sky Country

Capital: Helena

Size: 147,046 sq. mi. (380,849 sq km)

Population: 902,195

Statehood: Montana became the 41st state on November 8, 1889.

Electoral votes: 3 (2004)

U.S. representatives: 1 (until 2003)

State tree: ponderosa pine

State flower: bitterroot

State fish: Western meadowlark

Highest point: Granite Peak, 12,799 ft. (3,901 m)

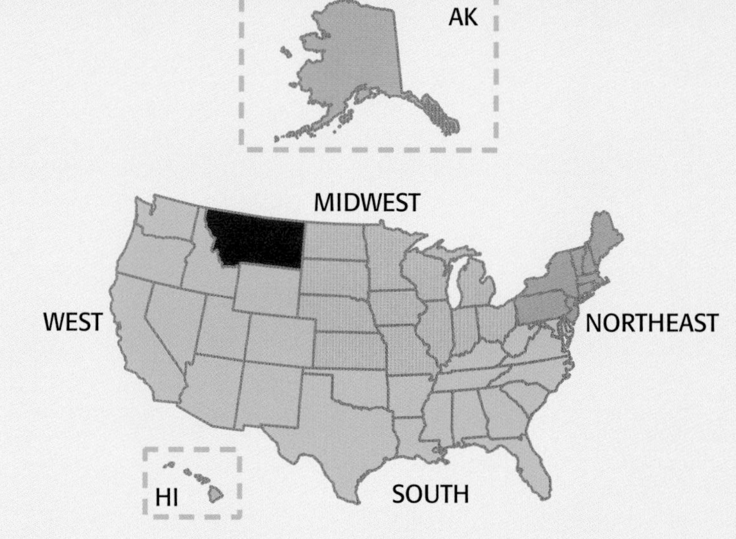

The Place

Montana is the fourth-largest state in the Unites States. It was one of the last states to be settled, and even today it retains a rugged and wild frontier character.

Montana is somewhat isolated by the

Montana's vast open spaces have helped earn the state the nickname, "Big Sky Country."

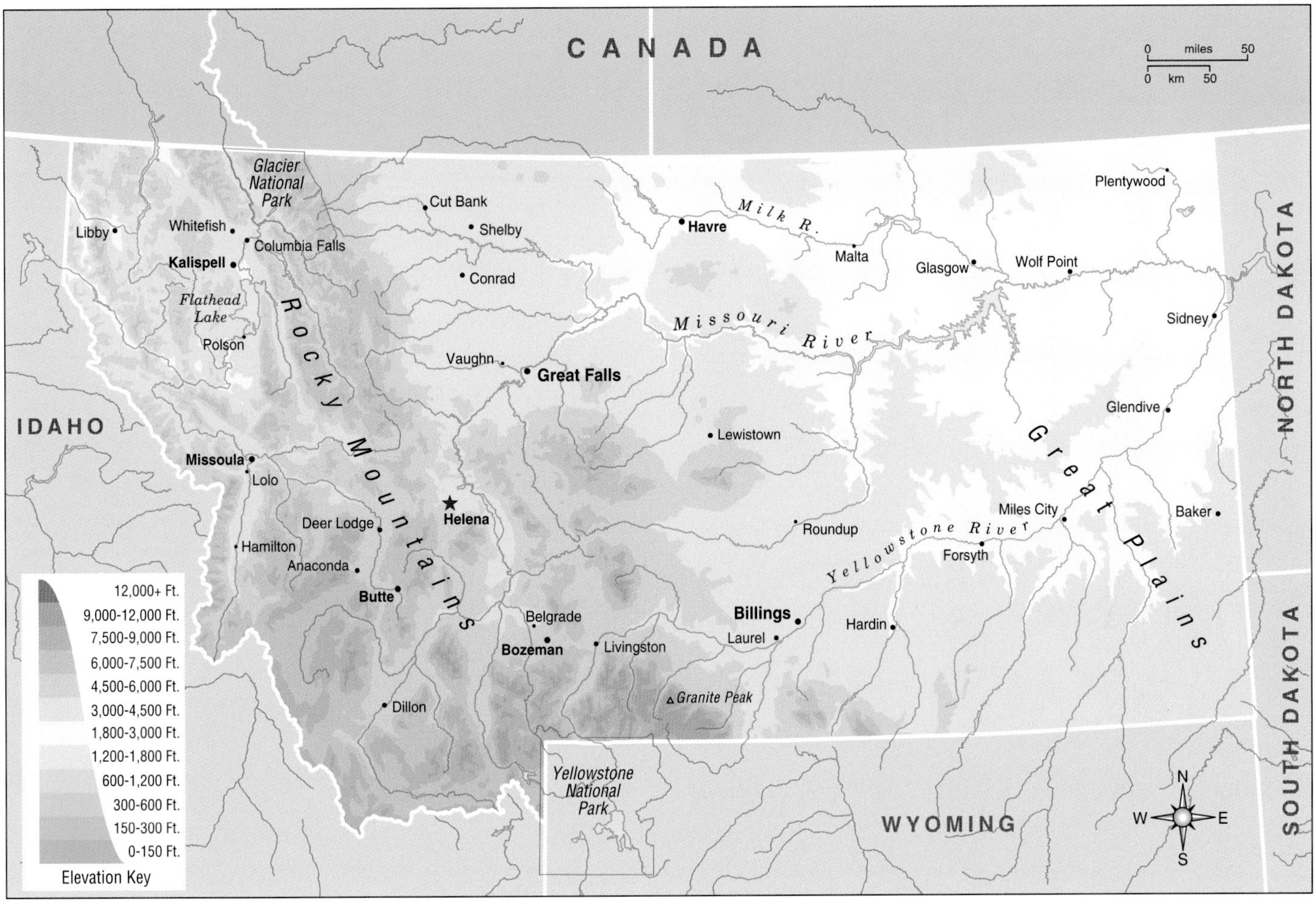

Rocky Mountains, which cover the western two-fifths of the state. The mountains are steep and densely forested, and many are snow-covered throughout the year. This area also has many crystal-blue lakes, such as Flathead Lake, which covers 189 square miles (490 sq km) in northwestern Montana. Valuable deposits of minerals including copper, gold, lead, platinum, silver, and zinc exist in the western mountain region.

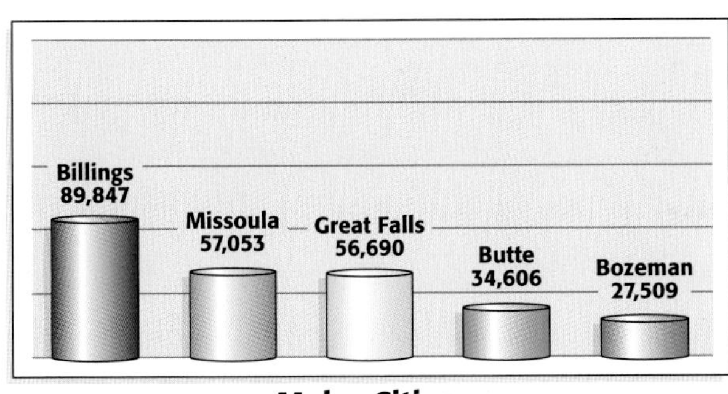

Major Cities

Eastern Montana is part of the Great Plains region, which stretches from Canada in the north all the way to Mexico in the south. This area has rolling hills, broad plains, fertile soil, and wide river valleys. A few small mountain ranges, such as the Bears Paw, Big Snowy, and Judith, cover parts of this area. The climate in the eastern plains of Montana is different from the cool, snowy climate of the west. Temperatures in the eastern prairie can be extreme—bitterly cold in the winter and hot in the summer.

The Blackfeet people of northern Montana were one of the tribes who originally inhabited the area.

The Past

Once the home of many different Native American tribes, Montana was not settled by whites until the 1860s. During the early 1800s, French trappers explored the area, and in 1803 the United States bought the land from France as part of the Louisiana Purchase.

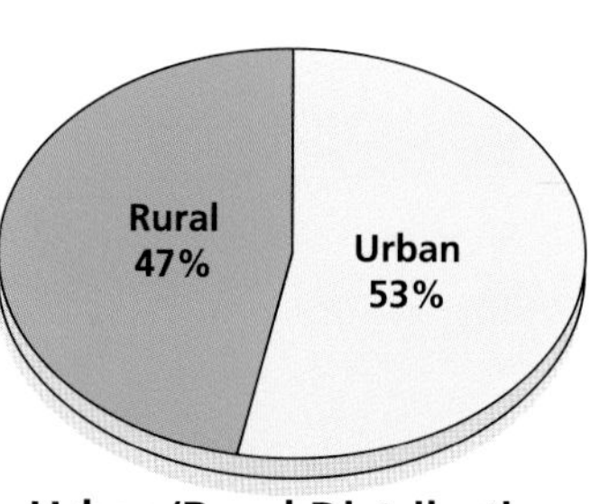

Urban/Rural Distribution

The cattle industry came to Montana's eastern plains in the 1850s, and railroads were quickly completed to ease cattle transport. Montana did not receive much attention, though, until 1862, when gold was discovered there and settlers rushed west to try to strike it rich. As Montana became more settled, the area's Native Americans fought to keep their lands.

In 1876, Sioux and Cheyenne wiped out a U.S. Army regiment led by General George Armstrong Custer in the Battle of

Facts and Firsts

- ★ There are more deer, elk, and antelope in Montana than people. The average square mile of land contains 1.4 elk, 1.4 pronghorn antelope, and 3.3 deer.
- ★ Forty-six of Montana's 56 counties are considered "frontier" and contain six or fewer people per square mile.
- ★ Montana has more species of mammals than any other state.
- ★ Montana has the largest grizzly bear population of the contiguous 48 states.
- ★ Yellowstone National Park, located in Montana and Wyoming, is the oldest national park in the world.
- ★ More people visit Glacier National Park than any other spot in Montana.
- ★ In 1888, Helena was home to more millionaires than anyplace else in the world.

the Little Bighorn. By the 1880s, however, most Native Americans had been forced out, and mining began in earnest. Montana's population grew rapidly as miners came from all over the United States to take advantage of the gold, silver, and copper resources of the region. In 1889, Montana was admitted to the Union.

Lumber and mining were keystones of Montana's industry until the Great Depression of the 1930s, when demand for goods dropped. World War II brought prosperity to Montana as the state provided food and metals for the war effort. Energy production took off after oil fields were discovered along the Montana–North Dakota border in the early 1950s. Tourism also grew and became an important source of revenue.

During the 1980s, economic problems slowed Montana's industrial growth, while technological advances in farming and mining cost many Montana residents their jobs.

Above: *A covered wagon pulls out onto the main street of Helena, Montana, in 1870, during its gold boom.*
Below: *The Little Bighorn Battlefield National Monument is located near Crow Agency, Montana.*

State Smart

The Little Bighorn Battlefield National Monument, which was designated as a national cemetery in 1879, is the oldest national monument in the United States.

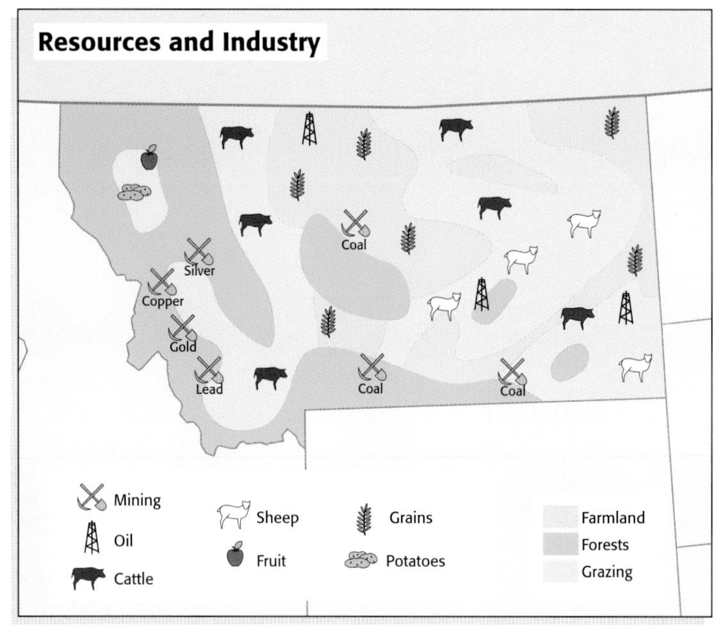

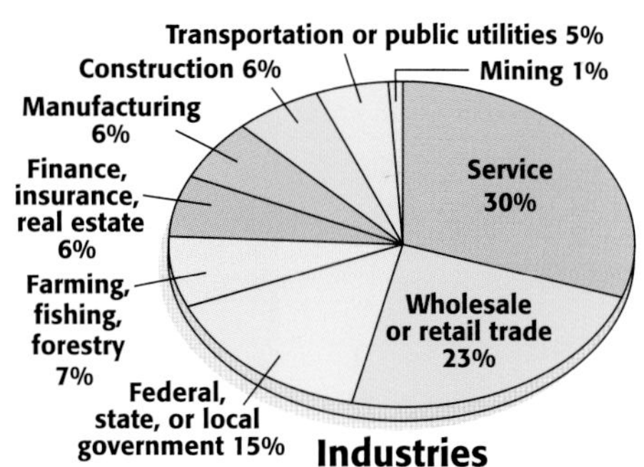

The Present

Montana remains one of the least populated and least developed states. Montana has retained its traditional industries—coal and petroleum mining continue to support the state's economy. Lumbering also remains a major industry, and today Montana processes much of its wood into products such as plywood, pencils, telephone poles, and prefabricated houses.

In the eastern plains, crop and livestock farming are important

The wilderness of Montana offers outdoor activities to tourists.

Born in Montana

- ★ **Dorothy Baker**, author
- ★ **Gary Cooper**, actor
- ★ **Chet Huntley**, television newscaster
- ★ **Myrna Loy**, actress
- ★ **Jeannette Rankin**, first woman elected to Congress
- ★ **Martha Raye**, actress

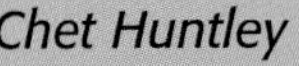

Chet Huntley

Grizzly bears (above) and buffalo (right) are both found in Montana.

revenue-producing activities for residents. Approximately 22,000 farms raise beef and dairy cattle; grow wheat, barley, and hay; and produce sugar beets. Food-processing industries prepare much of this food for world consumption. Montana encourages these industries and many others, including tourism.

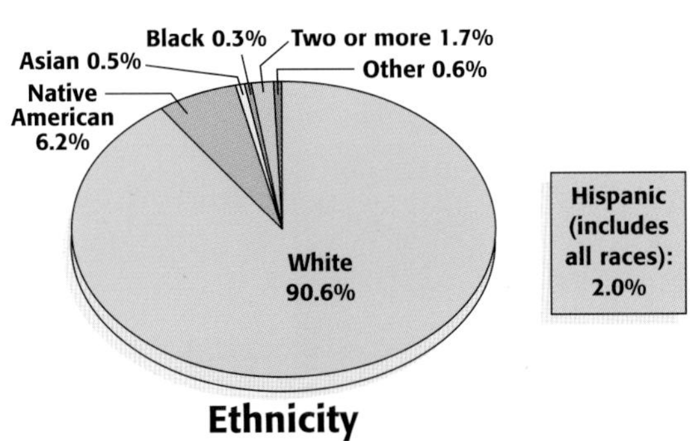

Ethnicity

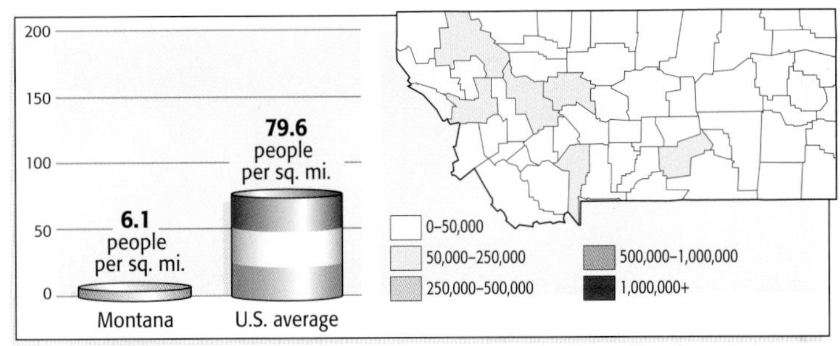

Population Density

Population by County

Nebraska

Equality before the law.

Land area rank
Largest state (1) — 15 — smallest state (52)

Population rank
Most people (1) — 38 — fewest people (52)

At a Glance

Name: Nebraska is from the Oto Indian word *nebrathka,* meaning "flat water."

Nickname: Cornhusker State

Capital: Lincoln

Size: 77,358 sq. mi. (200,358 sq km)

Population: 1,711,263

Statehood: Nebraska became the 37th state on March 1, 1867.

Electoral votes: 5 (2004)

U.S. representatives: 3 (until 2003)

State tree: cottonwood

State flower: goldenrod

State animal: white-tailed deer

Highest point: Johnson Township, 5,426 ft. (1,654 m)

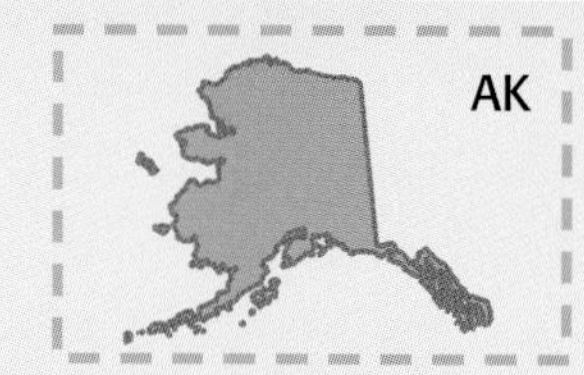

The Place

Nebraska is one of the Midwest states. Thousands of years ago, glaciers covered the eastern part of the state. These slow-moving ice forms left behind a rich layer of soil. Today, this fertile area is used for growing crops such as corn, soybeans, and sorghum.

The elevation of Nebraska rises gradually from

Settlers traveling west often stopped at Eagle Rock, Nebraska.

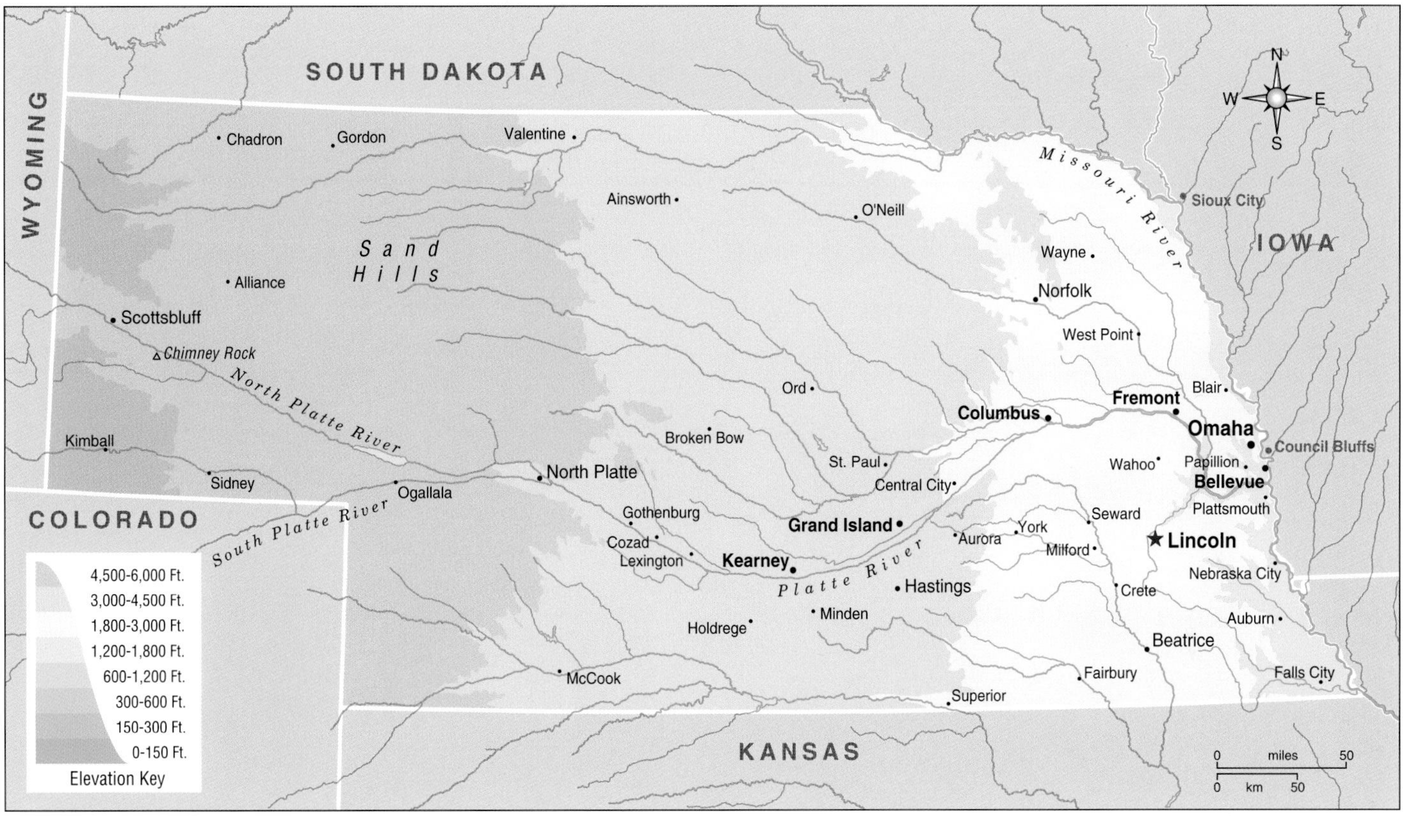

southeast to southwest in a series of rolling plateaus. The central region, called the Sand Hills, is an area of sand drifts covered with grass and small lakes. Western Nebraska is an area of plains, slightly drier than the plains of eastern Nebraska. This area is used for growing corn.

There are very few trees in Nebraska; only about 2 percent of the state is forested. Tall prairie grasses, especially bluestem, grow in eastern Nebraska, while short grasses grow in the drier western region. Nebraska's mineral products include natural gas, petroleum, sand, and gravel.

Nebraska's weather can be extreme. In the summer, the climate is hot and humid. Winters are cold and snowy. The region sometimes experiences violent thunderstorms, tornadoes, hailstorms, and blizzards.

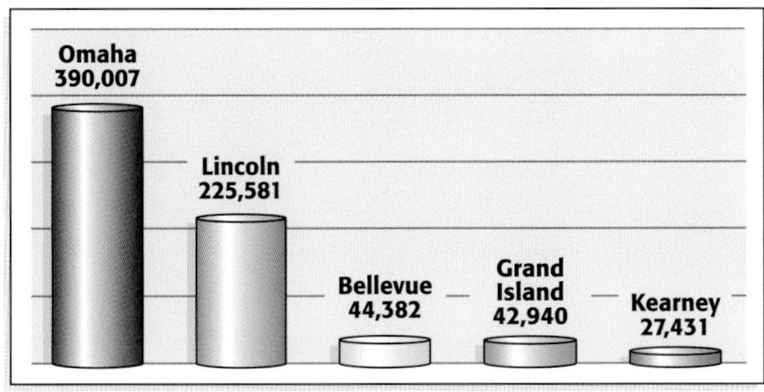

Major Cities

The Past

Stone tools found in Nebraska's soil suggest that Native American people lived there as long as 10,000 to 25,000 years ago. More recent groups, such as the Missouri, Oto, Pawnee, Sioux, and Omaha, were living in the region when Spanish explorers first arrived there in the late 1500s.

The area of Nebraska was alternately under Spanish and French control until it was sold to the United States in 1803 as

These Pawnee boys, standing outside their home in Loup Village, Nebraska, in 1871, were related to the Native Americans who lived in the region when Spanish explorers arrived in the 1500s.

part of the Louisiana Purchase. The government maintained Nebraska as a territory and prohibited white settlement until passage of the Kansas-Nebraska Act in 1854. That act allowed the newly established territories of Kansas and

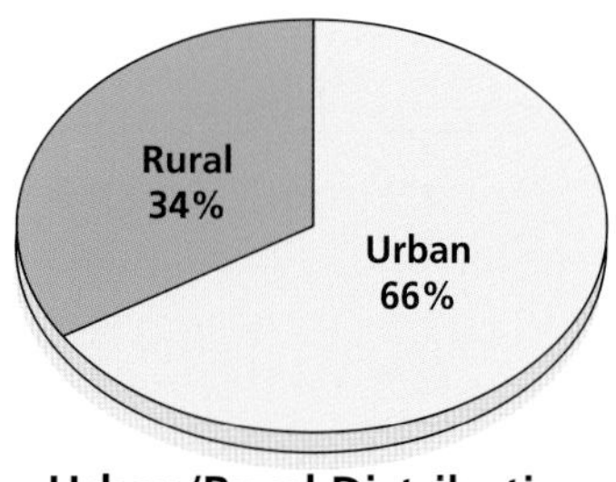

Urban/Rural Distribution

Facts and Firsts

- ★ Kearney is located exactly halfway between Boston and San Francisco.
- ★ Nebraska has more miles of river than any other state.
- ★ The world's largest known woolly mammoth fossil was found in Lincoln County in 1922.
- ★ The world's largest indoor rain forest is the Lied Jungle in Omaha.
- ★ Nebraska is the only state with a unicameral (one-house) legislature.
- ★ The Reuben sandwich originated in Nebraska.
- ★ Lincoln was the first city to use the 911 emergency system.

Sandhill cranes resting at the Platte River

Nebraska to choose whether they would permit slavery.

Settlers moved to the region and built houses out of prairie sod because there were so few trees. After the Homestead Act of 1862, which promised settlers free land if they would farm it, Nebraska's population grew steadily. In 1867, Nebraska entered the Union.

State Smart

Nebraska has the largest population of sandhill cranes of any state. For five weeks every year, about 500,000 cranes (75% of the world's total population) rest at the Platte River in Nebraska before continuing their migration.

Insects were a problem for farmers. Drought was also a problem until the 1890s, when farms began to use improved irrigation methods. Nebraska's farming industry continued to grow until the Great Depression of the 1930s, when the state again suffered from drought. During World War II, Nebraska's agricultural industry rebounded as farmers produced corn, oats, potatoes, and wheat in great quantities to contribute to the war effort.

The discovery of oil in the late 1930s also helped Nebraska's economy. New farm technology in the 1950s put many farmers

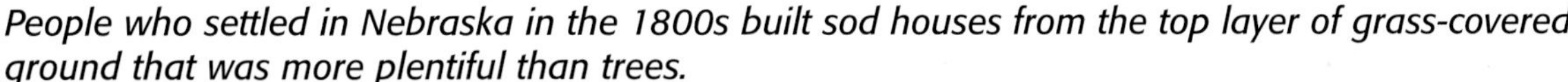

People who settled in Nebraska in the 1800s built sod houses from the top layer of grass-covered ground that was more plentiful than trees.

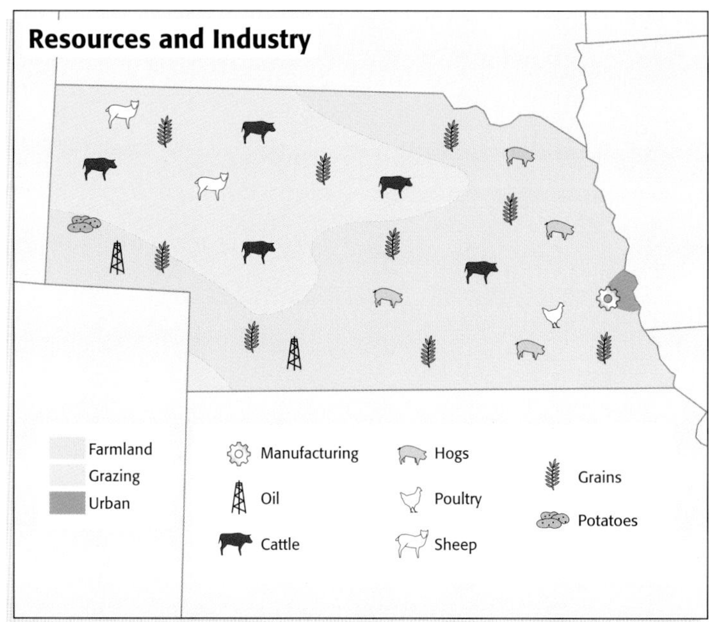

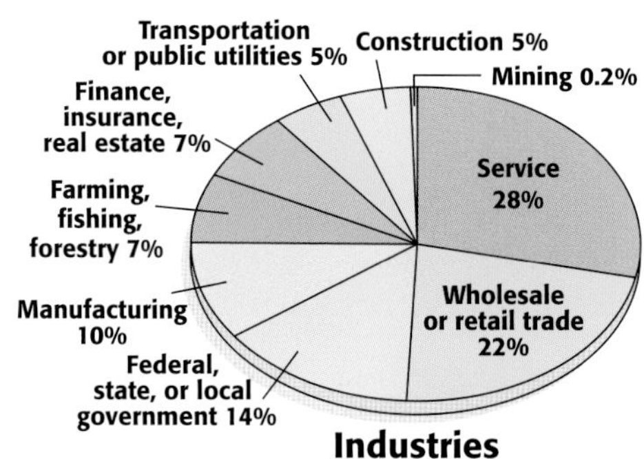

out of work, though, and as they began to move to the cities, Nebraska became more urban. Manufacturing and other urban industries expanded.

The Present

Today, farming continues to be the most important economic activity in Nebraska. About 95 percent of the state's land is used for growing crops, including wheat and corn, and raising cattle and hogs.

The food-processing industry, which prepares Nebraska's agricultural products for market, is very important to the state's economy. Meat and grain processing are centered in the Omaha area.

Nebraska companies manufacture scientific, medical, and surgical equipment as well as farm equipment. Omaha and Lincoln have become financial and

Above: *Omaha is a financial center of the Midwest.*
Below: *A Nebraska farmer harvests wheat.*

Born in Nebraska

- ★ **Grover Cleveland Alexander**, baseball player
- ★ **Fred Astaire**, dancer and actor
- ★ **George Beadle**, Nobel Prize winner and geneticist
- ★ **Marlon Brando**, actor
- ★ **Warren Buffett**, investor
- ★ **James Coburn**, actor
- ★ **Henry Fonda**, actor
- ★ **Gerald Ford**,U.S. president
- ★ **Bob Gibson**, baseball player
- ★ **Malcolm X**, civil rights advocate
- ★ **Nick Nolte**, actor
- ★ **Red Cloud**, Native American rights advocate
- ★ **Mari Sandoz**, author

Above: *Malcom X;* below: *Gerald Ford*

transportation centers of the Midwest. Mutual of Omaha, one of the nation's largest health insurance companies, is headquartered in Omaha. Both Omaha and Lincoln have railroad and trucking companies that move products from the Midwest all over the country.

Ninety-five percent of the land in Nebraska is used for agriculture. Rural communities such as Gordon, near the Sand Hills, may use one-room schoolhouses.

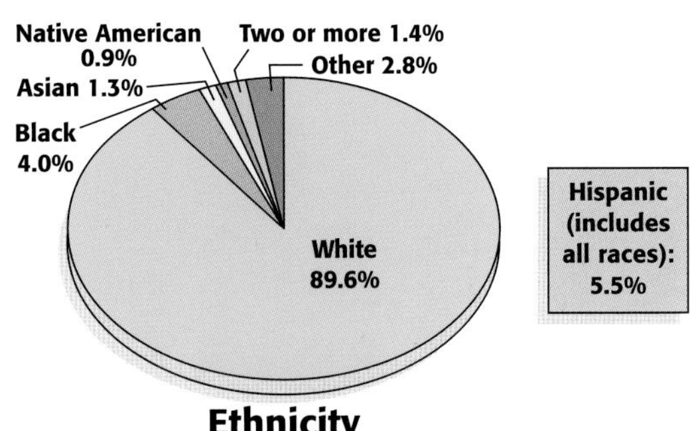

Ethnicity

Hispanic (includes all races): 5.5%

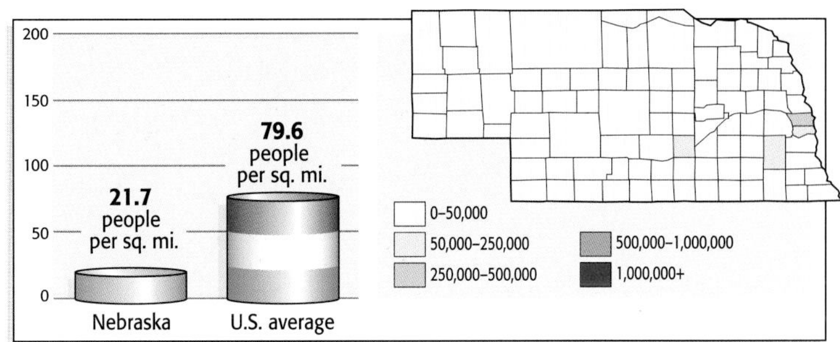

Population Density

Population by County

Nevada

All for our country.

Land area rank *Largest state (1)* — 7 — *smallest state (52)*

Population rank *Most people (1)* — 35 — *fewest people (52)*

At a Glance

Name: Nevada means "snowcapped" in Spanish.
Nicknames: Sagebrush State, Silver State
Capital: Carson City
Size: 110,567 sq. mi. (286,367 sq km)
Population: 1,998,257
Statehood: Nevada became the 36th state on October 31, 1864.
Electoral votes: 5 (2004)
U.S. representatives: 3
State trees: single-leaf piñon and bristlecone pine
State flower: sagebrush
State animal: desert bighorn sheep
Highest point: Boundary Peak, 13,140 ft. (4,005 m)

Nevada's large desert area has poor soil but rich mineral resources.

The Place

Nevada is one of the mountainous states of the West. Most of Nevada is located within a large desert area known as the Great Basin. The northeastern corner of the state is a lava-made plateau full of steep ridges and streams. The land flattens into prairie close to the state's border with Idaho.

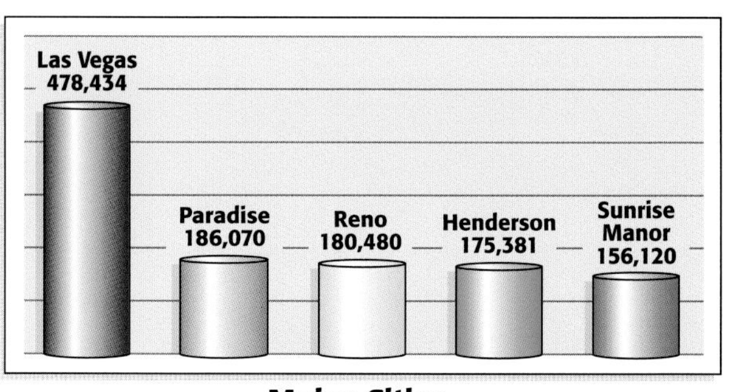

Major Cities

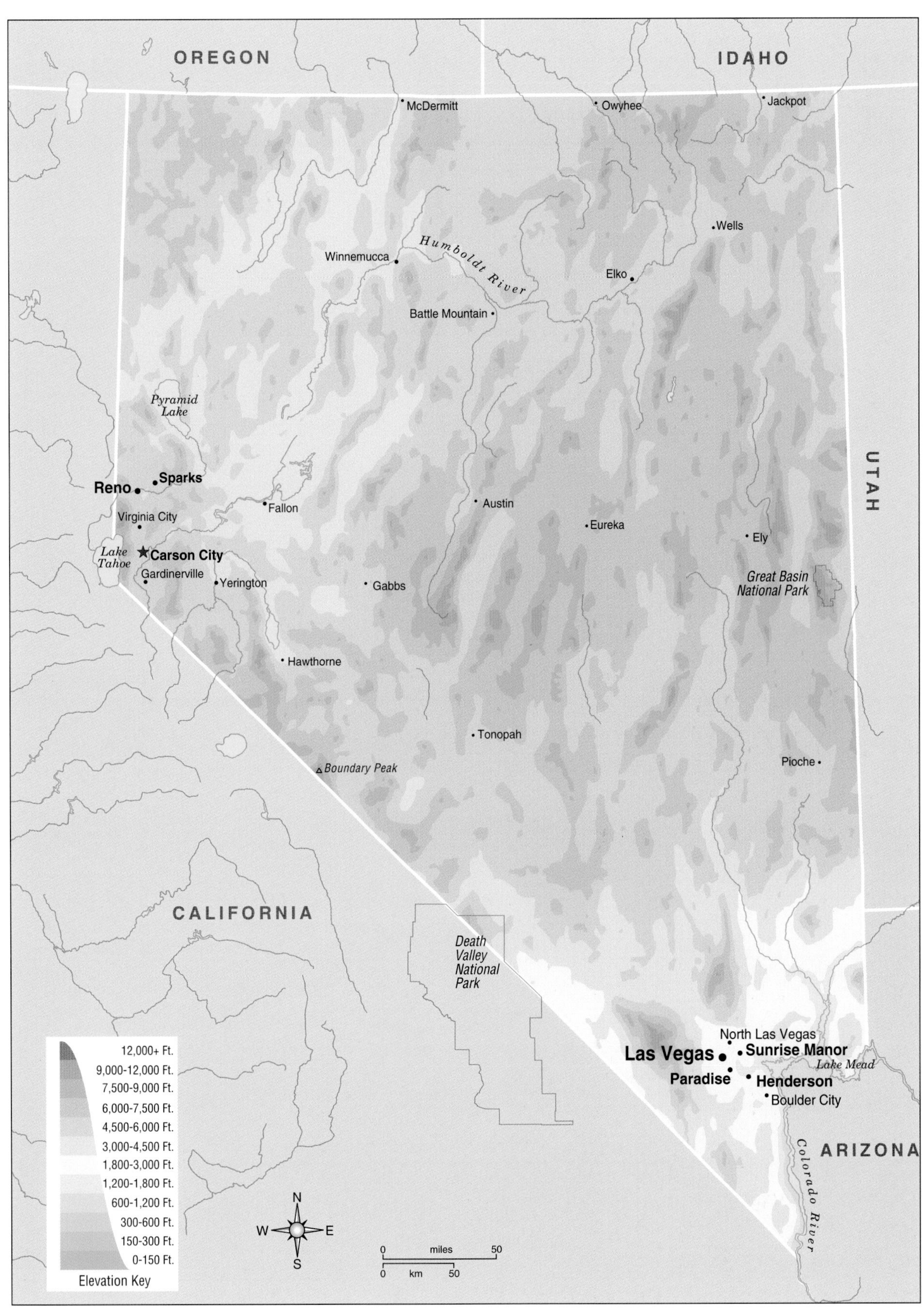
OREGON
IDAHO
UTAH
CALIFORNIA
ARIZONA
McDermitt
Owyhee
Jackpot
Wells
Humboldt River
Winnemucca
Elko
Battle Mountain
Pyramid Lake
Reno
Sparks
Fallon
Virginia City
Austin
Eureka
Ely
Lake Tahoe
Carson City
Gardinerville
Yerington
Gabbs
Great Basin National Park
Hawthorne
Tonopah
Boundary Peak
Pioche
Death Valley National Park
North Las Vegas
Las Vegas
Sunrise Manor
Lake Mead
Paradise
Henderson
Boulder City
Colorado River
12,000+ Ft.
9,000-12,000 Ft.
7,500-9,000 Ft.
6,000-7,500 Ft.
4,500-6,000 Ft.
3,000-4,500 Ft.
1,800-3,000 Ft.
1,200-1,800 Ft.
600-1,200 Ft.
300-600 Ft.
150-300 Ft.
0-150 Ft.
Elevation Key
N
W
E
S
0 miles 50
0 km 50

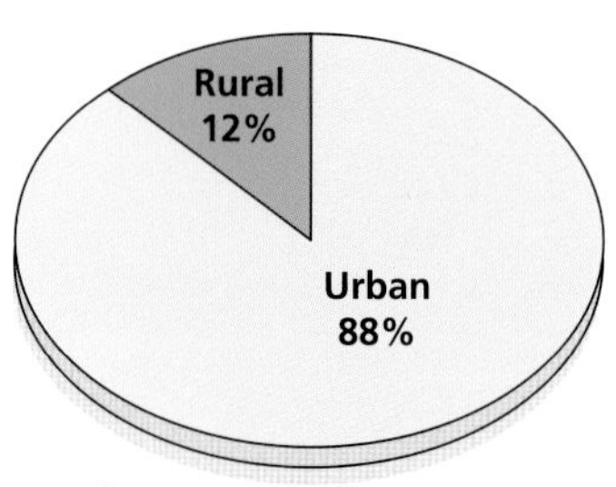

Urban/Rural Distribution

The Sierra Nevada is a rugged mountain range that cuts across the south and west of Nevada. Lake Tahoe is the most famous lake in this region. Other smaller mountain ranges cover the rest of Nevada. Grasses grow in many of the valleys between Nevada's mountains, where cattle often graze.

The regions of Nevada all have different weather. The northern and mountainous parts have long, cold winters and hot summers, and winter is milder in the south and west.

Since Nevada has poor soil, its most important resources are its varied mineral deposits, which include copper, mercury, gold, silver, and petroleum.

Hoover Dam outside of Las Vegas

THE PAST

Nevada has one of the longest and richest Native American histories of any state. Cave paintings from thousands of years ago have been found in this region. The first Europeans arrived in Nevada in the 1770s, when the Spanish claimed it as part of the

Facts and Firsts

- ★ Nevada has more mountain ranges than any other state.
- ★ Nevada's lakes are home to some unique species of fish, like the cui-ui, a large sucker from Pyramid Lake, and the Devils Hole pupfish from Devils Hole. These fish are found nowhere else in the world because they were isolated in lakes thousands of years ago when prehistoric rivers dried up.
- ★ The U.S. government owns about 80 percent of Nevada's land, the largest percentage of any state.
- ★ Nevada produces more gold than any other state. In the world, it is second only to the country of South Africa.
- ★ Hoover Dam in Nevada was the biggest single public works project in the history of the United States. It contains about 4.5 million cubic yards (3.4 million cu m) of concrete—enough to pave a two-lane highway from San Francisco to New York City.
- ★ In 1999, Nevada had 205,726 slot machines for gambling—one for every 10 state residents.

territory of Mexico. Fur traders from Canada and the eastern United States also made their way to Nevada during the early 1800s.

Nevada became part of the United States at the end of the Mexican-American War in 1848. Soon after, a group of Mormons who sought religious freedom settled in Nevada. They supplied provisions to prospectors who traveled to California in search of gold.

Major settlement in Nevada was slow until the Comstock Lode, a huge deposit of silver, was discovered near Carson City in 1859. The area became a thriving mining center, where life was dangerous, expensive, and often lawless.

Nevada became a state in 1864, during the Civil War. It was admitted to the Union with the support of President Abraham Lincoln, who wanted another free state that would help pass his antislavery proposals.

After the Civil War, the federal government reduced the amount of silver used in its coins, and as a result, many Nevada mines failed. Once-thriving mining towns became ghost towns as people left the state to find work elsewhere. During the next 80 years, prices for mined goods rose and fell unpredictably because of the Great Depression and two world wars. As mining declined, however, cattle ranching became more important.

In 1931, the Nevada legislature made gambling legal in the state. After World War II, tourism began to increase as visitors took advantage of the legal gambling in Las Vegas and Reno and the beautiful scenery around Lake Tahoe, Nevada's most famous resort.

State Smart

Nevada is the driest state. It receives an average of 9 inches (23 cm) of rain each year.

A deserted ghost town is a trace of Nevada's mining past.

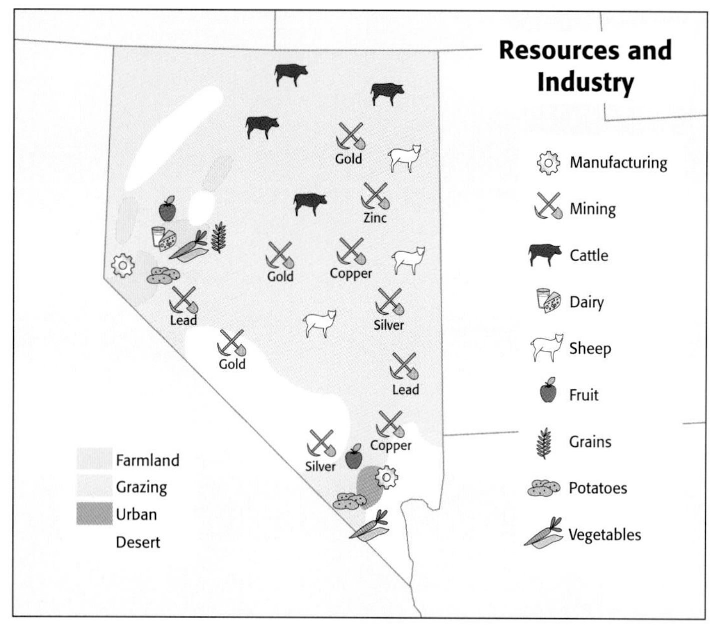

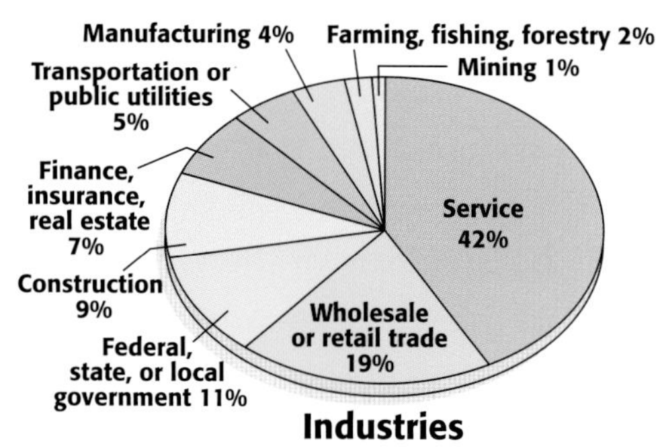

The Present

Today, Nevada is most famous for Las Vegas and Reno, the sites of huge hotels, nightclubs, and casinos. Nevada has the loosest gambling laws of any state. Each year, more than 40 million tourists spend billions of dollars in Nevada.

Sports, ranches, and fishing resorts also attract many people to Nevada. The service industries around the tourist centers of Las Vegas and Reno contribute about one-third of the entire state's yearly income. More than four-fifths of Nevada residents and many people from other states also live in these metropolitan areas because of the availability of service industry jobs.

Despite the importance of tourism to Nevada's economy, mining remains one of the state's chief industries. Nevada produces almost two-thirds of all the gold mined in the United States and mines more silver than any other state.

Lake Tahoe (below, left) and Las Vegas (below, right) are two of Nevada's greatest tourist areas.

Born in Nevada

- ★ **Andre Agassi**, tennis player
- ★ **Robert Caples**, painter
- ★ **Abby Dalton**, actress
- ★ **Michele Greene**, actress
- ★ **Sarah Winnemucca Hopkins**, author and Paiute interpreter
- ★ **Thelma "Pat" Nixon**, first lady
- ★ **Lute Pease**, cartoonist and Pulitzer Prize winner

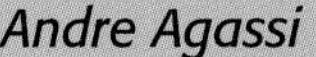

Andre Agassi

Petroleum, gravel, and sand are also valuable products. Many of these minerals are used to support Nevada's manufacturing industries, which process meat; make concrete, computer, and electronic equipment; and publish printed materials. Raising livestock is also a chief economic activity. Most farms operate near the Colorado River, where irrigation enables the growth of crops.

Chuck wagons race at a rodeo. Rodeos are popular events in Nevada.

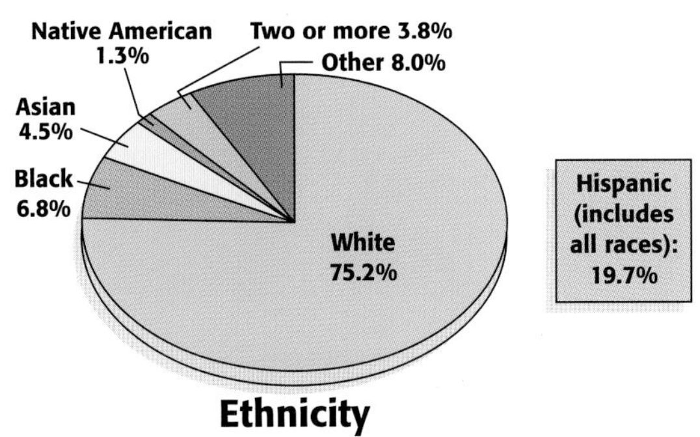

Ethnicity

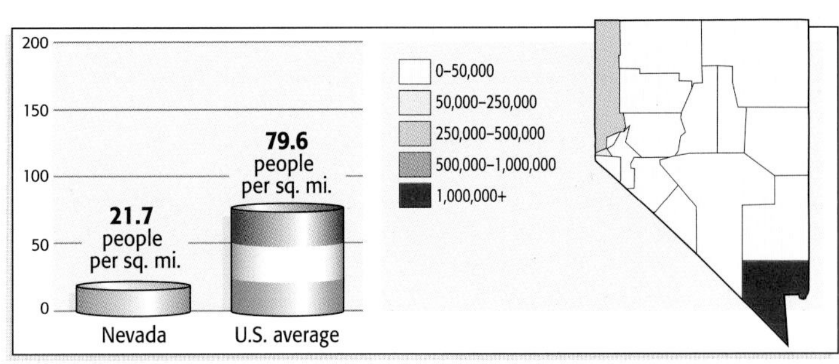

Population Density

Population by County

New Hampshire

Live free or die.

Land area rank
Largest state (1)

Population rank
Most people (1)

At a Glance

Name: New Hampshire was named for the English county of Hampshire.

Nickname: Granite State

Capital: Concord

Size: 9,283 sq. mi. (24,044 sq km)

Population: 1,235,786

Statehood: New Hampshire became the ninth state on June 21, 1788.

Electoral votes: 4 (2004)

U.S. representatives: 2 (until 2003)

State tree: white birch

State flower: purple lilac

State reptile: red spotted newt

Highest point: Mount Washington, 6,288 ft. (1,917 m)

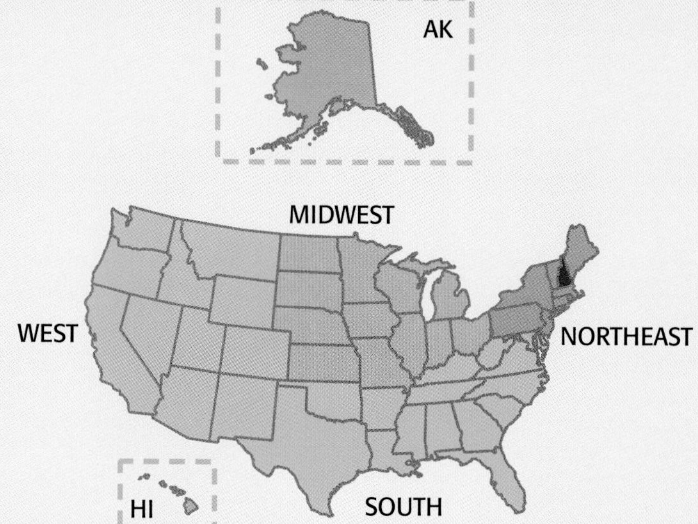

The Place

New Hampshire is one of the six New England states. Its 13-mile coastline on the Atlantic Ocean is the shortest coastline of any state bordering an ocean. The land along the coast is flat, and its rivers and streams attract large numbers of migrating ducks and geese.

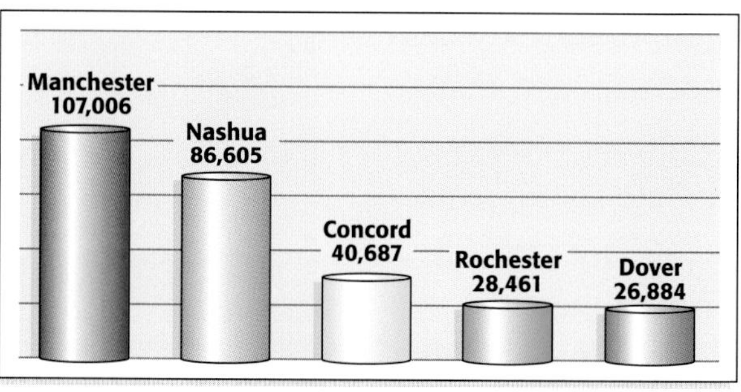

Major Cities

Portsmouth, one of the few coastal cities in New Hampshire, sits at the mouth of the Piscataqua River where it empties into the Atlantic Ocean.

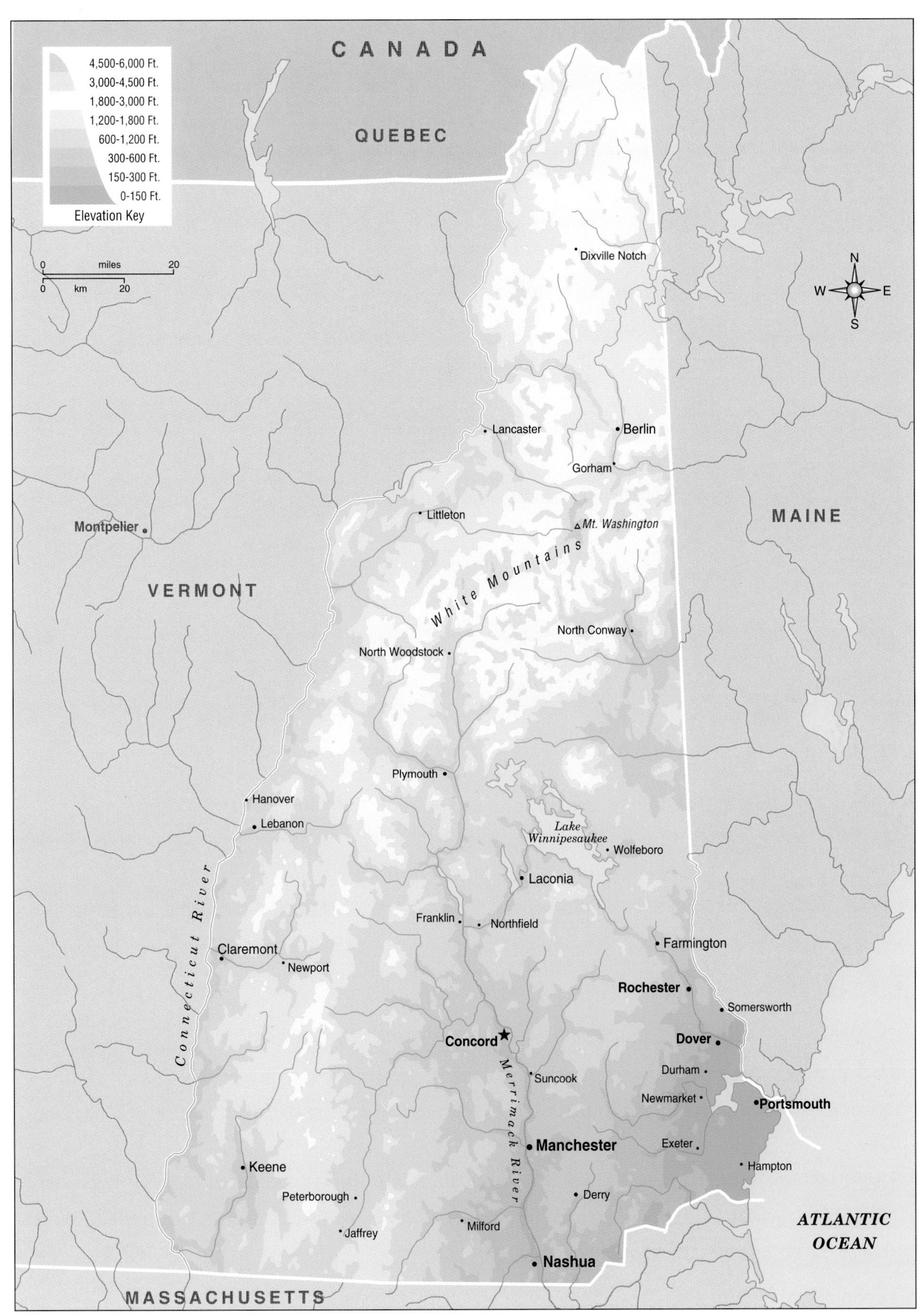
CANADA
QUEBEC
4,500-6,000 Ft.
3,000-4,500 Ft.
1,800-3,000 Ft.
1,200-1,800 Ft.
600-1,200 Ft.
300-600 Ft.
150-300 Ft.
0-150 Ft.
Elevation Key
0 miles 20
0 km 20
N
W
E
S
Dixville Notch
Lancaster
Berlin
Gorham
Littleton
Mt. Washington
Montpelier
MAINE
White Mountains
VERMONT
North Conway
North Woodstock
Plymouth
Hanover
Lebanon
Lake Winnipesaukee
Wolfeboro
Laconia
Connecticut River
Franklin
Northfield
Farmington
Claremont
Newport
Rochester
Somersworth
Concord
Dover
Merrimack River
Suncook
Durham
Newmarket
Portsmouth
Manchester
Exeter
Keene
Hampton
Peterborough
Derry
ATLANTIC OCEAN
Milford
Jaffrey
Nashua
MASSACHUSETTS

New Hampshire winters are snowy.

New Hampshire's weather is cool year-round. Summers are fairly dry, but winters are snowy, especially in the north and west. The pleasant summer weather and snowy winters attract many visitors to the White Mountains, which are located in northern New Hampshire. The Presidential Range of the White Mountains has the highest peaks in New England.

Large amounts of granite give New Hampshire its nickname, the Granite State. New Hampshire's natural resources include a variety of minerals, but only sand and gravel are mined to any extent.

Most of southern New Hampshire is covered by a series of fertile valleys, beautiful lakes, and forested hills—about 85 percent of the entire state's land is forested. The Connecticut River stretches along the western border of New Hampshire, where there is rich farmland.

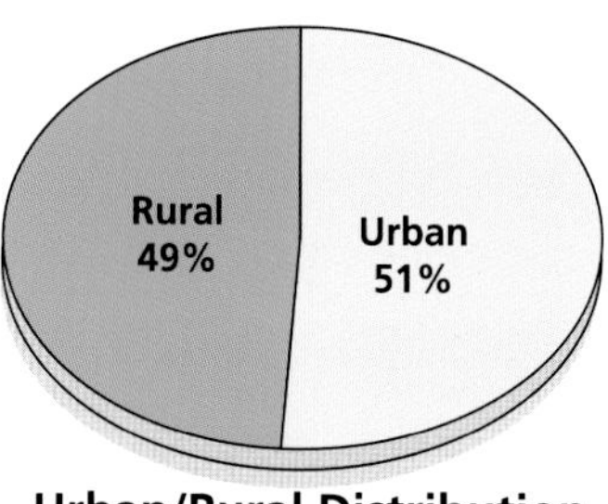

Urban/Rural Distribution

The Past

New Hampshire was first explored and settled by the English in the 1600s. Colonists found about 5,000 Native Americans, mostly Algonquian groups, living there. These Native Americans allied with French colonists

Facts and Firsts

- ★ In 1719, the United States's first potato was planted at Londonderry Common Field.
- ★ New Hampshire was the first of the 13 original colonies to declare independence from England.
- ★ The first women's labor strike in the United States took place at the Dover Cotton Factory on December 30, 1828.
- ★ In 1833, Peterborough established the first free public library in the United States.
- ★ In 1905, New Hampshire became the first and only state to host end-of-war negotiations for foreign countries. In that year, the treaty ending the Russo-Japanese War was signed in Portsmouth.

from Canada to fight against the British during the French and Indian War.

Before the first battles of the Revolutionary War were fought (in Massachusetts), the first armed attack against the British took place in New Hampshire. New Hampshire was the first colony to write a state constitution. This constitution went into effect in 1776, shortly before the Declaration of Independence was signed.

Colonial New Hampshire was primarily a rural agricultural society, and remained agricultural through the Revolutionary War. In the 1860s, during the Civil War, industry increased in the state, as shipyards and mills began to expand. The textile, woodworking, and leather industries also grew. Ship and submarine manufacturing gave the economy a boost during World Wars I and II. By the end of the 20th century, many rural parts of New Hampshire had become urban and industrialized.

State Smart

The Haverhill-Bath Covered Bridge, built in 1829, is the oldest covered bridge still in use in the United States.

Below: *The Haverill-Bath bridge is the oldest covered bridge in America.* Above right: *Concord, the capital of New Hampshire, depicted here in 1835, remained a rural community until the Civil War began.*

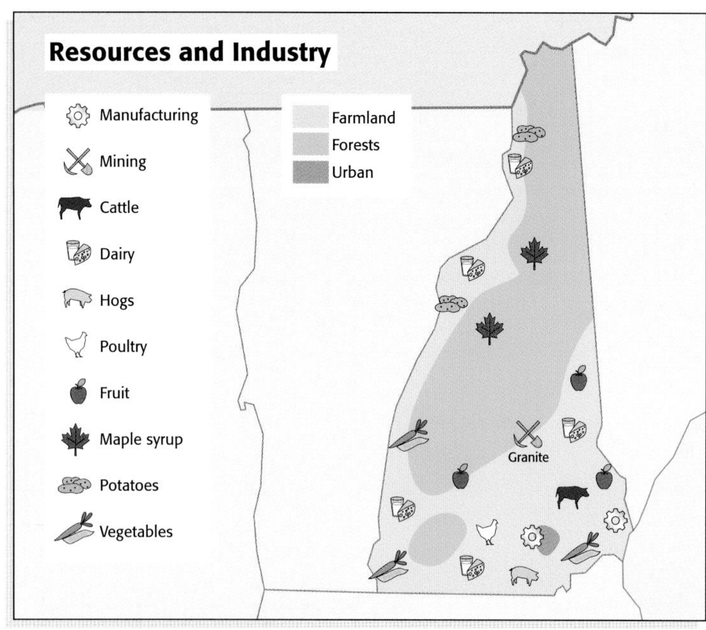

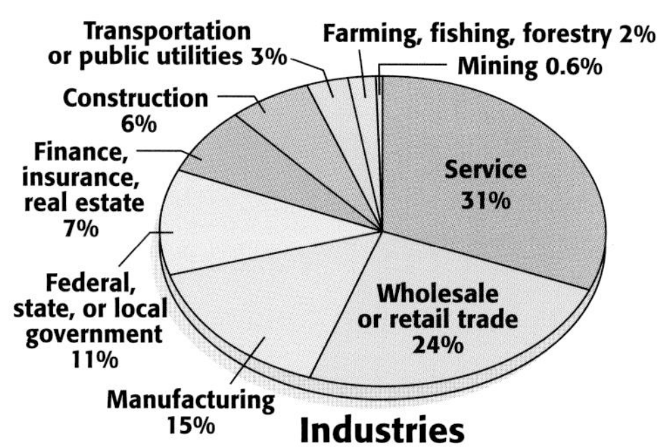

The Present

Today, only about 7 percent of New Hampshire's land is farmland. Many of the state's approximately 2,900 farms produce dairy products.

New Hampshire maintains a system of low taxation and has no income or sales tax, so many businesses and residents have been attracted to the state. New Hampshire's manufacturing industries have become vital to its economy. The state produces many different kinds of machinery—especially computer parts. It also produces electrical equipment such as military communications systems, scientific instruments such as navigational equipment, and medical instruments.

Tourism has also become an important source of income. New Hampshire's

Below left: *New Hampshire's famous fall foliage.* Below right: *Visitors to New Hampshire may hike up Mt. Washington, the highest peak of the White Mountains.*

Born in New Hampshire

- ★ **Salmon P. Chase**, jurist
- ★ **Charles Anderson Dana**, editor
- ★ **Mary Baker Eddy**, founder of the Christian Science Church
- ★ **Daniel Chester French**, sculptor
- ★ **Horace Greeley**, journalist and politician
- ★ **Sarah J. Hale**, author, editor, and feminist
- ★ **John Irving**, author
- ★ **Franklin Pierce**, U.S. president
- ★ **Alan Shepard**, astronaut
- ★ **Harlan F. Stone**, jurist
- ★ **Daniel Webster**, statesman

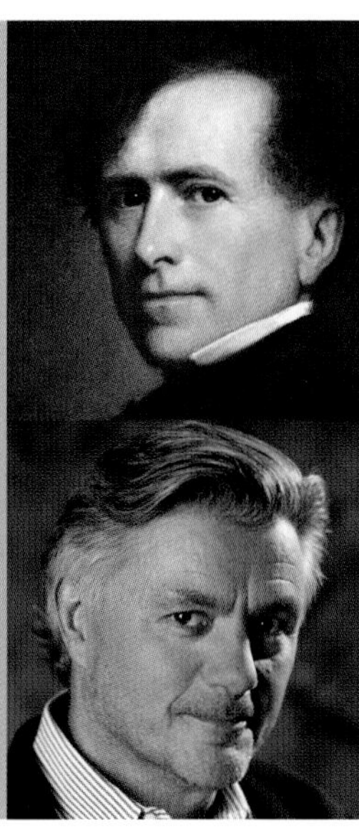

Above: *Franklin Pierce;* below: *John Irving*

mountains, beaches, and lakes attract many vacationers, and its colorful foliage brings thousands of visitors to the state every fall. Tourists visit many popular ski resorts during the winter months. Revenue from tourism has helped New Hampshire finance many public service projects that are not supported by taxes, such as road construction and schools.

Dartmouth College in Hanover.

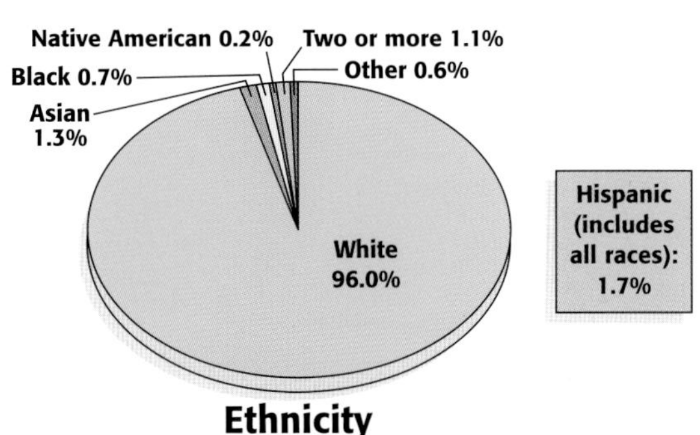

Ethnicity

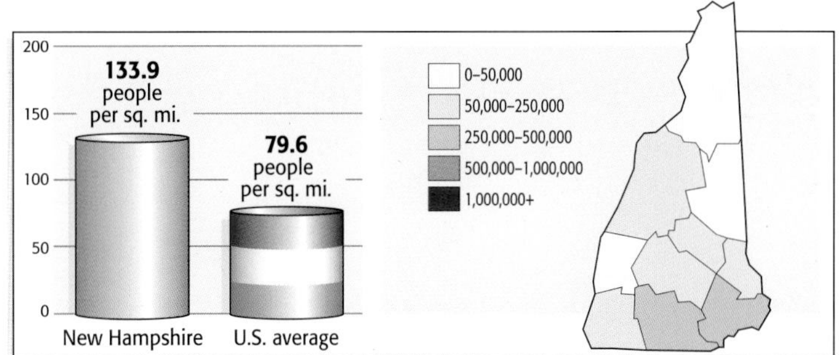

Population Density

Population by County

New Jersey

Liberty and prosperity.

Land area rank *Largest state (1)* — 46 — *smallest state (52)*

Population rank *Most people (1)* — 9 — *fewest people (52)*

At a Glance

Name: New Jersey was named after Jersey, an island in the English Channel.

Nickname: Garden State

Capital: Trenton

Size: 7,790 sq. mi. (20, 175 sq km)

Population: 8,414,350

Statehood: New Jersey became the third state on December 18, 1787.

Electoral votes: 15 (2004)

U.S. representatives: 13 (until 2003)

State tree: red oak

State flower: purple violet

State insect: honeybee

Highest point: High Point, 1,083 ft. (550 m)

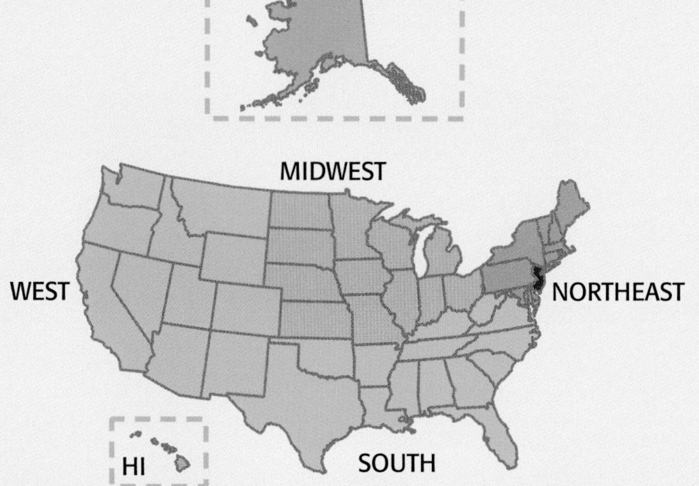

The Place

New Jersey is one of the Mid-Atlantic states. It is the fourth-smallest state in the United States, bigger than only Rhode Island, Delaware, and Connecticut. New Jersey is located between New York and Pennsylvania. The Delaware River marks the state's western border, while the

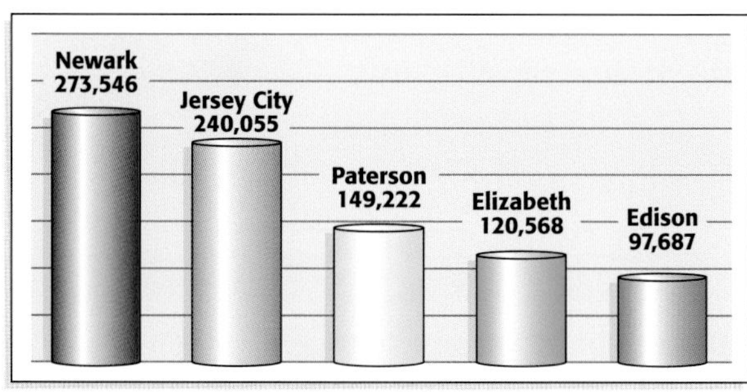

Major Cities

Atlantic City is a popular beach resort on the East Coast.

4,500-6,000 Ft.
3,000-4,500 Ft.
1,800-3,000 Ft.
1,200-1,800 Ft.
600-1,200 Ft.
300-600 Ft.
150-300 Ft.
0-150 Ft.
Elevation Key
High Point
Delaware River
Kittatinny Mountain
Sussex
Highland Lakes
Franklin
NEW YORK
Hudson River
Newton
Ramsey
Pompton Lakes
Ridgewood
Paramus
Hopatcong
Paterson
Wayne
Hackensack
Flanders
Dover
Clifton
Passaic
Belvidere
Montclair
Nutley
Morristown
Livingston
Union City
Washington
Madison
Newark
New York
Hoboken
Phillipsburg
New Providence
Jersey City
High Bridge
Elizabeth
Bayonne
Rahway
Bridgewater
Carteret
PENNSYLVANIA
Piscataway
Edison
Flemington
Somerset
Perth Amboy
New Brunswick
Sayreville
East Brunswick
Hazlet
Old Bridge
Middletown
Lambertville
Princeton
Jamesburg
Rumson
Red Bank
Eatontown
Long Branch
Ewing
Freehold
Trenton
Asbury Park
Neptune City
Belmar
Bordentown
Manasquan
Lakewood
Point Pleasant
Willingboro
Lakehurst
Delaware River
Mount Holly
Philadelphia
Brown Mills
Toms River
Camden
Cherry Hill
Gloucester City
Oak Valley
Somerdale
Blackwood
Glassboro
Pennsville
Clayton
Hammonton
Tuckerton
Beach Haven
Salem
DELAWARE
Egg Harbor City
Buena
Vineland
Pomona
Absecon
Bridgeton
Brigantine
Millville
Pleasantville
Atlantic City
N
W
E
S
Somers Point
Ocean City
Woodbine
Sea Isle City
Delaware Bay
ATLANTIC OCEAN
Cape May Court House
Avalon
Villas
Wildwood
Cape May
0 miles 20
0 km 20

Hudson River separates New Jersey from New York in the northeast.

New Jersey has a 130-mile (209-km) coastline on the Atlantic Ocean. Salt marshes, shallow lagoons, and meadows cover much of the area near the coast. The land in the center of the state is fertile farmland. New Jersey has more than 800 lakes and ponds, and its many rivers provide power for the state's large cities, which include Newark, Paterson, Elizabeth, Trenton, and Camden.

About two-fifths of New Jersey is covered by forests. Most of the forested area is in the northwestern corner of New Jersey, in the Appalachian Mountains. The Delaware Water Gap, where the Delaware River cuts through the mountains, is one of the most scenic natural formations in the region. The grassy Appalachian Valley is the largest valley in the area and is ideal for grazing dairy cattle.

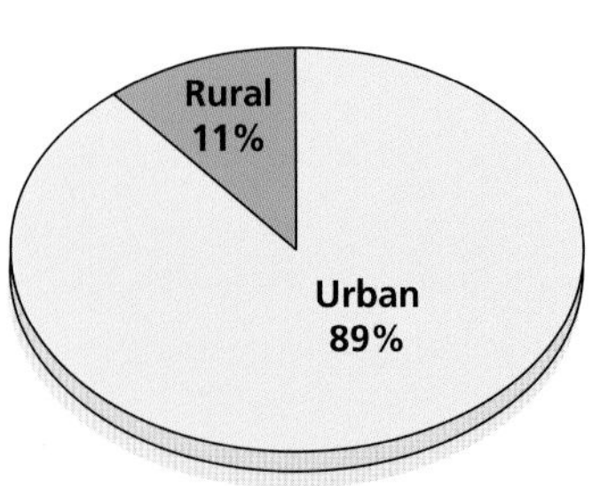

Urban/Rural Distribution

New Jersey has warm-to-hot summers and cold winters, with more moderate temperatures along the coast. New Jersey's most valuable mineral resources are granite, traprock, sand, and gravel.

Giovanni da Verrazano explored the New Jersey coast in the 16th century.

The Past

Before Europeans settled in New Jersey, the land was home to around 8,000 Native Americans, who came to be known as the

Facts and Firsts

- ★ Cape May is the oldest seashore resort in the United States.
- ★ Atlantic City has the longest boardwalk in the world. Built in 1896, it stretches for 4.5 miles (7.2 km) along the Atlantic coast.
- ★ New Jersey is the only state to have all of its counties classified as metropolitan areas.
- ★ New Jersey has the densest system of highways and railroads in the country.
- ★ New Jersey is a leading state in chemical production, and chemicals are the state's leading manufactured product.
- ★ Two-thirds of the world's eggplants are grown in New Jersey.

Delaware. Italian navigator Giovanni da Verrazano, working for the king of France, reached New Jersey's coast in 1524. Henry Hudson explored New Jersey as part of his Hudson River expedition for the Netherlands in the early 1600s. The earliest settlers came from the Netherlands and Sweden to trade furs. Fearing competition from the Swedes, the Dutch quickly pushed them out, and New Jersey became part of the Dutch colony of New Netherland.

In 1664, the English drove out the Dutch and took control of New Netherland, which they renamed New York and New Jersey. The governor of New York also ruled New Jersey until 1738, when Lewis Morris became the first governor of the New Jersey colony.

Because of New Jersey's central location, Patriot and British forces engaged in almost 100 Revolutionary War conflicts there. The colony was the site of many key battles, including the battles of Trenton, Princeton, and Monmouth.

After the Revolutionary War, New Jersey quickly became one of the first industrialized states. By 1792, Paterson was an important center for the manufacture of textiles. In 1804, New Jersey began to pass legislation to gradually free its slaves, but there was significant pro-South sympathy in the state. It was one of only three states that voted against the reelection of President Abraham Lincoln in 1864.

In the late 1800s, the construction of new canals and railroads helped Camden, Elizabeth, Jersey City, Newark, Trenton, and Passaic to become major manufacturing centers. New Jersey became the home of many large industrial businesses. Thousands of European immigrants came to work in New Jersey factories.

New Jersey suffered through unemployment and economic hardship during the Great Depression. During World War II, however, the state's electronics and chemical industries grew as the state supplied communications equipment, ships, weapons, and ammunition for the country's military operations.

During the mid–20th century, many New Jersey residents left the industrial cities to live in the country. Many people

State Smart

In 2000, New Jersey surpassed Connecticut as the state with the highest per capita (per person) income.

George Washington led troops at the Battle of Princeton.

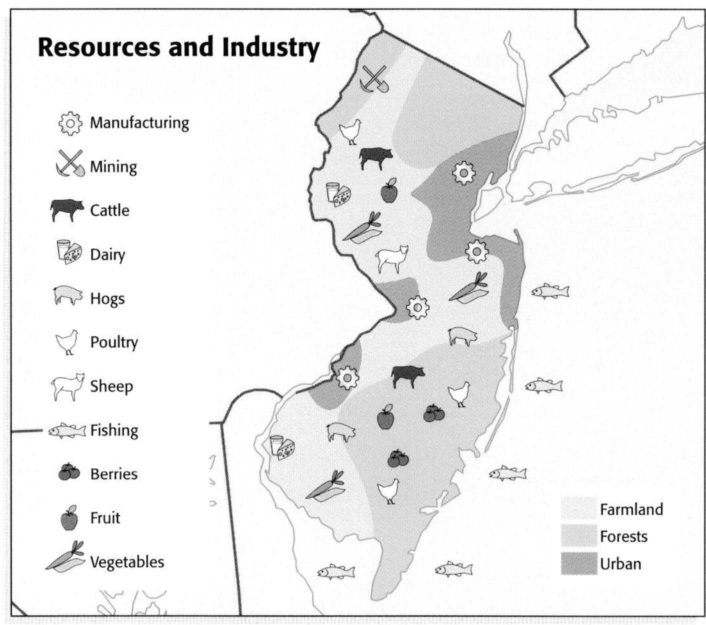

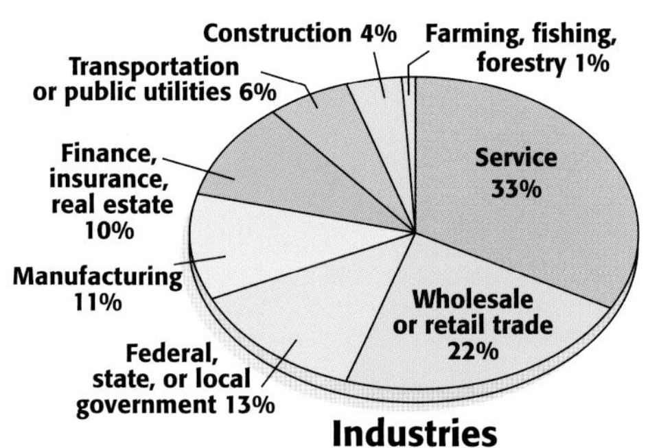

who worked in the large cities of New York and Philadelphia also moved to New Jersey's suburbs, which quickly became overpopulated. The expanding population had a negative impact on the environment and strained the resources of the state government, which needed revenue to pay for roads, schools, and social assistance.

The Present

With about 89 percent of its residents living in urban areas, New Jersey has the highest population density of any state, with an average of 1,098 people per square mile. Its manufacturing centers produce electronics, paper and printed products, and processed food. New Jersey is one of the leading states in the production of chemicals and pharmaceuticals.

New Jersey's location between New York and Philadelphia brings business to the state, and its transportation system moves goods and people between those two cities and all over the world. New Jersey's airport in Newark is one of the busiest international airports in the world.

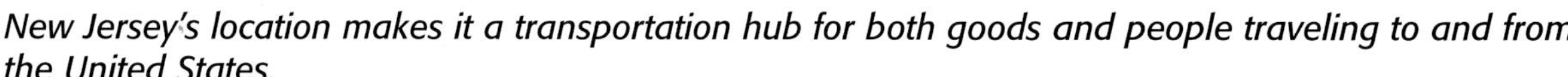
New Jersey's location makes it a transportation hub for both goods and people traveling to and from the United States.

Born in New Jersey

- ★ **Bud Abbott**, comedian
- ★ **Charles Addams**, cartoonist
- ★ **Jason Alexander**, actor
- ★ **William "Count" Basie**, bandleader
- ★ **Joan Bennett**, actress
- ★ **Jon Bon Jovi**, musician
- ★ **William J. Brennan Jr.**, jurist
- ★ **Aaron Burr**, political leader
- ★ **Grover Cleveland**, U.S. president
- ★ **James Fenimore Cooper**, author
- ★ **Lou Costello**, comedian
- ★ **Stephen Crane**, author
- ★ **Allen Ginsberg**, poet
- ★ **Jerry Lewis**, comedian and actor
- ★ **Anne Morrow Lindbergh**, author and aviator
- ★ **Norman Mailer**, author
- ★ **Dorothy Parker**, author
- ★ **Paul Robeson**, singer and author
- ★ **Philip Roth**, author
- ★ **H. Norman Schwarzkopf**, general, U.S. Army
- ★ **Frank Sinatra**, singer and actor
- ★ **Bruce Springsteen**, musician
- ★ **Alfred Stieglitz**, photographer
- ★ **Meryl Streep**, actress
- ★ **William Carlos Williams**, physician and poet

Top to bottom: *Grover Cleveland, Stephen Crane, Meryl Streep*

New Jersey is a leading agricultural state. The Garden State grows flowers that are sold all over the country, dairy farms produce milk and cheese, while produce farms grow a variety of fruits and vegetables, such as apples, asparagus, lettuce, and sweet corn.

Thousands of tourists visit the resorts along New Jersey's Atlantic coastline every year. Atlantic City is the most famous of these resort towns, where casinos, hotels, stores, and restaurants flourish.

A family fishes along the New Jersey shore.

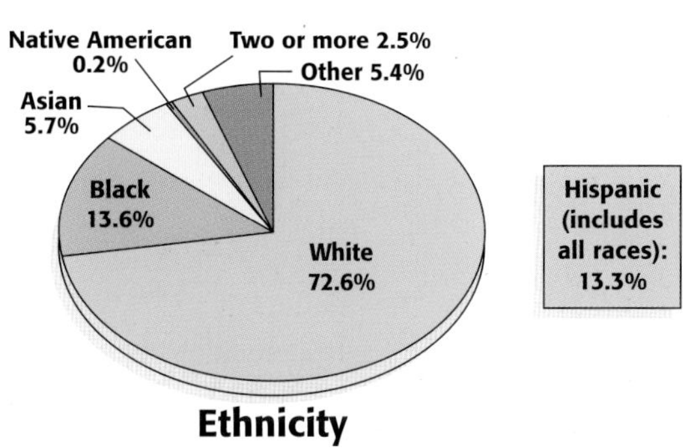

Ethnicity

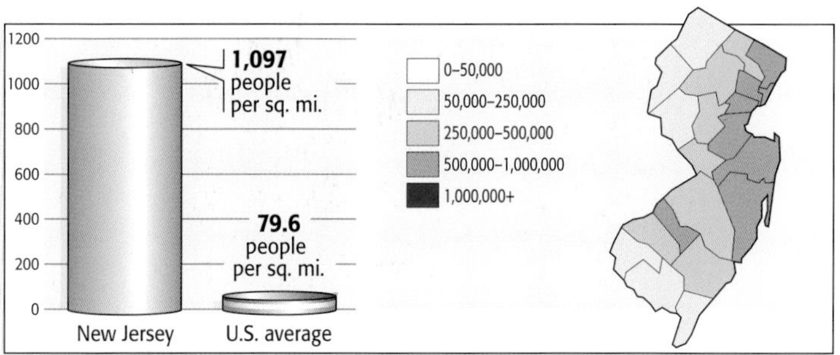

Population Density

Population by County

New Mexico

Crescit eundo (It grows as it goes).

Land area rank *Largest state (1)* — 5 — *smallest state (52)*

Population rank *Most people (1)* — 36 — *fewest people (52)*

At a Glance

Name: New Mexico was named after Mexico by Spanish explorers in the 16th century.

Nickname: Land of Enchantment

Capital: Santa Fe

Size: 121,598 sq. mi. (314,939 sq km)

Population: 1,819,046

Statehood: New Mexico became the 47th state on January 6, 1912.

Electoral votes: 5 (2004)

U.S. representatives: 3 (until 2003)

State tree: piñon

State flower: yucca

State animal: black bear

Highest point: Wheeler Peak, 13,161 ft. (4,011 m)

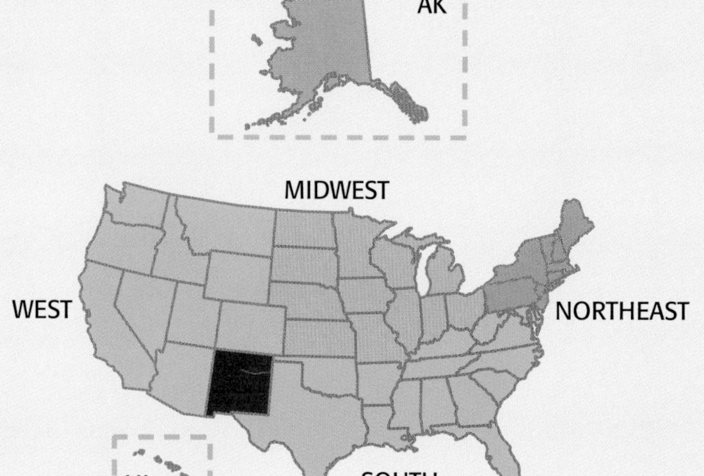

The Place

New Mexico, a southwestern state, is the fifth-largest state in area but is one of the least populated. The eastern third of New Mexico is part of the Great Plains, and irrigation has made parts of this area into good farmland. The Rocky Mountains extend through the middle of New Mexico.

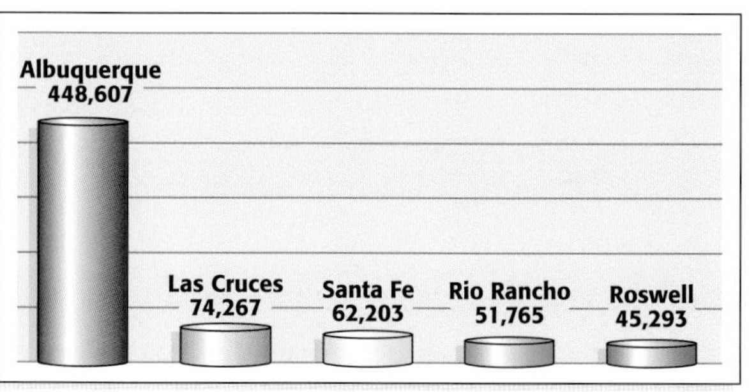

Major Cities

Eastern New Mexico is part of the Great Plains.

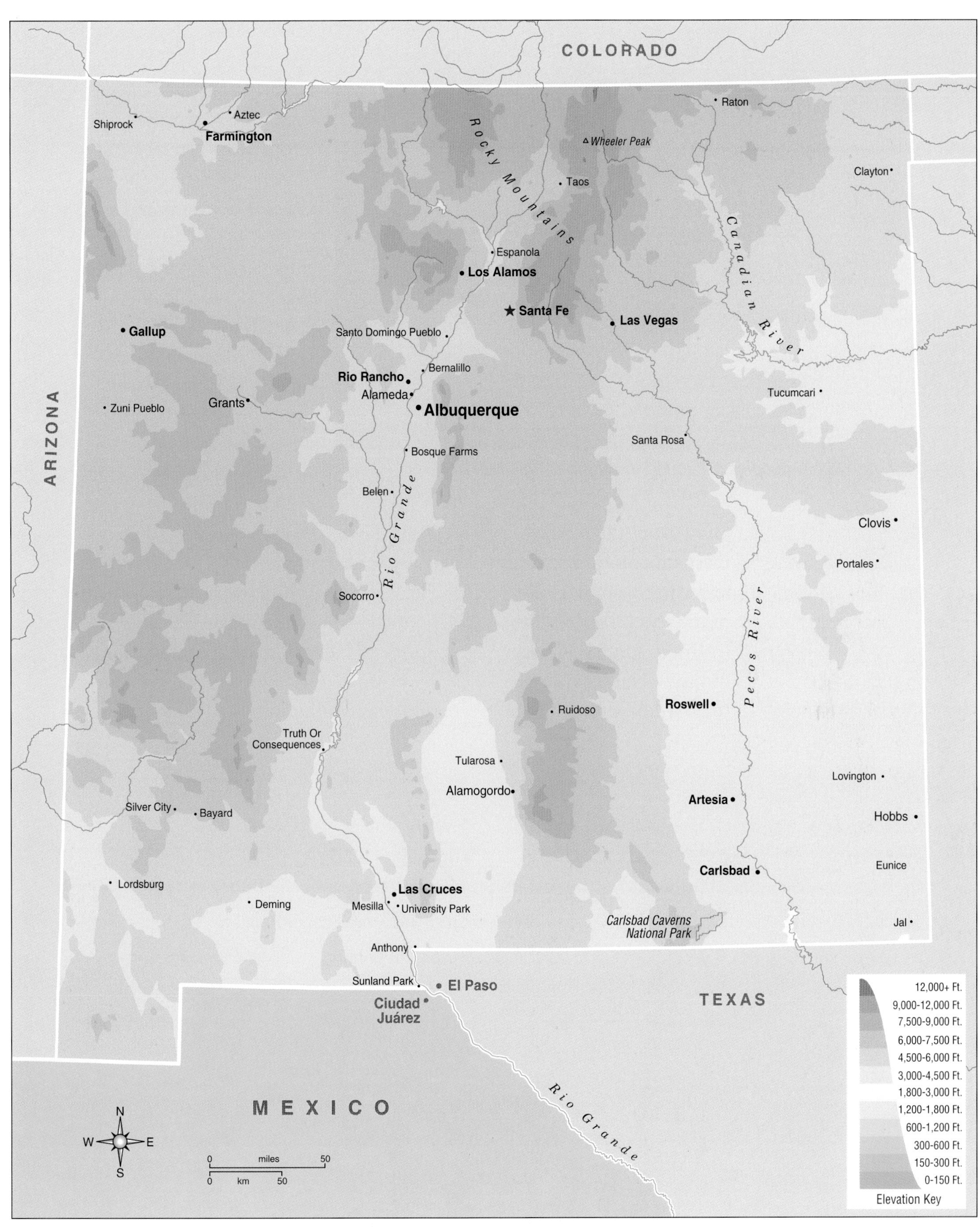
COLORADO
ARIZONA
TEXAS
MEXICO
Raton
Shiprock
Aztec
Farmington
Rocky Mountains
Wheeler Peak
Taos
Clayton
Canadian River
Espanola
Los Alamos
Santa Fe
Las Vegas
Gallup
Santo Domingo Pueblo
Bernalillo
Rio Rancho
Alameda
Albuquerque
Zuni Pueblo
Grants
Tucumcari
Santa Rosa
Bosque Farms
Belen
Rio Grande
Clovis
Portales
Socorro
Pecos River
Ruidoso
Roswell
Truth Or Consequences
Tularosa
Alamogordo
Lovington
Artesia
Silver City
Bayard
Hobbs
Eunice
Carlsbad
Lordsburg
Las Cruces
Deming
Mesilla
University Park
Carlsbad Caverns National Park
Jal
Anthony
Sunland Park
El Paso
Ciudad Juárez
N
W
E
S
0 miles 50
0 km 50
12,000+ Ft.
9,000-12,000 Ft.
7,500-9,000 Ft.
6,000-7,500 Ft.
4,500-6,000 Ft.
3,000-4,500 Ft.
1,800-3,000 Ft.
1,200-1,800 Ft.
600-1,200 Ft.
300-600 Ft.
150-300 Ft.
0-150 Ft.
Elevation Key

Ruins from the Pueblo peoples are found throughout New Mexico.

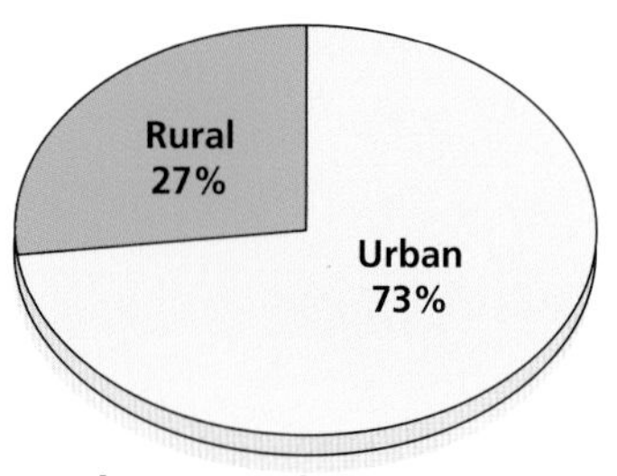

Urban/Rural Distribution

Snow from the tops of these mountains provides water for crop irrigation in the Rio Grande valley.

To the south and west of the Rockies, toward the borders with Arizona and Mexico, are more isolated mountain ranges. Desert basins lie between some of these mountains. The northwestern corner of New Mexico is the most unusual, with rugged valleys, plains, canyons, cliffs, and flat-topped hills called mesas. (*Mesa* is Spanish for "table.")

New Mexico has few lakes, but forests cover about one-fourth of the state. Desert plants, including cactus and sage, are common in the driest regions. New Mexico's climate is warm and dry, and the state receives less than 20 inches (51 cm) of rain or snow each year. The northern mountains receive the majority of New Mexico's precipitation.

New Mexico has plentiful deposits of oil, natural gas, and uranium.

Facts and Firsts

- ★ Santa Fe, at 7,000 feet (2,134 m) above sea level, is the highest capital city in the United States. Its Palace of Governors, built in 1610, is the oldest government building in the United States.
- ★ The Taos Pueblo, outside the city of Taos, has been occupied for more than 900 years.
- ★ In several small, isolated villages in north-central New Mexico, including Truchas, Chimayo, and Coyote, some residents still speak a form of 16th-century Spanish that is extinct in the rest of the world.
- ★ Three-quarters of New Mexico's roads are unpaved. The climate is so dry that these roads do not wash away.
- ★ New Mexico's state flower, the yucca, can be woven into rope, baskets, and sandals.
- ★ In 1945, the first atomic bomb, which was manufactured in Los Alamos, was tested at the White Sands Testing Site outside of Alamogordo.
- ★ More than one-third of New Mexican families speaks Spanish at home.

The Past

New Mexico has been the home of Native Americans for more than 10,000 years. One of the most advanced Native American groups, the Anasazi, built cliff dwellings that still stand today. One of these dwellings, the Pueblo Bonito, was an apartment building–like structure with between 600 and 700 rooms. Descendants of the Anasazi, the Pueblo, still live in New Mexico today.

The Spanish explored New Mexico in the 1530s after they had traveled from Florida to Mexico. Upon their return to Europe, they told stories of seven mythical cities made of gold that referred to New Mexico. The lure of riches attracted other explorers, and a Spanish colony was established near the Chama River in 1598. The Spanish imposed forced labor, taxation, and the Roman Catholic religion on the native peoples, who revolted and attacked the Spaniards.

In the 1700s, trappers from the American East made their way into New Mexico. They were friendly with the Mexican government, which took control of New Mexico in 1821. The United States won New Mexico from Mexico in 1848. In 1850, New Mexico became a U.S. territory. Fighting between the native peoples and Mexican and American settlers took place during this entire period.

Native American unrest lasted until 1886, when the Apache leader Geronimo surrendered to the United States. Fighting between the new settlers was common also, as outlaws such as Billy the Kid fought sheriffs like Pat Garrett, the sheriff of Lincoln County.

During the late 1800s, new railroads linked New Mexico with the rest of the country, and the territory enjoyed a mining and cattle boom. In 1912, New Mexico entered the Union as a state.

State Smart

The Kodak International Balloon Fiesta, held every October in Albuquerque, is the largest balloon festival in the world.

New Mexico became a possession of the United States after the Battle of Buena Vista led to the American victory in the war with Mexico in 1848.

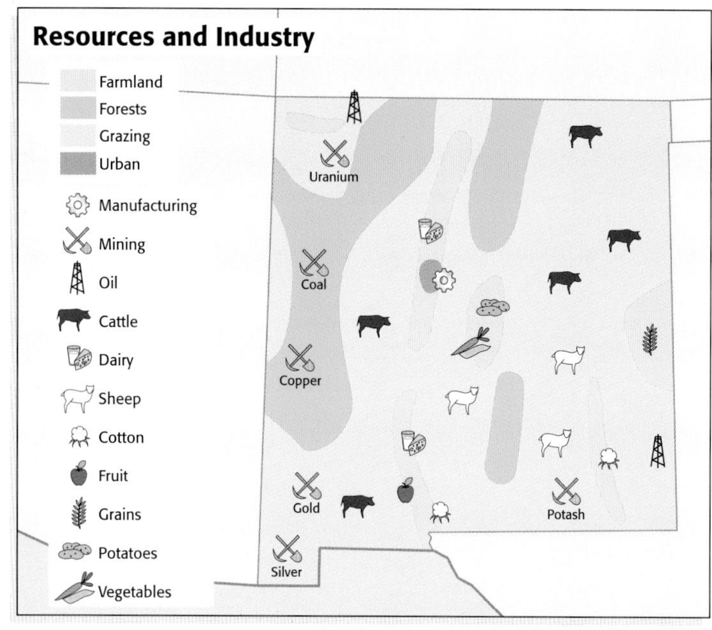

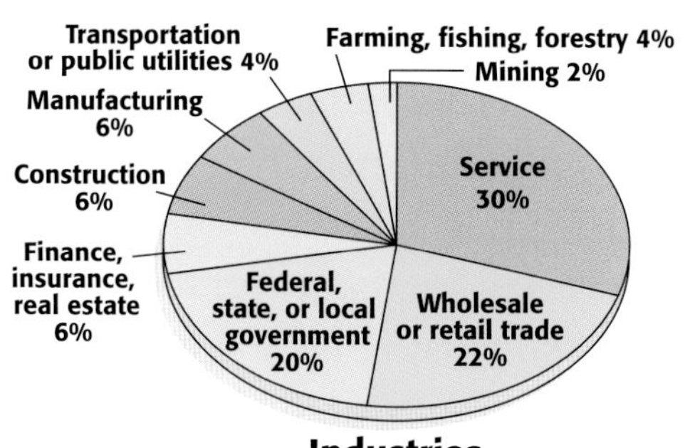

Cattle ranching was the most common occupation in the state until the 1920s, when oil was discovered. In 1930, the famous Carlsbad Caverns became the site of a national park, and brought tourists to the state.

New Mexico played an important role in World War II, when the first atomic bombs were built at Los Alamos, a nuclear science research center. Scientific research conducted at Los Alamos National Laboratory in the 1940s and 1950s led to growth in many of New Mexico's industries. Another boost to the economy came from the tourist industry, which grew during the 1960s and 1970s with the construction of winter sports resorts.

New Mexico's economy was hurt in the early 1990s when the U.S. government curtailed spending on military research, but growth in the tourism and manufacturing industries helped the state to recover.

Albuquerque is New Mexico's largest city.

Born in New Mexico

- ★ **John Denver**, singer and songwriter
- ★ **Conrad Hilton**, hotel executive
- ★ **Peter Hurd**, artist
- ★ **Maria Martinez**, artist
- ★ **Demi Moore**, actress
- ★ **Bill Mauldin**, political cartoonist
- ★ **Al Unser**, auto racer
- ★ **Linda Wertheimer**, radio journalist

Maria Martinez

The Present

Today, scientists at Los Alamos continue to conduct research, but their studies are now on nuclear energy. Nuclear weapons research is performed at Sandia National Laboratory in Albuquerque. Large plants located near Albuquerque produce military communications equipment and computer chips.

Mining and manufacturing are other key industries in New Mexico. Mines bring millions of gallons of oil and natural gas from the ground. Companies in the state produce chemicals, clothing, petroleum products, and primary metals.

Cattle ranching continues to be New Mexico's most important agricultural activity. Farms, which occupy about 55 percent of New Mexico's land, grow hay, chili peppers, pecans, cotton, onions, and wheat.

New Mexico, with its rich, colorful history, unique scenery, and winter sports, attracts thousands of tourists every year. As more people are attracted to the state because of its warm, dry climate, New Mexico has become one of the country's fastest-growing states.

Pueblo woman and child

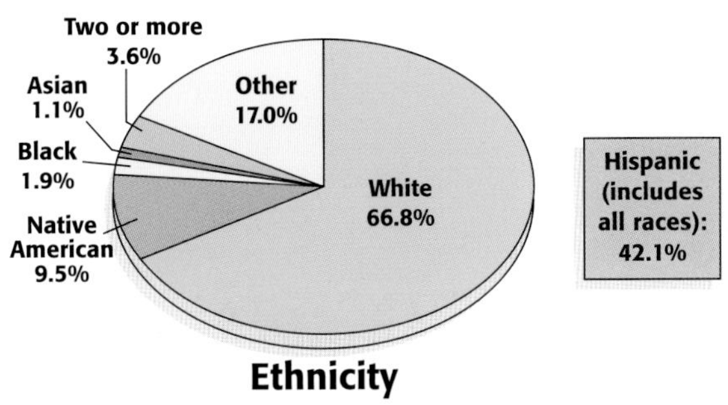

Ethnicity

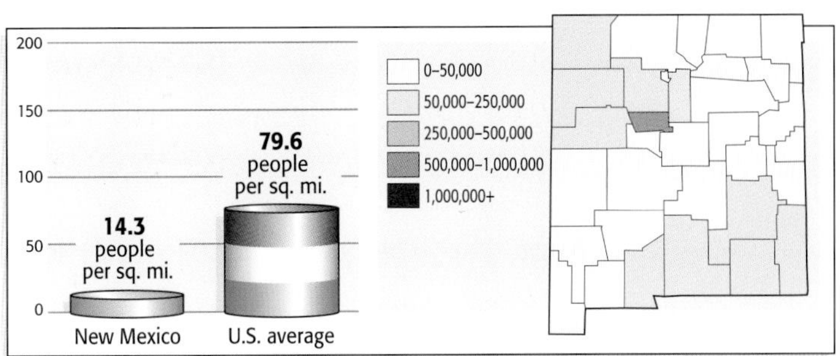

Population Density

Population by County

New York

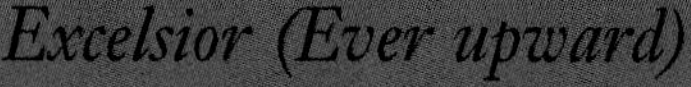

Excelsior (Ever upward).

Land area rank *Largest state (1)* — 30 — *smallest state (52)*

Population rank *Most people (1)* — 3 — *fewest people (52)*

At a Glance

Name: New York was named in honor of England's Duke of York.

Nickname: Empire State

Capital: Albany

Size: 49,112 sq. mi. (127,200 sq km)

Population: 18,976,457

Statehood: New York became the 11th state on July 26, 1788.

Electoral votes: 31 (2004)

U.S. representatives: 31 (beginning in 2003)

State tree: sugar maple

State flower: rose

State animal: beaver

Highest point: Mount Marcy, 5,344 ft. (1,629 m)

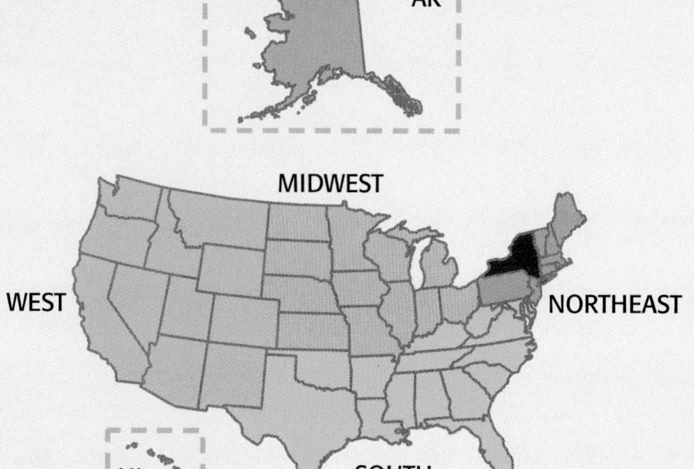

The Place

New York is one of the Northeast states. More than 11,500 years ago, New York was covered by a sheet of ice that was up to two miles (3.2 km) thick. This sheet of ice rounded off New York's mountains, deepened its valleys, and left a layer of rich soil in some parts of the state.

The eastern part of New York is a region of rounded hills and forests. There are some high peaks, which are extensions of the Berkshire Mountains in Massachusetts. The Hudson River cuts through this part

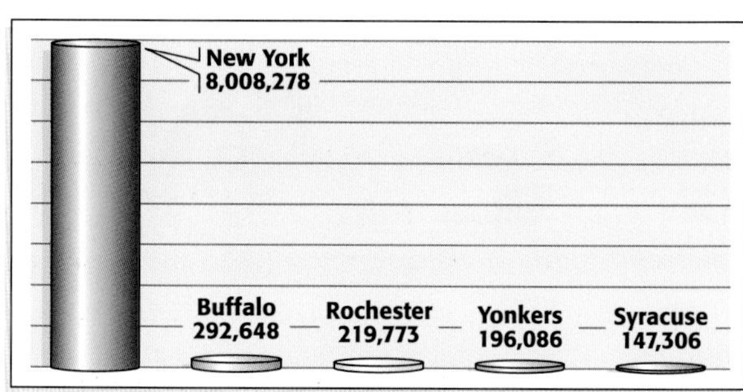

Major Cities

New York City is a major U.S. metropolis.

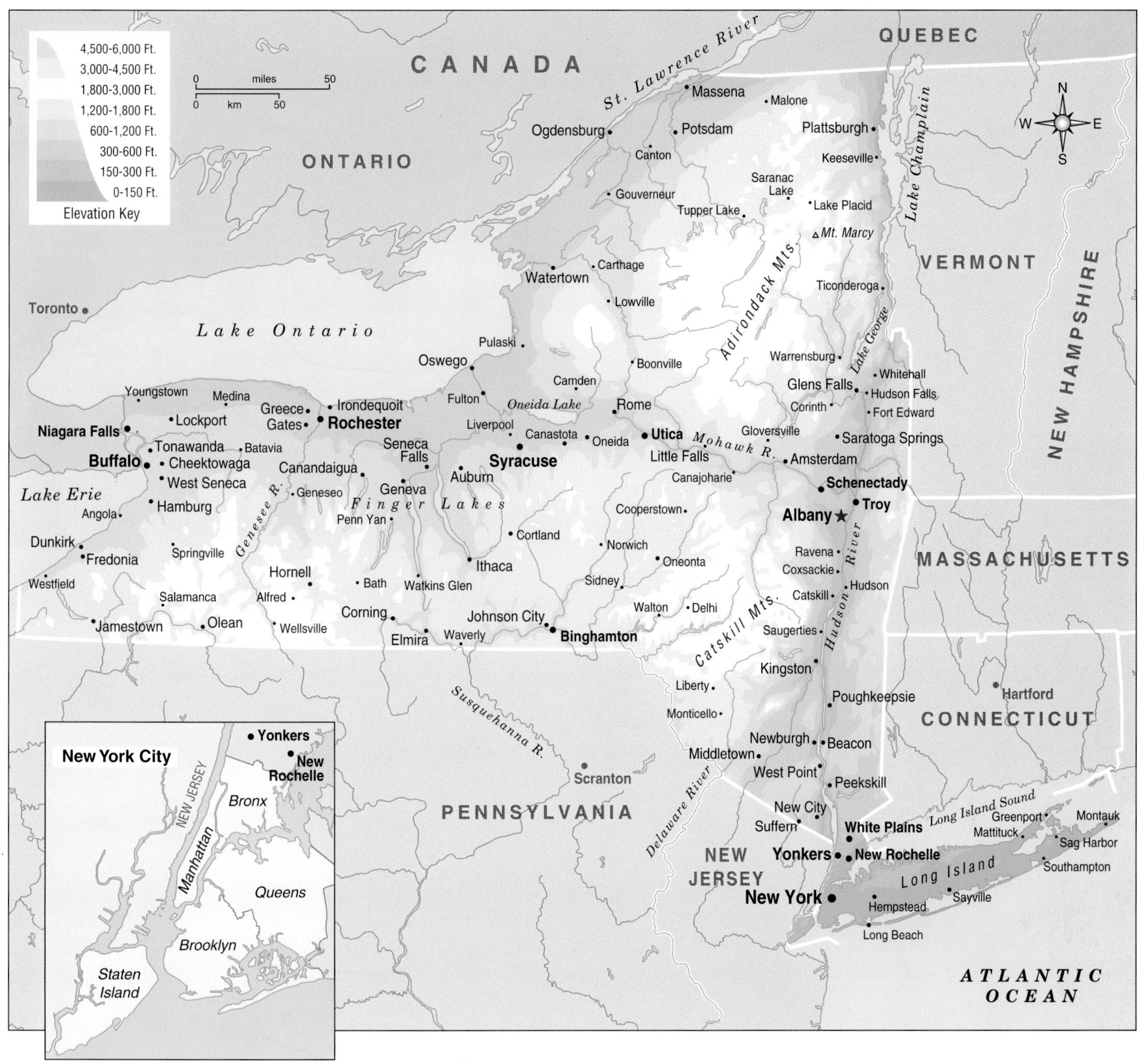

of the state from north to south, and in its valley is some of the most fertile land in New York. Northern New York is home to the St. Lawrence River, which forms part of the United States' boundary with Canada.

To the northeast is the Adirondack Upland, a rocky, mountainous region with many streams, waterfalls, and lakes, such as Lake Champlain and Lake Placid. In the Appalachian Plateau, Ice Age glaciers deepened the valleys that eventually filled with water and became the Finger Lakes region.

In the south and east of this plateau are the Catskill Mountains. Northwestern New York is the site of the famous Niagara Falls, which is on the New York–Canada border between Lakes Erie and Ontario. In the southern part of the state is Long Island, a long, low island that is part of the Atlantic Coastal Plain.

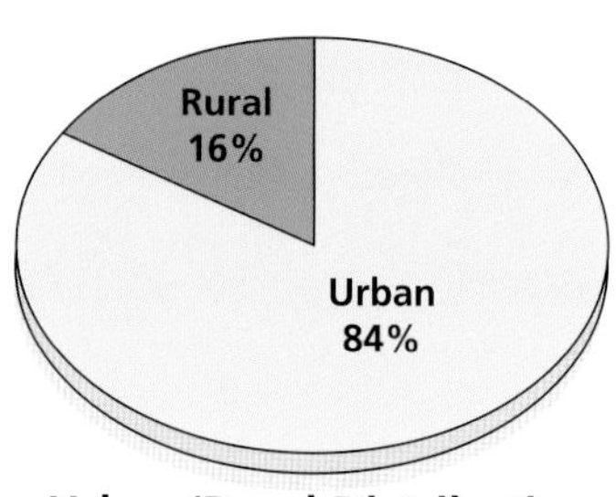

Urban/Rural Distribution

Temperatures vary among the different parts of New York. The weather is much cooler to the north, in the Adirondack Mountains, than to the south, on Long Island. The Adirondacks also receive more snow than the south, but the snowiest part of New York is the region around the Great Lakes. In this area, moisture from the water brings heavy winter snowfall to cities like Syracuse, Rochester, and Buffalo.

Mineral resources are varied throughout the state. New York contains lead, talc, zinc, garnet stone, clay, salt, and petroleum deposits.

The Past

New York was home to the two largest Native American groups, the Algonquian and Iroquois, when explorer Henry Hudson claimed the region for the Netherlands in 1609. Looking for a water route to Asia, Hudson explored the areas of both New York and New Jersey. Dutch settlers soon arrived and they called their new territory New Netherland. They traded fur, built farms, and established the city of New Amsterdam, which became New York City. Also in 1609, explorer Samuel de Champlain claimed the northern part of New York for France.

New Amsterdam, now New York City, was founded by the Dutch in the early 1600s.

In 1664, English king Charles II decided that he wanted New Netherland, so he sent

Facts and Firsts

- ★ New York City has more than 230 miles (370 km) of subway track.
- ★ Adirondack Park is bigger than Yellowstone, Yosemite, Grand Canyon, Glacier, and Olympic parks combined.
- ★ Milk is New York's leading agricultural product. There are more than 18,000 cattle farms in the state.
- ★ New York City was the first capital of the United States. President George Washington took his oath of office on the balcony of Federal Hall in 1789.
- ★ The *New York Post*, started by Alexander Hamilton in 1803, is one of the oldest-running newspapers in the country.
- ★ New York had the first railroad in the United States. The Mohawk and Hudson Railroad began running for 11 miles between Albany and Schenectady in 1831.
- ★ Gennaro Lombardi opened the country's first pizzeria in 1905 in New York City.

troops to New Amsterdam, where the Dutch surrendered without a fight. England won northern New York from the French at the end of the French and Indian Wars in 1763, and New York became one of 13 British colonies. The English renamed the colony for the Duke of York, the king's brother.

New Yorkers and other colonists began to resent English policies, and the American Revolution began in 1775. New York's central location along the Hudson River made it an important strategic point, and about a third of all the battles fought during the Revolution took place in the area.

From 1785 to 1790, New York City was the capital of the United States. New York, which entered the Union in 1788, was settled rapidly. By 1810, it was the most populous state. (It remained so until the 1960s, when California's population surpassed it.)

During the early 1800s, a need grew for better transportation between the state's coastal region and its interior. Work began on a series of railroads and canals, including the Erie Canal.

During the Civil War, New York provided more troops, supplies, and money to the Northern cause than any other state, despite the pro-Southern views of many residents. After the war, domestic and international trade expanded, and New York quickly became the industrial, financial, and cultural capital of the nation.

By the turn of the 20th century, job-seeking immigrants from all over the world were pouring into New York City, which caused the city's population to explode. The Great Depression of the 1930s brought hardship and unemployment, but New York's industrial cities rallied during World War II to supply the materials needed for the war effort in Europe.

State Smart

The Verrazano-Narrows Bridge, which connects Brooklyn with Staten Island, has the longest single-suspension span of all bridges in the United States. Its main span is 4,260 feet (1,298 m) and is suspended 230 feet (70 m) above New York Harbor.

In 1946, the United Nations chose New York City as its home. The Lincoln Center for the Performing Arts opened in the 1960s and began to showcase some of the nation's greatest cultural achievements.

During the 1970s, a loss of manufacturing jobs hurt the state's economy, and financial problems were particularly acute in New York City. Recovery was aided by growth in the service industries. Present-day challenges for New York include the need to address environmental problems such as industrial

New York City's population exploded with immigrants at the turn of the 20th century.

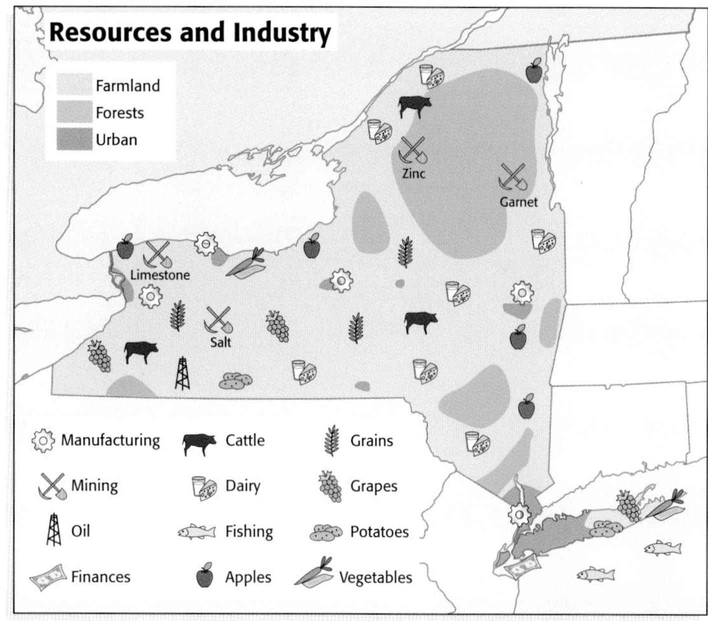

toxic waste, and social problems including drug abuse, crime, and an expanding prison population.

The Present

New York City is the financial, banking, publishing, fashion, and communications center of the United States. It is the city with the largest population in the United States, and one of the largest cities in the world. Almost a million tourists visit New York City every day.

Manhattan is home to cultural staples

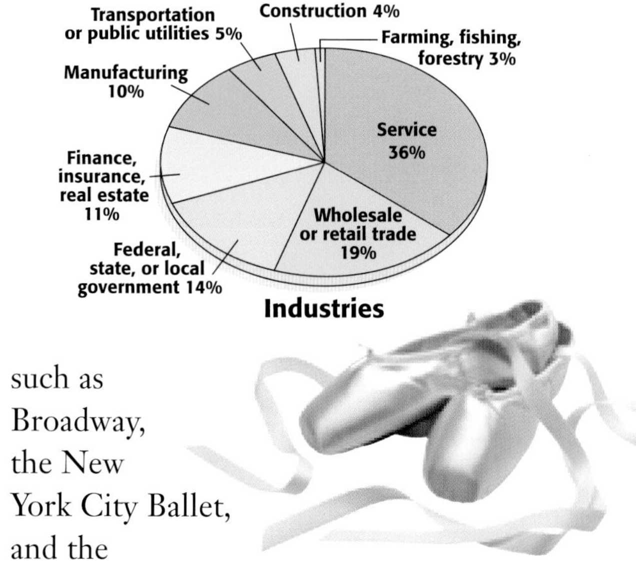

such as Broadway, the New York City Ballet, and the Metropolitan Museum of Art. The New York Stock Exchange is the largest securities exchange in the world. Property values in Manhattan are some of the highest in the world.

New York is, however, more than just New York City. There are more than 25,000 industrial plants throughout the state. Cities such as Rochester, Buffalo, and Albany are vital manufacturing centers and produce computers, heating and cooling machinery, and scientific and medical equipment.

New York also has nearly 36,000 farms and is one of the leading dairy states. Eggs and poultry, hay, and corn are also important

Below left: *Niagara Falls is a world-famous landmark.* Below right: *Cross-country skiers enjoy the Adirondack region.*

Born in New York

- ★ **Kareem Abdul-Jabbar**, athlete
- ★ **Woody Allen**, director and actor
- ★ **Lucille Ball**, actress and comedian
- ★ **Humphrey Bogart**, actor
- ★ **James Cagney**, actor
- ★ **Maria Callas**, soprano
- ★ **Aaron Copland**, composer
- ★ **George Eastman**, inventor
- ★ **Millard Fillmore**, U.S. president
- ★ **Lou Gehrig**, baseball player
- ★ **George Gershwin**, composer
- ★ **Julia Ward Howe**, poet and reformer
- ★ **Washington Irving**, author
- ★ **Henry James**, author
- ★ **Michael Jordan**, basketball player
- ★ **Julius "Groucho" Marx**, comedian
- ★ **Herman Melville**, author
- ★ **Ethel Merman**, singer and actress
- ★ **J. Pierpont Morgan Jr.**, industrialist
- ★ **Ogden Nash**, poet
- ★ **Eugene O'Neill**, playwright
- ★ **Colin Powell**, general, U.S. Army
- ★ **Anne Frances "Nancy" Reagan**, first lady
- ★ **John D. Rockefeller**, industrialist
- ★ **Norman Rockwell**, painter and illustrator
- ★ **(Anna) Eleanor Roosevelt**, first lady, humanitarian
- ★ **Franklin D. Roosevelt**, U.S. president
- ★ **Theodore Roosevelt**, U.S. president
- ★ **Jonas Salk**, polio researcher
- ★ **Margaret Sanger**, women's rights activist
- ★ **Jerry Seinfeld**, actor and comedian
- ★ **Elizabeth Cady Stanton**, women's rights activist
- ★ **Barbra Streisand**, singer and actress
- ★ **Martin Van Buren**, U.S. president
- ★ **Mae West**, actress
- ★ **Edith Wharton**, author
- ★ **Walt Whitman**, poet

Top to bottom: *Lou Gehrig, Lucille Ball, Colin Powell, Michael Jordan*

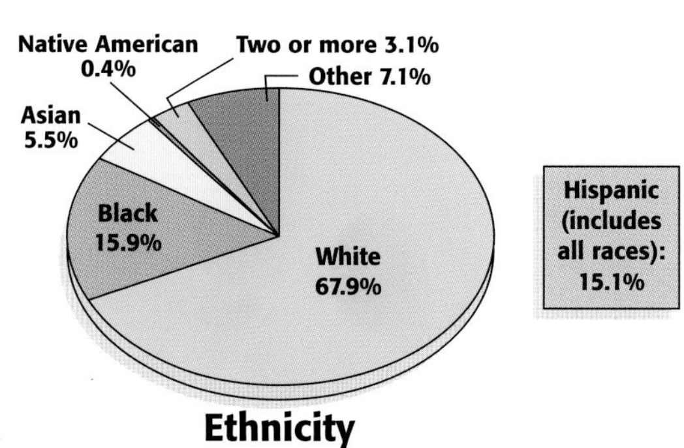

Ethnicity

farm products. Apples are the state's leading fruit crop. New York's commercial fishing industry, especially in Long Island Sound, supplies huge amounts of shellfish—mostly clams, lobsters, oysters—as well as flounder, sea trout, and striped bass.

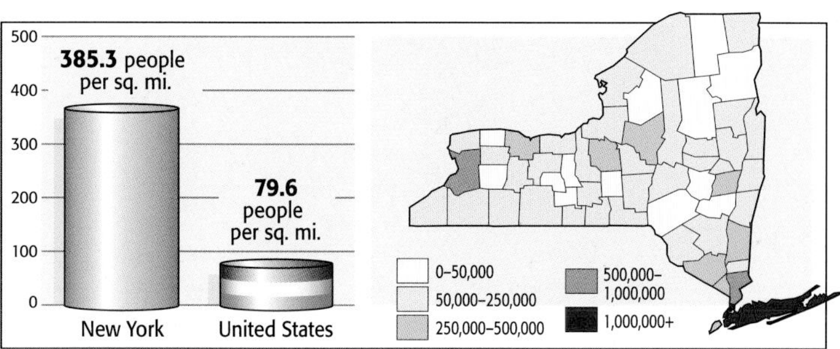

Population Density **Population by County**

North Carolina

Esse quam videri (To be, rather than to seem).

Land area rank *Largest state (1)* — 28 — *smallest state (52)*

Population rank *Most people (1)* — 11 — *fewest people (52)*

At a Glance

Name: North Carolina was named after King Charles I of England. (The Latin word for the name *Charles* is *Carolana*.)

Nicknames: Tar Heel State, Old North State

Capital: Raleigh

Size: 52,672 sq. mi. (136,421 sq km)

Population: 8,049,313

Statehood: North Carolina became the 12th state on November 21, 1789.

Electoral votes: 15 (2004)

U.S. representatives: 13 (2003)

State tree: longleaf pine

State flower: flowering dogwood

State reptile: box turtle

Highest point: Mount Mitchell, 6,684 ft. (2,037 m)

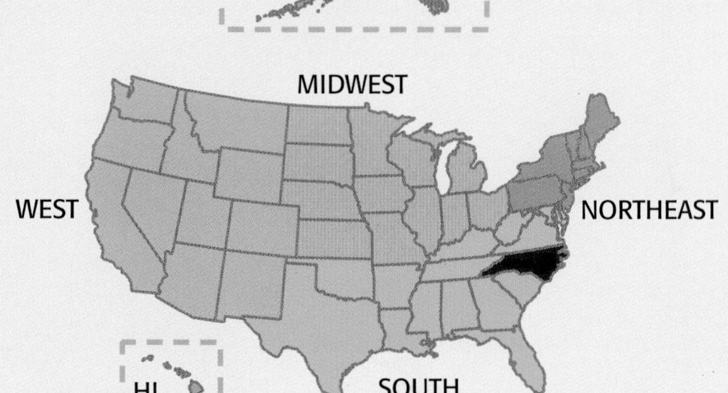

The Place

North Carolina is one of the southern states along the Atlantic Ocean. Its land along the coast is low and marshy. One of the largest marshes in this part of North Carolina is the Dismal Swamp in the northeastern part of the state.

The Outer Banks of North Carolina jut out into the Atlantic Ocean and form Cape Fear, Cape Lookout, and Cape Hatteras.

Cape Hatteras is part of the Outer Banks along the Atlantic Ocean.

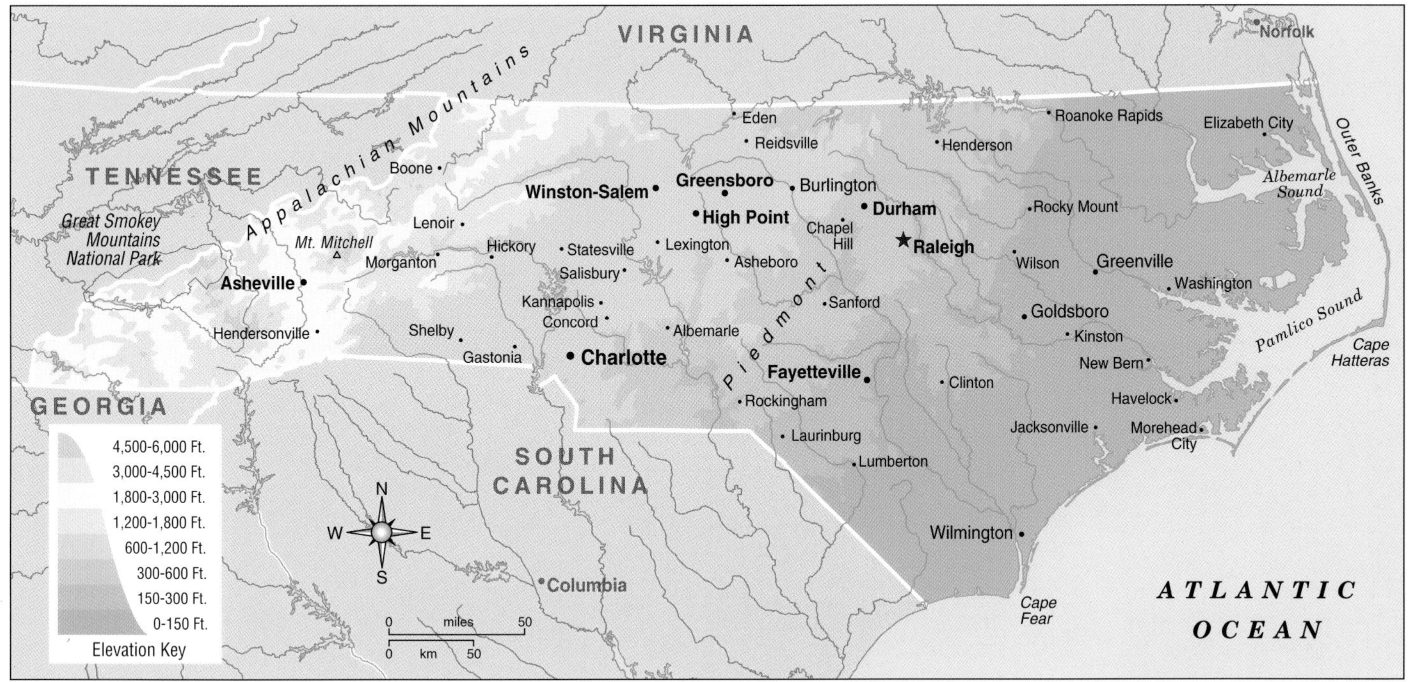

The Outer Banks are shifting sandbars and have caused many shipwrecks. Hurricanes and tropical storms are common along the Outer Banks.

The Piedmont, the rocky middle section of North Carolina, slopes upward from the east until it meets the mountainous region of western North Carolina. The largest mountains in this part of the state are in the Blue Ridge range; there are also smaller ranges that are part of the Appalachian Mountains in western North Carolina. Southwestern North Carolina has many beautiful waterfalls, including Whitewater Falls, which is one of the tallest in the eastern United States.

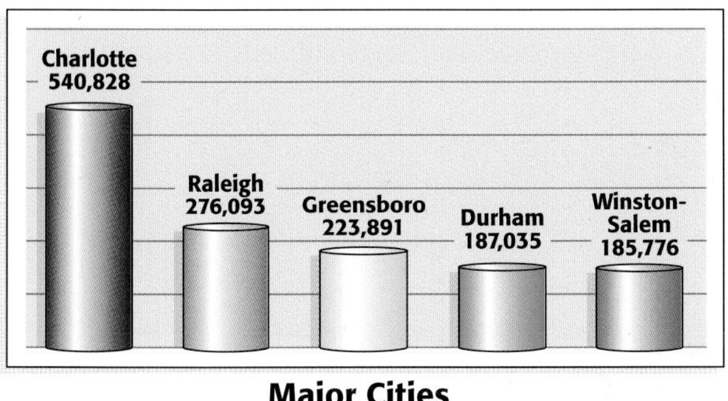

Major Cities

North Carolina's climate varies greatly throughout its regions. Summers are hot and humid and winters are mild in southeastern North Carolina, but winters are considerably colder in the western mountains. The mountains also receive more rain and snow.

North Carolina's greatest resources are its soil, which is most fertile in the central and western coastal plain, and its minerals. North Carolina has deposits of more than 300 different minerals and rocks, including feldspar, gneiss, sand, gravel, clay, limestone, granite, phosphate rock, and lithium.

The Past

North Carolina was once home to Cherokee, Hatteras, Catawba, Chowanoc, and Tuscarora tribes, but it is most famous as the site of the first English colony. Although the French and Spanish explored various parts of North Carolina, it was the British who began a colony at Roanoke Island in 1585. This first colony experienced

The Native American Secotan people, whose village in North Carolina is shown in a 16th-century illustration, knew the colonists on Roanoke Island.

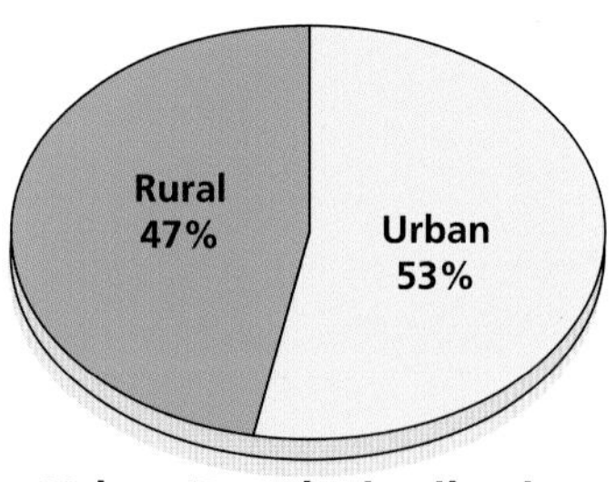

problems, and settlers were forced to return to England the next year. Another settlement was tried again in 1587, but when Governor John White arrived from England in 1590, he found that the whole colony (more than 100 people) had disappeared. The fate of the "Lost Colony" is still a mystery.

Colonists from Virginia started the first permanent settlement in North Carolina in 1650. By 1710, settlements had spread south along the coast. In 1711, Native Americans who resented the theft of their lands attacked several settlements, where they burned homes and crops and killed settlers. In 1713, the colonists defeated the native tribes.

In April 1776, North Carolina became the first colony to vote for independence at the Continental Congress. During the

Facts and Firsts

★ Roanoke Island, off the coast of North Carolina, was the site of the first English colony in the United States. It was established in 1585. The colony was unsuccessful, and a second colony established in 1587 vanished without a trace.

★ In 1898, pharmacist Caleb Bradham of New Bern invented the soft drink Pepsi, which was trademarked in 1903.

★ Near Kitty Hawk on December 17, 1903, Orville and Wilbur Wright made the first successful airplane flight.

★ In 1916, Pinehurst became the site of the first miniature golf course.

★ The Venus flytrap plant grows in select boggy areas in North Carolina.

★ North Carolina grows more tobacco and sweet potatoes and raises more turkeys than any other state. It also leads the country in furniture, brick, and textile manufacturing.

The University of North Carolina at Chapel Hill

Revolutionary War, North Carolina sent soldiers to fight the British in South Carolina, Virginia, and Georgia.

During the 1830s, the western region of the state was settled, and manufacturing and mining expanded. The agriculture industry also grew as many plantations were established that produced tobacco and other crops.

When the Civil War began in 1861, North Carolina was reluctant to fight. Although the state remained part of the Union at first, North Carolina eventually seceded with the other Southern states. During the Civil War, about one-fourth of all Confederate soldiers killed were from North Carolina.

Before the Civil War, North Carolina's plantations had relied heavily on slave labor. After the war ended, plantations were quickly divided into smaller farms, and soon North Carolina was growing tobacco and cotton at rates equal to before the war. Industry also grew, as manufacturers turned out textiles and furniture.

State Smart

In 1795, the University of North Carolina at Chapel Hill became the first state-supported university in the United States.

The Great Depression brought hard times, and many workers in North Carolina lost their jobs as farms and businesses failed. World War II, however, brought economic recovery as North Carolina's textile mills supplied the military forces with more textiles than any other state. During the 1950s, North Carolina began to attract other industries and continued its shift from a rural, agricultural society to a more urban economy. In 1956, three of North Carolina's largest universities combined their research resources to form the Research Triangle Park, a renowned industrial research center.

Orville and Wilbur Wright made the first successful airplane flights at Kitty Hawk, North Carolina, in 1903.

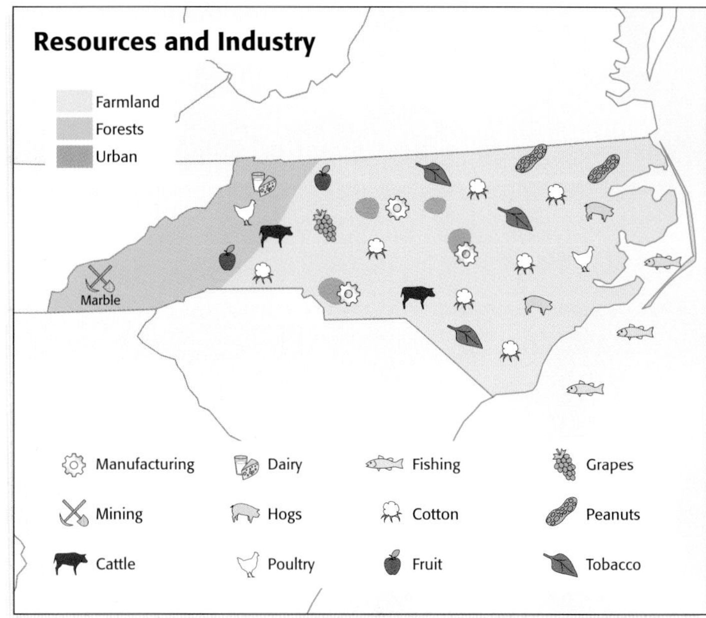

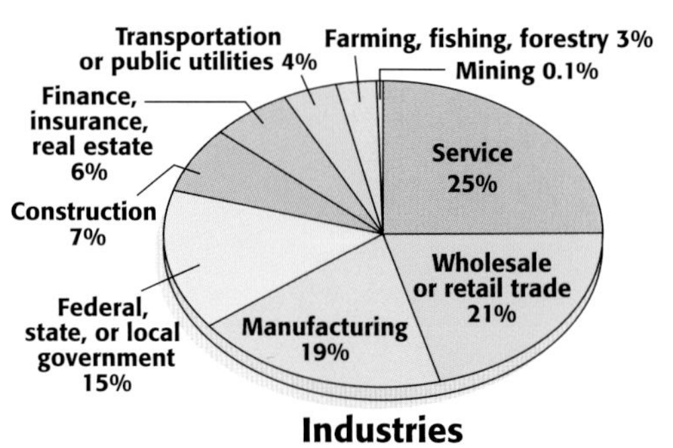

In the 1960s, the practice of segregation (separation of whites and blacks) caused racial tension in North Carolina and throughout the rest of the South. Demonstrations and protests eventually led to the passage of civil rights laws that prohibited the segregation of public facilities. During the 1970s, North Carolina school districts began to use busing to achieve racial integration.

THE PRESENT

North Carolina is the largest producer of tobacco and tobacco products, textiles, and furniture in the United States. Textile factories in North Carolina make about half of the nation's hosiery. North Carolina's newer products include chemicals and pharmaceuticals, computers, construction equipment, and electrical equipment. Charlotte has become a leading financial center and home to some of the nation's largest banks.

North Carolina also produces various agricultural products. Although tobacco continues to be its primary crop, North Carolina also grows soybeans, corn, and many other fruits and vegetables. North

Below left: *Four college students in Greensboro, North Carolina, protested segregation, in 1960, by holding a sit-in at a luncheon counter where only whites were served.* Below right: *Furniture-making is a big North Carolina industry.*

Born in North Carolina

- ★ **David Brinkley**, newscaster
- ★ **John Coltrane**, jazz musician
- ★ **Virginia Dare**, first person born in America to English parents
- ★ **Elizabeth "Liddy" Dole**, politician
- ★ **Ava Gardner**, actress
- ★ **Richard Gatling**, inventor
- ★ **Andy Griffith**, actor
- ★ **O. Henry (William Sidney Porter)**, author
- ★ **Andrew Johnson**, U.S. president
- ★ **Charles Kuralt**, television journalist and author
- ★ **Ray Charles "Sugar Ray" Leonard**, boxer
- ★ **Dolley Madison**, first lady
- ★ **Thelonious Monk**, pianist
- ★ **Edward R. Murrow**, commentator and government official
- ★ **James K. Polk**, U.S. president
- ★ **Thomas Wolfe**, author

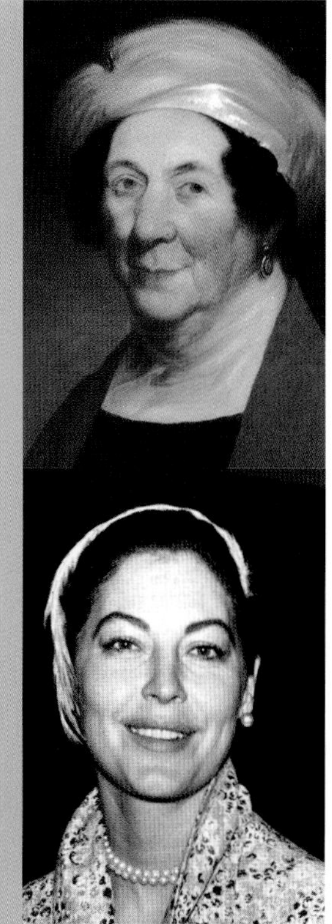

Above: *Dolley Madison;* below: *Ava Gardner*

Carolina is also one of the leading producers of peanuts and sweet potatoes.

Fishing off the Atlantic coast is another important industry and brings in millions of dollars every year. North Carolina's aquaculture industry raises catfish, crayfish, and trout in artificial ponds and streams.

Many of the nation's largest banks have headquarters in Charlotte.

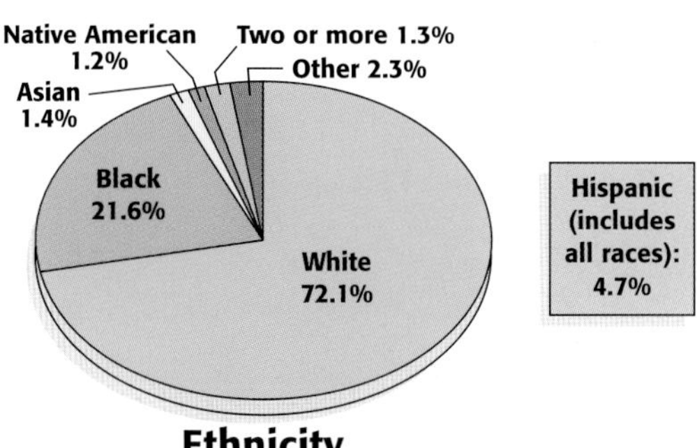

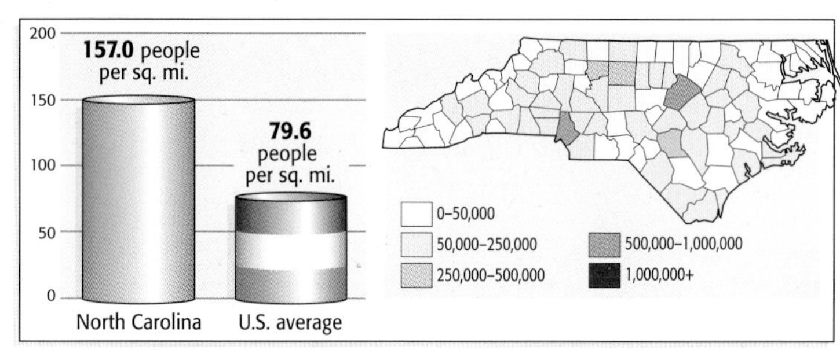

North Dakota

Liberty and union, now and forever, one and inseparable.

Land area rank *Largest state (1)* — 17 — *smallest state (52)*

Population rank *Most people (1)* — 47 — *fewest people (52)*

At a Glance

Name: *Dakota* is a Sioux word that means "friends" or "allies."

Nicknames: Sioux State, Flickertail State, Peace Garden State, Rough Rider State

Capital: Bismarck

Size: 70,704 sq. mi. (13,123 sq km)

Population: 642,200

Statehood: North Dakota became the 39th state on November 2, 1889.

Electoral votes: 3 (2004)

U.S. representatives: 1 (until 2003)

State tree: American elm

State flower: wild prairie rose

State fish: northern pike

Highest point: White Butte, 3,506 ft. (1,069 m)

The Place

North Dakota is an agricultural state in the Midwest. It is located in the geographic center of North America and borders Canada. The fertile Red River Valley, which lies in the bed of an ancient glacial lake, Lake Agassiz, is located in the eastern part of the state along the Minnesota border.

The Missouri River at Bismarck

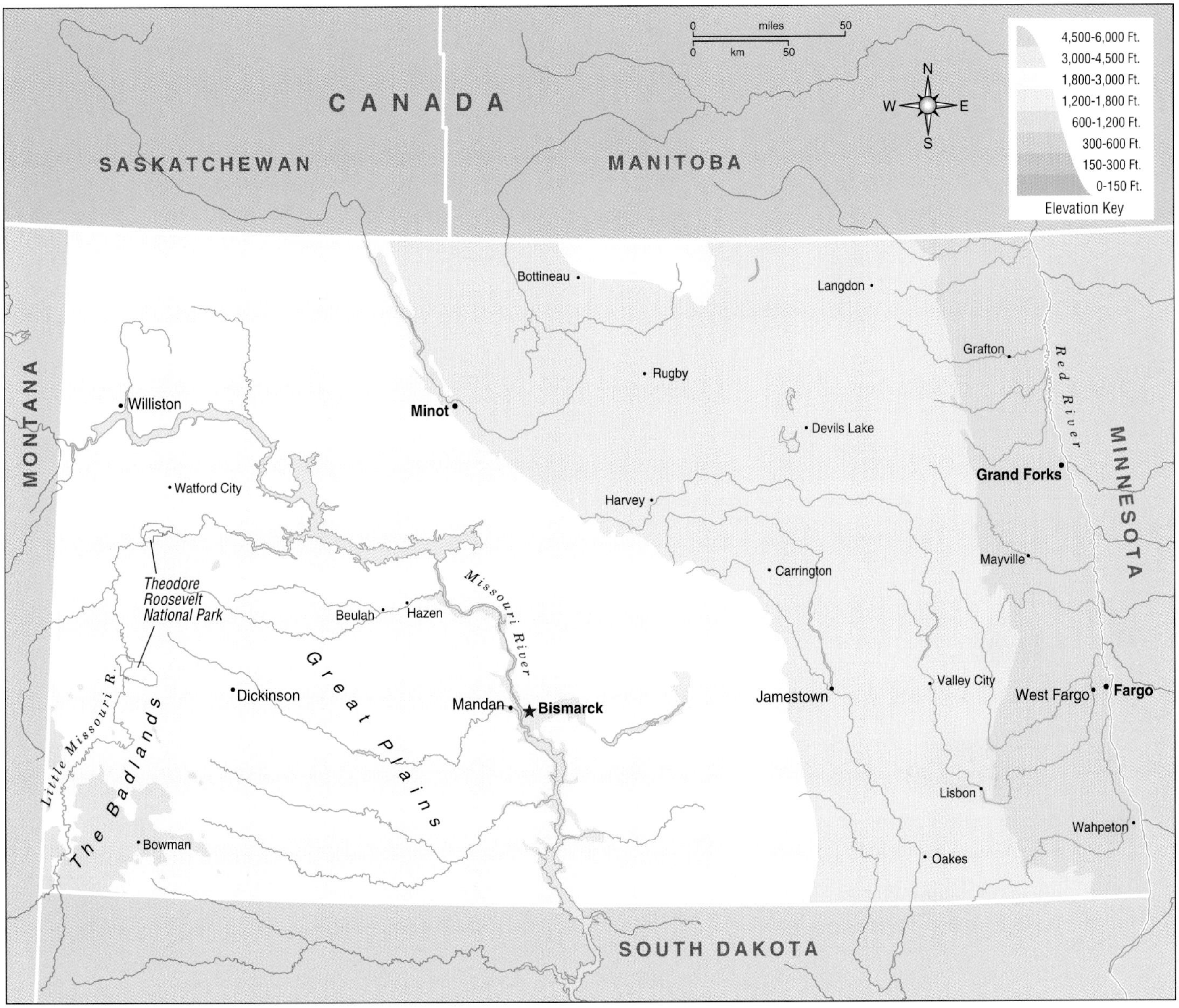

A large plain, flattened and carved by glaciers 11,500 years ago, is located in the west. Southwestern North Dakota is part of the Great Plains region that extends from Canada to Texas. This hilly highland area is primarily used for grazing cattle.

North Dakota's most prominent rivers are the Missouri and the Red Rivers. The Badlands region of the Little Missouri River is located in southwestern North Dakota. This 190-mile (306-km) -long stretch of land is a sandstone, shale, and clay valley carved out by the movement of water and wind. Buttes, domes, pyramids, and other natural formations rise from the floor of the valley.

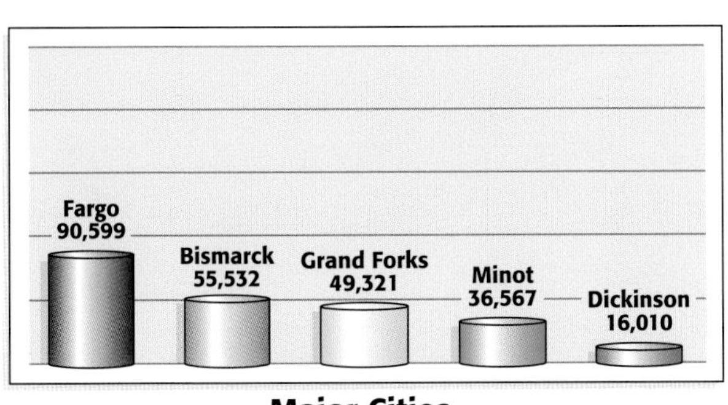

Major Cities

The Mandan, members of the Sioux family, lived in earthen homes like this one in North Dakota.

The climate of North Dakota is warm, dry, and pleasant in the summer but can be snowy and harsh in the winter. The southeast region of the state receives the most rain and snow, while the western region receives the least.

Western North Dakota has large deposits of petroleum and one of the largest beds of lignite coal in the world. North Dakota also has large amounts of sand and clay.

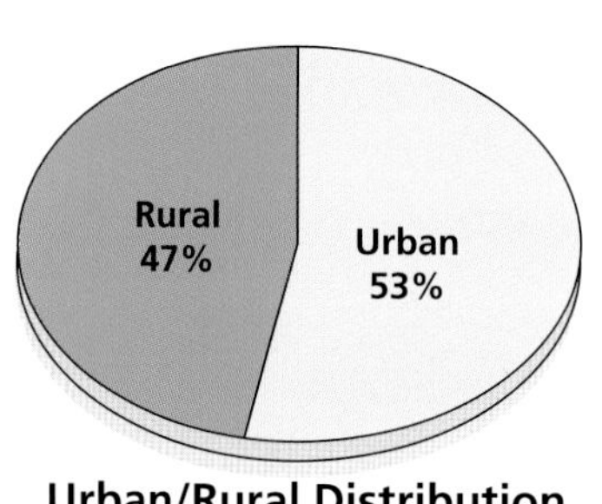

Urban/Rural Distribution

The Past

North Dakota was once the home of legendary Native American leaders Sitting Bull and Gall. North Dakota was first claimed by France (as part of its Canadian land) and later by Spain. Like much of the Midwest, North Dakota was reclaimed by the French in 1800. The United States bought most of the area from France in 1803 as part of the Louisiana Purchase, then acquired the rest of North Dakota from England in 1818.

At that time, the area was sparsely populated and had very few European settlers. In 1863, the U.S government opened the Dakota Territory to homesteading, and settlers were given free land in the territory if they agreed to farm it. Angry Sioux tribes started to attack settlers' villages. These attacks did not end until 1881, when Sioux leader Sitting Bull voluntarily surrendered to the U.S. Army.

Facts and Firsts

- ★ The geographic center of North America is near Rugby.
- ★ Milk is the official beverage of North Dakota.
- ★ The largest state-owned sheep research center in the United States is at North Dakota State University's research station in Hettinger.
- ★ More sunflowers are grown in North Dakota than in any other state.

Sitting Bull

Several families from the East bought huge farms and became rich on the profits they made from growing wheat. Soon, other settlers came to try to profit from farming. Transportation in the region improved with the construction of railroads, and more people were able to travel to North Dakota to settle the land.

In 1889, North Dakota was admitted into the Union. North Dakota's population expanded rapidly after statehood. Farming continued to grow until the Great Depression of the 1930s, when low food prices hurt North Dakota's agricultural economy. The economy recovered during World War II, however, when North Dakota farms supplied the U.S. military with food.

During the late 1940s, low food prices and advances in machinery left many farm workers jobless. Some people moved to cities to find work, which increased North Dakota's urban population.

State Smart

North Dakota has the world's largest cow statue, Salem Sue, which stands more than 38 feet (11.6 m) high. North Dakota also has the world's largest buffalo statue, which weighs 60 tons.

Salem Sue, standing in New Salem, is the largest statue of a cow in the world.

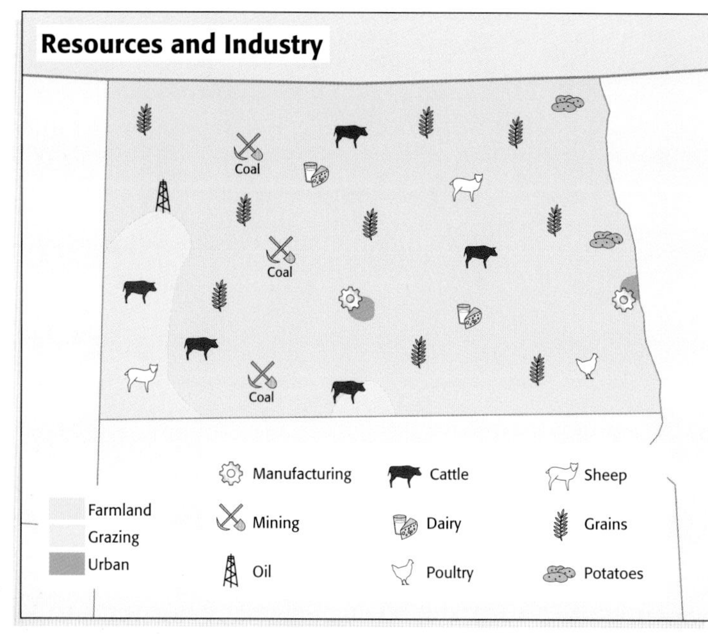

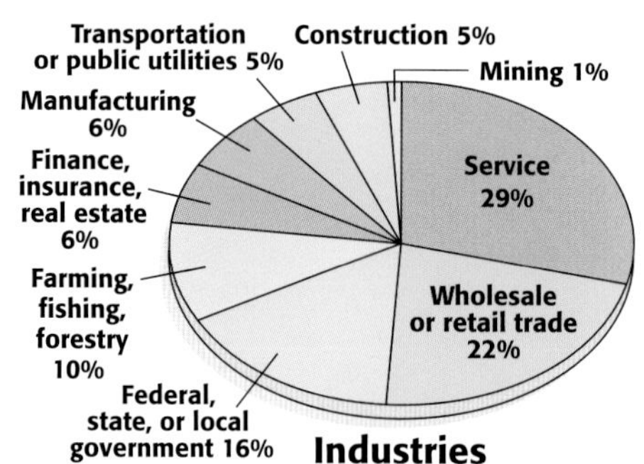

The Present

During the 1980s and 1990s, the government sought to attract new, nonagricultural industries to the state. North Dakota's economy, however, remains more dependent on agriculture than any other state's except South Dakota's. About 90 percent of North Dakota's area is farmland. The state's farms produce flaxseed, sunflowers, barley, oats, and sugar beets. North Dakota also produces more honey than any other state.

Agricultural jobs are less available as machinery performs more and more of the work. North Dakota has tried hard to attract a larger variety of businesses and industries, but its location—far from east–west trade routes and other densely populated areas—has hurt the effort.

Below left: *Farms take up about 90 percent of the land in North Dakota.* Below right: *Beekeeping carrying crates stacked in a field. North Dakota leads the country in producing honey.*

Born in North Dakota

★ **Warren Christopher**, statesman
★ **Angie Dickinson**, actress
★ **Carl Ben Eielson**, aviator and explorer
★ **Dr. Leon O. Jacobson**, researcher and educator
★ **Louis L'Amour**, author
★ **Peggy Lee**, singer
★ **Eric Sevareid**, television commentator
★ **Edward K. Thompson**, magazine editor
★ **Lawrence Welk**, band leader

Above: *Peggy Lee;* below: *Warren Christopher*

Besides agriculture, North Dakota's economy relies on key industries such as food processing and the manufacture of farm equipment and machinery. Coal, oil, and natural gas production help to balance the state's economy.

Many children in North Dakota grow up on farms that have belonged to their families since the homesteading of the mid-1800s.

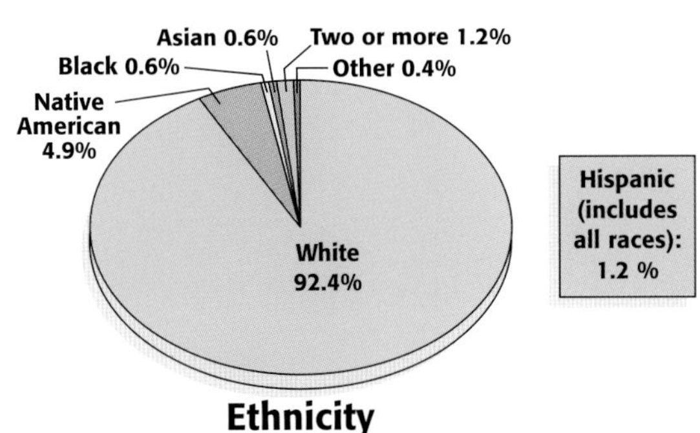

Ethnicity

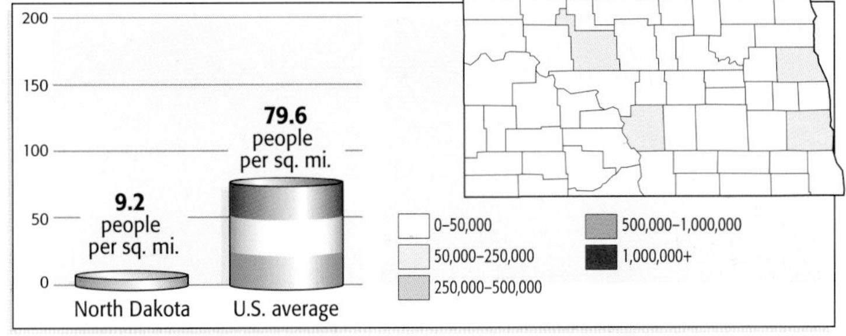

Population Density

Population by County

Ohio

With God, all things are possible.

Land area rank
Largest state (1) — 35 — *smallest state (52)*

Population rank
Most people (1) — 7 — *fewest people (52)*

At a Glance

Name: *Ohio* is an Iroquois word for "fine or great river."

Nickname: Buckeye State

Capital: Columbus

Size: 41,330 sq. mi. (107,040 sq km)

Population: 11,353,140

Statehood: Ohio became the 17th state on March 1, 1803.

Electoral votes: 20 (2004)

U.S. representatives: 19 (until 2003)

State tree: buckeye

State flower: scarlet carnation

State insect: ladybug

Highest point: Campbell Hill, 1,549 ft. (472 m)

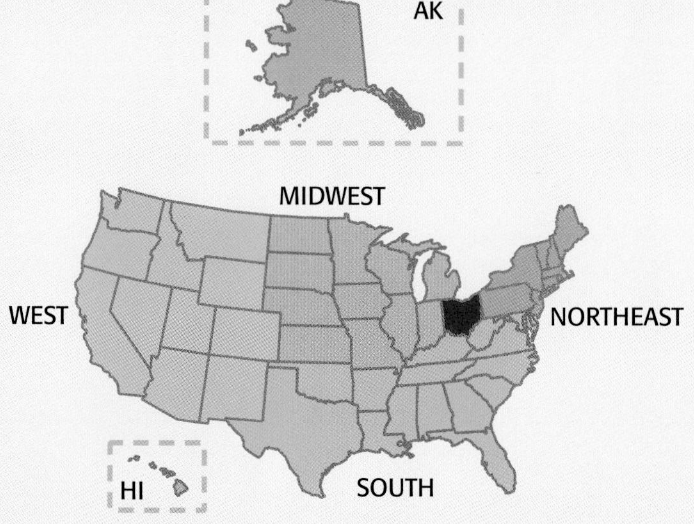

The Place

Ohio is one of the Great Lakes states. More than 11,500 years ago, glaciers and ice moved over the land and covered all of the area except for the southeastern corner. These glaciers helped form Ohio's present terrain by smoothing down mountains, digging

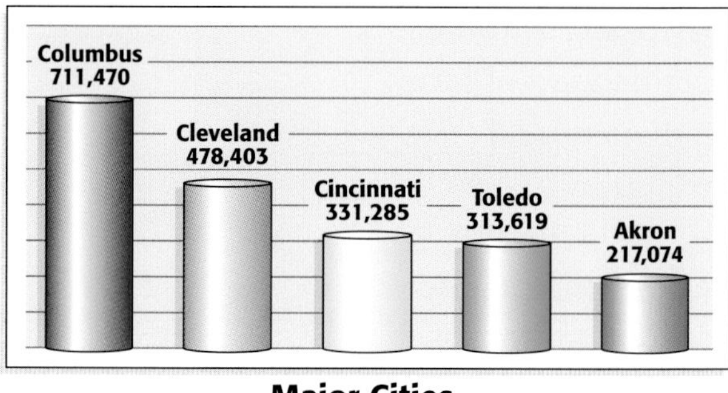

Major Cities

Fertile valleys make Ohio farmland, such as pictured here, well suited for growing crops.

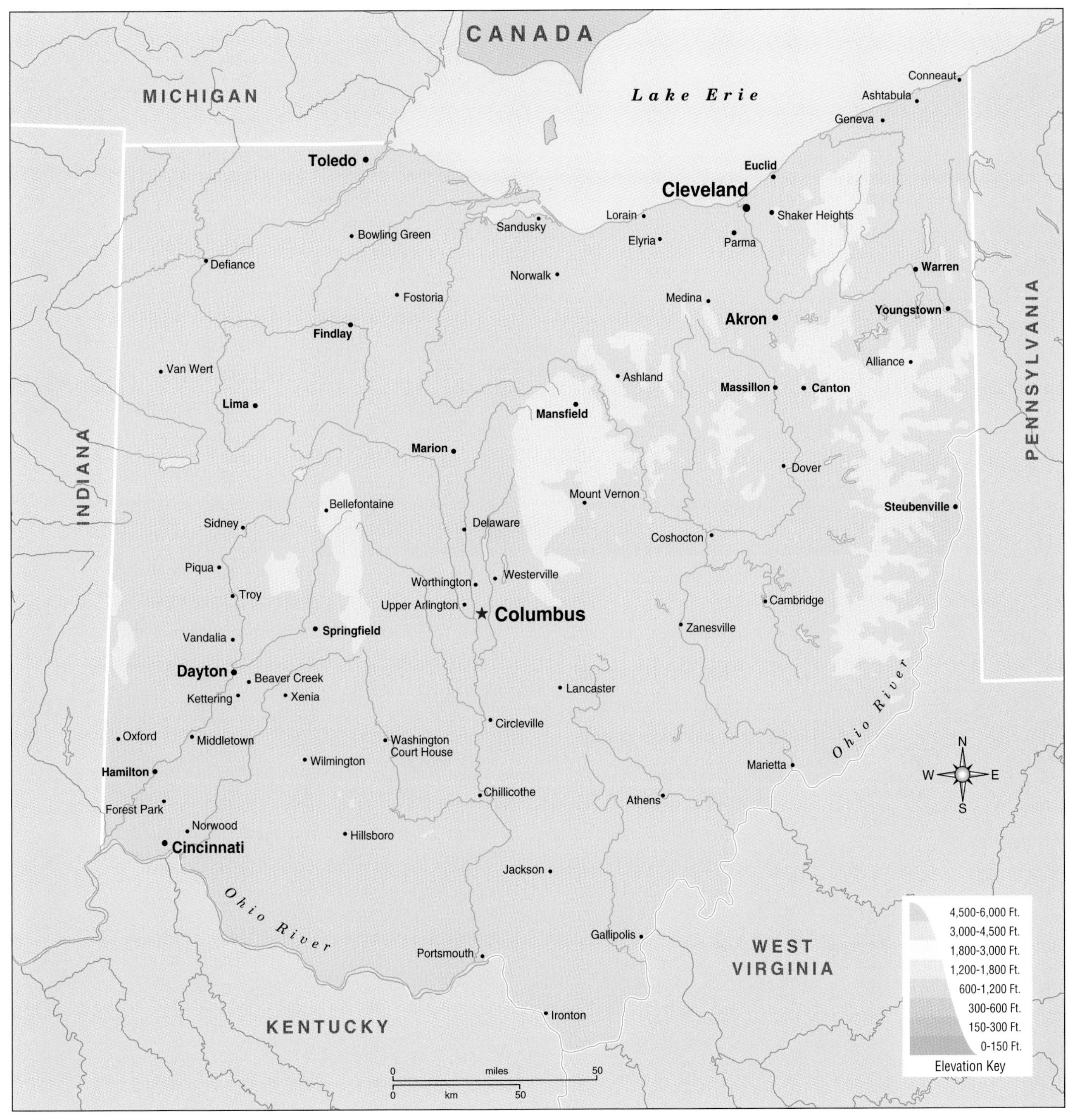

valleys, and depositing a rich top layer of soil. Some of this fertile land is found along the shore of Lake Erie, in a narrow region of low, level plains broken only by a few hills. Lake Erie forms Ohio's northern border.

Plains cover western Ohio. This prairie is the easternmost section of the Great Plains region that covers most of the Midwest. The land has good soil and is level with a few rolling hills.

The eastern half of Ohio is part of a plateau in the Appalachian Mountains. The southern part of the state is a rugged, steep region that is mostly forested. The very

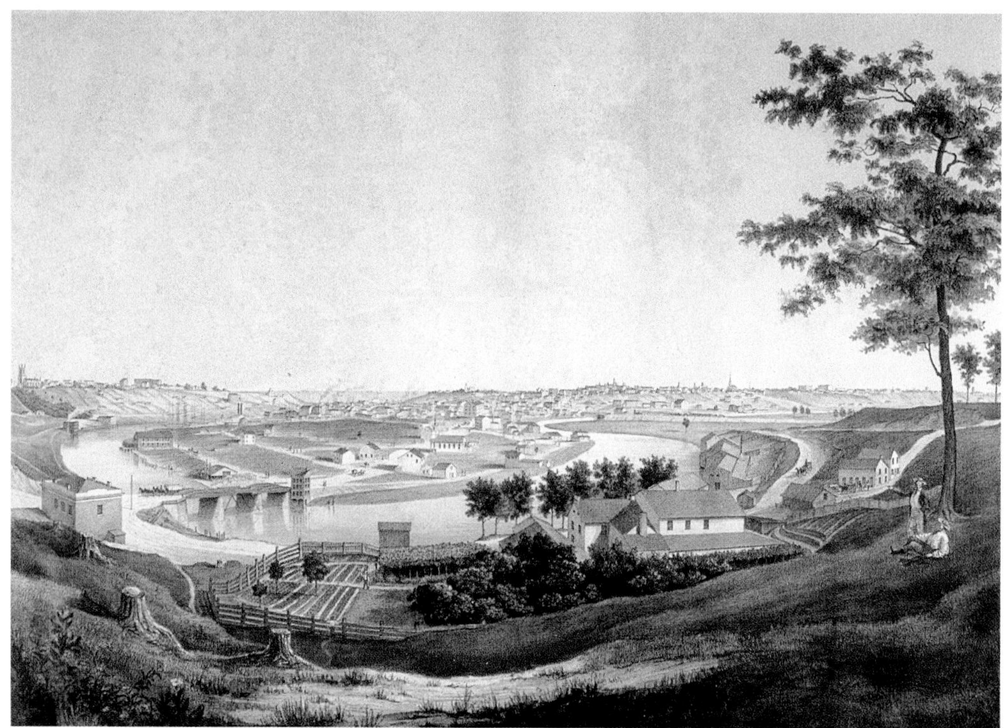

Cleveland, depicted here in 1851, developed along Lake Erie.

Ohio's primary natural resources are fertile soil, powerful rivers, and rich mineral deposits. The Appalachian Plateau has trees, clay, coal, natural gas, oil, and salt.

Winter in Ohio is cold, but summer is hot and humid. Southwestern Ohio receives more rain than other parts of the state, while the shore of Lake Erie is the driest area. During the winter, northeastern Ohio receives the greatest snowfall amounts in the state.

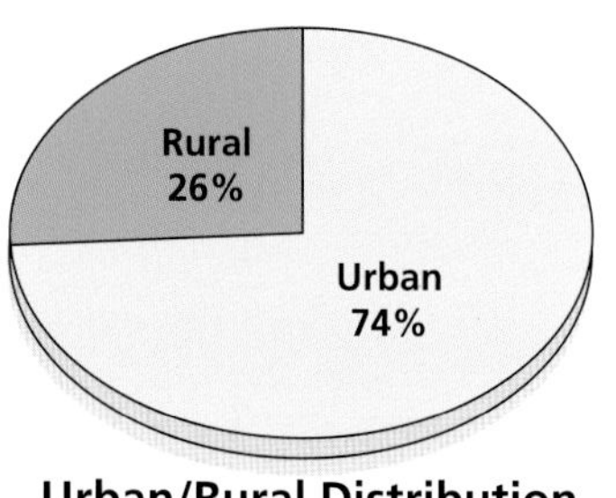

Urban/Rural Distribution

south of Ohio, known as the Bluegrass Region, is a triangular section of gently rolling, grassy hills that begin in Kentucky. The Ohio River forms most of the Kentucky–Ohio border.

The Past

More than 6,000 earth mounds, forts, and other formations made by prehistoric Native Americans called Mound Builders

Facts and Firsts

- ★ Half of the U.S. population lives within a 500-mile radius of Columbus, the capital of Ohio.
- ★ Oberlin College, established in 1833, was the first interracial and coeducational college in the United States.
- ★ In 1914, the first electric traffic signal lights in the United States were installed in Cleveland.
- ★ In 1869, the Cincinnati Red Stockings became the nation's first professional baseball team. The name has since been shortened to the Cincinnati Reds.
- ★ Seven U.S. presidents were born in Ohio: Ulysses S. Grant, Rutherford B. Hayes, James A. Garfield, Benjamin Harrison, William McKinley, William H. Taft, and Warren G. Harding.
- ★ Ohio produces more garden and greenhouse plants than any other state.

are located throughout Ohio. When the first French explorers arrived from Canada, these people had long since disappeared and been replaced by a number of smaller tribes, including the Delaware and Shawnee.

The French engaged the help of these Native Americans in fighting the British, who claimed all the territory extending inland from their eastern colonies in North America. In 1763, the French gave up the fight and gave all their colonies east of the Mississippi River to Britain. Britain lost these colonies to the Americans during the Revolutionary War. In 1788, colonists from New England built the first permanent white settlement in the territory of Ohio, at the town of Marietta. Ohio became a state in 1803.

State Smart

The fastest roller coaster in the United States is the Millennium Force, located at Cedar Point Amusement Park in Sandusky. It can reach a top speed of 92 miles per hour and is 310 feet (92 m) tall.

The Louisiana Purchase, which included the Mississippi River, quickly made Ohio an important center of trade. The construction of railroads and the Erie Canal increased prosperity in the state. Factories and mills were built along Ohio's rivers. Trade exploded during the Civil War, as Ohio provided coal, iron, and other supplies for the Union army.

Ohio manufactured parts for the war planes that were flown in World War II.

Ohio's industrial strength grew during World Wars I and II, when the state manufactured aircraft, ships, tires, and weapons for the U.S. military. By the end of World War II in 1945, manufacturing had become Ohio's most important industry.

During the 1960s and 1970s, Ohio suffered from low funding for public education, and several districts had to close schools. In 1971, a new income tax was imposed to fund Ohio's state government services.

Years of prosperous industry brought pollution from industrial waste. During the last two decades of the 20th century, Ohio cleaned up many of its rivers and lakes, which were badly polluted from this waste.

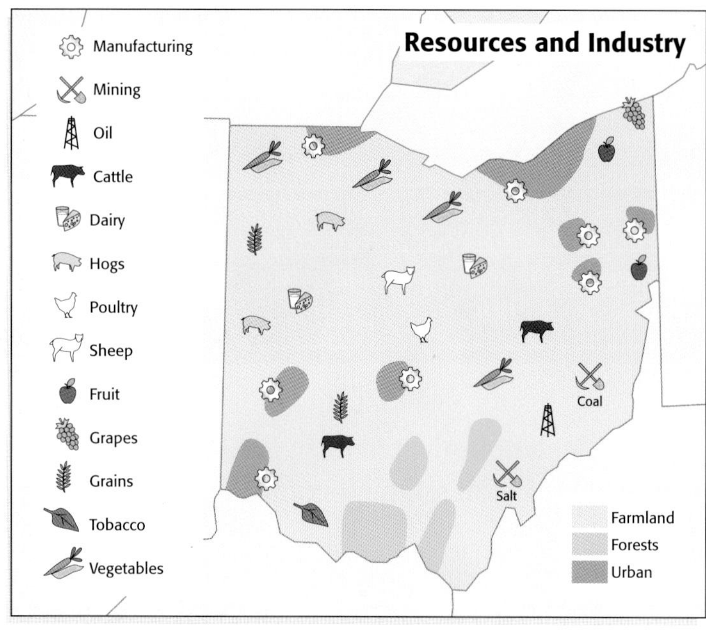

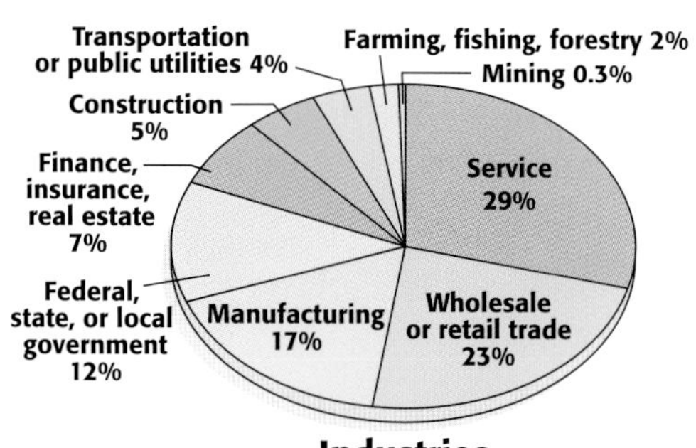

The Present

Ohio is one of the country's leading manufacturing states. Manufacturing is the state's single most important economic activity, and transportation equipment such as automobiles, aircraft, and their parts are Ohio's most valuable products. Ohio also produces machinery such as heating and cooling equipment.

Ohio's two largest cities, Columbus and Cleveland, are more than just manufacturing centers: Columbus is the home of Battelle Memorial Institute, one of the largest research and development centers in the world. Cleveland is one of the country's leading health care and financial centers.

About half of Ohio is farmland. Field crops, including corn and soybeans, account for most of the state's agricultural income, but milk and other dairy items are also valuable products. The state is a leading producer of hogs, and Ohio farmers produce more wool than any other state east of the Mississippi River.

Ohio suffers from a number of economic problems, including declining crop and livestock prices and increased foreign competition in the steel industry. In recent years, some businesses have left the state. Pollution of Lake Erie and the state's rivers is an ongoing concern.

Below left: *The pollution of Lake Erie is an ongoing concern.* Below right: *Columbus is a center for scientific research and development.*

Born in Ohio

- ★ **Neil Armstrong**, astronaut
- ★ **Kathleen Battle**, opera singer
- ★ **George Bellows**, painter and lithographer
- ★ **Ambrose Bierce**, journalist
- ★ **Erma Bombeck**, columnist
- ★ **Hart Crane**, poet
- ★ **George Armstrong Custer**, general, U.S. army
- ★ **Dorothy Dandridge**, actress
- ★ **Doris Day**, singer and actress
- ★ **Clarence Darrow**, lawyer
- ★ **Ruby Dee**, actress
- ★ **Rita Dove**, U.S. poet laureate
- ★ **Hugh Downs**, television broadcaster
- ★ **Thomas A. Edison**, inventor
- ★ **Clark Gable**, actor
- ★ **James A. Garfield**, U.S. president
- ★ **John Glenn**, astronaut and senator
- ★ **Ulysses S. Grant**, general and U.S. president
- ★ **Zane Grey**, author
- ★ **Warren G. Harding**, U.S. president
- ★ **Benjamin Harrison**, U.S. president
- ★ **Rutherford Hayes**, U.S. president
- ★ **Robert Henri**, artist and teacher
- ★ **William Dean Howells**, author and critic
- ★ **William McKinley**, U.S. president
- ★ **Chloe Anthony "Toni" Morrison**, author
- ★ **Paul Newman**, actor
- ★ **Jack Nicklaus**, golfer
- ★ **Annie Oakley**, markswoman
- ★ **Norman Vincent Peale**, author
- ★ **Edward "Eddie" Rickenbacker**, aviator and war hero
- ★ **Roy Rogers (Leonard Frank Sly)**, actor and singer
- ★ **Arthur M. Schlesinger Jr.**, historian
- ★ **William Tecumseh Sherman**, general
- ★ **Steven Spielberg**, director
- ★ **Gloria Steinem**, feminist and writer
- ★ **William H. Taft**, U.S. president
- ★ **Tecumseh**, Shawnee chief
- ★ **James Thurber**, author and cartoonist
- ★ **Orville Wright**, aviator
- ★ **Cy Young**, baseball player

Top to bottom: *Ulysses S. Grant, Annie Oakley, John Glenn, Toni Morrison*

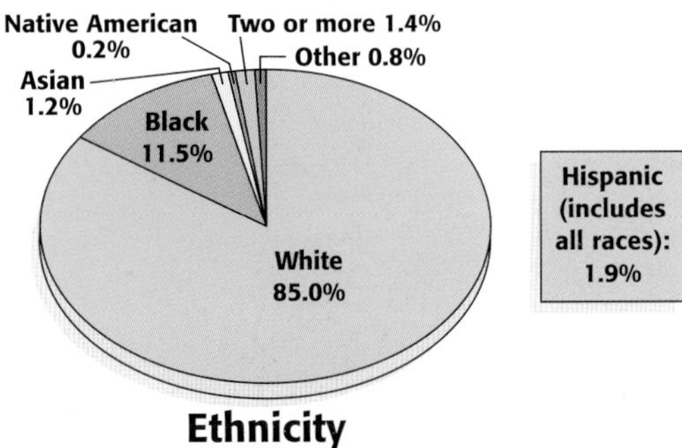

Ethnicity

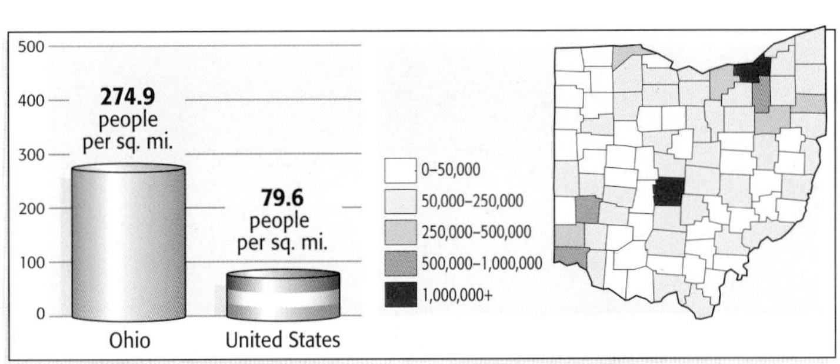

Population Density

Population by County

Oklahoma

Labor omnia vincit (Labor conquers all things).

Land area rank *Largest state (1)* 18 — *smallest state (52)*

Population rank *Most people (1)* 27 — *fewest people (52)*

At a Glance

Name: Oklahoma comes from the Choctaw words *okla humma*, which mean "red people."

Nickname: Sooner State

Capital: Oklahoma City

Size: 69,903 sq. mi. (181,048 sq km)

Population: 3,450,654

Statehood: Oklahoma became the 46th state on November 16, 1907.

Electoral votes: 7 (2004)

U.S. representatives: 6 (until 2003)

State tree: redbud

State flower: mistletoe

State animal: American bison

Highest point: Black Mesa, 4,973 ft. (1,516 m)

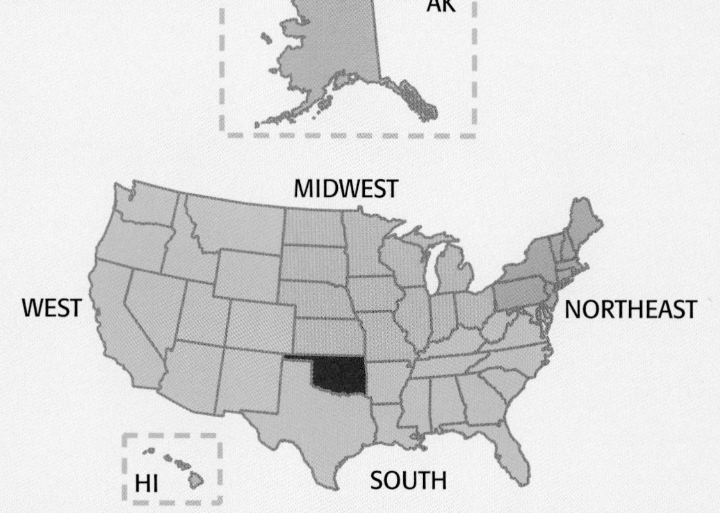

The Place

Oklahoma is a southwestern state located close to the center of the continental United States. It has a variable terrain, with hilly slopes in the Ozark Mountains in the northeast, fertile plains in the Red River Region, and sandstone ridges that form the Ouachita Mountains in the southeastern corner near Arkansas.

Scenic Veterans Lake is located in the Chickasaw National Recreation Area in southern Oklahoma.

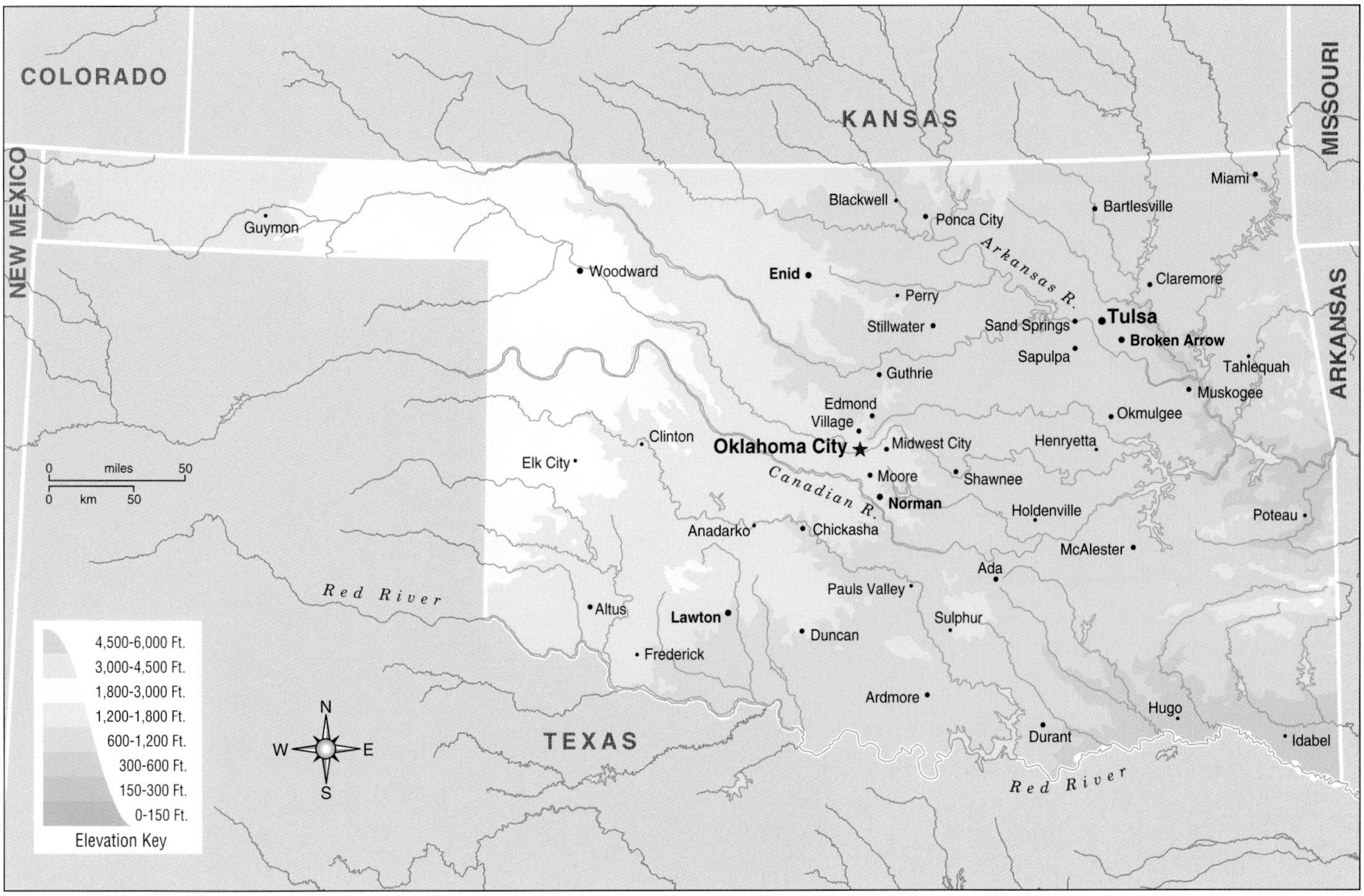

The middle region of Oklahoma has forested hills with rich deposits of oil and plains with fertile soil for farming. South-central Oklahoma is home to the Arbuckle Mountains. Over millions of years, these once-tall mountains have been so eroded by wind and weather that the peaks are low and rounded, with many unusual rock formations. To the southwest are the Wichita Mountains, which are higher peaks made of granite. Oklahoma's Panhandle, the part of the state that juts out to the west, is a region of level prairie.

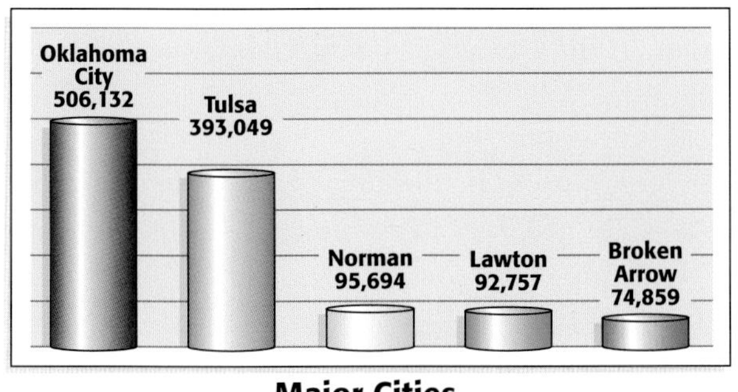

Major Cities

Oklahoma's two major rivers are the Red and the Arkansas. The state's most important resources are its large areas of fertile soil and prairie grasses, and deposits of petroleum, natural gas, and coal.

Most of Oklahoma has a warm climate, which is important for the state's largely agricultural economy. Northwestern Oklahoma is cooler and receives more snow in the winter. Oklahoma's Panhandle is the state's snowiest region.

The Past

Oklahoma's plains were once the home of huge herds of bison that provided food and

Settlers raced each other in Oklahoma Territory on the first day that Indian lands were made available to the white homesteaders, in 1889.

supplies to many Native American peoples, including the Arapaho, Cheyenne, Comanche, Kiowa, Pawnee, and Wichita. In 1541, the first Europeans to reach the area were Spanish explorers in search of gold. Finding none, they quickly passed through. The French claimed the Oklahoma region in 1682. Although the Spanish regained control in 1762, the French eventually retook Oklahoma and in 1803 sold it to the United States as part of the Louisiana Purchase.

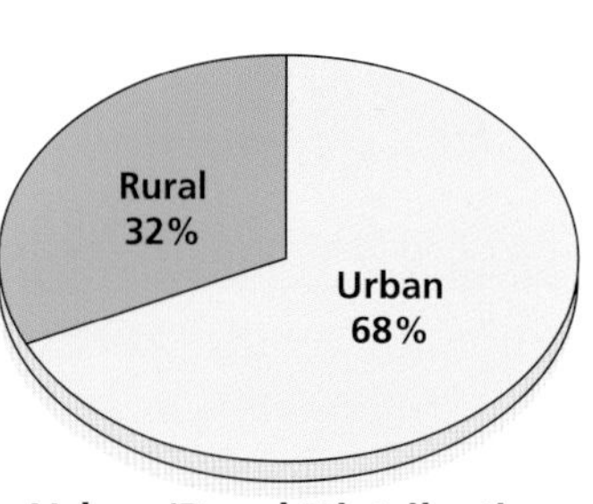

Urban/Rural Distribution

Since few white settlers lived in the area, the U.S. government forced many Native American tribes to give up their lands in the East and relocate to Oklahoma. Between 1830 and 1842, many Native Americans became ill and died during the forced migrations. For the Cherokee, the westward route came to be known as the Trail of Tears.

Soon the territories that surrounded Oklahoma began

Facts and Firsts

- ★ Oklahoma has about twice as many artificially created lakes as it has natural lakes.
- ★ Thirty-nine Native American tribes have headquarters in Oklahoma.
- ★ The largest independently owned Native American newspaper in the United States is the *Native American Times* in Tulsa.
- ★ Sylvan Goldman invented the shopping cart in Oklahoma.
- ★ In 1935, the first automatic parking meter, invented by Carl C. Magee, was installed in Oklahoma City.
- ★ Okmulgee hosts a pecan festival every June, and the town holds the world's record for the world's largest pecan pie—42 feet (13 m) in diameter.

to fill with settlers from the East, who sought good, inexpensive land to farm. Texas cattle ranchers pressured the U.S. government to open Oklahoma to settlement so that they could drive their cattle straight through from Texas to Kansas. The government resisted until 1889, when it bought more than 3 million acres of land (1.2 million ha) from Creek and Seminole tribes and opened the area to settlement. About 50,000 people moved into Oklahoma on the first day that the land was opened. In the same year, Oklahoma's first oil well began operation near Chelsea.

Two of the most famous eras in Oklahoma's history were dramatized in the musical play *Oklahoma!* and John Steinbeck's novel *The Grapes of Wrath*. The musical *Oklahoma!* depicts the years after Oklahoma was opened to settlement, when farmers and cattle ranchers competed for control of the land. *The Grapes of Wrath* portrays a more difficult time—the drought and economic hardship of the Dust Bowl during the Great Depression. During this time, thousands of farm families lost their money and land and left for California to look for work.

After the Great Depression, oil production increased in Oklahoma, and today there is even an oil well on the grounds of the State Capitol. (The well ended production in

State Smart

The 45th Infantry Division Museum in Oklahoma City is the largest state military museum in the United States. It covers more than 12.5 acres (5 ha).

Thousands of Oklahoma farmers and their families, like the one shown here, moved west during the Dust Bowl of the 1930s.

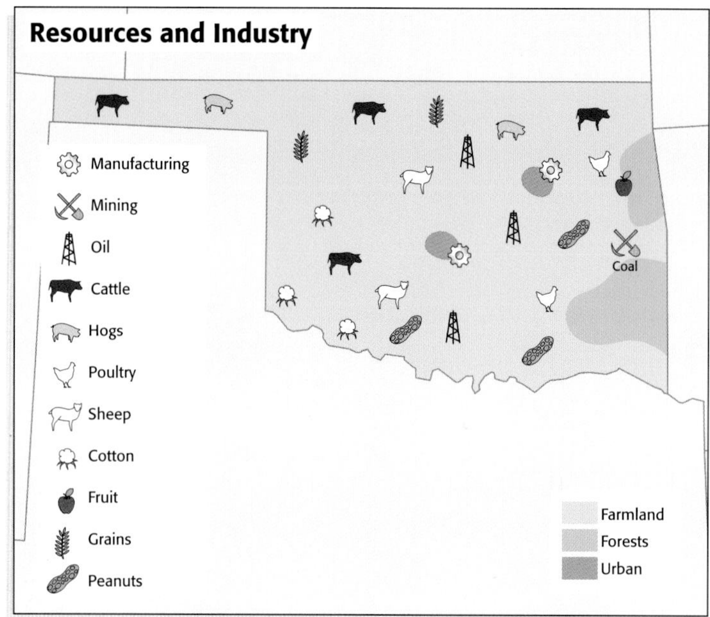

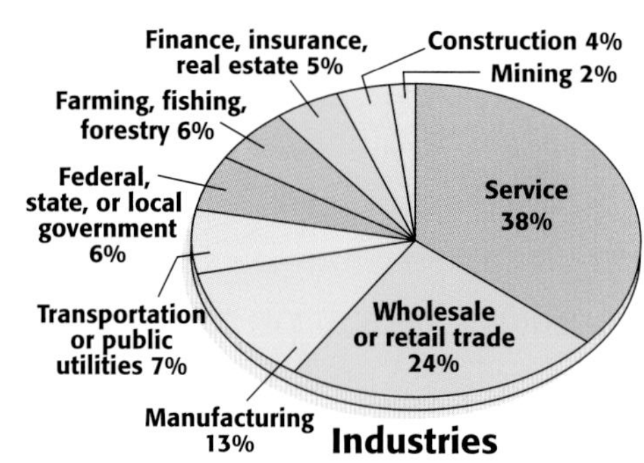

1986 but remains as a tourist attraction.) Oklahoma became increasingly urban as factories were built, and dams were constructed to provide hydroelectric power to new industries. The Federal Aviation Administration (FAA) built an aeronautics center in Oklahoma City in the 1960s, which furthered Oklahoma's industrial economy.

In 1995, Oklahoma was the scene of tragedy when a terrorist bomb destroyed Oklahoma City's Murrah Federal Building and killed 168 people.

The Present

Because of its location midway between the East and West Coasts, Oklahoma is a major transportation and distribution center for manufactured goods. Factories in Oklahoma produce computer and electronics equipment,

Below left: *A cowboy herds cattle in the Oklahoma Panhandle.*
Below right: *Oklahoma is a major transportation center.*

Born in Oklahoma

★ **John Berryman**, poet
★ **Garth Brooks**, singer
★ **L. Gordon Cooper**, astronaut
★ **Iron Eyes Cody**, actor
★ **Ralph Ellison**, author
★ **James Garner**, actor
★ **Chester Gould**, cartoonist
★ **Woody Guthrie**, singer and composer
★ **Roy Harris**, composer
★ **Ron Howard**, actor and director
★ **Jean Kirkpatrick**, U.S. public official
★ **Wilma Mankiller**, chief of the Cherokee nation
★ **Mickey Mantle**, baseball player
★ **Reba McEntire**, singer
★ **Bill Moyers**, journalist
★ **Will Rogers**, humorist
★ **Maria Tallchief**, ballerina
★ **Jim Thorpe**, athlete
★ **Alfre Woodard**, actress

Above: *Jim Thorpe,* below: *Ron Howard*

Wilman Mankiller was the first woman to serve as principal chief of the Cherokee Nation of Oklahoma. Inset: *Cherokee headquarters in Tahlequah*

machinery, automobiles, rubber and plastic products, and heating and refrigeration equipment.

Oklahoma has remained a largely agricultural state, with farms covering about three-quarters of its area. Many cattle ranches operate throughout the state. Oklahoma has more than 5 million beef cattle; other livestock include chickens, hogs, and turkeys. Oklahoma is a leading producer of wheat and hay.

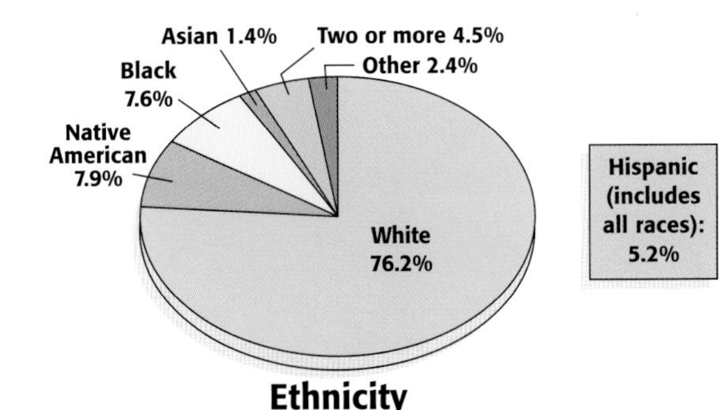

Ethnicity

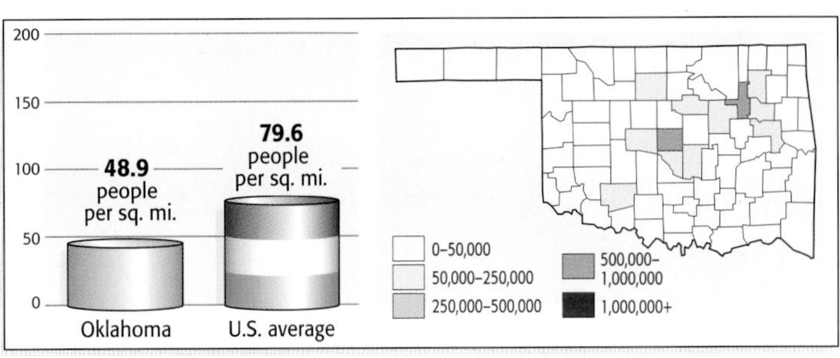

Population Density **Population by County**

Oregon

She flies with her own wings.

Land area rank *Largest state (1)* — 10 — *smallest state (52)*

Population rank *Most people (1)* — 28 — *fewest people (52)*

At a Glance

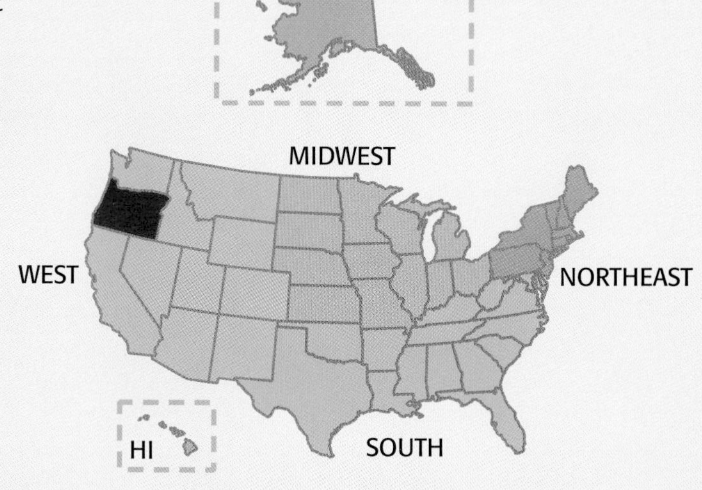

Name: The exact origin of Oregon's name is unknown, but it may have come from the Native American name for one of the area's rivers—the Ouragon.

Nickname: Beaver State

Capital: Salem

Size: 97,052 sq. mi. (251,365 sq km)

Population: 3,421,399

Statehood: Oregon became the 33rd state on February 14, 1859.

Electoral votes: 7 (2004)

U.S. representatives: 5 (until 2003)

State tree: Douglas fir

State flower: Oregon grape

State insect: swallowtail butterfly

Highest point: Mount Hood, 11,239 ft. (3,426 m)

The Place

Oregon is one of the Pacific Northwest states. Oregon has a steep, rugged coastline with many bays and harbors. Two large mountain ranges, the Coast and the Cascade, run down the length of Oregon. The Coast Range includes the shortest of Oregon's mountains. The state's highest

The Columbia River carved out the Columbia Gorge in northern Oregon.

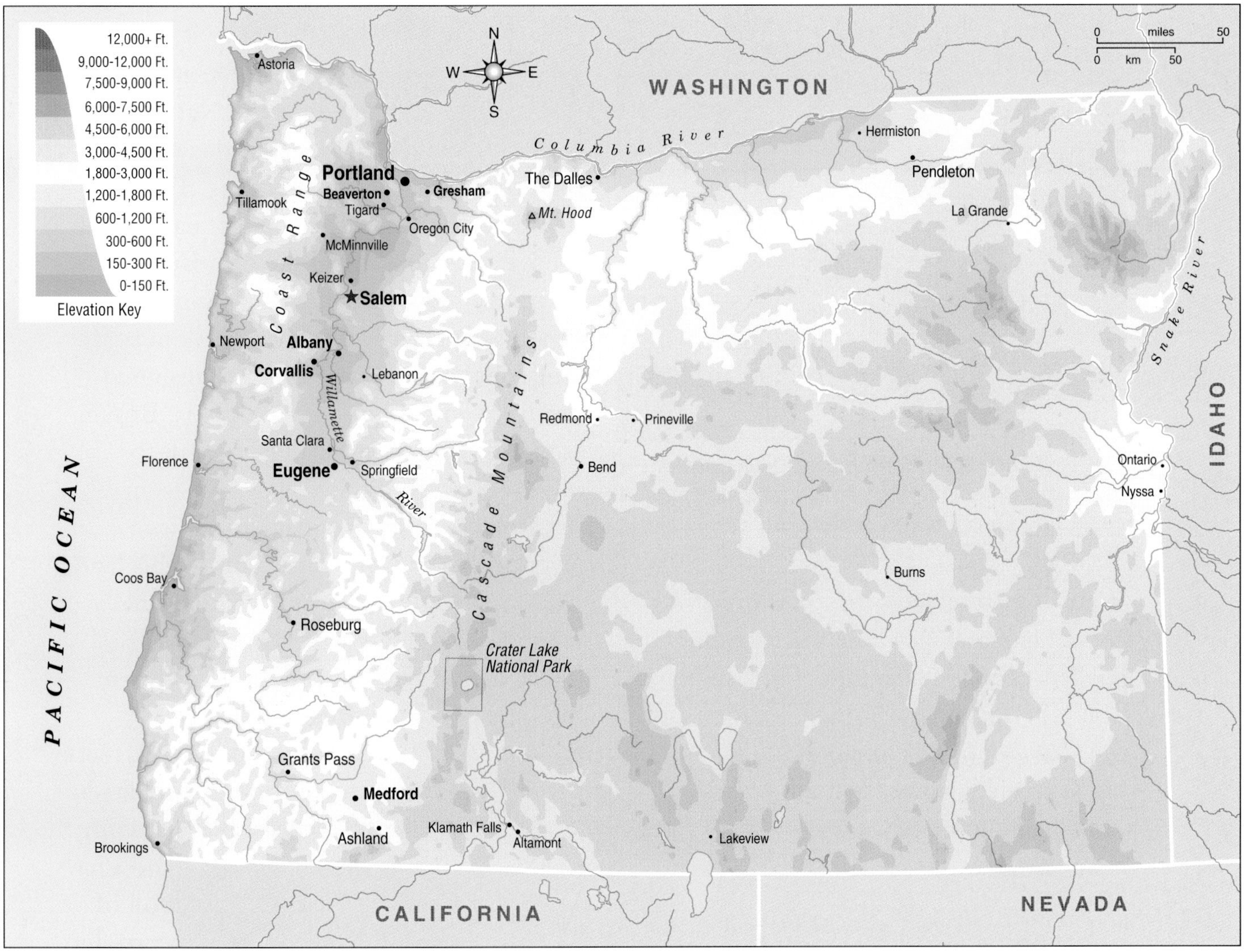

mountain, Mount Hood, is part of the volcanic Cascade Mountains. Crater Lake, which rests at the top of an inactive volcano, is located in the Cascades, as are many waterfalls. The Klamath Mountains, in the southwestern corner of Oregon, have some of the state's thickest forests and best mineral deposits.

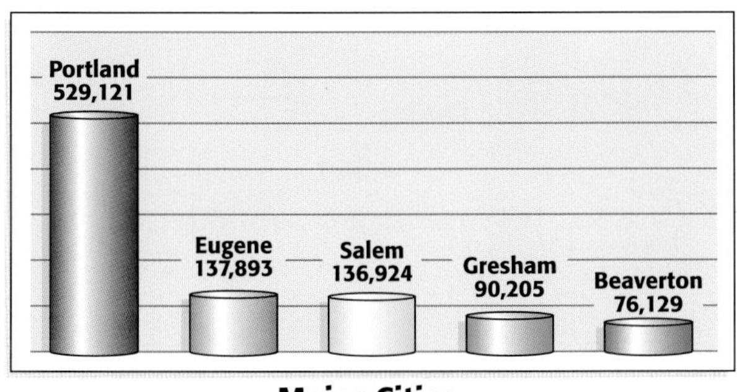

Major Cities

The Willamette Valley lies between the Coast and Cascade Ranges and contains some of Oregon's most fertile farmland. The Willamette River runs through this valley, which is also an industrial center and home to more than half the state's population. The Columbia River, which forms the border between Oregon and Washington, is the state's largest river. Water from the Columbia River and its tributaries provides energy for much of the state.

Oregon's climate is greatly affected by the mountain ranges. Moist winds from the

This sculpture in Portland honors Sacagawea, the Native American interpreter who accompanied Lewis and Clark though present-day Oregon.

Pacific Ocean cool as they pass over the coastal mountains, where the moisture condenses and falls as rain. The winds are drier after passing over the Cascades, and the area east of this mountain range receives almost no rain.

Oregon's most valuable resources are trees, fertile soil, sand and gravel, limestone, natural gas, diatomite, clays, coal, and some gemstones.

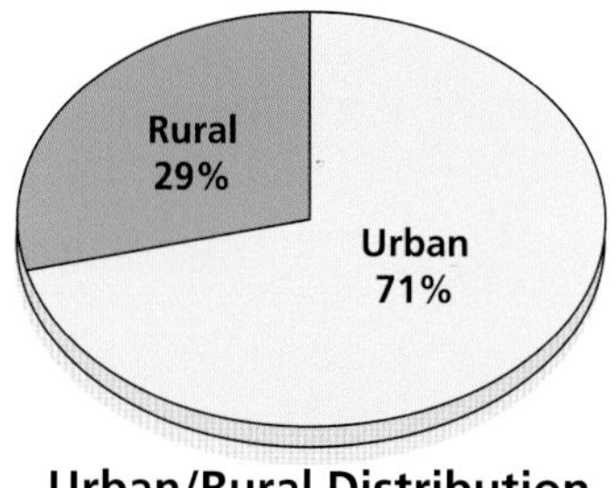

Urban/Rural Distribution

The Past

Many of Oregon's towns, rivers, and natural formations are named for the Native American tribes that lived in the area before the arrival of Europeans. The Chinook, Tillamook, Bannock, Paiute, and Nez Percé are some of these native peoples.

In the 1500s, the Spanish became the first Europeans to reach the Oregon coast, but control of the territory was disputed until the mid-1800s. Spain, Russia, Britain, and the United States all laid claim to different parts of the West Coast from California to Alaska. Spain and Russia eventually gave up their claims to this land, and in 1846, President James Polk finally negotiated a treaty with Britain that fixed the United States's northern boundary at the present-day border with Canada.

Before the mid-1800s, there were few European settlers in the Oregon area. Fur trading was the region's only industry. The first large migration of settlers to Oregon occurred in 1843, when about 900 settlers

Facts and Firsts

- ★ Oregon's Crater Lake is the nation's deepest lake—1,932 feet at it deepest point. It was formed more than 7,000 years ago in the crater of an ancient volcano.
- ★ The Heceta Head Lighthouse in Lane County is thought to be the most photographed lighthouse in the United States.
- ★ Oregon is the only state with a double-sided state flag. One side shows a shield, designed to represent Oregon; the reverse side has a picture of a beaver.
- ★ The world's largest log cabin was built in Portland in 1905 for a fair that celebrated the centennial of the Lewis and Clark expedition. The cabin burned down in 1964.
- ★ Oregon is the only state with an official state nut, the hazelnut.

came from the East along the Oregon Trail and settled in the Willamette Valley.

During the years that followed, more and more people began to settle in Oregon, California, and the area that would become the state of Washington. Native Americans clashed with these settlers in a series of wars between 1847 and 1877. In the late-1800s, after the Civil War, Oregon's population grew as former soldiers looking for inexpensive land settled in the West. Population growth also took place as a result of the construction of transcontinental railroads, which made travel to the West Coast easier.

During World War II, Portland became a major port for shipment of supplies to Russia and for U.S. troops in the Pacific. In the 1950s, huge dams were built on the Columbia River to provide inexpensive hydroelectric power for new industry. Many people moved to cities, where they worked in factories that manufactured goods such as electrical equipment, machinery, and metals.

In the early 1980s, Oregon suffered its worst economic decline since the Great Depression of the 1930s. A period of nationwide economic problems caused a decrease in the construction of new homes and businesses, and many Oregon lumber mills closed.

State Smart

Sea Lion Caves is an underwater cave system that is more than 360 feet (110 m) long—the longest sea cave system in the world.

Above: *An engraved stone marks the end of the Oregon Trail.* Below: *Sea lions rest on the rocks of Sea Lion Caves, a cavern that is 11 miles north of Florence, Oregon, on the coast..*

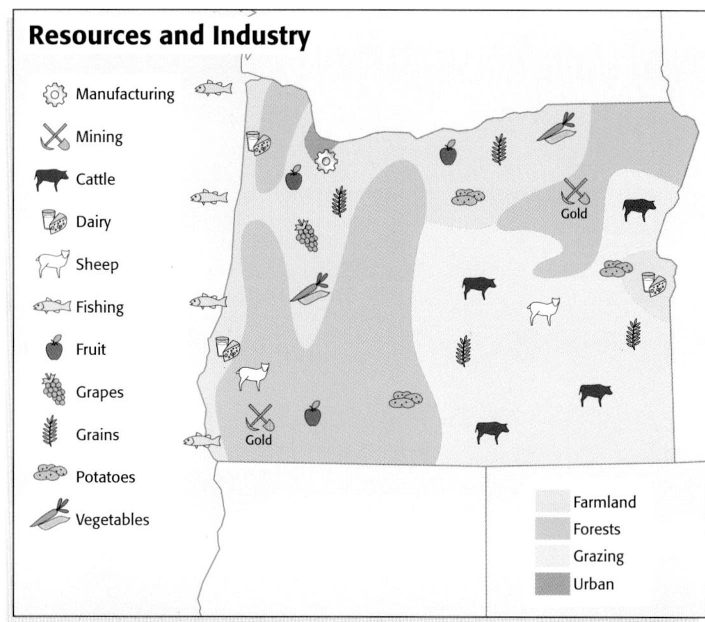

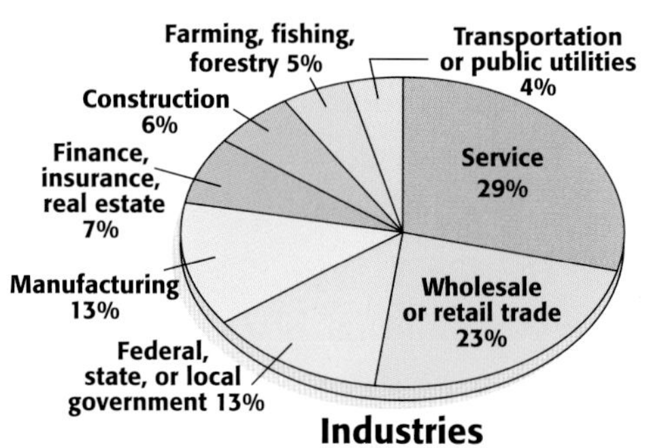

The Present

During the late 1980s and early 1990s, expansion of a variety of industries helped diversify Oregon's economy. While Oregon produces 10 percent of all the nation's lumber, manufacturing and service industries have surpassed wood products in importance. Factories in the Willamette Valley make such products as computer microprocessors and printer parts.

Production of agricultural goods, such as fruit, nursery plants, nuts, and wine, has increased. Orchards in the Hood and Rogue River Valleys grow fruit that is shipped all over the world. Irrigation from Oregon's large rivers allows farmers to grow potatoes, sugar beets, and wheat. Irrigation has also enabled the dry region east of the Cascade Mountains to be used for raising cattle, thanks to irrigation.

The Willamette Valley is the center of Oregon's agriculture, trade, and industry. Oregon's two largest cities, Portland and

Below left: *Mt. Jefferson is a part of the Cascade Mountains.* Below right: *Portland is a major seaport.*

Born in Oregon

- ★ **James Beard**, food expert
- ★ **Raymond Carver**, writer and poet
- ★ **Matt Groening**, cartoonist
- ★ **Chief Joseph**, Nez Percé chief
- ★ **Edwin Markham**, poet
- ★ **Phyllis McGinly**, poet
- ★ **Linus Pauling**, chemist
- ★ **John Reed**, poet and author
- ★ **Carl "Doc" Severinsen**, band leader
- ★ **Norton Simon**, art collector
- ★ **Sally Struthers**, actress

Above: *Chief Joseph;* below: *Matt Groening*

Salem, are located in this rich valley. Portland's location at the meeting site of the Willamette and Columbia Rivers has made it a major seaport. There, foreign cars are brought into the United States, and wheat and wood products are shipped to the rest of the world. Nike, the shoe manufacturer, has headquarters in nearby Beaverton.

Tourism has earned Oregon the nickname Pacific Wonderland. Oregon's natural wonders attract millions of visitors each year.

Cannon Beach on the Pacific Coast in northwest Oregon offers spectacular views for tourists.

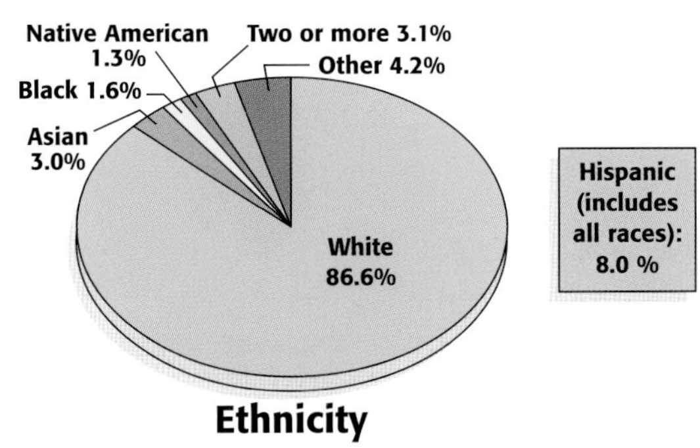

Ethnicity

Hispanic (includes all races): 8.0 %

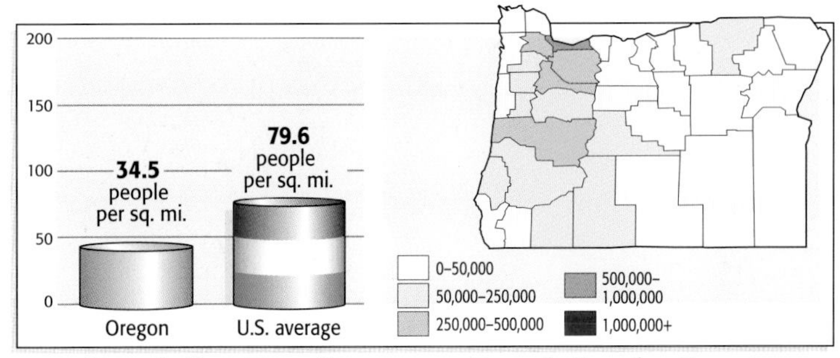

Population Density

Population by County

Pennsylvania

Virtue, liberty and independence.

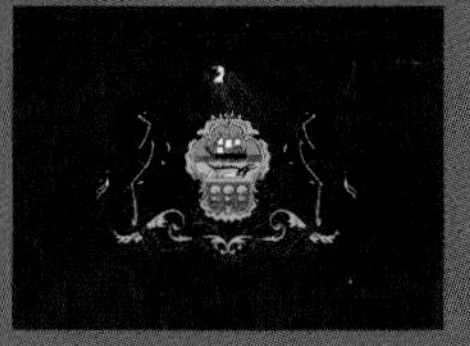

Land area rank *Largest state (1)* — 33 — *smallest state (52)*

Population rank *Most people (1)* — 6 — *fewest people (52)*

At a Glance

Name: Pennsylvania was named by King Charles II of England in honor of Admiral Sir William Penn, the father of William Penn, who governed the area. The name means "Penn's woods."

Nickname: Keystone State

Capital: Harrisburg

Size: 45,310 sq. mi. (117,351 sq km)

Population: 12,281,054

Statehood: Pennsylvania became the second state on December 12, 1787.

Electoral votes: 21 (2004)

U.S. representatives: 21 (until 2003)

State tree: eastern hemlock

State flower: mountain laurel

State dog: Great Dane

Highest point: Mt. Davis, 3,213 ft. (979 m)

The Place

Pennsylvania is in the Mid-Atlantic region of the United States. The western and northern areas of the state are part of the Appalachian Mountain Plateau, a high region of hills, valleys, and mountains that extends from Maine to Alabama. The Pocono Mountains are in the northeastern part of the plateau; the Allegheny Mountains are at the eastern edge. The western area of the Appalachian Plateau has many coal deposits and oil fields.

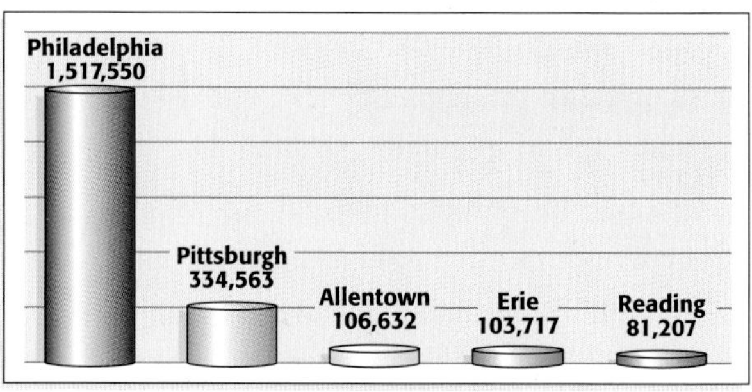

Major Cities

A man fishes in one of the many rivers in Pennsylvania.

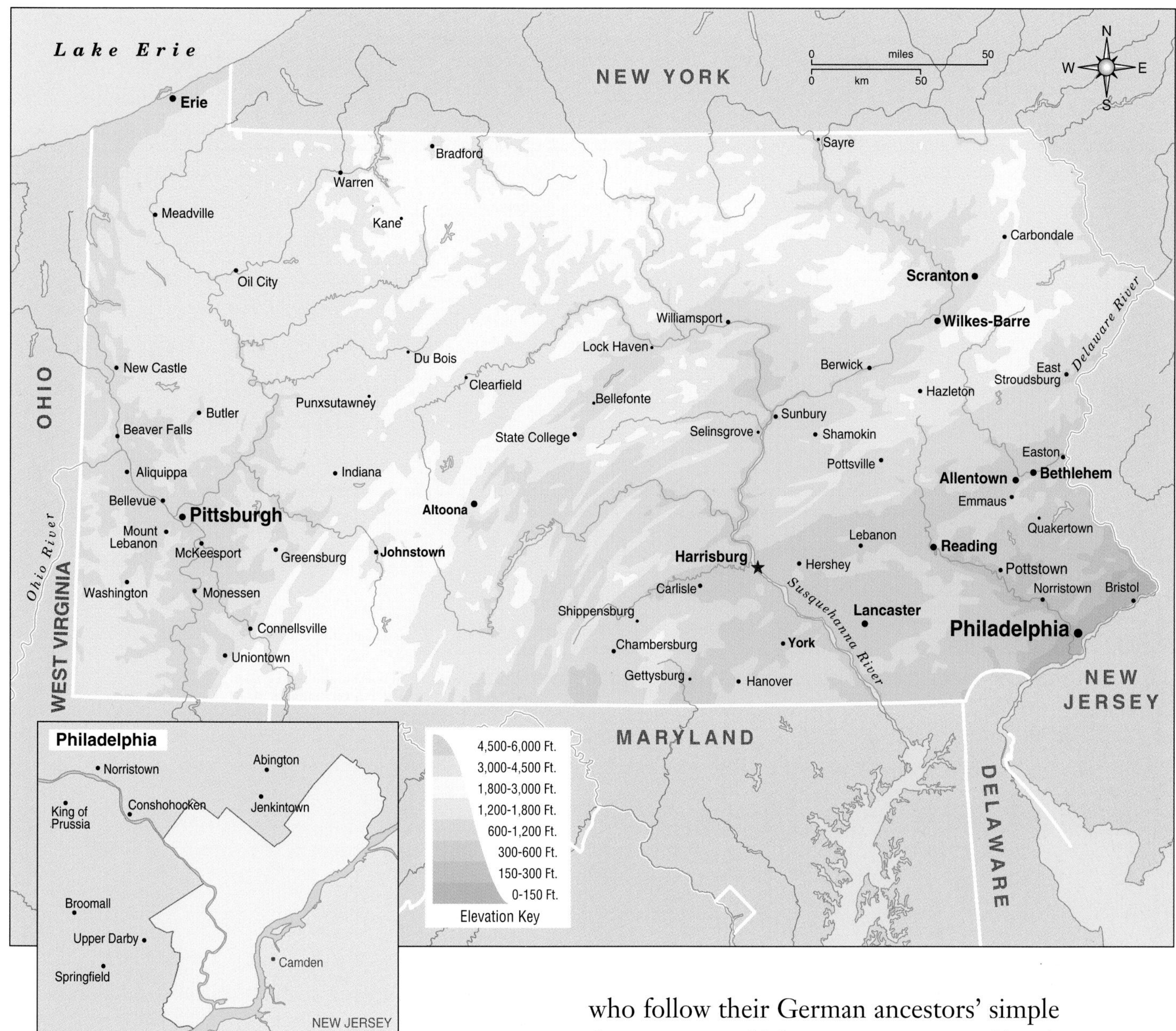

Pennsylvania's greatest mineral resources are its many varieties of coal. Much of southern and eastern Pennsylvania is farmland. A region known as the Piedmont is made up of rolling plains, low hills, and valleys that contain some of the most fertile land in the country. This area, in the eastern part of the state, is also home to the Pennsylvania Dutch, a group of people who follow their German ancestors' simple farming way of life. A narrow strip of level, fertile land that crosses the southeastern corner of the state is part of the Atlantic Coastal Plain.

About three-fifths of Pennsylvania is forested, and several rivers, including the Susquehanna and Delaware, cross the state. Pennsylvania's weather is generally moist, with cold winters and warm summers. Temperatures vary greatly throughout the state. Western Pennsylvania is the coldest, snowiest part of the state.

The U.S. Constitution was created during the Constitutional Convention, held in Philadelphia in 1787.

THE PAST

Pennsylvania, especially the city of Philadelphia, played a prominent role in America's history. The area now known as Pennsylvania was originally home to several different tribes of Iroquois and Algonquians. Henry Hudson, who explored Pennsylvania in 1609, claimed the region for the Dutch, who held it until the British took over in 1664. Pennsylvania was part of a territory that included New York and New Jersey until 1681. At that time, English king

Facts and Firsts

- ★ Pennsylvania is the only one of the original 13 colonies that does not border the Atlantic Ocean.
- ★ In 1776, the Declaration of Independence was signed in Philadelphia, and in 1787, the U.S. Constitution was signed there as well.
- ★ From 1790 to 1800, Philadelphia was the capital of the United States. The city was the site of the first presidential mansion.
- ★ Betsy Ross of Philadelphia is believed to have made the first American flag with stars and stripes, which was adopted by Congress in 1777.
- ★ Philadelphia became the home of the country's first daily newspaper, *The Pennsylvania Packet and General Advertiser*, in 1784.
- ★ In 1859, Edwin L. Drake began drilling the world's first oil well in Titusville.
- ★ In 1909, Pittsburgh became the site of the world's first baseball stadium, Forbes Field.
- ★ The first Internet emoticon, the Smiley :), was created in 1980 by a computer scientist at Carnegie Mellon University in Pittsburgh.
- ★ Rockville Bridge in Harrisburg is the longest stone arch bridge in the world.

Charles II gave Pennsylvania to William Penn as repayment for debts owed to Penn's father. Penn was a member of the peaceful Quaker religion. He became known for his religious tolerance and fairness to Pennsylvania's Native Americans. His descendants controlled the area until the Revolutionary War.

Many important events took place in Pennsylvania during the last quarter of the 18th century. The Second Continental Congress met at Philadelphia in 1775, and the Declaration of Independence was written there in 1776. In 1787, the first U.S. Constitution was also drafted and signed there.

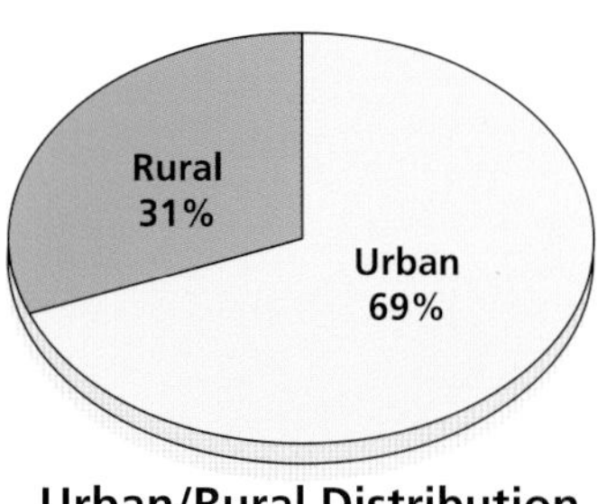

Urban/Rural Distribution

After the American Revolution, Pennsylvania became a leading industrial state. By 1860, Philadelphia produced many of the nation's textiles, leather, and iron, while Pittsburgh was a leading producer of glass and iron. New railroads helped many Pennsylvania factories supply materials for the Union army during the Civil War.

In the decades following the Civil War, Pittsburgh became the largest steel producer in the United States. Pennsylvania also produced huge amounts of coke, a kind of coal used in industry. The availability of jobs attracted thousands of European immigrants to the state.

During World War II, Pennsylvania factories produced cement, clothing, coal, petroleum, ships, steel, and weapons for the U.S. military. During the 1950s, however, Pennsylvania's industry was hurt by competition from other steelmakers, a declining demand for coal, and the departure of many textile mills for the South.

State Smart

Hershey Chocolate North America, headquartered in Hershey, is the largest candy producer in the United States, with yearly sales of more than $245 million.

In 1979, an accident at the Three Mile Island nuclear power plant near Harrisburg almost caused the release of toxic radiation into the area. Although a disaster was prevented, the incident raised concerns about the safety of nuclear power plants and resulted in the adoption of new regulations throughout the United States.

For many years, Pittsburgh was a center of the steel industry.

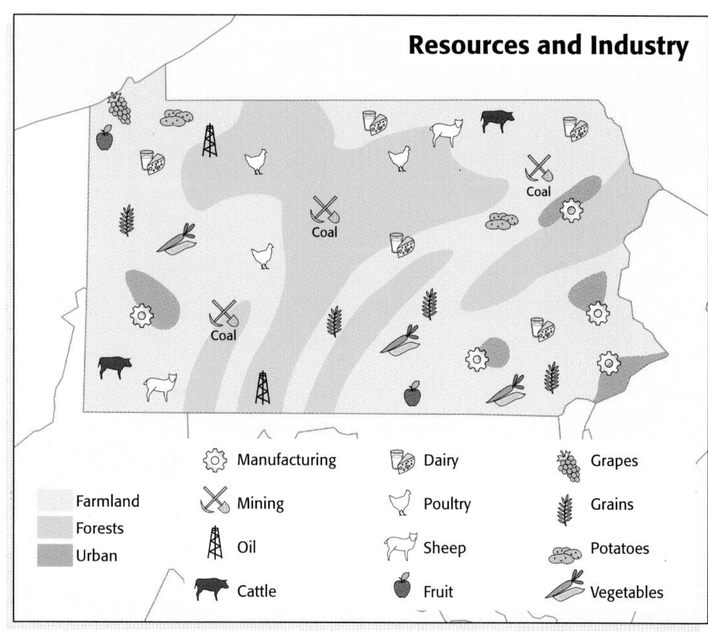

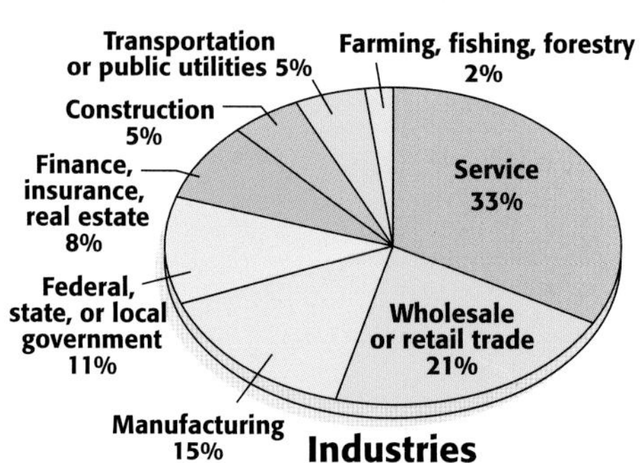

The Present

Pennsylvania's steel-making industry never fully recovered from its problems in the 1950s. Although Pennsylvania continues to produce large amounts of steel, the state has encouraged development of other industries. Chemicals, processed food, computer components, and electrical equipment are now Pennsylvania's chief manufactured products. The Hershey Foods factory in southeastern Pennsylvania is the largest chocolate and candy factory in the world. Pharmaceuticals and other chemicals are made in the Pittsburgh and Philadelphia areas. The Binney & Smith Company, maker of Crayola crayons, has headquarters in Easton.

Philadelphia and Pittsburgh redesigned their downtown centers and historic sites during the 1990s to attract new businesses and increase tourism. Many tourists come to

Below left: *Elfreth's Alley, the oldest residential street in the United States, attracts thousands of visitors to Philadelphia each year.* Below right: *Pittsburgh is an important center for the research and development of medicines.*

Born in Pennsylvania

- ★ **Louisa May Alcott**, author
- ★ **Marian Anderson**, opera singer
- ★ **Maxwell Anderson**, playwright
- ★ **Samuel Barber**, composer
- ★ **John Barrymore**, actor
- ★ **Ed Bradley**, television anchorman
- ★ **James Buchanan**, U.S. president
- ★ **Alexander Calder**, sculptor
- ★ **Rachel Carson**, marine biologist and author
- ★ **Mary Cassatt**, painter
- ★ **Bill Cosby**, comedian and actor
- ★ **Tommy Dorsey**, bandleader
- ★ **W.C. (William Claude) Fields**, comic actor
- ★ **Stephen Foster**, songwriter and composer
- ★ **Robert Fulton**, inventor
- ★ **Martha Graham**, dancer and choreographer
- ★ **Milton Hershey**, chocolate maker
- ★ **Reggie Jackson**, baseball player
- ★ **Gene Kelly**, dancer and actor
- ★ **Grace Kelly**, Princess of Monaco
- ★ **George C. Marshall**, general
- ★ **Margaret Mead**, anthropologist
- ★ **Andrew Mellon**, financier
- ★ **Joe Namath**, football player and sportscaster
- ★ **Arnold Palmer**, golfer
- ★ **Robert E. Peary**, explorer
- ★ **Man Ray**, artist
- ★ **Betsy Ross**, seamstress
- ★ **B.F. Skinner**, psychologist
- ★ **Will Smith**, actor and musician
- ★ **Gertrude Stein**, author
- ★ **James "Jimmy" Stewart**, actor
- ★ **John Updike**, novelist
- ★ **August Wilson**, playwright and poet
- ★ **Andrew Wyeth**, painter

Top to bottom: *Mary Cassatt, Rachel Carson, Margaret Mead, Ed Bradley*

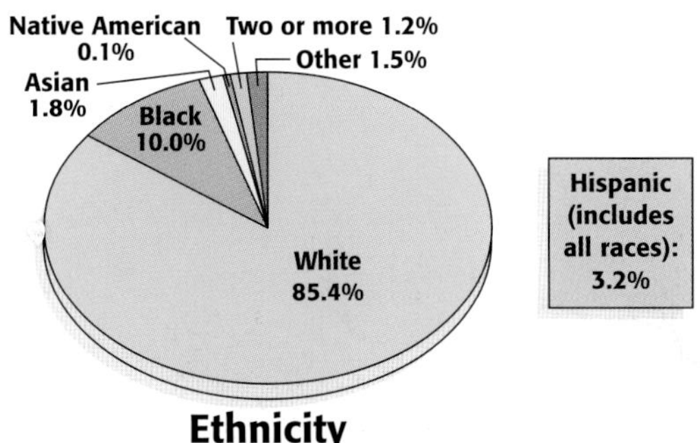

Ethnicity

Philadelphia to see the State House (where the Declaration of Independence was drafted), the Liberty Bell, and other Revolutionary War sites of interest. The Pennsylvania Dutch country, settled by members of the Amish and Mennonite religious groups, has retained a plain, simple way of life and is another popular tourist destination.

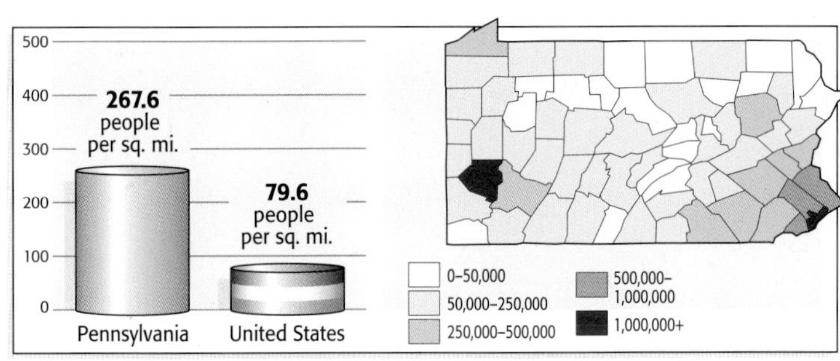

Population Density **Population by County**

Rhode Island

Hope.

Land area rank
Largest state (1)

Population rank
Most people (1)

At a Glance

Name: Some historians believe that Rhode Island was named by a Dutch navigator who called it Roode Eylandt ("red island") because of its red clay. Rhode Island may also have been named for the Greek Isle of Rhodes.

Nicknames: Ocean State, Little Rhody

Capital: Providence

Size: 1,212 sq. mi. (3,142 sq km)

Population: 1,048,319

Statehood: Rhode Island became the 13th state on May 29, 1790.

Electoral votes: 4 (2004)

U.S. representatives: 2 (until 2003)

State tree: red maple

State flower: violet

State bird: Rhode Island Red

Highest point: Jerimoth Hill, 812 ft. (247 m)

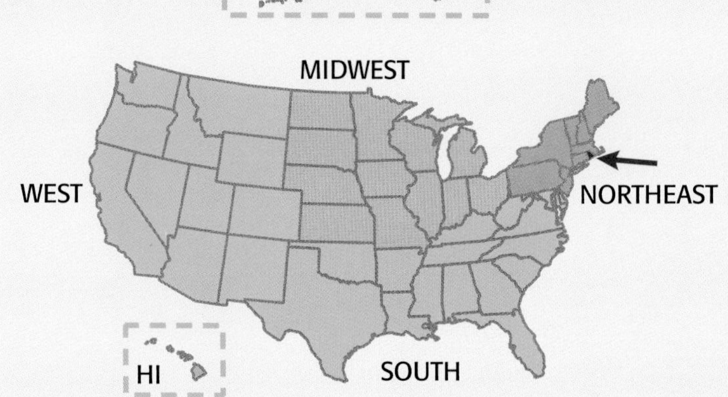

The Place

Rhode Island is one of the New England states. It is located on the Atlantic coast between Massachusetts and Connecticut. The Narragansett basin, which surrounds Narragansett Bay, is a lowland area with carbon deposits that stretch into southeastern

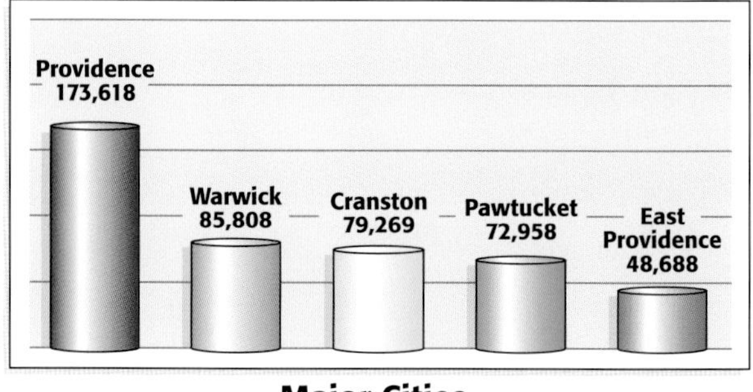

Major Cities

Rhode Island has miles of coastline and many lighthouses, such as this one at Watch Hill.

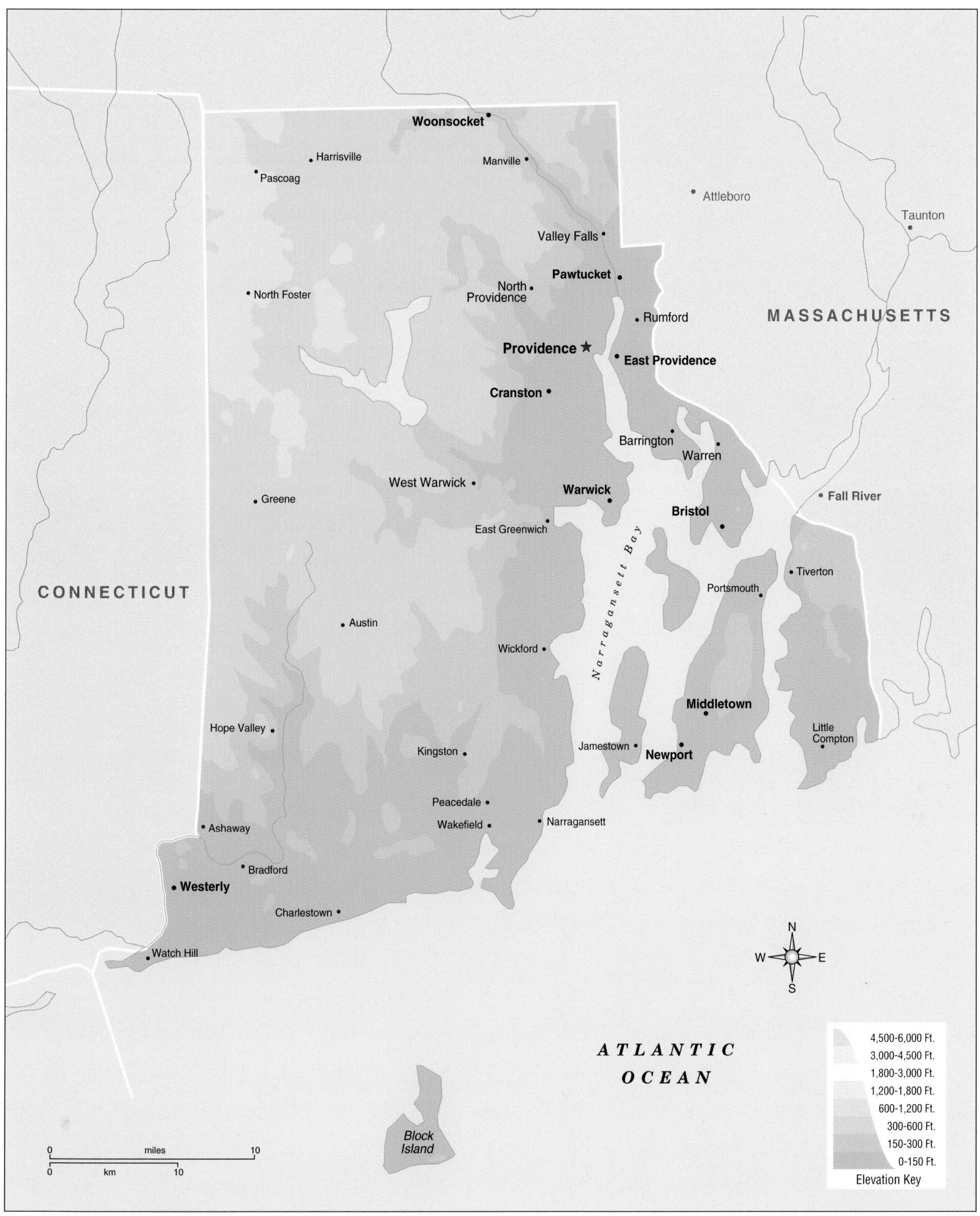

Massachusetts. Narragansett Bay extends about 28 miles (45 km) inland from southern Rhode Island. It starts at Providence, where it meets the Blackstone River. Narragansett Bay has several islands, including Aquidneck, which is the largest and the site of historic Newport; Conanicut Island, home to Jamestown; and Prudence Island. (Aquidneck Island is what the early Europeans named Rhode Island; the

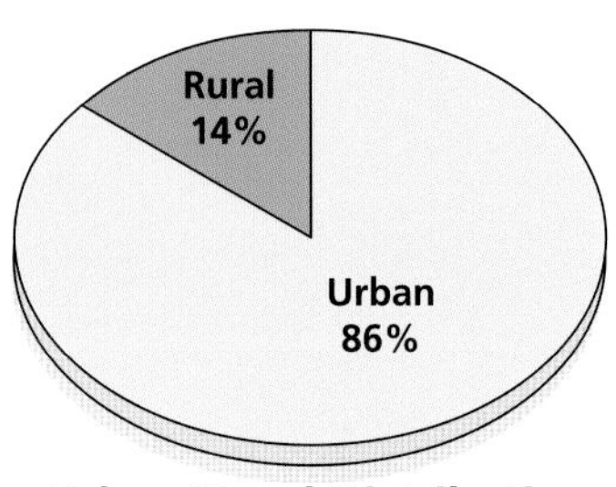

Urban/Rural Distribution

mainland became known as Providence Plantations.)

Rhode Island's coastline, which stretches from Point Judith to Watch Hill, has beaches, lagoons, and salt marshes. Inland, the state has many lakes and a rolling, hilly surface. More than half of Rhode Island is covered with forests, yet the state is very urbanized. Providence is the capital of Rhode Island and is also the state's largest city. Other notable cities are Warwick, Cranston, Pawtucket, and Newport.

Rhode Island's coast is lined with resorts noted for their swimming and boating facilities. Block Island, located 10 miles (16 km) off the shore of Rhode Island, is also part of the state.

The Past

Around 1524, explorer Giovanni da Verrazano first visited the area that is today Rhode Island. In 1614, Dutch explorer Adriaen Block explored the region. Roger Williams, who was banished from the Massachusetts Bay Colony, established the first settlement in the area at Providence in 1636. He used land he purchased from Native Americans of the Narragansett tribe.

Roger Williams established Providence.

In 1638, Puritans bought Aquidneck Island from the Narragansetts. There they established a settlement called Pocasset,

Facts and Firsts

- ★ Rhode Island's official name is the State of Rhode Island and Providence Plantations. It's the smallest state but has the longest name.
- ★ Rhode Island was the first colony to take military action against England in the years before the American Revolution, when colonists sank the English ship *Gaspee* in Narragansett Bay in 1772. Rhode Island was also the first colony to officially declare itself independent of England on May 4, 1776.
- ★ Rhode Island was the last of the original 13 colonies to become a state.
- ★ Roger Williams, the founder of Rhode Island, is credited with establishing the policies of freedom of religion, freedom of speech, and freedom of public assembly, which are contained in the First Amendment to the Constitution.
- ★ The oldest schoolhouse in the United States, built in 1716, is located in Portsmouth.
- ★ The Touro Synagogue in Newport, built in 1763, was the first Jewish synagogue in the United States. It is home to the oldest Torah in North America. Newport is also home to the International Tennis Hall of Fame, which has the oldest grass tennis courts in the United States.
- ★ Bristol holds the record for the longest-running, unbroken series of Independence Day observances in the United States. The town held its first celebration in 1785.

which was later renamed Portsmouth. Newport was founded in 1639 on the southwest side of the island, and Warwick was settled on the western shore of Narragansett Bay in 1643. The four towns united under a single charter in 1647.

Newport was the commercial center of the colony until the American Revolution. The area generated money through the trade of rum, slaves, and molasses. Narragansett Bay became a notorious haven for smugglers.

During the 1760s, colonists reacted against British laws that restricted trade and imposed taxes on the colonies. In 1772, Patriots protested by burning the British ship *Gaspee* near Providence.

After the Revolution, Rhode Island experienced bankruptcy and currency difficulties. Shipping, which had contributed greatly to the state's economy, was hard hit by President Thomas Jefferson's Embargo Act of 1807 and by competition from larger ports such as those at New York and Boston. The decline of shipping sparked the beginning of Rhode Island's industrial era. Samuel Slater built the first successful American cotton-textile mill in Pawtucket in 1790. Waterpower from Rhode Island's rivers led to the rapid development of manufacturing.

As Rhode Island industry grew, mill towns increased in population, and Providence surpassed Newport as the commercial center of the state. Mills and mill owners dominated Rhode Island's political and economic life into the 20th century. English, Irish, and Scottish settlers began arriving in large numbers in the first half of the 19th century. French Canadian immigration began around the time of the Civil War. At the end of the 19th century, many Poles, Italians, and Portuguese moved to Rhode Island.

State Smart

Rhode Island is the smallest state in area. It is only 48 miles (77.2 km) long and 37 miles (59.5 km) wide.

Slater's Mill in Pawtucket was the first successful cotton mill in the United States.

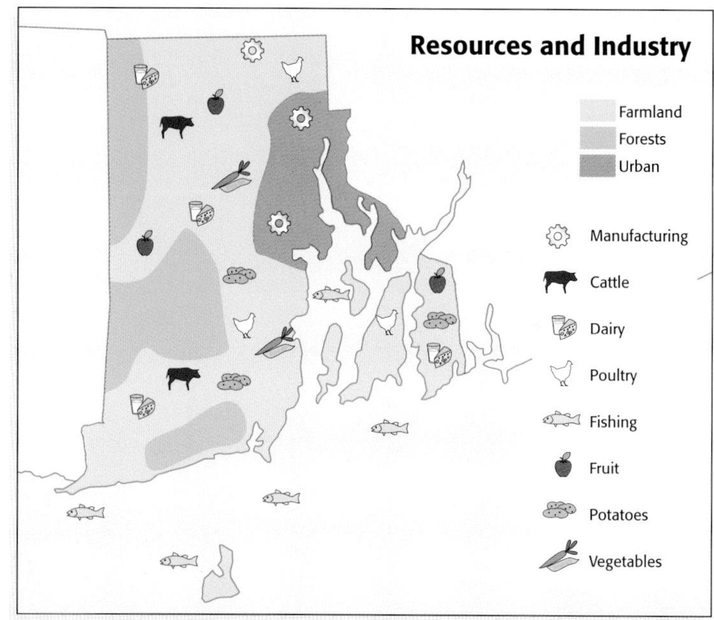

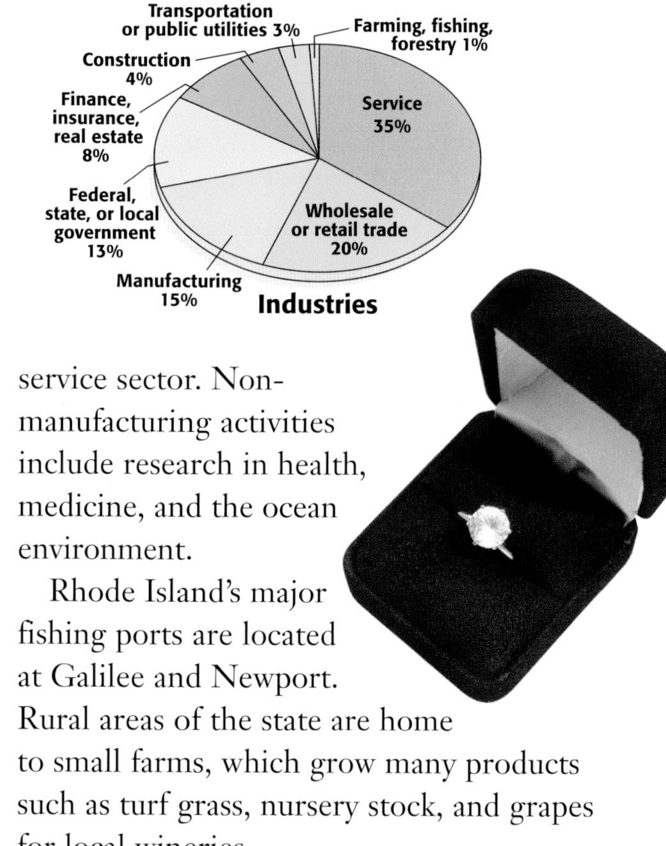

The Present

Rhode Island is the smallest of the 50 states and is densely populated and highly industrialized. Today, Rhode Island is a major center for the manufacture of jewelry. Electronics, metal, plastic products, textiles, and construction of boats and ships are other important industries. Since the 1970s, however, the state's economy has shifted away from manufacturing and toward the service sector. Non-manufacturing activities include research in health, medicine, and the ocean environment.

Rhode Island's major fishing ports are located at Galilee and Newport. Rural areas of the state are home to small farms, which grow many products such as turf grass, nursery stock, and grapes for local wineries.

Tourism generates more than a billion dollars in revenue for Rhode Island each year. Newport was the summer capital of high society in the mid-19th century, and today it remains a popular tourist destination.

Below left: *A dead whale lying on a beach in Narragansett Bay is dissected by Rhode Island scientists who study the ocean environment.* Below right: *Newport, Rhode Island, is a popular harbor for sailboat enthusiasts.*

Born in Rhode Island

- ★ **George M. Cohan**, actor and dramatist
- ★ **Sarah DeCosta**, athlete
- ★ **Nelson Eddy**, actor and singer
- ★ **Nathanael Greene**, Revolutionary War general
- ★ **Thomas H. Ince**, film producer
- ★ **Galway Kinnell**, poet
- ★ **Irving R. Levine**, news correspondent
- ★ **Ida Lewis**, lighthouse keeper
- ★ **Matthew C. Perry**, naval officer
- ★ **Oliver Hazard Perry**, naval officer
- ★ **King Philip (Metacomet)**, Native American leader
- ★ **Gilbert Stuart**, painter
- ★ **Sarah Helen Whitman**, poet
- ★ **John Wilbur**, Quaker leader
- ★ **Leonard Woodcock**, labor leader

Above: *Gilbert Stuart;* below: *Irving R. Levine*

Other popular destinations for visitors are the Roger Williams Park and Zoo in Providence, Slater's Mill in Pawtucket, Revolutionary War general Nathanael Greene's Homestead in Coventry, the Newport mansions, Block Island, and the many beaches and campgrounds in the southern half of the state.

Block Island is a relaxing vacation spot 12 miles off the coast of Rhode Island.

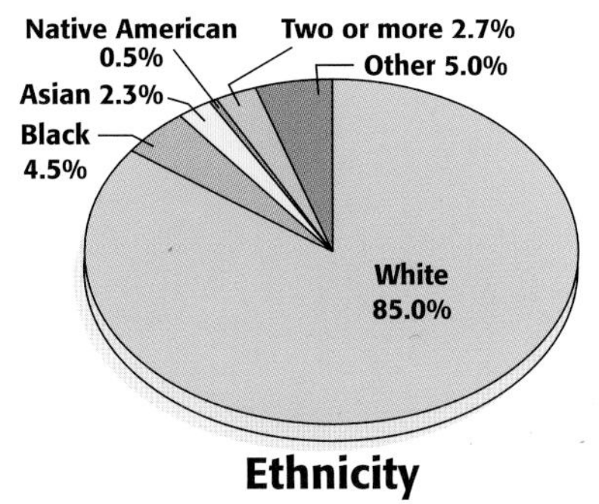

Hispanic (includes all races): 8.7%

Ethnicity

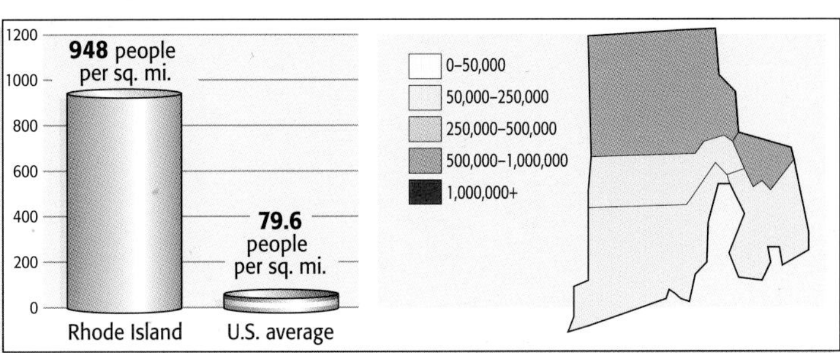

Population Density

Population by County

South Carolina

Dum spiro spero (While I breathe, I hope).

Land area rank *Largest state (1)* — 40 — *smallest state (52)*

Population rank *Most people (1)* — 26 — *fewest people (52)*

At a Glance

Name: South Carolina was named after King Charles I of England.

Nickname: Palmetto State

Capital: Columbia

Size: 31,117 sq. mi. (80,593 sq km)

Population: 4,012,012

Statehood: South Carolina became the eighth state on May 23, 1788.

Electoral votes: 8 (2004)

U.S. representatives: 6 (until 2003)

State tree: palmetto

State flower: yellow jessamine

State fish: striped bass

Highest point: Sassafras Mountain, 3,560 ft. (1,085 m)

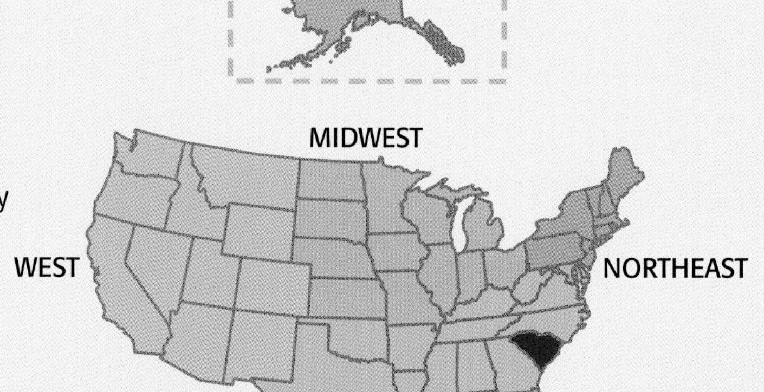

The Place

South Carolina is the smallest of the states in the Deep South. The southeastern two-thirds of South Carolina is part of the Atlantic Coastal Plain, which stretches along the Atlantic coast from Maine to Florida. South Carolina residents call the

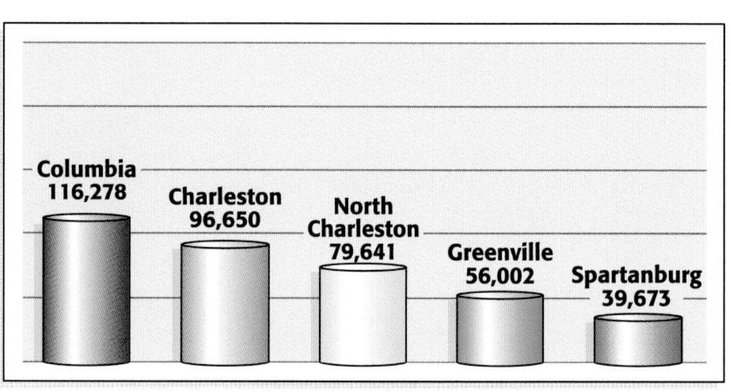

Major Cities

An avenue of oak trees greets visitors to a Boone Hill plantation in the Low Country of southeast South Carolina.

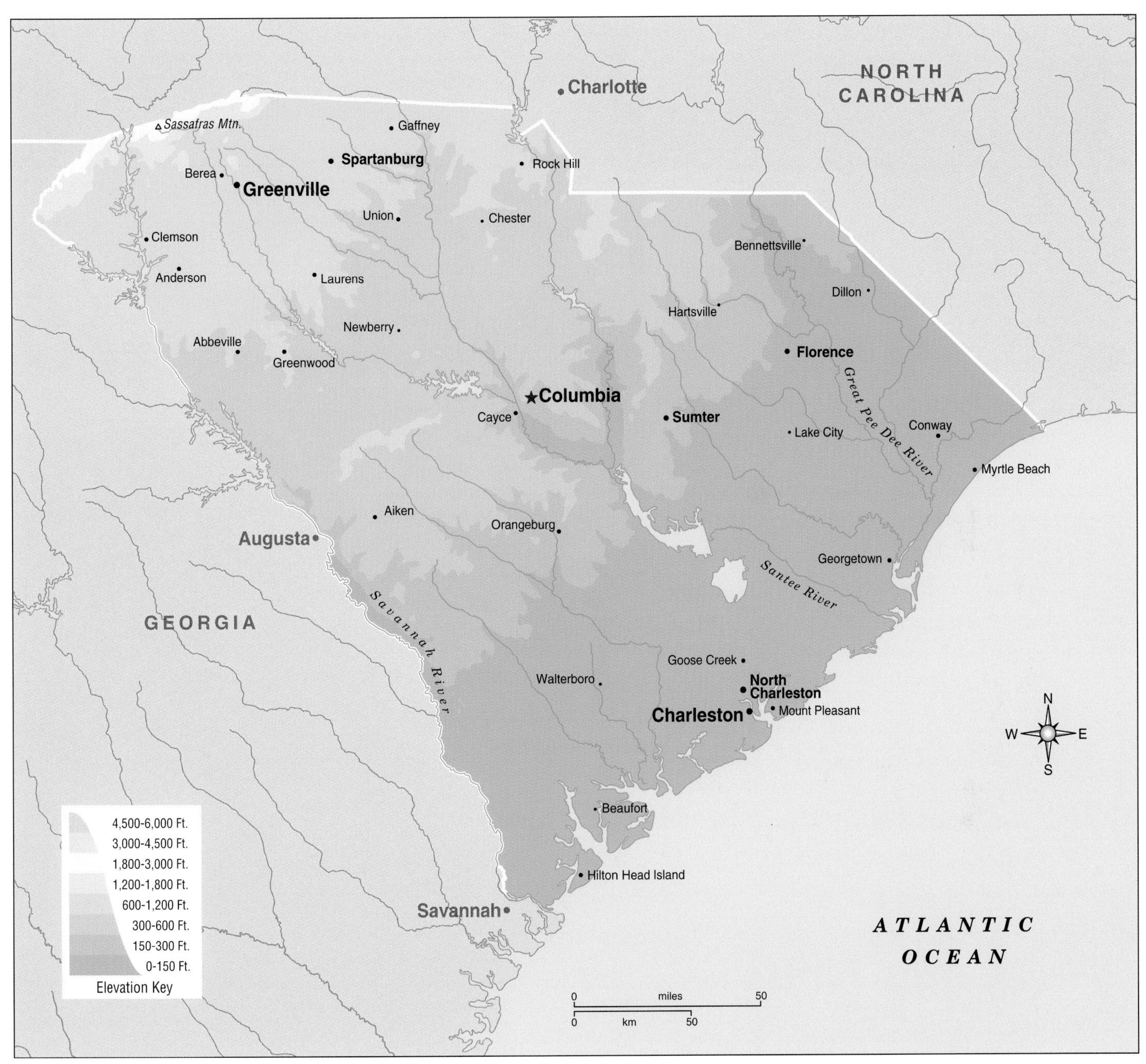

low but sometimes hilly southeast the Low Country. This area has good soil, rivers, swamps, and some pine forests. There are also sand hills left behind from the time when eastern South Carolina was under the Atlantic Ocean.

Western South Carolina is known as the Upcountry, because it is a region of hills that gradually rise into mountains in the northwest corner. Most of South Carolina's major rivers cross through the middle of the state to the Atlantic Ocean and provide good sources of energy.

The Blue Ridge Mountains, part of the Appalachian Mountain system that extends from Maine to Alabama, cross South Carolina in its most northwestern region. The forested Blue Ridge Mountains of South Carolina are lower than the mountains of the same chain in North Carolina.

South Carolina has a warm, subtropical climate. South Carolina receives little snow, and the small amount it does receive usually falls in the mountains. Subtropical plants, such as palmettos and yuccas, grow along the coast. South Carolina has large deposits of clay, limestone, sand, talc, gravel, gold, granite, and topaz.

An African American family poses on Smith's Plantation at Beaufort in 1862.

The Past

The first European settlement in the United States may have been founded in South Carolina. In 1526, Lucas Vasquez de Aylion, from the colony of Santo Domingo on the island of Hispaniola, started a Spanish settlement named San Miguel de Gualdape on the coast of either present-day South Carolina or Georgia. The settlement lasted less than a year.

England claimed control of all of North America in the early 1600s. Under English control, present-day South Carolina, North Carolina, and Georgia comprised a territory named Carolana that was granted to

Facts and Firsts

- ★ In 1861, the first battle of the Civil War took place at Fort Sumter.
- ★ South Carolina's official state amphibian is the spotted salamander.
- ★ At 411 feet (125 m), the Upper Whitewater Falls is the highest waterfall in the eastern United States.
- ★ Sumter is home to the largest ginkgo farm in the world.
- ★ The Duncan Park baseball stadium in Spartanburg is the oldest minor league stadium in the country.
- ★ Myrtle Beach, one of the most popular resort destinations on the East Coast, is in the center of the Grand Strand, a 60-mile (96-km) stretch of South Carolina's best beaches.
- ★ At the Riverbanks Zoological Park in Columbia, more than 2,000 animals live in re-created habitats without cages.

English noble Sir Robert Heath. Heath did not settle Carolana; King Charles II of England sent the first permanent colonists there in 1669.

During the Revolutionary War, colonists won two battles in South Carolina that helped turn the tide of war against the British. Important American victories took place during the Battle of Kings Mountain in 1780 and at Cowpens in 1781.

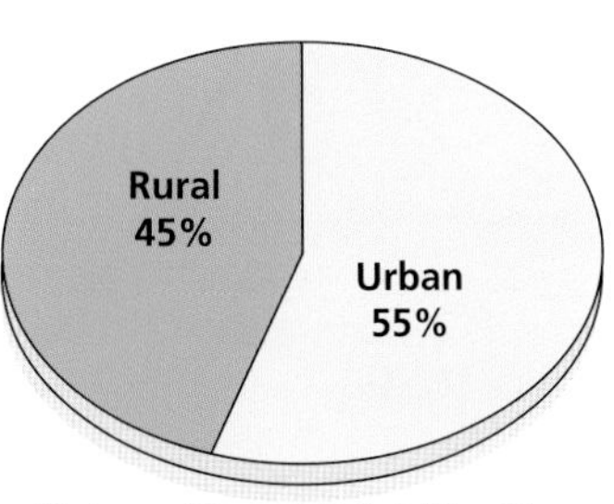

Urban/Rural Distribution

After the Revolution, South Carolina strongly supported the right of each state to make its own laws and control its own affairs. This belief led South Carolina to be the first state to secede from the Union during the Civil War. The first shots of the war were fired at Fort Sumter in 1861.

Before the Civil War, South Carolina's economy depended on large plantations worked by slaves. After the South's defeat and the abolition of slavery, South Carolina's farms were hurt by competition from farms in the West. The state turned to industry, and built textile mills that ran on hydroelectric power from the area's many rivers.

As South Carolina continued to industrialize throughout the 20th century, large river dams were built to supply the necessary energy. In 1953, the Savannah River Plant, one of the first nuclear power plants, was built near Aiken.

State Smart

The Charleston Museum is the oldest museum in the United States. Built in 1773, the museum's many displays showcase the rich history of the city of Charleston.

Parts of Charleston were devastated during the Civil War.

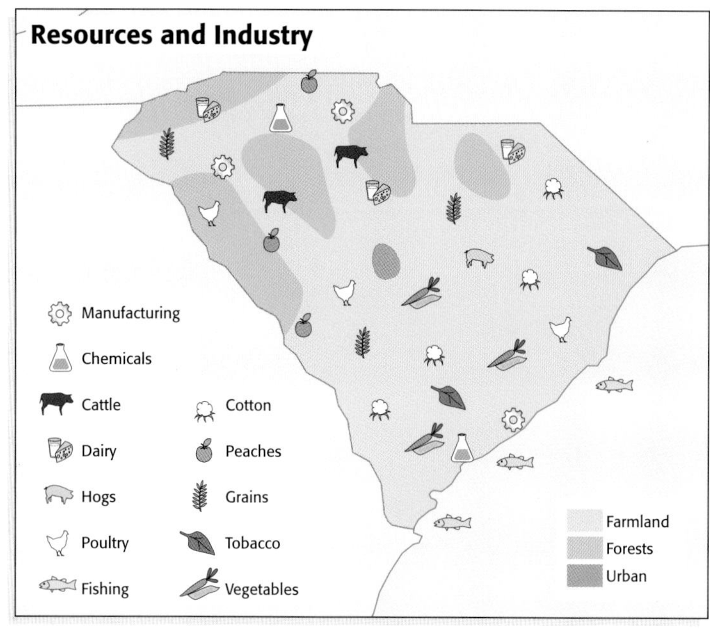

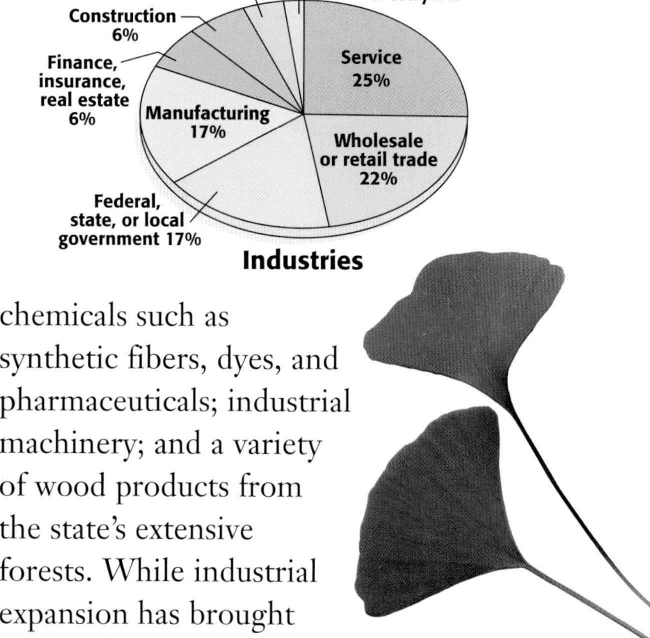

The Present

The growth of its factories and manufacturing industries during the 20th century helped South Carolina to become an important industrial center. Today, South Carolina is one of the leading textile-producing states, with approximately 500 textile factories that produce goods such as acrylic, cotton, polyester, silk, and wool cloth. South Carolina industries also manufacture chemicals such as synthetic fibers, dyes, and pharmaceuticals; industrial machinery; and a variety of wood products from the state's extensive forests. While industrial expansion has brought jobs and economic growth to the state, it has also caused serious air and water pollution problems.

Many traditional agricultural activities, such as growing tobacco, raising broilers (young chickens), and growing crops like cotton, soybeans, and corn, continue today. Approximately one-fourth of South Carolina's land is used for farming, and the

Below left: *South Carolina is known for its antebellum architecture.* Below right: *Raising broilers (young chickens) is a traditional agricultural activity in South Carolina.*

Born in South Carolina

- ★ **John C. Calhoun**, statesman
- ★ **Althea Gibson**, athlete
- ★ **Dizzy Gillespie**, jazz musician and composer
- ★ **DuBose Heyward**, poet, playwright, and novelist
- ★ **Jesse Jackson**, civil rights leader
- ★ **Eartha Kitt**, actress, singer, and dancer
- ★ **Francis "Swamp Fox" Marion**, soldier
- ★ **Ronald McNair**, astronaut
- ★ **John Rutledge**, jurist
- ★ **Strom Thurmond**, senator
- ★ **Charles Townes**, physicist
- ★ **William Westmoreland**, general
- ★ **Vanna White**, television personality

Above: *John Calhoun;* below: *Ronald McNair*

state ranks as one of the leading tobacco producers in the United States.

South Carolina maintains strong ties to its history. Antebellum (pre–Civil War) homes and plantations near Charleston attract many tourists who want to experience historic South Carolinian life and farming. Myrtle Beach and Hilton Head are two of the most popular beach resort areas in the United States.

Antebellum homes line the historic Charleston Harbor in Charleston, South Carolina.

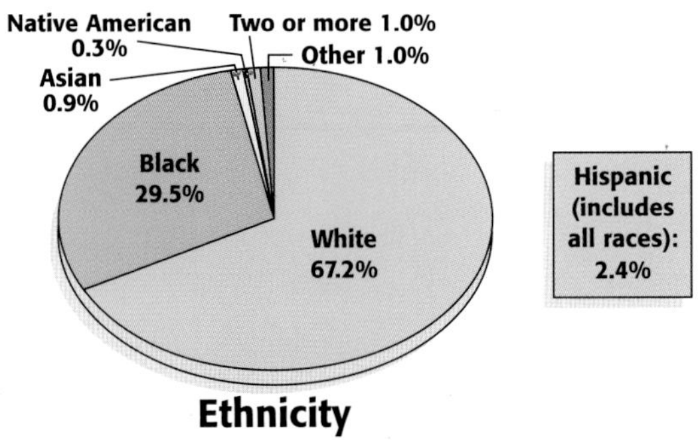

Ethnicity

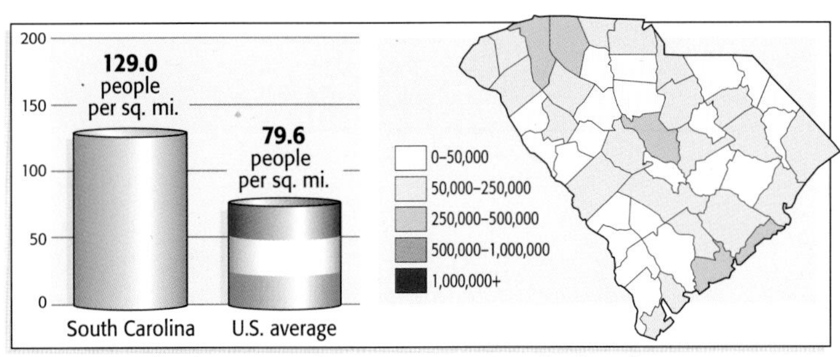

Population Density

Population by County

South Dakota

Under God, the people rule.

Land area rank *Largest state (1)* 16 ——— *smallest state (52)*

Population rank *Most people (1)* 46 ——— *fewest people (52)*

At a Glance

Name: *Dakota* is a Sioux word meaning "friends" or "allies."

Nicknames: Coyote State, Mount Rushmore State

Capital: Pierre

Size: 77,121 sq. mi. (199744 sq km)

Population: 754,844

Statehood: South Dakota became the 40th state on November 2, 1889.

Electoral votes: 3 (2004)

U.S. representatives: 1 (until 2003)

State tree: Black Hills spruce

State flower: American pasqueflower

State animal: coyote

Highest point: Harney Peak, 7,242 ft. (2,207 m)

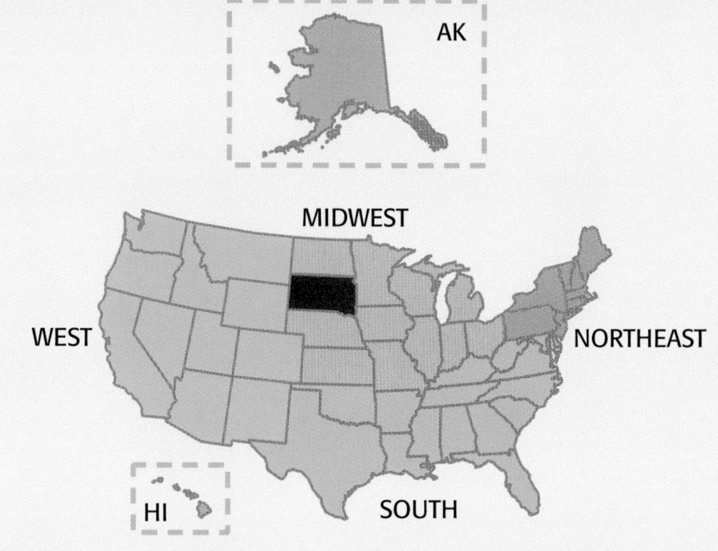

The Place

South Dakota is one of the fertile Midwest states. South Dakota is often called the Land of Infinite Variety because of its landscape, which includes wide rivers, deep canyons, rolling plains, the Black Hills, and the Badlands.

The Missouri River divides South Dakota roughly into eastern and western halves. The river's dams provide energy and

The Badlands, regions of unique rock formations, are located in southeastern South Dakota.

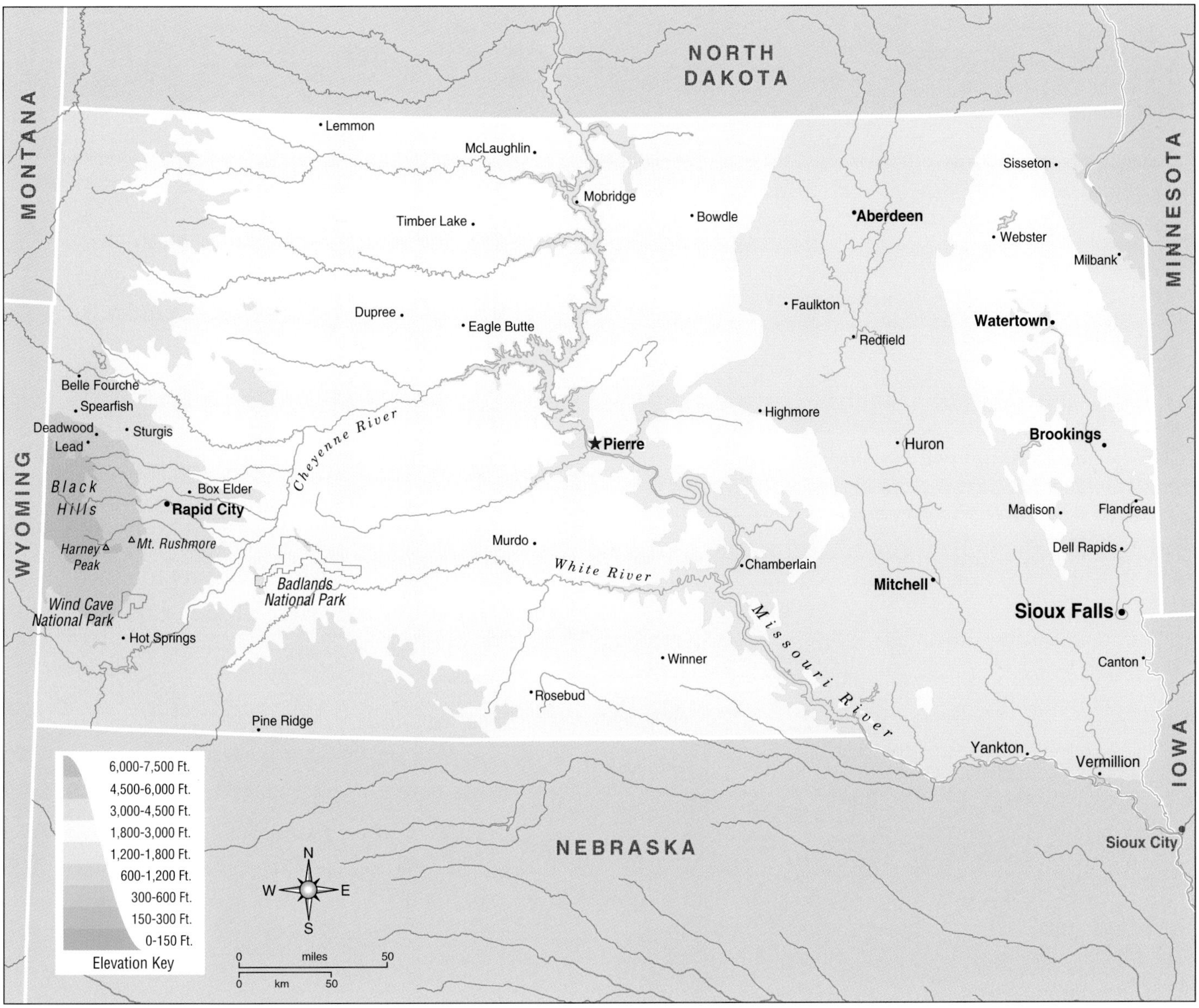

water for irrigation. East of the Missouri River, ancient glaciers carved the land into low hills and small lakes. The soil in this

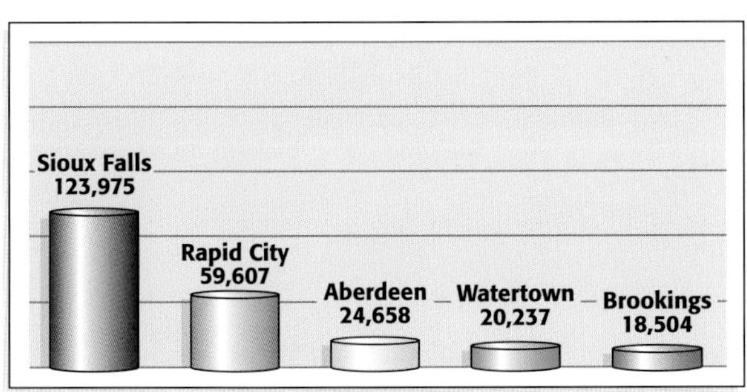

Major Cities

area is the most fertile in the state. To the west of the Missouri River is the Great Plains region, an area of canyons, gorges, buttes (flat-topped hills standing alone), and plains.

The Black Hills, which rise from the middle of the prairie to form peaks, canyons, and unusual rock formations, are located in the southwest. South Dakota's best forests and mineral deposits, especially of gold, are found in the Black Hills. Some of the most famous badlands (or regions of

Above: *A Lakota camp near Pine Ridge, in 1891*
Below: *Settlers to South Dakota in the 1850s created difficulties with the Native Americans.*

unique rock formations carved by wind and water) are located southeast of the Black Hills. South Dakota has few forested areas, except in the Black Hills.

South Dakota's climate can be unpredictable. Summers are usually hot and dry, and winters are cold and snowy. Rich, fertile soil and minerals such as gold and petroleum are South Dakota's most abundant resources.

The Past

During the 1700s, bison provided food, clothing, and shelter to Sioux, or Dakota, tribes who roamed South Dakota following the herds. The first white persons to claim the Dakota territory were French explorers from Canada. For a few years, however, the area was under Spanish rule, and then was returned to the French, who sold present-day North and South Dakota to

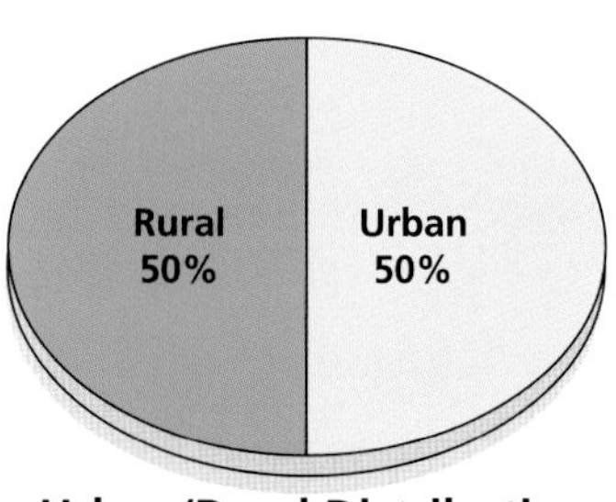

Urban/Rural Distribution

Facts and Firsts

- ★ Belle Fourche is the geographical center of the United States, including Alaska and Hawaii.
- ★ The highest mountain in the United States east of the Rockies is Harney Peak, which stands 7,242 feet above sea level in the Black Hills.
- ★ The third-longest known cave in the world is Jewel Cave, which is named after the sparkling calcite crystals that run throughout it.
- ★ The most endangered land mammal in North America, the black-footed ferret, has been reintroduced to the wild in the Sage Creek wilderness area.
- ★ South Dakota is home to only one kind of venomous snake, the prairie rattlesnake.
- ★ South Dakota is home to the largest bison herd in the United States. The herd is privately owned by Triple-U Enterprises near the city of Pierre.

the United States in 1803 as part of the Louisiana Purchase.

Settlers from the East, attracted by the fur trade established by the French, came to South Dakota and established the first permanent settlement in the region in 1817. In the 1850s, settlers moved into eastern South Dakota and began to farm. Wars with Native Americans, particularly Red Cloud's War (named for Sioux chief Red Cloud), slowed settlement in the 1860s.

In 1874 and 1876, the discovery of gold in western South Dakota set off a gold rush. The town of Deadwood quickly became an important center for prospecting. Life there was wild and dangerous, and Deadwood was home to such legendary people as Wild Bill Hickok and Calamity Jane.

The rush of new prospectors and settlers threatened some Native Americans. Leaders, such as Sitting Bull and Crazy Horse, and their followers attacked white settlements. In 1877, the U.S. government took possession of the Black Hills and forced many Sioux to live on reservations, where they had to give up their former lifestyle of following the bison herds. Some Sioux started a new religion known as the Ghost Dance, which was intended to restore their old way of life. The U.S. government misinterpreted the Ghost Dance as a further threat to white settlers. In 1890, federal troops killed 300 Sioux in a massacre known as Wounded Knee.

The rush of farmers and speculators continued during the 1880s. To meet the growing demand by miners and townspeople for meat, cattle ranchers moved into the open land west of the Missouri River. During the next 40 years, South Dakota experienced times of great prosperity followed by economic depressions caused by droughts, grasshopper plagues, dust storms, or low food prices.

To decrease its dependence on farming, South Dakota undertook efforts to broaden its economy. During the 1950s, the state built hydroelectric dams along the Missouri River to provide irrigation and energy for

State Smart

In 1927, sculptor Gutzon Borglum designed Mount Rushmore, which took 14 years and cost $1 million to complete. It has the largest figures of any statue in the world. Considered the world's greatest mountain carving, Mount Rushmore displays the faces of four U.S. presidents as a tribute to democracy.

The Corn Palace in Mitchell, built in 1921, has exterior murals made from corn, grain, and grasses.

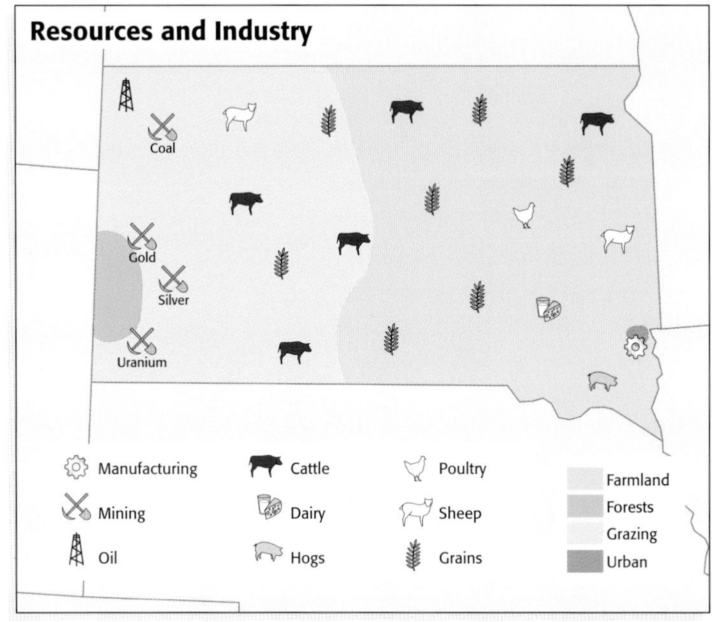

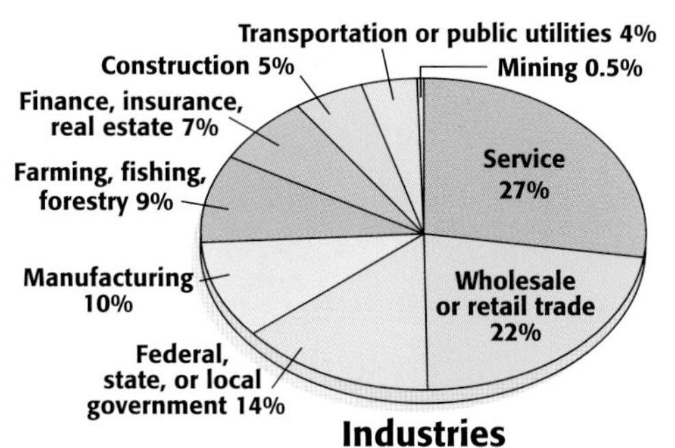

new industries. These dams created new lakes that began to attract thousands of tourists to South Dakota every year. Tourism ranked second only to agriculture in importance to the state's economy.

In 1980, the U.S. Supreme Court directed the U.S. government to pay the Sioux more than $100 million for the theft of their land in the Black Hills in 1877. The Sioux refused to accept the money and continue today to fight for the return of their former land.

The Present

Despite its industrial growth, South Dakota continues to be the leading agricultural state. Its economy is more dependent on farming than that of any other state. About nine-tenths of South Dakota's land is farmland. Half of this area, especially in western South Dakota, is pastureland, used to graze cattle, hogs, lambs, and sheep.

South Dakota is a leading beef cattle producer. Crop farms in the north, south, and east grow corn, soybeans, wheat, flaxseed, hay, oats, and rye. Many factories throughout South Dakota process these farm products for sale around the world.

South Dakota continues to develop its mineral resources. The Homestake Gold Mine near the city of Lead produced large amounts of gold from its opening in 1876

Below left: *Cowboys relax after a day of herding.* Below right: *Mt. Rushmore is one of the world's most recognized landmarks.*

Born in South Dakota

- ★**Sparky Anderson**, baseball manager
- ★**Gertrude Bonnin (Zitkala-Sa)**, Sioux writer
- ★**Tom Brokaw**, television newscaster
- ★**Crazy Horse (Tashunka Witko)**, Oglala chief
- ★**Mary Hart**, television host
- ★**Hubert H. Humphrey**, U.S. vice president
- ★**Cheryl Ladd**, actress
- ★**Ernest Orlando Lawrence**, physicist
- ★**George McGovern**, politician
- ★**Sitting Bull (Tatanka Yotanka)**, chief of Hunkpappa Sioux
- ★**Mamie Van Doren**, actress

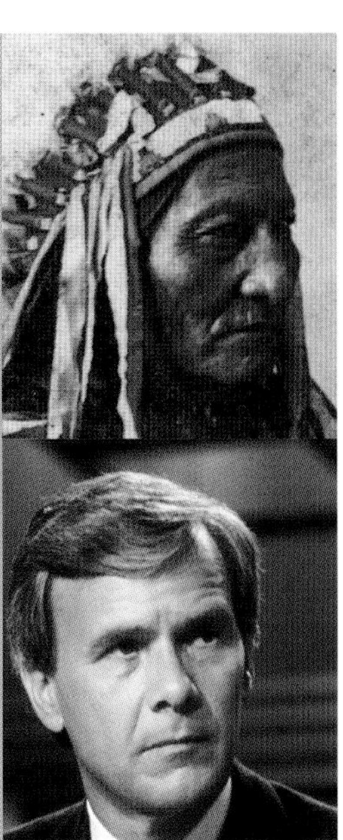

Above: *Sitting Bull;* below: *Tom Brokaw*

until its closure in 2001; the state is still a leading producer of gold. Petroleum was discovered in the 1950s and is second in importance among South Dakota's mineral products.

Industries begun in recent decades produce items including computers and computer components, medical instruments, lumber, and transportation and construction equipment. Tourism has also grown considerably, and millions of people visit South Dakota's lakes and the Black Hills, where they can see Mount Rushmore, the gigantic mountain carving of presidents George Washington, Thomas Jefferson, Abraham Lincoln, and Theodore Roosevelt. Residents have begun work nearby on an even larger statue of Sioux leader Crazy Horse.

The coyote, South Dakota's state animal, is found primarily near the Missouri River and in the Black Hills.

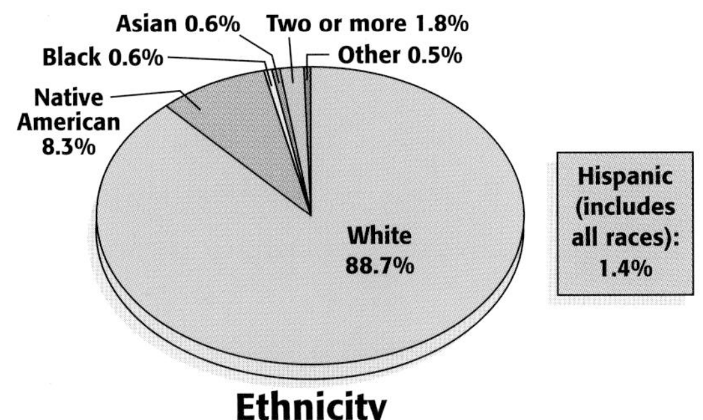

Ethnicity

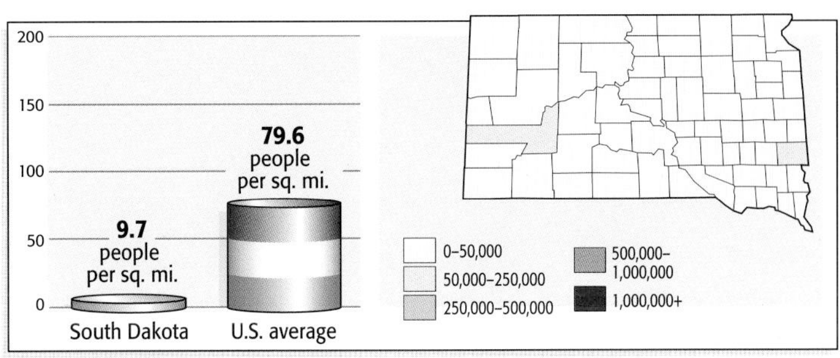

Population Density

Population by County

Tennessee

Agriculture and commerce.

Land area rank
Largest state (1)
34 — *smallest state (52)*

Population rank
Most people (1)
16 — *fewest people (52)*

At a Glance

Name: The region may have been named after Tanasie, a group of Cherokee villages on the Little Tennessee River.
Nickname: Volunteer State
Capital: Nashville
Size: 42,146 sq. mi. (109,158 sq km)
Population: 5,689,283
Statehood: Tennessee became the 16th state on June 1, 1796.
Electoral votes: 11 (2004)
U.S. representatives: 9 (until 2003)
State tree: tulip poplar
State flower: iris
State animal: raccoon
Highest point: Clingmans Dome, 6,643 ft. (2,025 m)

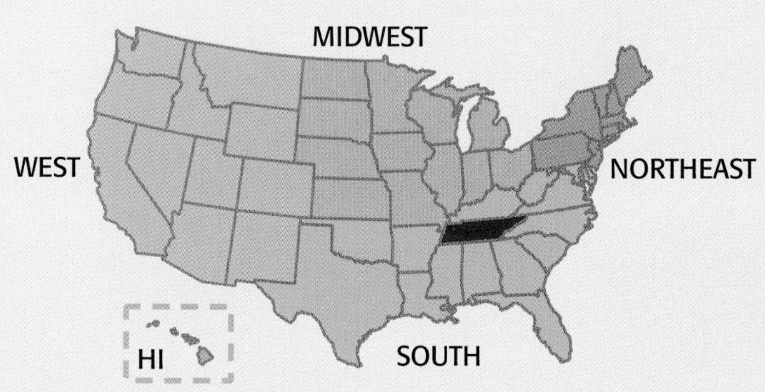

The Place

Tennessee is located in the south-central United States and is bordered by Kentucky and Virginia to the north, North Carolina to the east, Georgia, Alabama, and Mississippi to the south, and, across the Mississippi River, Arkansas and Missouri to the west. The Blue Ridge Mountains, which contain large forests and valuable minerals, form part of Tennessee's border. To the west of the Blue Ridge Mountains are fertile valleys and rocky cliffs. Nashville lies in a large, fertile basin with extensive phosphate deposits. Land around the Mississippi River is mostly low and rich near the Mississippi Delta but

The Blue Ridge Mountains form part of Tennessee's eastern border.

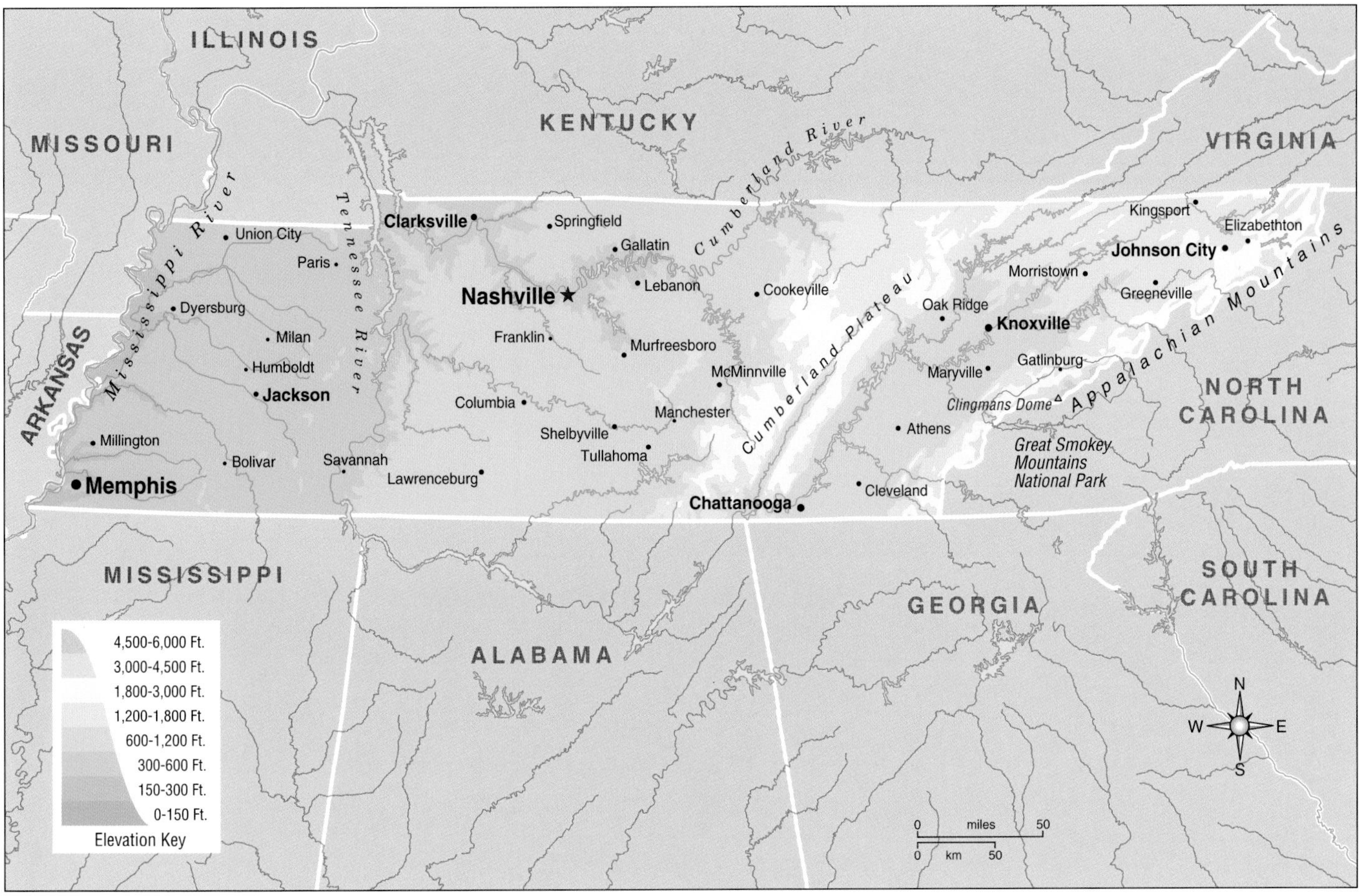

hilly in other places. Tennessee's climate is warm and subtropical. The Blue Ridge Mountains are cooler and snowier than the lower plains of western Tennessee.

In eastern Tennessee, fluorite, marble, and zinc are common minerals. Deposits of limestone, phosphate, and zinc are found in central Tennessee, while coal is common in the hills around the Blue Ridge Mountains.

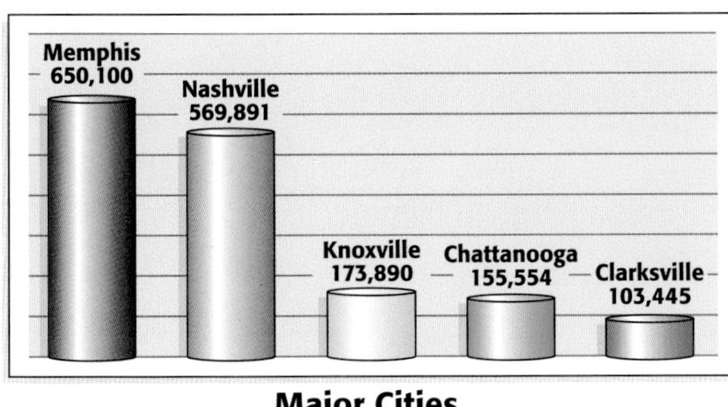

Major Cities

The Past

Artifacts indicate that the earliest inhabitants of the area were prehistoric Mound Builders. When Hernando de Soto led the first Spanish explorers into Tennessee in 1540 on his journey to the Mississippi River, he encountered Cherokee, Shawnee, Creek, and Chickasaw tribes. De Soto died in 1542 without starting a settlement. In 1673, the first English and French explorers reached the Tennessee region. These countries fought for control of the area, but the English eventually won in 1763 in the French and Indian Wars.

The first permanent settlers began to move into Tennessee from Virginia and North Carolina. In 1775, Daniel Boone started a new trail to western Tennessee

Andrew Jackson, standing right, came to Tennessee as a young lawyer and made his political career there.

and beyond, which opened this area to settlement. Tennessee was a part of North Carolina and did not become a separate state until after the Revolutionary War.

Large plantations worked by slaves were built in central and western Tennessee, while eastern Tennessee remained slave-free. Three future presidents were prominent in Tennessee politics: Andrew Jackson, James K. Polk, and Andrew Johnson.

During the Civil War, Johnson attempted to keep Tennessee in the Union. When Tennessee became the last state to secede from the United States, Johnson left the state to serve as Abraham Lincoln's vice president. After Johnson became

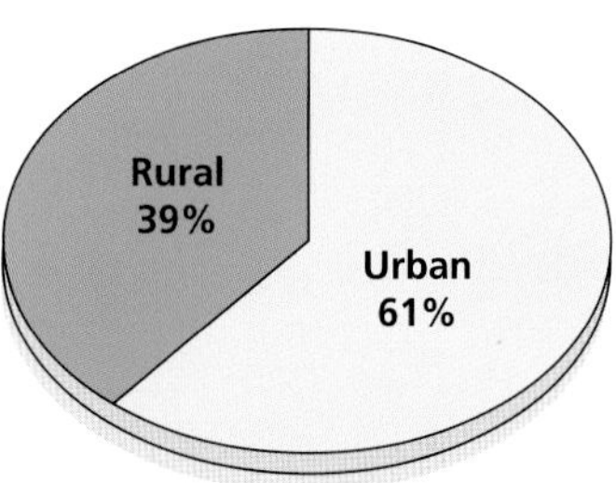

Urban/Rural Distribution

Facts and Firsts

- ★ Tennessee, along with Missouri, shares its borders with the largest number of other states—a total of eight.
- ★ There are more than 3,800 caves in Tennessee.
- ★ The Lost Sea in Sweetwater is the largest underground lake in the country.
- ★ In the winter of 1811, the largest earthquake in U.S. history shook northwestern Tennessee. Reelfoot Lake in Obion was created as a result of the earthquake.
- ★ Legendary railroad engineer Casey Jones, who was killed when his train crashed in 1900, lived in Jackson, where today there is a museum in his honor.
- ★ Nashville's *Grand Ole Opry* is the longest continuously running live radio program in the world. It has been broadcast every Friday and Saturday night since 1925.
- ★ Graceland, Elvis Presley's home in Memphis, is the second-most visited house in the United States. Only the White House attracts more visitors.
- ★ Shelby County has more horses per person than any other county in the United States.
- ★ The sale of cotton made Memphis an important port city on the Mississippi River. Even today, the Memphis Cotton Exchange handles about one-third of the nation's cotton every year.

president, Tennessee was the first state readmitted to the Union, in March 1866.

After the Civil War, Tennessee's plantations were divided into smaller farms. Without slave labor, farms lost their former prosperity. New industries began to grow. Coal mining and textile production increased.

In 1925, the state attracted attention for the Scopes trial, which involved a lawsuit against a biology teacher who was charged with illegally teaching evolution instead of the Bible's creation story. The state law that banned the teaching of evolution in public schools was not repealed until 1967.

In 1942, during World War II, the U.S. government built an atomic energy and nuclear physics facility near Oak Ridge, where scientists conducted research on the atomic bomb. The facility's existence was kept secret from most of the country until the summer of 1945.

New dams were built to provide abundant and inexpensive hydroelectric power and Tennessee became less agricultural and more urban. Nashville emerged as the center of the country music industry.

In the 1950s and 1960s, Tennessee and many other states suffered from racial problems caused by segregation, which denied African Americans the same rights as whites. In April 1968, when civil rights leader Dr. Martin Luther King Jr. traveled to Memphis to support striking sanitation workers, he was shot and killed. King's assassination prompted Tennessee lawmakers to enact civil rights legislation there.

State Smart

The Tennessee Lady Volunteers NCAA basketball team has won more games than any other NCAA basketball team in the country. Home games attract sellout crowds of more than 15,500 spectators.

Below left: *Women atop Lookout Mountain, scene of the Battle Above the Clouds during the Civil War;* below right: *Tennessee is the home of the leading U.S. women's college basketball team, the University of Tennessee Lady Volunteers.*

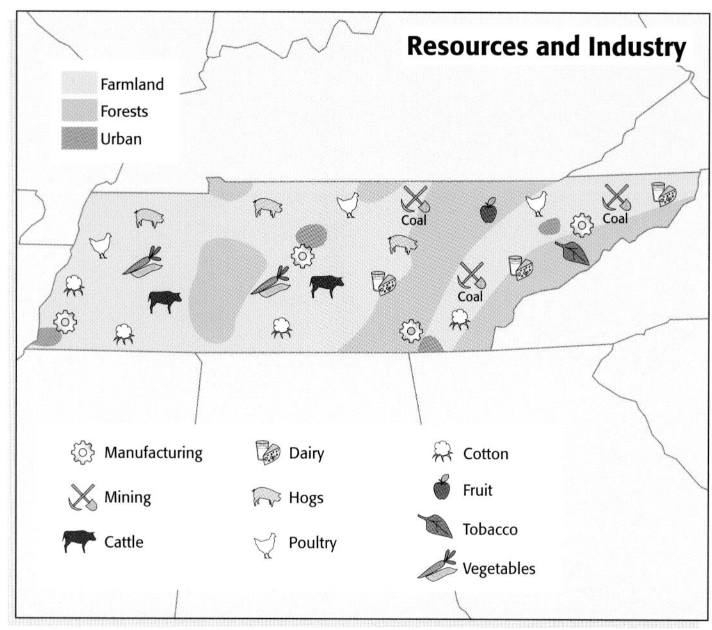

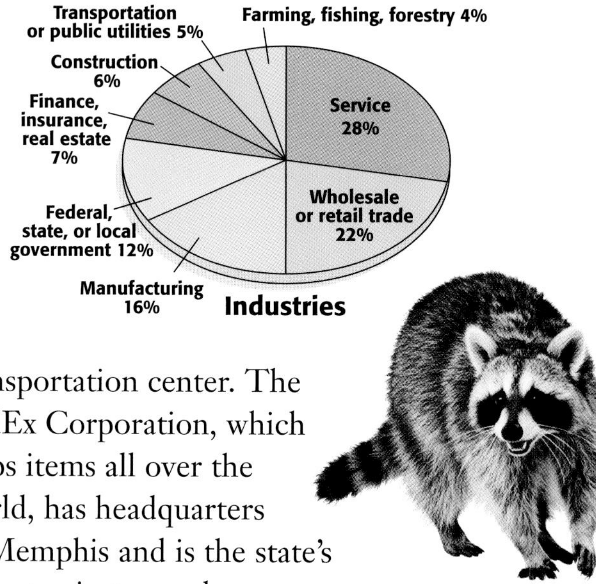

The Present

Today, more Tennessee residents live in cities than on farms, and manufacturing is Tennessee's most important industry. Paints, pharmaceuticals, and soaps are the state's leading products. The manufacture of transportation equipment is also a major industry. Tennessee factories produce boat and airplane parts, and car manufacturers Saturn and Nissan have large plants in Spring Hill and Smyrna. Because of its central location, Memphis is an important transportation center. The FedEx Corporation, which ships items all over the world, has headquarters in Memphis and is the state's largest private employer.

Food and beverage processing is another important source of revenue. The state's major products include bread, cereals, flour, beer, whiskey, and soft drinks.

Despite the state's shift to an industrial economy, approximately half of Tennessee's land is still devoted to farming. Horse farms are common, and the Tennessee walking horse breed was developed in central Tennessee. Cattle, dairy products, and hogs are principal farm commodities. Cotton is the leading crop in western Tennessee, just as it was before the Civil

Below left: *Nashville is the second largest city in Tennessee.* Below right: *A Tennessee farmer harvests corn.*

Born in Tennessee

- ★ **Davy Crockett**, frontiersman
- ★ **David G. Farragut**, first American admiral
- ★ **Aretha Franklin**, singer
- ★ **Morgan Freeman**, actor
- ★ **Isaac Hayes**, musician
- ★ **Estes Kefauver**, legislator
- ★ **Dolly Parton**, singer
- ★ **Minnie Pearl (Sarah Ophelia Colley Cannon)**, singer and comedienne
- ★ **Wilma Rudolph**, athlete
- ★ **Sequoyah**, Cherokee scholar and educator
- ★ **Cybil Shepherd**, actress
- ★ **Tina Turner**, singer
- ★ **Alvin York**, World War I hero

Above: *Wilma Rudolph;* below: *Dolly Parton*

War, and Memphis is one of the nation's centers of cotton trading. Farmers throughout the state grow tobacco, soybeans, and corn. Tomatoes, snap beans, apples, and peaches are Tennessee's chief fruits and vegetables.

Tennessee has begun to exploit its mineral resources, and crushed stone is its most valuable mineral, followed by zinc and coal.

Tourism is on the rise in Tennessee. It has long been a popular destination due to attractions such as the Great Smoky Mountains National Park. Tennessee is also known for its music festivals, where bluegrass, blues, and country musicians play their music. Nashville is the nation's country music capital, while Memphis is a hub for blues and jazz.

Bluegrass, blues, and country are all popular forms of music in Tennessee.

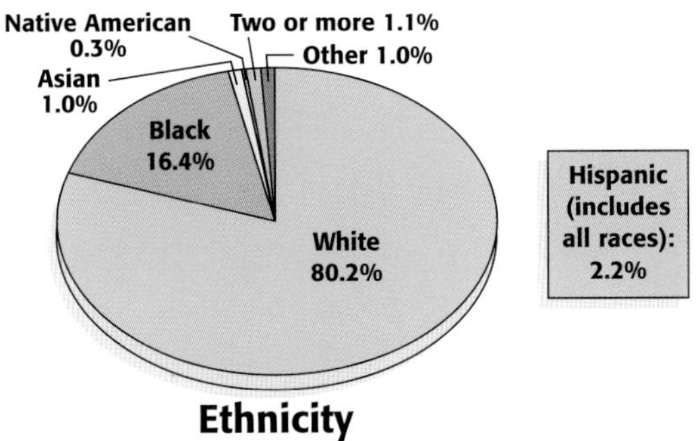

Ethnicity

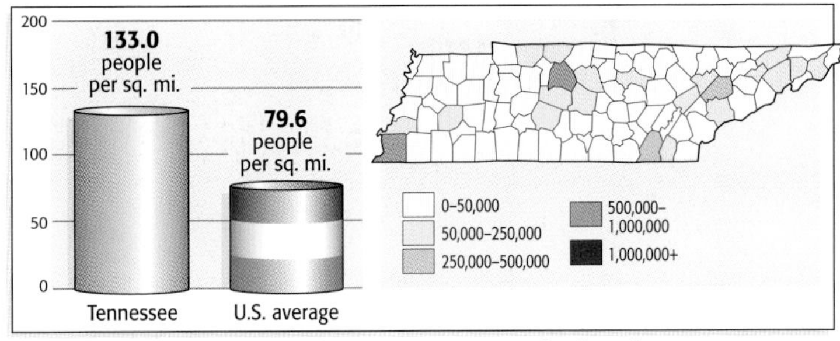

Population Density

Population by County

Texas

Friendship.

Land area rank
Largest state (1) 2 — *smallest state (52)*

Population rank
Most people (1) 2 — *fewest people (52)*

At a Glance

Name: *Texas* is a Spanish version of a Native American word meaning "friends" or "allies."

Nickname: Lone Star State

Capital: Austin

Size: 266,874 sq. mi. (691,201 sq km)

Population: 20,851,820

Statehood: Texas became the 28th state on December 29, 1845.

Electoral votes: 34 (2004)

U.S. representatives: 30 (until 2003)

State tree: pecan

State flower: bluebonnet

State bird: mockingbird

Highest point: Guadalupe Peak, 8,749 ft. (2,667 m)

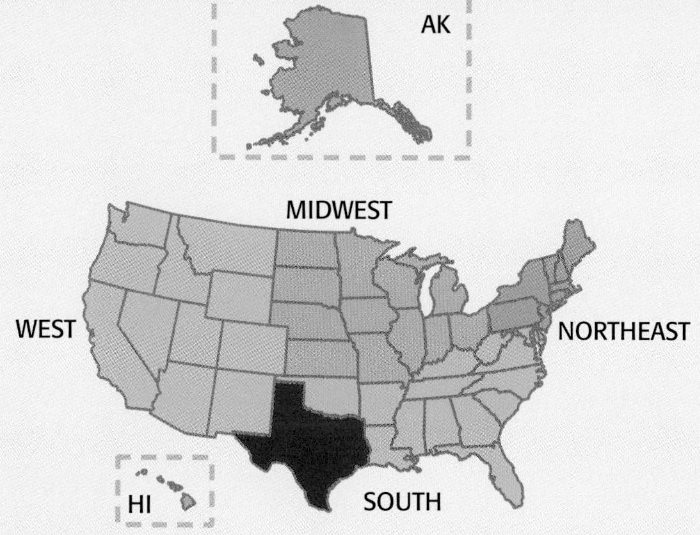

The Place

As the second-largest state in the United States, Texas is larger than Illinois, Indiana, Iowa, Michigan, and Wisconsin combined. Land along the Gulf of Mexico coast is low and has subtropical weather. The Rio Grande, which ends in the Gulf of Mexico and forms part of the boundary between the United States and Mexico, is surrounded by some of the most fertile soil in Texas. Toward the interior of Texas, the land is characterized by rolling plains, with a number of hills and forests. Under the fertile soil of these plains lie oil deposits that have made Texas the nation's leader in the production of petroleum.

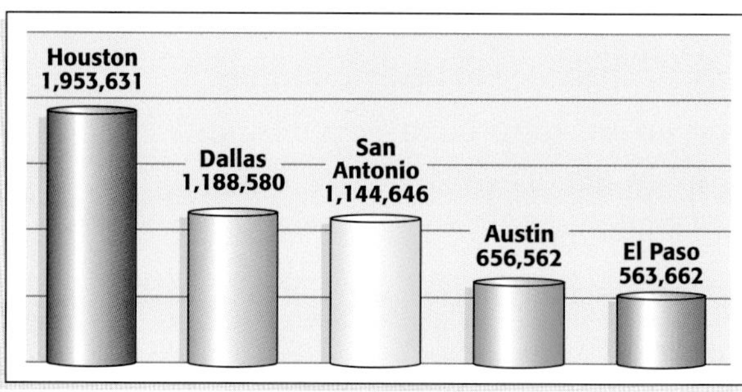

Major Cities

The Great Plains region reaches down from Canada into Texas and forms the state's Panhandle, or the region where it runs along New Mexico and Oklahoma. The western

Houston, near the Gulf of Mexico, is a center for the oil industry.

Panhandle is treeless grassland; the southern Panhandle lies above the underground Permian Basin, the site of the state's best deposits of oil and natural gas. Western Texas consists of dry and level plains crossed by spurs, or extensions, of the Rocky Mountains known as the Guadalupe, Davis, and Chisos Ranges. A number of sandbars lie off the coast of Texas, including Padre Island.

About 15 percent of Texas is forested, and more than 500 kinds of grasses grow in

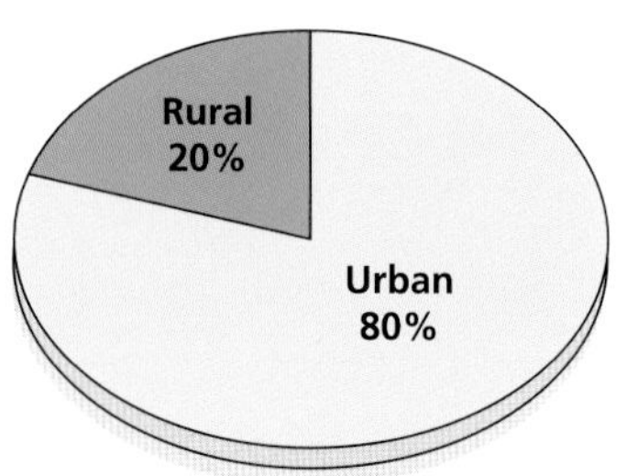

Urban/Rural Distribution

the state. The greatest mineral resources are oil and natural gas. Texas also benefits from fertile soil, which enables farmers to grow many kinds of crops.

Climate varies throughout the state. The Rio Grande Valley is the warmest place in Texas; the coldest area is the Panhandle in the northwest. The Gulf Coast has a warm, humid climate with mild winters; central Texas is mild, but northeastern Texas is cold. More rain falls in the eastern portion of Texas than the other regions.

The Alamo, in San Antonio, was the site of an 1834 battle between American settlers and Mexican soldiers.

The Past

Spain was the first European country to claim the area that is now Texas. Explorers who traveled northward from Spain's Mexican settlements in 1519 returned with tales of fabulous gold and silver deposits. The Spanish sent many expeditions to look for "golden cities" known as the Seven Cities of Cibola. In 1682, Franciscan friars built the first Spanish settlements in Texas—Catholic missions near present-day El Paso. Very soon, most of Texas was part

Facts and Firsts

- ★ Texas is the second-largest state in the United States, smaller than only Alaska. Texas's King Ranch is bigger than the entire state of Rhode Island.
- ★ Texas is the only state that has been part of six different nations, including Spain, France, Mexico, the Republic of Texas, the Confederate States, and the United States. Texas was once an independent country and therefore is the only state to have entered the United States by treaty instead of territorial annexation.
- ★ Three of the 10 most populous U.S. cities are in Texas: Houston, Dallas, and San Antonio.
- ★ Texas produces more cotton, cattle, and sheep than any other state.
- ★ Texas is home to the largest herd of whitetail deer in the United States.
- ★ Central Texas is sometimes called the Silicon Valley of the South because it is home to major computer companies such as Dell and Compaq.
- ★ In 1885, the soft drink Dr. Pepper was invented in Waco.

of Mexico. Although the French began to explore northern Texas in 1685, their attempts to settle there were unsuccessful.

In 1821, Mexico won its independence from Spain, and Texas then became part of the country of Mexico. Mexico gave permission for a growing number of Americans to settle in the area. Mexican officials soon became alarmed, however, because American settlements grew rapidly. In 1834, Mexican general Antonio Lopez de Santa Anna overthrew Mexico's government and made himself dictator. American settlers were outraged, and revolted against the new Mexican leader. Texas rebels lost a bloody battle at the Alamo, a Spanish mission, but a small army led by Texas hero Sam Houston later captured Santa Anna's forces at San Jacinto. In 1836, the Republic of Texas was founded, with Houston as president.

When Texas joined the United States in 1845, an outraged Mexican government contested the state's borders. The United States, easily provoked into war, gained Texas and other southwestern lands as a result of victory in the Mexican-American War.

In 1861, Texas left the Union to join the Confederacy during the Civil War. After the war ended in 1865, cattle ranches became numerous in Texas, and cowboys drove their cattle north to railroad centers in Kansas and Missouri to be shipped east. Oil was discovered in 1866, which prompted the construction of oil refineries and manufacturing plants. Between 1900 and 1920, railroads and irrigation systems were completed.

Texas industries continued to expand during World War II, when the state was the training site for more than a million American soldiers. In 1962, the National Aeronautics and Space Administration (NASA) established a Manned Spacecraft Center at Houston, which is now the control center for all piloted space missions. This facility, renamed the Lyndon B. Johnson Space Center in 1973, helped attract many other space research facilities and corporations to Texas during the following decades.

State Smart

Texas has about 225,000 farms, more than any other state. These farms cover three-quarters of the state's land.

Above: *The cowboy population on Texas ranches increased after the Civil War.*
Below: *NASA's Lyndon B. Johnson Space Center in Houston is the control center for all piloted space missions.*

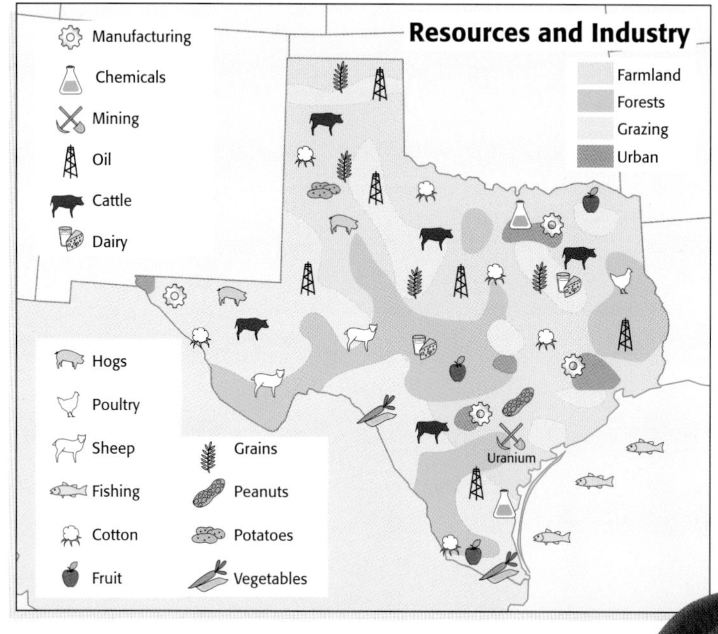

Industries

Transportation or public utilities 5%
Farming, fishing, forestry 4%
Mining 2%
Construction 6%
Finance, insurance, real estate 8%
Service 29%
Manufacturing 10%
Wholesale or retail trade 22%
Federal, state, or local government 15%

The Present

Texas is the second-most populous state, after California. People of many backgrounds and races live there. A large majority of the Texas population lives in metropolitan areas, including Houston, Dallas, and San Antonio.

Texas's natural resources have helped to make it one of the wealthiest states. Texas leads the country in oil production—drilling and refining about one-third of the nation's oil—and natural gas mining.

The agricultural industry contributes to the state's economy, and Texas has more farmland than any other state. Mild winters and rich grasses allow cattle to graze outdoors year-round, and as a result, Texas produces more beef cattle than any other state. Northeastern Texas has a number of dairy farms, while the central plains and the Panhandle have most of the state's hog farms. Cotton is the leading agricultural crop, and Texas produces more of it than any other state. Corn, hay, rice,

Below left: *Dallas is home to the headquarters of many retail and transportation companies.* Below right: *Mild weather allows cattle to graze outdoors year-round in Texas.*

Born in Texas

★**Alvin Ailey Jr.**, dancer and choreographer

★**Mary Kay Ash**, cosmetics entrepreneur

★**Gene Autry**, singer and actor

★**Carol Burnett**, comedienne

★**Laura Welch Bush**, first lady

★**Joan Crawford**, actress

★**Dwight D. Eisenhower**, U.S. president and general

★**Buddy (Charles Hardin) Holly**, musician

★**Howard Hughes**, industrialist and film producer

★**Lyndon B. Johnson**, U.S. president

★**Tommy Lee Jones**, actor

★**Janis Joplin**, singer and composer

★**Scott Joplin**, composer

★**Willie Nelson**, singer

★**Sandra Day O'Connor**, jurist

★**Quanah Parker**, last chief of the Comanche

★**Selena (Quintanilla) Pérez**, singer

★**Katherine Ann Porter**, novelist

★**Dan Rather**, television newscaster

★**Robert Rauschenberg**, artist

★**Nolan Ryan**, athlete

★**Sissy (Mary Elizabeth) Spacek**, actress

★**Rip Torn**, actor

Top to bottom: *Lyndon B. Johnson, Sandra Day O'Connor, Laura Bush*

and wheat also grow well on the plains of Texas.

Although Texas's economy has traditionally depended on its production and processing of oil and natural gas, unrelated industries have flourished during recent decades. Major retail stores, including J.C. Penney, 7-Eleven, and Radio Shack, have headquarters in the Dallas–Fort Worth area. Important transportation companies, such as Continental Airlines and American Airlines, are also headquartered there. Texas companies produce benzene, ethylene, fertilizers, propylene, and sulfuric acid in plants along the Gulf Coast. Factories also manufacture computer and office equipment. Texas Instruments, which produces calculators, electronics equipment, and military communications systems, has factories throughout Texas.

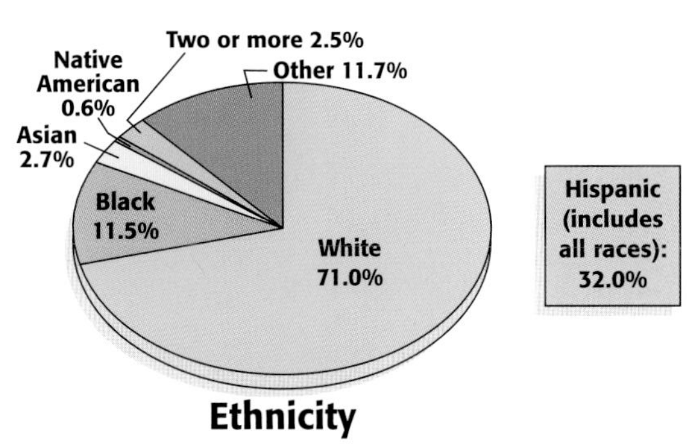

Ethnicity

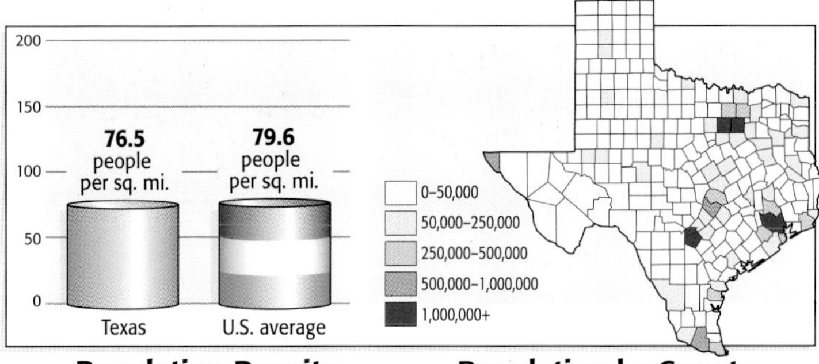

Population Density

Population by County

Utah

Industry.

Land area rank
Largest state (1)
11 — *smallest state (52)*

Population rank
Most people (1)
34 — *fewest people (52)*

At a Glance

Name: Utah was named for the Ute tribe. *Ute* means "higher up."

Nickname: Beehive State

Capital: Salt Lake City

Size: 84,904 sq. mi. (219,902 sq km)

Population: 2,233,169

Statehood: Utah became the 45th state on January 4, 1896.

Electoral votes: 5 (2004)

U.S. representatives: 3 (until 2003)

State tree: blue spruce

State flower: sego lily

State animal: Rocky Mountain elk

Highest point: Kings Peak, 13,528 ft. (4,123 m)

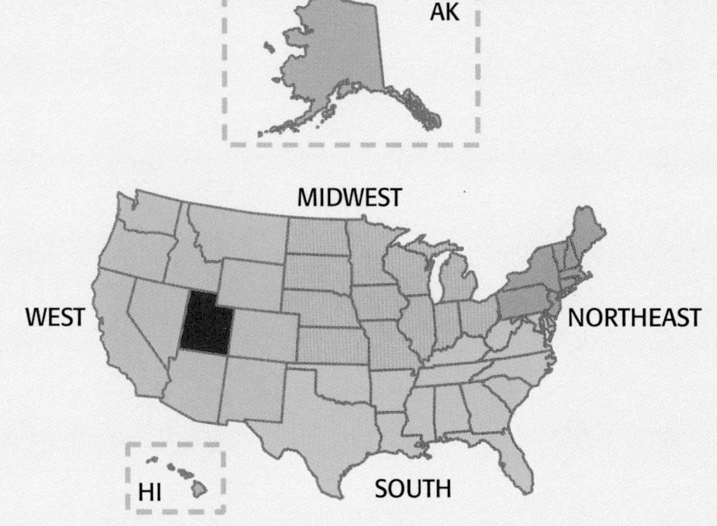

The Place

Utah is a mountainous western state. Two of its mountain ranges, the Uinta and Wasatch, are part of the Rocky Mountain chain. The Uinta Range, which extends from Colorado to Salt Lake City, is the only range in the Rockies to run from east to west. This range has many lakes and canyons

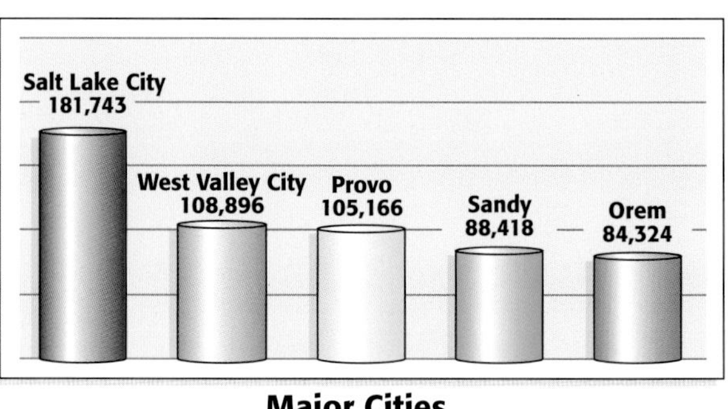

Major Cities

Utah's capital, Salt Lake City, is set in the Uinta Range of the Rocky Mountains.

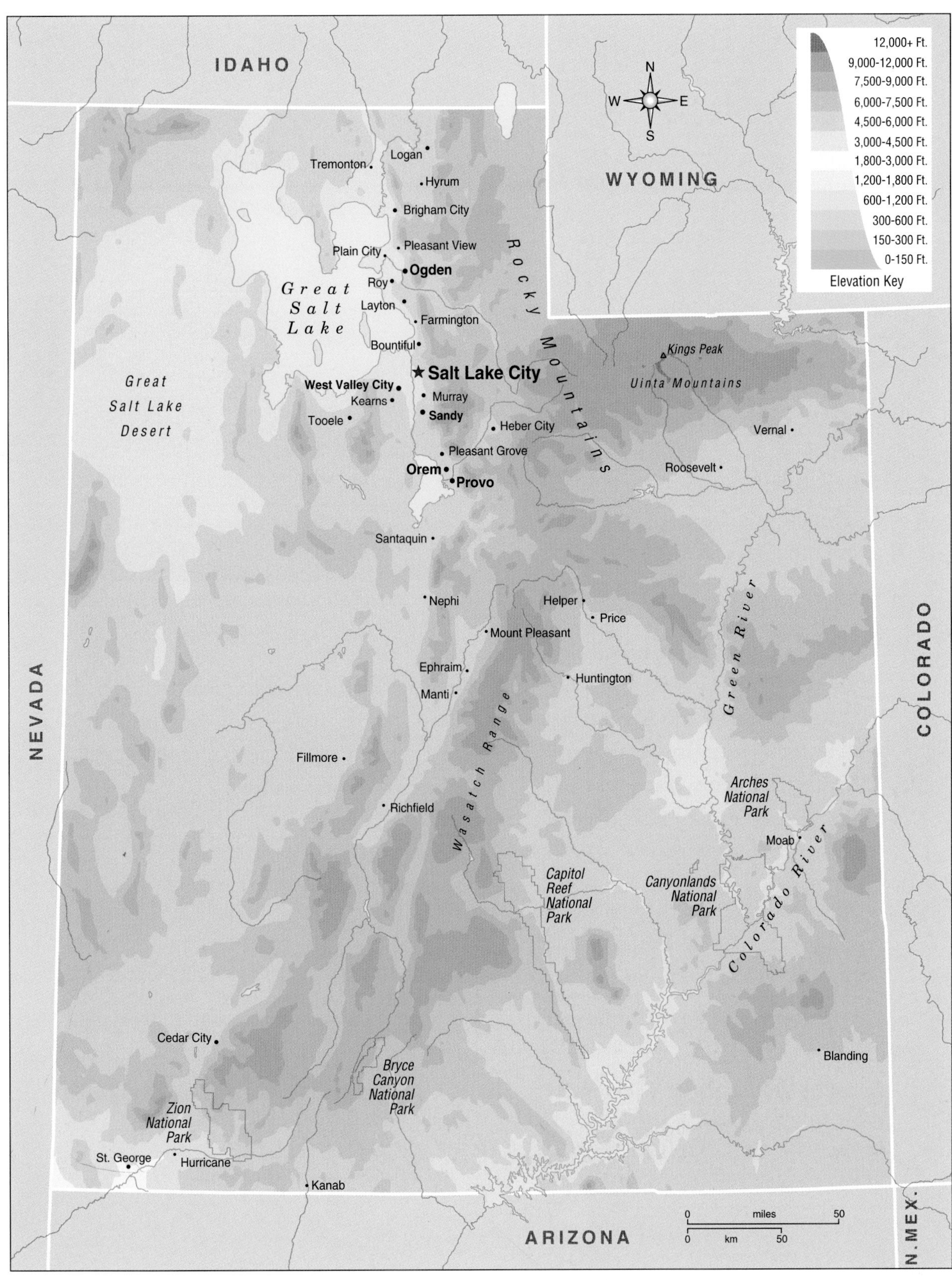

that were carved by glaciers thousands of years ago. Canyons in the Wasatch Range provide water to many of Utah's cities.

Western Utah is part of a dry basin that extends through several states. The area includes small mountain ranges and the

Great Salt Lake, the largest natural lake west of the Mississippi River. Southwest Utah is desert, although the southwestern region is the lowest, most fertile part of Utah. Southern and eastern Utah has deep canyons and high plateaus. The Abajo and La Sal Mountains cover southeastern Utah where it meets Arizona, Colorado, and New Mexico.

A huge freshwater lake, which scientists call Lake Bonneville, once covered the area of present-day Utah. The lake gradually shrank over time, leaving isolated lakes and ponds, including the Great Salt Lake.

Utah's climate is generally dry, and one-third of its land is desert. Summers can be hot, and winters are usually not snowy, except in the northeastern mountains. The Colorado River, the largest in Utah, provides energy and water to irrigate farms in drier parts of Utah. Utah has valuable deposits of coal, uranium, oil, and natural gas, as well as copper, gold, silver, and magnesium.

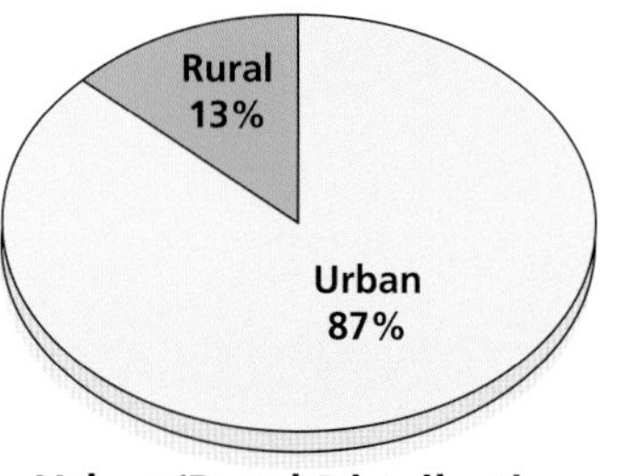

Urban/Rural Distribution

Remains of an Anasazi structure in Anasazi State Park, at Boulder, Utah.

Facts and Firsts

- ★ Utah's mountain peaks, with an average height of 11,222 feet (3,420 m), are the highest in the United States.
- ★ Utah's Great Salt Lake, the state's most famous natural feature, has an area of about 1,600 square miles (4,200 sq km), with an average depth of 13 feet (4 m).
- ★ The first railroad to cross the entire United States was completed at Promontory in 1869, when the Union Pacific Railroad (being built from the East Coast) met the Central Pacific Railroad (being built from the West Coast).
- ★ The first department store in the United States, Zions Co-operative Mercantile Institution, was established in Utah in the late 1800s.
- ★ Approximately 70 percent of Utah residents are Mormons, or members of the Church of Jesus Christ of Latter-Day Saints.
- ★ Utah has the highest literacy rate (94%) of any state.

The Past

Utah was once home to a Native American group known as the Anasazi, who built homes, apartment-like structures, and even cities in the rocky cliffs of Utah and other states. When the first Spanish explorers arrived in 1765 from Mexico, they found several Native American tribes living in the area of Utah. The Spanish were not interested in settling in Utah, but in 1811, other settlers came to Utah to trade furs. By 1830, American travelers were crossing Utah to journey from New Mexico to California.

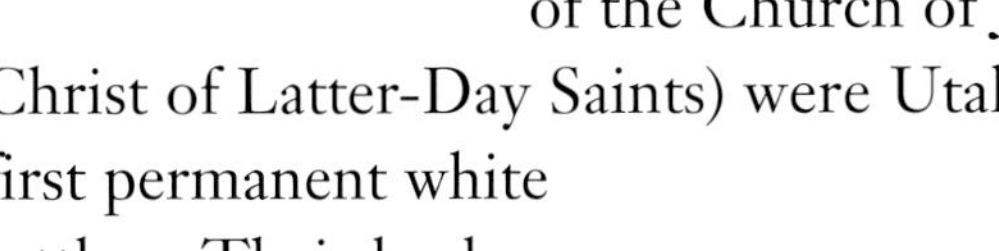

Brigham Young led Mormons to Utah.

Mormons (members of the Church of Jesus Christ of Latter-Day Saints) were Utah's first permanent white settlers. Their leader, Brigham Young, led the religious group to the Great Salt Lake in 1847 to avoid persecution in the East. At the time, Utah belonged to Mexico, but the United States attained the region during the Mexican War, which ended in 1848.

Mormons from all over the world immigrated to Utah and built farms, despite Native American protests. The population grew, and Utah asked to be admitted to the Union. Congress, however, refused to allow Utah to become a state, in part because of the Mormon practice of polygamy (one man having more than one wife).

In October 1861, the first transcontinental telegraph line was completed when cable from the East met cable from the West in Salt Lake City. Then, in 1863, gold and silver were discovered. A transcontinental railroad, completed in Utah less than a decade later, allowed gold, silver, and other items to be more easily shipped from the area. Utah adopted a new constitution that outlawed polygamy and was finally admitted as a state of the Union in 1896.

State Smart

Utah has the largest natural stone bridge in the world. Made of sandstone, Rainbow Bridge is 290 feet (88 m) high and 275 feet (84 m) wide.

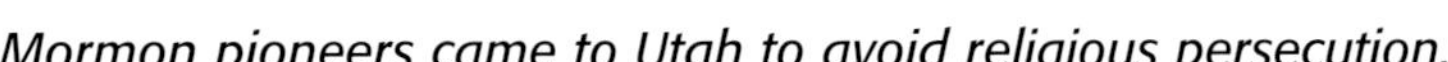

Mormon pioneers came to Utah to avoid religious persecution.

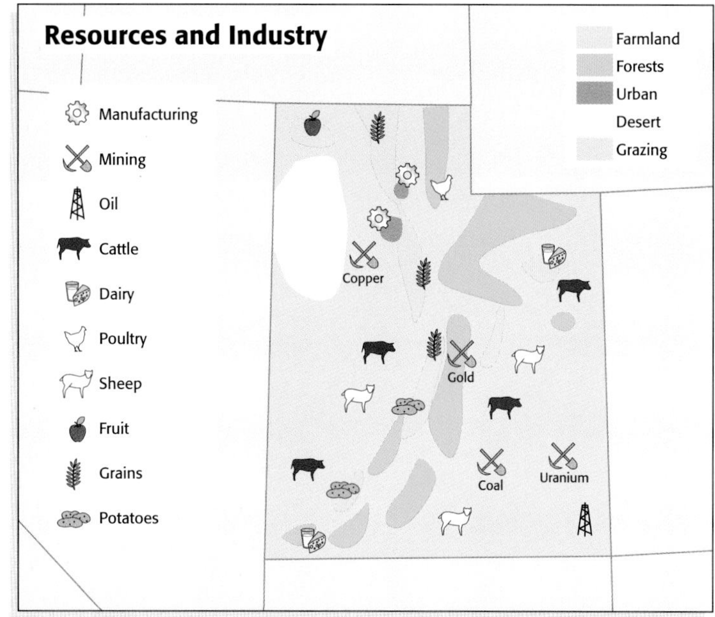

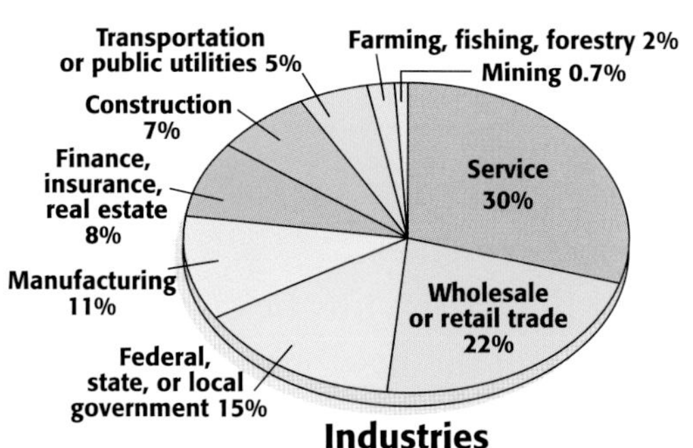

The expansion of Utah's railroads encouraged the growth of agricultural industries such as cattle ranching and farming, which required good transportation. The introduction of new mining techniques improved Utah's copper yield, and the state's mines supplied metals to the Allies during World War II. Several military bases were built in Utah, which became a center of missile and steel production.

Tourism became important to Utah's economy as mountain ski resorts attracted more visitors during the 1950s and 1960s. Large population growth during the 1970s and 1980s, however, strained Utah's economic and environmental resources, and the state struggled to fund public schools and limit industrial expansion into undeveloped wilderness areas.

The Present

The federal government owns two-thirds of Utah's land, and several military bases, including Hill Air Force Base, are located in Utah. Private industry has expanded since World War II, and today Utah produces rocket propulsion systems for

Below left: *Utah farmers grow fruit-bearing trees, such as pear trees.* Below right: *Utah's beautiful scenery attracts tourists.*

Born in Utah

- ★ **Maude Adams**, actress
- ★ **Roseanne (Barr)**, actress
- ★ **Butch Cassidy (Robert Leroy Parker)**, outlaw
- ★ **Philo Farnsworth**, inventor
- ★ **Harvey Fletcher**, physicist
- ★ **John Gilbert**, actor
- ★ **J. Willard Marriott**, restaurant and hotel chain founder
- ★ **Merlin Olson**, athlete and announcer
- ★ **Donny Osmond**, singer and actor
- ★ **Marie Osmond**, singer and actress
- ★ **Ivy Baker Priest**, U.S. treasurer
- ★ **Robert Walker**, actor
- ★ **James Woods**, actor
- ★ **Loretta (Gretchen) Young**, actress

Above: *Philo Farnsworth;* below: *Donny and Marie Osmond*

spacecraft and weapons, air bags for automobiles, beverages, dairy products, baked goods, metal products such as sheet metal, and machinery.

Utah's coal mining industry thrives, especially when shortages of oil from foreign countries affect the U.S. energy supply. Utah's second-most valuable mineral is copper, which is mined near Salt Lake City.

New irrigation techniques make it possible for farmers to raise cattle and sheep and grow hay, wheat, apples, peaches, pears, barley, and corn in parts of Utah that used to be desert. These irrigation techniques have prompted debate, however, because many Utah residents worry that irrigation of desert land puts a strain on Utah's natural ecological system. Conservationists are concerned about the opening of more land to industrial and agricultural development.

Snowbird is a popular ski resort.

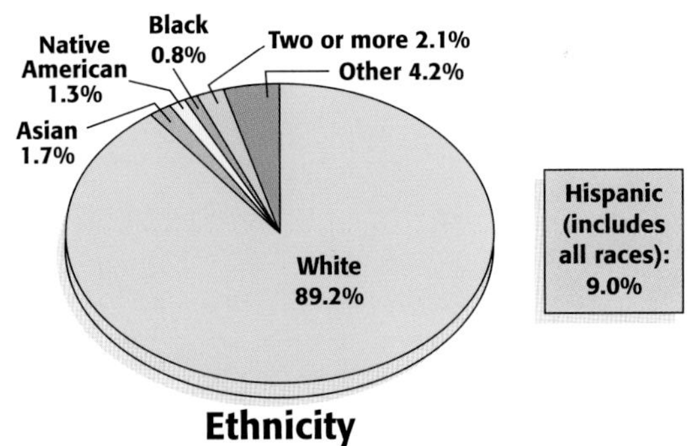

Ethnicity

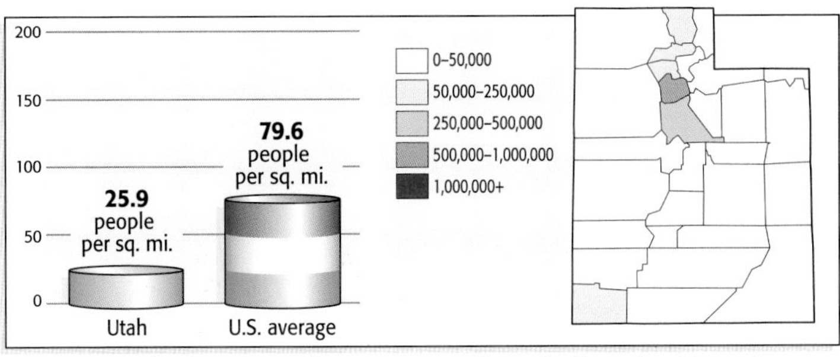

Population Density

Population by County

Vermont

Freedom and unity.

Land area rank
Largest state (1)
Population rank
Most people (1)

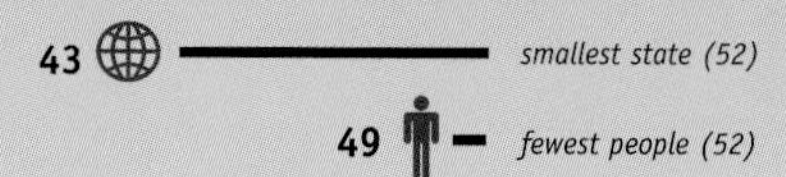

At a Glance

Name: Vermont is a combination of the French words *vert* and *mont*, which mean "green" and "mountain."
Nickname: Green Mountain State
Capital: Montpelier
Size: 9,615 sq. mi. (24,903 sq km)
Population: 608,827
Statehood: Vermont became the 14th state on March 4, 1791.
Electoral votes: 3 (2004)
U.S. representatives: 1 (until 2003)
State tree: sugar maple
State flower: red clover
State bird: hermit thrush
Highest point: Mount Mansfield, 4,393 ft. (1,339 m)

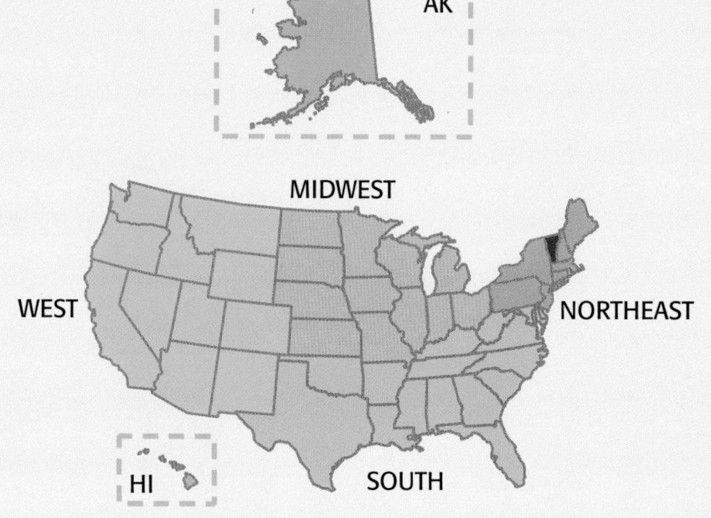

The Place

Although Vermont is the only New England state without a coastline on the Atlantic Ocean, about half of Vermont is bordered by water. The Connecticut River forms Vermont's eastern border, and Lake Champlain, the largest lake in New England, forms much of Vermont's western

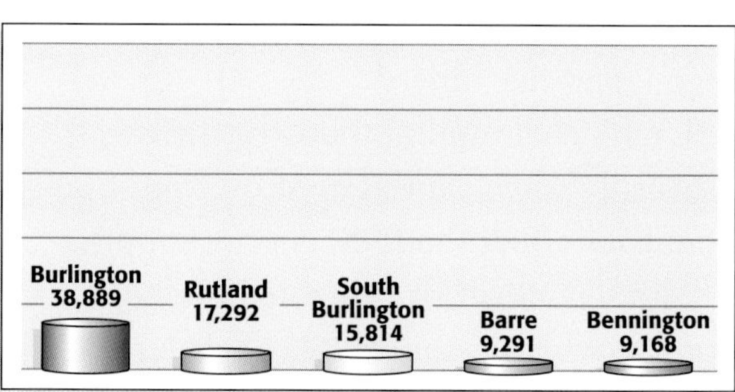

Major Cities

Colorful autumns in Vermont attract many tourists to the state every year.

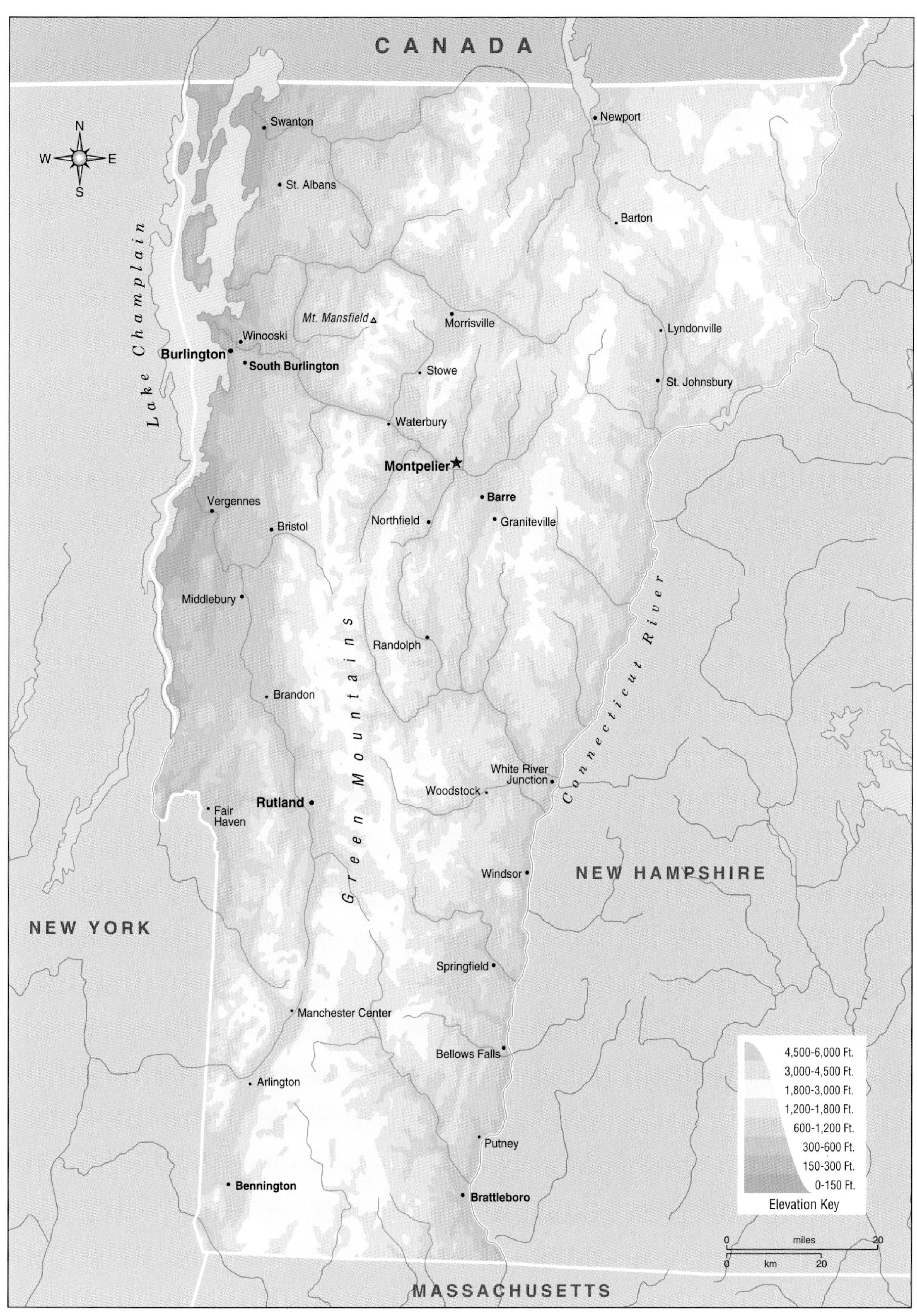
CANADA
N
W
E
S
Swanton
St. Albans
Newport
Barton
Lake Champlain
Mt. Mansfield
Morrisville
Lyndonville
Winooski
Burlington
South Burlington
Stowe
St. Johnsbury
Waterbury
Montpelier
Barre
Vergennes
Bristol
Northfield
Graniteville
Middlebury
Green Mountains
Randolph
Connecticut River
Brandon
White River Junction
Woodstock
Rutland
Fair Haven
Windsor
NEW HAMPSHIRE
NEW YORK
Springfield
Manchester Center
Bellows Falls
Arlington
Putney
Bennington
Brattleboro
4,500-6,000 Ft.
3,000-4,500 Ft.
1,800-3,000 Ft.
1,200-1,800 Ft.
600-1,200 Ft.
300-600 Ft.
150-300 Ft.
0-150 Ft.
Elevation Key
0 miles 20
0 km 20
MASSACHUSETTS

border. Several islands in Lake Champlain are part of Vermont, and the valley that surrounds the lake has some of Vermont's richest farmland.

The Green Mountains, located in the center of the state, have deposits of granite, marble, slate, and talc. Vermont's tallest peaks are in the Green Mountains. Northeastern Vermont has mountains made of granite, and southwestern Vermont is covered by a small extension of the Taconic Mountains, which extend into Massachusetts.

About three-quarters of Vermont's land is forested. The climate is cold, with short, cool summers and long, snowy winters. Vermont's mountains are usually cooler and receive more snow than the rest of the state.

Urban 32%
Rural 68%

Urban/Rural Distribution

The Past

Before the arrival of white settlers, Vermont was the home of several tribes of Algonquian and Iroquois, who fought with each other for control of the region. In 1609, French explorer Samuel de Champlain was the first European to reach present-day Vermont. In 1690, Jacobus de Warm and troops of British soldiers established a fort at Chimney Point, near Middlebury. Vermont's location, between the French colonies in present-day Canada and England's American colonies, made it an important strategic point. English colonists from Massachusetts moved into the Vermont region in 1724 and built Fort Dummer to guard Massachusetts from French and Native American attacks.

Samuel de Champlain

In the mid-1770s, during the French and Indian Wars, the French and their Native American allies were defeated, and the English took firm control of Vermont. Both New York and New Hampshire fought for the right to settle Vermont, but

Facts and Firsts

- ★ Vermont, which was once part of New Hampshire and New York, was the first state admitted to the Union after the original 13 colonies.
- ★ Montpelier, with a population of less than 9,000 people, is the smallest state capital in the United States. It is also the only capital without a McDonald's restaurant.
- ★ Vermont produces nearly 3 billion pounds of milk annually.
- ★ During the 1890s, writer Rudyard Kipling lived in Vermont.
- ★ Vermont produces more maple syrup, monument granite, and marble than any other state.

Vermont's Ethan Allen (left, with sword) led his Green Mountain Boys to victory at Ft. Ticonderoga during the Revolutionary War.

in 1775, the Revolutionary War broke out and settlers from both states joined forces to fight the English.

During the war, Vermont's Green Mountain Boys, led by Ethan Allen, were a strong fighting force. After the Revolution, Vermont was an independent republic called New Connecticut. In 1791, the area was admitted to the Union as the 14th state.

A canal built in 1823 connected Lake Champlain with the Hudson River in New York. Vermont farmers quickly became rich raising sheep and shipping their wool all over the country. After the Civil War, however, Vermont's agriculture declined as farmers left to settle farming territories in the Midwest or to work in city factories.

During the late 1800s, industry expanded, and Burlington developed into an important port city where lumber from Canada was shipped to the West. Tourism also flourished as resorts and vacation camps were built. In 1911, Vermont became the first state to have an official bureau of tourism.

Vermont's industry grew even more during World War II, as factories produced supplies for the U.S. military. Several small corporations moved into Vermont after the war, and the 1950s and 1960s were a time of industrial and urban expansion. Tourism continued to be extremely important to the state's economy.

State Smart

Vermont is home to the oldest coral reef in the United States. It was left behind by a shallow sea more than 480 million years ago, when North America was still close to the equator.

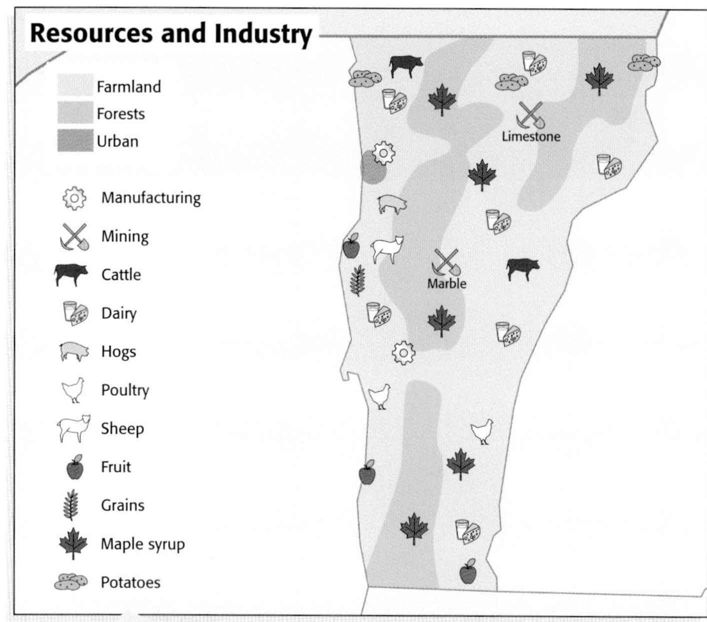

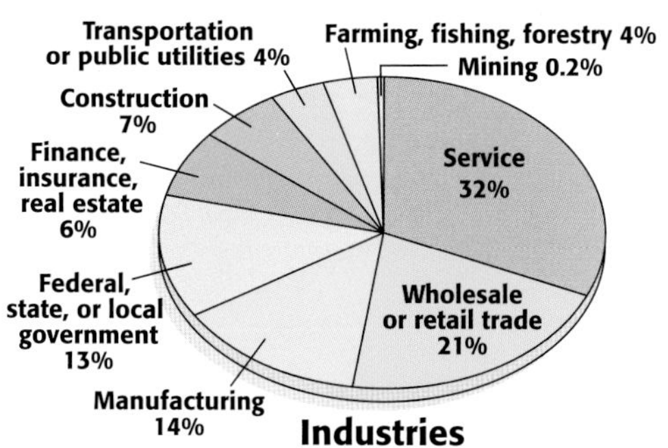

Many Vermonters were concerned about the growth of manufacturing and tourist activities in the state; they wanted to maintain Vermont's rural identity. In 1970, Vermont passed one of the first laws that allowed a state's government to prevent industrial and tourist development.

The Present

Vermont's government has worked to preserve Vermont's natural beauty and rural character. Today, Vermont has the third-smallest population in the United States, larger than only Alaska and Wyoming. It has the smallest percentage of people living in cities, because much of Vermont's economy depends on agriculture.

Tourism is centered in the Green Mountains region, which attracts millions of vacationers from New York and the other New England states annually. Service industries, which supply health care, dining, and hotel accommodations to visitors, contribute significantly to Vermont's economy.

Below left: *Much of Vermont is rural in character.* Below right: *A worker at the IBM factory in Burlington*

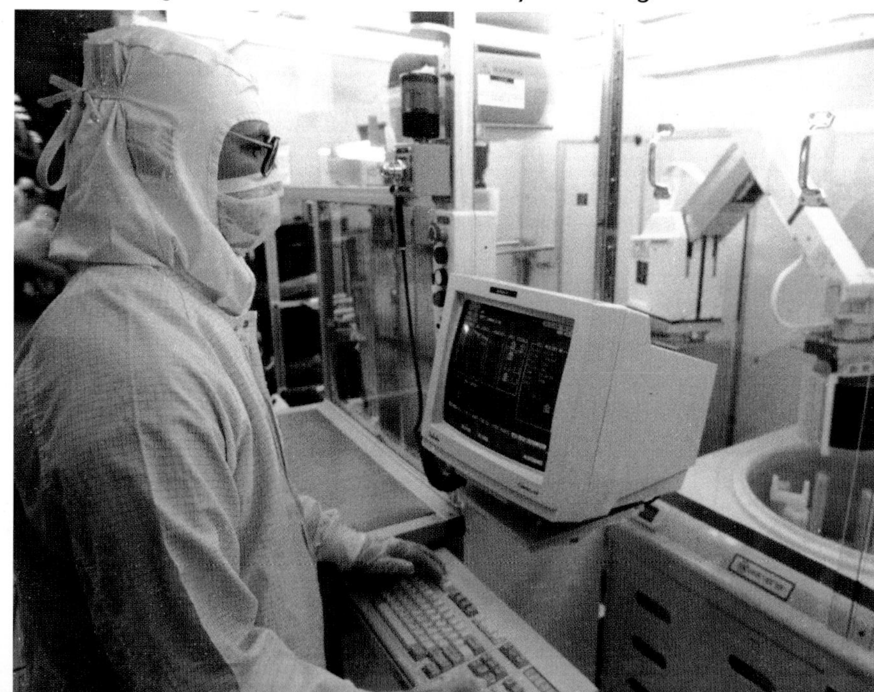

Born in Vermont

★ **Chester A. Arthur**, U.S. president
★ **Orson Bean (Dallas Frederick Burrows)**, actor
★ **Calvin Coolidge**, U.S. president
★ **George Dewey**, admiral
★ **John Dewey**, philosopher and educator
★ **Stephen A. Douglas**, politician
★ **James Fisk**, financial speculator
★ **Richard Morris Hunt**, architect
★ **William Morris Hunt**, artist
★ **Elisha Otis**, inventor
★ **Joseph Smith**, religious leader
★ **Henry Wells**, pioneer expressman
★ **Brigham Young**, religious leader

Above: *John Dewey*, below: *Chester Arthur*

Vermont residents disagree on how much of Vermont should be opened to new businesses and industries. Some Vermonters have urged the state to allow new business development, and growth of Vermont's manufacturing industries has resulted. The IBM Corporation, which produces computers and electrical equipment, has a large factory in Burlington. Other factories make batteries, ovens, transformers, books, newspapers, metal products, and machine tools.

Attempts to retain Vermont's rural character have also been successful. The state is famous for agricultural products, especially maple syrup, and dairy products such as cheddar cheese and ice cream.

The Battleground covered bridge attracts tourists who stay in Green Mountain resorts.

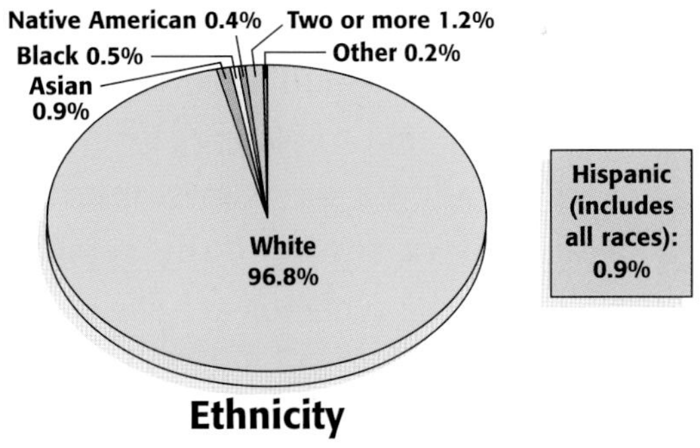

Ethnicity

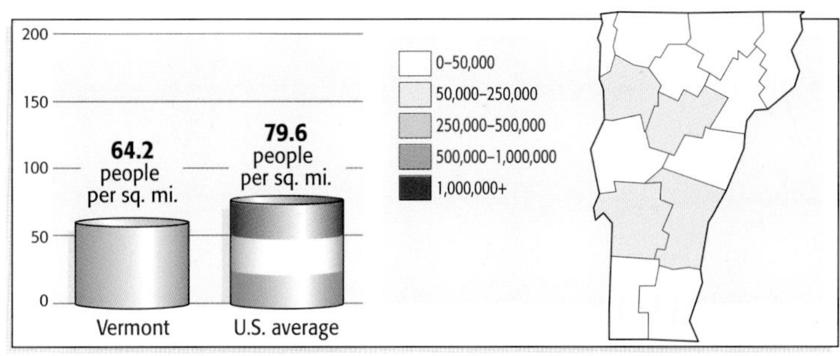

Population Density

Population by County

Virginia

Sic semper tyrannis (Thus always to tyrants).

Land area rank
Largest state (1)
36 — *smallest state (52)*

Population rank
Most people (1)
12 — *fewest people (52)*

At a Glance

Name: Virginia was named for Queen Elizabeth I of England, who was known as the Virgin Queen because she never married.
Nicknames: Old Dominion, Mother of Presidents
Capital: Richmond
Size: 40,598 sq. mi. (105,149 sq km)
Population: 7,078,515
Statehood: Virginia became the 10th state on June 25, 1788.
Electoral votes: 13 (2004)
U.S. representatives: 11 (until 2003)
State tree: dogwood
State flower: dogwood
State dog: American foxhound
Highest point: Mount Rogers, 5,729 ft. (1,746 m)

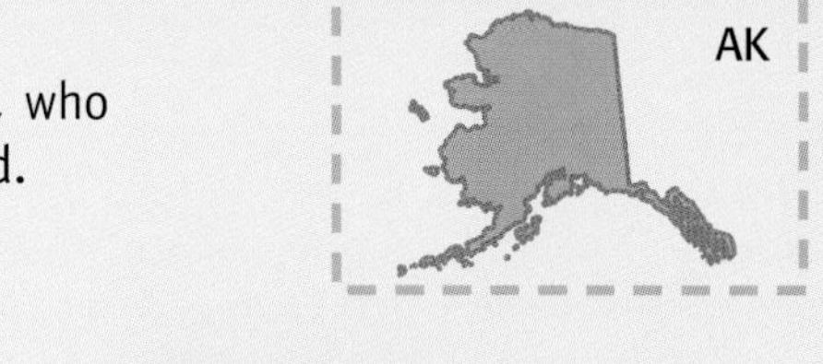

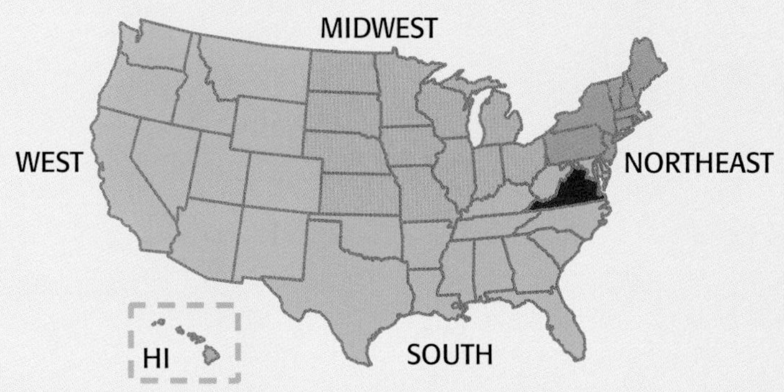

The Place

Virginia is a southern state that is bordered by the Atlantic Ocean. The Chesapeake Bay, an inlet of the Atlantic Ocean, divides Virginia's coast into a western mainland and a peninsula called the Eastern Shore. Virginia's shore is called the Tidewater because ocean water sometimes flows up into the rivers that empty into the Atlantic. Land in this part of Virginia is marshy, with several swamps. The largest one is Dismal Swamp in the southeast.

Western Virginia is a series of plateaus and ridges formed by the Appalachian Mountains, which stretch from Alabama to Maine. Virginia's Great Valley, a series of connecting river valleys, is part of this region. Many of the plateaus are sliced by deep gorges and covered with trees.

The Natural Bridge in the Shenandoah River Valley of the Blue Ridge Mountains near Lexington, Virginia.

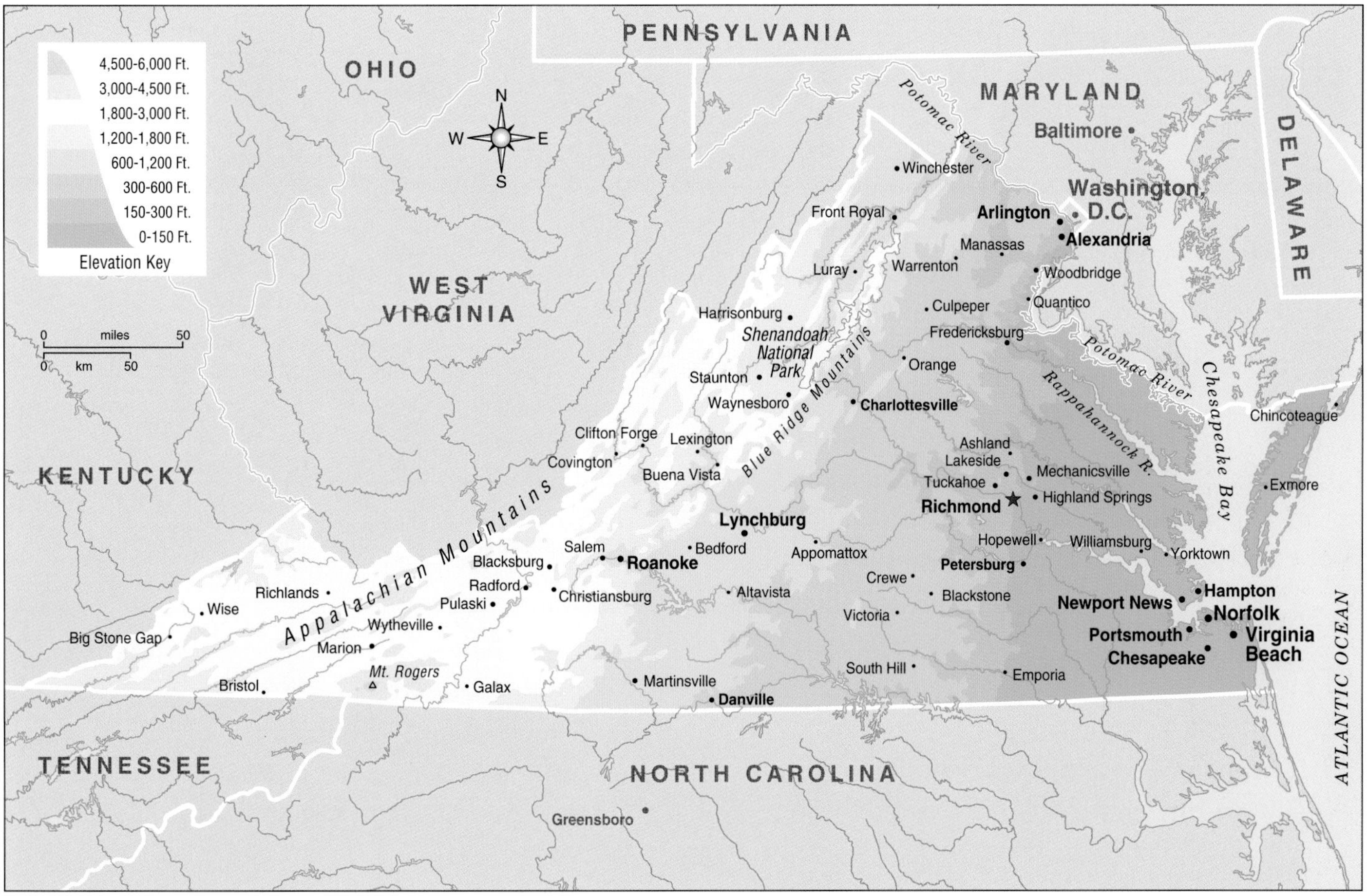

Between western and central Virginia are the Blue Ridge Mountains, also part of the Appalachian system. Central Virginia is made up of high, rolling plains that gradually become lower as they slope to the east. Many rivers in this area empty into the Chesapeake Bay.

Virginia's climate is generally mild, but cooler in the mountainous western region, which receives the most snow. This area also has Virginia's largest deposits of coal, the state's most valuable mineral resource. Other minerals include granite, limestone, shale, soapstone, marble, gypsum, natural gas, and petroleum.

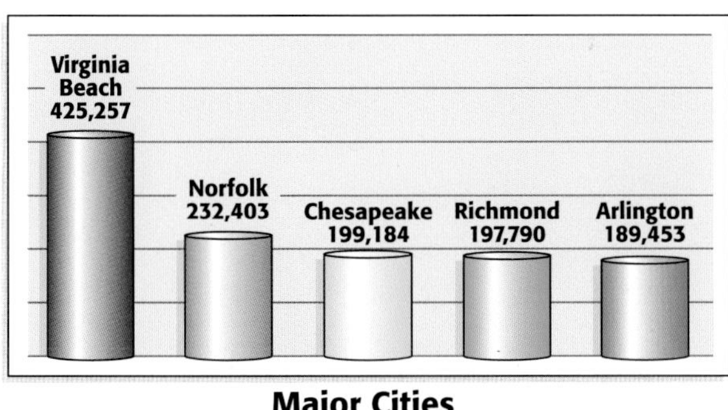

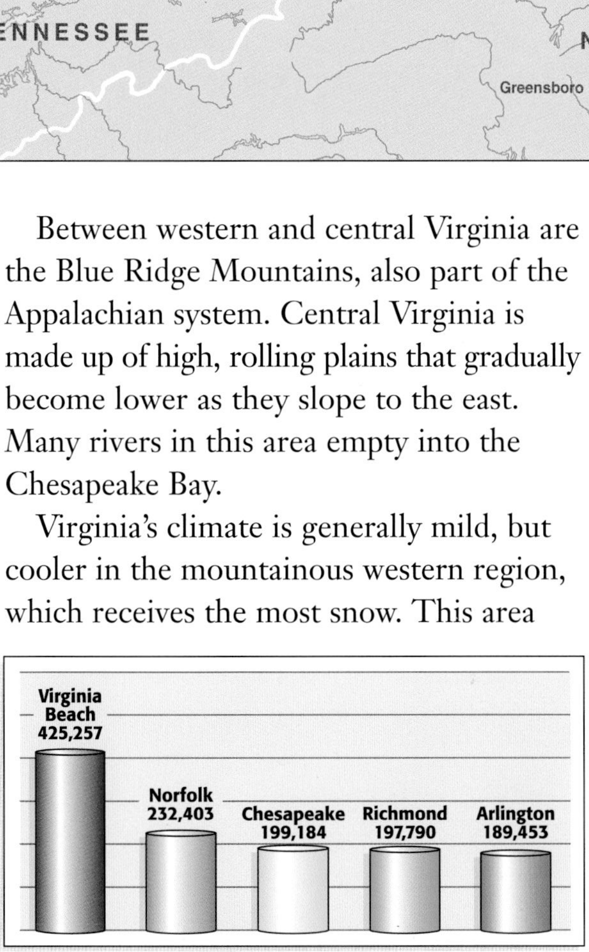

Major Cities

The Past

Virginia has played a central part in the history of the United States. In 1584, Sir Walter Raleigh attempted to establish the first English settlement in North America at Roanoke Island, off the coast of what is now North Carolina. Although the settlement failed, King James I sent another group of colonists to Vi ginia. This second attempt was successful, and in 1607 the colonists founded Jamestown, the first permanent English settlement in America.

Native American woman, Pocahontas, married John Rolfe of the Jamestown colony.

The colonists grew tobacco and shipped it to Europe. In 1624, King James I made Virginia a royal colony. Profitable trade stimulated population growth, and settlers began to move west and explore. As more colonists moved to western Virginia, Native Americans, aided by the French, began to retaliate by attacking settlements.

When the Revolutionary War began, many Virginia residents remained loyal to England. Others, however, wanted independent control of trade and economic affairs in the colony. Two of the most well-known supporters of American independence—Patrick Henry and Thomas Jefferson—were from Virginia. Virginia was the site of some of the most important battles of the American Revolution, including the final battle at Yorktown that led to England's surrender. Four of the first five presidents of the United States—George Washington, Thomas Jefferson, James Madison, and James Monroe—were Virginians.

Above: *George Washington*
Below: *Thomas Jefferson*

During the Civil War, Virginia initially did not want to secede

Facts and Firsts

- ★ Jamestown, founded in 1697, was the first successful English settlement in the American colonies. The site of the Jamestown settlement now lies on an island because, over time, it has been cut off from the mainland by water.
- ★ The College of William and Mary, founded in 1693, is the second-oldest college in the nation. Only Harvard University (in Massachusetts) is older.
- ★ Six first ladies were born in Virginia: Martha Washington, Martha Jefferson, Rachel Jackson, Letitia Tyler, Ellen Arthur, and Edith Wilson.
- ★ Kentucky and West Virginia were once part of Virginia.
- ★ Richmond, Virginia's capital, was also the capital of the Confederacy during the Civil War. More Civil War battles were fought in Virginia than in any other state.
- ★ Today, Virginia is the home base for the U.S. Navy 's Atlantic Fleet.
- ★ The Pentagon, located in Arlington, is the world's largest office building and has more than 68,000 miles (108,800 km) of internal telephone lines.

(withdraw from the Union), but the state felt pressure from others in the South to defend a state's right to pass its own laws. When Virginia decided to secede from the Union, many people in western Virginia refused and set up an independent government. In 1863, these independent counties were declared by President Abraham Lincoln to be the separate state of West Virginia.

The city of Richmond served as the capital of the South through much of the Civil War. Important battles were fought throughout the state at such places as Bull Run, Chancellorsville, and Fredericksburg. The Civil War, like the American Revolution, ended in Virginia. In 1865, Confederate general Robert E. Lee surrendered to Union general Ulysses S. Grant at Appomattox Court House.

Virginia's modern industries were established after the Civil War. During the 1880s, factories made cigarettes, cotton textiles, and ships. Progress was slow, however, especially during the 1920s and 1930s, when many Virginians moved to other states in search of better employment.

State Smart

Virginia is known as the "birthplace of presidents" because more U.S. presidents were born there than in any other state. Those eight presidents are George Washington, Thomas Jefferson, James Madison, James Monroe, William Henry Harrison, John Tyler, Zachary Taylor, and Woodrow Wilson.

In the 1940s, government and military workers settled in Virginia, just outside of the nation's capital of Washington, D.C. The population boomed, tourism increased, and industry expanded.

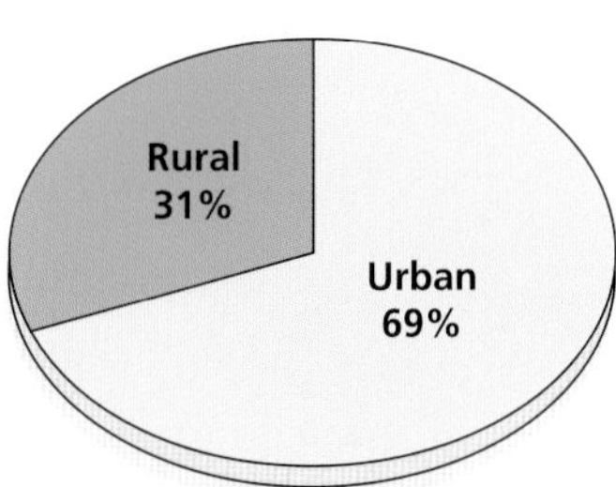

Urban/Rural Distribution

Virginia, like most other states, had racial conflicts in the 1950s and 1960s. Some segregated school districts resisted compulsory integration, and even closed schools rather than end segregation.

Fredericksburg lay in ruins after the Civil War battle that took place there.

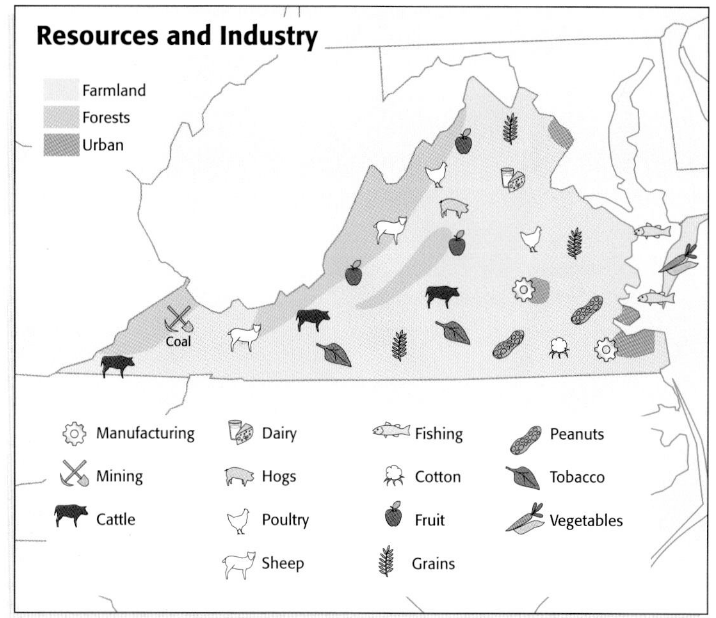

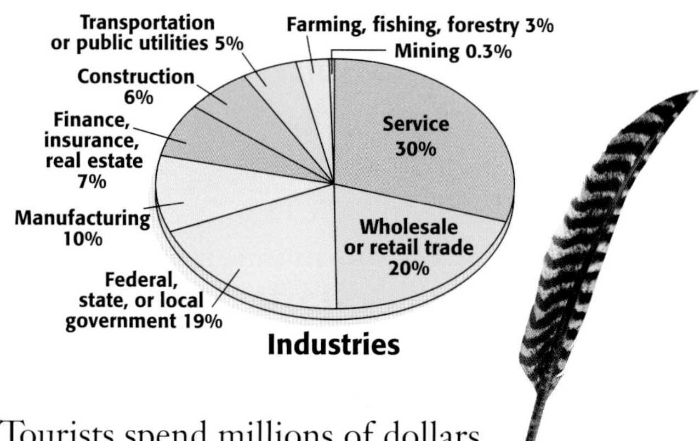

By the 1970s and 1980s, the arrival of more people and businesses in Virginia began to threaten plants and animals in the Chesapeake Bay and surrounding areas. Virginia undertook efforts to clean polluted areas and protect wildlife.

The Present

Virginia's location along the Chesapeake Bay has traditionally benefited the state's economy. Good soil for tobacco planting, combined with access to the ocean, helped make the colony rich and continues to bring prosperity to the state.

Tourists spend millions of dollars every year to see sights such as Revolutionary and Civil War battlegrounds, Colonial Williamsburg, George Washington's home at Mount Vernon, Thomas Jefferson's home at Monticello, and Arlington National Cemetery, where President John F. Kennedy is buried.

A number of government offices are located in Virginia because of the state's proximity to Washington, D.C. The Pentagon, the headquarters of the Central Intelligence Agency (CIA) and the Department of Defense, and many military bases are located in northeastern Virginia. Many people who work in the capital choose to reside in Virginia.

Access to the Chesapeake Bay and the many rivers that flow into it has also helped ensure Virginia's industrial success. Businesses in Virginia manufacture products

Below left: *The Pentagon contains the offices of the Department of Defense and is situated in Arlington, across the Potomac from Washington, D.C.* Below right: *Farmland in Madison County*

Born in Virginia

- ★ **Arthur Ashe**, tennis player
- ★ **Warren Beatty**, actor and director
- ★ **Richard E. Byrd**, explorer
- ★ **Henry Clay**, statesman
- ★ **Ella Fitzgerald**, singer
- ★ **William H. Harrison**, U.S. president
- ★ **Patrick Henry**, statesman
- ★ **Sam Houston**, political leader
- ★ **Thomas Jefferson**, U.S. president
- ★ **Robert E. Lee**, Confederate general
- ★ **Meriwether Lewis**, explorer
- ★ **Shirley MacLaine**, actress
- ★ **James Madison**, U.S. president
- ★ **John Marshall**, jurist
- ★ **Cyrus McCormick**, inventor
- ★ **James Monroe**, president
- ★ **Pocahontas (Matoaka)**, daughter of Native American chief Powhaten
- ★ **Walter Reed**, army surgeon
- ★ **Bill "Bojangles" Robinson**, dancer
- ★ **George C. Scott**, actor
- ★ **James "Jeb" Stuart**, Confederate army officer
- ★ **Zachary Taylor**, U.S. president
- ★ **Nat Turner**, leader of slave uprising
- ★ **John Tyler**, U.S. president
- ★ **Booker T. Washington**, educator
- ★ **George Washington**, U.S. president
- ★ **Woodrow Wilson**, U.S. president
- ★ **Tom Wolfe**, journalist

Top to bottom: *Richard Byrd, Arthur Ashe, Ella Fitzgerald*

such as synthetic cloth, pharmaceuticals, cigarettes, peanut butter, soft drinks, boats and ships, automobile parts, and rubber. Rivers that flow into the bay also provide water for Virginia's farms, which produce chickens, beef cattle, milk, turkeys, hogs, tobacco, potatoes, and apples.

Mt. Vernon, on the Potomac River, was the home of George and Martha Washington.

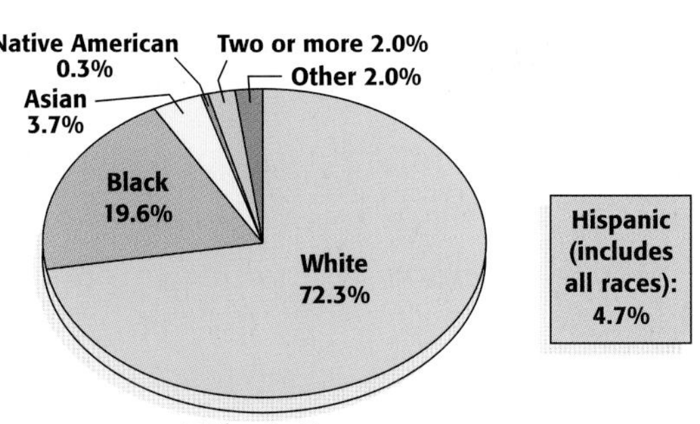

Ethnicity

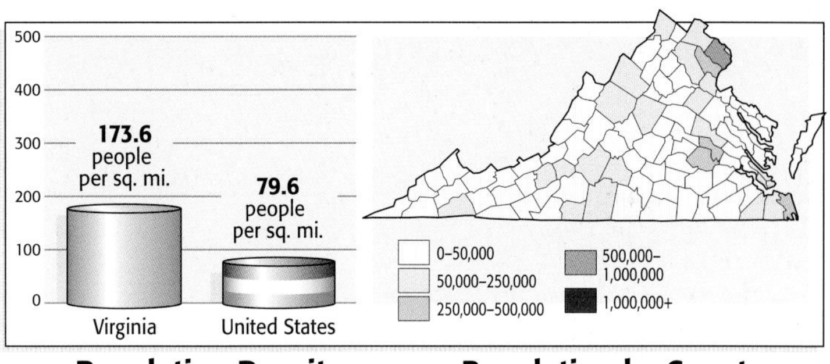

Population Density

Population by County

Washington

Alki (By and by).

Land area rank *Largest state (1)* 20 — *smallest state (52)*

Population rank *Most people (1)* 15 — *fewest people (52)*

At a Glance

Name: Washington is named after President George Washington

Nickname: Evergreen State

Capital: Olympia

Size: 68,126 sq. mi. (176,446 sq km)

Population: 5,894,121

Statehood: Washington became the 42nd state on November 11, 1889.

Electoral votes: 11 (2004)

U.S. representatives: 9 (until 2003)

State tree: western hemlock

State flower: western rhododendron

State fish: steelhead trout

Highest point: Mount Rainier, 14,410 ft. (4,392 m)

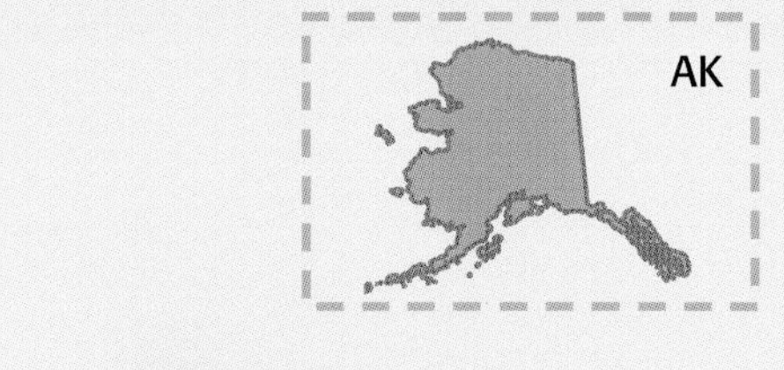

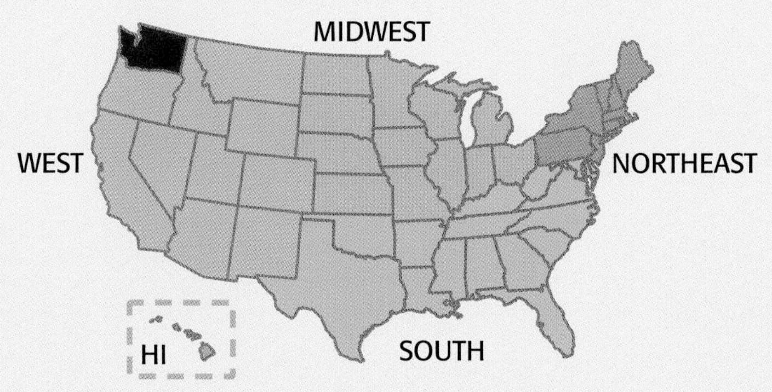

The Place

Washington is a Pacific Northwest state located on the U.S. border with Canada. Washington's location makes it a prime jumping-off point for travel to and from Asia and Alaska by land, sea, and air.

Washington's landscape varies greatly throughout the state. In the rugged northwest are the snowcapped Olympic Mountains, one of the least explored areas in the United States. The Cascade Mountains, which divide western and eastern Washington, are located in the south. These mountains, part of a chain that extends from Canada to northern California, include several volcanoes, such as Mount

Mount Rainier is a snow capped dormant volcano in the Cascade Mountain chain.

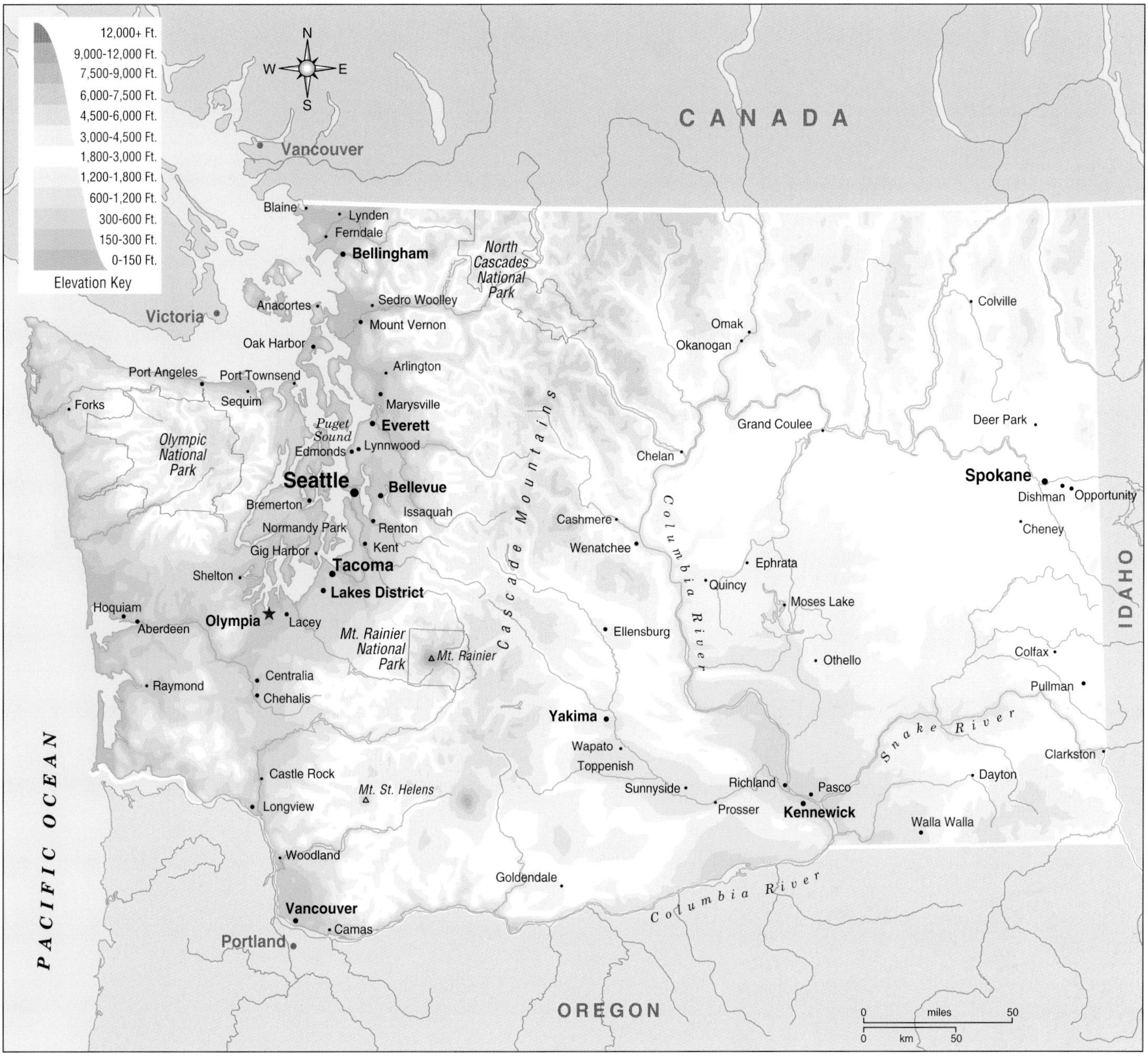

St. Helens and Mount Rainier. The Cascade Mountains block much of eastern Washington from rain or snow, and as a result, the Columbia Basin to the east of the Cascades is semidesert. Rivers provide water for agriculture, except in the very southeastern corner of Washington, where the rich soil holds huge amounts of water.

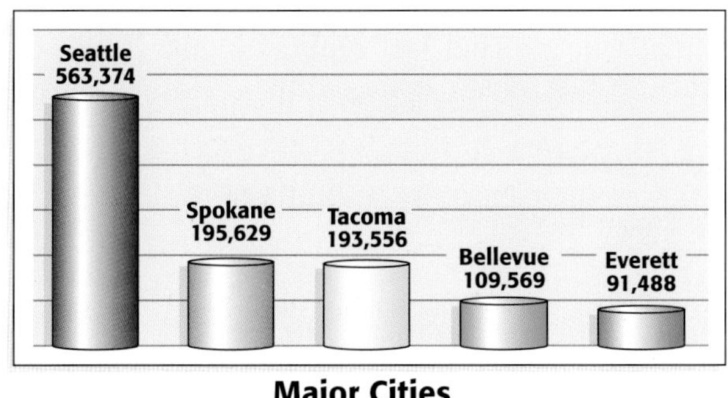

Major Cities

The Rocky Mountains run through the northeastern corner of Washington. Between the Olympic Mountains and the Cascade Mountains lies Puget Sound, a large bay of the Pacific Ocean. Most of

Washington's population is concentrated near Puget Sound.

The Columbia River is the largest river in Washington and one of the largest in the United States. It provides water to many areas of Washington that are normally too dry for farming. Moist winds from the Pacific Ocean make the Olympic Peninsula one of the wettest places on Earth. The ocean also keeps temperatures in western Washington mild. Eastern Washington has warm summers and cold winters.

A Native American attorney of the Quinault people carries on his ancestors' feeling for Washington's beauty.

The Past

A mild climate and an abundance of Pacific Ocean fish made western Washington a desirable home for Native American tribes. The first Europeans to reach Washington probably traveled up the Pacific Coast from California in the 1500s.

Spain, France, England, and Russia all claimed rights to the region during the late 1700s. Washington remained mostly unsettled until 1810, when British and American fur traders moved into the region. The United States was already an independent nation, but Britain contested the country's northern boundary and claimed many of the northern lands, including Washington. The boundary was not officially determined until 1846,

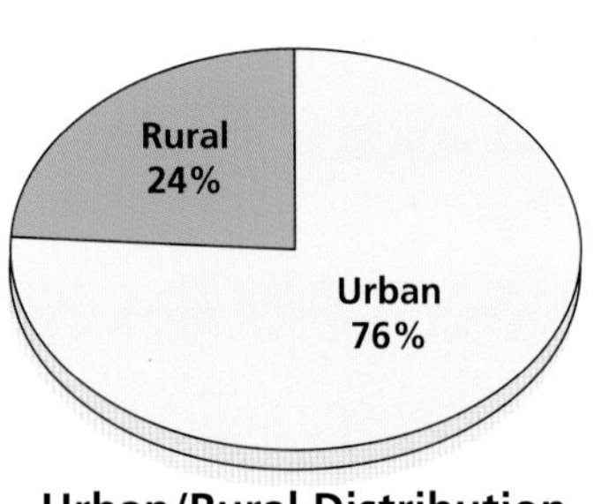

Urban/Rural Distribution

Facts and Firsts

- ★ Washington is the only state named after a U.S. president.
- ★ The most northwestern point in the lower 48 states is Cape Flattery, located on Washington's Olympic Peninsula.
- ★ Mount Rainier, the highest point in Washington, is a dormant volcano that last erupted about 2,000 years ago.
- ★ There are more glaciers in Washington than in all other continental 48 states combined.
- ★ The world's first revolving restaurant was built in Seattle's Space Needle in 1961.
- ★ Starbucks, the world's biggest coffee shop chain, opened its first shop in Seattle's Pike Place Market in 1971.

when a treaty set the present northern border of Washington.

The discovery of gold in present-day Oregon and Idaho brought many new American settlers to the northwestern United States after 1860, but settlement in Washington did not drastically increase until the transcontinental railroad was completed in 1883. The new railroad allowed Washington residents to ship cattle, minerals, lumber, and food to the East.

By 1900, much of Washington's dry land was being irrigated for farming. Wheat fields and fruit orchards replaced much of the state's open cattle range. Gold rushes in Alaska around the same time drew additional settlers, and Seattle, which is located near Puget Sound, became a chief supply center and a major port city.

During World War I, Washington's economy prospered as the state supplied forest products, food, and ships for the war effort. Although the Great Depression of the 1930s took a toll on industry, the state's economic activities rebounded and hit a new high during World War II. Lumber and manufacturing industries provided ships, aircraft, and nuclear weapons to the U.S. military. In 1943, the U.S. government built Hanford Works in southeastern Washington as a site for nuclear research. After the war, many workers stayed in Washington and found employment in new aluminum and aircraft factories.

State Smart

Washington produces more apples than any other state—an average of 4.9 billion per year.

During the second half of the 20th century, lumber and agriculture became less important, and Washington grew more urban. In the 1960s, the Boeing Company, a major aircraft manufacturer, moved into the Seattle area and drew workers from all over Puget Sound. The tourism industry was boosted by the completion of the Space Needle, an observation tower built for a world's fair in Seattle in 1962.

Washington suffered from a natural disaster in 1980, when the long-dormant volcano Mount St. Helens erupted. The eruption resulted in 57 deaths and caused billions of dollars in damage to southwestern Washington.

Below left: This stone marks *Washington's border with Canada which was decided in 1846.*
Below right: *Mount St. Helens in southwestern Washington erupted in 1980 and caused 57 deaths.*

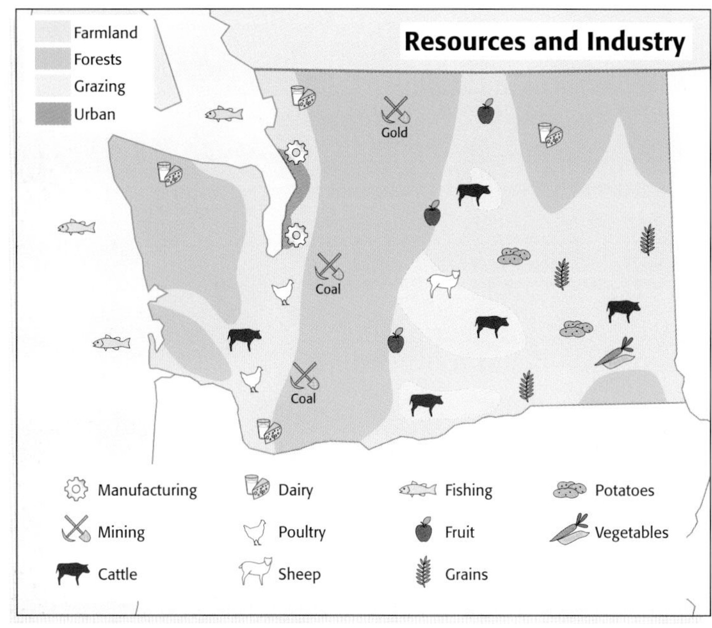

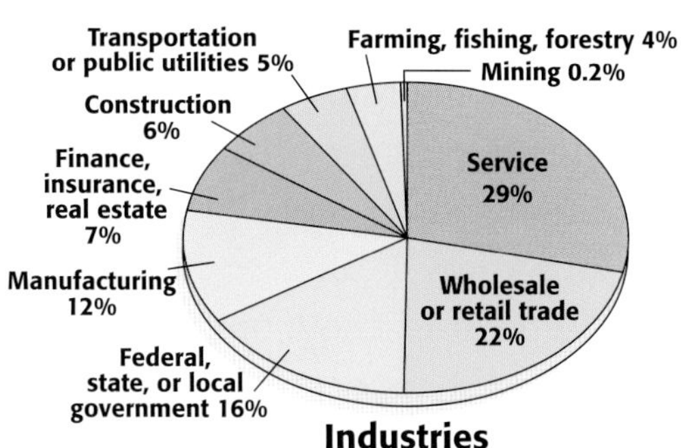

The Present

Washington is today a leader in many industries. The Microsoft Corporation and other software companies are located throughout the Seattle–Tacoma area. Boeing continues to manufacture airplane parts in Seattle and all over the rest of the state. The U.S. Navy's shipyard in Bremerton is one of the largest shipyards on the Pacific Coast. Washington is home to Nordstrom, one of the largest clothing store chains in the United States, and Starbucks, the largest retail coffee vendor in the nation.

Timber is Washington's most valuable agricultural product. Washington's agricultural industry, although not as important as it once was, has benefited from better irrigation on the Columbia River, and about half of Washington is farmland. Wheat is Washington's leading field crop, and only Idaho grows more potatoes. Cattle and dairy farms also dot the state. Washington grows more apples and pears than any other state.

Below left: *The Grand Coulee Dam taps the power of the Columbia River.* Below right: *The Space Needle distinguishes the Seattle skyline.*

Born in Washington

★**Carol Channing**, singer and actress
★**Kurt Cobain**, musician
★**Judy Collins**, singer
★**Bing (Harry Lillis) Crosby**, singer and actor
★**Merce Cunningham**, dancer and choreographer
★**Frances Farmer**, actress
★**Bill Gates**, software executive
★**Jimi Hendrix**, guitarist
★**Chuck Jones**, animator
★**Gary Larson**, cartoonist
★**Mary McCarthy**, novelist
★**Robert Motherwell**, artist
★**Patrice Munsel**, opera singer
★**Seattle**, chief of the Suquamish
★**Francis Scobee**, astronaut
★**Hillary Swank**, actress

Above: *Bill Gates;* below: *Jimi Hendrix*

State officials are working to address serious environmental problems caused by development in Washington's industrial and agricultural activities. Some dams on Washington's rivers that provide hydroelectric power and water for crops also prevent salmon from swimming upstream to mate, and as a result, Washington's salmon population is in danger. Also, officials discovered in the 1980s that underground tanks at the Hanford Works research site were leaking radioactive waste and polluting the Columbia River. A cleanup plan was initiated in 1989.

Pike's Market in Seattle is popular with residents and visitors.

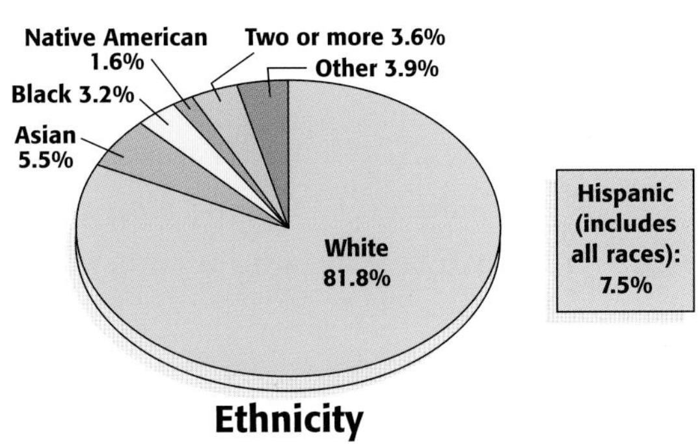

Ethnicity

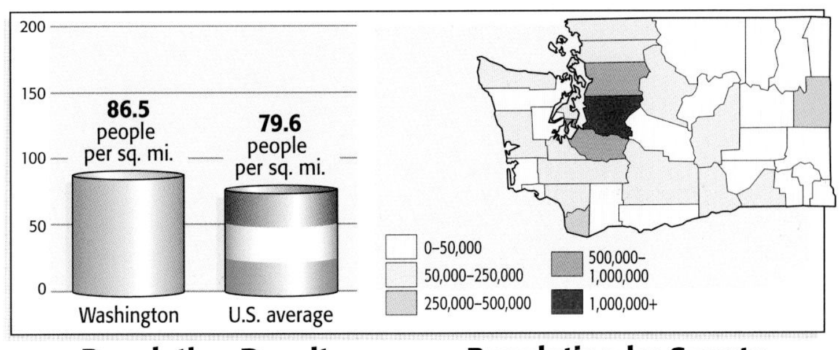

Population Density

Population by County

West Virginia

Montani semper liberi (Mountaineers are always free).

Land area rank *Largest state (1)*

Population rank *Most people (1)*

At a Glance

Name: West Virginia was once part of Virginia, which was named for England's Queen Elizabeth I. She was known as the Virgin Queen because she never married.

Nickname: Mountain State

Capital: Charleston

Size: 24,231 sq. mi. (62,759 sq km)

Population: 1,808,344

Statehood: West Virginia became the 35th state on June 20, 1863.

Electoral votes: 5 (2004)

U.S. representatives: 3 (until 2003)

State tree: sugar maple

State flower: big rhododendron

State animal: black bear

Highest point: Spruce Knob, 4,861 ft. (1,482 m)

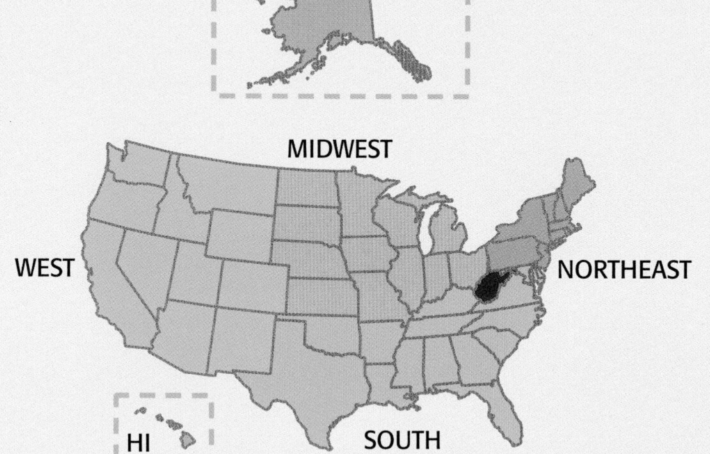

Glade Creek Grist Mill in the Blue Ridge Mountains of West Virginia

The Place

West Virginia is an eastern state that does not border the Atlantic Ocean. West Virginia is irregularly shaped because most of its borders follow natural features such as rivers and mountains. A narrow strip of land called the Northern Panhandle runs northward between Ohio and Pennsylvania, while the Eastern Panhandle runs north-eastward between Maryland and Virginia.

West Virginia is known as the Mountain State because so little of its land is flat. In

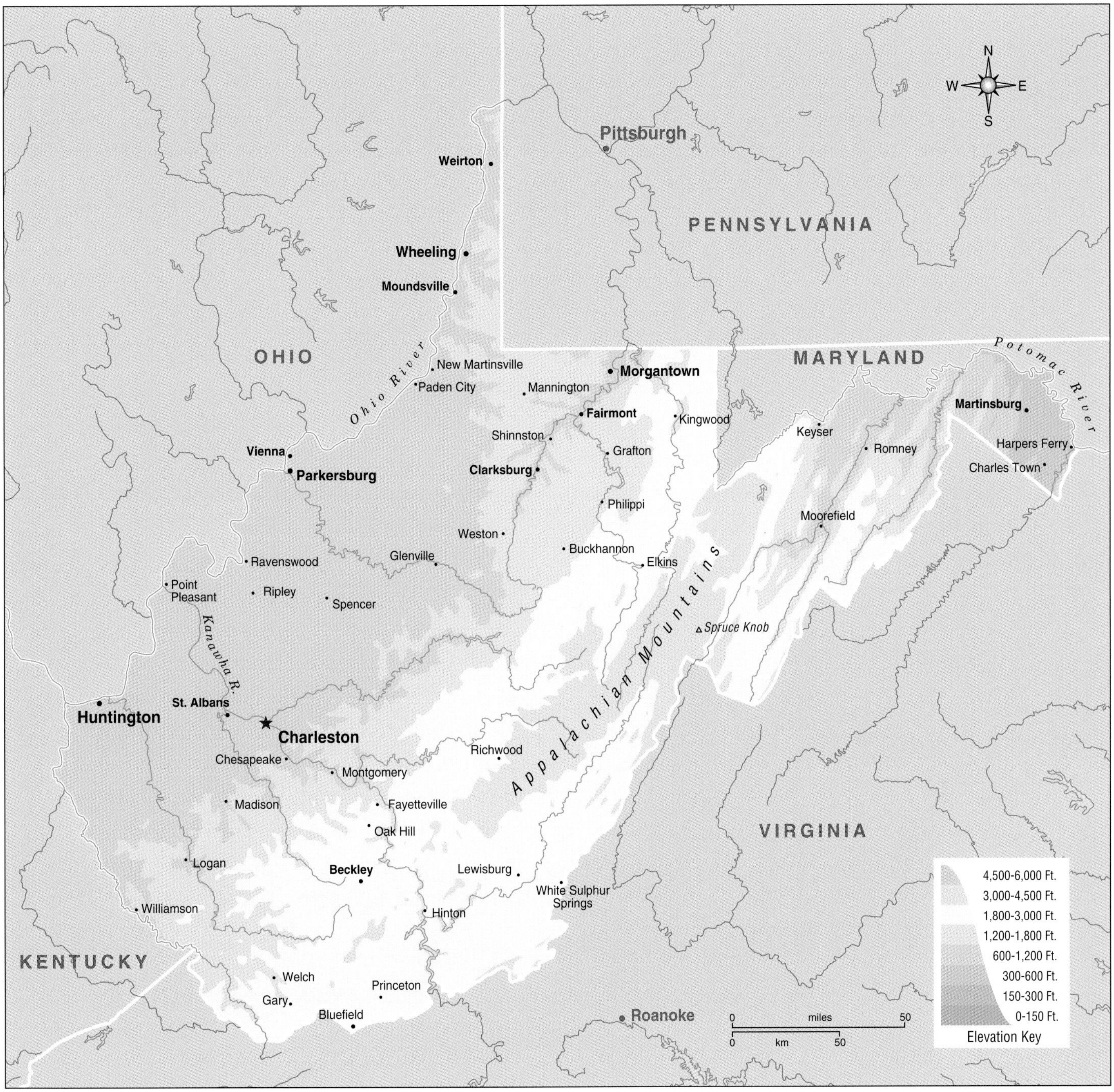

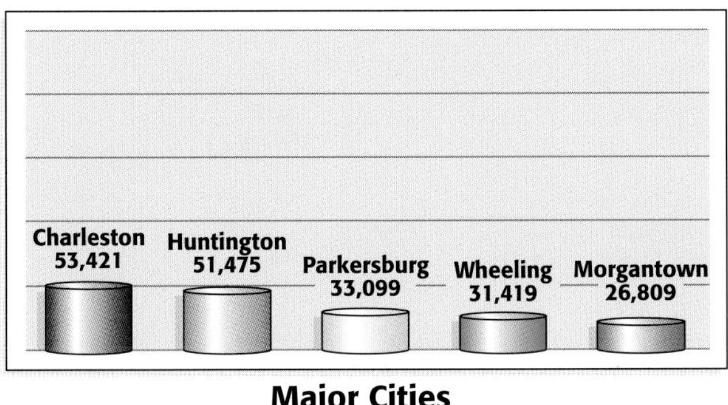

Major Cities

fact, West Virginia is one of the most rugged states in the East. The Appalachian Mountains cover all of the eastern and central parts of West Virginia, which was once the mountainous western half of Virginia. The Blue Ridge and Allegheny Mountains run through eastern West Virginia.

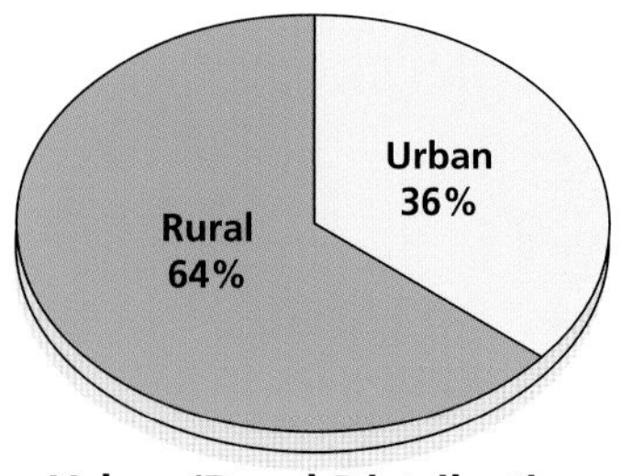

Urban/Rural Distribution

The western third of West Virginia is made up of rolling hills and narrow valleys. West Virginia's western river valleys have the most fertile soil in the state, as well as deposits of natural gas and petroleum. The Ohio River flows along the state's western boundary with Ohio.

West Virginia's summers are warm; the valleys are typically warmer than the mountainous areas. Rainfall is plentiful throughout the state and sometimes causes flash floods that damage homes and property in lower valleys. The mountains sometimes get as much as 100 inches (250 cm) of snow in a year.

The Past

Around 14,000 years ago, various groups of Native Americans hunted large animals such as bear and deer in the West Virginia area. In later times, native peoples such as the Woodland built large earthen burial mounds. By the 1700s, when European settlers reached West Virginia, disease and warfare had killed many of the Native Americans there.

The first European settlers who came to present-day West Virginia were searching for new farmland, but in 1742, explorers discovered the area's large coal beds, and settlers began moving to the land to mine the coal. During the Revolutionary War, Native American tribes frequently raided these white settlements. After the American Revolution and the War of 1812, manufacturing expanded as West Virginians began to produce items they had formerly bought from England, such as iron.

In 1788, the Virginia Colony, which included West Virginia, became a state. In the decades that followed, present-day West Virginia became increasingly unlike eastern Virginia. While the eastern region was dominated by large cotton plantations that relied on slave labor, western Virginia was made up of small family farms. The eastern plantation owners controlled the

Facts and Firsts

- ★ West Virginia has an average altitude of 1,500 feet (457 m), the highest average altitude east of the Mississippi.
- ★ Forests cover almost 80 percent of West Virginia.
- ★ West Virginia is home to the world's largest sycamore tree, on the Back Fork of the Elk River in Webster Springs.
- ★ West Virginia is the only state that became independent by declaration of the president of the United States.
- ★ West Virginia was the first state to implement a sales tax on the goods it sold and traded. The tax went into effect June 1, 1921.
- ★ West Virginia has the oldest population in the United States. The state's median age is nearly 39.

Confederate general Stonewall Jackson was born in the part of Virginia that became West Virginia

state's government and promoted policies that hurt the western farmers.

When the Civil War broke out in 1861 and Virginia decided to withdraw from the Union, residents of western Virginia called for an official separation. In 1863, President Abraham Lincoln declared West Virginia a separate, official state. West Virginia remained in the Union, although some natives, such as Confederate general Thomas "Stonewall" Jackson, stayed loyal to the South.

After the Civil War, West Virginia's mining industry exploded, and the state became a leading producer of coal, oil, and natural gas. Manufacturers made chemicals, glass, iron, and steel from these resources. In the early 1900s, the coal mining industry experienced labor problems as poorly paid workers fought with mine owners to form unions for better wages

West Virginia's manufacturers produced supplies for World War II during the 1940s, but after the war, the mining industry again declined. Factories stopped using coal for power and new mining techniques reduced the need for workers. These trends combined to put many of West Virginia's miners out of work. West Virginia's population decreased as workers left the state to look for jobs. The decline continued until the 1970s, when government programs aided West Virginia's economy, and an international oil shortage helped the coal industry. The gains of the 1970s were reversed in the 1980s, however, when coal prices fell and unemployment rose. The 1990s brought some improvement, as the timber and tourism industries became more profitable and federal projects created jobs in the state.

State Smart

The New River Gorge Bridge in Fayetteville is the world's longest single-span steel arch bridge. Its arch length is 1,700 feet (518 m). The bridge's height is 876 feet (267 m) above the New River, making it the second-highest bridge in the country.

West Virginia participated in the Great Strike against the B&O Railroad in August 1877, by blocking engines at Martinsburg.

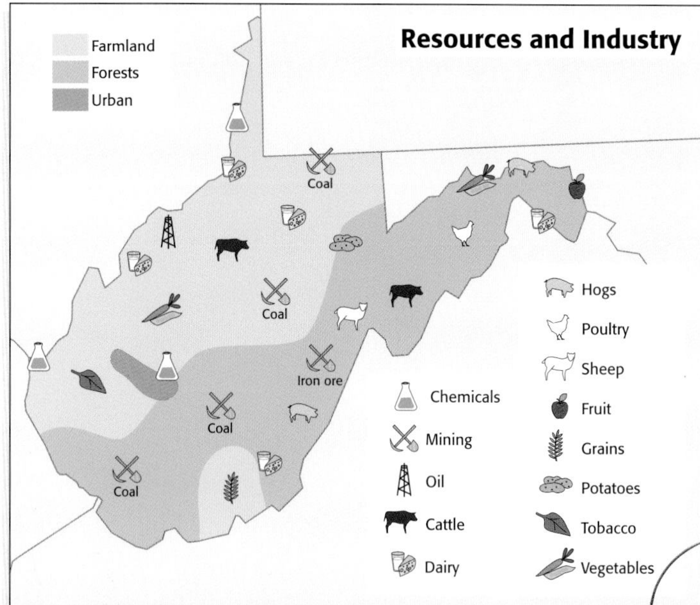

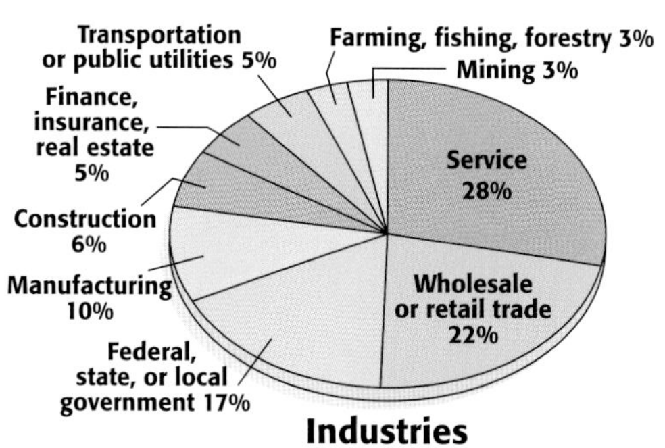

The Present

Today, most of West Virginia's revenue comes from the service industry, which includes schools, restaurants, hotels, and retail trade. In the past, West Virginia's economy was heavily dependent on mining. Because of downturns in the coal industry, many West Virginians lost their jobs, and the state received little tax revenue. Since the 1960s, the federal government has provided assistance to West Virginia to improve health services, schools, and transportation.

West Virginia has started to expand some industries and encourage new business growth. Manufacturing plants in cities along the Ohio River use coal to make iron and steel. Factories in the Kanawha and Ohio River Valleys produce chemicals, and both DuPont and General Electric have large plants in the western Ohio Valley. Other factories use West Virginia's deposits of sand and gravel to make glassware and pottery.

Agriculture is an important economic activity, and about a quarter of the state is

Below left: *The black bear is the official state animal of West Virginia.* Below right: *Despite downturns in the industry, mining technology continues to improve.*

Born in West Virginia

- ★ **George Brett**, athlete
- ★ **Pearl S. Buck**, author
- ★ **Homer Hickam Jr.**, engineer and author
- ★ **Thomas "Stonewall" Jackson**, Confederate general (was Virginia at that time)
- ★ **John S. Knight**, publisher
- ★ **Don Knotts**, actor
- ★ **Dwight Whitney Morrow**, banker and diplomat
- ★ **Mary Lou Retton**, gymnast
- ★ **Walter Reuther**, labor leader
- ★ **Eleanor Steber**, opera singer
- ★ **Lewis L. Strauss**, naval officer and scientist
- ★ **Cyrus Vance**, secretary of state
- ★ **Jerry West**, basketball player and coach
- ★ **Charles "Chuck" Yeager**, test pilot and air force general

Above: *Chuck Yeager;* below: *Mary Lou Retton*

farmland. Broilers, or young chickens, are West Virginia's most important agricultural product.

To further balance its economy, West Virginia has encouraged the development of tourism, and the state's lakes, forests, mountains, and historic towns have become popular with visitors.

Glass manufacturers use West Virginia sand to blow glass.

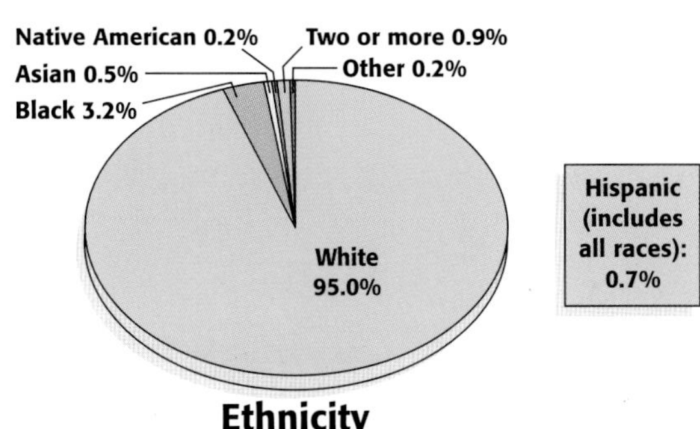

Ethnicity

Hispanic (includes all races): 0.7%

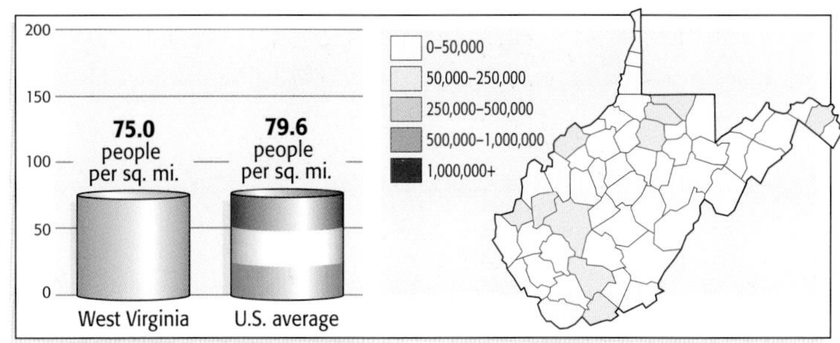

Population Density

Population by County

Wisconsin

Forward.

Land area rank *Largest state (1)* — 26 — *smallest state (52)*

Population rank *Most people (1)* — 18 — *fewest people (52)*

At a Glance

Name: Wisconsin is believed to be taken from one of three possible Indian words—Ouisconsin, Mesconsing, or Wishknosing. The words' meanings are unclear.

Nickname: Badger State

Capital: Madison

Size: 56,145 sq. mi. (145,414 sq km)

Population: 5,363,675

Statehood: Wisconsin became the 30th state on May 29, 1848.

Electoral votes: 10 (2004)

U.S. representatives: 9 (until 2003)

State tree: sugar maple

State flower: wood violet

State peace symbol: mourning dove

Highest point: Timms Hill, 1,951 ft. (595 m)

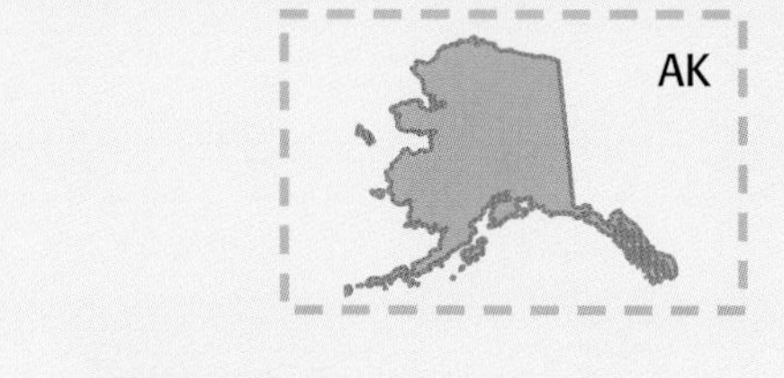

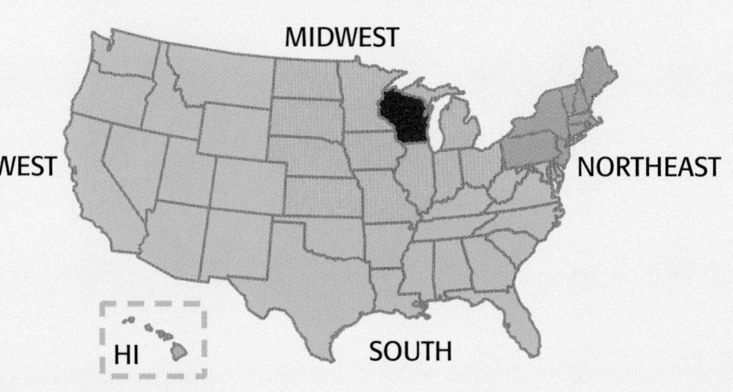

The Place

Wisconsin is a Midwest state located along the Great Lakes. Wisconsin borders Lake Michigan in the east and Lake Superior to the north. Wisconsin's most populous city, Milwaukee, is on the shore of Lake Michigan.

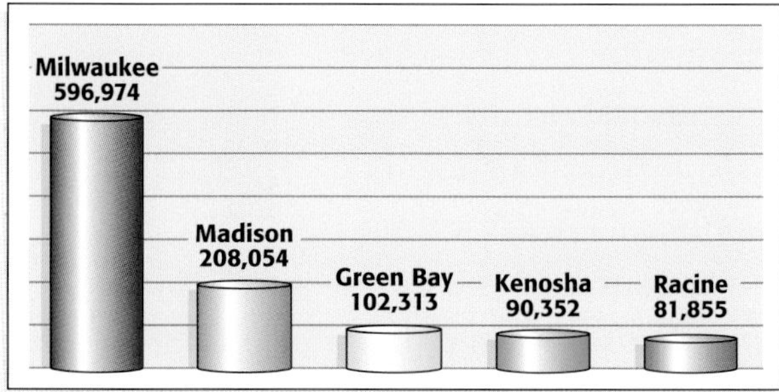

Major Cities

The Mississippi River forms part of Wisconsin's western border.

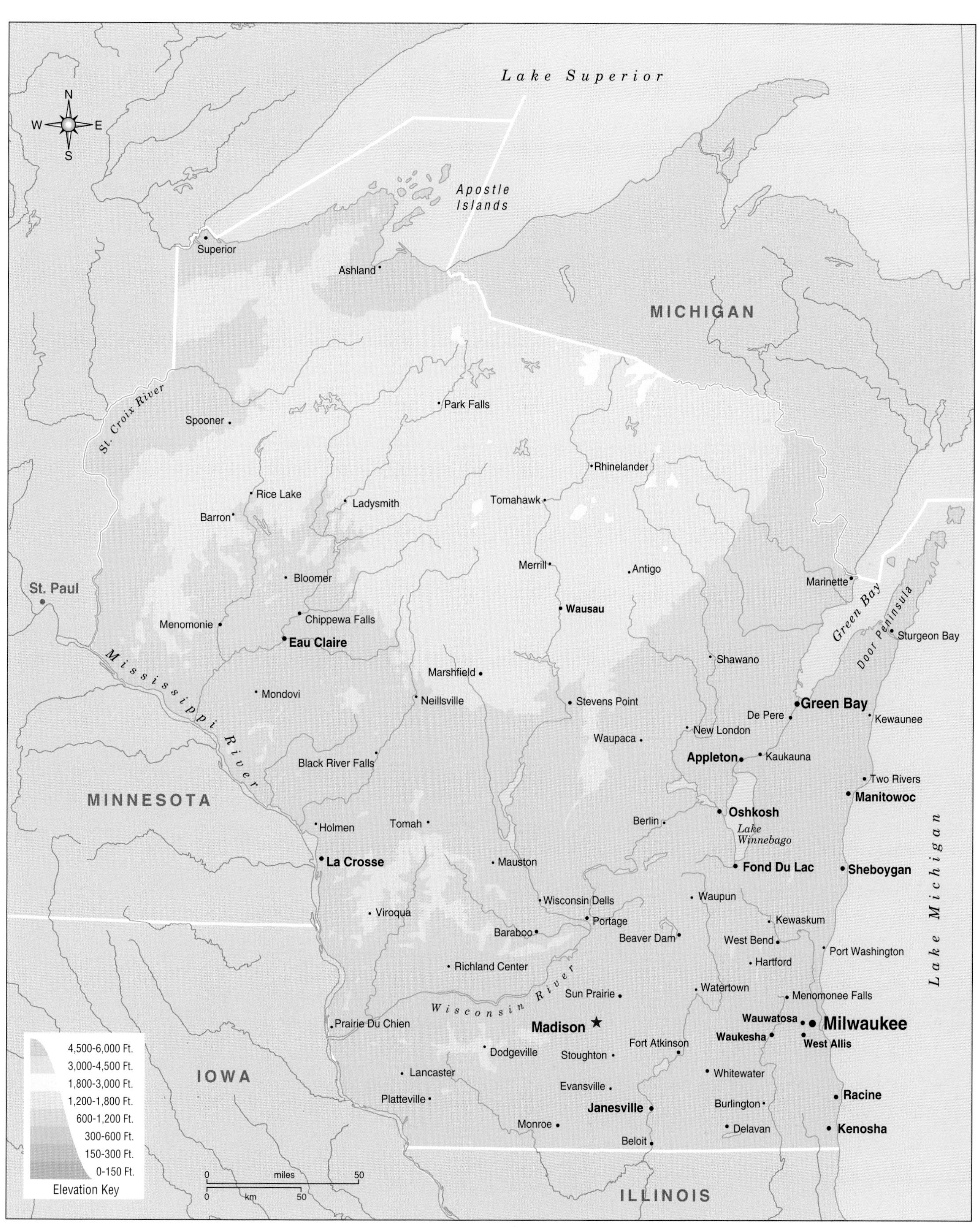

Lake Superior
N
W
E
S
Apostle Islands
Superior
Ashland
MICHIGAN
St. Croix River
Park Falls
Spooner
Rhinelander
Rice Lake
Ladysmith
Tomahawk
Barron
Merrill
Antigo
Bloomer
Marinette
St. Paul
Wausau
Green Bay
Door Peninsula
Sturgeon Bay
Menomonie
Chippewa Falls
Eau Claire
Mississippi River
Shawano
Marshfield
Mondovi
Neillsville
Stevens Point
Green Bay
De Pere
Kewaunee
New London
Waupaca
Appleton
Kaukauna
Black River Falls
Two Rivers
Manitowoc
MINNESOTA
Oshkosh
Berlin
Lake Winnebago
Holmen
Tomah
La Crosse
Mauston
Fond Du Lac
Sheboygan
Lake Michigan
Waupun
Wisconsin Dells
Viroqua
Portage
Kewaskum
Baraboo
Beaver Dam
West Bend
Port Washington
Hartford
Richland Center
Watertown
Sun Prairie
Menomonee Falls
Wisconsin River
Wauwatosa
Milwaukee
Prairie Du Chien
Madison
Waukesha
West Allis
Fort Atkinson
Dodgeville
Stoughton
4,500-6,000 Ft.
3,000-4,500 Ft.
1,800-3,000 Ft.
1,200-1,800 Ft.
600-1,200 Ft.
300-600 Ft.
150-300 Ft.
0-150 Ft.
Elevation Key
IOWA
Lancaster
Whitewater
Evansville
Platteville
Racine
Janesville
Burlington
Monroe
Delavan
Kenosha
Beloit
0 miles 50
0 km 50
ILLINOIS

Southeastern Wisconsin has the most fertile soil in the state. Central and western Wisconsin are characterized by gently rolling plains, while northern Wisconsin is dotted with many small lakes. The land around Lake Superior is a level plain that gradually rises. Southwestern Wisconsin is full of steep hills, ridges, and limestone bluffs along the Mississippi River.

The Menominee people, original inhabitants of Wisconsin, built lodges like this one out of bark.

Approximately 15,000 lakes and waterfalls are located throughout Wisconsin, and almost half the state is forested. Wisconsin's summers are warm but short, and its winters are usually long and snowy. Along the edges of Lakes Michigan and Superior, moist winds keep temperatures more moderate. Southeastern Wisconsin is the state's warmest region.

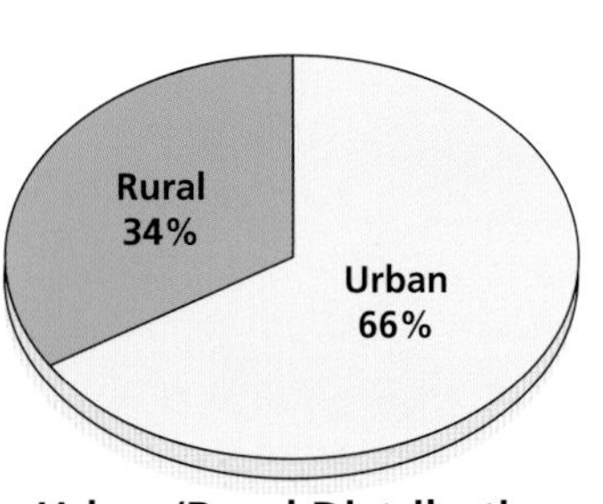

Urban/Rural Distribution

Wisconsin's greatest natural resource is its fertile soil. The state also has deposits of sand, gravel, dolomite, granite, iron, lead, copper, and zinc.

The Past

Many of Wisconsin's names for its towns, counties, and natural features come from Native American groups that lived there

Facts and Firsts

- ★ Southwestern Wisconsin's Kickapoo River, which twists and turns for nearly 120 miles (196 km), is often called "the most crooked river in the world."
- ★ Wisconsin produces about one-third of the cheese and about one-quarter of the butter produced in the United States.
- ★ Wisconsin has the oldest state constitution of any state west of the Allegheny Mountains. The document went into effect in 1848.
- ★ Wisconsin was home to the nation's first hydroelectric power plant, which began harnessing the energy of the Fox River in 1882.
- ★ In 1884, Baraboo was the site of the first Ringling Brothers Circus.
- ★ Seymour, which claims to be the birthplace of the American hamburger on a bun (which first was made there in 1885), boasts a Hamburger Hall of Fame. Seymour holds an annual Burger Festival in August with a hamburger-eating contest and a hamburger parade.

State Smart

Wisconsin hosts Summerfest—the biggest annual music festival in the country. It takes place every June in Milwaukee, and about one million people attend it.

before the arrival of Europeans. The three largest of these groups were the Winnebago, Dakota, and Menominee.

The first European explorer was the Frenchman Jean Nicolet, who arrived in 1634 from French Canada in search of a water route to Asia. In 1660, Father Rene Menard, the first French missionary, arrived and established a mission near present-day Ashland. Soon others came to the region to trade furs with the Native Americans. In 1754, the French and Indian Wars began, and the French and their Native American allies fought the British for control of North America. France lost control of Wisconsin, as well as most of its land east of the Mississippi River, to the British.

The Wisconsin area remained under British rule until the Revolutionary War ended in 1783, when Wisconsin's land became part of U. S. territory. In the 1820s, lead ore was discovered in southwestern Wisconsin. Settlers began to arrive from all over the country to mine the ore, which was used to make paint and shot for guns and cannons.

By 1848, when Wisconsin became a state, its population had increased dramatically as settlers came to seek opportunities on the frontier. Many settlers fought hard for the Union cause during the Civil War. By 1870, dairy farming had become Wisconsin's leading economic activity, and farmers joined together to work in cooperatives, or large groups.

One of the most famous periods in Wisconsin's history began around the turn of the century. In 1900, Robert M. La Follette was elected governor, and Wisconsin's Progressive Era began. During the next 50 years, Wisconsin was the first state to pass many laws designed to protect workers and citizens. Wisconsin was the first state to hold direct primary elections, open a library for state legislators, regulate railroads and utilities, provide pensions for retired teachers, introduce kindergarten for children, end the death penalty, and establish a minimum wage for workers.

In the 1950s, Wisconsin's agricultural industry declined in economic importance. Increased imports of beef from other countries and the American public's switch to a lower-fat diet hurt Wisconsin's beef and dairy farms. At the same time, manufacturing became more important to the

The Pabst mansion in Milwaukee was built by a family of successful brewers.

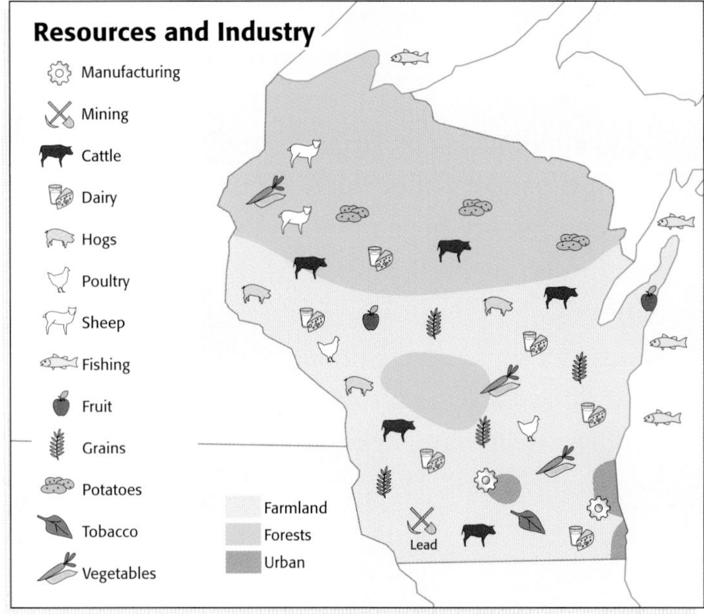

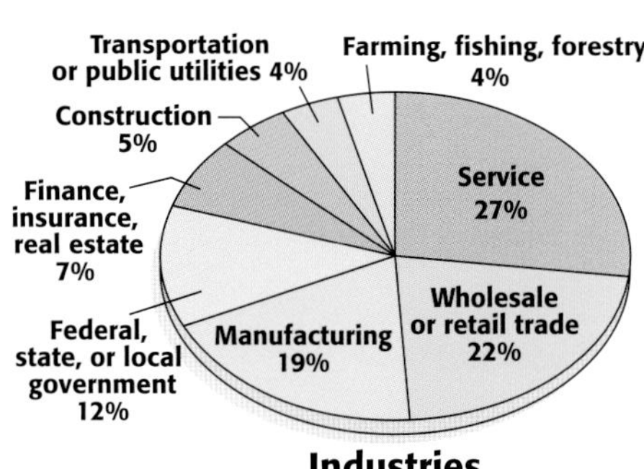

economy, and the population moved from rural to metropolitan areas.

To pay for education, welfare, and other social services, Wisconsin introduced its first sales tax in 1961. A state lottery was adopted in 1987 to help raise government revenue.

The Present

Manufacturing is now Wisconsin's most profitable activity. Machinery (including engines, power cranes, and heating and cooling equipment) is the leading manufactured product. Wisconsin also manufactures paper products such as cardboard and tissue paper.

Manufactured food products include cheese and butter. Wisconsin also produces most of the country's ice cream. Canned vegetables and beer are other important food products processed in Wisconsin.

Wisconsin is most famous for its dairy farms, which provide more than half of the state's farm income. Fertile, grassy land helps Wisconsin remain a leading milk producer, even though the number of dairy farms has decreased during the past 50 years. Beef cattle and hogs are valuable

Below left: *Milwaukee is a chief port for the Midwest.* Below right: *Wisconsin is famous for its dairy farms.*

Born in Wisconsin

- ★ **Don Ameche**, actor
- ★ **Roy Chapman Andrews**, naturalist and explorer
- ★ **Carrie Chapman Catt**, woman suffragist and peace advocate
- ★ **Tyne Daly**, actress
- ★ **Eric Heiden**, athlete
- ★ **Woodrow "Woody" Herman**, bandleader
- ★ **Robert La Follette**, politician
- ★ **Alfred Lunt**, actor
- ★ **Frederic March (Frederick Mcintyre Bickel)**, actor
- ★ **John Ringling North**, circus director
- ★ **William Joseph "Pat" O'Brien**, actor
- ★ **Georgia O'Keefe**, artist
- ★ **William H. Rehnquist**, jurist
- ★ **Spencer Tracy**, actor
- ★ **Thorstein Veblen**, economist
- ★ **Orson Welles**, actor and producer
- ★ **Thornton Wilder**, author
- ★ **Frank Lloyd Wright**, architect

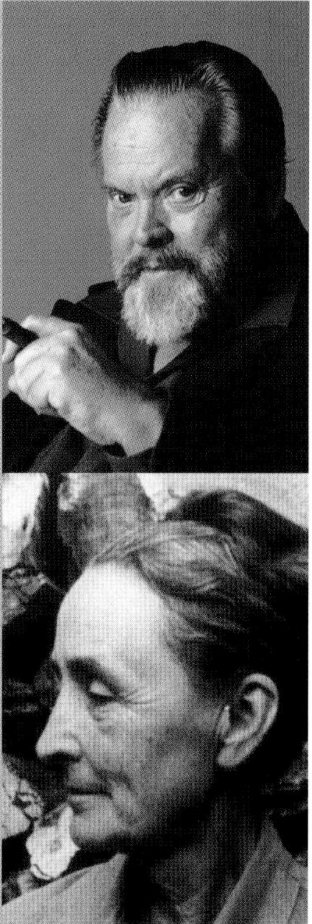

Above: *Orson Welles;* below: *Georgia O'Keeffe*

livestock products. Wisconsin farmers grow corn, hay, barley, tobacco, wheat, apples, raspberries, and other produce.

Milwaukee is a chief port and shipping center for the Midwest. The city also ranks as a leading center of finance and health care.

Wisconsin faces challenges in meeting the funding needs of health care, education, and welfare programs. Revenue from new taxes and new industries, however, is helping to offset the losses caused by the decrease in dairy farming.

A young Wisconsin girl cares for her pony.

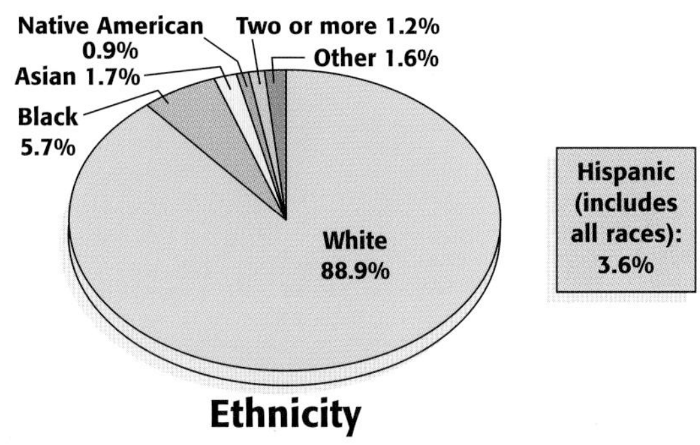

Hispanic (includes all races): 3.6%

Ethnicity

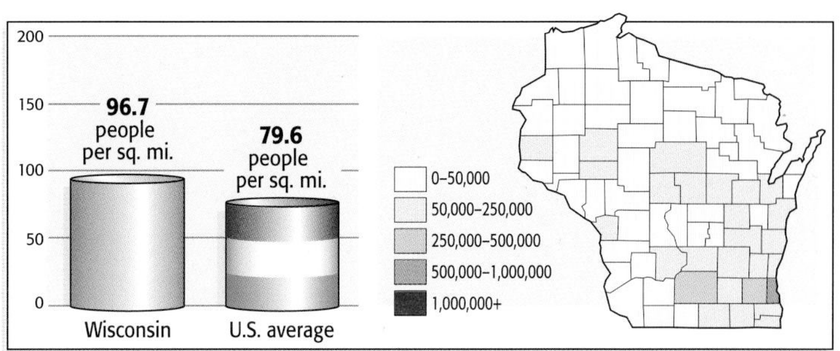

Population Density

Population by County

Wyoming

Equal rights.

Land area rank *Largest state (1)* — 9 — *smallest state (52)*

Population rank *Most people (1)* — 50 — *fewest people (52)*

At a Glance

Name: Wyoming comes from an Algonquian phrase meaning "large prairie place" or "at the big plain."

Nicknames: Equality State, Cowboy State

Capital: Cheyenne

Size: 97,818 sq. mi. (253,349 sq km)

Population: 493,782

Statehood: Wyoming became the 44th state on July 10, 1890.

Electoral votes: 3 (2004)

U.S. representatives: 1 (until 2003)

State tree: cottonwood

State flower: Indian paintbrush

State bird: meadowlark

Highest point: Gannett Peak, 13,804 ft. (4,207 m)

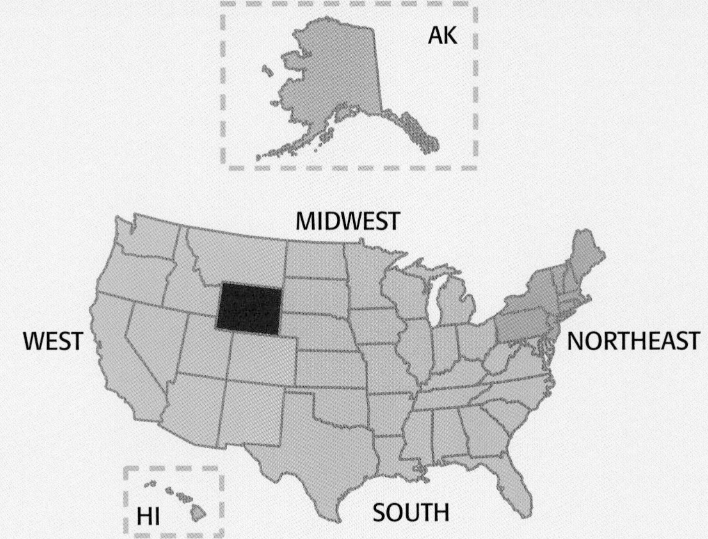

The Place

Wyoming is located on the border of the Midwest and West. The Great Plains cover eastern Wyoming and meet the Rocky Mountains in the center of the state. The Continental Divide cuts through Wyoming, from the northwest corner to the south-central area of the state. Water on the eastern side of the divide flows to the Atlantic Ocean; water on the western side drains into the Pacific.

Eastern Wyoming is a region of fertile soil that is covered by grasses and crossed by small rivers. In the state's northeast

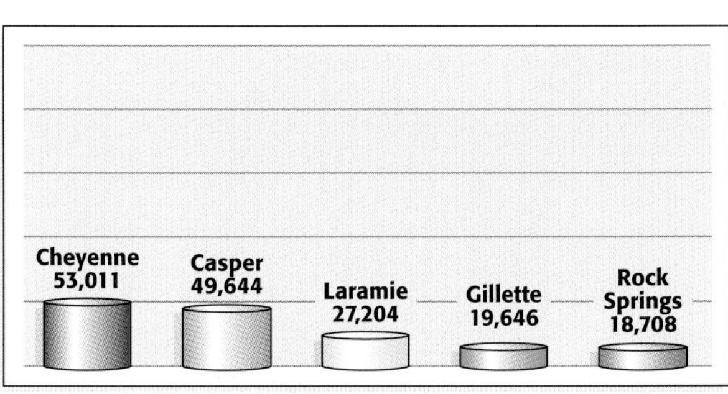

Major Cities

Devil's Tower is a landmark in the Black Hills of Wyoming.

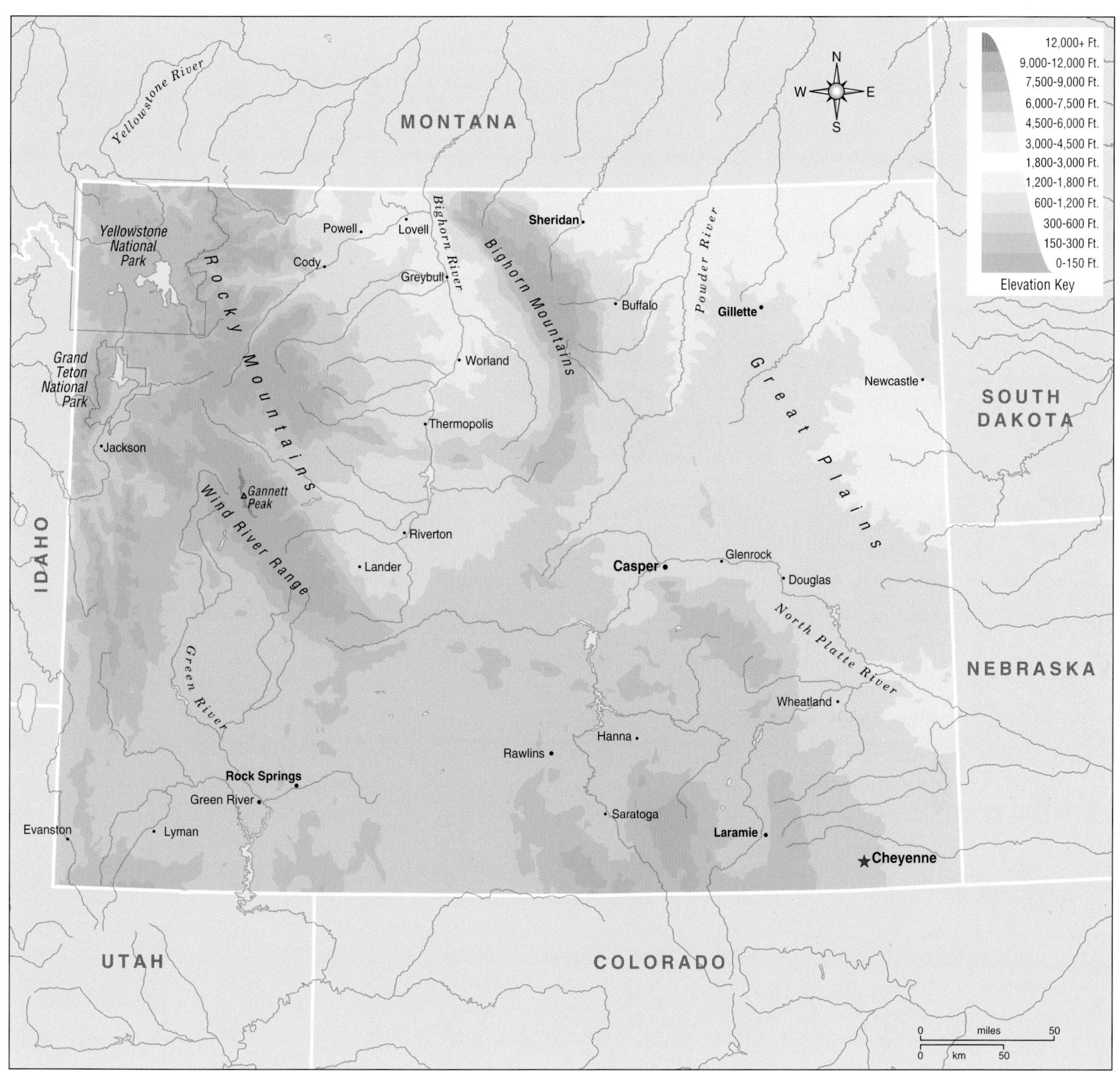

corner is the Black Hills, a mountain range that stretches into South Dakota. The Rocky Mountains, which extend into western Wyoming, are made up of many smaller ranges, including the Bighorn, Laramie, Wind River, Granite, Snake River, and Teton Ranges. Low basins, such as the Bighorn and Powder River basins, lie between these ranges.

Three of the largest river systems in the United States begin in the mountains of Wyoming. The Missouri River flows north and east, while the Green River, the primary source for the Colorado River, begins in the Wind River Mountains. The Columbia River system begins with the Snake River, which has cut rugged gorges through western Wyoming.

Wyoming's climate is dry and warm in the summer but cold in the winter, especially at higher elevations. The state's greatest mineral resources are petroleum and natural gas, but Wyoming also has clay, coal, sodium carbonate, uranium, gold, and limestone deposits.

Native Americans in what is now Wyoming hunted buffalo for many of their needs.

The Past

After the last Ice Age ended more than 11,000 years ago, large herds of bison roamed the Great Plains. Many Native American groups followed the bison herds, which provided meat, tools, clothing, and shelter, to the eastern prairies of Wyoming.

French explorers may have visited Wyoming during the 1700s, but the area did not receive much attention until 1803, when the United States purchased present-day Wyoming as part of the Louisiana Territory. Settlers came in search of furs, and in 1812, a passage through the mountains was discovered and named South Pass. In 1833, oil was discovered in Wind River Basin. The government soon purchased the few forts that had been built in Wyoming by fur traders.

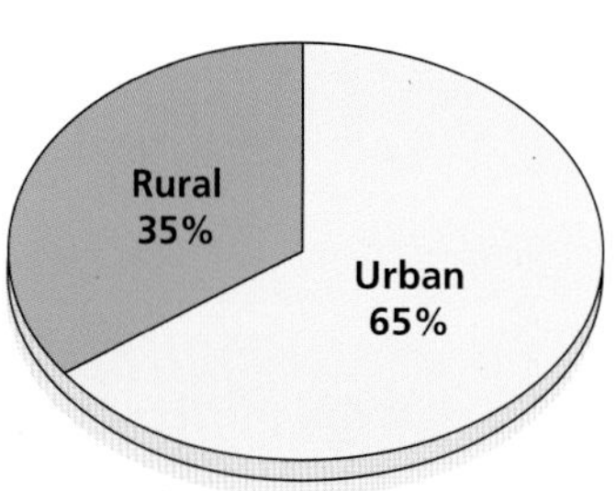

Urban/Rural Distribution

By the 1840s, settlers from the East began to pass through Wyoming by way of South Pass to reach California. The Oregon, Mormon, and California Trails, which crossed Wyoming, were main routes to the West.

Facts and Firsts

- ★ With only 493,782 residents, Wyoming has the smallest population of all of the states.
- ★ Wyoming is home to Black Thunder, the largest coal mine in the United States.
- ★ Wyoming was home to the first national monument, Devils Tower, which was dedicated in 1906.
- ★ Wyoming was the first state to allow women to vote, in 1869.
- ★ The J.C. Penney department store chain began in Kemmerer in 1902.

At first, Native Americans of the Midwest plains were happy to help and trade with the settlers. As increasing numbers of pioneers crossed Native American lands, however, they scared away the bison herds, set huge grass fires in the plains, and brought disease. Conflict broke out between the settlers and the native tribes. Many pioneers crossed through Wyoming and admired its beauty, but only a few stayed to settle the land.

In 1867, the Union Pacific Railroad entered Wyoming, and in 1869, the territory became the first to allow women to vote. Yellowstone National Park was created in 1872, when the national government bought a huge piece of land in Wyoming. Because of the park, tourism grew immediately.

Oil wells were built in the 1880s, but it took several years for the oil industry to achieve prosperity. Ranchers in eastern Wyoming, who raised cattle for shipment to the East, supported the territory's economy and controlled its politics until the late 1880s.

After Wyoming became a state in 1900, settlers flocked to the area. Disputes broke out between newly arrived sheep ranchers and the established cattle ranchers. Wyoming's population began to climb greatly when the national government gave away free Wyoming farmland as part of the Homestead Acts of 1909, 1912, and 1916.

By the middle of the 20th century, Wyoming's mining industry had overtaken agriculture in importance to the state's economy. Trona, which contains sodium carbonate, and uranium were discovered in the 1950s and prompted new industrial growth. In the 1960s, a steel company built an iron ore processing plant in Sunrise. Other manufacturers followed this lead, and coal and petroleum mining expanded.

Between 1970 and 1980, Wyoming's population grew by almost 42 percent as people moved to the state to work in the mining industries. This rapid population growth caused problems such as housing shortages during the 1980s. Many communities struggled to provide services, health care, and education to the newly increased population.

State Smart

Yellowstone National Park, which is located mostly in Wyoming, was the country's first national park. It was established in 1872.

Women vote in Cheyenne. Wyoming Territory allowed women to vote before any other U.S. state or territory.

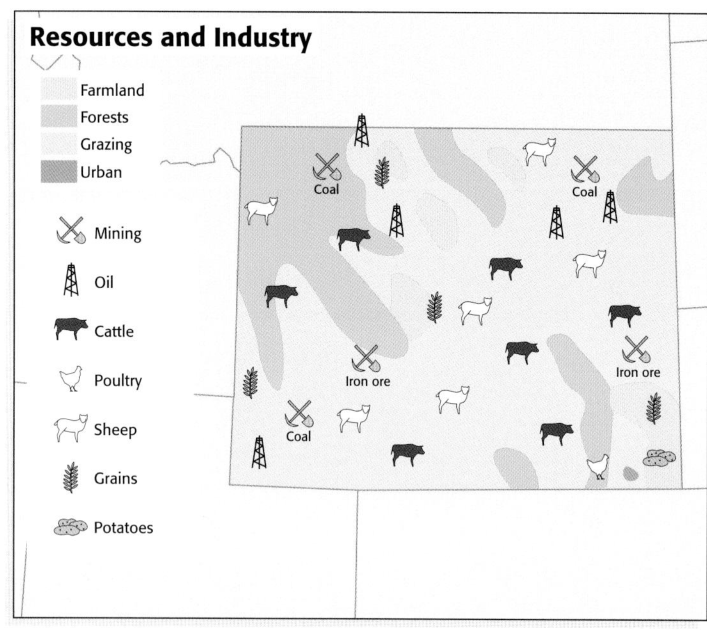

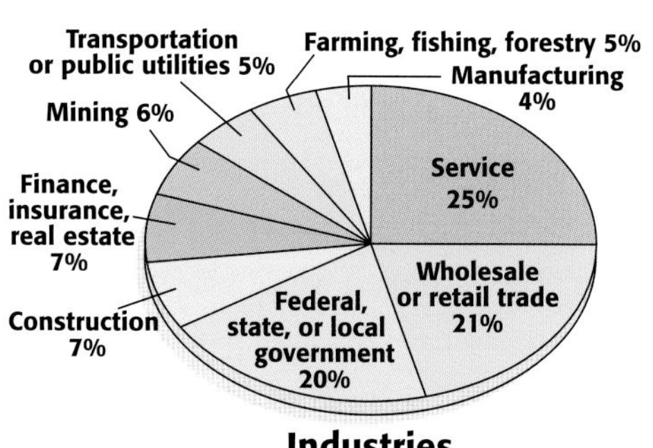

The Present

Wyoming has the smallest population of any state. Even Cheyenne, the largest city in Wyoming, has only about 50,000 residents. The U.S. government owns more than half of Wyoming's land and strictly controls its development. The national government monitors logging, cattle grazing, and mining on all of Wyoming's public land. This land also includes national parks, Native American reservations, and military sites. The Francis E. Warren Air Force Base in Cheyenne controls one of the nation's most important long-range missile systems.

Because the government owns so much of Wyoming's land, government jobs are integral to Wyoming's economy. Mining also continues to be of critical importance, and the mining industry employs many of Wyoming's workers. Wyoming receives more revenue from mining than any other state. Oil drills dot many parts of Wyoming's terrain, and the state leads all others in coal production. Cattle

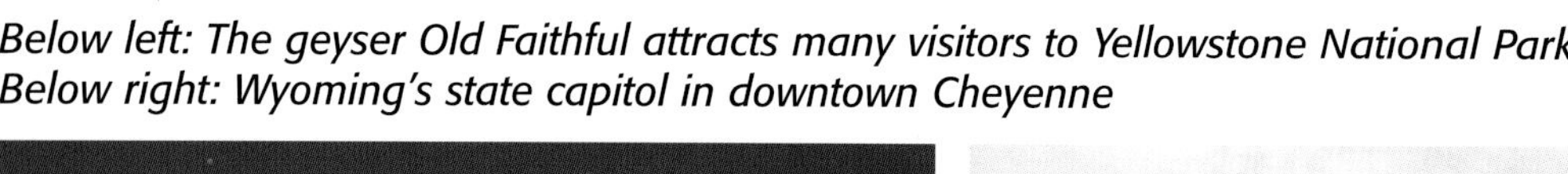

Below left: The geyser Old Faithful attracts many visitors to Yellowstone National Park.
Below right: Wyoming's state capitol in downtown Cheyenne

Born in Wyoming

★**Jim Geringer**, governor
★**Curt Gowdy**, sportscaster
★**Leonard S. Hobbs**, inventor
★**Patricia MacLachlan**, author
★**Jackson Pollock**, artist

Jackson Pollock

Wyoming's cattle ranching tradition makes rodeo popular in the state.

ranching is yet another activity that is important to the state's economy.

The national parks, too, employ many of Wyoming's workers. Grand Teton and Yellowstone parks feature scenery and mineral springs that attract millions of tourists, campers, and wilderness enthusiasts every year.

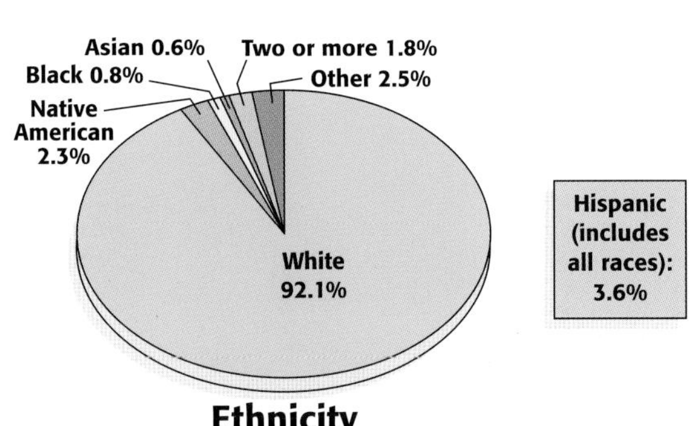

Ethnicity

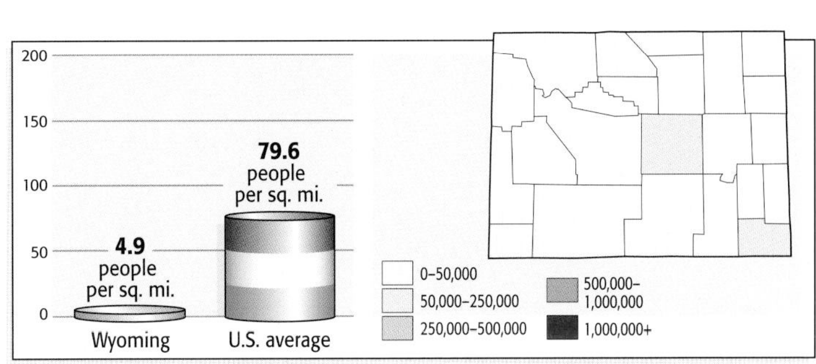

Population Density

Population by County

District of Columbia

At a Glance

Government: The District of Columbia has been the seat of the U.S. government since 1800, and a municipal corporation since February 21, 1871.

Area: 68.25 sq. mi. (177 sq km)

Population: 572,059

Electoral votes: 3

U.S. Representatives: 1 (nonvoting)

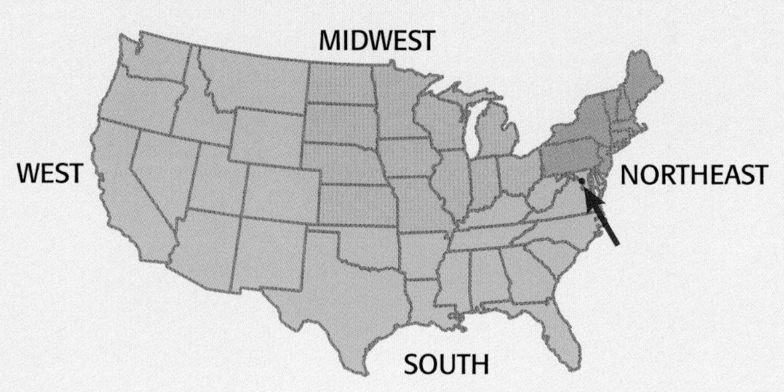

The Place

The city of Washington covers the entire District of Columbia, an independent section of the country controlled by the federal government. Washington, D.C., is part of the southeastern United States and lies between Maryland and Virginia. The Potomac River separates Washington, D.C., from Virginia.

The U.S. Capitol, White House, Smithsonian Institution, Washington Monument, Lincoln Memorial, and many other government and cultural offices are located in northwestern Washington, D.C. Portions of this area are known as the Mall. Other areas of Washington, D.C., are residential.

The idea of a tribute to George Washington was conceived in 1791, but the Washington Monument (pictured) did not open to the public until 1888.

The Past

After the Revolutionary War ended in 1783, Congress looked for a site to build a permanent, independent capital. This plan caused much disagreement because every state wanted to have the nation's capital built on its land. It was decided that the capital should be built on federal land, and an area near the Potomac River was chosen. In 1791, Congress asked President George Washington to select the exact site of the future capital.

Washington chose land that was part of both Maryland and Virginia, and those states agreed to donate it. Washington then hired French engineer Pierre Charles L'Enfant to design the layout of the capital. When work was completed and the federal government moved to its new home in

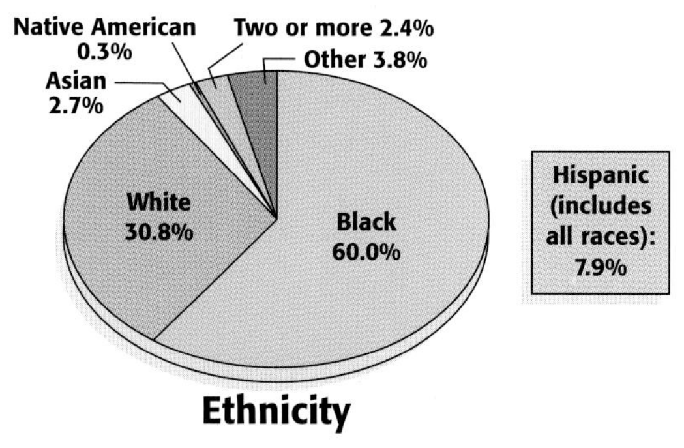

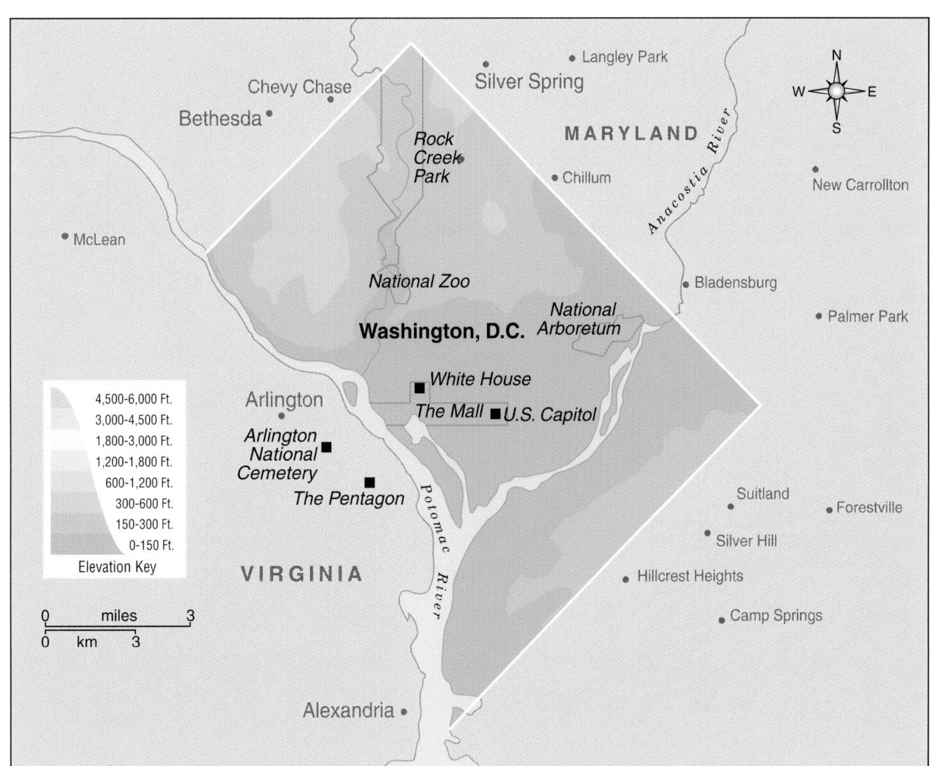

1800, the commissioners named the city Washington and the entire region the District of Columbia.

Washington developed slowly, and in 1846 the federal government returned the land that Virginia had donated. Washington expanded, however, especially in times of national crisis, such as wars and economic depressions. During the Civil War, the Union stationed large numbers of troops in the city to protect it from Confederate attack. Thousands of refugee slaves also flocked to the city.

Another period of growth occurred in 1917, when the United States entered World War I. During the Great Depression of the 1930s, thousands of government jobs were created. This job boom contrasted sharply with the devastating unemployment suffered in other cities. U.S. involvement in World War II again stimulated Washington's growth.

The White House is the residence of the U.S. president.

In 1970, Congress made it legal for the city of Washington, D.C., to have a representative in the House of Representatives who may vote only in committees. In 1973, Congress also allowed the city of Washington to elect its own local officials, including a mayor.

The Present

Today, government and its related services are the primary industry in Washington, D.C., and most residents work in government-related offices. Many government workers live outside the city, in suburban Maryland and Virginia.

The capital's economy thrives on tourism. Millions of visitors are attracted each year to the capital's historic buildings, monuments, museums, libraries, and other cultural institutions. Washington has an extensive public transportation system and is served by three major airports for commercial traffic.

American Samoa

At a Glance

Name: *Samoa* is a native Polynesian word.
Capital: Pago Pago
Size: 77 sq. mi. (199 sq km)
Population: 67,084 people
Statehood: Unincorporated
Electoral Votes: 0
U.S. Representatives: 1 (nonvoting)

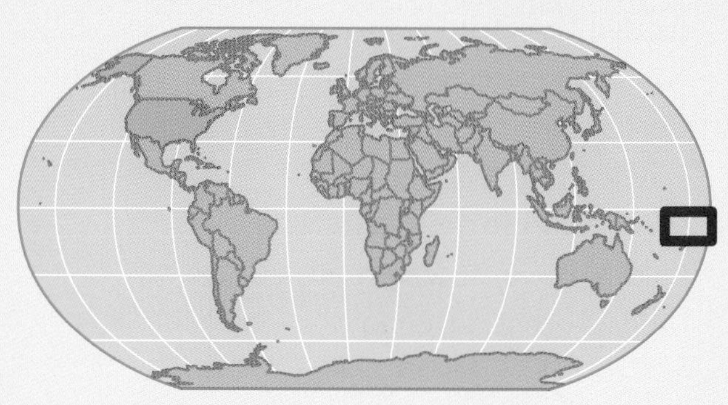

The Place

American Samoa is a group of seven islands located about 2,600 miles (4,184 km) southwest of Hawaii. The U.S. federal government administers the islands, which are named Tutuila, Aunuu, Ofu, Olosega, Tau, and Rose. The seventh island, Swains, is privately owned by an American family that has lived there since 1856.

The capital of American Samoa, Pago Pago, is located on the island of Tutuila and has one of the most beautiful harbors in the South Pacific Ocean. Old coral reefs form Rose and Swains Islands, and extinct volcanoes form the remaining islands. Most of American Samoa is mountainous, and only about a third of the islands can be used for agriculture. The best soil lies in the valleys between the mountains. American Samoa has a tropical climate and receives more than 200 inches (508 cm) of rainfall every year.

The Past

Polynesians settled American Samoa more than 2,000 years ago. They arrived in boats from eastern Melanesia and settled on the habitable islands. In 1722, European explorers visited the islands. Later, in 1878, the islanders agreed to allow the United

Pago Pago has one of the most beautiful harbors in the South Pacific Ocean.

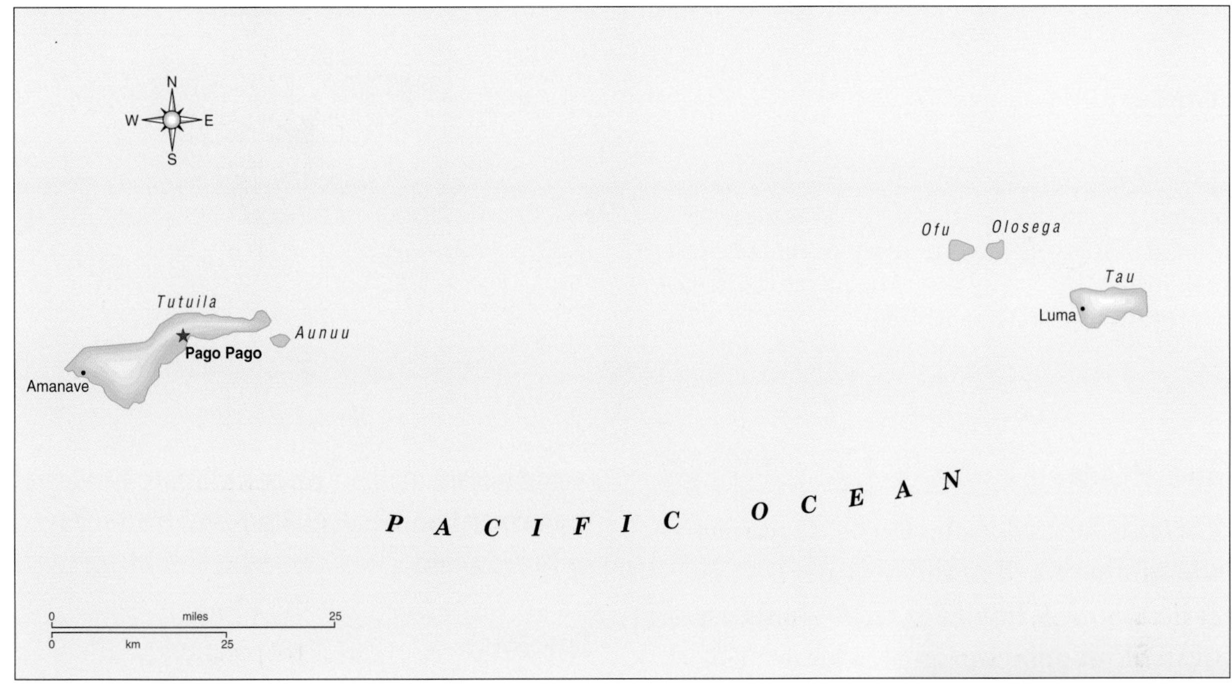

States to use Pago Pago as a naval repair station.

The United States began to trade with the Polynesians, and in 1899, the United States, Britain, and Germany signed a treaty that divided the Samoa Islands among them. At first, the U.S. Navy directly governed American Samoa. The Department of the Interior took over this role in 1951 and continued to appoint governors until 1978, when American Samoans first elected a governor of their own choosing.

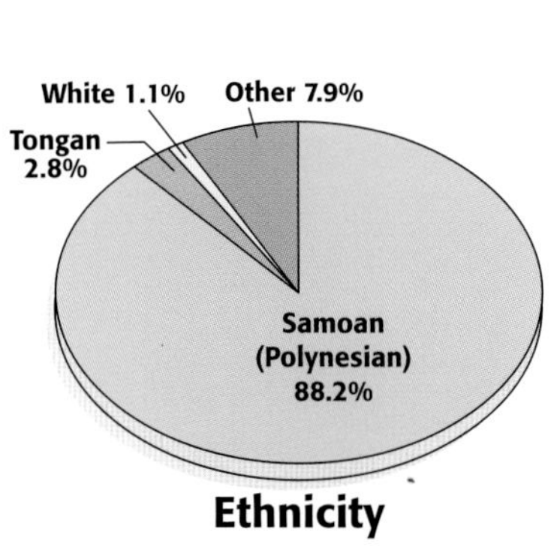

The Present

American Samoa is an unincorporated territory of the United States. Its residents are not U.S. citizens, but they can travel freely throughout the United States.

American Samoan residents do not pay taxes to the United States, but they receive considerable amounts of financial aid from the U.S. government.

American Samoa has a strong economy based on fishing. Approximately 96 percent of American Samoa's exports are fish or fish products. American Samoa also produces coconuts, bananas, and taro in its most fertile regions. Since 1960, when the first resort and large airport was built, travel to the islands has increased.

A father and son travel a path lined with tropical vegetation.

Guam

At a Glance

Capital: Hagatna (Agana)
Size: 209 sq. mi. (541 sq km)
Population: 157,557
Government: Unincorporated territory of United States
Electoral votes: 0
U.S. Representatives: 1 (nonvoting)

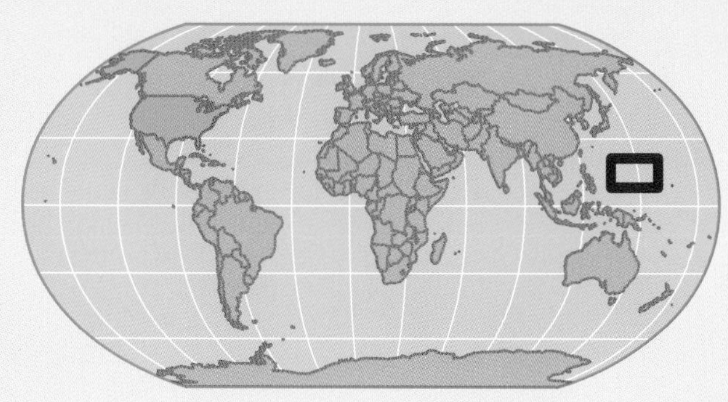

The Place

Guam is located in the Pacific Ocean at the southern end of the Mariana Islands. It lies about 1,300 miles (2,100 km) east of the Philippines in an area known as Micronesia.

Guam has many coral reefs, as well as a mountain range formed by volcanoes in the south. The northern part of the island consists of a limestone plateau. Guam's largest town is Tamuning, and Apra Harbor is the island's chief port.

Typhoons, or devastating ocean storms, often strike the island, and earthquakes occur occasionally. Guam's climate is warm year-round and especially rainy from May to November.

The Past

Chamorros, or groups from Southeast Asia, were the first known people to migrate to Guam, arriving sometime before 1500 B.C. Portuguese explorer Ferdinand Magellan was the first European to arrive in Guam, in 1521. Spain claimed Guam in 1565 but did not actively govern it until 1668.

After Spain lost the Spanish-American War in 1898, it gave up Guam to the

The coral reefs near Agana, Guam's capital and chief harbor, break up waves before they reach the shore.

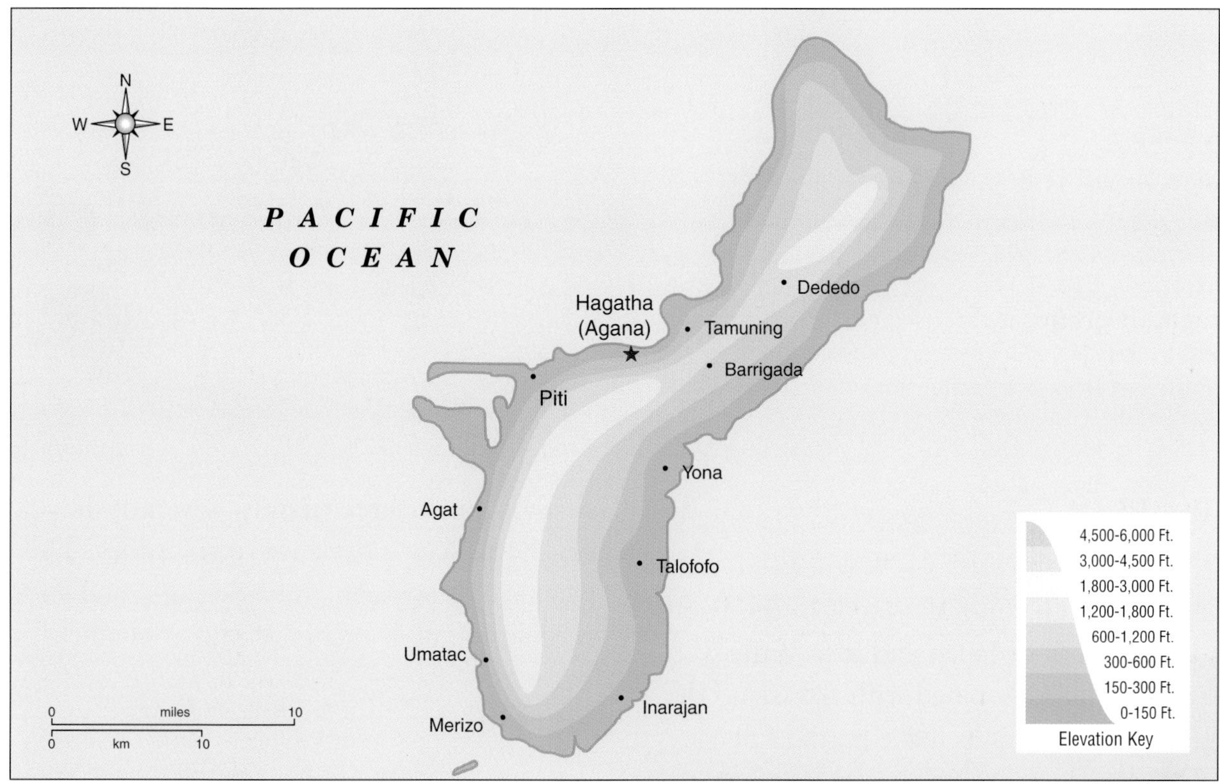

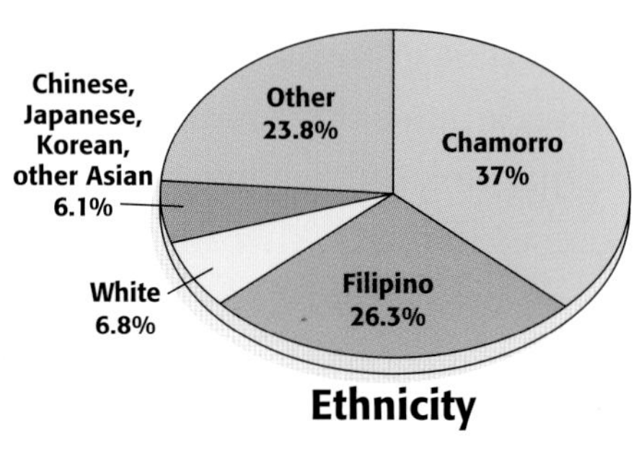

United States and sold the Northern Mariana Islands to Germany. The U.S. Navy was responsible for handling Guam's affairs until the Japanese took it over in 1941, during World War II. The United States reclaimed Guam in August 1944. In 1950, when the United States made Guam a territory and transferred control to the U.S. Department of the Interior, Guam's residents became U.S. citizens.

In 1954, the U.S. military used about one-third of Guam's land to build Andersen Air Force Base. Guam first elected its own governor in 1970, and in 1972, sent a delegate to the U.S. House of Representatives. Guam's representative can vote in committees but not in general House floor votes.

The Present

Tourism and related industries produce the largest part of Guam's income. More than 500,000 tourists, mostly from Japan, visit Guam each year.

The United States has a strong presence in Guam, and the U.S. military is Guam's second-largest source of income. About one-sixth of Guam's workforce is employed by the U.S. military.

Agriculture and fishing are minor economic activities. Coconuts, sweet potatoes, taro, and tuna are the most common agricultural and fish products of Guam.

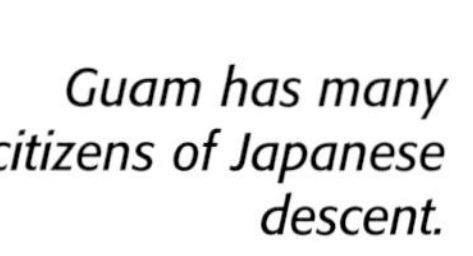

Guam has many citizens of Japanese descent.

Northern Mariana Islands

At a Glance

Nickname: America's Best Kept Secret
Capital: Saipan (38,896)
Size: 184 sq. mi. (477 sq km)
Population: 74,612
Statehood: Unincorporated
Electoral votes: 0
U.S. Representatives: 1 (nonvoting)

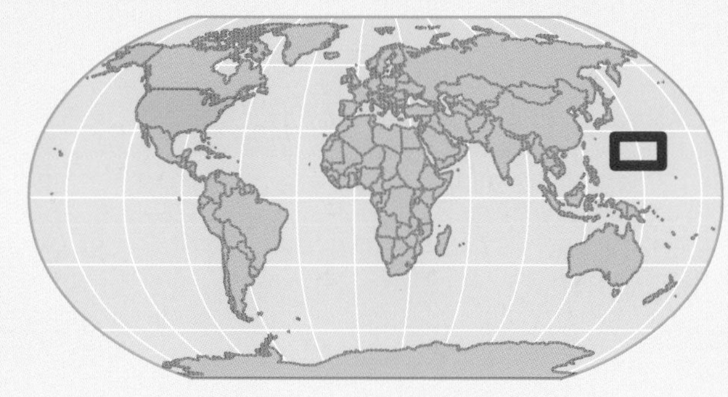

The Place

The Commonwealth of Northern Mariana Islands is a chain of 16 islands in the Pacific Ocean, south of Japan and east of the Philippines. Combined with the island of Guam, these islands make up the full Mariana Islands. The Mariana Islands are part of the region in the Pacific Ocean known as Micronesia.

The largest island in the Northern Marianas is Saipan, which is also the capital. The second-largest island is Tinian; Rota is the third largest. Most of the population lives on these three islands. Seven of the northern islands have active volcanoes. The islands have a warm climate year-round and receive about 84 inches of rain annually.

A fisherman walks on the beach on Saipan, largest of the islands.

The Past

A group of people known as the Chamorros first began to settle in the Northern Marianas around 1500 B.C. Another group, known as the Carolinians, first came to the Marianas after 1815, when typhoons (huge storms) washed out their homes in lower Micronesia.

The first European to see the Mariana Islands was Portuguese explorer Ferdinand Magellan in 1521. Spain quickly claimed the region, but did not settle the area until 1668. The islands were ruled successively by Spain, Germany, and Japan. Japan controlled the Northern Mariana Islands until 1944, when the United States took them over as a United Nations trusteeship during World War II. In 1975, the United States allowed the Northern Mariana Islands to choose

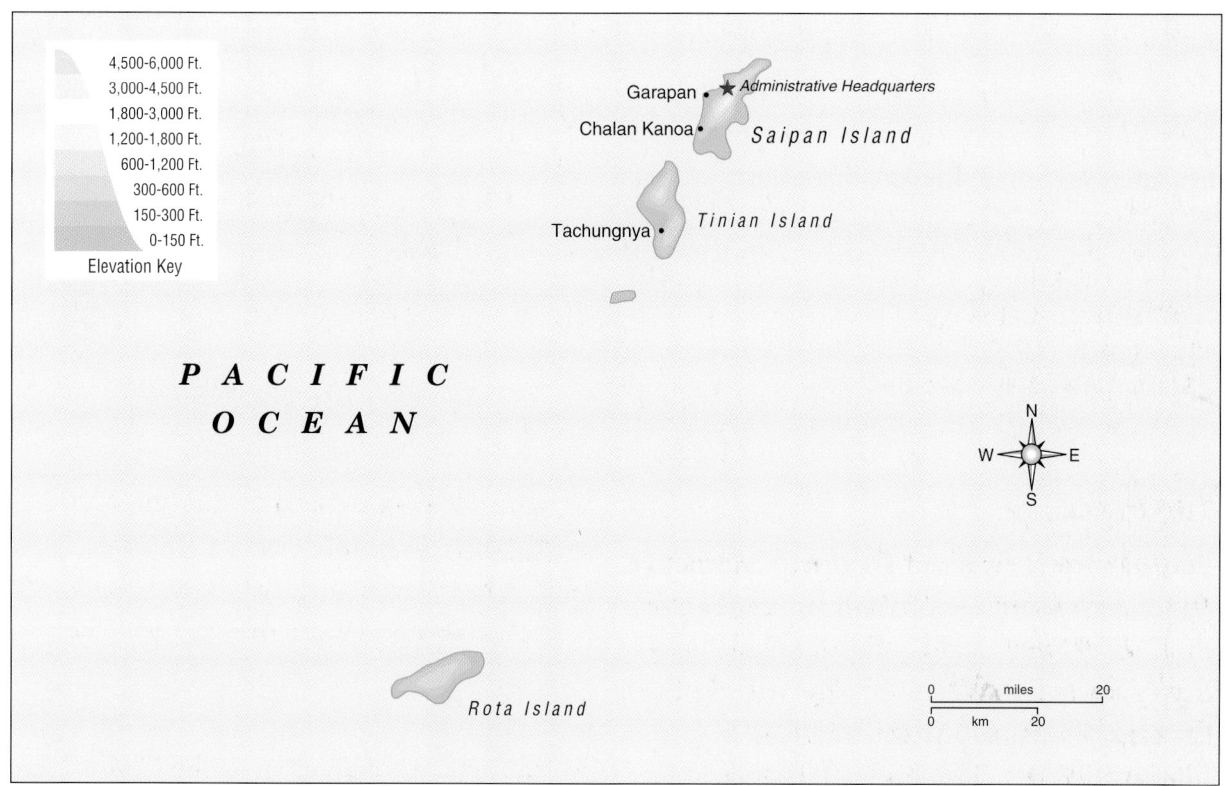

its own government officials, and it became a U.S. commonwealth in November 1986.

The Present

Residents of the Commonwealth of Northern Mariana Islands are considered U.S. citizens, but they cannot vote in presidential elections. They have one representative in the U.S. House of Representatives, but this representative can vote only in committees. The Northern Mariana Islands' government is made up of a 9-member senate and a 15-member house of representatives, and the three largest islands have mayors. The United States provides defense and handles international relations for the islands.

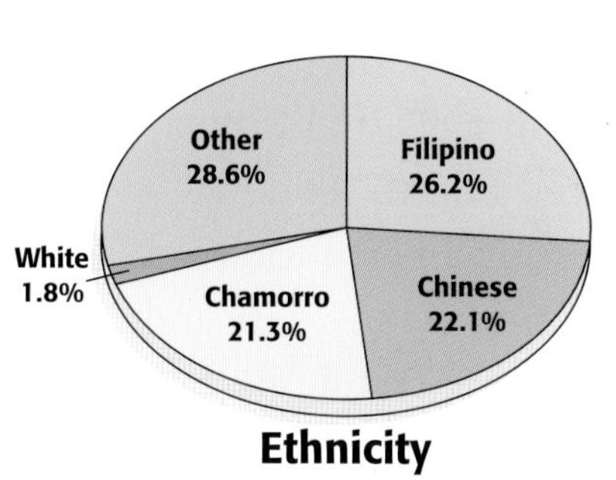

Ethnicity

The island of Saipan is the capital of the Northern Mariana Islands and is home to about 90 percent of its population. Saipan contains the seat of government, a busy seaport, and an international airport.

The economy is based on tourism, manufacturing, and agriculture. Tourism is the largest industry. The islands manufacture textiles, and agricultural exports include vegetables, beef, and pork. Government jobs are also critical to the economy of the Northern Mariana Islands.

Descendants of Carolinians celebrate a wedding with a feast.

Puerto Rico

At a Glance

Name: *Puerto Rico* means "rich port" in Spanish.
Capital: San Juan
Size: 3,515 sq. mi. (9,103 sq km)
Population: 3,808,610
Statehood: Unincorporated
Electoral votes: 0
U.S. Representatives: 1 (nonvoting)

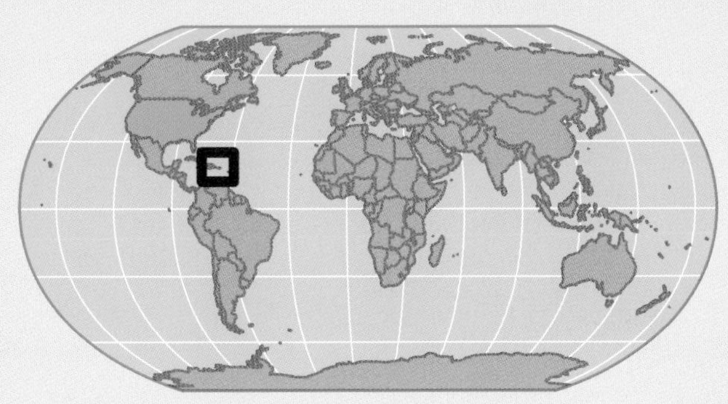

The Place

Puerto Rico is an island about 1,000 miles (1,600 km) southeast of Florida, between the United States and South America. Puerto Rico also includes many smaller islands; the largest are Vieques, Mona, and Culebra. Puerto Rico lies partly in the Atlantic Ocean and partly in the Caribbean Sea.

Puerto Rico has fertile soil, a subtropical climate, and sandy beaches. The island has regions of low land, valleys, and foothills, and the Cordillera Mountains cross south-central Puerto Rico. Puerto Rico's climate is humid in many places, and some areas experience powerful storms daily. During the summer and fall, hurricanes can cause serious devastation. Mild ocean breezes keep summer temperatures in Puerto Rico relatively cool.

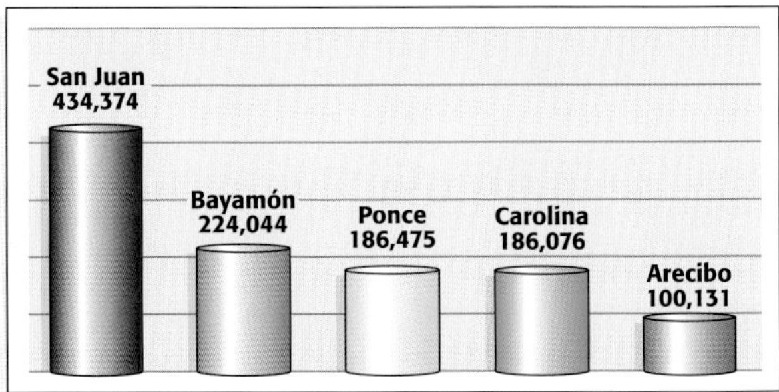

Major Cities

A man sells produce along a mountain road in Naranjito. The fertile soil and combination of tropical heat and rain are good for crops.

The Past

Puerto Rico is the island on which Christopher Columbus first landed in 1493, during his second voyage to North America. Columbus claimed Puerto Rico for Spain, and it remained a Spanish possession until 1898, when Spain surrendered Puerto Rico to the United States at the end of the Spanish-American War.

In 1917, Congress passed legislation that made Puerto Ricans citizens of the United States, and in 1947, the U.S. government allowed Puerto Rico to elect its own governor. Puerto Rico wrote its own constitution in 1950, and became a self-governing commonwealth in 1952. Although Puerto Ricans are

U.S. citizens, they cannot vote in presidential elections. They elect one representative to the U.S. Congress, but this representative can vote only in committees.

At around the same time, many Puerto Ricans moved to the U.S. mainland to find better job opportunities. This migration slowed during the 1960s and 1970s, when Puerto Rico experienced tremendous industrial growth. In both 1993 and 1998, Puerto Ricans voted to remain a commonwealth of the United States instead of becoming a state or an independent country.

Other 1.2%

Hispanic (of any race) 98.8%

Ethnicity

The Present

Manufacturing is Puerto Rico's chief industry, and factories produce pharmaceuticals, processed sugar, electrical equipment, machinery, and clothing. Livestock products include milk, poultry, and beef, while farmers grow coffee, pineapples, bananas, sugarcane, avocados, and coconuts. Fishing is another important industry, with an annual catch valued at around $21 million.

Tourism is the second-most developed industry on the island; every year millions of vacationers come from the U.S. mainland and other countries to visit Puerto Rico's white, sandy beaches and to experience the island's unique Hispanic culture.

Puerto Rican artist Juan Alindato carries on the tradition of mask-making.

U.S. Virgin Islands

At a Glance

Government: Unincorporated; purchased by the United States in 1917
Size: 136 sq. mi. (352 sq km)
Population: 122,211
Electoral votes: 0
U.S. Representatives: 1 (nonvoting)

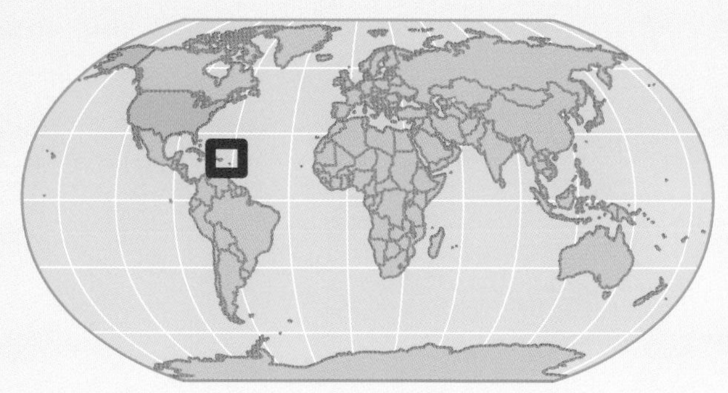

The Place

The Virgin Islands are two groups of islands in the Atlantic Ocean, 40 miles (64 km) east of Puerto Rico. They are part of a long island chain known as the Lesser Antilles. One group of islands—St. Croix, St. John, St. Thomas, and some smaller islands—is a U.S. territory and is known as the U.S. Virgin Islands. The second group belongs to Great Britain and is known as the British Virgin Islands.

Of the American islands, only St. Croix, St. John, and St. Thomas are inhabited. St. Croix is the largest of the islands in both area and population. Most of the American islands, except St. Croix, are rugged and hilly. The islands' most important mineral resource is basalt, used to make concrete. The climate is tropical, and flowers and trees flourish. Ocean winds keep the temperature moderate year-round.

Cruise ships line the harbor at St. Thomas.

The Past

Although Christopher Columbus claimed the Virgin Islands for Spain in 1493, the Spanish used the islands solely to hide royal treasure from pirates. The English and Dutch finally settled the islands in 1625, and for the next few hundred years, the English, Dutch, Spanish, and French fought for control of the area. Eventually, in 1917, these three islands were sold to the United States for $25 million. In 1927, the U.S. government passed legislation that made residents of these Virgin Islands citizens of the United States. In 1954, the United States allowed the U.S. Virgin Islands to have its own legislature, and in 1968 the people were given the right to elect their own governor.

The Present

The United States retains a large presence in the U.S. Virgin Islands. More than one

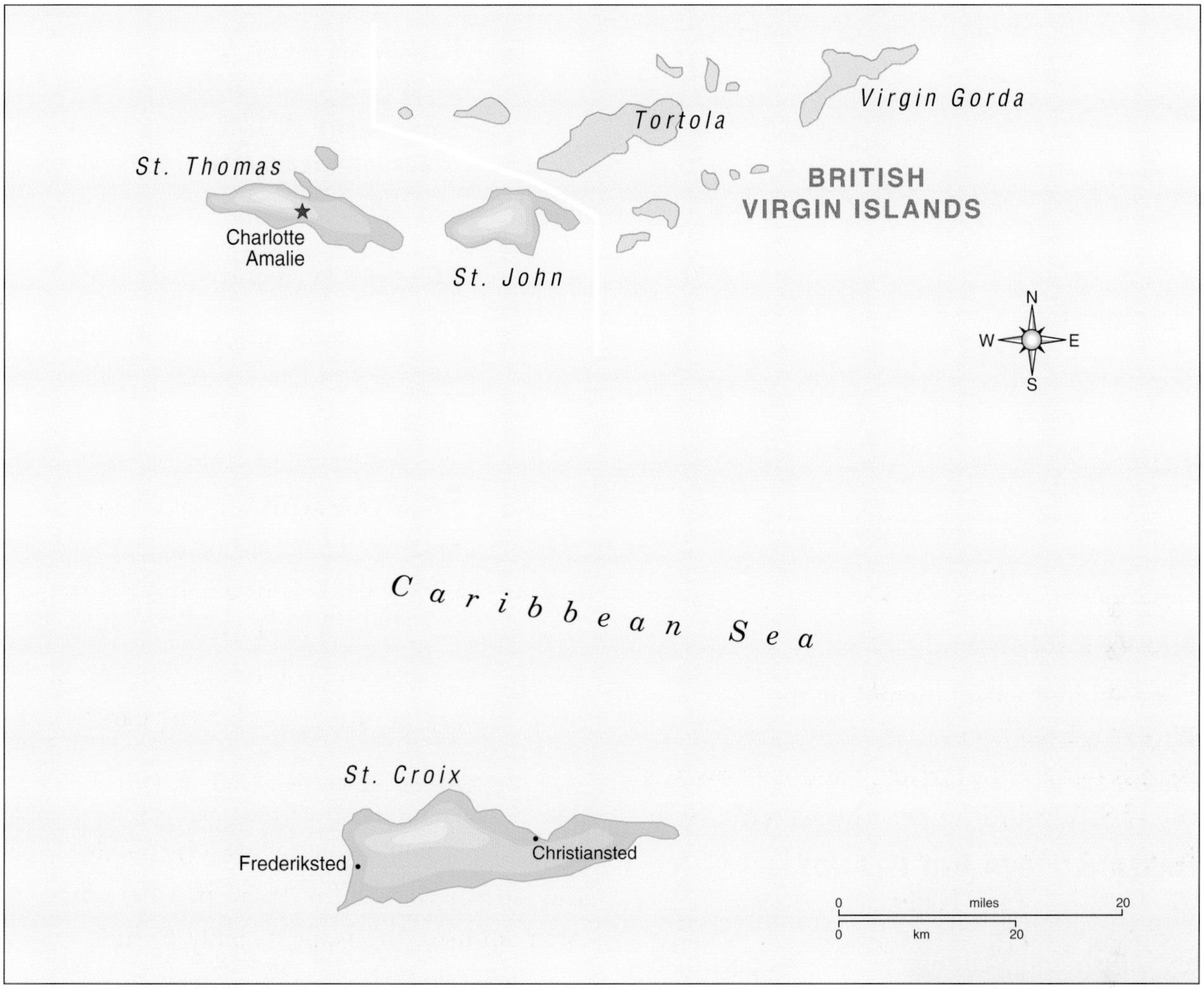

Virgin Gorda
Tortola
St. Thomas
BRITISH VIRGIN ISLANDS
Charlotte Amalie
St. John
N
W
E
S
Caribbean Sea
St. Croix
Frederiksted
Christiansted
0 miles 20
0 km 20

million tourists, many of them from the mainland United States, vacation there every year. The scenery, weather, and beaches draw visitors from all over the world to the islands, especially St. Croix. The carnival held on St. Thomas every April is a major tourist attraction.

The island has rum distilleries, oil refineries, and factories that produce aluminum ore, knitted goods, thermometers, perfume, and watches. Most of the food must be imported because farms on the island cannot support visitors and residents.

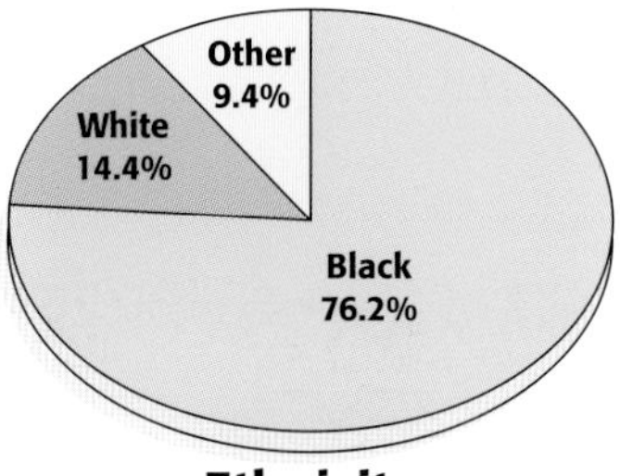

Other 9.4%
White 14.4%
Black 76.2%

Ethnicity

Less than 1 percent of U.S. Virgin Island residents are farmers. The soil is fertile, however, and farmers raise beef and poultry, as well as vegetables.

A resident of St. John demonstrates basketweaving in front of an 18th-century mill on a sugar plantation.

U.S. Possessions

NAVASSA ISLAND

Uninhabited island owned by the United States

Area: 2 sq. mi. (5.2 sq km)

BAKER & HOWLAND ISLANDS

Unincorporated territories administered by the U.S. Fish and Wildlife Service as part of the National Wildlife Refuge

Official Name: British Indian Ocean Territory
Area: 0.5-0.6 sq. mi. (1.40-1.60 sq km), each

JARVIS ISLAND

Uninhabited territory of the United States

Area: 1.7 sq. mi. (4.5 sq km)

JOHNSTON ATOLL

Area: 1.1 sq. mi. (2.8 sq km)
Population: 1100
Government: unincorporated territory of United States.

KINGMAN REEF

Area: 0.4 sq. mi. (1 sq km)
Government: privately owned and administered by the U.S. Department of the Navy

MIDWAY ISLANDS

Uninhabited, unincorporated territory of the United States

Area: 2.4 sq. mi. (6.2 sq km)

PALMYRA ATOLL

Area: 4.6 sq. mi. (11.9 sq km)
Government: privately owned and administered by the U.S. Department of the Navy

WAKE ISLAND

Area: 2.5 sq. mi. (6.5 sq. km)
Population: no indigenous inhabitants; U.S. military personnel left the island, but some civilians remain
Government: unincorporated territory of United States, administered by the U.S. Air Force

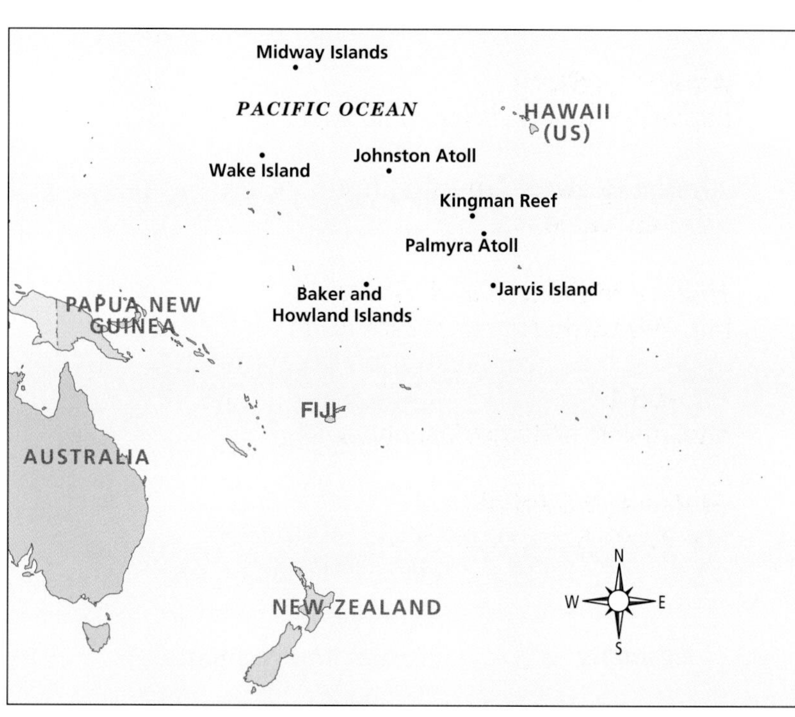

For More Information

Alavezos, Gus. *Stuck on the U.S.A.: Fascinating Facts about the 50 States.* New York: Grosset & Dunlap, 2000.

Aten, Jerry. *50 Nifty States.* Columbus, OH: Good Apple, 2002.

Bennett, William J., editor. *The Children's Book of America.* New York: Simon & Schuster, 1998.

Davidson, James West. *The American Nation: Beginnings through 1877.* Berkeley Heights, NJ: Prentice Hall, 1997.

Garraty, John Arthur. *The Story of America.* New York: Holt, Rhinehart, & Winston, 1994.

Hakim, Joy. *A History of US.* New York: Oxford University Press, 2002.

Ross, Wilma S. *Fabulous Facts about the 50 States.* New York: Scholastic Trade, 1989.

Sobel, Syl. *Presidential Elections and Other Cool Facts.* Happauge, NY: Barron's Juveniles, 2001.

Stienecker, David L. Glassman, Bruce, editor. *First Facts about the States.* Woodbridge, CT: Blackbirch Press, 1996.

Waldman, Carl. *Encyclopedia of Native American Tribes.* New York: Checkmark Books, 1999.

Websites

America's Story
http://www.americaslibrary.gov/cgi-bin/page.cgi

Archiving Early America
http://earlyamerica.com/

History of Women in America
http://www.wic.org/misc/history.htm

Info-USA
http://usinfo.state.gov/usa/infousa/

States and Capitals
http://www.50states.com/

INDEX

PHOTO CREDITS

Cover: Digital Stock, PhotoDisc; Back cover: PhotoDisc, PhotoSpin; Interior: page 16 © Dan Brothers/Alabama Bureau of Tourism & Travel; pages 18, 19, 20, 21 © Karim Shamsi Basha/Alabama Bureau of Tourism & Travel; page 16, 22, 25, 26, 28, 31, 32, 33, 34, 44, 45, 48, 49, 50, 52, 55, 62, 68, 70, 73, 74, 75, 80, 82, 86, 87, 92, 98, 100, 104, 111, 112, 116, 117, 118, 122, 124, 127, 128, 129, 130, 134, 136, 139, 142, 146, 152, 154, 158, 160, 164, 170, 171, 172, 176, 177, 181, 182, 188, 190, 194, 195, 196, 198, 200, 206, 208, 213, 218, 220, 223, 224, 226, 230, 235, 236, 237, 238, 242, 248, 250, 254, 256, 259, 261, 266, 268, 270, 271, 272, 284, 285, 290, 291, 295, 296, 298, 302, 304, 308, 310, 314, 316, 326 © PhotoDisc; page 19, 27, 33, 39, 51, 56, 57, 60, 61, 63, 67, 69, 73, 74, 75, 81, 84, 85, 93, 97, 98, 99, 102, 104, 105, 110, 111, 114, 115, 117, 121, 122, 123, 126, 127, 128, 129, 132, 134, 141, 146, 147, 148, 151, 153, 157, 158, 159, 165, 169, 171, 175, 183, 184, 188, 189, 192, 195, 201, 207, 210, 211, 212, 213, 214, 219, 223, 231, 237, 243, 249, 252, 253, 254, 255, 261, 266, 267, 279, 284, 291, 294, 297, 302, 303, 307, 309, 318, 319, 320, 321, 322, 323, 324, 325, 327 © CORBIS; page 21, 24, 25, 31, 36, 43, 45, 63. 66, 85, 87, 93, 96, 121,141, 153, 157, 168, 216, 225, 228, 229, 258, 267, 271, 285, 313 © Library of Congress; page 21, 225 © NASA; page 26, 58, 68, 81, 164, 166, 171, 178, 180, 183, 186, 206, 242, 244, 260, 278, 285, 290, 291, 295, 309 © Corel Corporation; page 27 © Emory Kristof/National Geographic Society Image Collection; page 30, 109, 163, 225, 265, 289 © National Archives; page 35, 37, 38, 39 © Arkansas Department of Parks & Tourism; page 37, 54, 55, 57, 75, 78, 91, 92, 93, 94, 97, 99, 102, 117, 129, 141, 144, 145, 162, 165, 170, 177, 187, 189, 193, 194, 195, 204, 205, 207, 211, 213, 222, 225, 231, 234, 237, 241, 243, 246, 249, 255, 262, 266, 267, 273, 277, 282, 285, 286, 288, 291, 301 © Blackbirch Press Photo Archives; page 40, 76, 106, 182, 202, 260, 272 © PhotoSpin; page 42 © California Section, California State Library; page 46 © Gunnison County Lodging Tax Panel; page 51 © Collection of the Supreme Court of the United States; page 51 © Robert Royem Photography; page 56 © Sikorsky Aircraft; page 64, 69, 79, 242, 272, 280, 296, 317 © Digital Stock; page 72 © Sun Valley Photography/nativestock.com; page 75 © Bettmann; page 88, 90, 91, 92 © Illinois Department of Commerce and Community Affairs; page 105, 261 © Nate Salzburg/Denver Public Library/Western History Department; page 108, 153, 156, 315 © Hulton Archive; page 115, 116, 117 © Kentucky Department of Travel Development; page 120, 139, 199, 241, 264, 283, 301, 306 © North Wind Picture Archives; page 132, 133, 134, 135 © Maryland Office of Tourism; page 135, 273 © Collection of the Supreme Court of the United States; page 138, 140, 141 © Massachusettes Tourism Department; page 147 © St. Paul Dispatch; page 165 © Simpson College; page 169 © Southwest Parks and Monuments Association; page 174 © Smithsonian Institute; page 175 © Nebraska Department of Economic Development; page 217 © South Dakota Historical Society; page 217 © North Dakota Tourism; page 231 © Tom Gilbert; page 232 © Oregon Tourism Commission; page 235 courtesy Oregon Sea Lion Cave; page 243 © Beinecke Rare Book and Manuscript Library, Yale University; page 247 © Jim McElholm; page 248, 265, 279, 284, 303, 314, 315 © AP/Wide World; page 255 © EyeWire; page 273 © Frank Muto/LBJ Library Collection; page 274, 276, 278, 279 Courtesy of Frank Jensen/Utah Travel Council; page 277, 312 © Denver Public Library; page 288 © National Portrait Gallery; page 297 © Microsoft Corporation;